T0140112

Lecture Notes in Computer Science　750

Edited by G. Goos and J. Hartmanis

Advisory Board: W. Brauer　D. Gries　J. Stoer

Jorge L. Díaz-Herrera (Ed.)

Software Engineering Education

7th SEI CSEE Conference
San Antonio, Texas, USA, January 5-7, 1994
Proceedings

Springer-Verlag
Berlin Heidelberg New York
London Paris Tokyo
Hong Kong Barcelona
Budapest

Series Editors

Gerhard Goos
Universität Karlsruhe
Postfach 69 80
Vincenz-Priessnitz-Straße 1
D-76131 Karlsruhe, Germany

Juris Hartmanis
Cornell University
Department of Computer Science
4130 Upson Hall
Ithaca, NY 14853, USA

Volume Editor

Jorge L. Díaz-Herrera
Software Engineering Institute, Carnegie Mellon University
Pittsburgh, PA 15213-3890, USA

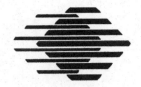

Carnegie Mellon University
Software Engineering Institute

CR Subject Classification (1991): D.2, K.3.2

ISBN 3-540-57461-1 Springer-Verlag Berlin Heidelberg New York
ISBN 0-387-57461-1 Springer-Verlag New York Berlin Heidelberg

© Springer-Verlag Berlin Heidelberg 1994
Printed in Germany

Typesetting: Camera-ready by author
Printing and binding: Druckhaus Beltz, Hemsbach/Bergstr.
45/3140-543210 - Printed on acid-free paper

Preface

The seventh Conference on Software Engineering Education was held in San Antonio, Texas, on January 5-7, 1994. This annual conference is sponsored by the Educational Products Program of the Software Engineering Institute, a federally funded research and development center of the U.S. Department of Defense. For the last three years, it has also been held in conjunction with the Association for Computing Machinery and the IEEE Computer Society. The conference is a forum for discussion of software engineering education and training among members of the academic, industry, and government communities. The technical motivation behind the CSEE series has been putting the *engineering* into software engineering—applying the principles and methods of traditional engineering disciplines to software engineering—and the 7th CSEE continues this focus.

The quality of the accepted contributions is excellent. Out of 87 submissions, the program committee carefully selected 37 papers, 1 panel, and 4 tutorials for presentation. The program committee consisted of the following:

William W. Agresti, *MITRE*

Mark A. Ardis, *AT&T*

Maribeth B. Carpenter, *Software Engineering Institute*

Michael B. Feldman, *George Washington University*

Gary Ford, *Software Engineering Institute*

David Garlan, *Carnegie Mellon University*

Rosalind L. Ibrahim, *Software Engineering Institute*

William Richardson, *United States Air Force Academy*

Keith R. Pierce, *University of Minnesota, Duluth*

David C. Rine, *George Mason University*

Carol A. Sledge, *Software Engineering Institute*

In addition to the above people, the following were referees:

Jim Armitage, William Bail, Marilyn L. Bates, Daniel M. Berry, David Budgen, David W. Bustard, James E. Cardow, Neal S. Coulter, Joseph F. Delgado, Jorge L. Diaz, Merlin Dorfman, Henry A. Etlinger, Richard P. Evans, Eduardo B. Fernandez, Robert Firth, Frank L. Friedman, Norman E. Gibbs, Chris A. Gustafson, Anthony Hall, Daniel E. Hocking, James W. Hooper, Robert R. Korfhage, Leslie Lander, Jeffrey A. Laskey, Patricia K. Lawlis, Timothy J. Lulofs,

Michael J. Lutz, Peter H. Lutz, Nancy R. Mead, Linda M. Northrop, Jeff Offutt, John A. Ogden, Mike Overstreet, F. G. Patterson, Jr., Marie Silverthorn, Raj Tewari, Richard H. Thayer, James E. Tomayko, Judy A. Vernick, John Werth, Laurie Honour Werth, Shirley A. Williams, Bryant W. York.

As is usual with an undertaking of this size and scope, nothing would have been accomplished without an excellent support staff. The level of success is due to the efforts of Mary Ellen Rizzo, more than anyone else, for her tireless work in handling administrative matters, including tracking papers, referees, and final manuscripts. Bernadette Chorle and Jane DeSimone kept the budget and provided continuity. The expert advice and support of Helen Joyce, Wendy Rossi, and others in the Events group made it possible for this conference to run so smoothly. My sincere thanks to them, the program committee, the reviewers, and all who have contributed to the conference.

Pittsburgh, Pennsylvania

August 1993

Jorge L. Diaz-Herrera

Conference Chair, 7th CSEE

Contents

Keynote Address:

Designing a Discipline of Software Design

Peter J. Denning
George Mason University
Department of Computer Science
Farifax, Virginia 22030-4444

Abstract. Software engineering is not a discipline. Its practitioners cannot systematically make and fulfill promises to deliver software systems judged by their customers as usable and dependable, on time and fairly priced. The illusion that software engineers possess a discipline has produced the major breakdown called the software crisis.

The central claim explored here is that the standard engineering design process produces a fundamental blindness to the domains of action in which the customers of software systems live and work. The connection between measurable properties of the software and the satisfaction of those customers is, at best, tenuous. We propose a broader interpretation of design that is centered on observing the work processes of a community of customers in a domain and connecting those processes to supportive software technologies. The skill that a designer needs to have to observe work processes and begin making the connections is here called ontological mapping. This skill can be learned and is the basis of a discipline of software design.

Session 1:
Undergraduate Software Engineering Education

A Two-Semester Undergraduate Sequence in Software Engineering: Architecture & Experience
David B. Boardman and Aditya P. Mathur, Purdue University, West Lafayette, Indiana

Software Engineering in an Undergraduate Computer Engineering Program
Terry Shepard, Royal Military College of Canada, Kingston, Ontario, Canada

When the Golden Arches Gang Aft Agley: Incorporating Software Engineering into Computer Science
Kenneth L. Modesitt, Western Kentucky University, Bowling Green, Kentucky

A Two-Semester Undergraduate Sequence in Software Engineering: Architecture and Experience*

David B. Boardman   Aditya P. Mathur

July 14, 1993

Abstract

A two-semester sequence in Software Engineering has been offered to Computer Science undergraduates at Purdue University since the fall of 1991. An attempt was made to balance the teaching of theory and practice of software engineering and provide the students with an opportunity to apply some of the techniques learned in the classroom to a controlled development project. The project was selected from an industrial setting and the product developed was returned to industry. We describe the architecture of the offering and our experience during the first offering in Fall 1991 and Spring 1992.

1 Introduction

The growing demand for professionals with a knowledge of principles, techniques, and tools of software engineering (SE) has led several universities to offer courses or degree programs in this area. We describe the architecture of and experience with a two-semester sequence in SE for seniors at Purdue University that was offered starting Fall 1991. Our success with this offering leads us to believe that our offering can serve as a model or a basis for other institutions contemplating a course in SE. This by no means implies that there is no scope for improvement in our future offerings. We point out deficiencies in our past offering.

. The remainder of this paper is organized as follows. The next section traces the evolution of this course. The architecture and execution of the course is described in Section 3. We provide sufficient information for a reader to plan a similar offering. Details of the course appear in a technical report [11]. Course handouts given to students during Fall 91 and Spring 92 are included in two appendices at the end of this report. Various evaluation components for grading the students are listed in Section 4. Lessons learned in the planning and execution of the course are summarized in Section 5.

2 Historical background

An undergraduate course in SE has been offered at Purdue since Spring 1986. Until its redesign, this was a one semester 4-credit course. During a single semester, the students were taught principles, methods, and tools of SE. In addition they were assigned a term project. The term project involved

---

*This work was supported in part by an educational supplement from the National Science Foundation No. CCR 9102311. The authors are with Software Engineering Research Center and Department of Computer Sciences, Purdue University, W. Lafayette, IN 47907. Aditya P. Mathur can be contacted at (317)494-7822 or via email at apm@cs.purdue.edu. David Boardman can be contacted via email at boardman@cs.purdue.edu.

the development of a complete product starting from requirements definition to the final product including complete documentation at each stage of the life cycle.

During the initial semesters there was noticeable enthusiasm amongst the students. Gradually, however, the enrollment dropped. From Spring 1986 until Spring 91 the semester enrollment had dropped from 43 to 12. Three different instructors had offered the course a total of 11 times with an average enrollment of 25 per semester. A subsequent informal analysis, triggered by declining enrollments, revealed that "too much class work" was the overwhelming reason why students were staying away from this course. The students were not prepared to spend the many hours required for an optional 4-credit course. The amount of time they spent probably distracted them from this course to other options in the department. It was this analysis that motivated the design of the 2-semester long course in SE discussed in in the remainder of this paper.

3 Course design

The 2-semester sequence in SE consists of two separate though highly interrelated courses. CS 404 Software Engineering I is offered during the fall semester and CS 405 Software Engineering II is offered during spring. CS 404 is a required prerequisite for CS 405. Each course consists of three lecture hours per week and carries 3-credits. There are no scheduled laboratory hours for the courses. There is one suggested prerequisite, namely CS 352 Programming Languages and Compilers, which gives students an opportunity to work on a fairly complex program (a 2000 line compiler written in C). We feel that this experience better prepares a student to appreciate the need for software engineering. The architecture of the two courses is depicted in Figure 1. The courses have been organized into two distinct, though related, layers of educational material. As shown in the figure, these layers are called theory and practice. The practice layer is further divided into a project layer and a tools layer. The theory layer consists of principles and methods of SE. The practice/project layer consists of a 2-semester long project in which students apply some of the material they acquire from the theory layer. The practice/tools layer consists of tool-based assignments. Description of different layers appears below.

3.1 Theory layer

The theory layer, taught during lectures, comprises principles and methods of SE and is supported by textbook and selected research articles. Table 1 lists the components in the theory layer and the reference material used by students.

A broad selection of topics is covered during the lectures. These include topics that the students are likely to use when they join a software house after graduation as well as topics which are less likely to be used. For example, knowledge on topics in software design and testing is likely to be useful in a student's software development career while knowledge gained in symbolic execution and proofs of correctness is less likely to be used in practice. However, even a cursory knowledge and an appreciation of formal methods, prepares a student for circumstances wherein such methods may be in use. The hours devoted to each topic reflect a utilitarian viewpoint that underlies the design of the course. This is not to indicate that one topic is more important than the other but it does reflect the current reality in the world of software development.

The division of topics between the two semesters is also based on their relative complexity and the utility of the knowledge acquired. Thus, for example, estimation of software reliability was covered during spring and software testing was covered during fall. This division provides us with time during the fall semesters to be devoted to other interactions with students described below.

Not all topics covered are dealt with in the recommended textbook [4]. Specifically, for the following topics cited research papers and reports were recommended readings: (i) data flow testing [2, 8], (ii) mutation testing [1, 3], and (iii) documentation [9]. The textbook did serve well for

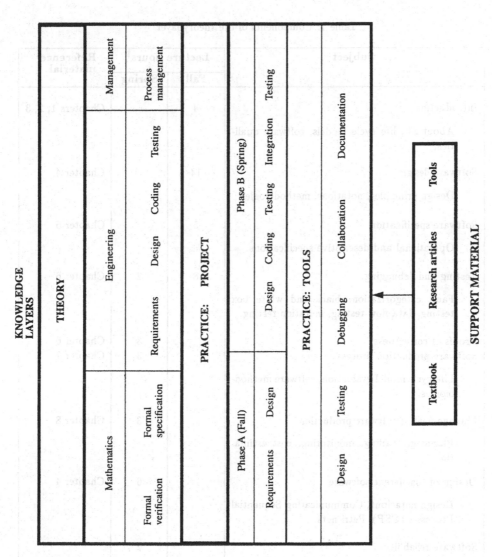

Figure 1: Multi-layered architecture of a 2-semester sequence in software engineering at Purdue University.

Table 1: Components of the theory layer

Subject	Lecture hours[†]		Reference[‡] material
	Fall	Spring	
Introduction	4		Chapters 1, 2, 3
About SE, life cycle models, software qualities.			
Software design	14		Chapter 4
Design principles, notations, methodologies.			
Software specification	5		Chapter 5
Operational and descriptive specifications.			
Testing and debugging	8	2	Chapter 6
Fault categorization, black and white box testing, data flow testing, mutation testing.			
Proofs of correctness		3	Chapter 6
Software production process		3	Chapter 7
Life cycle model evaluation, software methodologies.			
Management of software production		3	Chapter 8
Planning, staffing, monitoring, cost estimation.			
Design of concurrent software		6	Chapter 4
Design notations, Communicating Sequential Processes (CSP), Petri nets.			
Software reliability		2	
Research issues	1	1	
Miscellaneous	3	2	
Total	**35**	**23**	

† Each lecture is of 50 minutes duration.
‡ Chapter numbers are from the textbook used [4]. Other reference material is listed in the text.

almost the entire 2-semester course. It ranked high when evaluated by the students and was used again during the second offering of this course starting Fall 1992.

3.2 Practice layer: project

A year long project, starting in the fall semester and continuing until the end of the spring semester, is a key element of the course. To account for the fact that not all students who take the course during fall will return during spring, the project is divided into two parts. The specification and design phases of the project are completed during fall. Detailed design, coding, testing, integration, and documentation are carried out during spring. Note that the design phase appears during both semesters for reasons outlined below. Students have to spend more time on the project during spring than during fall. This is the primary reason why less hours are devoted to the theory layer during spring than during fall.

3.2.1 Rationale for project selection

There are several choices to be made when preparing a project for such a course. The choices we faced are illustrated by the following questions: (1) Should the project require development of a new product or the enhancement of an existing product? (2) Should the product have industrial relevance?, and (3) Should there be a single or multiple projects?

To answer question (1) above, we relied on our belief that most established software houses are constantly upgrading some existing software. When a project is initiated, it is more often an enhancement of an existing product than the design and development of a product from scratch. Thus a graduating senior who decides to take up a SE career is likely to be in a situation where an existing product is being enhanced. This would imply that experience in reading and understanding existing code and implementing enhancements would be valuable to a student. Further, most computer science students do get experience in developing a new product, albeit simple and not well engineered, in other courses such as compilers and operating systems. This led us to decide that the project should require the students to enhance an existing product. We note that Shaw [13] has pointed out the teaching of *programming from scratch* as a shortcoming of the current software curriculum in most universities.

As an answer to question (2) we decided to consider a project that had industrial relevance. We conjectured that such a project might result in some form of interaction with an industrial user. In turn, such an interaction would serve to boost the student's motivation to complete the project in a professional manner.

Considering the fact that the course would have about forty students, we decided on a single project (3) as against multiple projects. The prime motivation was to keep the time spent in interaction with students to within reasonable limits. Multiple projects would have required preparing different handouts for each project during the semester. As this was the first time this course was offered, we decided not to take the risk of multiple projects. Instead, we argued, variety could be injected into a single project in several innovative ways. Thus, we decided to enhance one existing product. The variety was brought about by providing students with a choice of which enhancements to make.

To summarize, we decided on a single project that required the enhancement of an existing product. The selected product was originally developed in industry and was in use. Variety in the project was brought about by making available a list of enhancements from which the students had to select a few to implement.

Table 2: Modules in ATAC

Type	Size (in total lines of code)
Pre-compile-time	6766
Compile-time	10,468
Run-time	725
Post-run-time	2493

3.2.2 Overview

The project was to enhance an existing testing tool called ATAC (Automatic Test coverage Analysis for C)[1]. ATAC measures the data flow coverage obtained when a C program is executed on elements of a set of test cases. ATAC measures four coverages: block, decision, p-use, and c-use. Definitions of these terms and details about ATAC may be found in [6]. The entire source of ATAC was made available to all students. The structure of ATAC and its functioning from a user's point of view was explained. Table 2 lists the four major modules in ATAC and their size. The implementation was to be carried out on Sun/3 and Sun/4 workstations made available to the students by the Computer Science Department.

ATAC was in use at Purdue prior to the offering of this course. We were familiar with the strengths and weaknesses of this tool. Keeping these in view, we divided the project into two parts. The first part required every group to understand and *document* a minimum amount of ATAC code. The minimum lines of code to be documented was set to $N * 500$, N being the number of group members. Documentation was to be carried out using the CWEB system of documentation [9]. CWEB is a version of WEB for C programs which treats code and comments as one entity. It can be used to generate a TEX file for printing code in a readable format and also to generate a file consisting of compilable C code. We postulated two advantages of the documentation activity. First, students will read code that they have to understand anyway in order to modify it in the second part of this project. Second, generated documentation for ATAC will simplify any future modifications. In its original form ATAC had no technical documentation.

The second part of the project required enhancing ATAC along two dimensions. One dimension was characterized by performance improvement and the other by additional features. A list of enhancements were designed which when implemented would improve the usability of ATAC. This list, and an estimate of the relative complexity of each enhancement, appears in Table 3. There were three types of enhancements. Type C required compile time changes, Type R required run-time changes, and type P required post-run time changes to ATAC. There was no enhancement that required changes to pre-compile time code in ATAC. Enhancements R1 and R2 were performance related. The remaining enhancements were intended to improve ATAC's functionality.

Groups, formed as described below, were advised to select enough enhancements so that the total complexity of their selection was at least 100. For example, it was sufficient to select only enhancement C2 as its relative complexity is 100. The modules selected for documentation by a group were directly related to the enhancements selected by that group. Details of various enhancements appear in the course handout [11]. The complexity numbers were purely subjective and were estimates by the author based on several years of experience with software development.

---

[1]ATAC is a Bell Communications Research proprietary tool given, under license, to Purdue University. It has been developed by Bob Horgan and Saul London.

Table 3: Proposed enhancements to ATAC and their relative complexity.

Enhancement	Relative complexity
C1: Selective instrumentation	15
C2: Interprocedural data flow analysis	100
C3: ALL-DU path coverage	75
R1: Trace file optimization	20
R2: Trace file splitting	20
P1: Tabular display of coverage data	20
P2: Coverage tracking	30
P3: Function coverage	15
P4: Frequency profile computation	15

3.2.3 Student grouping

During the fall semester a total of 37 students took the course. The class was instructed to organize into small groups of 3 to 5 members within the first week. This resulted in a total of 9 groups. Each group was required to make selections for enhancements to be carried out and the modules to be documented.

During the spring semester a total of 14 out of 37 students from fall registered for the course. These remaining students were divided into 3 groups consisting of 5, 4, and 5 members each. Regrouping was done based on the grouping during the previous semester. Thus, students who had selected a similar set of enhancements were grouped together. No student had to take on a task of implementation and enhancement that he or she had not selected during fall. One individual from the class volunteered to be responsible for the entire task of integrating the three products that would be developed by each of the three groups.[2] In addition to participating in the group activities, the task of this individual was to (i) interact with all groups, (ii) identify potential integration problems, and make specific recommendations to groups to avoid such problems, and (iii) integrate the three products into one usable enhanced version of ATAC.

3.2.4 Schedule: Fall

During the fall semester, all groups were required to complete the documentation of selected modules. In addition, they were required to complete the design of the modules that they would add to or modify in ATAC for the selected enhancements. The end of fall deliverables for each group consisted of: (i) CWEB documentation of selected modules, (ii) design documentation, and (iii) complete project logs. Whereas CWEB documentation and the design report were to be turned-in one per group, each student was expected to maintain an individual project log.

Each group was expected to turn in its own reports and files. Code documentation was to be turned in as a compilable CWEB source file. Guidelines were laid out to help groups produce a fairly uniform design document. The design document was required to contain: (i) the design expressed in the Textual Design Notation (TDN) and Graphical Design Notation (GDN) elaborated in the textbook used for the course[4], (ii) a list of modules in ATAC that will need modification and a description of this modification, and (iii) algorithms in pseudo-code. It was suggested that the project log contain dated entries such as: (i) brief description of the task performed e.g. *Examined the* atac_i *module* or *discussed the data structure used for maintaining block coverage information* or *Could not figure out the behavior of module xyz!*, (ii) approximate time spent in that activity,

---

[2]Dave Boardman, one of the authors, was responsible for all integration work.

Table 4: Project schedule

Week	Event
	Fall
5	Presentation: preliminary design
13 and 14	Presentation: final design
	Spring
2	Overview presentations-I (initial)
3	Overview presentations-II (final)
4	Progress presentations
5	Design review, Group I
	Design review, Group II
	Design review, Group III
6	Integration issues, Design report due
7	Progress presentations; Design report returned
8	Code review, Group I
	Code review, Group II
	Code review, Group III
10	Progress presentations
11	Progress presentations
12	Code review, Group I
	Code review, Group II
	Code review Group III
13	Integration issues
14	Progress presentations
15	Project demonstrations;Final report due (first draft)
	Final report (first draft) returned
16	Late project demonstrations (5% loss of grade)
	Revised final report due

and (iii) any other comments relevant to the project or course. It was recommended that the log be maintained in LaTeX [7] format. To check on group progress, all students were informed that logs could be requested for examination by the instructor without significant prior notice.

In addition to the reports to be submitted at the end of the semester, all groups were required to make two short presentations during the semester. As shown in Table 4, these presentations were scheduled during the 5th and 13th week of the semester. Most groups did not have any formal design by the 5th week. However, they had understood some of the modules that were supposed to be documented. At the time of second presentation, each group had completed the design.

3.2.5 Schedule: Spring

Substantially more time was devoted to the project during spring than during fall. As evident from Table 4, at least one class hour was devoted to the project almost every week. During the spring the schedule was tighter and enforced more strictly than in the fall. Figure 2 shows the project schedule for various activities during spring. Detailed schedule with exact dates [11], was provided to the class on the first day of the semester.   The deliverables at the end of the spring semester

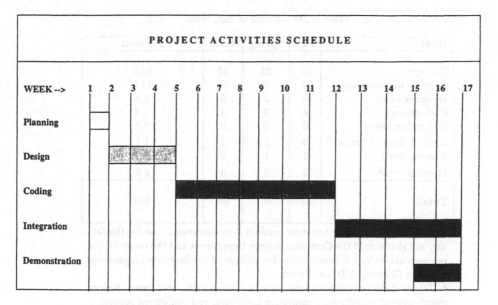

Figure 2: Schedule of various project related activities during Spring 92. Even though integration was originally scheduled starting the 12th week, integration related activities actually took place throughout the development.

were: (i) a final report on the project to be submitted by each group, (ii) the final product in the form of documented code, and (iii) a public demonstration of the final product.

The final report, one per group, was essentially a revision and extension of the design report completed during the previous semester. The report was required to contain the following information: (i) design of the enhancements implemented by the group, (ii) size and time to completion of each module listed together with their estimates obtained at the start of the spring semester, (iii) details of how the system was tested; each module was required to be tested to obtain 100% block and decision coverage with the help of ATAC, and (iv) a brief manual, in the Unix man-page style, of the enhanced ATAC. The code turned in by each group was to be documented using CWEB.

3.2.6 Execution and delivery

At the start of the course it was decided that the entire project would be monitored and steered in a scheduled manner. The following methods were used for monitoring and steering the project: (i) design presentations, (ii) design reviews, (iii) code reviews, (iv) product demonstrations, and (v) private meetings between the instructor and the groups. Except for private meetings, all presentations, reviews and demonstrations had deadlines that were announced at the start of each semester. There were no reviews or demonstrations during fall.

Table 5 shows the time devoted to formal presentations during the two semesters. In all a total of about 38% of the class time was devoted to the project. We do not have any estimates of the time spent by individual students and groups on the project. However, it seems obvious that groups spent significantly more time on the project during spring than in fall.

Table 5: Distribution of class time.

Item	Fall	Spring	Total	Percent
Theory	35	22	57	63.3
Progress presentations	6	7	13	14.5
Design reviews	0	3	3	3.3
Code reviews	0	3	3	3.3
Integration issues	0	2	2	2.2
Product demonstrations[†]	0	1	1	1.1
Examinations	1	1	2	2.2
Miscellaneous[‡]	3	3	6	6.6
Total:	45	45	90	100

[†] In addition there were two more product demonstrations, one for the faculty and students of the Computer Science Department and the other for the representatives from industries that are affiliates of the Software Engineering Research Center (SERC) at Purdue.
[‡] This includes announcements regarding homework, tool-based assignments, project guidelines, presentation guidelines, and evaluation reports.

Presentations: During fall, each group had to present their design twice. There was no formal in-public design review. Based on meetings with each group, one interim project report, and one final project report, the instructor kept track of the progress made by each group. During spring, much greater effort and planning went into project monitoring. Every Monday we scheduled either a progress presentation by each group or a design or code review. Progress presentations were 15 minutes in duration. Each group was expected to outline the progress made and point out potential problems. The entire class participated in the discussions. The class was, in particular, on the lookout for potential integration problems due to incompatibilities introduced by the three designs.

Design review: Each group was subjected to one 50-minute design review. During the review each group presented their design and the underlying rationale. In all cases the design was a modification of the one proposed during the previous semester. The entire class, the instructor, and the grader participated in design reviews as *external* participants. Note that members of all groups were well versed with the internal architecture of ATAC. Thus, the participation provided useful inputs to the group presenting the design. An intermediate report containing the final design was submitted by each group.

The notion of *design divergence* was introduced to students at the start of the semester. Design divergence meant the divergence of design from what was developed during the previous semester. Four factors that could lead to design divergence were identified. These were: (i) need to integrate code developed by various groups, (ii) change in group structure, (iii) meticulous examination of the previous design, and (iv) design reviews. Divergence was explicitly recorded by the integration manager. There were discussions on how such divergence could have possibly been avoided in the earlier design. The causes for such divergence were later classified as (i) error in requirements analysis, (ii) lack of prototyping of various screens, (iii) concerns of efficiency, and (iv) incorrect understanding of the existing system (in this case ATAC). Thus, for example, here is a brief description of a design change that resulted due to infeasible requirements:

The original definition of "selective instrumentation" was to be able to instrument individual lines of code. This turned out to be infeasible because a variable could be defined in uninstrumented code and later used in instrumented part of the code. This would not produce any useful information. By the second design report it was decided that selective instrumentation should apply only to functions.

Code reviews: Each group was subjected to two code reviews. To assist groups in planning for code review, specific guidelines were given. These guidelines are reproduced in Table 6. A group was required to demonstrate executable code by tracing and explaining it to the entire class. For this to be feasible, a 26" TV monitor was connected to a workstation. Saber-C[12] was used for tracing the code. One member of the group controlled code tracing using Saber-C commands and another member pointed to code segments and data structure values to explain how the code worked. Each code review required meticulous planning on the part of a group. During planning group members considered (i) example(s) to be used for tracing the code, (ii) communication between the persons at the workstation and TV, and (iii) any handouts to be given to the audience prior to the review. The audience watched for (i) code quality (error checking possible errors, etc.), (ii) variations from the design finalized earlier, and (iii) problems that may arise during integration. At the time of the first code review no group had the entire functionality implemented. All groups had their products completed by the time of the second review.

Testing: Each group was required to test their code in three steps. First, functional testing was to be performed to ensure that all the enhancements implemented by the group were functioning as expected. This testing generated a test set T_f. T_f was then evaluated using the existing version of ATAC to determine block and decision coverages. In the second step a test set T_b was constructed by adding test cases to T_f so as to achieve "almost" 100% block coverage. Blocks that contained code to process erroneous OS function call errors or were difficult to execute, such as malloc failure processing, were not required to be covered. In the third step, T_b was modified to obtain T_d which covered all decision except the ones corresponding to blocks mentioned above. Though most of the errors were discovered during functional testing, coverage measurement and improvement did reveal the "tough" errors that may have otherwise remained unnoticed.

Demonstration: The final demonstration, to the students and faculty of the Computer Science Department, was carried out using the same set up as used for the code reviews except that code tracing was not used. Instead, the audience was given a product demonstration as if this was a new version of an existing product. Thus, the rationale underlying each enhancement was presented before demonstrating the workings of the product. The entire demonstration was carried out by the integration manager with the help of one member selected from a group. However, all groups cooperated with the integration manager during the long hours that went into planning and preparation. The above demonstration was repeated for the representatives of the affiliates of Software Engineering Research Center at Purdue. The original developers of ATAC were also present at this demonstration.

Delivery: The entire class was quite excited about the prospects of their *class* product being delivered to industry for evaluation and possible use. The product and a video tape of the demonstration given to industrial affiliates was delivered to Bellcore. We reproduce below the comments received from one of the originators of ATAC at Bellcore [5]:

Table 6: Code review guidelines.

Demonstrate	Description	Steps to follow
Functionality	To explain (a) what the program does and (b) convince the participants that it does so correctly.	State functionality, construct sample test inputs, apply inputs to the program, show sample output.
Logic and data structures	(a) To explain the algorithm and data structures used, (b) prompt the participants to ask devious questions, (c) accept challenges from the participants and show, if possible, that the code will not crash or enter into an infinite loop.	Construct sample input; trace the program for this input, use incremental tracing by dividing the program into meaningful code segments and trace segment-by-segment; explain what each segment does; begin with a simple path and then move to more complex paths through the program.
Environment	To (a) explain how the code has been or will be integrated into the existing version of ATAC, (b) to prompt the participants to compose devious conditions that may arise in the environment, and (c) show, if possible, that malfunctioning of the environment will not cause the code to get confused.	Explain the environment in which the code appears and how the environment interacts with the code.
Reliability	To demonstrate how well the program has been tested.	Convince the participants of high program reliability with data from testing and logic of the program.
Robustness	To convince that the program will behave gracefully under various unexpected conditions.	Construct test cases that represent boundary conditions (e.g. an empty input file) and demonstrate the infallibility of your code to such inputs.

I received the video and have watched it twice. The work your students have done is remarkably well conceived. The architecture of the trace management function is exactly right, and, judging from the demo, the implementation is excellent as well. Some of the features added to ATAC have been requested by our users at Bellcore including, function coverage, individual function instrumentation, frequency counting, and summary displays for p- and c-uses. Everything you have done has enhanced the value of ATAC. I doubt that a professional development team could have done a better job. This contribution is of great value to Bellcore. Congratulations!

3.2.7 Product integration

As mentioned earlier, a single student, titled "integration manager", was given the responsability of overseeing the development and integration of the course project. It was important that this person could clearly abstract the details of each enhancement to devise a smooth development plan and integration procedure. Figure 3 gives an overall view of the flow of product development. ATAC was obtained from Bellcore. Three different groups generated three different versions of enhanced ATAC; the integration manager integrated the three versions into one usable enhanced ATAC. The enhanced ATAC was delivered to Bellcore. The role of the integration manager and the integration process used are summarized below.

Design and Development: Throughout development the integration manager acted as a liaison between the different design groups. If one group was considering a change to a common data structure it was the responsability of the integration manager to lead discussion regarding the affects on other enhancements. In this project the majority of the data structure modifications generated few conflicts between the groups and required little mitigation.

However, when a conflict did arise the integration manager would devise a procedure to integrate the conflicting enhancements. This would assure compatability when the enhancements were merged at the end of the semester integration sessions.

Final Sessions: As each enhancement took shape the integration manager set goals with each group regarding the date of integration for each of the enhancements. During these sessions each enhancement was merged into a single integrated version of ATAC. The session was led by the integration manager outside the regular class hours and attended by the student(s) responsible for providing the given enhancement. The following procedure was meticulously followed during each of these sessions.

1. The student(s) would provide a listing of modified source files with their modifications underlined.

2. The on line source files of the integrated version would be archived using RCS (revision control system)[14]. This provided the ability to revert to any of the previous integration sessions if necessary.

3. The current integrated version of the source file and the students' modified source file would be run through diff [3] and the results were recorded into an integration log.

4. The integration manager would then compare the students underlined modifications to the results generated by diff. This was to insure that the student had not missed underlining any of their modifications.

5. Modified code was copied from the students source into the integrated version manually.

6. Functional testing was performed to insure that the enhancement was successfully integrated.

7. The integrated version was released to the course grader for final testing.

Problems: The following problems proved significant :

- *Meeting Deadlines* - If one group or student did not have their enhancement completed by the suggested deadline it delayed the integration of the entire project.

- *Intergroup Communication* - During development, getting groups to provide a consistent interface to modules under development presented many problems. More than once a group was forced to delay progress until a supporting group provided additional information regarding changes to shared data structures.

---

[3] A UNIX utility to display line-by-line differences between pairs of text files.

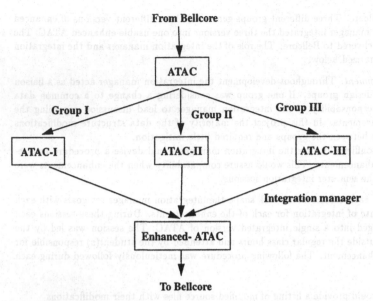

Figure 3: Product development flow and integration. Arrow labelling indicates the group or individual responsible for developing the product.

- *Integration Sessions* - These were tedious and provided several opportunities to inject human errors. It was easy to leave out statements required even though several redundant checks were inherent to the process.

3.3   Practice layer: tools

Software engineers are almost invariably using one or more *process related* tools during software development. In the commercial world we come across tools that cater to almost every phase of the software life cycle. In this course we selected a set of tools from what was available to us at Purdue. This resulted in tools for documentation, design, testing, debugging, and source code revision control. Table 7 lists the tools that were made available to students. For the purpose of tool-based assignments, a laboratory consisting of HP workstations was used. Mothra was the only tool which required the use of Sun workstations.

Wherever possible, a tool based assignment was given to familiarize each student with a specific tool. For example, students were asked to determine if a mutation adequate test set could be developed that will *not* detect an error in a given program. A solution to this exercise required the use of Mothra[1] a mutation testing tool. Students learned how to use Mothra and also realized how difficult it is to *not* detect an error when a mutation adequate test set is being constructed.

Except for Mothra, all tools learned through assignments were also used by students during project work. For example, CWEB was used for documenting the ATAC code, ATAC was used to test the code developed, and RCS was used within each group to control various revisions of the code developed. Mothra could not be used during code testing because it accepts Fortran programs whereas the project required code development in C.

Table 7: Tools used.

Tool name	Semester	Purpose
ATAC	Fall	Data flow testing
CWEB	Fall	Integrated programming and documentation
LATEX	Fall	Report writing and documentation
Mothra	Fall	Mutation testing
RCS	Fall and Spring	Revision control
Saber-C‡	Spring	Debugging
Spyder†	Spring	Debugging using dynamic slicing
Teamwork†	Fall	Requirements and design

† The tool was demonstrated to students. There was no assignment based on this tool.
‡ This tool was used extensively by all groups during testing, debugging, and code reviews.

4 Student evaluation

During both semesters, the emphasis was more on "practical" aspects of SE. A midterm and a comprehensive final examination were given in each semester. During these examinations the students were tested for their knowledge in topics covered during lectures relating to concepts, techniques, and the mathematics.

Table 8 lists various course evaluation components and their relative weights. During spring, the project was given relatively more importance than other components of the course. This is evident in the 25% and 75% of the grade allocated to the project, during fall and spring, respectively. A project report was required during the spring and was graded as part of the final product demonstration.

5 Lessons learned and concluding remarks

In the end, this course was a satisfying experience for the instructor and appeared to be so for most students. The course had a rating of 4.1 and 4.8 on a scale of 1 to 5, during fall and spring, respectively. The instructor had a rating in the top 5% of the undergraduate instructors in the department. The students came to the course wanting to learn what SE is all about. Most, specially those who went through the spring semester also, thought they learned it well. Below are some of the lessons we learned from this offering.

1. It is important to plan the entire one year course at the beginning and clearly explain the plan to the class. The importance of precisely laid out schedules cannot be overemphasized.

2. Without a significant project component this course may have little value. A project of direct industrial relevance provides additional motivation.

3. Close and frequent monitoring of the project is important for its success.

4. When used in the project, material taught in the lecture classes helps the student appreciate its utility, strengths, and weaknesses.

Table 8: Components used for students evaluation.

Component	Fall	Spring
Written examinations	45	20
Midterm	20	
Final	25	20
Assignments	35	5
Written home work	10	5
Tool based assignments	25	
Project	20	75
Project reviews	10	
Final project report	10	
Planning		10
Design		20
Code		25
Final product demonstration		20
Total	100	100

5. Regardless of what and how we teach documentation, very few students seem to document their code willingly.

6. It is difficult to motivate topics that require mathematical maturity such as formal verification and specification.

7. Availability of design tools would have improved the students' ability to document their designs and appreciate the strengths and weaknesses of such tools.

8. Setting "smaller" goals during development would have helped insure meeting intermediate deadlines.

9. Integration sessions could be greatly improved with the availability of automated integration tools or formal integration methods.

The course turned out to be particularly weak in the area of requirements and design. Even though these topics were covered during the lectures, the students did not gain any experience in the use of tools in these areas. The project laid out the requirements quite clearly. In some cases clarifications were requested by students and readily provided by the instructor. In a fewer cases the students had to struggle with the requirements before they decided that a given requirement was infeasible. Other than in these few situations, there was no challenge in the requirement analysis part of the project.

Though object oriented design was discussed during lectures, the students did not get to actually develop any design using object oriented design (OOD) techniques. The product they were enhancing was itself not designed using OOD methods. Thus, it was not clear how students could use this technology while enhancing such a product. The problem was further compounded by the fact that the essential data structures in ATAC were used without any significant modification. This is not to imply that OOD cannot be used for enhancing a product that is itself not designed using OOD. It would have probably required more thought and planning at the time of project formulation.

The non-availability of a fully equipped laboratory completely or partly dedicated to the course proved to be a major irritant during the day-to-day operations of the course. Workstations (Sun/3 an Sun/4) used by students were either shared by researchers in the department or too few of them were available (HP 900 workstations). This often resulted in frustrations amongst students due to the unusually slow response from the workstation. Further, not all tools were available on the same type of workstation. This also created confusion as students maintained their work files in different file systems. We therefore conclude that a fully equipped laboratory is essential for the course described here.

Handouts used in this course are listed in [11]. Both Mothra and ATAC are very useful tools in an SE course. The integration of tools that were the outcome of research at SERC into the SE course turned out to be beneficial for the students in the course and to some researchers. The interactions between research and teaching and the benefits thereof are described in more detail in [6]. ATAC is available on a limited basis to universities. Mothra is in public domain and is available from Purdue.[4]

Acknowledgements

A significant credit for the success of this course is due to the students of CS 490S and CS 490T (These course numbers were later changed to CS 404 and CS 405, respectively). Software Engineering I and Software Engineering II respectively, offered during Fall 1991 and Spring 1992. Students of CS 490T deserve special credit for their courage to attend this course and be subjected to the rigor imposed throughout the semester. These are: Chris Benes, Cheryl Greiner, Wes Hart, Tad Lin, Michael Manley, Carolyn Moore, Shirley Liao, Angelin Ng, Chris Reifel, Kelly Roberts, Howard Shum, and Mike Spitzer. Susan Evans ably handled all the tool based assignments and some other chores during the entire course. Ronnie Martin made suggestions to improve the preliminary version of this paper. Bob Horgan and Saul London of Bellcore were always ready to answer questions on the phone. They provided the much needed encouragement and, of course, the source code of ATAC. Our sincere thanks go to to all these individuals.

References

[1] B. J. Choi, R. A. DeMillo, E. W. Krauser, A. P. Mathur, R. J. Martin, A. J. Offutt, H. Pan, and E. H. Spafford, "The Mothra toolset," *Proceedings of Hawaii International Conference on System Sciences*, HI, January 3-6, 1989.

[2] L. A. Clarke, A. Podgruski, D. J. Richardson, and S. Zeil, "A formal evaluation of data flow path selection criteria," *IEEE Trans. on Software Engineering*, Vol. 15, No 11, pp 1318-1332, November 1989.

[3] R. A. DeMillo, R. J. Lipton, and F. G. Sayward, "Hints on test data selection: Help for the Practicing Programmer," *Computer*, Vol. 11, No. 4, April 1978.

[4] C. Ghezzi, M. Jazayeri, D. Mandrioli, *Fundamentals of Software Engineering*, Prentice Hall, New Jersey, 1991.

[5] J. R. Horgan, Bellcore, *Personal Communication*.

[6] J. R. Horgan and A. P. Mathur, "Assessing tools in research and education," *IEEE Software*, May 1992, pp 61-69

---

[4]To obtain a copy of ATAC contact J. R. Horgan at Bellcore (jrh@bellcore.com). To obtain Mothra, contact R. J. Martin at Software Engineering Research Center, Purdue University (rjm@cs.purdue.edu).

[7] L. Lamport, A document preparation system: LATEX User's guide & reference manual, Addison-Wesley Publishing Company, Reading, MA, 1986.

[8] J. W. Laski and B. Korel, "A data-flow oriented program testing strategy", *IEEE Trans. on Software Engineering*, Vol. SE-9, No. 3, May 1983, pp 347-354.

[9] S. Levy and D. E. Knuth, "The CWEB system of structured documentation," *Technical Report*, UMSI 91/56, February 1991, University of Minnesota Supercomputing Research Institute, MN.

[10] A. P. Mathur, "On the relative strengths of data flow and mutation testing," *Proceedings of the Ninth Annual Pacific Northwest Software Quality Conference*, October 7-8, 1991, Portland, OR.

[11] D. B. Boardman and A. P. Mathur, "A 2-semester undergraduate sequence in software engineering: architecture and experience," Technical Report SERC-TR-140-P, May 1993, Software Engineering Research Center, Purdue University, W. Lafayette, IN 47907.

[12] Using Saber-C, Version 3.0, Saber Software Systems, Inc., Cambridge, MA, 1986.

[13] M. Shaw, "We can teach software better," *Computing Research News*, September 1992.

[14] W. F. Tichy, "An introduction to the Revision Control System," in Unix Programmer's Manual, Supplementary Documents 1, USENIX Association, November 1986.

Software Engineering in an Undergraduate Computer Engineering Program

Terry Shepard

Department of Electrical and Computer Engineering
Royal Military College of Canada
Kingston, Ontario, K7K 5L0
Canada

Abstract. This paper describes one way to include software engineering in undergraduate computer engineering. A description of the context is given, to help readers relate it to their own situations. The need for software engineering in all branches of engineering is clear, but it is difficult to find space in undergraduate curricula. This is illustrated with reference to an electrical engineering curriculum. A set of six software engineering courses is described, as are three other courses that are relevant to students deciding on the software option. Some of the factors that led to the choices made are discussed. Three of the software courses are in the core of computer engineering, while three are taken only by students specializing in software.

1 Introduction

The Royal Military College of Canada (RMC) is a university of about 700 students, owned and operated by the Canadian Department of National Defence. Undergraduates must meet academic, military, physical fitness and official language requirements to obtain a degree. RMC also offers Master's and Ph.D. degrees. On the academic side, RMC is primarily an engineering school, although it does offer other degree programs. It does not offer a computer science program. This may have made it easier to introduce software engineering into its computer engineering program. It offers 7 different undergraduate programs in engineering. The focus of this paper will be on recent changes to the curriculum of one of these, computer engineering. These changes are still being implemented, so there has been no opportunity yet for evaluation of the results.

RMC's engineering programs are based on a common core in the first two years of the four year program. Courses are offered on a semester basis. The academic component of this core includes courses in mathematics, physics, chemistry, english or french composition and literature, history, psychology, materials, drawing, and computer science. The computer science courses emphasize numerical methods and elementary data structures and algorithms using Pascal. The change to Pascal is recent, as all the engineering departments except Electrical and Computer Engineering preferred to continue using Fortran, and can still advance legitimate arguments in favour of Fortran. The exact selection of courses is less interesting than the near impossibility of gaining access to the first two years for any significant amount of new material in support of either software or computer engineering. In some ways, this is a blessing, as it ensures that the students receive a well rounded and solid education in the traditional fundamentals of engineering, something that is often lacking in computer science programs. [1]

Of all the branches of engineering, computer engineering is the most amenable to the inclusion of software engineering. The major rationale is that computer hardware projects are typically 85% software. Engineers from other branches are nonetheless faced with an ever increasing need to understand the basic techniques of software engineering, especially as they relate to safety critical applications of software in systems they design. They generally view software at something for which the mathematically based design techniques of the kind they are used to in their own branch of engineering do not exist. Curricula in civil, mechanical, electrical, chemical and other branches of engineering are generally well established, and have very little room for software engineering courses.

The norm for software engineering in many computer engineering curricula is a single overview course, plus two or three courses such as structured programming, data structures, real-time system design, or operating systems. These courses are often concerned with making things work at low levels of detail, so the software engineering perspective tends to be lost. It is easy to teach computer students the truth of the maxim that "the devil is in the details", but it is necessary to get past these details. Finding that balance is one of the challenges of teaching computer and software engineering. The alternative sometimes employed in computer science programs, which is to suppress details in actual teaching, assuming that students will learn enough on their own or with minimal help, is not feasible in a curriculum with 37 or more contact hours per week.

The rest of the paper is organized as follows. An overview of the curricula for computer and electrical engineering at RMC is given. This is followed by a more detailed description and discussion of 9 courses selected for their relevance to the software engineering option. Then the alternatives and rationales for some of the curriculum choices made are given, after which there is a brief discussion of the poor availability of textbooks and design tools to support software engineering courses. Finally, some issues are raised relating to engineering certification, and conclusions are presented.

2 Curriculum overview

Third year computer and electrical engineering both include two military leadership courses, an arts elective, engineering economics, a two semester course on differential equations and complex variables, an introductory control course (with a material science course as an alternative for the computer engineers), second language training (English or French, as appropriate), physical education and drill. This leaves 4 slots open for computer engineering courses in each semester. Each slot is 5 hours (three lecture and two lab periods per week), or 20 hours out of about 37 total hours of classroom time each week. The choices made to fill these slots are shown in Table 1.

There is only one course that differentiates the two programs in the fall term, while there are two differentiating courses in the winter term. One of them, the Modelling and Simulation of Digital Systems course, is available again to the electrical engineers as an option in fourth year. It would have been a nice option from a software engineering viewpoint to make the Computer System Design course available in the same way, but Computer Program Design is a prerequisite, so this is not possible.

Table 1. 3rd YEAR PROGRAM			
	Computer Engineering	Common Courses	Electrical Engineering
F A L L		Circuit Fundamentals	
		Logic Design	
		Computer Organization (Assembly Language)	
	Computer Program Design		Energy Conversion
W I N T E R		Electronic Devices	
		Interfacing Techniques	
	Computer Systems Design		Systems and Signals
	Modelling and Simulation of Digital Systems		Applied Electromagnetics

Fourth year computer and electrical engineering both include two military leadership courses, a history course, an arts elective, second language training, physical education and drill. A fourth year design project takes two hours per week in the fall semester, and 6 in the winter semester. This leaves 25 hours per week in the fall, and 20 hours in the winter. The choices available to fill these slots are shown in Table 2. There is more commonality in fourth year than might appear at first glance: the VLSI design course is available to both, and, as mentioned above, the third year Modelling and Simulation of Digital Systems course is available to electrical engineers in fourth year.

The lack of space in the electrical engineering curriculum is most evident in the number of options available in the winter semester of fourth year. What is not shown, but adds to the difficulty, is the prerequisite relation among courses.

There is a computer applications course in the electrical engineering program, but the focus of that course is on interfacing computers to electrical machinery and learning to program in C. The result is that there is virtually no software engineering in electrical engineering. One effect is to open a path for students who are not interested in software to specialize in digital hardware to some extent. Computer engineers can take more digital hardware courses than electricals can, but they must then take the three core software engineering courses. The desire to open such a path, and the curriculum pressure from traditional electrical engineering courses, are the two main reasons that it is difficult to

Table 2a: 4th YEAR PROGRAM - Fall Term

Computer Engineering		Common Courses	Electrical Engineering		
		Electronic Circuits			
		Project			
Computer Architecture			Computer Applications		
Communications for Computer Engineers			Communication Theory		
Software Engineering I			Control Systems I		
Hardware	Software		Choose one:		
VLSI design	Object Oriented Techniques		VLSI Design	Emag and Prop	Mach and Power

Table 2b: 4th YEAR PROGRAM - Winter Term

Computer Engineering		Common Courses	Electrical Engineering	
		Project		
Computer Communications			Choose 4 of the courses below:	
Choose 2 courses by choosing specialization:			Modelling and Simulation of Digital Systems	
Hardware	Software		Communications and Electronics	Control and Power
Digital Systems Architecture	Software Engineering II		Microwave Circuits & Devices	Power Distribution
Digital Systems Design	Real-Time Embedded Sys Design		Signal Processing in Communications	Computer Measurements and Appl'ns
			Computer Communications	Control Systems II
Choose 1 of the courses below:			Circuits for Communications	Modelling and Control of AC Machines
Robotic Control				Digital Control
Power Semiconductors				
Computer Graphics				
Database Management				
Digital Signal Processing Hardware and Applications				
Out of Department Course				

introduce more software engineering into the electrical engineering curriculum. The curriculum pressure also makes it difficult to offer the full set of digital systems courses to the electrical engineers.

3 Description and Discussion of Selected Courses

3.1 Computer Program Design

The aim of this course is to expose the student to basic computer program design techniques, which will serve as a basis for later software related courses. The course also serves as an introduction to the Ada language, which is the main vehicle used to illustrate design concepts studied in the course. Students gain hands-on experience in Ada, by implementing some of the structures and algorithms discussed in class. Students are exposed to the basics of software engineering, including requirements, program design, coding, testing, validation and maintenance, but at this stage, the emphasis is on algorithms, data structures and implementation. More flesh is added to this skeleton in the first of the two software engineering courses in fourth year.

Much of the material in this course would be found in courses in first or second year in a conventional computer science curriculum. In engineering curricula, especially those following a tradition of one or two common years for all branches, this is more difficult to achieve. It could be argued that a course like this one should be a minimum to ensure that engineers in all branches have a better appreciation of how to develop reliable large software systems. The problem is that this course does not go far enough to achieve that purpose, and it is impossible to convey good software design practices for large systems to students who have not taken a course like this one.

The course takes advantage of being Ada-based to teach concepts that are more difficult to illustrate using languages such as C or Pascal. This is evident in the detailed list of topics for the course:

Introduction to Ada. Software reuse. Strong typing. Structured programming. Compilation units, separate compilation, libraries. Pre-defined data types: integers, reals, enumeration types, arrays, records, pointers, files. User-defined types. Universal numbers and conversions. Objects. Control structures. Modules, functions and procedures. Abstract data types. Overloading. Exceptions. Testing and debugging. Stub and driver programs. Basic data structures, including linear lists, queues, stacks, linked lists. Linear and binary search. Binary tree search. Insertion sort, binary sort, merge sort, quick sort. Hashing. Relative efficiency of algorithms.

3.2 Modelling and Simulation of Digital Systems

This is a digital hardware design course. Topics include a review of fundamental concepts, system level design, functional abstraction and decomposition, partitioning, and documentation. VHDL is introduced and then used to support this design methodology. Students first analyze and design combinatorial and sequential circuits. This experience is later used in the design of more complex digital systems such as intelligent memory parts, microsequencers, microcontrollers, device controllers and microprocessors.

Many examples are presented in class, and reinforced by using VHDL design and simulation tools. The formal material is presented using an integrated lecture, demonstration and hands-on practical exercises approach. The latter portion of the course is dedicated to laboratory work on assigned problems.

For computer engineers, this course is offered in third year to allow more advanced digital design courses to build on it in fourth year. The electrical engineers can take this course in fourth year. They do less design than the computer engineers do, because, lacking an Ada background, they must spend more time learning VHDL. The computer engineers are familiar with Ada when they start this course, which makes it easier for them to learn VHDL and to appreciate its partitioning techniques. There is reinforcement of the idea that hardware design is similar to software design in many ways.

VHDL differs from Ada primarily in the way it treats the timing behaviour of objects. It introduces notions of simulation timing, concurrent control structures (WHEN, WHEN-ELSE, WITH-WHEN,...), and signals and attributes. This focus on timing is essential in hardware design, as circuits will not work reliably if their timing characteristics are wrong. In the design of software that must meet hard timing requirements, this is equally true, but the techniques for ensuring that a software design will meet timing requirements when it is implemented are much less well developed than similar techniques are for hardware. It is also worth noting that the level of circuit complexity that can be dealt with in this course is relatively low. A typical example of laboratory work is the design, simulation, implementation and testing of an edge triggered RS flip-flop with delay, setup and hold times. This is in fact complex from the student's perspective, but the functionality of the end product is low compared to the functionality of the end products of software courses at the same level.

3.3 Computer System Design

This is a replacement for a conventional computer science operating systems course, which typically has its roots in the design of time-sharing systems, where resource management is driven by different factors than it is in embedded systems.

The aim is to study basic issues in the design of computer systems, with emphasis on strategies for the allocation of resources shared among a number of tasks. The course begins with a discussion of the need for sharing of resources among concurrent activities in computer systems, and of how effective concurrency on a single CPU can be achieved through the use of tasks that share the CPU. Other resources that must be shared include devices, memory, and files. Practical experience is achieved by a series of programming problems intended to illustrate aspects of resource management in each of these areas. Ada, C and 80x86 assembler are used as the programming languages. Topics covered in the practical work include the Ada rendezvous, low level device management, a device driver in Ada, low level context switching, and process synchronisation in C. An object based approach to programming is emphasized in the practical work.

Experience with Ada tasking in this course, even using a low end Ada compiler that runs on a PC, introduces the students to many concepts that are important in the design of real-time systems, including independent threads of control, synchronization and mutual exclusion, the difficulty of scheduling and the need for control of scheduling, the tendency to sequentialize tasks that are intended to be executed in parallel, and the influence of tasking overheads in determining run-time efficiency.

3.4 VLSI Technologies and Design

This course deals with integrated circuit technologies, including bipolar and CMOS, and with the IC development cycle. It covers comparative analysis; representation (behavioral, structural and physical); IC lithography and fabrication steps; design rules and layout techniques; I/O structures; digital subsystems; IC design flow and design tools; VLSI subsystems (programmable logic arrays: mixed notation stick diagrams; basic concept of a PLA generator; static RAM: basic cell operation and layout, overall architecture and operation; dynamic memories; Read Only memory); and IC Design Flow (specification; technology selection; design approach; design verification; CAE tools; testing).

While there is a strong hardware component to this course, there is also a systems approach to both the design of the circuits implemented as part of the practical work for the course, and in terms of the professional design tools used, which are part of the Mentor Graphics suite of tools. It is worth observing that the students use the Mentor Graphics tools for a number of courses, and so they become thoroughly familiar with them. On the software side, it is not possible to have such a unified set of tools, simply because there is not enough agreement on what the tools should do. In later courses on the hardware side, there is a greater emphasis on high level system design. Because of scheduling and prerequisites, these courses are not available to software specialists.

Practical work includes simulation and analysis of CMOS circuits, layout and layout verification of standard cells, placement and routing of standard cells, and design examples from circuit to layout.

3.5 Design Project

In this course, groups of 2-4 students design and construct a prototype system to satisfy selected criteria against which actual performance is evaluated. Oral progress reports are required along with a written final report and formal examination by a board of staff members. In computer engineering projects, emphasis is placed on software specification, documentation and management techniques. There is also a requirement that the design project be an integrative project, involving several aspects of the whole curriculum, so a pure software project would have difficulty being accepted.

Students usually find their design project to be the most satisfying of all the courses taken, and at the same time the most difficult and demanding.

Students are judged on their ability to reach an appropriate engineering solution to a problem. They must

a. assess a problem, define it in engineering terms, and negotiate the terms and scope of the project with a supervisor;

b. apply academic knowledge to the formulation of possible solutions;

c. evaluate the feasible solutions and choose a realistic and effective solution;

d. produce a detailed design within the constraints of available components and the characteristics of real devices;

e. develop, integrate, prototype or otherwise show the feasibility of a design;

f. measure the performance of the product against the design specifications, and;

g. communicate status at all stages of the project, both orally and in written form.

Preliminary work on the project is completed during the fall term. This includes a statement of work, a performance specification, and a proposed testing plan. A review of the applicable literature and formulation of an action plan are required. The winter term is given over to completing the design, and to constructing, testing, evaluating and documenting the solution. This course reinforces the engineering approach to software.

3.6 Software Engineering I

This is the cornerstone of the six software courses. The two software courses in third year lead up to it, and it is the basis for the remaining three courses. The approach is to teach specific techniques for the different stages of a conventional software process in the first 60% of the course, using small examples to illustrate each technique, and then to spend the remaining 40% of the course on a larger example to illustrate more clearly how and why the techniques become more important as the system gets larger.

The general approach is motivated by the work of David Parnas (e.g. [2]). The course was described at this conference last year [3]. A version of the course has been taught at the University of Victoria for the past 7 years, and it was taught for the first time at RMC in 1991/92. A text for the course will be available in 1994 [4].

Topics covered include: The software engineering problem. The search for approaches that will provide an order of magnitude improvement in productivity. Mathematical logic as a basis for specification. The importance of reviews and inspections to improve productivity. An overview of software development approaches. A rational software process: requirements, decomposition into modules using the information hiding principle, module interface specifications based on mathematical logic and abstract state, program specifications using predicates on concrete state expressed as variables in a particular language, implementation, test plans, testing using a testing tool. Criteria for module interface design. Language support for modules. Modules as finite state machines.

3.7 Software Engineering II

This course offers a selection of topics in software engineering. It is closer to traditional courses in software engineering offered in many computer curricula. There is some discussion of data flow and other diagram based methods of software design, primarily on the basis that the students should be aware of these methods, and know their limitations.

Topics covered include: Software process models and alternative steps in the process, including prototyping. Reusable components. Changing software in response to new requirements. Software maintenance and reverse engineering. Version control and configuration management. Software metrics. Predicting reliability. Trustworthy vs reliable software. Tools that support software development.

3.8 Object-Oriented Techniques

The aim of this course is to expose the student to the object-oriented paradigm. The modules introduced in Software Engineering I are really objects by another name, but the focus there is on mathematically based specification techniques, while the focus in this course is on analysis, design, implementation, and relationships among objects. The student learns how to break down a problem using object-oriented analysis, with an emphasis on the management of complexity in the problem domain using data and procedural abstraction, encapsulation, and association. The analyzed problem domain gives way to an engineered software solution using object-oriented design. Design trade-offs involving performance, code reuse, and clarity are discussed. Students use the C++ programming language to acquire practical experience in the implementation of object-oriented designs.

Students are introduced to the concepts of multiple inheritance and polymorphism. Other topics covered include linking analysis to design, design criteria for class coupling, cohesion, and clarity, and criteria for the selection of object-oriented languages. There is also some material on such diverse topics as human-computer interaction and task management (identifying event-driven tasks, identifying clock-driven tasks, priority tasks, identifying a coordinator, real-time issues)

3.9 Real-Time Embedded System Design

A course of this kind appears fairly frequently in computer engineering programs. The students taking the curriculum described in this paper exceptionally well prepared for this kind of course. The major weakness of this area, inevitably reflected in any course, is a lack of well-established mathematically based methods to deal with the timing properties of real-time computer systems. In practice, timing behaviour is usually dealt with after implementation, and problems are solved by tweaking the code, reducing functionality, or using faster processors. This course largely reflects that practice, although a variety of emerging techniques are being considered for inclusion in the course. Among these techniques are language based techniques for schedulability analysis, rate monotonic analysis, and static scheduling techniques.

Topics covered include: Definition, structure, and properties of embedded real-time systems. Typical applications. Review of related concepts, including tasking models, context switching, interrupts, and the Ada rendezvous. Specification and design methods for real-time systems. Applicable CASE (Computer-Aided-Software-Engineering) tools. Specification and verification of timing. Scheduling and schedulability analysis. Real-time operating systems, kernels, and programming languages. Fault tolerance, critical races, deadlock and livelock. Host-target development. Distributed systems.

4 Laboratory Work

Practical laboratory work is a major part of the work required in all of the courses described above. Typically, two to three weeks are allocated for each of five or six laboratory projects. Projects are often done in groups of two or three students, with the aim of giving the students experience in working as members of a team.

5 Alternatives and reasons for choices

VLSI Design is opposite Object Oriented Techniques (OOT) at the point where the hardware and software streams split in the fall term of fourth year. The reason is interesting: both courses are perceived as being very popular. For students with a hardware bent, the VLSI course integrates many of the courses that they have taken up to that time. For students interested in software, the opportunity to learn more about inheritance, polymorphism and C++ is attractive. There was some pressure to use Smalltalk in the OOT course, on the basis that it makes OO concepts clearer. On the other hand, there are those who feel that inheritance and polymorphism as presented in Smalltalk are not essential to the use of objects in software development, and some of that point of view is part of the OOT course as well, reinforced by the student's knowledge of Ada. Ada 9X will be considered for future versions of the course.

An alternative considered for the OOT course was a language paradigms course. The main difficulty was that language paradigm courses seem either to spread themselves thinly among many languages used as examples, or to choose a single language like LISP to illustrate all the paradigms. Neither alternative is attractive in an engineering context.

Many courses that are standard in computer science programs do not appear in this program. A few, like computer graphics and data base management, are available choices for the elective course in fourth year. The main reasons for this decision are that the space is filled with more traditional engineering courses, and if expertise in these other areas is needed, the graduates of this program will be able to work with graduates of computer science programs.

A future potential modification to the six courses presently offered is to find a place for a software architecture course [5]. The problem is that this would mean cutting out something else, or putting software architecture among the group of courses like computer graphics and data bases, of which the student can choose just one. The problem with the latter alternative is that only the students in the software engineering stream would have the necessary background to take the course, and they would then not have a final year elective if they chose to take software architecture. Another alternative is to put some software architecture material into Software Engineering II.

The notations and concepts of mathematical logic are introduced as needed in the other courses. If there were space, it would be better to have a course on mathematical logic for software engineers, since it is not part of traditional engineering mathematics. There is little need to teach finite automata, as the students are exposed to finite state machines in other courses.

The optional control course in third year is intended to be taken by all students taking the software option. The materials science course complements the VLSI course.

6 Textbooks and Tools

It will come as no surprise that the textbook situation is generally unsatisfactory for all of these courses. For example, in the computer program design course, there is a large selection of Pascal based texts for the data structures and algorithms part of the course, but no satisfactory Ada based text has been found. The Pascal based texts tend not to deal with the software engineering issues that can be illustrated using Ada.

In some of the courses, there are as many as five texts. This is an indication of the unconventional nature of these courses, and of the immaturity of the field. In some cases, the only alternative available is to use a collection of papers and professor's notes. A new text will be used this fall for Software Engineering I, which will improve matters for that course [4].

On the hardware side of computer engineering, the design tool support is excellent. The main tool is the Mentor Graphics package, which is used in a number of courses. On the software side, standard tools like editors, browsers and compilers are available, but they are of limited value in doing design. Many of the design tools (CASE tools) that are available on the software side are of questionable usefulness in the software stream. In some cases, exposure to CASE tools helps students to understand the underlying weaknesses of the design techniques supported by the tools, and to see first hand the lack of support provided for the whole design process. The students love to use debugging tools, but they are taught to avoid them if at all possible once they have mastered a language, and to use inspection instead, followed by testing. A testing tool developed at the University of Victoria is used for module testing. Tools in other areas, like configuration management and documentation support prior to coding, are almost entirely lacking for the approaches taught.

7 Certification Issues

Engineering certification is important for safety critical systems. The RMC baccalaureate degree programs in Electrical and Computer Engineering are accredited by the Canadian Engineering Accreditation Board of the Canadian Council of Professional Engineers. There is no certification of the software stream, although it is assumed that it will be acceptable when RMC is next accredited in the fall of 1993. The engineering community has generally viewed programming as being like drafting, and so has been reluctant to give engineering credentials to computer science programs. This is slowly changing.

Change is slow because the software engineering field is not ready for accreditation, since agreement on what constitutes the basic core of material to be taught at the undergraduate level has yet to be reached. The change may come about in computer engineering since making the transition from accreditation in one area (computer engineering) to accreditation in another (software engineering) may be easier than it would be to get acceptance of engineering accreditation for computer science.

8 Conclusion

While it is still too early to seriously propose an undergraduate degree in software engineering, the curriculum discussed in this paper goes some distance in that direction for the particular branch of software engineering concerned with the development of embedded systems. There is in fact a terminology problem, as there really is no single discipline of software engineering. People who develop MIS systems for business use would find many of the courses presented in this curriculum unnecessary, and would need many courses not presented here. For software systems that are safety critical, the designer must be willing to accept responsibility in the same way that a civil engineer accepts responsibility for the design of a bridge. The curriculum presented in this paper improves the qualifications of individuals to accept such responsibility, but better design techniques are needed, particularly with respect to the real time behaviour of software. Extending a software engineering competence to other branches of engineering appears to require an additional qualification beyond the bachelor's level, as there is not enough flexibility in traditional engineering programs to accommodate more software courses. This suggests that graduate programs in software engineering should be available for students who do not have an undergraduate computing degree.

References

[1] David Lorge Parnas, "Education for Computing Professionals", IEEE Computer, V. 23, No. 1, January 1990, pp. 17-23

[2] David Lorge Parnas and Paul Clements, "A Rational Design Process: How and Why to Fake It", IEEE Transactions on Software Engineering, V. SE-12, N. 2, February 1986, pp. 251-257

[3] Terry Shepard and Dan Hoffman, "On Teaching the Rational Design Process", Proceedings of the 1992 SEI Conference on Software Engineering Education, San Diego, October 1992, Springer Verlag, LNCS V. 640, pp. 44-62

[4] Daniel Hoffman and Paul Strouper, Software Design and Verification, to be published by McGraw Hill

[5] David Garlan, Mary Shaw, Chris Okasaki, Curtis M. Scott and Roy F. Swonger, "Experience with a Course on Architectures for Software Systems", Proceedings of the 1992 SEI Conference on Software Engineering Education, San Diego, October 1992, Springer Verlag, LNCS V. 640, pp. 23-43

When the Golden Arches Gang Aft Agley: Incorporating Software Engineering into Computer Science

Kenneth L. Modesitt, Ph.D.

Head, Department of Computer Science
Western Kentucky University
Bowling Green, KY 42101

"Press On: Nothing in the world
can take the place of
PERSISTENCE.
• Talent will not -- Nothing is more
  common than unsuccessful men [sic]
  with talent.
• Genius will not -- Unrewarded
  genius is almost a proverb.
• Education alone will not -- The world
  is full of educated derelicts.
Persistence and determination alone
are omnipotent."
      [McDonald's Ad, 1989]

"But Mousie, thou art no thy lane,
In proving foresight may be vain;
The best-laid schemes o' mice an' men
   Gang aft agley,
An' lea'e us nought but grief an' pain,
   For promis'd joy!
      [5]

Abstract. The incorporation of software engineering into an existing university computer science curriculum involves major cultural and content changes. Considerable persistence is required (note the golden arches), yet even the best laid plans do not always suffice (note quotation from famous poem by Burns). This is particularly true for those departments which have a strong mathematics emphasis -- a common phenomenon in many comprehensive universities (M.S. granting) today. Despite the major challenges involved in such change, the rewards are many. The beneficiaries include: current students, graduates, employers, computer science faculty, the university. and society.

Significant aspects of cultural change are discussed: stimulus, rewards, change types, impact on courses, continuation requirements, and required resources. Examples of the last item include: Professional Advisory Board, Student Advisory Board, industry experience for faculty, state-of-the-art tools from industry-$110,000, capital funds from the university-$60,000, and capital funds from industry-$20,000.

OUTLINE

1. Current program
2. Stimulus for change
3. Rewards for change
   Student
   Graduate
   Faculty
   Western Kentucky University
   Employer
   Society
4. Change requirements
   Entire software lifecycle
   Program management skills
   Advanced software tools: types, vendor-supplied, extent of use
   Teamwork
   Communication skills
5. Impact of change requirements on specific courses
   CS 1
   CS 2
   CS 3
   Software Engineering I
   Software Engineering II
   Research Methods
   All Courses following SWE I
6. Continuation requirements
   Faculty enthusiasm and flexibility
   Three options for majors
   Mathematics and statistics
   Technical writing
   Introductory course on computer science discipline
7. Required resources
   Counsel and advice
   Software tools
   Hardware platforms
   Faculty
   Space
   Instructional materials
8. Summary

1 Current Program

The Department of Computer Science at Western Kentucky University was established in 1983, after being part of the Department of Mathematics and Computer Science, and the Department of Mathematics before that since 1971. It currently enrolls about 250 undergraduate majors, and has about 25 students seeking a M.S. degree. The total number of graduates is approaching 500, virtually all employed in industry, and scattered over 27 states and 8 countries.

The program requires 40 hours of coursework in computer science as of 1991, as a requirement for CSAB accreditation (site visit was in October, 1992). There are three options at the undergraduate level: scientific applications, business applications, and systems. The systems and scientific ones require a mathematics minor, whereas the business one requires the first calculus course.

The original faculty were primarily Ph.D.s in Mathematics, with one early C.S. Ph. D. (1971) being a founding member. In the last two years, two new assistant professors have been added, both with a Ph.D. in C.S. The department head (the author) arrived in 1988 with a Ph.D. in C.S. (1972).

2 Stimulus for Change

Software engineering is a required skill of computer science students. The Bureau of Labor Statistics predicts a demand for 900,000 by 1995, vs. a supply of only 600,000. Customers world-wide in business, industry, and government are applying considerable pressure to software developers. Such customers want powerful, reliable, easy-to-use software products to be developed and maintained within reasonable costs and time. People have similar expectations for other products, such as computers, bridges, aircraft, VCRs, etc.. Therefore, they are not terribly interested in our replies of "but we are very new at this!" Perhaps we should stop considering software as a product, and re-think our paradigm as a service, as one author has recently suggested [23].

Many people and agencies tell us of the importance of software engineering proficiency for our students. Specific examples include alumni, employers (of graduates and cooperative education students), professional advisory boards, professional organizations (ACM), and accrediting agencies (professional such as the Computing Sciences Accreditation Board, and regional such as the Southern Association of Schools and Colleges) [6, 22]. We have a professional responsibility as academics to let the people and agencies know what we can do in response, given the state-of-the-art and other constraints. That is, we can use the engineering method and tell them of our "strategy for causing the best change in a poorly understood or uncertain situation within available resources" [13, 14].

This stimulus is already well understood at the graduate level in computer science. Two of the three post-graduate institutions of the author now offer a M.S. in software engineering. Others, such as St. Thomas and the University of Houston, are also appearing.

3 Rewards for Change

Who benefits from the incorporation of software engineering into the curriculum of a computer science department? There are six entities which accrue advantages: current students, graduates, faculty, the university, employers, and society.

3.1 Rewards for the Students

She benefits immediately upon learning and using new software engineering skills. Within the current course, she will be able to become both more effective and efficient, including abilities to:

> give better estimates of required resources,
> concentrate more on analysis and design rather than coding,
> look for available and reusable components,
> manage her time more effectively,
> participate as a member of a successful team,
> become involved in all phases of the software development life cycle
> (analysis, design, code, documentation, testing, quality, etc.) as
> either a developer or as part of an inspection team,
> choose/use appropriate software tools, e.g., CASE, project management,
> be aware of potential risks in the final product and will have
> notified the user/manager, and
> be aware of and use underlying theory, as understood in class and in
> the professional literature.

The rewards to the student will accrue most quickly the earlier she is introduced to and uses the state-of-the-art practices in software engineering. CS 1 and CS 2 are certainly *not* too early for practicing most of the skills planning, time management, teams, tools, etc.

In the software engineering courses, all of the above objectives are emphasized. Projects are chosen so that the students have the widest possible exposure to all the skills required throughout the entire software cycle, including reverse software engineering. See Appendix A for course objectives, syllabus, and projects. Teams are typically of the size likely in industry (four to five), and project management qualities are practiced. The front end of the lifecycle includes needs assessment, feasibility, RFPs, proposals, etc. CASE tools are used and evaluated extensively.

3.2 Rewards for the Graduates

The graduates of a computer science program in which software engineering has been incorporated have a far better chance of becoming employed in the career of their choice soon after graduation. They will have demonstrated a firm grasp of the theoretical areas of computer science, as well as the engineering concerns of producing a reliable and useful artifact within available resources. Many of the standard methods, processes, and tools used by professional software engineers will be part of the toolkit of our new graduates. Therefore they will feel they are contributing sooner and more effectively.

Surveys of our alumni have been used to ascertain their success in this area.

3.3   Rewards for the Computer Science Faculty

Faculty will gain first-hand experience in the development and use of software within industry as a result of taking advantage of sabbaticals, externships, summer programs with industry and government, and other similar programs.   They will have the opportunity to see the role of software engineering in current software development, and to note any deficiencies. They could then consult on other, perhaps better, methods. They can prepare and present related professional works.   Grants from the cooperating industries could be used to support graduate students, professional workshops, or as seed for larger grant competition, e.g., NSF and NASA. Such research and scholarly activity is receiving increased emphasis in universities, even comprehensive ones, and is a larger factor in promotion and tenure.

Because faculty will have had hands-on industry experience, they can assign more realistic projects and homework, *and* be able to assist their students.   Also, their students will have had previous experience with planning, controlling and developing more sophisticated systems.   More demanding assignments will accomplished successfully.   So, although faculty are being encouraged to perform scholarly research, they are likewise expected to be very good teachers.   Collaboration with industry promotes both!

3.4   Rewards for the University

Alumni who are excellent performers for their employers provide multiple rewards to Western Kentucky University.   Some alumni, believing they have received a quality education in computer science, will contribute financially for equipment and scholarships. The employers likewise are more likely to provide fiscal assistance.   Faculty who generate peer-reviewed publications are increased assets to the university.   Service by faculty to the local and regional software developers and users also strengthens the role in the community.

3.5   Rewards for the Employer

The learning curve for our graduates with software engineering experience will be shorter. They will become more productive, and at a faster rate, than those with no such experience.   They will understand and use the important skills of teamwork, advanced tools, management and communication, lifecycles, and software quality assurance.   The graduates will be prepared to assume additional technical and/or managerial responsibilities more readily.

Numerous studies show employers have expectations which our graduates meet [8, 19]. Such studies show that an educated graduate is highly-valued. Training is also of interest. Training is the acquisition of specific skills, usually transient, necessary to perform given tasks of interest to the employer.   The software industry really does understand the similarities and distinctions between education and training.   Consequently, they do not expect our graduates to be "up-to-speed" on every aspect of a particular, perhaps unique, approach to software development. They fully expect to train new graduates in specific areas.

Graduates will also have additional expectations of their employer, i.e., assistance with advanced education, professional development opportunities, multiple-track career paths, access to state-of-the-art tools, good libraries, challenging assignments, and professional supervisors. Surveys of employers will be used to ascertain success.

3.6 Rewards for Society

Our graduates with software engineering backgrounds will be contributing, self-sufficient, and interdependent members of society. The products they build will be higher quality (e.g., less susceptible to failure), and thus the cost to society will be less. This is the "best" definition of quality seen to date by this author.

"Quality is the cost to society after the product is shipped (or service rendered)." [24]

A very recent major event is of special import to software development. The Technology Reinvestment Project is to "stimulate the transition to a growing, integrated, national industrial capability which provides the most advanced, affordable, military systems and the most competitive commercial products." [25] One of the major technology focus areas is "software development methods, tools, and environments." This entire effort involves collaboration among higher education, industry and major agencies of the federal government.

4 Change Requirements Across the Curriculum

The incorporation of software engineering into a computer science curriculum is quite different than simply adding a course on graphics. Although the approval process is the same for the two courses, the changes are far more substantive, more likely to encounter resistance; hence the requirement to be extremely patient, diligent and persistent, just as the McDonald's quotation indicates. The major changes include increasing the emphasis on the following: complete software lifecycle, project management skills, state-of-the-art software tools, teams, and communication skills.

4.1 Complete Software Lifecycle

There has been much written about the lifecycle, so there is little point of repeating it here. Pressman gives a good overview in his excellent textbook [21]. Only a few highlights are pointed out. One variant is given in Figure 1.

41

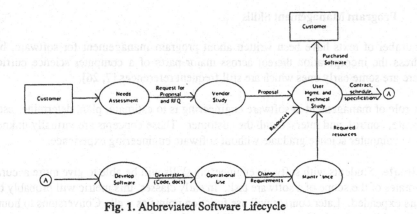

Fig. 1. Abbreviated Software Lifecycle

Figure 2 shows a current snapshot of effort spent on the software lifecycle, once a decision is made to build the product.

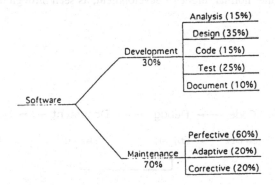

Fig. 2. Time Allocation for Software Development/Maintenance

Students will understand that programming qua coding is a very small and shrinking component of the software lifecycle. The role of coding stressed so heavily in education of 10-30 years ago pales quickly with quantum increases in memory size and processor speed. To be sure, size and speed are important, but it is no longer appropriate to sacrifice other software qualities for their sake, e.g., maintainability, reliability, ease-of-use, etc. Students will encounter, first-hand, the expensive problems our previous emphasis on coding has caused, in terms of difficult-to-maintain systems. Consequently, they will understand the increased emphasis on analysis and design.

Students will also understand that we do not, in fact *must not*, start from scratch in each and every development effort. What engineering products would exist today if our predecessors made no use of reusable components for bridges, planes, computers, skyscrapers, power plants, cars, etc.? The dramatic increase in object-oriented methodologies will be apparent.

Finally, the critical role of designing software to be easy-to-change will be emphasized. The dominant role of perfective maintenance is ample evidence of the dire need to design for change. This is a distinguishing feature of software and will not be extinguished with a "silver bullet" [3].

4.2   Program Management Skills

A number of texts have been written about program management for software, but few address the incorporation thereof across major parts of a computer science curriculum. There are some early ones which are still frequent references [7, 26].

The role of management in software engineering is to estimate, plan, determine resources, allocate, control, and interact with the customer. These concepts are virtually unknown to a new computer science graduate without software engineering experience.

Estimate. Students with software engineering skills will be able to give more accurate estimates of the scope of a software task. In early classes, this metric will probably be hours expended. Later courses will use function points as well. Conversions to hours, days, and line of code if appropriate, will be made as well.

Plan. Planning which tasks are necessary for successful development will be an acquired skill. See Figure 3 for the "normal" mode of development, as seen through the eyes of a beginning student.

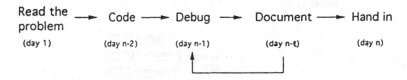

Fig. 3. "Normal" student view of software life cycle

It is obvious that this is inexcusable and woefully inadequate, even for a beginning student. The steps of the software lifecycle as discussed earlier will be detailed, and several processes will be added: risk analysis, management (progress and final report, lessons learned), SQA, and configuration management. Where appropriate, requests for proposals (RFPs and RFQs), proposals, and contracts will be used. The role of risk assessment, including contingency plans, will receive special consideration, esp. since it is probably missing from their previous experience. The admonition of Burns from many years before still holds true: "the best laid plans o' mice and [software engineers] gang aft agley." Students will understand the importance of heuristics and uncertainty inherent in this non-algorithmic process.

Determine resources. The students, as a team, will determine various resources available to them. Engineering judgement for this task will begin to accrue over time. Such resources include: customer (e.g., instructor), calendar time, individual skills, communication modes (phone, bulletin boards, e-mail), methods, and tools (languages, operating systems, hardware, debuggers, profilers, metric evaluators, CASE, program management, fourth generation languages, knowledge-based systems for prototyping, and libraries -- both program and university types).

Allocate tasks to resources. Allocation of tasks to the various resources is a key management step. Students will make use of standard formats such as person- loading tables, Gantt charts, work breakdown structures, person- loading vs. phase graphs, etc. These will be used to schedule people, tasks, computer resources, tools, and other resources such that the final reliable product is delivered to the customer on time and within budget.

Control process. Controlling the development process is a major management responsibility. Keeping individuals on track, providing assistance when they veer is critical. Ensuring a continuing means for customer input is essential. Internal progress reports, based on individual logbooks, must occur periodically to lessen unwelcome surprises.

Interact with the customer. The importance of maintaining close contact with the customer cannot be underestimated. Numerous studies have shown the expensive tragedies which befall developers who fail in this critical arena. Therefore, project teams develop a strong sense of responsibility for this task. One of the most obvious is during the final report presentation to the customer, with a prototype demonstration, validation testing and other contract deliverables. The contract deliverables normally include the following: program source code, executable code, documentation (user -- hard copy and on-line, installation, maintenance, design and analysis -- CASE format), and training plan. The final oral presentation includes the following: final cost and schedule, anomalies, lessons learned (including accuracy of risk analysis) and product demonstration.

4.3   State-of-the-Art Software Tools

Current use of state-of-the-art software tools is very limited in computer science courses. This section addresses several issues related to the shortcoming and how it may be overcome. After a short introduction on types of tools, a tactic for acquiring such tools is given, involving careful planning and thoughtful vendors. Finally, the issue of software tools, qua tools, for computer science faculty who have a strong mathematics background is addressed.

Types of tools. Currently, it is common for students in their first software engineering course to have previous primary experience only with tools of the same genre experienced by students in the 1970s -- a tragic commentary. These include Pascal, data structures and assembly language for the IBM 360/370. That is, the formal requirements are CS1, CS2 and CS3. Because only three courses are prerequisites, the software tools which are familiar to all students are also limited. These are compilers, assemblers, operating systems (VMS, CMS, and maybe DOS), editors, and perhaps some debuggers. Perhaps we should require additional courses, but to do so would delay the software engineering course, and work against our desire to incorporate the objectives thereof as soon as possible in the curriculum. Another option is to make use of sophisticated tools in CS1, CS2, and CS3. See Section 5.

The above list of compilers, etc. is simply not adequate for computer science students, let alone graduates. The use of tools in the software industry has grown rapidly in the last decade, and we must be more responsive to our customers. Example areas of advanced tools include: libraries of reusable components, user interface prototyping, metric analyzers, profilers, 4GLs, structured analysis and structured design tools, SA to SD converters, code generators, dynamic analyzers, expert system building tools, configuration management, test harnesses, test generators, regression testing, program management, presentation graphics, computer-baced training and of course word processors! Any recent copy of any professional software engineering periodical will list articles on these and many more.

Vendor-supplied tools. Can computer science graduates be expected to have working knowledge of all of these advanced software tools? It is doubtful, and certainly not as a result of one software engineering course. However, our graduates should have hands-on experience with most of these, and in a wide variety of courses. Consequently, over $110,000 worth of state-of-the-art software tools from 39 vendors has been obtained at *no cost* to the university. See Appendix B.

The arrangement with each vendor is for students in one or more courses to evaluate formally several of these tools, write a formal evaluation of the product, and submit it to the vendor. The Multi Element Component Comparison Analysis (MECCA) model of Tom Gilb has been used with considerable success for such evaluations over a period of several years [9]. The instructor also receives a copy to grade, after the student gives a formal class presentation. The vendor then responds, often by sending an updated version. It is frequently the case that student recommendations appear as features in the new version. This "win-win" same process of departmental-vendor cooperation has been used since 1984 at two different universities. *Not once* has a vendor recalled a product!

The CASE and program management tools receive the most use in the software engineering course. This is appropriate as the course emphasizes analysis, design, and management skills. Were the course structured more along the lines of a single large project, as Bruegge describes [4], a wider suite would be employed, esp. testing and configuration management ones.

Extent of tool use. The department has often addressed a "meta" question re: the use of software tools, other than the standard ones used for the last 20 years, in our courses. There is little doubt that other universities face similar concerns. There are two issues involved:

> 1. science "vs." engineering and
> 2. computer science "vs." management information systems.

Science "vs." engineering: In a computer science department which grew primarily out of the mathematics discipline, it has been difficult for such faculty to encourage students to make use of advanced tools as quickly as those faculty who also have an engineering background. [As a footnote, the recent advent of Mathematica has turned this around for many math departments!] There is a persistent belief that students must create these self-same tools from scratch -- an approach which is definitely not engineering oriented. The "truth," as perceived by the author, is for students and faculty throughout the curriculum to: use existing state-of-the-art software tools, evaluate them and determine weaknesses and strengths, be able to extend the tool features (maybe do so later), and determine new tools required for new areas of computer science.

The famous quote by Richard Hamming, as heard by the author at the Fall Joint Computer Conference in 1968, is appropriate here.

> "In other professions, they build on each other's shoulders; in computer science we build on each other's toes!"

Let's not build on toes in the future. A decade ago, the author recommended the following strategy: "Give powerful tools to creative people and stand back" [17]. The recommendation is even stronger today!

Computer science "vs." management information systems (MIS): The other reason for hesitancy in using state-of-the-art tools in computer science courses may be a local anomaly, but has been noticed in several universities. When the computer science department at Western Kentucky University was being formed, the MIS discipline wanted some portions of the program. There is a perception that MIS is primarily a user of software tools for business, whereas computer science is a builder of software tools. Again, the "truth" is that computer science is indeed a builder of state-of-the-art software tools, in conjunction with users. However, to become the best possible developer, computer science students must be aware of and use existing state-of-the-art software tools. Tony Hoare made this same point about use of tools almost two decades ago in an excellent article about software engineering.

> "An engineer respects his tools and demands from them the highest precision, convenience, quality, and reliability." [10]

4.4 Teamwork in Software Development

The day of the guru who single-handedly and on-time developed a software system for the customer is history. With few exceptions, it is improbable that the system had the complexity and reliability requirements of large systems today. True, she probably completed the final integration testing the night before the due date, as noted in so many humorous tidbits. This phenomenon was very much a part of our past over the last 30 years, and can be vouched for, based on personal employment experience with four major software developers.

However, it is not the way successful systems are developed today. Current software systems are built by teams of developers. Any software professional today will confirm this, including the Professional Advisory Board at Western Kentucky University. Our hundreds of alumni also provide ample evidence in their returned surveys. National and international journals and conferences abound with evidence that successful software today is developed in a team environment.

It is therefore, not a great leap of faith to suggest that students in a computer science curriculum should have a wide variety of team experiences. These can and should occur in all three courses which are prerequisites to the software engineering course: CS1, CS2, and CS3. See section 5.

When students who have been through a CS1,2,3 sequence with such a recommended background reach the software engineering course, they would have ample evidence that coding is not the same as software development, an all-too-common current myth. The myth is alive and well in several of our students. As an example of how one student sees computer science, after completing the first three courses, his (abbreviated) answer to a final exam question from the software engineering course in the spring of 1992 is given below.

> Q: "What is the difference between software engineering and computer science?"

> A: "Computer science just deals with programming. CS people just get a project and work on it... Software engineers first meet with a customer to define the project objectives and scope..."

Students entering the software engineering course would be well- prepared to concentrate on the front end of the software lifecycle. They would have good experiences with the technical parts of the back end of the cycle and be familiar with the advantages (many!) and disadvantages (few) of teamwork.

Unfortunately, the "what is" snapshot of prerequisite courses differs from the "what should be" scenario. Our current students have virtually no formal team experiences prior to the software engineering course (even though some are graduating seniors!). Collaboration had usually been discouraged, for fear of being accused of plagiarism by faculty. Obviously, collaboration should probably be discouraged on examinations and individually- assigned projects. Moreover, most current students do not understand the role of design-prior-to-coding, and of black box testing. Nor are they familiar with documentation, other than internal coding style conventions.

However, they are bright, industrious, and creative, so we work with where they are, not where we wish they were.

How is a team selected? It is *not* by pairing those who happen to sit together on the first day of class! At the beginning of the term, the students work on a small project with one or two others. Each student does an exercise telling of her background, schedule, and computing equipment. Later, they prepare resumes and fill out applications for a fictitious software development company (owned by the instructor). A formal interview is held and they specify what role in the development process they prefer and which they do not want to do. Later, they are asked with whom they would like to work, and with whom they do not want to work. The instructor then makes team assignments for the first large projects based on these and other factors, e.g., year in school, cooperative education experience, personalities, etc. For the last project, the students can choose their own teammates. A thoughtful monograph on cooperative learning at the university level gives several excellent additional techniques for forming teams [11].

By the end of the term, students are very convinced of the essential nature of teamwork skills. They have no trouble believing Boehm's findings that team makeup is the biggest contributor to software productivity, after the size of the product 2].

A related phenomena, noticed over 25 years of using teams, is the close personal relationships often generated as a result. On several occasions, graduates and other students have returned to relate that they began close friendships during the intense team projects. Several actually were married and continue to send holiday greeting cards!

4.5 Communication Skills

Both written and oral communication skills are used extensively in a software engineering course. The communication occurs among students as they play the roles of client, employer, manager, employee, and peer, so they have ample opportunity to practice!

Upon completion of the software engineering course, students have had extensive practice in communicating with others. The personal experience of the author in industry and field trips to local industry are convincing testimony to the essential nature of such a skill. Students, upon graduation, will use the skills to persuade decision makers in industry regarding a product or creative idea. This importance is reinforced constantly by our Professional Advisory Board, alumni, employers, and professional publications. In fact, the department has felt so strongly about communication skills that it has required a technical writing course, requiring oral presentations, of all majors since 1983.

Students gain many valuable insights by "walking in the shoes of another," both as a customer and a project manager. As a project manager, they deal with employees (fellow team members) who do not show up for scheduled meetings, or are late with their development component, or who have a family or work emergency. Similarly, as a customer, they see exactly what can happen when a developer does not meet contract requirements, is late or over-budget in product delivery, gives a sloppy presentation, does not solicit customer input for long periods of time, or gives lame excuses for product reliability.

In addition to formal communication modes, informal ones also play a vital role. Electronic mail among team members and/or a bulletin board between customer and developer are such examples. A detailed log of all activities is required of each student, and reviewed at random intervals by the instructor.

Formal presentations to the customer are stressed. These include: initial contract, progress report, final report, lessons learned, and product demonstration. A video tape is made of the final presentation, and is put on reserve for future classes, as well as to aid in evaluation.

5   Impact of Change Requirements on Specific Courses

Prerequisite courses to the software engineering course are CS1, CS2, and CS3.

5.1 CS1 (Algorithms)

Team experiences can begin at the CS1 level with a team of two: one who designs an algorithm, and the other who codes from the design. Another assignment would have the students switch roles, and add a third member in charge of testing. This testing would be done at a functional level (black-box), as well as at code level (white-box). The latter would be performed after the code is written, but before execution. Variations on this theme would have all of the team participate in inspections at all levels: design, code, and testing. In this way, some aspects of software quality assurance (SQA) would become second nature by the end of the course. The "cute" idea of software bugs would be replaced by preventing defects, i.e., a failure which is not so cute! Software quality would begin to receive a natural emphasis in this very first course.

5.2 CS2 (Data Structures) and CS3 (Assembly Language)

The skills mentioned for CS1 would continue to be emphasized. Additionally, the concept of reusability is introduced. Packages for various data structures are perfect examples and easily modularized. An introduction to object-oriented design and programming is a good fit here. The maintenance portion of the lifecyle can be addressed easily in a small team environment. Have one team develop a set of queue routines for the VAX. The other team would exercise adaptive maintenance and port these packages to Turbo Pascal on a personal computer. After downloading, any changes required would be noted. These could include the code as well as all documentation (installation, user, design, and test). The extent of such changes could be a factor in the grade of the first team.

In all three courses which are prerequisites to the software engineering one, a team of students could develop a small stand-alone application. Another small team would then evaluate the system with respect to criteria such as: ease of installation, ease of learning, ease of use (user interface), adequacy of documentation, ease of maintenance (adaptive, corrective, perfective), software reuse, power, and efficiency (speed and size).

For the CS3 Assembly language course, PC assembly language could be used and then offer IBM 360/370 assembly language as a bi-term (8 week) course afterwards. This would reflect the vast increase in PC use.

5.3 CS 360: Software Engineering I

See Appendix A for a complete syllabus, objectives, and projects.
The objectives of this first course are to:
1. add skills missing from earlier courses, where the backend of the lifecycle was emphasized,
2. introduce front-end skills (needs assessment, customer, analysis, analysis-to-design),
3. involve extensive team experiences,
4. involve extensive hands-on CASE experiences,
5. demonstrate the vital importance of frequent customer interaction,
6. exercise communication skills extensively,

7. emphasize the many aspects of software quality, and
8. practice management skills.

5.4 CS 460: Software Engineering II

This is a follow-on course requiring software engineering I as a prerequisite. It has not yet been taught at this university, so only the catalog copy is given here.

> "An example of the critical theoretical problems underlying software engineering, including the rigorous treatment of software metrics, cost-estimating, object-oriented design, real-time systems, automatic programming, reliability and software safety, and verification and validation."

5.5 CS 476/G: Research Methods

This is a follow-on course requiring software engineering I as a prerequisite. Students do an entire project from conception to delivery, as recommended in the recent article by Bruegge. This course has been taught many times over the years, covering a wide variety of topics, e.g., object-oriented vs. classical development techniques, graphics, simulation, etc. The catalog copy is reproduced here.

> "The languages, programming techniques and skills acquired in the sequence of core courses in the undergraduate program are applied to the analysis and design of computer-based systems. Top-down design techniques are applied in one or more large-scale programs which require attention to the documentation, communication, and interfacing or modules in a team project. These techniques are essential in most large-scale research applications of computers."

5.6 General Suggestions for all Follow-on Courses

Such courses, in addition to the two above, include artificial intelligence, data base management systems, and operating systems. The suggestions are numerous: utilize more team development to reflect realistic industry practice; allocate more class time to collaborative learning and less to lecture; utilize more state-of-the-art software tools, e.g., CASE; use library resources extensively, esp. current periodicals and conferences; require more writing and oral communication; have students submit papers to professional conferences; encourage more independent study and practicum and cooperative education courses; increase the use of object-oriented methods (analysis, design, programming); add a course on human-computer interaction, esp. graphic user interfaces; exercise the analysis component of software development prior to design; try to involve real customers, e.g., for courses on data bases, graphics, advanced data structures; consider lowering the graduate-level course on mathematical foundations for undergraduates; beef up a follow-on graduate-level course on mathematical foundations; strengthen the theory component of all computer science courses, esp. as it might relate to software engineering.

6 Continuation Requirements

Kaufman writes of the need for "continuation requirements" as well as "change requirements" in order to move from "what is" to "what should be" [12]. That is, not everything is broken, so decisions must be made about what is being done correctly at the current time. These are some suggestions re: the current computer science program:

1. Maintain enthusiastic, diligent, flexible, competent full-time faculty.
2. Maintain the three options for undergraduate majors.
3. Maintain the math minor for systems and scientific options.
4. Strengthen the statistics component.
5. Keep the technical writing requirement.
6. Keep the new course on Introduction to Computer Science, as a way of showing that computer science is not equal to software engineering is not equal to coding.

7 Required Resources to Affect the Desired Changes

A number of resources are required, in order to bring about the changes necessary to incorporate software engineering into the existing computer science curriculum. These vary in type and source. By now, the reader is aware that the incorporation of software engineering into the curriculum involves considerably more than the relatively straight-forward process associated with adding a new course to a university catalog. Software engineering is considerably more pervasive. Consequently, the required resources are also more significant than adding a few books to the library.

The resources required include: counsel, tools, hardware, faculty, space, and instructional material. The format for most of them is in a simple form, listing the resource required and the supply sources thereof.

7.1 Counsel

We require lots! Otherwise, we will be in a similar situation to the marvelous horse-shoe maker who was the world's most productive producer, until one day, there was no market for the product! We would ignore outside advice at the risk of our very livelihood. Some of the most valuable counsel comes from the following sources:

Computer science alumni. These number nearly 500 who have graduated since 1976. We send out alumni newsletters on an annual basis. Every three years, a survey is enclosed.

Computer Science Professional Advisory Board. This was initiated in 1990, and currently has nine members from around the city, state, and region. They meet twice a year and give advice on all issues, from curriculum to equipment. See Figure 4 for the current roster.

Organization	Year Joined
Ashland Petroleum	1991
Bell South	1990

Brown and Williamson	1992
Desa International	1990
Humana Corporation	1991
Logan Aluminum	1990
Marshall Space Flight Center, NASA	1992
R. R. Donnelley and Sons	1991
TransFinancial BanCorp	1990

Fig. 4. Computer Science Professional Advisory Board
1992-93

Computer Science Student Advisory Board. This board was initiated in 1989, and has representatives from every class, as well as non-traditional, graduate students, cooperative education, and part-time. Their suggestions often involve changes to the curriculum.

Employers. The first survey will be done in the fall of 1993, and will occur every four years thereafter.

Cooperative education employers. We obtain feedback from these at the end of every term. Normally, there are about 30 students/year.

Computing Sciences Accreditation Board. This agency composed of representatives from both ACM and IEEE has provided a great stimulus in all areas of instruction: curriculum, faculty, equipment, students, and university resources. Curriculum 91 has also been particularly helpful [1].

7.2 State-of-the-art Software Tools

These include: vendors (see Appendix B for a list of 39 such); University grants, alumni donations, and national grants.

7.3 State-of-the-art Hardware Platforms

These include ones available with support from the University and the Professional Advisory Board.

7.4 State-of-the-art Faculty

This resource, of course, is primarily from the University initially, i.e., new hires. However to retain such faculty, other investments are required from the University: professional development funds, travel funds, and less committee overhead to permit time for research and scholarly activity. Likewise, industries can assist with externships during the summer, sabbaticals during the school year, and summer hires. Finally the faculty must avail themselves of such resources as continuing education, e.g., ACM, IEEE, and the National Technological University [20]

7.5 State-of-the-art Classroom, Laboratory, Faculty, and Department Offices

The University must allocate space and money to furnish these.

7.6 State-of-the-art Instructional Materials

This can come from faculty, publishers (textbooks, multi-media, video tapes), and integrated learning system publishers (computer-based learning material, computer-managed learning systems, and authoring systems).

8 Summary

The incorporation of software engineering into an existing university computer science curriculum involves major cultural change. Considerable persistence is required, yet even the best laid plans do not always suffice. This is particularly true for those computer science departments which have a strong mathematics emphasis -- a common phenomenon in many comprehensive universities (M.S. granting) today. Despite the major challenges involved in such change, the rewards are many. The beneficiaries include: current students, graduates, employers, computer science faculty, the university, and society.

Not all of the changes discussed in this paper have yet borne fruit. Therefore, the reader is cautioned that this is more of a "what should be" picture, than a "what is" one. Students and faculty associated with the course are just beginning to make significant differences.

Persistence, a champion, receptivity to faculty concerns, and sensitivity to industry needs are some of the requirements for success in the incorporation of software engineering, as a pervasive component, into an existing computer science program heavily mathematical in nature. However persistence does not guarantee anything! Therefore, it will be no surprise if, like the field mouse in Burns' famous poem almost two centuries ago, our best laid plans "gang aft agley" (oft go astray).

References

1. ACM, *Curriculum '91*, ACM Press, New York, 1991.

2. Boehm, B., *Software Engineering Economics*, McGraw-Hill, 1986.

3. Brooks, B., "No Silver Bullet: Essence and Accidents of Software Engineering, " *Computer*, IEEE, April, 1987, pp. 10-19.

4. Bruegge, B. "Teaching an Industry-Oriented Software Engineering Course," *Software Engineering Education*, SEI Conference, Springer/Verlag, October, 1992.

5. Burns, R., "To A Mouse, on Turning Her up in her Nest with a Plough, November, 1785," *The Poems and Songs of Robert Burns*, p. 125.

6. Computing Sciences Accreditation Board, "Criteria for Accrediting Programs in Computer Science in the United States," June, 1992.

7. DeMarco, T., *Controlling Software Projects*. Yourdon Press, 1982.

8. Frailey, D. "CS Employers: What They Want," *Syllabus on Computer Science*, Syllabus Press, Sunnyvale, CA, Spring, 1992, pp. 8-9.

9. Gilb, T., *Principles of Software Management*. McGraw-Hill, 1989.

10. Hoare, C.A.R., "The Engineering of Software: A Startling Contradiction," *Computer Bulletin*, December, 1975.

11. Johnson, D. W., R.T. Johnson, and K. A. Smith, *Cooperative Learning: Increasing College Faculty Instructional Productivity*. ASHE-ERIC Higher Education Report No. 4, 1991.

12. Kaufman, R., *Identifying and Solving Problems*. Third Edition, University Associates, San Diego, CA, 1982.

13. Koen, B., *Definition of the Engineering Method*. American Society for Engineering Education, Washington, D.C., 1985.

14. Koen, B., "The Engineering Method and the State-of-the-Art," *Engineering Education*, April, 1986, pp. 570-674.

15. Modesitt, K., "Computer-based Learning, Expert Systems, and Software Engineering: Advanced Tools for Engineering Education Now and in 2001," *International Journal of Applied Engineering Education*, Tempus Publications, vol. 7, No. 6, 1991, pp. 452-455. Also presented at the *Frontiers in Education Conference*, American Society for Engineering Education, Vienna, 1990, and at Bond University, Gold Coast, Queensland, Australia, 1990.

16. Modesitt, K., Computer Science in the Real World: Expert Systems, Software Engineering, and Computer-based Learning: Engineering of Complex Reliable Software Systems, and How Computers Can Help People Learn to Build Them. Two-week series of invited lectures given to the Department of Computer Science and Engineering, University of Science and Technology, Beijing, People's Republic of China, June, 1991.

17. Modesitt, K., "Computer Based Learning: Important Problems, Creative People, and Powerful Affordable Tools," *Journal of Computer-Based Instruction*, Vol. 9, May, 1983, pp. 26-33. *IEEE International Conference on Consumer Electronics*, June, 1983, pp. 206-207. Also *Association of Educational Data Systems (AEDS) National Conference*, 1983, pp. 213-217; *National Society for Performance and Instruction (NSPI) National Conference*, 1983.

18. Modesitt, K. "Software Engineering Training for TI Middle Management," Invited Presentation for *ACM National Conference*, 1980.

19. Moore F. and P. Purvis, "Meeting the Training Need of Practicing Software Engineers with the Defense System Electronics Group," *Texas Instruments Technical Journal*, May-June, 1989, pp. 61-67.

20. NTU, "NTU Celebrating Five Years," NTU UPLINK, National Technological University, Vol. 5., Num. 4, April, 1990.

21. Pressman, R., *Software Engineering: A Practitioner's Approach*, Third Edition, McGraw-Hill, 1992.

22. SACS, Criteria for Accreditation: Commission on Colleges. Southern Association of Colleges and Schools, 1988.

23. Shapiro, M., "Software is a product ... NOT!" *IEEE Computer*, September, 1992, p. 128.

24. Taguchi, G. and M.S. Phadke, "Quality Engineering Through Design Optimization," *Proceedings of the Globecom 84 Meeting*, IEEE Communication Society, 1984, pp. 1106-1113.

25. Technology Reinvestment Project, "Program Information Package for Defense Technology Conversion, Reinvestment, and Transition Assistance, Arlington, VA March 10, 1993.

26. Yourdon, E., *Tools and Techniques of Modern Software Engineering*. Yourdon Press, 1987.

Western Kentucky University   Appendix A   Professor Ken Modesitt
Computer Science Department   Thompson Central 137A
Spring, 1993   745-4642
Office Hours: by appointment   MODESITT@WKUVX1 (Bitnet)
      (not 45' before class)

COMPUTER SCIENCE 360-001
SOFTWARE ENGINEERING I
11:45 a.m. - 12:45 p.m. TR(F)

SUBJECT MATTER
The modern development cycle is examined via software engineering: needs
assessment, requirements analysis, user interface, design, construction,
test, maintenance/enhancement. Current methodologies and tools: data
dictionary, data flow diagrams, structured walkthroughs, teams, program
management. Case studies involving automated CASE and expert systems.

PREREQUISITE: CS 242 (Assembly Language)

GOALS
"Build useful and reliable software more quickly and cheaply."
The objectives of this course are to:
1. add skills missing from earlier courses, where the back-end of the
   software lifecycle was emphasized
2. introduce front-end skills (needs assessment, customer interaction,
   estimation, analysis, design, analysis-to-design)
3. have extensive collaborative learning experiences (teams)
4. have extensive hands-on CASE experiences
5. demonstrate the vital importance of frequent customer interaction
6. exercise communication skills extensively
7. emphasize the many aspects of software quality
8. practice time management skills
9. make extensive use of library resources
10. MAKE MISTAKES AND LEARN FROM THEM!

A more detailed listing uses Bloom's taxonomy* for the cognitive domain
(1)knowledge: the student will be able to define, recognize, and recall
   concepts related to software engineering, e.g.[req. anal]: data flow
   diagram, data dictionary, funct. specs, decision table, pseudo-code,
   structured spec, performance spec, MECCA chart; [test]: black/white/grey
   box testing, acceptance test; [design]: structure chart, FMEA, inspect.
   play-throughs; [mgmt]: Gantt & person-loading charts, demos;
   [quality]: metrics, SQA; [tools]: CASE, proj. mgmt; [future]: knowledge
   based systems, rapid prototyping
the student will be aware of existing products which address the above
   concepts and other productivity tools

(2)comprehension: the student will be able to compare and contrast major
   concepts related to software engineering, esp. as they compare to
   programming and computer science

(3)application: the student will be able to apply methodologies and
   existing tools for the modern software development cycle

(4)analysis: the student will be able to analyze a customer's need, and the
   proposed solutions, designs, and testing procedures of their own and
   others

(5) synthesis: the student will be able to construct a useful requirements analysis, design document, and testing procedure for a customer's problem

(6) evaluation: the student will be able to evaluate various products, including analyses, designs, testing procedures, problems, applications, physical products, and professional articles

* Bloom, B., et.al.,(eds) <u>Taxonomy of Educational Objectives, Handbook I Cognitive Domain</u>. David McKay, New York, 1956.

Affective: the student will communicate professionally via oral and written means to peers, the instructor, and perhaps others outside the class ("customers")
the student will actively participate as a member of a variety of different teams, e.g., customer, developer.

<u>NON-GOALS!!</u>
Extensive coding, professor "reading" text to students

<u>ATTENDANCE POLICY</u>
I assume you are here to learn by whatever legitimate means you can. I am here to help you to the best of my ability. If you do not come to class, I am much less likely to be able to help. Positive attitudes toward attendance and the classroom are desirable.

<u>METHODOLOGY</u>
Syllabus (see attached)

Lectures by instructor and other students

Projects - both team and individual

Resources
books, journals, popular magazines, Computer-aided software engineering (CASE) tools, Knowledge-based systems, peers, instructor, others, computer equipment, computer-based learning systems

<u>EVALUATION</u>
Continual for both professor and student with built-in checkpoints
Student

homework	quizzes	projects	attend	mid-term+final	course (%)	
15%	10%	55%	5%	15%	90.0 - 100	= A
					80.0 - 89.9	= B
					70.0 - 79.9	= C
					60.0 - 69.9	= D
					<60.0	= F

Quizzes: Usually prior to a chapter (in-class, open notes, closed book)
     Normally given <u>prior</u> to classroom discussion: really a "pre-quiz"
Mid-term and final: normally include take-home as well as in-class.

Professor
     mid-course and end of term using free-form, MECCA model, and WKU form

Late Project/Homework Grading Policy
(Make-ups only for documented medical/personal emergencies)

On-time(class beginning)	One class day late	Two	> Two
Full-credit	80%	50%	0%

Western Kentucky University   Spring, 1993
Computer Science Department   Professor Ken Modesitt

COMPUTER SCIENCE 360-001
SOFTWARE ENGINEERING I

COURSE SYLLABUS

Texts: Software Engineering: A Practitioner's Approach by Pressman,
     McGraw-Hill, Third Edition, 1992
     BriefCASE: The Collegiate Systems Development Tool, version 2.0,
     by Crow, South-Western, 1990
     VAX Users Manual, newest edition, ACRS
Software Engineering textbooks and articles
     indexed by author: on reserve in the Science Library
Older software engineering articles (400+) indexed by topic, keyword,
     and author: on the back wall of the Science Library

	READINGS
TOPIC ORDER	[CHAPTER]
The impact of software	[1,2]
The software crisis and the "aging software plant"	
Overview of software engineering	
Project management and metrics	
Discussion of projects	[3,4]
Planning software projects: introduction	
Software Risks	1 wk.
Computer system engineering	[5]
Hardware and software issues	
Allocation	
Good software	1 wk
Project planning and organization	[6]
Software cost and schedule estimation	
Cost models	
Risk analysis	
Analysis fundamentals	[7,8]
Object-oriented analysis	
Introduction to data flow techniques	
Exam #1	
Formal paper assigned	
Elements of Software Design	[10,11]
Fundamental concepts	
Architectural, data and procedural design	
Data Flow Design	
Data structure oriented design	
User interface design	[14]

58

Software quality assurance and reliability   [17]

Testing Methods   [18]
White box, black box

Testing Strategies   [19]
Debugging

Exam #2

Maintenance   [20]

Software Configuration Management   [21]

Future Methodologies   [22-24]

Final Exam

Reading: see reserve reading list for each topic

COMPUTER PROJECTS (Most will involve class room presentations)   WEEKS
Overlap will occur!

Black box testing   1

Maintenance: corrective, perfective, adaptive   1

[BriefCASE exercises   3]

Evaluation of commercial Project Management Tools: PC/Mac   1

Evaluation of student-developed Computer-aided Registration Systems   1
    (CAR) and Advising Systems (CADS) using MECCA evaluation model

Academic support system
    Perfective and Adaptive maintenance of CAR   3
    Development of Computer Assisted Advising System (CADS)   4
    Integration of CAR and CADS   1

Evaluation of CASE Tools   2
    [Excelerator, DesignAid, Anatool, MacBubbles, Visible Analyst]

*Simple Knowledge-based System   2
    [1st Class]

*Extra Credit

Western Kentucky University   Appendix B   May, 1993
Computer Science Department   Professor Modesitt

COURSE-RELATED SOFTWARE OBTAINED FOR PERSONAL COMPUTERS

CAD, COMPUTER-BASED LEARNING, COMPUTER-AIDED SOFTWARE ENGINEERING (CASE),
DATA BASES, EXPERT SYSTEM BUILDING TOOLS, FOURTH GENERATION LANGUAGES,
GRAPHICS, INTEGRATED PACKAGES. PROGRAMMING LANGUAGES, PROJECT MANAGEMENT

PRODUCT	MANUFACTURER	INITIAL LOAN DATE	UNIT PRICE	COPIES	PRICE ($)
COMPUTER-AIDED DESIGN (CAD)					
AUTOCAD	Autodesk, Inc.	89	3,200	1	3,200
CADD,Level 5	Generic Software	89	500	1	500
CADD,Level 1/Mac	Generic Software	89	150	1	150
TOTAL FOR CAD				3	3,850
COMPUTER-BASED LEARNING					
AUTHORWARE	Authorware	89	8,000	1	8,000
PCD3 Authoring	The Roach Organization (TRO	91	10,000	1	10,000
PLATO (Pilot Test on LAN)	TRO	91	100,000	1	110,000
TOTAL FOR CBL				3	118,000
COMPUTER-AIDED SOFTWARE ENGINEERING (CASE)					
Anatool/Mac	Adv. Logical SW	89	700	1	700
BriefCASE vers. 2.0	SouthWestern	89	50	1	50
Design Aid	Nastec	88	7,000	2	14,000
Excelerator vers. 1.9	Index Technology	88	9,000	1	9,000
IEW/Design Workstation	KnowledgeWare	90	10,100	1 + 4 site licenses	10,100
IEW Construction Workstation	KnowledgeWare	90	10,100	1 + 4 site licenses	10,100
MacBubbles/Mac vers. 2.0	StarSys	89,91	800	1	800
ProMod (+CAP, RESOURCE, etc.)	ProMod	88	10,500	1	10,500
Visible Analyst Workbench	Visible Systems	91	4,000	1	4,000
TOTAL FOR CASE TOOLS				10	59,250

PRODUCT	MANUFACTURER	DATE	UNIT PRICE	COPIES	PRICE ($)
DATA BASES -- INTEGRATED					
Object View Version 2.0	KnowledgeWare (Client/Server)	93	2,800	1	2,800
TOTAL FOR DATA BASES -- INTEGRATED				1	2,800
EXPERT SYSTEM BUILDING TOOLS					
1stClass-HT (Hypertext)	1stClass	89	2,500	1	2,500
1stClass	1stClass	88	500	1 +Site License	500
Darwin II	Novacast SoftCenter (SW)	91	1,000	1	1,000
Expert Ease	Knowledgelink	88	600	2	1,200
ExTran	Knowledgelink	88	3,000	2	6,000
Fusion	1stClass	88	1,500	1	1,500
Level5/PC	Information Builders	89	700	1	700
Level5/Mac	Information Builders	89	700	1	700
M.4	Cimflex Teknowledge	92	1,000	1	1,000
PC/Beagle	Warm Boot, Ltd.	88	1,000	1	1,000
Personal Consultant + (TI SCHEME)	Texas Instruments	88	3,000	1	3,000
Rule Master 3 (Turbo C)	Radian Corporation	90	595	1	595
Super Expert	Novacast	88	1,000	1	1,000
VP-Expert	Paperback Software	88	100	1	100
X-Pert Rule	Attar Software	88	1,000	1	1,000
Xi Plus	Expertech	88	1,300	1	1,300
TOTAL FOR EXPERT SYSTEM BUILDING TOOLS				18	23,095
FOURTH GENERATION LANGUAGES (4GL)					
PRO-C	Vestronix	89	675	1	675
TOTAL FOR 4GL				1	675
GRAPHICS					
Mac Flow	Mainstay	92	350	1	350
Showplace-MacRenderMan	Pixar	92	1,000	1	1,000
TOTAL FOR GRAPHICS				2	1,350

PRODUCT	MANUFACTURER	DATE	UNIT PRICE	COPIES	PRICE ($)
INTEGRATED PACKAGES					
Q&A, vers.2.0	SYMANTEC	89,91	350	1	350
TOTAL FOR INTEGRATED				1	350
PROGRAMMING LANGUAGES					
Dr. Pascal	Visible Software	89	90	2	180
Matlab & Simulab	Math Works	92	4,000	1	4,000
Minitab: Simulation	Minitab, Inc.	90	400	1	400
TK Solver Plus -Num Anal/Mac	Universal Technical Systems	90	600	1	600
TOTAL FOR PROG. LANG.				5	5,180
PROJECT MANAGEMENT					
Cocomo1	Cocomo	90	300	1	300
INFORMATION MANAGER/Mac	AEC Management	90	700	1	700
FAST-TRACK SCHEDULE/Mac	AEC Management	90,92	200	1	200
MacProject	Claris	92	500	1	500
MacSchedule	Mainstay	92	300	1	300
ON TARGET Windows	SYMANTEC	91	700	1	700
PAC-MICRO	AGS Management	88	1,000	1	1,000
SECOMO	IITRI	89	500	1	500
SPQR/20	Pressman	92	50	1	50
TIME-LINE Version 5.0	SYMANTEC	89,91	700	1	700
TOTAL FOR PGM MGMT				10	5,250
GRAND TOTAL				55	110,500
39 manufacturers				Pilot:	110,000

Session 2:
Tools of the Trade

Cohesive Use of Commercial Tools in a Classroom
Janusz Zalewski, University of Texas of the Permian Basin, Odessa, Texas

Ada Reusable Software Components for Teaching Distributed Systems
Yvon Kermarrec, ENST de Bretagne, Cedex, France and Laurent Pautet, Dassault Electronique, Saint Cloud, France

Using Commercial CASE Environments to Teach Software Design
Thomas B. Horton, Florida Atlantic University, Boca Raton, Florida

Cohesive Use of Commercial Tools in a Classroom*

Janusz Zalewski

Dept. of Computer Science
University of Texas of the Permian Basin
Odessa, TX 79762-0001
(915)367-2310
zalewski_j@utpb.pb.utexas.edu

Abstract. *This paper presents a set of integrated commercial tools (both software and hardware), for use in courses on real-time systems and software engineering. A background for adopting such a set of tools is given and team projects, in which these tools have been used, are also outlined.*

1 Introduction

Current recommendations on software engineering curricula, as well as sample programs offered by various universities, as investigated by this author, do not mention the use of tools in classrooms (whether undergraduate or graduate). It is hard to disagree, however, that the use of tools in the academic environment may significantly improve both the curriculum in general and the particular software enginering programs. Yet, the reports on such undertakings are not very common.

This author looked at the potential use of tools in a classroom, from one particular perspective, while developing a real-time systems course. This course is viewed as a part of the broader software engineering curriculum and it is believed that the related experience is applicabile to the use of such tools throughout the entire curriculum.

This paper first outlines a model for teaching undergraduate real-time systems courses. The model, presented in details elsewhere [20], uses ACM/IEEE-CS "Computing Curricula 1991" framework to describe the course contents, and is based on a four-layer paradigm for such a course, comprised of: real-time development methodologies, programming languages, operating system kernels, and bus architectures. The motivation for this course and for the use of tools is given next, followed by the description of criteria used for tool selection. Examples of student projects which use these tools are presented, and finally lessons learned and prospects for improvements and extensions are discussed.

---

* Work supported by DARPA, Contract No. MDA972-92-J-1023; performed while the author was with Southwest Texas State University, San Marcos, Texas.

2 Motivation and Educational Objective

The primary motivation to undertake this project was the lack of appropriate curriculum for a real-time systems course. Growing market demand for real-time systems engineers resulted in two major consequences: first, in better visibility of deficiencies of current educational practices in this area, and second, in overwhelming request for guidance from educators. Neither one of the two most direct sources for such guidance, ACM/IEEE "Computing Curricula '91", in general, or specifically the Software Engineering Institute, currently provide such guidance. In practice, no curriculum exists which would be broadly applicable.

Searching for hints to shape his own real-time systems course, the author has reviewed syllabi of similar courses taught at several other universities [9,10,11,13,15], and found them very valuable but not broad enough to fit well into his own environment. Therefore the author defined his own paradigm for such course, which is based on his extensive industrial practice and contact with first year college graduates. The basic assumption is that developing real-time systems is one part of the traditional software process, comprising all phases of the life cycle, particularly requirements specification, design, and implementation. This leads to a four-layer model, viewed as part of the software process, with development methodologies as a foundation (Fig. 1). The implementation phase splits into three different layers: programming languages, operating system kernels and hardware architectures.

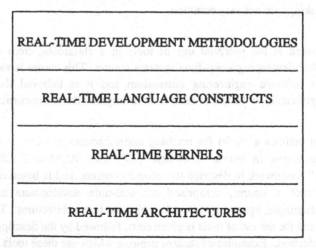

Fig. 1. Four-layer Paradigm of Real-Time Systems

An interesting feature of this model is that it can be used to teach real-time systems, not only from the software engineering perspective (viewed in a top-down manner), but also in a bottom-up manner which is used more traditionally in electrical engineering schools. Moreover, particular implementations of such course do not have to cover the entire spectrum; they may include only two or three top layers, if implementing the top-down view, or two or three bottom layers, if implementing the bottom-up view.

The question of tools arises immediately for two reasons. First, for the course material organized in the form of knowledge units, corresponding lab units are needed to support practical understanding of concepts. Using only compilers in classrooms is not sufficient and replacement for paper-and-pencil projects for trasmitting knowledge is more than desirable. The obsolete technology of teaching we use in classrooms needs improvements. Secondly, it was realized that in such a course, which clearly prepares students to enter industry, good industrial practice must be taught. This is consistent with the pressure from both students and industrial companies which hire them [18]. Use of tools in classes offers, first of all, a tremendous advantage for graduates to know tools in job search and pursue their industrial careers, as well as a significant course enhancement, making it more attractive.

All of this supports the view that using tools in class is indispensible, especially when combined with the educational objective to prepare students to start successful careers in industry.

An important question must be answered, before starting to use tools in class: buy or develop them? Although some educators seem to endorse the view of developing rather than buying them [14], this author's position is that, in a real-time systems course, developing tools for real-time systems somewhat looses the point of real-time requirements.

3 Tool Selection Criteria and Integration

Tools hierarchy should follow the accepted paradigm. This means that the notion of tools should not only include software tools but equipment as well. The top down approach to teaching real-time systems determined the tool selection method, to start from the tools supporting real-time development methodologies. The criterion for including a particular development methodology was its industrial maturity, which translates into a book or several major papers published.

3.1 High-Level Tools

The initial approach was to investigate the availability of public domain tools for methodologies known to be successful and thoroughly documented in textbooks. Two such sources have been identified [1,3], accessible via file transfer protocol (ftp), but neither was feasible to port to author's environment; the first because it is hosted on Sun workstations, not available at that time, and the second because of being based on Objective C, also unavailable.

The following primary criteria were formulated and used for selection of commercial tools:

1. Simultaneous support for both major categories of real-time development methodologies: classical structured development for real-time systems and object-oriented development.
2. Simulation capabilities on the specification or design level.
3. Code generation option.
4. Possibility and ease of interfacing to tools from other vendors.

A few secondary criteria were also considered. Compatibility with a variety of languages, operating systems, and hardware platforms is important in classes. In particular, high-level tools should not preclude use of various implementation languages. Support for multiprocessor and distributed systems would also be a plus. Support for the entire process, which normally is one of the most important criteria, was not included here, as the issue goes far beyond the scope of a real-time systems course. Another important criterion, cost of tools, was considered only after the primary selection was made, and included considerations on educational discounts for all preferred products.

In the next step, several commercially available and widely used tools were cosidered, among them ObjecTime (ObjecTime Inc., Ottawa, Canada), Statemate (iLogix Inc., Burlington, MA), StP (Interactive Development Environments, San Francisco, CA), Teamwork (Cadre Inc., Providence, RI), VRTXvelocity (Ready Systems, Sunnyvale, CA). The simulation tool which seemed to best meet our requirements was SES/workbench (from SES, Austin, TX), which is a very powerful tool for real-time systems simulation, both hardware and software, and has interfaces to Teamwork and StP through its SES/steps. CDIF standard [6] (CASE Data Interchange Format), which defines the structure and content of a transfer that may be used to exchange data between two CASE tools, was selected as a tool interface vehicle.

3.2 Lower-level Tools

Following the basic paradigm, three kinds of tools are needed to support teaching on the implementation layers: the programming language, the kernel and the hardware.

This course focuses on the use of Ada, because Ada offers significant advantages in teaching real-time systems by integrating several concepts: concurrency, exceptions, standard way of mixing languages, interrupt handling on the application level, device register access, and priorities. Criteria for selecting an Ada compiler, which are equally applicable to choosing compilers of other programming languages, included:

- support of the wide range of real-time concepts
- integration with the real-time kernel
- best potential for portability of applications
- running on a variety of architectures.

Regarding real-time kernels, this author extensively studied currently available commercial products as a member of the POSIX.4 committee [16] (real-time extensions of Unix) and while working in the industrial setting [2]. The following criteria were used in the selection process:

- compliance with Unix
- tasks mapped to threads
- results of existing benchmarks
- ease of writing device drivers
- support for modern scheduling concepts (such as rate monotonic scheduling)
- network support (not a real-time issue, but to facilicate access.)

Of very few kernels which offer support for priority inheritance, such as VxWorks (Wind River Systems, Alameda, CA) or LynxOS (Lynx Real-Time Systems, Campbell, CA), the one which runs on multiple architectures, including Intel 80x86 and Motorola 680x0, has a better chance to be adopted in the academic environment.

For real-time hardware architectures, two categories of tools were considered. First, simple boards for the PC compatibles or Macintoshes, such as analog/digital I/O boards (from National Instruments, Austin, TX, or Keithley, Taunton, MA), digital signal processor boards with additional availability of Ada compilers, and microcontrollers. The second category includes a cross section of advanced multiprocessor buses: VMEbus, Multibus II, and Futurebus+. The selection criteria for choosing the bus may include:

- implementation of real-time arbitration protocols
- support for Intel/Motorola/RISC architectures
- support for cache coherence protocols
- good educational support
- connectivity to other buses and links.

The second category needs much more investment in equipment and was dropped from initial purchase considerations at this stage, but not entirely from the course (even in this edition). Rather than purchasing equipment, an excellent teaching vehicle has been identified and obtained, and used in class: Futurebus+ self-paced instruction tape [5].

3.3 Tools Integration

Tool integration is not easy even in the industrial settings. Figure 2 presents the environment which has been set up according to the paradigm for teaching this course, as a result of the tool selection process.

The key element of it is the Teamwork tool set, especially the part supporting the HOOD methodology (Hierarchical Object-Oriented Design [12]). It produces designs which can be used for simulation on SES/workbench, generates the regular Ada code (also in languages C and Fortran, this however is not used at the moment), and has a PC tool OpenSelect/HOOD (from Meridian, Irvine, CA) interfaced to it. Using SES/steps tool the Teamwork designs can be semi-automatically transferred to SES/workbench for simulation, but this option has not been checked yet (only beta version of SES/steps for Teamwork existed at the time of this writing).

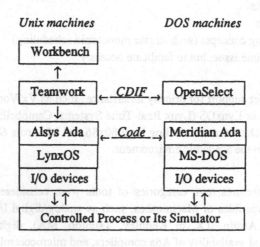

Fig. 2. Tools Integration Environment

Not pictured on the diagram are two important extensions for future use, not yet incorporated into the course: TMS320 digital signal processor board (from Texas Instruments, Houston, TX), for which an Ada compiler hosted on VAX is supplied by Tartan Laboratories (Monroeville, PA), and multiprocessor transputer boards, from Computer Systems Architects (Provo, UT) with an Ada compiler from Alsys (Burlington, MA).

4 Sample Projects

Once the tools are there, their use in classrooms becomes the major issue. High-level tools demonstrate their usability and power only in relatively complex projects, and their use cannot be started from scratch with unprepared students. The author's approach to this problem, discussed in details elsewhere [17], encompasses three steps in helping students to acquire knowledge: demos and exercises first, team projects next. The rationale for this is to prepare students to gradually get some necessary familiarity with new technology and leave them enough time, at the beginning of the course, to learn how to use tools. Technically, this approach can be characterized as follows: watch and repeat the demos, then work individually on simple exercises, and finally work in teams to solve a significant problem.

Demos may include a presentation of a well understood example. A good example to start with, the cruise control system, was chosen because it is well described in several publications [7], and is delivered as a sample problem with the Teamwork tool set. It is presented first in a lecture and then students work on it individually in the lab learning how to use the tool.

As exercises one can use relatively simple, individual, projects based on concepts of concurrent programming, such as those discussed in [17] or more involved, which build on this knowledge, such as multitasking simulation of Ethernet, network synchronization in Ada, data acquisition benchmark, or more advanced, requiring some special knowledge, such as trie search. The selection depends on the level of the student group, and is more clear after first demos and simple exercises are done. An important consideration is that students have several presented exercises to choose from. They are also allowed to work in pairs, building the groundwork for the team project later on.

Regarding more complex projects, which are the ultimate goal of this class, there are plenty of different realistic examples. They vary from a simple vending machine to a complex air traffic control system, and are relatively well described in the literature. For a comprehensive list, see [20] or contact the author. Author's own industrial experience concentrated on safety related applications and similar lab projects were also developed:

- Radiation Detection System [17]
- Message Broadcast System [17]
- Water Boiler Controller [8]

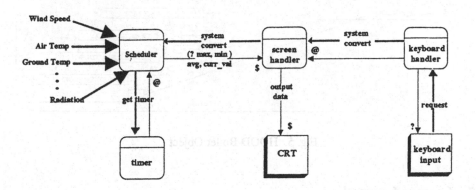

Fig. 3. Radiation Detection System Design

The Radiation Detection System design (Fig. 3) was developed earlier without tools, using SCOOP-3 [4] methodology, and implemented in Ada and C++, on the VAX/VMS. It is a good vehicle for comparison with a newer HOOD design and Ada implementation for LynxOS, as an alternative to replace the cruise control example. Water boiler controller (Fig. 4 and 5), as a part of the entire power generating station, was developed from scratch, implemented and tested using a simplified boiler simulator obtained from the Institute of Risk Research (Waterloo, Ontario, Canada).

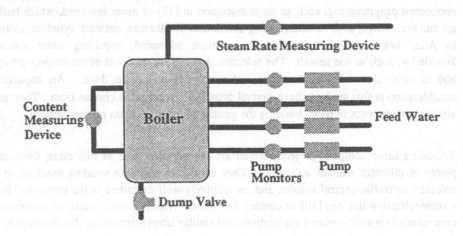

Fig. 4. Boiler Configuration

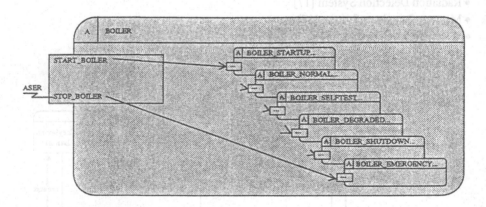

Fig. 5. HOOD Boiler Object

5 Lessons Learned

Early experiences with the use of these tools in a small class (10 students) are summarized below.

Starting to use a tool in a comprehensive way in class means a radical change of technology, which causes problems for both students and instructors. Students who used to apply compilers as the only class tools have significant problems with the use of higher level tools. The author's approach with stepwise introduction via demos and exercises helps a bit, but a smoother approach is necessary. Just as use of programming languages early in computer science curriculum helps students to gain familiarity with these tools, software engineering tools must be introduced as early.

A very positive observation is that transmitting knowledge by means of tools is very effective, provided a question mentioned in former paragraph is resolved. Students learn concepts much quicker and more profoundly by using notations from respective methodologies and apply them using real tools in projects. Notational and diagrammatic techniques are mastered automatically, just like a programming language.

For projects which take the entire semester for the whole class without the use of tools, it takes one person a semester to complete such a project with the use of tools (in this case, applying HOOD and Ada). The time to complete the project is an order of magnitude faster, mostly at the cost of intensive work on learning how to use the tool.

From the point of view of engineering, the controlled real-time equipment plays a major role in teaching in the lab. The approach taken here, to substitute hard equipment by a good simulator running on the PC compatible, works relatively well.

It is essential to determine prerequisites for this course. From the point of view of earlier preparation for the use of tools, only software engineering is recommended as a required prerequisite, for which programming in Ada should be required in turn. However, ideally a course like this should have also prerequisites in areas of operating systems and computer architecture. For example, in the author's environment, for a course CS4364 Real-Time Computing Applications, a combination of the following courses would serve as an ideal prerequisite:

- CS3398 Software Engineering - to prepare for the real-time development methodologies
- CS4368 Survey of Computer Languages - to prepare for the real-time language components
- CS4328 Operating Systems - to prepare for the kernels component
- CS3408 Introduction to Computer Architecture - for the hardware component.

6 Conclusion

After completion of the major milestone, it is clear that commercial tools may play a significant role in software engineering education, provided they are well integrated for class use. They are relatively expensive but affordable in small quantities, including maintenance, assuming major academic discounts are given.

The proposed course model, and its supporting set of tools and projects is fairly complete but still needs improvement. It is planned to continue developments by further integrating the tools and adding more lab exercises and projects in areas of real-time langauges and kernels, for example:

• Rewrite a simple C kernel in Ada
• Prove that a set of tasks meet their deadlines [19]
• Compare Ada and C++ implementations for sample design
• Port HOOD module using CDIF.

Examples of projects and exercises will be made availabe through ftp and on AdaNET. Future work will include extensions towards parallel computing (using Ada and Occam on transputers) and more focus on software safety.

One problem which could not be adequately solved was that of finding a textbook. At the moment, no such book exists on the market, which in addition to presenting major methodologies would provide comprehensive examples of the usage of tools supporting these methodologies.

References

[1] Berzins V., Luqi, *Software Engineering with Abstractions*. Addison-Wesley, Reading (MA), 1991

[2] Botlo M., J. Zalewski, *An Evaluation of VxWorks Version 5.0*. CERN Mini and Micro Computer Newsletter, No. 32, pp. 15-18, October 1991

[3] Buhr R.J.A., *Practical Visual Techniques in System Design with Applications to Ada*. Prentice-Hall, Englewood-Cliffs (NJ), 1990

[4] Cherry G., *Software Construction by Object-Oriented Pictures - Specifying Reactive and Interactive Systems*. Thought**Tools, Canandaigua (NY), 1990

[5] DEC, *Futurebus+ Concepts*. Self-Paced Instruction Course, Magnetic Tape 6250BPI, Order No. EY-N377E-MA-001, Digital Equipment Corp., Maynard (MA), 1993

[6] EIA, *CDIF - Framework for Modeling and Extensinbility*. Interim Standard EIA/IS-81, Electronic Industries Association, Washington (DC), July 1991

[7] Gomaa H., *Software Design Methods for Real-Time Systems. Curriculum Module*. Report SEI-CM-22, Software Engineering Institute, Pittsburgh (PA), December 1989

[8] IRR, *Specification for a Software Program for a Boiler Water Content Monitor and Control System*. Institute for Risk Research, Waterloo, Ontario, Canada, January 1992

[9] Liu J., *Real-Time Systems*. Lecture Notes, Dept. of Computer Science, University of Illinois at Urbana-Champaign, Fall 1991/92

[10] Mead N., M. Shaw, *Essential Issues in Real-Time Systems*. Draft Syllabus, Course No. SEI 5316, Software Engineering Institute, Pittsburgh (PA), Private information, May 1992

[11] Mok A., *Real-Time Systems*. Short Course Lecture Notes, Dept. of Computer Sciences, University of Texas at Austin, January 1992

[12] Robinson P.J., *Hierarchical Object-Oriented Design*. Prentice-Hall, Englewood Cliffs (NJ), 1992

[13] Shaw A., *Real-Time Systems*. Course Outline, University of California 23rd Annual Institute in Computer Science, August 1993

[14] Schwarz J.J., J.J Skubich, P. Swed, M. Maranzana, *Real-Time Multitasking Design with a Graphical Tool*. Proc. First IEEE Workshop on Real-Time Applications, New York, May 11-12, 1993, Computer Society Press, Los Alamitos (CA), 1993

[15] Volz R., *Real-Time Computing.* Course No. CPSC 489 Syllabus, Texas A&M University, College Station, TX, September 1991

[16] Zalewski J., *An Independent Comparison of Three Real-Time Kernel Standards: ORKID, ITRON, and POSIX.4*. Submitted to Microprocessing and Microprogramming, 1992

[17] Zalewski J., *A Real-Time Systems Course Based on Ada*. Proc. ASEET 7th Annual Ada Software Engineering Education and Training Symposium, pp. 25-49, Monterey, CA, January 12-14, 1993

[18] Zalewski J., *IEEE Draft P-1074 Mapped on a Parallel Model: A Teaching Vehicle for Software Development*. Proc. Workshop on Directions in Software Engineering Education, pp. 125-134, L. Werth and J. Werth (Eds.), 13th International Conference on Software Engineering, Austin, TX, May 12-16, 1991

[19] Zalewski J., *What Every Engineer Needs to Know on Rate Monotonic Scheduling. A Tutorial*. Submitted for publication, 1993 (Draft available from the author)

[20] Zalewski J., *A Model for Teaching Real-Time Systems in the Academic Environment*. Unpublished draft.

Ada Reusable Software Components for Teaching Distributed Systems

Yvon Kermarrec[1] and Laurent Pautet[2]

[1] ENST de Bretagne - BP 832
F 29 285 Brest Cedex - France
kermarrec@enstb.enst-bretagne.fr
[2] Dassault Electronique
55, Quai Marcel Dassault
F 92 214 Saint Cloud - France
pautet@inf.enst.fr

Abstract. This paper presents our experience in developing a toolset for distributed applications in Ada in an educational environment. Our students are trained to become top level engineers in the telecommunications domain. Their curriculum is quite broad and computer science is only one subject among others. We are aware that most of them will consider a computer as an ordinary tool. Moreover, their education is twofold : on the one hand, they must be taught the foundations in order to deal with complex situations, on the other hand, they must train and develop their practical skills. We believe software components to be an interesting solution for these students as they can use them as building blocks to produce complex systems and these components emphasize software engineering benefits.

1 Introduction

Local area networks are becoming more and more common. Each machine in such a system has its own local memory and each machine may communicate with its neighbors using a communication facility (e.g. Ethernet). This is what we call a distributed system. Advances in hardware and communication facilities go together with a decrease in price. Distributed systems are becoming more and more interesting and viable for industrialists and academics. But what about programming a distributed system in an educational context ? What about using it for performance improvement or for increased reliability ? We have to admit that the software industry does not address these issues very well. This implies that designing an application for a distributed system requires an enormous effort. In our University, we teach these subjects (parallel architectures, methodologies for large system design, distributed control paradigms) and we did have a set of workstations. But we did not make the students experiment these techniques in real situations because we do not have enough time and because we would have to start from the very beginning.

Thus, in order to make our teaching evolve, we have decided to design a set of reusable software components which address the previous issues. Our aim is to make a toolset which can be similar to what we can find in various repositories for sequential programming. These components are basic blocks which can be plugged together in order to design larger systems which could not be obtained so easily from scratch. These software components offer basic primitives and complex operations which are basic units for building distributed systems. Approaching networks and distributed systems with the idea of reusability provides our students with a complete toolset which allows them to have a better understanding of the subjects studied.

Moreover, these components illustrate all the benefits of software engineering to the students : documentation, reusability, abstraction. All these notions will be present in their professional lives. For the design of these components, we also have industrial requirements. Thus these components can be used in real applications. Nevertheless, performance and optimization are not our major criteria; making them usable for students is our aim.

The next sections of this paper detail our existing software components. We shall explain why they were necessary in the educational context and why they can be used in real industrial applications. We shall consider two groups of components : the first ones we call basic components and the others we call elaborate components. We present their interests for education and their possible use in industrial projects. We give examples which illustrate the simplicity and power of expression of our software components. Finally, we conclude with research in progress and projects for the future.

2 Teaching distributed techniques

In the previous section we expressed our aim : developing a set of software components which can be used at student level as well as professional level. These software components must also be designed in order to ease the development of applications which involve networks and distributed techniques.

2.1 Ada as our programming language

Ada has been chosen as the support for teaching in computer science. We selected it because it offers software engineering concepts and an interesting tasking model. Students use it to program basic algorithms and to do larger projects : e.g. designing a switching board and control of a train set. We shall not go into the details of all the benefits of Ada [3] [4] but we prefer to outline one subject: reusability.

"Ada Style" [9] highlights Ada features which are to be used in order to design reusable software components : e.g. modularity, information hiding, separate compilation, type model and genericity. This document presents also the criteria which are to be fulfilled :

- Reusable parts must be understandable.
- Reusable parts must be of the highest possible quality.
- Reusable parts must be adaptable.
- Reusable parts should be independent.

Nevertheless, when it comes to system programming in Ada, the programmer is faced with numerous difficulties :

- Calling an external subprogram written in a foreign language implies reading technical compiler documentation in order to transmit parameters, for example.
- Interfacing with operating system primitives is not immediate in Ada. One has to realize that these primitives usually block the calling process. As in most Ada implementations, one Ada program (and not just one task) is supported by a process; the result of a system call is the blocking of the entire program (and not just the calling task). Coping with such situations requires deeper knowledge of Ada, operating systems and network primitives.
- Accessing primitives of the underlying operating system can also be tedious. There is nothing complex to program but for each primitive to be called the programmer may have to write two or three Ada declaration specifications and pragmas.
- Programming in Ada system applications requires specific knowledge of this language (representation clauses and other system features, in particular). Leaving the student alone with these problems does not encourage him to move ahead, wastes his time and makes him tackle specificities which are far related from the original aim (e.g. network communication and distributed system programming).

2.2 Components for networks

Networks and communication protocols are part of our students' curriculum. Up until recently, the practical studies were restricted to basic data transfer between machines. This was the case since they also had to learn at the same time the communication facilities of the underlying operating system and C as a new programming language. Moreover, they also had to deal with Unix features like "fork".

At this level, we faced a challenge and a dilemma : either Ada is a general language and we can program a wide range of applications with Ada and its tasking model is well suited to system programming, thus it is worth teaching it to our students ; or these assertions are (partly) false and what about choosing another programming language that will be more suitable to our students in their professional activities ?

Network programming in real applications is an area in which software development is often more difficult than it should be [8]. Providing a reusable code to access a network is one of our primary goal. With such components the students and the programmers are spared from dealing with low level details and the applications can also be programmed more quickly and more efficiently.

One of our aims is to develop software components which can be used to access Unix interprocess communication mechanisms like pipes, sockets and streams (TLI) [16]. Our restriction to Unix is linked to the fact that this is the most widely used operating system which is available on our machines. (We will see later that we can also deal with other platforms.)

These software components must provide the same services and the same interface as the interprocess communication mechanisms (IPC). This requirement will help the student to make a smooth transition between abstract knowledge and practical developments. Moreover, if this requirement is fulfilled then the technical documentation for these IPC mechanisms can also be used as the technical documentation for these software components.

We also want to develop high level software components which offer communication services in networks. Here our criterion is transparency as we do not want the user to be concerned with the underlying protocol or IPC. This software component must offer a high level interface and elaborated services : e.g. synchronous/asynchronous operations and time limited primitives. It can also take advantage of lower level components which can access network facilities.

2.3 Components for parallel programming

Parallel programming is another daunting task since the programmer usually has a sequential approach. The programmer has to deal with multiple activities which communicate and synchronize. Thus programming such a system induces new complex errors such as deadlock, livelock, starvation, and so on. Moreover, new dedicated tools are required in order to tackle these subjects. We have isolated tools which implement semaphores, schedulers which can be used to schedule activities in a simulation context and components which allow concurrent access to a terminal, and so on.

We will not go into the details of these components as their specifications are well known. In our educational context, they are used as basic elements to simulate complex systems like roundabouts with various priority models. These experiments allow students to realize how necessary it is to design a parallel application with a clear approach since, if they do not, deadlock situations or other troubles will appear.

2.4 Components for distributed programming

Distributed programming is also taught to our students but there are almost no applications nor practical developments. The reason is quite simple for distributed systems : we have to tackle networks with high level languages. One approach is to simulate the network in order to avoid these troubles but here also the students are faced with the classical difficulties of this sort of programming : e.g. expressing asynchronous communication with synchronous primitives, simulating a network with a given set of properties. All the features are quite interesting but they require a large amount of time even to express the simplest application.

Moreover, simulation of such a distributed system well illustrates the concepts but it does not address execution in real situations : i.e. execution on a distributed system composed of several machines. Also, simulating a distributed system does not address implementation issues that the students will face in industry. We have already produced a set of software components which implement distributed control [12] and we would like to reuse parts of this previous work.

2.5 Software components as one of our solutions

For the previous subjects, the teacher and the students are frustrated. The teacher cannot ask the students to test and implement the concepts taught because of time. And this is certainly a flaw in the curriculum. A deadlock situation is a neat theoretical concept but facing it in real developments illustrates the imperative of using firstly an adequate design methodology and then adequate validation tools.

Thus for both subjects (networks and distributed system programming) we need software components which can be used by our students in order to illustrate the concepts they are being taught. Students have to learn how to reuse as it is done in industry instead of starting from scratch. We have another criterion as we also want these software components to be adequate for industrial developments. This implies a minimum of efficiency and scalability and being aware of the preoccupations of the industrial world. Nevertheless, software components are only part of the solution. Software components alone will not solve everything but they can reduce complexity and make people concentrate on parallel and distributed programming instead of wasting time with low level details.

3 Basic components

Basic components are key components in our repository. They can be used directly by the programmer to access a low level primitive and they can be used indirectly by higher level components as they implement lower level services.

3.1   Interprocess communication components

We shall not present the details of these components. As mentioned above, we have restricted ourselves to the Unix world. Thus, we have produced software components which address interprocess communications through files, pipes, sockets and streams. The specifications of these components are inspired from interfaces of the Unix world since Unix offers more or less the same interface whatever the peripheral kind is [17]. Therefore the related technical documentation can be used when integrating these components in a system. These specifications are also related to Ada as they are similar to the specifications of Ada I/O packages (e.g. Text_Io).

As one can imagine strict portability of these components cannot be obtained directly. Thus we used a conditional compilation tool to ease the adaptability of these components. With such an approach, these components are now available using three different Ada compiler technologies on various platforms. Unanticipated changes to fit a given environment are limited to subprogram interfaces.

3.2   A high level network interface

To reduce the complexity of developing large concurrent systems in Ada, many groups such as CIFO or ExTRA have proposed specification packages to provide extended and sophisticated primitives ([5] and [7]). In this context, ExTRA has produced a specification package for generalized I/O operations. In many operating systems, inter-program communication is considered as a common I/O operation. We chose a similar approach for accessing the network; the latter is viewed as a common driver of the system.

In [10] we present more detailed information about our implementation and the inherent interests of this software component. In particular, with Devices (the name of a package specified by ExTRA) we have a common high level interface to reach any network or any Unix IPC and still take into account the specific needs of real time applications. ExTRA defines the notion of communication request and communication device and specifies various synchronous/asynchronous operations to handle requests. Figure 1 shows the structure of the communication package.

4   More elaborate components

4.1   A component for virtual distributed shared memory

There is no shared memory in a distributed system such as a set of workstations connected with a network. Therefore, message based communication is the sole means of exchanging information with the other nodes. As mentioned by H. Bal et al. in [2] "it may seem to be unnatural to use shared data for communication and synchronization in a distributed system". Nevertheless, if we still want the

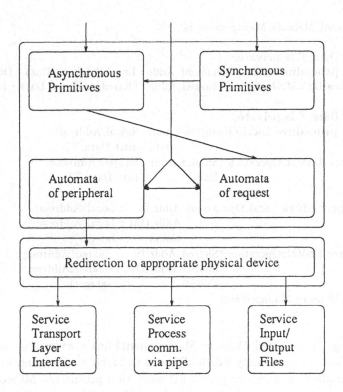

Fig. 1. *Structure of the communication package*

programmer to benefit from the shared memory programming paradigm [1], we have to design a distributed shared virtual memory (DSVM) by implementing a software layer based upon :

- the local memory of each machine,
- a set of adequate protocols which can transmit data between machines and which guarantees memory consistency.

We chose Li and Hudak's distributed algorithm [14] as a starting point because it presents several interesting points :

- Copies of a memory page can be transmitted if there will be only read operations on the given page.
- Memory page ownership is dynamic.
- An invalidation protocol guarantees memory consistency.
- We have extended the application domains of this algorithm by introducing a new approach for page replacement [11] making it suitable for embedded systems.

The Ada specification of this software component is as follows :

```
package Shared_Memory_Management is
   generic
      type Data_T is private;
      with procedure Local_Operation( Addr : Local_Address; Data : Data_T);
   procedure DSVM_Operation (Shared_Addr : Shared_Address; Data : Data_T);
   generic
      type Data_T is private;
      with procedure Local_Operation (Addr : Local_Address;
                                      Data : out Data_T);
   procedure DSVM_Operation (Shared_Addr : Shared_Address;
                             Data        : out Data_T);
   generic
      with procedure Local_Operation( Addr_In   : Local_Address;
                                      Addr_Out  : Local_Address;
                                      Count     : Integer);
   procedure DSVM_Operation (Shared_Addr_In    : Shared_Address;
                             Shared_Addr_Out : Shared_Address;
                             Count           : Integer);
end Shared_Memory_Management;
```

This package (i.e. Shared_Memory_Management) has a wide range of applications. This is due to genericity which allows us to tackle a wide range of domains: from the simplest to more complex synchronization primitives. Moreover, it allows the programmer to benefit from the shared memory programming paradigm which can present immediate solutions to numerous problems. This is done without deep knowledge of the internal behavior of the component : its properties and its facilities are reachable directly. (DSVM uses facilities offered by Devices; this is another illustration of reusability in our system).

4.2   Components for distributed control

With Devices and Shared_Memory_Management, we have two software components which propose both shared memory programming paradigm and message based communication paradigm. Thus the programmer can choose the more adequate model depending on the application.

These components are the core of our software library for distributed system programming as they offer communication means at the application level. Thanks to reusability in Ada, we have integrated them in several applications. One issue addressed deals with distributed control algorithms which we will consider later in the example section.

They are three ways to reuse our distributed control software components :

– The first one is the simplest as it is a sequential simulation context. This approach is well known and we will not go into the details.

- The second approach is also related to simulation as we want the students to experiment with these sorts of algorithms but the target is a distributed system. In the next section, we give examples of such a simulation.
- The third one is certainly the most interesting, as it aims at designing distributed control agencies which can also be considered as service providers (see figure 2). Let us take an example : a distributed control algorithm which implements a service like mutual exclusion. There are many algorithms in this domain. They are different from each other because of their internal features, their complexity, their different behavior in a fault situation, etc... but they share a common point as there is a notion of controller. Firstly, a controller makes an interface between the network and the application level; secondly, it implements the distributed control with the other controllers which are run by the participating nodes of the network. Thanks to all our software components, we have designed several stand-alone servers for services like mutual exclusion and stable property detection. They are modules and they communicate with each other in order to implement the control. They offer communication channels to their environment so that application programs can ask for a given service.

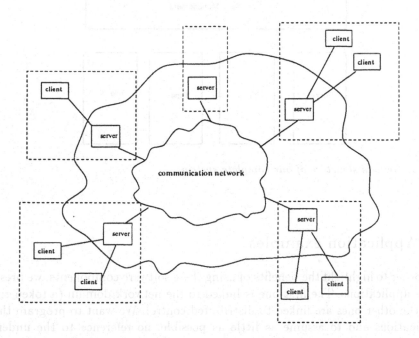

Fig. 2. *A service provider for mutual exclusion*

4.3 Architecture of our system

Figure 3 shows the structure of our complete system. In the lower part, one can recognize the basic components. And in the upper layer, we can find high level components which use the services of the basic components.

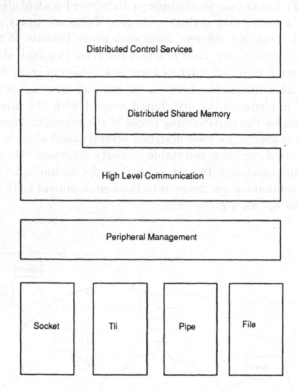

Fig. 3. *General structure of our complete system*

5 Application examples

In order to highlight the benefits of using these software components, we present three applications. The first one is linked to the network domain (a token ring) and the other ones are linked to distributed control. We want to program these applications and to assume as little as possible: no reference to the underlying communication protocol, no reference to the number of nodes in the network and no reference to their names. Thus we decided to use our high level communication component. It fulfills our previous requirements since there is a configuration file which describes the protocol to be used and the participating nodes in the domain. This guarantees the portability of the application on various networks and eases software developments. Since communication channels are defined with logical names, one does not need to recompile the application even if the communication kind or the participating nodes have changed. For example, the application run in a configuration composed of three workstations as depicted in figure 4.

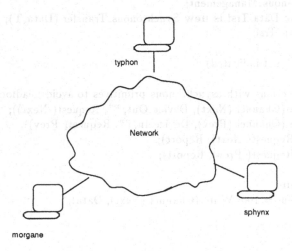

Fig. 4. *A target system for a distributed computation*

5.1 Token ring

This example is a very classical one of computation in a network: we make a token travel between several nodes connected in a logical ring. The token carries a value which is decreased when a node gets the token. Once the value is set to 0, the token travels once more between the nodes in order to terminate the application.

The following Ada code is extracted from a program which is to be run on several workstations connected with Ethernet. All the nodes execute the same code. The topology is set to be the easiest one : a logical ring. Nevertheless, one has to note that even this simple situation can be tricky and difficult for a non expert or a student. For example, using synchronous primitives for ring establishment induces deadlock unless the programmer breaks symmetry in the code. Here we use asynchronous primitives as our solution.

```
procedure Token_Ring is
    type Data_T is record
        Token : Integer32 ;
        Term : Integer32 ;
    end record;
    type Index is ( Prev, Next);
```

```
      Host : constant String := Unix_Interface.Gethostname;
      Channel : array (Index) of Device_Type := (others => Null_Device);
      Request : array (Index) of Device_Request := (others => Null_Request);
      Data : Data_T;

      use Asynchronous_Management;
      package Sync_Data_Trsf is new Synchronous_Transfer (Data_T);
      use Sync_Data_Trsf;
begin
- initialization ....(not indicated)

- Open the connections with asynchronous primitives to avoid deadlocks
      Open_Initiate (Channel (Next), Device_Out, "", Request( Next));
      Open_Initiate (Channel (Prev), Device_In, "", Request( Prev));
      Open_Wait (Request( Next), Report);
      Open_Wait (Request( Prev), Report);

      if Owner then
          Data.Token := 100; Write (Channel (Next), Data);
      end if;

- algorithm starts
      loop
          Read (Channel (Prev), Data);
          if Integer (Data.Token) /= 0 then
                  Data.Token := Data.Token - 1);
                  Write (Channel (Next), Data);
          else
              if Integer (Data.Term) /= N_Site then
                      Data.Term := Data.Term + 1);
                      Write (Channel (Next), Data);
                  end if;
                  exit;
              end if;
          end loop;
- Close the connections with asynchronous primitives to avoid deadlocks
      Close_Initiate (Channel (Next), Request( Next));
      Close_Initiate (Channel (Prev), Request( Prev));
      Close_Wait (Request( Next), Report);
      Close_Wait (Request( Prev), Report);
end Token_Ring;
```

5.2 Distributed computation using a shared memory

The class of distributed algorithms, we are interested in, deals with distributed control. Our aim is to implement standard services which are to be used in distributed applications [15]: e.g. mutual exclusion, deadlock detection, termination detection and many others. Besides the application level, these services can be used at system level as they provide basic services to implement higher level services.

Distributed activities have means of communicating with our basic communication components : by message with Devices and by shared data with our DVSM component. As an example, we programmed a mutual exclusion algorithm written by Dijkstra [6]. We are aware that this algorithm is not optimal and presents several drawbacks as far as fault tolerance is concerned. Nevertheless, we selected it because of its inherent simplicity and because it is well known.

In the algorithm, we have several nodes and each of them has a distinct identity (My_Id). These nodes are connected by a logical ring. There is an array of flags which stores one value per node. Each node can access its associated value (My_Value) and the value of its neighbor (Neighbor_Value).

One node will get the mutual exclusion privilege as soon as the following condition is true.

$$(My\_Id = 0 \text{ and } My\_Value = Neighbor\_Value) \text{ or}$$
$$(My\_Id /= 0 \text{ and } My\_Value /= Neighbor\_Value)$$

This algorithm is not symmetrical since the node whose identity is 0 has a special role. One major drawback of this algorithm is that mutual exclusion is transferred from one node to its successor on the logical ring. Therefore, one node can receive the right to enter mutual exclusion even if it does not need it. We have not initialized the flags as our DSVM component initializes the shared memory to 0.

The following program is executed on several Sun workstations. It is to be noted that in the application code there is no reference to topology. In this example, we have only illustrated the principles of the algorithm : each node will terminate as soon as it has received the mutual exclusion privilege 5 times.

```
procedure Mut_Exc_Dijkstra_74 is
    My_Id, Nb_Nodes          : Integer32;
    Object_Shared_Address    : Shared_Address := 10;
    My_Value, Neighbor_Value : Integer32;
    package Int_Io is new Text_Io.Integer_Io (Integer32);
begin
    Init_Shared_Memory;
    Mono_Text_Io.Put ("Nodes : "); Int_Io.Get (Nb_Nodes);
    Mono_Text_Io.Put ("Id : "); Int_Io.Get (My_Id);
    loop
- mutual exclusion prelude
        loop
            if My_Id = 0 then
                Copy (Object_Shared_Address + (Nb_Nodes - 1) * 4, Neighbor_Value'ADDRESS, 4
                Copy (Object_Shared_Address, My_Value'ADDRESS, 4);
```

```
      else
          Copy (Object_Shared_Address + (My_Id - 1) * 4, Neighbor_Value'ADDRESS, 4)
          Copy (Object_Shared_Address + My_Id * 4, My_Value'ADDRESS, 4);
      end if;
      exit when (My_Id = 0 and My_Value = Neighbor_Value)
                or (My_Id /= 0 and My_Value /= Neighbor_Value);
      delay 0.1;
  end loop;

      - in mutual exclusion
          Mono_Text_Io.Put_Line (" In mutual exclusion");
          delay 0.1;

      - mutual exclusion postlude
          if My_Id = 0 then
              My_Value := My_Value + 1;
              Copy (My_Value'ADDRESS, Object_Shared_Address, 4);
              exit when My_Val = 5;
          else
              Copy (Neighbor_Value'ADDRESS, Object_Shared_Address + My_Id * 4, 4);
              exit when Neighbor_Value = 5;
          end if;
      end loop;
      Stop_Shared_Memory;
  end Mut_Exc_Dijkstra_74;
```

5.3 Lamport's distributed control algorithm

Here we consider distributed control algorithms which are aimed at offering services at the application level (e.g. mutual exclusion) and aimed at distributing control (e.g. deadlock detection). Thanks to our previous developments in the simulation of distributed control algorithms [12], we can reuse our previous components almost immediately in a distributed context.

Lamport's algorithm [13] is the first distributed solution to a very classical problem : the strict ordering of events in a distributed system. Each message is time stamped with the help of a monotonous logical clock. This logical clock is incremented upon every internal event and when a received message carries a higher time stamp. Finally, Lamport introduces a strict order between events and this order is based upon the time stamps of the events and the node identities. As an illustration of this mechanism, Lamport implements it to deal with mutual exclusion in distributed systems: one node will have the privilege as soon as its request is the oldest (in Lamport's sense).

The principles of the algorithm are quite simple :

− This algorithm is aimed at distributed systems which are composed of nodes and each of the nodes has a distinct identity.

- The network must be reliable and the connection topology be complete (i.e. there is a communication channel between any two nodes).
- Each node maintains a logical clock which is used to time stamp messages.
- Each node maintains a data base of received messages.
- When a node wants to enter mutual exclusion; it broadcasts a request message. It will be allowed to enter mutual exclusion when its request is the oldest.
- When a node releases the mutual exclusion, it broadcasts a message.
- When a node receives a request message, it replies to this request message by sending an acknowledgment.

As explained in the previous sections, it is almost impossible for a student to succeed in implementing a simulation algorithm for an algorithm like Lamport's and then make it run on a distributed architecture. With the help of our software components, the student only has to deal with the algorithm to the exclusion of almost everything else.

The architecture of the system which implements Lamport's algorithm is depicted in figure 5. The main program is as follows :

```
procedure Mutex_Lamport is
    subtype Id_Site is Integer range 1 .. 10;
    subtype Time_Stamp is Natural;
    type Kind is (Free, Ack, Nul, Request);
    type Message_Type is record
        Kind_Message : Kind;
        Date : Time_Stamp;
        Origin : Id_Site;
    end record;

    Device : array (Id_Site) of Device_Type := (others => Null_Device);
    N_Site : Integer := 0;
    My_Identity : Id_Site;

    use Asynchronous_Management;
    package Sync_Data_Trsf is new Synchronous_Transfer (Message_Type);
    use Sync_Data_Trsf;

    procedure Broadcast_Message (Mess : Message_Type; My_Id : Id_Site) is separate;

- Specification of the controller task
    task Controller is
        entry Mutex_Req;
        entry Mutex_Free;
        entry Init (Id : Id_Site);
        entry Receive_Message (Message : Message_Type);
    end Controller;
```

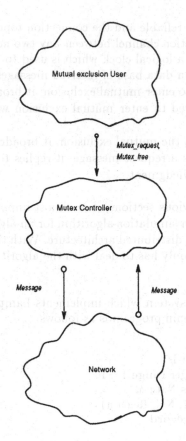

Fig. 5. *Architecture of Lamport's system*

```
    task body Controller is separate;
    procedure Init is separate;

begin
    Init;
    Controller.Init (My_Identity);
    loop
        Sync_Data_Trsf.Read (Device (My_Identity), Received_Message);
        Controller.Rec_Message (Received_Message);
    end loop;
end Mutex_Lamport;
```

The core of the algorithm is implemented by what we call a controller. Firstly, it makes an interface between the network and the programmer; secondly, it sets up Lamport's techniques with the other controllers which are run by the participating nodes of the network. A controller is run by an Ada task. The body of the controller can be found in the annex.

The next section of code simulates a user which from time to time needs to be granted the mutual exclusion privilege. For simulation purposes, this task mentions random number generators.

```
generic
    type Id_Site is range <>;
    My_Number : Integer;
    with procedure Mutex_Free;
    with procedure Mutex_Request;
package User_Mutex is
    task User;
end User_Mutex;

with Simulation; use Simulation;
package body User_Mutex is
    task body User is
    begin
        loop
            Duration_Between_Services;
            Put_line (" I require mutex");
            Mutex_Request;
            Put_line(" I get mutex");
            Duration_Of_Service;
            Put_line(" I free mutex");
            Mutex_Free;
        end loop;
    end User;
end User_Mutex;
```

6   Conclusions

Our aim was to develop a set of reusable software components which can be used in an educational context and in industry. We have reached our goal since these components are used as basic building units to design more complex systems. These components ease software development and allow students to experiment in-situ network and distributed system programming. Various issues are addressed (synchronous/asynchronous communication, real time requirements, network interfaces, distributed control algorithms,...) and both distributed system paradigms are made available.

This effort and the design of a library are continuing, extending the potentialities of the set of reusable components. Students participate in this project actively. Moreover, the specification of our message based communication component has been produced by a set of industrial developers. This implies that our software components can be used in an industrial context.

As mentioned earlier, the teaching in our University must be twofold : both theoretical and practical. We have found that these components are quite adequate in this context and also that they put the emphasis on software engineering. The notion of components is quite similar to what is available in electronics, for example, and the students are familiar with a built-in approach. With these software components students can easily practice the complex domains of system programming (network and distributed system) and still benefit from all the good features of Ada as a programming language. Moreover, since the students no longer need to tackle issues beyond their domain, they can reserve time and energy for more interesting problems and to go further into their learning. As such, our software components fulfill even our most ambitious targets.

These components are also used in a research context since we are involved in the distribution of Ada applications. It was no easy performance to design and implement these components so that they can address all the points mentioned and so that they can be reusable and adaptable to various platforms. But the results are invaluable since they allow us to tackle other research domains.

References

1. G. Andrews and F. Schneider. Concepts and notations for concurrent programming. *ACM computing surveys*, 15(1):3–44, 1983.
2. H. Bal, J. Steiner, and A. Tanenbaum. Programming languages for distributed computing systems. *ACM computing surveys*, 21(3):260–322, september 1989.
3. G. Booch. *Software engineering with Ada*. Benjamin-Cummings Publishing Company, 1983.
4. R. Buhr. *System design with Ada*. Prentice Hall, 1984.
5. CIFO working group. Asynchronous co-operation mechanisms (with reference memory model). *Catalog of Interface Features and Options for Ada run time environment*, july 1991. Realease 3.0.
6. E.W. Dijkstra. Self-stabilizing systems in spite of distributed control. *Communication of ACM*, 17(11):643–644, November 1974.
7. ExTRA working group. Proposed draft standard for real-time Ada extensions, december 1991. specific Input/Output chapter, release 1.0, version 1.0.
8. M. Hillman. A network programming package in Eiffel. In Jean Bezivin et al., editor, *TOOLS 2 Proceedings of the Second International Conference*, pages 541–551, Paris, France, 1990.
9. K. Johnson, E. Simmons, and F. Stluka. *Ada quality and style : guidelines for professional programmers*. Software Productivity Consortium, 1991.
10. Y. Kermarrec and L. Pautet. Ada communication components for distributed and real time applications. In *Proceedings of the TRI Ada 92 conference*, Orlando, Florida, November 1992. ACM SigAda.
11. Y. Kermarrec and L. Pautet. A distributed shared virtual memory for Ada 83 and Ada 9X applications. In *Proceedings of the TRI Ada 93 conference*, Seattle, Washington, September 1993. ACM SigAda.
12. Y. Kermarrec and R. Rannou. Simulation experiments with Ada. In *Proceedings of the 19th Modeling and Simulation Conference*, Pittsburg, May 1988. IEEE, ISA and SCS.

13. L. Lamport. Time, clocks and the ordering of events in a distributed system. *Communication of ACM*, 21(7):558–565, july 1978.
14. K. Li and P. Hudak. Memory coherence in shared virtual memory systems. *ACM transactions on computer systems*, 7(4):321–359, november 1989.
15. M. Raynal. *Distributed algorithms and protocols*. John Wiley, 1988.
16. W. Richard Stevens. *Unix network programming*. Prentice Hall Software series, 1990.
17. K. Thompson. Unix implementation. *Bell System Technical Journal*, 57(6):1–10, 1978.

Annex : body of task controller (Lamport's algorithm)

```
separate (Mutex_Lamport)
task body Controller is
    My_Identity : Id_Site;
    Table_Message : array (Id_Site) of Message_Type := (Id_Site => (Nul, 0, Id_Site'FIRST));
    Logical_Clock : Time_Stamp := 0;
    Sent_Message, Received_Message : Message_Type;

    function Mutex_Granted return Boolean is
        H1 : Time_Stamp := Table_Message (My_Identity).Date;
        H2 : Time_Stamp;
    begin
        for J in Id_Site'First .. N_Site loop
            H2 := Table_Message (J).Date;
            if H1 > H2 or ((H2 = H1) and (My_Identity > J)) then
                return False;
            end if;
        end loop;
        return True;
    end Mutex_Granted;

- This procedure is executed to free mutual exclusion
    procedure Postlude is
    begin
        Sent_Message := (Free, Logical_Clock, My_Identity);
        Broadcast_Message (Sent_Message, My_Identity);
        Table_Message (My_Identity) := Sent_Message;
        Logical_Clock := Logical_Clock + 1;
    end Postlude;

- The node may update its clock upon the reception of a message
    procedure Logical_Clock_Update (Message : Message_Type) is
    begin
        if Message.Date > Logical_Clock then
            Logical_Clock := Message.Date;
        end if;
        Logical_Clock := Logical_Clock + 1;
    end Logical_Clock_Update;
```

```
– Incoming messages are handled according to their kind
    procedure Handle_Message (Message : Message_Type) is
    begin
        Logical_Clock_Update (Message);
        case Message.Kind_Message is
            when Request =>
                Table_Message (Message.Origin) := Message;
                Sync_Data_Trsf.Write (Device (Message.Origin),
                    Message_Type'(Ack, Logical_Clock, My_Identity));
            when Free => Table_Message (Message.Origin) := Message;
            when Ack =>
                if Table_Message (Message.Origin).Type_Message /= Request then
                    Table_Message (Message.Origin) := Message;
                end if;
            when others => null;
        end case;
    end Handle_Message;
begin
    accept Init (Id : Id_Site) do My_Identity := Id; end Init;
    loop
        select
            accept Mutex_Free; Postlude;
        or
            accept Mutex_Req do
                Broadcast_Message (Message_Type'(Request, Logical_Clock,
                    My_Identity), My_Identity);
                Table_Message (My_Identity).Kind_Message := Request;
                Table_Message (My_Identity).Date := Logical_Clock;
                Logical_Clock := Logical_Clock + 1;
                while not (Mutex_Granted) loop
                    accept Receive_Message (Message : Message_Type) do
                        Received_Message := Message;
                    end Receive_Message;
                    Handle_Message (Received_Message);
                end loop;
            end Mutex_Req;
        or
            accept Receive_Message (Message : Message_Type) do
                Received_Message := Message;
            end Receive_Message;
            Handle_Message (Received_Message);
        end select;
    end loop;
end Controller;
```

Using Commercial CASE Environments to Teach Software Design

Thomas B. Horton

Department of Computer Science and Engineering
Florida Atlantic University
Boca Raton, FL 33431   USA
E-mail: tom@cse.fau.edu

Abstract. This paper describes a course developed to teach software design with a focus on the use of computer-aided software engineering (CASE) environments. Commercial CASE tools were acquired and used in a classroom environment in response to the needs expressed by local industry. The paper assesses the benefits and problems associated with placing emphasis on CASE tools in a software engineering course. Using mature CASE environments brings one kind of realism to the students' project experience, but the complexity of learning a design methodology and complex tools places limits on the scope of design projects that can be assigned. Design recovery tools show promise for helping students learn design principles. In addition, assignments in which students carried out independent assessments of various CASE tools were found to be very valuable opportunities for students to practice written and oral expression, in addition to broadening their knowledge of CASE.

1 Introduction

Companies developing software are increasingly willing to make use of computer-aided software engineering (CASE) tools in their development process. Many are beginning to expect that the graduates produced by today's universities should not only know the fundamentals of software engineering but also have some experience in putting these skills into practice. This lies behind the recent interest in team- and project-oriented software engineering courses. In our local area, there is some evidence that this expectation also extends to include some knowledge and experience with automated support of software development. This paper will address our department's success in the development a software engineering course that combines teaching design and the use of the type of commercial CASE tools that local companies employ in their own development process.

About five years ago several companies in the area suggested that our department include the use CASE tools in our curriculum in some manner. At that time we were beginning to expand our course offerings in software engineering, and we decided to develop a course with a strong CASE emphasis while seeking funding for the hardware and software resources needed. In 1989 we submitted a proposal entitled "An Undergraduate CASE Laboratory" to the National

Science Foundation (NSF) Instrumentation and Laboratory Improvement (ILI) Program. Eighteen months later this proposal was funded. In the interim, the two Motorola sites in our area agreed to set up a classroom with workstations on our campus to be used for employee training purposes and for our own academic courses. Since Spring 1991, a university course using CASE has been taught four times in either the Motorola lab and the NSF-funded lab that succeeded it. The courses have focused on teaching principles of design, structured design and CASE topics using commercial UNIX CASE tools like Interactive Development Environments' Software through Pictures (known as StP). The course has included a design project by student teams.

The issues discussed in this paper should interest educators considering the use of CASE in their courses. In addition, companies considering on-site training of their employees or supporting the use of CASE at a local university may benefit from some of the lessons learned. This paper is structured as follows. First, the goals of our course on software design using CASE are described. Second, a few issues regarding the hardware and software environment needed for the lab are discussed. (More details on this topic appear in an appendix.) Third, the design component of the course is discussed and evaluated. Finally I will assess the value of one of the major principles behind this course: students should have exposure to the kind of mature commercial tools and environments that are used by companies that have committed to CASE.

2   The Course and its Goals

The proposal to the NSF's ILI Program included several goals, all centered on providing a realistic laboratory environment for teaching undergraduates software engineering using modern tools and techniques for development. Two courses were proposed: the first focusing on design, and the second focusing on implementation. (This paper describes only the first of these two courses.) The focus of the undergraduate design course has been narrowed in several ways since the NSF grant was awarded. First, I seek to teach the general principles of software design and one specific design methodology, structured design. Second, students should have a realistic development experience that includes team projects. Third, the course will emphasize the use of commercial tools to support design and also to give students some exposure to other roles CASE plays in software development.

In our degree program, the current undergraduate course, CEN 4060 – Software Engineering with CASE, is an elective that most students take during their senior year. At this time a course in data structures is the only prerequisite, but we are currently reviewing our software engineering offerings and may require our software engineering survey course as a prerequisite for CEN 4060. The current catalog description is as follows:

> General aspects of software design (e.g. the context of design, modularity, system decomposition, information hiding), plus detailed study of a

particular design methodology (such as Structured Design or Object-Oriented Design). Use of UNIX computer-aided software engineering (CASE) tools to create designs and recover the design of existing code.

Students come into this course with a reasonable knowledge of C programming, but without a strong background in the principles of software engineering. They have varying experience on the department's UNIX computer systems. The course meets 3 hours a week in the workstation lab/classroom; there is no separately scheduled lab session.

This course has now been taught four times, in slightly different forms. In Spring '91 and Fall '92, it was taught to about 18 undergraduates each term using the Motorola-funded Apollo workstation lab and focused almost completely on structured analysis and design. In Fall '92 the course moved into the NSF-funded Sun workstation laboratory which can support 28 students. The course changed to some degree after this move. Less emphasis was placed on teaching structured analysis, a design recovery tool was introduced, and a number of other CASE tools were available for students to use, evaluate and describe in written and oral reports.

A variant of this course was offered during Spring '93 at the graduate level. Students in this course had taken a graduate-level survey course in software engineering, so a basic knowledge of analysis and design principles could be assumed. This allowed us to address more broad issues involving CASE, including tool assessment, integration methods and standards. Students were also able to explore tools outside the area of structured design. Some had taken a graduate course in object-oriented design (using Rumbaugh's OMT methodology), and these students worked with tools that supported OO methods. Other students worked in local industry where they had access to other tools which they assessed and reported on. These included sophisticated configuration management systems, change control systems, debugging environments for their company's parallel architectures, project planning tools, etc. These students enjoyed applying what they had learned in class about tool assessment to the tools being used in their own company, and the class benefited from hearing about a wider range of tools than we have at the university.

3 An Overview of the Lab Environment for the Course

Appendix A contains many details about the hardware and software environment used to support the course. This section gives a minimum amount of detail needed to understand the detailed descriptions of the use of CASE in the design course that follow.

As noted earlier, our course has been taught in two different UNIX workstation labs. In each lab two students share a workstation in a classroom environment while the professor lectures or demonstrates software on an instructor's machine. In one lab, the instructor's demonstrations could be viewed by the class on a projection screen in the front of the classroom. However, in the current lab environment a cheaper and more effective system has been found: a public-domain software package called **xmx** that allows all UNIX workstations in a classroom running X Windows to display everything that appears on the instructor's machine. (More details on this issue can be found in the appendix.) The ability for students to watch an instructor or student demonstrate a CASE tool "live" has been found to be extremely effective in bringing students up to speed on a given tool.

The major CASE environment used in this course is a product called Software through Pictures (StP), developed by Interactive Development Environments (IDE). (Other tools used for the course will be described in Sect. 5.2.) StP is fundamentally an upper CASE tool, supporting structured analysis, structured design, information modeling and other methods. It supports version control and document preparation (driven by document templates, including DOD 2167A, and supporting export to FrameMaker or Interleaf). It generates a data dictionary that is supported by a relational database management system. IDE has added a number of other components to the StP suite of tools, including a design recovery environment for C that will be described later.

If one is unfamiliar with CASE tools and the CASE marketplace there is a risk of "sticker shock" when pricing tools, particularly for multiuser platforms. The price for StP is in the neighborhood of $10,000 for some industry customers, but this falls on the boundary between a low and medium price for a tool according to a taxonomy described an SEI technical report, *A Guide to Classification and Assessment of Software Engineering Tools* [2]. However, IDE has had an excellent program for academic institutions who use their tools for classes; each year we pay about the cost of annual maintenance for one workstation (several thousand dollars) and in return receive a site license. Other tool vendors have similar programs for universities (but did not at the time we started), so potential academic customers should not necessarily give up on acquiring commercial tools just because of the high list price.

4 Teaching Design and Student Design Projects

A major purpose for acquiring laboratories was to teach software design. This section describes how teaching design has benefited from the use of CASE in our course. Some of the teaching methods are described and compared with the goals described in recent publications advocating projects in software engineering courses. Also, a course in software design is a good opportunity to require students to practice their oral and written communications. Finally some conclusions are drawn about difficulties students encounter in learning software design and about whether or not the course's goal of providing a realistic design experience has been met.

One may justifiably question the decision to use structured design in teaching the course, since many people believe object-oriented methods hold more promise. Structured design is certainly quite old (in computing years), but until recently it has been generally true that most commercial CASE environments only supported methodologies developed in the 1970s and 1980s. There are several reasons I have chosen to stay with structured design in this course. First, it is a natural follow-on to the concepts of top-down design, information hiding, structured programming, etc. that are taught as programming concepts in every CS1 and CS2 course. Students have learned these concepts but only think of them in relation to programming-in-the-small. Therefore in my course the concepts of design in general can be introduced without introducing a major paradigm shift for the students. Structured design is then used to illustrate these concepts and to allow the students to create high-level designs of large systems that could possibly be implemented using the languages and techniques that they know. (My personal belief is that educators should introduce the concepts of analysis and design and the structured methodologies early in the curriculum, at the same time as concepts like structured programming are being taught. Then object-oriented methods can be introduced later in junior- and senior-level classes as an alternative to the "traditional" approach.) Other reasons for not choosing to use object-oriented methods in this course are that most local companies interested in our CASE courses do not use OO methods yet, and also my own relative inexperience with OO methods. However, the reader may have noticed that the catalog description for CEN 4060 that was listed earlier gives us the option to use object-oriented methods in the future.

Students in the course are required to buy one textbook plus photocopies of the tutorial chapters from IDE's documentation for StP. In choosing a textbook from which to lecture, the instructor is faced with a difficult choice. At the undergraduate level there are more books for a more general course in software engineering (organized around the software development life-cycle) than for a course specializing in design. Mynatt's *Software Engineering with Student Project Guidance* [4] was used for one term. But while it contains reasonable sections on analysis and design, with some examples of structured analysis and design, more focus was required. The only alternative I have found is the book I am currently using, Meilir Page-Jones' text, *The Practical Guide to Structured Systems Design* [5]. The text has an applied approach throughout; this is both a strength and a weakness. A more serious problem for our students is that the book is dated and is also oriented towards information systems. (Many examples are about things like transaction processing systems and at times reference Cobol.) In some ways this reflects the nature and history of structured design. For these reasons, I attempt to supplement the text with other sample problems that are more relevant to what is taught in our other courses and to the problems faced by our local companies (for whom many of our students work).

Page-Jones handles requirements analysis in the same manner I have decided is most appropriate for this course. Rather than teach students to carry out structured analysis in depth, students learn enough to be able understand dataflow diagrams (DFDs), process specifications and data modeling techniques when they see them in specifications. In the first versions of the undergraduate course, we attempted to teach both structured analysis and design thoroughly; there was not time to do both and learn how to use the CASE environments. I have concluded that the topic of design includes more than enough for one

CASE-based course, and that students are well-served by focusing on this one development phase. The outputs of structured analysis are quite useful as part of specifications that are given to the students; they define the major data objects and the major processes/functions that the students should include in their designs.

4.1 Design Projects

After experimenting with different strategies for the project component of this course, I believe that a course with a significant emphasis on CASE is probably not suitable for large team projects as described in the software engineering education literature. In reference to the taxonomy given by Shaw and Tomayko [7], our course most closely fits the "Small Group Project" model. There is, however, a distinction between this course and the description of the typical course in that model: projects in my course are solely design projects, and by no means include implementation and testing. While this in many ways lowers the chance or meeting our stated goal of providing a realistic development experience, we believe that students receive a realistic view of the design experience and that this is of value as they enter industry to program or maintain systems. (Our department has recognized that one course cannot accomplish all our goals, and in the coming year we will offer an undergraduate elective course in the style of the "Project Only" model as a follow-on to our Software Design with CASE course.)

For these reasons, we attempt to assign student projects that are small but realistic. This is not easy, but one strategy is to describe a system that is made up of several related subsystems and to go through the design of one of the subsystems as a class example. This also has the benefit of initially providing them some of the high-level analysis and design representations (dataflow diagrams, structure charts, data models, etc.) to get them started. In choosing a design project for use in an undergraduate course, it seems best to choose applications that are very familiar to the students; otherwise the class spends too much time and energy just understanding what the problem is. (This, of course, is an important lesson in itself but does not seem like the best use of class time for this course.) Like many others, I have used course scheduling or registration systems for projects. One project that has been successful is a simple information retrieval system for small documents (such as abstracts or newspaper articles). After seeing the instructor's design of the subsystem that handles queries to the index, the students are asked to design the subsystem that handles index creation and updates. The system requirements specify only a very simple user interface. (Experience shows that student projects work best if their requirements specify only a very simple user interface.) Students also receive descriptions of primitive modules that give low-level access to index files.

Student projects that require that a large number of data items be identified and defined have been found to be less likely to be successful educational exercises. This is in part due to the fact that most CASE tools for structured analysis and design require a significant amount of effort to fully model each data item. Again, this is a realistic situation that must be addressed in industry when design methodologies are employed, but a large number of student projects have become bogged down by this process. Again, one could argue that this is a natural consequence of using a process-oriented design methodology like structured design. There may be some truth in this, but it appears that the primary problem is the difficulty and improbability of really achieving our objective of a realistic experience for students who are design novices in a class that lasts 15 weeks.

4.2 Design Reviews

In the course students are normally required to complete two significant design assignments. The first is done in groups of two, and is primarily to give them a chance to learn the CASE tools and to have a first attempt at structured design. The second project is substantially larger, and students work in groups of four or five. There will be six or seven groups working on this second project, and two or three of the teams are required to participate in a design review (or walkthrough) in front of the class. All team members participate in the design review, and in addition at least one member from another team plays the role of a reviewer brought in from outside the development group. (The students on the other teams who do not participate in reviews give individual oral reports on other CASE tools, as described below.) Each review lasts about 30 minutes, with the team asked to go through the highest-levels of their design (focusing primarily on their structure charts) and also to review the low levels of at least one subsystem in detail.

Students are given one lecture on design reviews that begins with the presentation of the SEI's video on code inspections [1]. Page-Jones' text also includes an appendix devoted to reviewing structured designs. The undergraduates enjoy the video's presentation of some problems of group dynamics, and everyone enjoys watching them mimic some of these problems in their own "performances." In the future I plan to conduct at least some of these reviews well before the due date of the projects so that the teams (and the other teams) can benefit from the close review and see the benefits of iteration in the design process. This component of the course has been very valuable. Educators in science and engineering need to help students learn to communicate effectively in their own subject area. In addition, presentation of this topic gives further reinforcement to a critical lesson for this course (and any other undergraduate software engineering course) — that the professional software practitioner is much more than just a "coder."

4.3 Assessment of the Course's Design Component

In assessing the success of the course's design component, the reader should first consider to what degree we have succeeded in providing a realistic design experience. It certainly uses an established methodology, has a team orientation (including group design reviews), and makes use of mature commercial CASE environments. As noted before, in some sense the nature of the design projects themselves probably do not provide all the components of "realism" that most want out of a project course as described by Shaw and Tomayko [7] and others. On the other hand, our department has concluded that all this is not possible in single course and that a design course is valuable in its own right. Our solution is to introduce a follow-on course in which students will make use of the design concepts, techniques and tools in a project-only software engineering course.

After teaching 90 students in these courses, the following observations can be made about teaching students design. First, our students have great difficulty with abstraction in almost any situation. They desperately want to code something, even when they cannot exactly describe particular details of problem they are trying to solve and even without being able to give a high-level description of how they are going to implement a solution. Second, many students do not understand the nature of a specification. Even after hearing lectures and correctly answering exam questions on this topic, one can give them a project specification and in return receive the solution to something significantly different. Regarding structured design, students are not as skilled in factoring a system into modules as I expected. A large number of students have a tendency to "overfactor:" to make every single action an individual module. This is an interesting contrast to students' programming habits, where they often do not factor enough activities into separate functions or procedures. This tendency seems to be due to two different factors. The bad students sometimes view structure charts as if they were like flowcharts, with a node in the graph for each activity. The better students take all structured design's lessons of modularity etc. to heart and then tend to overcompensate.

Educators should structure their design projects to allow for more iteration. This is often difficult for a university instructor because of time requirements and constraints related to grading. But without this iteration, students are once again reinforced in their view that development (of code, designs, etc.) is a process in which they have no further responsibility for a deliverable after they complete it.

Students also suffer because there are not enough good examples of design for them to study and analyze. Most CASE tools (e.g. IDE's StP, Cadre's Teamwork, Popkin's System Architect) come with some examples, but in most cases these are either incomplete or simplistic. I have not seen one that comes with any kind of requirements statement other than the structured analysis representations. Students learn to program in part because the iteration of the code/compile/test cycle gives feedback about what works in developing a solution for a problem. Without a similar iterative process for learning good design, we must fall back on teaching principles from a text and teaching from examples. Educators and CASE trainers would all benefit if complete designs (made up of a detailed requirements statement along with structure charts, data models, module specifications or whatever representations are required for the methodology used) were collected and made freely available in a format that is independent of the specific tool used to create the design. The relatively recent introduction of commercial design recovery tools (discussed in more detail in Sect. 5.1) may help in this regard.

There are also a number of comments and conclusions that can be made about the use of CASE tools like IDE's Software through Pictures for teaching design. First, the learning curve is quite steep for students no matter how good the tool is. Students are learning design concepts, a particular methodology and a tool all in the same course. If the tool is introduced at the same time as the methodology, some students confuse the tool with the method. In recent versions of the course I have quickly marched students through most of Page-Jones' book on structured design (using pop quizzes as a whip) before teaching them how to use StP. During this time groups of students draw simple structure charts etc. on the board or on large sheets of paper taped to the classroom walls; these are then viewed by the entire class for evaluation and comment.

In choosing tools for use in classes, instructors should look carefully at the documentation that comes with the tool. One thing is certain about this documentation: for mature tools like StP or Cadre's Teamwork, there will be a lot of it. Stand-alone tutorials for each tool that work through complete examples are absolutely necessary. These do not have to include every feature for the underlying methodology but must definitely include all configuration and set-up needed for a user's environment. While many tools have such tutorials, not all do, and instructors are strongly advised to write their own if they choose to use such a tool. Another factor to consider about documentation is availability and copying. How will you get documentation into the students' hands? IDE has an extremely enlightened policy stated on copyright page of every manual: owners of the tool are free to make copies for use on their site. For our course, students purchase copies of the tutorial chapters of the documentation from the university copy center. Complete manual sets are then made available in the laboratory for reference.

Other characteristics of the tool should be considered by the instructor before assigning projects using a CASE tool like Software through Pictures. One of the reasons for using a CASE tool is its ability to use methodology-dependent semantic information in editing and checking diagrams and data dictionary entries. If the students are to be required to make use of the tool's ability to to perform checks on diagrams and the data dictionary, instructors should evaluate how much effort is required to make this exercise useful. StP, for example, provides very detailed checking, but requires that the user provide detailed information for every data couple or dataflow in the diagrams; otherwise, the tool produces pages of error messages. I have concluded that the effort involved in specifying a system completely enough to make use of the consistency checking is not worthwhile for student exercises using this tool. (This is not to say that consistency checking in general is not worthwhile, or that StP's functions in this area are not very good.) Other tools (for example, Popkin's System Architect under OS/2) provide simpler checking with some benefit but without unreasonable extra effort on the part of the student.

Similar comments apply to a CASE tool's multi-user capabilities. StP allows the users in a team to access data and diagrams for a single project, but not in the most straightforward manner. (StP's best technique for this involves setting up a special UNIX account for each team, with special groups ids and permissions, etc.) Once all this is accomplished the tool provides valuable diagram locking facilities, version control, etc. To this point I have decided that the overhead and administration for these desirable features is not worth the benefit for student projects in this class. Students have therefore copied project files back and forth across user accounts or made arrangements to share access to one single account. (But I am not completely satisfied with my decision and may change this in the future.)

Finally, the system designs created with CASE tools can contain a large number of diagrams and text. A complete report of something like a student registration system can run to 80 pages of laser printer output. This causes a number of problems, most notably a large additional expense (paper, toner cartridges, etc.) for the course. After teaching this course for four semesters, I have found it much easier to grade the design assignments on-line, browsing the diagrams, data dictionary and module/process specifications using the tool itself. (Students give me access to the directory tree under which the system is stored, and I make an archive copy of all the files in this directory tree.) While this saves one printed copy of the complete assignment, students still want to print a few diagrams or even the entire design at certain times (to take home before a design review, for example). Because of the fiscal constraints that most university departments operate under, instructors who are considering the use of CASE should consider these issues related to output.

5 Exposing Students to Commercial Tools

To some extent the course's goal of exposing students to mature, commercial CASE tools can be assessed independently of an evaluation of the success of the design component. This aspect has certainly been successful in one way: students are eager to take the course, believing that knowledge of CASE tools makes them more valuable on the job market. (Indeed, several students who have taken the course have received good job offers after graduation from some of the local companies that use CASE tools similar to those taught in the course.) I feel that both undergraduate and graduate students benefit if the course places some emphasis on CASE topics beyond simply creating structured designs. First, through a discussion of vertical tools used in other phases of software engineering, their knowledge of that phase is reinforced by seeing what activities in that phase are supported by automation. In addition, these tools are large and sophisticated software applications, many of which have similar or identical functionality. This provides an opportunity to discuss what makes one software application better than another and to express such opinions through oral and written communication.

5.1 Design Recovery Tools

IDE has a product that works with Software through Pictures called the C Development Environment (CDE). This became available when the course was first offered in NSF-funded laboratory during Fall '92. CDE has the ability to take existing C source code and create an StP "system" directory containing structure charts, Jackson data structure diagrams and data dictionary entries. In order to use CDE, users must also have purchased one of several C development environments sold by vendors other than IDE, such as CenterLine's tool, CodeCenter (formerly SaberC). CDE and CodeCenter are integrated with StP's normal diagram editors to provide a powerful system for looking at and revising existing C code. CodeCenter provides a windowed execution and debugging environment (similar in flavor to BorlandC++ for DOS). Once a software system has been processed by CDE, a user can browse through the structure charts that reflect the system's implementation, call up the code itself in CodeCenter with a simple mouse action on the structure chart, modify the code and regenerate the design. By using StP in the normal manner, one can access all components of the design. All diagrams, reports and even code can be output in a structured report format. This report is created as a FrameMaker or Interleaf document; the documentation application is also integrated with the other tools. (These reports can easily be 100 pages, even when code is not included.)

For educational use, this design recovery tool was used in several ways. When we received the tool in the midst of the Fall '92 course, students had completed their design projects, and they were simply given an assignment to insure that they tried this tool on the tutorial that came with the tool. The next term in the graduate course, students explored CDE and then used the way the four tools (CDE, CodeCenter, StP, and FrameMaker) worked together as a starting point for discussing the topic of tool integration. In future terms I plan to use this tool to recover the designs of existing software systems in order to illustrate aspects of good design and bad design while lecturing from Page-Jones' text. This will also help students better understand the relationship between design representations (structure charts, data structure diagrams, data dictionary entries) and the source code that will eventually implement a design. (As noted earlier when discussing overfactoring, some students have problems with this.) Then when doing design, they will be able to know how a structure chart describes a system before it is implemented because they have seen examples of structure charts that describe working systems implemented in a language they know, C.

5.2 Tool Assessment Project

A final assignment in the course allows students to explore, evaluate and report on another CASE tool besides the IDE products used for the design projects and the design recovery assignment. Through funding by IBM Corporation and the State of Florida High Technology and Industry Council, several other commercial tools have been acquired and made available for this assignment. In addition, a few public-domain tools have been been deemed suitable for this assignment. (The individual tools are described below.)

Since the course's major focus is software design, most of these tools are upper CASE tools that support analysis and design. Three or four students evaluate each tool, and each of them prepares a short written report as follows:

1. The completion of a worksheet made up of the questions listed in Fig. 1. This is based on the tool taxonomy provided in a SEI report on tool classification and assessment [2].
2. A one or two paragraph high-level description of the tool. The size limit for this section is strictly enforced, encouraging the students to put some effort into writing a description that is both concise and informative. I ask them to imagine that this description would appear in a magazine or be presented to a manager who wished to know more about the tool.
3. A rating from 1 to 10 in four categories: ease of use, power and performance, robustness and functionality. Students are given a brief overview of the meaning of these categories, again using the descriptions given in the SEI tool assessment report.
4. A one-page report describing their personal experiences and evaluation of the tool, perhaps justifying the ratings given in the previous section.

The students who did not participate in the design reviews before the class then make 10-minute oral presentations of their reports (usually two students for each tool). Since a few other students have also evaluated the same tool, and since all the students have used StP for analysis and design, there are usually good questions and interesting discussions on the relative merits of each tool and the methods and criteria for assessing a CASE tool.

The CASE tools used for this assignment include:

1. Cadre's Teamwork, a set of products very similar in functionality and maturity to IDE's Software through Pictures. We own a single-license for running this tool on an IBM PS/2 running OS/2.
2. Popkin's System Architect. This is an upper CASE tool that supports a large number of analysis and design methodologies (including Coad/Yourdon's and Booch's OO methods). We again have a single-user version of this tool running under OS/2. This tool and Teamwork provide the students with good comparison points for a discussion about StP, its functionality, ease of use, etc. Many students initially complain about StP, mostly because they are using it to do something that is new and unnatural for them. (At least by using other tools they sometimes learn that what they really dislike is not the tool itself but the methodology used or the fact that they are required to design.)
3. EasyCASE Plus running under DOS. (This is the commercial version, not the public-domain version available on some archives.)
4. A public-domain testing tool, gct, that runs under UNIX. This is a modified version of the GNU C compiler that uses branch testing techniques (and others) to determine how thoroughly a set of test data exercises a C program.

Tool Assessment Worksheet
Provide short answers for each of the following items.

1. Tool Category:
2. Hardware Platform:
3. System Software Platform:
4. Tool Cost (including per user cost, educational cost, etc.):
5. Multiuser Capability:
6. Phases of Software Development Supported:
7. Associated Technique or Methodology:
8. Diagrams Supported:
9. Central Repository or Database:
10. Language Support:
11. Report Generation:

Subjective Judgements — rating from 1 (worst) to 10 (best):

12. Ease of Use:
13. Power/Performance:
14. Robustness:
15. Functionality:

Fig. 1. Worksheet for describing and classifying CASE Tools

5. **dbmalloc**, a publicly-available set of libraries that are linked with source code on UNIX and used to find memory leaks in C programs.

These last two tools give the few students who try them some exposure to vertical tools for testing. While these are not commercial tools, **gct** is of very high quality, and **dbmalloc** is similar in purpose to a number of commercial products available on the market. In the graduate version of the course several other tools became available and were used:

6. StructSoft's TurboCASE for the Apple Macintosh. Again, this is an upper CASE tool that supports a large number of analysis and design methodologies. Among its most interesting feature for educational use is a requirements traceability function.
7. Software Productivity Research's SPQR/20, a cost-estimation tool for DOS that is based on a function-point analysis technique.
8. GE Advanced Concepts Center's OMTool, a tool that supports the OMT object-oriented analysis and design methodology developed by Rumbaugh et. al. Our version runs under X Windows on the Suns.

TurboCASE and SPQR/20 are available to universities who use Pressman's software engineering textbook [6] at a very attractive special rate. (Contact your McGraw-Hill textbook representative or see the text's instructor's manual for more details.) The graduate class included some students with the background needed to evaluate OMTool and SPQR/20.

The tool exploration and assessment component of the course has proved very successful. Many students find exploring new tools particularly interesting, and as noted above the debate and discussion on a particular tool or type of tool is often lively. I strongly believe that the oral and written communication assignments are quite worthwhile, as many students do not seem to be getting this experience, especially with technical topics as the subject. The design recovery tool appears to have great promise for teaching structured design more effectively. It will be interesting to see if similar types of tools for object-oriented approaches will prove valuable as educators begin to teach OO methods. Of course we will have to find software artifacts that represent good OO design practice.

This phase of the course has a number of negative aspects, mainly for the instructor. Configuring and administering this many tools is very demanding on the instructor or on the department's support staff. (This is especially true for PC-based tools, where the careless or mischievous user can wipe out system configuration files.) It is impossible to learn each of these tools thoroughly, but the instructor must have explored each one to the extent that he or she can help students get started with the tool. Students may suffer from the fact that some of these tools run on machines in labs that are not as easily accessible as our UNIX machines. Like StP, most of these tools cannot be accessed from home via modems because of their user-interface requirements. Finally, while most of these tools have a fairly small initial purchase cost, some of them do require annual maintenance and license fees. As noted earlier, our department has been fortunate to receive grants and other funding to support CASE in our classes.

6 Conclusions

Experience with this course has shown that commercial CASE tools can play a important role in teaching university students aspects of software design. In addition, such tools can be used as a vehicle for achieving other desirable educational goals, such as development of technical writing and speaking skills. Using commercial tools leads to a number of advantages; the tools are full-featured and realistic (in the sense that they are the tools that many innovative companies use). In addition, there may be added benefits for a department's research programs; for example, a group in my department is implementing a system by which statements in a formal specification language are automatically generated from StP's data dictionary and diagrams. Disadvantages of commercial tools include: the typical high cost of acquisition and maintenance; the computing resources needed to support these environments; the complexity of tool configuration and administration; and, the possible steep learning curve for students.

Educators contemplating using CASE in software engineering courses should think carefully before committing to this style of course. Teaching with CASE as described in this paper is not for everyone. I have reasonably high skills as a "power-user" and systems administrator on both UNIX and DOS, and this has allowed me to make a large number of tools available to students. Instructors should consider how often they will teach a CASE-based course; if this is not going to be a regular offering, it may not be worthwhile to rely primarily on tools. Most of the instructional components described in this paper have been developed gradually over three or four semesters. If the student population is not very proficient and independent with regard to their computing environment, the instructor (or support staff) may be required to spend a lot of time getting students up to speed on a windowing system, operating system commands, etc. If multi-user and network capabilities are not particularly important, one might consider what I would describe as a rich but relatively easy-to-use tool such as TurboCASE for the Macintosh or System Architect for DOS or OS/2. Both these tools are quite professional, support a large number of methodologies, but do not require a large investment in cash or system administration.

There are several implications for industry, too. First, if companies desire universities to produce graduates who have experience with CASE, then they must be willing to support this by funding the acquisition and maintenance of tools, by assisting with system planning and configuration, and by helping educators learn the tools. (As noted earlier, we have been well-supported in this regard by the Motorola and IBM sites in our area.) In return these companies will have the opportunity to enroll their students in university courses that may have a direct and valuable benefit on software development in their corporation. About half of the graduate students in the course during the Spring '92 term were professional software developers employed by various local companies. Alternatively, companies can rely on the training courses offered by CASE tool vendors for customers who have purchased their products. These courses are certainly more expensive than tuition at our state university, and in at least one instance a student who had attended a training course reported that major principles of the design methodology were not being taught correctly in the vendor course.

There are two directions I wish to undertake that will lead to improvements to this course and also benefit other universities teaching software design. First, an archive site will be established (accessible over the Internet through anonymous ftp) that will contain software design projects. The archive is to be populated through contributions by educators. There will be a suggested contents and organization for contributions; submissions should include descriptions of the assignments, solutions, and even implementations if available. Information on each project will be will be organized so that files, documents and diagrams will be available in a general format that can be viewed or printed by most users (e.g. Postscript for diagrams) and also in the format specific to the tool that created the design. This would allow those using the same tool to access the design with the tool on their local site. If there are projects already stored on other sites, this site could store information describing these projects' contents and how to acquire them. Second, I plan to use IDE's design recovery tool to develop design recovery exercises for the current class. If carefully designed software systems in C can be found, then the CDE tool can be used to produce structure charts, data structure diagrams and data dictionary entries from the source code. It might also be desirable to develop a set of code-reading exercises based on these systems. All of this could be organized and formatted as described above and made available to other Internet users on the archive site.

Acknowledgements

The work described in this paper was supported by grant number CDA–9050963 from the National Science Foundation. In addition, we appreciate the matching contributions for this grant that were made by Sun Microsystems, the Florida Atlantic University Foundation and Florida Atlantic University. We also wish to thank Motorola sites in Boynton Beach and Plantation (especially Quiriro Balzano and Walt Davis) for supporting the establishment of advanced computing facilities at the university. Funding by IBM Corporation's Boca Raton site has allowed us to use CASE tools running in the OS/2 environment for this course. Thanks to the numerous CASE vendors who make special arrangements for universities, and special thanks to Interactive Development Environments, especially Paul Hale and Cam Collins. Finally, I wish to express my personal appreciation to Roy Levow, who co-authored the NSF grant proposal and helped teach the earliest version of this course.

References

1. Lionel E. Deimel. *Scenes of Software Inspections: Video Dramatizations for the Classroom.* Software Engineering Institute, Carnegie-Mellon University, Pittsburgh, CMU/SEI–91–EM–5, May 1991.
2. Robert Firth, Vicky Mosley, Richard Pethia, Lauren Roberts, William Wood. *A Guide to Classification and Assessment of Software Engineering Tools.* Software Engineering Institute, Carnegie-Mellon University, Pittsburgh, CMU/SEI–87–TR–10, August 1987.
3. J. P. Jacquot and J. Guyard. Seven Lessons to Teach Design. In James E. Tomayko (ed), *Software Engineering Education: Proceedings of the SEI Conference 1991*, pp. 195–204. Springer-Verlag, Berlin, 1991.
4. Barbee Teasley Mynatt. *Software Engineering with Student Project Guidance.* Prentice-Hall, Englewood Cliffs NJ, 1990.
5. Meilir Page-Jones. *The Practical Guide to Structured Systems Design*, 2nd ed. Yourdon Press, Englewood Cliffs NJ, 1988.
6. Roger S. Pressman. *Software Engineering: A Practitioner's Approach*, 3rd ed. McGraw-Hill Inc., New York, 1992.
7. Mary Shaw and James E. Tomayko. Models for Undergraduate Project Courses in Software Engineering. In James E. Tomayko (ed.), *Software Engineering Education: Proceedings of the SEI Conference 1991*, pp. 33–71. Springer-Verlag, Berlin, 1991.
8. Laurie Honour Werth. Industry-Academia Collaboration to Provide CASE Tools for Software Engineering Classes. In James E. Tomayko (ed.), *Software Engineering Education: Proceedings of the SEI Conference 1991*, pp. 245–256. Springer-Verlag, Berlin, 1991.

Appendix A: Computer Resources to Support the Class

This appendix gives an overview of the hardware and software environments that were acquired to support the design course. It also addresses some of the issues and problems that should be considered by educators seeking to make use of tools in the classroom. For our lab the acquisition of hardware and software was driven by several factors. First, for a variety of reasons our department is committed to a UNIX computer environment. Second, a goal of our course is to provide students with the same kind of tools used in industry (especially local companies). Finally, we took advantage of a number of special offers from software and hardware vendors.

As noted in the introduction, Motorola established a training laboratory on our campus in late 1990. This lab has 9 Apollo color DN3500 workstations, each shared by two students. The instructor uses the main server for the lab, an Apollo DN4500. The machines run Apollo's Domain/OS, are networked using a token ring network, and use a distributed file system (with disks on four machines). The server has a laser printer and is also attached to an overhead display system that could display either the server's screen or the output of a VCR on a screen at the front of the class. This network is identical to those used by many Motorola development groups at the time the lab was established. The NSF-funded has 14 Sun SPARC IPC color workstations, with a SPARC 2 serving as instructor station and server for a laser printer. Again, in the class setting two students share one workstation. Student files and applications software reside on a larger Sun server; all machines are attached to the campus ethernet. (Sun Microsystems sought to influence our decision about what kind of student stations to purchase by donating the server, which was the previous year's model, shortly after we received the NSF grant. It worked.)

Anyone in a university or a company who is considering teaching CASE in labs should be aware of the following issues you may face regarding computing environments. First, the operating system and user environment should be one with which the instructor and students are very familiar. You want to spend your energy teaching the design methodology and how the tool supports that methodology, not teaching system basics. This problem loomed large when the course was taught in the Apollo lab; the operating system (Domain/OS) and its windowing system were significantly different from what I knew and what the students knew (UNIX from Sun or HP with X Windows). Minor system administration issues that should have been simple (such as stopping a 100-page design document that was accidently sent to the laser printer) were often difficult because of my own lack of experience with Domain and possible configuration problems introduced by my department's support staff, who were also Domain rookies.

A second possible problem centers on networking and adequate hardware resources. As is almost always the case, we were trying to stretch our dollars in setting up these labs, and a major goal was to purchase the largest number of workstations in order to support the maximum number of students in the classes. Thus our workstations have not had adequate memory in either lab (the Apollos had 8 megabytes, while the Suns have either 12 or 16 megabytes). Similarly, file systems that are distributed across a network have many advantages, but some of the CASE tools' activities can suffer from (or cause) poor network performance. For example, the design recovery of a 6000-line system ran in just 30 minutes for one student who was logged in on the faster file server, but took about 4 hours for another student who ran it directly on one of the student workstations during a time of peak network usage. Similar problems were evident in the Apollo lab (in which 10 machines shared 4 disks) when 8 students simultaneously tried to generate a data dictionary.

In using a teaching lab, I have found it extremely beneficial to have some kind of system to allow students to all observe how the instructor is using an application. But great care must be taken to find something that is truly useful. The Apollo lab was equipped with a sophisticated overhead device that at that time sold for about $20,000. This projected onto a normal-sized projection screen at the front of the room. In the end, this system was an expensive disaster. Screen displays were never clear, despite regular on-site visits by vendor technicians to adjust the display system. Even in its best moments, text and small figures displayed by a CASE tool (in a structure chart, for example) were not readable on a normal-sized overhead screen. In recent years, display panels that hook into the port of a PC or UNIX machine and then lie across an overhead projector have become available. We evaluated one of these products for the Sun lab, and we concluded that it might perform adequately if we invested in a high-powered overhead projector. However, the limitation of the relative size of the screen at the front of the classroom still resulted in very poor readability of the text and symbols used in typical CASE tools being taught.

I have concluded that the best solution is software that allows one machine to drive the displays of all the networked machines in the teaching lab. For our Sun workstations running X Windows, we succeeded in using a "X multiplexor" package called xmx developed at Brown University and available for free on the Internet. The entire screen of each student station is taken over by the instructor's machine, and students can see all actions that the instructor performs, including mouse movements. This allows the instructor to walk-through the process of calling up a CASE tool, going through the initial steps of setting up a design project, invoking the editors to create diagrams or enter attributes, etc. Students appear to benefit from this exposure to how to use a tool before they start using it themselves, even when there are good tutorial documents. The xmx system has some disadvantages, however. Using it requires some detailed knowledge of the X Windows system (you have to use a script to start X servers on each student machine, then reset the instructor's DISPLAY variable, then start a new window manager, etc.) but some of this could perhaps be automated. Because of network performance bottlenecks, displaying dynamic graphics (such as a bouncing window demonstration) can bring your systems to a halt, but this was not found to be a problem for normal instructional use for CASE tools.

There were other minor problems related to teaching labs that we encountered. When a lab fills with warm student bodies, each of whom has their machine turned on, any room can become quite warm (and very claustrophobic if it is not large) unless the lab's cooling system can make rapid adjustments. (Ours does not, at least not until class is over.) While lecturing the instructor may also have to compete with the temptation of the computer sitting in front of each student. (Despite the obvious brilliance of most lectures, many students will still choose to read news or play Tetris!) Dynamically changing windows and system beeps can distract those in the class sitting near the guilty student, and the instructor must either be firm in requiring that the class resist this temptation or go to the trouble of finding software to lock up the student systems. (Networked UNIX systems are not normally turned off, but this would be the simplest option in a PC lab.)

Session 3:
Project-Oriented Courses

**Real-World Software Engineering:
A Spiral Approach to a Project-Oriented Course**
*Donald Gotterbarn and Robert Riser, East Tennessee
State University, Johnson City, Tennessee*

**Learning by Doing: Goals and Experience of Two
Software Engineering Project Courses**
*Melody Moore and Colin Potts, Georgia Institute of
Technology, Atlanta, Georgia*

**A "Just in Time" Course Framework:
Project-Oriented Courses**
*Edward C. Epp, The University of Portland,
Portland, Oregon*

**Project Courses at the NTH: 20 Years of
Experience**
*Rudolf Andersen, Reidar Conradi, John Krogstie,
Guttorm Sindre, and Arne Sølvberg, Norwegian
Institute of Technology, Trondhiem, Norway*

Real-World Software Engineering:
A Spiral Approach to a Project-Oriented Course[1]

Donald Gotterbarn and Robert Riser

East Tennessee State University
Johnson City, Tennessee 37604-0711

Abstract. A one-semester course cannot adequately cover the software development process and still provide meaningful project experience. We have developed and implemented a tightly- coupled two-semester undergraduate course which presents, in a *spiral form*, theory and practice, product and process. Coordinating the increase in depth of the lectures as topics are revisited repeatedly, with increasingly demanding projects, constitutes our spiral approach. Three projects differ in size, complexity, team structure, artifacts provided and delivered, and development methodologies. The projects are carefully choreographed to provide varied team experiences and allow each student to function in a variety of roles and responsibilities. The project framework provides a series of passes through the software development process, each pass adding to a body of common student experiences to which subsequent passes can refer. By the middle of the first semester students, individually and in teams, have begun accumulating their own "war stories"; some positive, some negative. This personalized knowledge provides a solid base for more advanced concepts and classroom discussion.

1 Introduction

Based on our experience teaching software engineering, we are convinced that a one-semester software engineering course cannot adequately cover all aspects of the software development process and still provide students with meaningful project experience. Current software engineering course models emphasize either the product or the process [Shaw 91]. These models rarely finish a realistic product or do so by marginal treatment of significant aspects of the life cycle and

[1] This project was partially funded by DARPA research grant DAAL03-92-G-0411.

premature immersion in implementation details. For example, while concentrating on implementation details, topics such as detailed design reviews, configuration management, and maintenance are not given adequate attention.

To address this problem, we have expanded and changed our undergraduate curriculum in software engineering. Integral to this effort we have incorporated lessons learned while developing and teaching software engineering courses at the graduate level. Moreover, we integrate graduate software engineering milestone reviews into the undergraduate software engineering classroom. A DARPA grant enabled us to complete development and implementation of a two-semester undergraduate course which presents, in a spiral form, theory and practice, product and process, throughout the tightly coupled two-semesters; mimicking a real-world software engineering process. [2]

Our course differs from other multi-semester courses in two ways. First, rather than separating theory and practice into different semesters [Adams 93]; we blend them throughout. Second, rather than mistakenly presenting the software development life cycle as two discrete pieces, analysis and design in one semester and code and test in the other, we more accurately model the iterative nature of software development. Our approach combines a thorough coverage of the software development process with realistic project experience.

This paper describes our course, related experiences, and lessons learned during its development and initial offerings.

2 The Approach

The two-course sequence is designed to present software engineering in a layered approach where "inter-related topics are presented repeatedly in increasing depth" [Ford 87]. Furthermore, the relationship of software engineering principles to software development is emphasized by the careful coordination of project and lecture stages [Shaw 91]. The combination of these two techniques, coordinating the increase in depth of the lectures with more demanding project experiences, constitutes our spiral approach.

The course is built around three projects which differ in several significant ways: size, complexity, team structure, artifacts provided and delivered, and

---

[2] The syllabus for the course is included as Appendix A.

development methodologies. The projects are carefully choreographed to provide varied team experiences and allow each student to function in a variety of roles and responsibilities.

In the first five weeks the students are rapidly introduced to the fundamental principles of software engineering and, while working in teams, they complete a modest development project. Despite the introduction of sound software engineering principles, the simplicity of the project allows student teams to concentrate on the end product rather than the development process and still achieve a modicum of success.

As the first project nears completion, a second, extended project with a real customer is introduced. It spans both semesters and requires revisiting concepts in depth that were merely touched upon in the first project. The large project is also a vehicle to introduce and utilize new concepts, such as detailed design and configuration management. The use of a real customer provides an opportunity to study more complex requirements and exposes students to problems which were not apparent in the small project. The added complexity, introduced by size, real customer, and intricate requirements, demands the use of more effective controlling disciplines and increased attention to the software process.

The third project requires the students to perform maintenance on an existing large software system. To mimic the typical industrial situation, these maintenance tasks are assigned while the students are still working on the large project. Work on the maintenance tasks and the large project overlap and they have a common due date. These tasks provide yet another opportunity to revisit and reinforce significant software engineering concepts, but this time from a maintenance perspective. Maintenance is treated as a complete software development task. Students can now understand the benefits of following good software engineering practices.

Finally, during a four-week assessment period, various formal methods, metrics, and tools are applied to the three course projects. In this assessment, both the processes and the products are evaluated to capture their strengths and weaknesses.

3 The Projects

In order to provide an instructional mechanism and realistic project experience we combine two models from [Shaw 91], the "small group project" and the "large project team" and supplement this with a set of maintenance tasks and a closing assessment period.

3.1 Project 1: The Modest/Toy Project

The requirements are provided and students are expected to specify, design, code, and test a solution. Toy projects recently used included a bottle and can recycling device, an automated fire and security alarm system, a kiosk vending machine system and an EMS-911 telephone exchange.[3] The toy project is scheduled for weeks 2 through 6 of the first semester. Since work must begin quickly, controlling disciplines are imposed upon the teams with minimum justification at this point. For example, students are immediately introduced to various lifecycle elements (scheduling, project organization, configuration management, quality assurance, and verification and validation techniques) by "living them" but only later are these topics formally addressed in lectures. While the project is implemented in a language familiar to the student, Ada specifications are introduced in high-level design.

These projects involve minimal logical complexity so that the students might devote their attention to the details of the design and development of the software. Students are asked to mimic a waterfall lifecycle. Teams are limited to four to six members each and we have found that instructors can successfully manage up to three different toy projects. Keeping track of the details of more than three simultaneous projects imposes a considerable burden without any benefit. Of course this means that for larger classes multiple teams will be working independently on the same project. There are some educational benefits to having several teams attempting the same project.

A democratic team organization is used for toy projects. At this point in the course, the instructor has inadequate knowledge of individual student's project-oriented skills to be able to place them in other organizational models. Because each project is relatively small, students approach it as individuals in an *ad hoc* fashion. Careful professorial management is required to minimize this mistake. As a means of tracking progress and focusing their efforts, a software project management plan (SPMP)[4], including scheduled product reviews and

---

[3] See Appendix B for some examples of such projects.

[4] A sample modest project management plan is contained in Appendix C.

deliverables, is provided. This software project management plan applies equally well to all of the toy projects.

Due to time constraints, we strongly recommend that the professor serve as the user for these projects. As the user, the instructor must assume a naivete about computing and only answer questions from the user perspective. We have found that it is helpful to declare which role --customer or professor-- is being assumed at any given time (e.g. during requirements clarification and formal reviews of deliverables). This is necessary to resist "professorial micro management" of projects. This over-management problem is further minimized by the involvement of other faculty in roles such as user, customer, staff, and reviewer.

In order to encourage meeting deadlines, we require regular team meetings. To help students who have not experienced task oriented meetings, we provide a task oriented team meeting report form[5]. We use this form to describe how to control and track tasks. Completed team meeting reports are required at the beginning of each week and any common problems are discussed with the class. Later this material is revisited in discussions of project status reports and assessment techniques.

The team meeting reports also serve as an early warning system for a variety of personnel problems. Even at this early stage, students sometimes shirk their responsibilities. We recommend team sizes of six students: if one or two students fail to contribute, or leave the team, it can still successfully function.

During this project, students are introduced to Ada through a "program reading methodology" [Deimel 90] using several artifacts developed especially for the course. At this point Ada is used only as a specification language. We have found John Herro's shareware tutorial, The Interactive Ada Tutor[6], to be useful as a self-paced introduction to Ada. As the toy project nears completion, a large project for a real customer is introduced.

The deliverables from each team's project include a requirements analysis document, a system design, the outline of a test plan which is traceable to the requirements, test cases, meeting reports, and an implemented system.

---

[5] A sample team meeting report form is contained in Appendix D.

[6] Useful introductory Ada tools include: [Herro 88], [Benjamin 91], and [Booch93].

3.2 Project 2: The Extended Project

Beginning with an initial request from a "real customer", students are expected to complete all aspects of a solution, from requirements engineering (elicitation, analysis, and specification) through implementation. This project begins in week five of the first semester and extends through week eleven of the second semester. Analysis and design, up through Ada specifications, are completed by the end of the first semester with detailed design, coding, and testing to follow in the second semester.

Several items introduced in project one are revisited and expanded upon here, including reviews, controlling techniques, software development standards, Ada as a software development tool, and development team organizations.

Internal project reviews are emphasized [Bruegge 91]. The SPMP for the extended project[7] requires reviews at appropriate places. For example, students experience for the first time a formal requirements review in the presence of a customer. The schedule includes time for them to modify their documents based on the reviews. Students are uncomfortable reviewing the work of their peers and uncomfortable presenting their work to peers. We address these two problems in several ways. The reviews are highly structured by providing the students with general guidelines for a review process and specifications for the content of preliminary and detailed designs[8]. We have found that it also helps to have another faculty member, who is carefully coached to assume an attitude of constructive criticism, participate in the reviews.

In some cases we have multiple reviews on the same day for teams which have an obvious vested interest in the other team's work. This interest, even if generated out of self-defense, guarantees careful prior attention to the material being reviewed. For example, the preliminary user manual review and the preliminary requirements review are scheduled for the same day. These reviews also provide ample opportunity for "planned spontaneity" on the part of the instructor. The multiple review approach insures that other viewpoints are heard and prompts an apparently spontaneous discussion of viewpoint analysis and resolution.

---

[7] A sample project management plan for extended projects is in Appendix E.

[8] The review guidelines and formats for detailed and preliminary design are contained in Appendix F.

A tool to help students overcome their concerns with reviews is an educational materials package from the Software Engineering Institute. The package includes a video-tape "Scenes of Software Inspections" and discussion aids. [Deimel 91] In less than 20 minutes, students see several dramatizations of common pitfalls in formal reviews. The presentation makes the pitfalls and the problems they generate obvious to the students. Each dramatization is intended to be followed by a discussion of how to avoid these pitfalls. This discussion reduces anxiety about reviews and develops an appreciation of appropriate review roles and behavior. The students are required to attend at least one formal review in our graduate software engineering program.

While Ada was introduced in the high level specification of project one, it is now used as a requirements specification and design tool. It is also the implementation language for the extended project. Following our spiral approach, the program reading methodology is continued. The examples and classroom exercises provided go into greater depth. In-class discussion of Ada syntax is minimized and there is a continued reliance on self-paced Ada tutorial materials, laboratory experiences, and the Ada Language Reference Manual [ANSI/MIL-STD-1815a, 1983].

We now justify the controls which were imposed in the toy project. Recognized standards, such as DOD, NASA, or IEEE models, are formally introduced and are required for all project documents and procedures. The size and complexity of the current project helps students appreciate the importance of all aspects of the standards, both managerial and technical, in controlling both process and product. The use of accepted controlling techniques is also reinforced.

The project team organization changes dramatically for this project. Rather than multiple projects with democratic teams, the entire class is organized to work on a single project and students assume roles on various functional teams, e.g., requirements, configuration management, testing, design, and programming. Several of these teams start work immediately following the client request.

New concepts are also introduced in project two, including rigorous controlling techniques such as configuration management, formal test plans, team walkthroughs and inspections, a matrix organization requiring inter-team and intra-team communication, verification and validation, software quality assurance, and requirements elicitation.

Configuration management is enforced. A configuration management plan is developed by a student selected as configuration manager. This plan is developed and presented to the class for review.[9] The revised plan is automated and in place prior to the development or submission of any other configuration items. From this point on, all documents submitted for formal review are immediately placed under configuration management and subsequent modifications must follow the configuration management plan.

The careful selection of a configuration manager (CM) greatly improves the chances for a successful project. The student selected as the CM is placed in a unique position among peers. The instructor, like other managers, must provide appropriate support and direction for the CM.

Because students have little exposure to formal test design and testing methods, we provide them with a sample test plan. Because the sample test plan is keyed to requirements and design, we use it to introduce traceability. Most students view testing simply as code verification. To address this narrow view we require that the test team begin work on its plan shortly after requirements analysis is underway. The degree of abstraction of the requirements forces the test team to treat testing as a complete lifecycle issue.

In addition to revisiting formal reviews, we add required team inspections and walkthroughs of their configuration items. These processes occur during team meetings. To give the widest possible range of experiences, the students are required to function in two different review roles on each team during the semester. Since each student is on two teams, they experience four different roles.

A significant aspect of this project is our employment of a matrix organization. The class is organized as a project team working on a single project. This resembles a functional organization. We make it resemble a matrix organization when we divide the class into several functional teams, as described above. Each student, with the exception of the CM, serves on at least two teams [Stuckenbruck 81]. The correct allocation of students to functional teams is critical for project integrity. For example, students should not be on both the coding and the test team. A critical guideline is that no student be assigned to two teams which are responsible for validating each other's work. Many teams act as cross checks on each other during development. For example, if at all possible there should be a user's manual team which meets independently with the user, while the requirements team meets with the customer. During the requirements review the user's manual team can be used to help validate the requirements. Appendix H

---

[9] A sample plan developed by a student is attached as Appendix G.

contains a model of a matrix organization for a class of fifteen students; a model for a class of twenty-five students has also been developed.

This methodology has the virtue of placing many students in leadership roles. Because teams which must communicate directly with each other have no common students, a higher level of precision is required in inter-team communications. They cannot rely on a student who is on both the sending and the receiving team to clarify document ambiguities. Although most students function as members of only two teams, they learn about the functions and products of the other teams through the review process.

The first semester takes this project through preliminary design review. Emphasis is placed on validation techniques for requirements and design. Successful deliverables, specified in Ada, from this semester become baseline documents for the second semester. The second semester begins detailed design and continues through acceptance testing. The deliverables from the class and teams have included: requirements documents from the requirements team; test plan and testing report from the test team; configuration management plan, change report log, system build report from the configuration manager; preliminary and detailed design documents from the respective design teams; meeting reports from all teams, and an implemented and accepted system.

3.3 Project 3: The Maintenance Project

Another major component of the second semester involves multiple maintenance requests applied to a large Ada artifact. This disciplined approach to maintenance gives the students experience needed by industry but rarely achieved in traditional software engineering courses.

Students perform major maintenance (including corrective, enhancement, and adaptive activities) on an existing software system. A maintenance configuration management plan which introduces version control techniques, and a maintenance project management plan is provided. The maintenance project is scheduled for weeks six through eleven of the second semester, overlapping the extended project. A variety of maintenance tasks, like those described by Engle, Ford, and Korson [Engle 89], are assigned. Without guidance students tend to revert to "code and fix" habits.

A new project organization is introduced here. The students are organized into chief-programmer teams [Brooks 82]. The choice of chief-programmer is based on our knowledge of the students' skills and attitudes demonstrated on the other course projects. Each team is given responsibility for different maintenance tasks [Callis 91]. These tasks, applied to a single large artifact, require inter-team communication and stronger change control, and introduce the problem of maintaining conceptual integrity. This new complexity provides new challenges to the student CM.

The maintenance project helps students see the utility of controlling techniques during original development. By equating maintenance and development the students revisit most of the concepts previously discussed. This third trip through the spiral makes it easier for them to work with a large unfamiliar artifact. Many students find this somewhat surprising and rewarding.

3.4 Project Assessment Period

Continuous assessment is integrated into all project activities using formal reviews and an emphasis on validation and verification throughout the life cycle. In addition, an extended closing assessment period is dedicated to appraising the strengths and weaknesses of the processes and products discussed and developed during the course.

This assessment period, based on the final phase of the Design Studio course from Carnegie Mellon's Master of Software Engineering curriculum [Tomayko 91], takes place during the final four weeks of the second semester. It also incorporates aspects of the lessons learned document of the NASA software development standard [NASA 86]. Students learn to be constructively critical of their own work and to be realistic about their plans. The major purpose is to determine to what degree the original project plans were realized and to discover shortcomings of the software product and, perhaps more importantly, the software process. The assessment includes an analysis of possible product improvements and a discussion of how to revise the product accordingly.

4 Innovations and Advantages of this Approach

This course provides a commercial-like environment where students work on multiple teams and team organizations, work on multiple projects, and assume different roles. This interplay of models accurately reflects what the students will encounter in industry. This setting is also modeled by using a variety of project types, namely, the "real client" and the "toy project" described by Bruegge, Cheng, and Shaw [Bruegge 91]. Our projects collectively meet the standards set forth by Shaw and Tomayko. For example, the large project has a real customer and a target audience. "A project with a real client is the best motivator" [Shaw 91]. But this project is only pursued after the students have completed a smaller project and have been exposed to the proper techniques of software development. Students will gain programming-in-the-large experiences on the extended project and on the maintenance project. Acquisition of new domain knowledge, another standard set forth by Shaw and Tomayko, is required to some extent in all three projects. Finally, configuration management tools appropriate to each type and size of project are used [Shaw 91]. These projects provide both a teaching mechanism and realistic project experience for the students.

Multiple modes of communication are experienced. The democratic model gives the students experience with a small project and intra-team communication. The matrix organization gives the students experience with inter-team communication. The maintenance project requires both of these forms of communication. All of these forms of communication are needed by the successful software engineer.

ETSU's College of Applied Science and Technology has an ongoing emphasis on written and oral communication skills. In all work for this course, including reviews, formal presentations and documents, the students are required to adhere to the standards as specified in the *Language Skills Handbook* [AST 90]. Reviews and presentations could be videotaped for review, development and evaluation.

Ada is used throughout all course activities. This is our students' first exposure to Ada. It is introduced early in the first semester using program reading techniques [Deimel 90]. For example, students learn to read Ada specifications as illustrations of simple designs. At the same time, Ada's complexities are progressively introduced by reading other Ada examples. In addition to program reading and extensive use of Ada examples, students learn to write high-level design specifications in Ada. A major objective is to have the students produce and validate a complete Ada specification of a large project by the end of the first semester. Students come to view Ada as more than an implementation language. During the second semester, the large project is implemented in Ada, and maintenance is performed on an existing Ada software system. We use *Ada Quality and Style: Guidelines for Professional Programmers* [SPC 91] as our Ada style guide.

Professional, ethical, and legal issues are integrated into both the lecture and laboratory components of the course. This is consistent with the recommendations of the IEEE/ACM Computer Society Task Force. Our model of the industrial setting provides a context in which to discuss a range of ethical situations not normally encountered in typical software engineering courses.

5 Conclusion

We have found this spiral approach to be an effective teaching and learning tool. The project framework provides a series of passes through the software development process, each pass adding to a body of common student experiences to which subsequent passes can refer. By the middle of the first semester students, individually and in teams, have begun accumulating their own "war stories"; some positive, some negative. This personalized knowledge provides a solid base for more advanced concepts.

Acknowledgements

We would like to acknowledge Dr. Suzanne Smith's contribution in the development of the research grant proposal used to support this work. East Tennessee State University provided institutional support throughout the project. A special debt is owned to the software engineering students who survived early versions of this course and helped us develop a better product. We would like to thank the Defense Advanced Research Project Office and the Ada Joint Program Office for their support of the improvement of software engineering curricula and the support by the U.S. Army Research Office.

References

[Adams 93] E. Adams, "Experiences in Teaching a Project-Intensive Software Design Course," Proceedings of the First Annual Rocky Mountain Small College Computing Conference, volume 8, number 4, March 1993, pp. 112-121.

[ANSI/MIL-STD-1815a, 1983] ANSI, American National Standard reference manual for the Ada programming language, ANSI, New York, New York, 1983.

[AST 90] School of Applied Science and Technology Language Skills Handbook, East Tennessee State University, 1990.

[Benjamin 1991] G. Benjamin, Ada Minimanual, to Accompany Appleby:Programming Languages, McGraw-Hill, Inc,New York, N.Y., 1991

[Booch 93] G. Booch, Software Engineering with Ada, Benjamin/Cummings Publishers, Menlo Park, CA, Forthcoming.

[Brooks 82] F. Brooks, The Mythical Man Month, Addison-Wesley, Reading, MA, 1982.

[Bruegge 91] B. Bruegge, J. Cheng, and M. Shaw, "A Software Engineering Project Course with a Real Client," CMU/SEI-91-EM-4.

[Callis 91] F.W. Callis and D.L. Trantina, "A Controlled Software Maintenance Project," Software Engineering Education, SEI Conference 1991, Pittsburgh, PA, October 7-8, 1991, Springer-Verlag, New York, NY, pp. 25-32.

[Deimel 90] L.E. Deimel and J.F. Neveda, "Reading Computer Programs: Instructor's Guide and Exercises," CMU/SEI-90-EM-3.

[Deimel 91] L.E. Deimel, "Scenes from Software Inspections," CMU/SEI-91-5.

[Engle 89] C.B.Engle, G. Ford, and T. Korson, "Software Maintenance Exercises for a Software Engineering Project Course," CMU/SEI-89-EM-1.

[Ford 87] G. Ford, N. Gibbs, and J. Tomayko, "Software Engineering Education: An Interim Report from the Software Engineering Institute," SEI-87-TR-8.

[Herro 88] John Herro, The Interactive Ada-Tutor, Software Innovations Technology, 1083 Mandarin Drive N.E., Palm Bay FL. 32905-4706

[Humphrey 88] W. S. Humphrey, "Characterizing the Software Process: A Maturity Framework," IEEE Software, March 1988, pp. 73-79.

[NASA 86] NASA Sfw-DID-41, "Lessons Learned Document Data Item Description."

[Shaw 91] M. Shaw and J. Tomayko, "Models for Undergraduate Project Courses in Software Engineering," Software Engineering Education, SEI Conference 1991, Pittsburgh, PA, October 7-8, 1991, Springer-Verlag, New York, NY, pp. 25-32.

[SPC 91] Software Productivity Consortium, Ada Quality and Style: Guideline for Professional Programmers, Software Productivity Consortium, Herndon, Virginia, 1991.

[Stoecklin 93] S. Stoecklin, Ada Laboratory Exercises, funded by a Darpa Grant 1993.

[Stuckenbruck 81] L.C. Stuckenbruck, A Decade of Project Management, Project Management Institute, 1981.

[Tomayko 91] J.E.Tomayko, "Teaching Software Development in a Studio Environment," SIGCSE Bulletin, volume 23, number 1, March 1991, pp. 300-303.

APPENDIX A
SYLLABUS - FIRST SEMESTER

COURSE DESIGN: Like an art studio or any development course students need a cursory acquaintance with the whole area before they can build items. Here, a layered approach is taken: visiting a subject at an introductory level as needed for early development, with successive revisits to the subject in greater depth corresponding to more complex construction.

Week 1:   Introduction to software engineering
   a) Definition, scope, objectives; relationship between computer science and software engineering; software as an engineered product.
   b) Current state of software engineering

Overview of the life cycle and controlling disciplines
   a) Life cycle phases; objectives, activities, deliverables
   b) Life cycle models
   c) Qualities of well engineered software

Introduction to team projects
   a) Project leadership; working in groups
   b) Team organization, meetings, techniques
   c) Team formation; initial meetings, establishment of meeting times

Written and oral communication skills

Week 2:   Overview of Controlling Disciplines
   a) Configuration management
   b) Software quality assurance
   c) Software verification and validation
   d) Relationship of a-c to team project 1

Presentation of Requirements for first team project
   a) Assignment of projects to teams
   b) Project management plan; project deliverables
   c) Test plans, verification and validation for projects

Week 3:   Introduction to software design: purpose, process, reviews
Structured design: methods, notations, tools
Introduction to ADA; ADA as a design notation
Team presentations of small project designs
Design standards: structural and environmental

Week 4:   Object-oriented design
a)   Introduction to object-orientation
b)   Review project as object-oriented
c)   Examples of project one objects in Ada and their relation to structured design

Week 5:   Verification for real projects
a)   Software quality assurance
b)   Software testing: overview, types, strategies
c)   Software safety

Week 6:   Preliminary Description of Acceptance Reviews
a)   Format and content of reviews
b)   Professional responsibility for product

Requirements engineering
a)   Elicitation of requirements; identifying and interacting with users
b)   Requirements analysis

Introduction to project 2: the client request

Week 7:   Team presentations and reviews of project one; submit specifications, designs, test histories, instruction manual, documented code and executable system

First Major Examination
Announce requirements team assignment and set up preliminary customer interview

Week 8:   Review Examination

Project 2 organization
a)   Matrix model: team roles, responsibilities, and deliverables
b)   Formation of teams; initial team meetings and establishment of meeting times

Continue discussion of requirements engineering
a)   Requirements specification: methods and notations
b)   Ada as a specification language

Week 9:   Continue discussion of requirements engineering
c)   Logical vs physical views
d)   CASE tools for analysis
e)   Analysis documents
f)   Assessment activities and role of controlling disciplines (CM, SQA, V&V) in requirements engineering

Week 10:   Requirements reviews of project two
                a)   Requirements team presentation
                b)   First drafts of user manual and of test plan, baselined requirements
                      placed under configuration control
                Introduce software development planning and milestones
                Introduce systems design
                a)   Design methods and strategies

Week 11:   Continue discussion of systems design
                b)   Characteristics of good design
                c)   Human engineering standards
                d)   Transition from analysis
                e)   Design fundamentals: modularity, structure, abstraction, information
                      hiding

Week 12:   Continue discussion of systems design
                f)   Design methods and tools: structured design, object-oriented design,
                      other design methodologies
                g) Ada and systems design
                Second Major Examination

Week 13:   Review of Examination
                Continue discussion of systems design
                h)   Preliminary design
                i)   Detailed design
                j)   Design documents
                k)   Standards- 2167a
                l)   Assessment activities and role of controlling disciplines (CM, SQA,
                      V&V) in design

Week 14:   Design Review of project two
                a)   Design team presentation
                b)   DUE: 2nd draft of user manual; 2nd draft of test plan
                Submission of Baselined Design for Project two
                User manual, test plan and design placed under configuration control

Week 15:   Final Preliminary design due
                Faculty assessment of final preliminary designs
                Professional and moral issues in design decisions

SYLLABUS - SECOND SEMESTER

Week 1: Introduction and review of semester 1
Review Project 2 specification and preliminary design documents (Requirements analysis and specification through preliminary design completed in 1st semester)
Reorganize project 2
a) Matrix model: team roles, responsibilities, and deliverables
b) Formation of teams: initial meetings, establishment of meeting times

Week 2: Detailed Design
a) Methods
b) Notations
c) Tools
d) Goals: flexibility, maintainability, cost, reliability, testability, reusability, etc.
Assessment: Formal and Informal Reviews {V&V}
a) Software quality assurance
b) Walkthroughs
c) Inspections

Week 3: Software implementation
a) Programming practices; standards
b) Programming environments and tools
c) Ada specifications and implementation
d) Comparison of implementation languages
Student walkthrough of detailed design

Week 4: Detailed Design Review of project two
a) Design team presentation
b) Submission of draft version 3 of user manual
c) Submission of draft version 3 of test plan
Submission of baselined detailed design for project two
Revised user manual, test plan and design placed under configuration control
Software Implementation, continued
d) Comparison of implementation languages
e) Assessment activities and role of controlling disciplines (CM, SQA, V&V) in implementation

Week 5: Final Detailed design due
Acceptance test plan due
Software project management
a) Software metrics
b) Estimation and scheduling
c) Organizational structures
Presentation of Configuration Management Plan

d) Project management plans
e) Professional and moral issues in project planning
Faculty assessment of final detailed design

Week 6: Software evolution/maintenance
    a) Evolution/maintenance considerations throughout the life cycle
    b) Types of maintenance: corrective, perfective, adaptive
    c) Maintenance tools and techniques
    d) role of controlling disciplines, change requests, discrepancy reports
Maintenance project and team assignments

Week 7: First major examination
Software evolution/maintenance, continued
    e) Assessment activities and role of controlling disciplines (CM, SQA, V&V) in maintenance

Week 8: Code inspections
Software testing and maintenance
    a)' regression testing
    b) integration testing
Team code inspections and reports due

Week 9: Unit testing and advanced test case design
Testing tools and test generators
User interface development
    a) design and human factors
    b) tools

Week 10: System test
Acceptance test presentations
Real-time systems
    a) design
    b) implementation and testing considerations

Week 11: Final Project 2 deliverables
Maintenance Project Due
Revisit Assessment activities and role of controlling disciplines (CM, SQA, V&V) in maintenance
Software safety: design, languages, maintenance, useability related to project 2

Week 12: Second Major Examination
Review Examination
Beginning of assessment period for all projects
Software Product Metrics using Project 2
    a) Complexity

137

        b)   Size
        c)   Estimation and scheduling

Week 13:   Software Product Metrics
        d)   Testing
        e)   Reusability
        f)   CASE tools
        Results of using metrics tools on project 2

Week 14:   Software Project Metrics
        a)   Estimation and scheduling
        b)   Staffing

Week 15:   Legal and ethical issues, professionalism
        a)   Professional ethics and responsibilities
        b)   Ethical issues
        c)   Professionalism
        Lessons learned document due

APPENDIX B

RECYCLING PROJECT DESCRIPTION

A system is needed to control a recycling machine for returnable glass bottles, plastic bottles and metal cans. The machine can be used by up to three customers at the same time and each customer can return all three types of items. These items come in various types and sizes. The machine must check which type of item was turned in so that it can print a receipt.   A receipt, which can be taken to a cashier, will be printed out. The total value of the items turned in will be printed on one line and the value of each item type will be printed on separate types for each line.

The machine has to be maintained so there is information for the maintenance operator which consists of the total quantity of each item type that has been turned in since the last time the totals were cleared. This information should be able to be printed out. In addition to these totals, the maintenance operator should be able to change the values assigned to individual item types. The machine has numerous mechanical functions which can go awry. The machine has an alarm which indicates that an item is stuck or that the receipt roll is out of paper.

To return items the customer first presses the receipt button to clear all totals. The system then places the items into the correct item type slots. With each item deposited the machine increases the daily totals and the customer totals for that item type. The customer presses the receipt button again to indicate the end of his transaction. The action prints the receipt and updates the daily totals.

The operator needs the ability to turn the alarm off, print the daily reports, and clear the report totals. Not only can the value of the items be changed, but because manufacturers regularly change their packaging, the operator must be able to change the allowable sizes for each item type. When items are stuck the customer is prevented from inserting more items but that customers totals are not lost. After the stuck item is cleared from the machine, the customer can continue to insert items which are added to his/her previous totals. (adopted from Jacobson, Ivar *Object Oriented Software Engineering*,1992).

APPENDIX B (cont)

KIOSK VENDOR PROJECT DESCRIPTION

A system is needed to control a kiosk vending machine that consists of three apparently separate vending machines that are actually under common control. The kiosk has three walls, each wall housing one vending machine. Each machine can dispense up to 32 different items and has its own coin slot, dollar bill slot, and selection panel. The coin slots accept quarters, dimes and nickels. The dollar bill slots accepts only one-dollar bills. The selection panels consist of a series of buttons, each showing a graphical representation of the item to which the button corresponds or an "empty" indicator.

To use any of the machines, a customer enters money, presses one or more buttons on the selection panel, and then presses a "dispense" button. Assuming sufficient money has been entered, the selected items are dispensed and the correct change returned. A customer can cancel a transaction at any time prior to hitting the "dispense" button and his/her money is returned. If a customer's requests cannot be honored, his/her money is also returned automatically.

All three machines are to have a common control system that keeps track of each machine's status including the total amount of money it has taken in, and the number of items dispensed (for each of the 32 different items). The money supply and money input is shared by the three machines and the system must keep track of the number of coins it has (quarters, dimes, and nickels), and number of dollar bills it has.

A maintenance operator services the kiosk frequently. The operator must be able to request a report of the kiosk status as well as the status of any of the individual machines. The operator must also be able to restock the machines, reprice items, and replenish and collect money.

There are several mechanical functions that can go awry and the existence of these problems are indicated by an alarm which is transmitted to the operator's pager. Alarm conditions always indicate the machine involved and the particular condition. Conditions include a stuck item, stuck coin or dollar bill slot, machine low on money or type of change, machine out of money, machine out of particular items, and machine or kiosk door open. The operator needs the ability to turn the alarm indicators off. Stuck items or coins disable the particular machine until it is serviced. The machine out of money condition disables the kiosk until it is serviced. A problem analysis report is generated monthly.

APPENDIX C

Software Project Management Plan - Small Project

Week, Class	CI Id	Description
1a		Requirements statement distributed
1b	CI-1	Requirements: abstract of project and detailed list of requirements
2b	CI-2	Analysis decisions completed: CD, DFD, and data dictionary
3a	CI-3	Design documents: system architecture - structure chart and external descriptions of modules and interfaces
	CI-4	Test plan: classes of tests for each requirement
3b		Presentation of design review
		Modify design and check coding standards
4a		Begin coding system and design of test cases
		Detailed architectural reviews
5a	CI-5	Test cases: specific tests, their input and expected output and their relation to requirements
		Code reviews and unit tests and corrections
6a		System testing and corrections to program
6b	CI-6	Documented source code
	CI-7	Executable code
7a	CI-8	Certified Acceptance Test: documentation of test cases and their relation to test plan; documentation of consistency of source code structure with architectural design; also include package of CI-1 through CI-6
		Presentation of system to customer

All presentation/review items are distributed to designated reviewers 24 hours prior to the presentation/review.

APPENDIX D

Project Team Meeting Report

TEAM: _____

Members Present: _____ _____

_____ _____

_____ _____

Location: _____

Date: _____ Start Time: _____ End Time: _____

Recording secretary: _____

_____AGENDA ITEM_____   PERSON RESPONSIBLE

1.

RESOLUTION:

2.

RESOLUTION:

3.

RESOLUTION:

4.

RESOLUTION:

APPENDIX E

Software Project Management Plan
Extended Project, Semester 1 (through Preliminary Design)

Week, Class	CI Id	Description
1a		Customer request presented.
1b		Team assignments announced and roles defined.
		Start development of configuration management plan (CMP), preliminary requirements (P_REQ), preliminary test plan (P_TP), and preliminary user's manual (P_UM).
3a	CI-1	CMP delivered and presentation to teams.
4a	CI-2	P_REQ delivered and presentation to teams and customer.
4b	CI-3	P_TP delivered and presentation to teams.
	CI-4	P_UM delivered and presentation to teams.
5a		Requirements review. Preliminary design begins.
5b	CI-5	Final revised requirements delivered and baselined.
7a		Preliminary design review. Detailed design begins.
9a	CI-6	Final preliminary design delivered and baselined.
9b	CI-7	Final test plan delivered and baselined.
9b	CI-8	Final user manual delivered and baselined.
10		Milestone acceptance review.

NOTE: All presentation/review items are distributed to designated reviewers 24 hours prior to the presentation/review.

APPENDIX F (cont)
Detailed (Critical) Design Review: Procedural and Data Design

* Correctness of algorithms within modules

* Review modules specifications,

* Review of module implementation sketches,

* (DDR checklist from Pressman):
  does algorithm accomplish its purpose?
  is the algorithm logically correct?
  is the interface consistent with the architectural design?
  is the logical complexity reasonable?
  has error handling been specified?
  is detail design amenable to implementation language?
  has maintainability been considered?

APPENDIX F
Design Review Guidelines and Formats

Preliminary Design Review: Architectural and Data Design
Module decomposition and dependency

* Customer present, designated secretary

* Logical Module Architecture
  - verbal description of each module, including:
    function of module
    interface to other module,
    requirement(s) related to module
  - interface descriptions, internal and external

* Narrative description of design partitioning

* Consistency Check

* Completeness Check

* Recovery Issues

* Quality issues:(simplicity, modularity, reliability...)

* Is user interface acceptable to customer

* Errors recorded for verification of correction during DDR

* (PDR checklist from Pressman):
  requirements reflected in software architecture,
  effective modularity-functionally independent modules,
  interfaces for modules and & external system elements,
  is data structure consistent with information domain,
  is data structure consistent with software requirements,
  have quality factors been explicitly assessed?

APPENDIX G

Configuration Management Plan

```
+----------------------------------------------------------------
|   PROJECT:            Third Eye Project
|   FILE NAME:          CM_PLAN.DOC
|   DOCUMENT NAME:   Configuration Management Plan
+----------------------------------------------------------------
|   PURPOSE:
|       This document describes the responsibilities of
|       Configuration Management.
+----------------------------------------------------------------
|   MODIFICATION HISTORY:
|       WHO:                     REV:              DATE:
|       Kellie Price
|           * Created initial revision of document.
+----------------------------------------------------------------
```

Computer and Information Sciences
Third Eye Project

Configuration Management Plan

Kellie Price

Table of Contents

1.   PURPOSE

The Configuration Management Plan defines the Configuration Management (CM) policies which are to be used in the Third Eye Project. It also defines the responsibilities of the project configuration manager.

2.   MANAGEMENT

2.1   CONFIGURATION MANAGER RESPONSIBILITIES

The first responsibility of the configuration manager is to develop and implement this Configuration Management Plan.

Throughout the project, the configuration manager will report directly to the customer. It is the configuration manager's responsibility to ensure that the project is implemented in a straight-forward and well-defined manner according to the customer's specifications and standards established by Configuration Management for this project.

2.2   ORGANIZATION

This project will be divided into 7 teams as follows:
(Refer to CM_TEAMS.DOC for the specific team assignments)

NOTE: All of the documents required of each team below are listed in the file CM_DOCS.DOC.

2.2.1   REQUIREMENTS TEAM

The Requirements Team is responsible for communicating with the customer in order to determine and well-define the software system requirements. The documents required of the Requirements Team are:

* Narrative description of system
* List of requirements (acceptance criteria)
* Context Diagram
* A series of leveled Data Flow Diagrams
* Data Dictionary
* Process Specifications

2.2.2 USER MANUAL TEAM

The User Manual team is responsible for producing all user documentation for the system. The documents required of the User Manual Team are:

* Preliminary format of user manual
* User Manual

2.2.3 TEST PLAN TEAM

The Test Plan team is responsible for designing subsystem and system tests. The documents required of the Test Plan Team are:

* Test plan

2.2.4 PRELIMINARY DESIGN TEAM

The Preliminary Design team is responsible for creating a preliminary design structure of the system based on the software system requirements. The documents required of the Preliminary Design Team are:

* An Object Model:
    * Complete object diagram
    * Class dictionary
    * Object-Requirements traceability matrix
* Ada Specifications for each object class

2.2.5 DETAILED DESIGN TEAM

This team is responsible for creating algorithms to implement the system structure. The documents required of the Detailed Design Team are:

* Data Structure Design using a data structure dictionary

* Algorithm Design using Nassi-Shneiderman models

* An object attributes and object operations traceability matrix

2.2.6 CODE & UNIT TEST TEAM

The Code & Unit Test team is responsible for producing source code for the algorithms produced by the Detailed Design Team, integration of the modules to produce a working system. The documents required of the Code & Unit Test Team are:

* Source code

2.2.7 TESTING TEAM

The Testing team is responsible for implementing the tests in the test plan and using them to test the system. The documents required of the Testing Team are:

* Test data
* Documented test results

3. CONFIGURATION MANAGEMENT ACTIVITIES

3.1 C.M. REQUIREMENTS DOCUMENTS

The configuration manager has provided documentation to assist the teams in meeting the C.M. requirements. This documentation is in a series of files which are available on the project file server. The C.M. requirements defined in these files are as follows:

DESCRIPTION	FILENAME
* Documents required by C.M.	CM_DOCS.DOC
* Document header info	CM_HEADR.DOC
* Document naming conventions	CM_NAMES.DOC
* Document format & standards	CM_FORMT.DOC
* Change request form format	CM_CHREQ.DOC
* Configuration item request procedure	CM_CIREQ.DOC
* Configuration item access procedure	CM_ACESS.DOC
* Configuration item change process	CM_CHPRO.DOC
* Configuration item baseline process	CM_BASLN.DOC

3.2 C.M. CONTROL

The configuration manager will provide the teams and team members controlled access to their respective configuration items. In order to have access, however, the teams and/or team members must provide the configuration manager with a written request for any desired configuration items as defined in the file CM_CIREQ.DOC.

4. CONFIGURATION MANAGEMENT RECORDS

All BASELINED Configuration Items and documents will be maintained on the project file server in a directory structure as defined in the file CM_FILES.DOC.

4.1 C.M. FILES
All Configuration Management files (including the requirements files listed in section 3.1) are listed below:

DESCRIPTION	FILENAME
* Configuration item access procedure	CM_ACESS.DOC
* Configuration item baseline process	CM_BASLN.DOC
* Configuration item change process	CM_CHPRO.DOC
* Change request form format	CM_CHREQ.DOC
* Configuration item request procedure	CM_CIREQ.DOC
* Original customer request	CM_CRQST.DOC
* Documents required by C.M.	CM_DOCS.DOC
* C.M. file directory structure	CM_FILES.DOC
* Change request form	CM_FORM.DOC
* Document format & standards	CM_FORMT.DOC
* Document header info	CM_HEADR.DOC
* Document naming conventions	CM_NAMES.DOC
* Document page header	CM_PGHDR.DOC
* Configuration Management Plan	CM_PLAN.DOC
* Software Project Management Plan	CM_SPMP.DOC
* Project team organization	CM_TEAMS.DOC

APPENDIX H

Matrix Organization - Extended Project, Semester 1
Class Size 15

TEAM	SIZE	MEMBERS	ALLOCATION NOTES
Requirements (RQ)	5	1,2,3,4,5	3-PD
Users Manual (UM)	3	6,7,8	1-PD
Test Plan (TP)	4	9,10,11,12	2-PD
Prelim. Dsgn (PD)	6	1,2,3,6,9,10	3-RQ, 1-UM, 2-TP
Tools (TL)	2	13,14	sole job
Config. Mgr (CM)	1	15	sole job

NOTES

1. The tools team members are dedicated exclusively to their service functions, including tools training and consultation. They do not serve on other teams during the first semester of the extended project.

2. With the exception of the configuration manager and members of the tools team, each student serves in multiple roles.

3. During the second semester of the extended project, a reorganization occurs into other teams, such as detailed design, code and unit test, installation, and acceptance test.

4. Following requirements baseline, two students from the requirements team are reassigned as designated reviewers and configuration control board members.

Learning by Doing: Goals and Experiences of Two Software Engineering Project Courses

Melody Moore and Colin Potts

College of Computing, Georgia Institute of Technology
Atlanta, Georgia 30332-0280

Abstract. In this paper, we describe two laboratory software engineering class series that are intended to teach the students 'reflection-in-action.' We offer the labs at undergraduate and graduate levels, and we present our experience and results from eight project quarters.

1. INTRODUCTION

Software engineering cannot be taught exclusively in the classroom. Because software engineering is a competence, not just a body of knowledge, any presentation of principles and experience that is not backed up by active and regular participation by the students in real projects is sure to miss the essence of what the student needs to learn. As Denning has argued [1], computer science and engineering degrees should be based at least in part on demonstrations of accomplishments and competencies. We have instituted undergraduate and graduate project sequences that are consistent with Denning's argument. In this paper, we describe our pedagogical goals in setting up these projects, report some early results, and discuss how we and others might continually improve the teaching of software engineering through project-based courses. We hope that the compromises between our goals and the ways in which we run the courses currently will interest educators who are planning similar courses.

1.1. Cultivating Reflective Practitioners

In an influential book, Donald Schon [2] presents evidence that experts in a range of professions from architecture to psychoanalysis exhibit what he calls reflection-in-action. Expertise, according to Schon, is the interplay of two competencies: core competencies that permit the practitioner to act and respond effectively in familiar problem situations, and reflective skills that let the practitioner reason about his or her skills and knowledge when the most immediate course of action seems likely to be unfruitful.

Translated into software engineering terms, Schon's distinction is between the type of competence that a designer uses when making frequent design decisions and the type of competence that leads the designer to reason about the design method itself. Skills of the first type are taught in the classroom and through small, focused exercises. Skills of the second type are extremely difficult to teach by instruction, because their effective deployment depends on the practitioner being sensitive to a wide range of contextual effects, some of them not within the realm of engineering at all. Cultivating this awareness, and knowing when to use a rigorous technique and when to trust one's instinct, is something that only comes with experience. Our position is that software engineering educators have a responsibility to accelerate that learning process and that this can best be achieved by means of integrating project classes into the curriculum.

1.2. Contrasting Pedagogical Goals of Instruction and Learning by Doing.

Our argument that project classes should be incorporated more fully into the curriculum is not new. It resembles the idea of the software engineering 'studio' [3]. In this paper, we focus on our three main pedagogical objectives in establishing our undergraduate and masters level project courses.

First, as explained above, we aim to educate reflective software engineering practitioners. These are people who not only know about techniques such as Z or object-oriented analysis, but have good judgment about when to apply them and with what degree of penetration and rigor.

Second, we want to produce graduates who are comfortable working in collaborative design teams and have developed appropriate interpersonal and management skills. We do not intend our courses to give the students a dose of the real world, like some unpalatable medicine; instead we aim to make students want to work collaboratively and to regard it as the normal and healthy way of doing design.

Finally, we wish to eradicate the idea that a design project is an individual or group possession from concept to implementation. Instead, we give students the experience of working on ongoing projects. Occasionally they join part way through and must reconstruct by detective work, reading and patient questioning the design decisions they were not around to make. In others, they initiate a project they cannot complete but must hand over to groups coming after them.

Over the last two years, we have translated these high-level pedagogical goals into concrete objectives for undergraduate and graduate labs. We have developed a sequence of elective undergraduate software engineering courses and have proposed a Masters degree in software engineering to the Board of Regents of our institution.

The undergraduate and graduate sequences have a strong laboratory emphasis. The undergraduate practicum (or "Real World Lab" as it has become known) and the graduate software engineering project course are both three-quarter course series. Projects are contributed by cooperating industry and academic organizations. Projects have real customers, real requirements, and real schedules. The philosophy is to emulate industrial software development organizations and practices as closely as possible in an educational and research laboratory setting. This lets us give the students a "real-world" educational experience and provides us with a source of realistic case studies for research.

We launched the undergraduate practicum in Fall 1992. The masters software engineering project course sequence has been taught for the first time during Winter and Spring, 1993.

1.3. Hypotheses about Educational Outcome

We are claiming that students will benefit in three specific ways from our project classes. Naturally, we have different expectations from our undergraduate and graduate students.

> (a) Students with project experience can better cope with size and complexity. The projects give our students experience with complex and unbounded problems. They have to learn that customers never define a problem unambiguously and that they must learn to bound problems for themselves. They work on problems that are too big for each of them to handle individually, not just because of the school schedule, but also because the problems are intrinsically suited to group work. They learn firsthand that what each of them produces or changes may have unpredictable ramifications on the progress of their colleagues.

(b) Students with project experience can exhibit autonomy and responsibility. They can make and justify design decisions. They can choose and blend methods and tools, rather than slavishly following the recommendations of the instructor's favorite textbook. And they must manage their own project and be accountable for their schedule.

(c) Students with project experience are flexible and can cope with the unexpected. Students work on problems that are not set as exercises by the instructor (and may also harbor big surprises for the instructor). Students therefore soon realize that the requirements will change and that they must do installation and maintenance work to guarantee a reliable and stable system infrastructure.

Because our courses are new and small, we can at this stage report only qualitative data that bear on these hypotheses. In the following section, we describe the undergraduate and masters project courses in more detail. In Section 3, we report our early experiences. Then, in Section 4, we discuss the implications of our observations.

2.   COURSE BACKGROUND AND PREREQUISITES

2.1.   Undergraduate Level

The newly revised Georgia Tech undergraduate curriculum for computer science [4] includes a requirement for a minimum two-quarter-long project course. Undergraduates must also choose at least one area of specialization, and the practicum serves to fulfill both the project requirement and the specialization area for Software Engineering. Students can participate in the practicum for up to three quarters; the first two quarters satisfy the design project requirement, and the last quarter is taken as a computer science elective to complete the specialization requirements.

We have designed the practicum for third and fourth year students who have already completed most of the basic courses in computer science. The prerequisite course, "Introduction to Software Engineering" (CS 3302), is an intensive project-centered course that covers the theoretical basis of software engineering and exposes students to every phase of the project life cycle.   The one-quarter-long team project incorporates requirements elicitation, preliminary design, a design review presentation, implementation, and independent testing. This course is an excellent preparation vehicle for the practicum, since we teach students many techniques, methods, and tasks required by the projects.

2.2.   Masters Level

The masters program in software engineering consists of one-quarter courses in the following subjects: Introduction to Software Engineering, Foundations of Software Engineering, Project Management, Requirements Analysis and Rapid Prototyping, Principles of Software Design, Human Computer Interface, Software Generation and Evolution, and Software Evaluation. (Other courses are also included for a total of 50 credit hours.) The first three lecture courses above are prerequisites for the project course. (From now on, we will refer to the project courses as the graduate 'lab', to be consistent with the undergraduate lab.)

Students do project work in before taking the lab. For example, the introductory course is taught by means of lectures and a group project. Depending on the nature of the application, the group project may involve programming. Usually, however, it emphasizes requirements specification, design and test planning. Other courses also have a heavy project emphasis.

2.3.   Early Experiences

The undergraduate Real World Lab has been operational for three quarters. We selected the original group from among the best performers in the Introduction to Software Engineering course, intentionally keeping the group small. All students who have been involved in the projects have either stayed with the Lab series or graduated. Following are the enrollment statistics:

- Fall Quarter 1992 (first offering)   5 students
- Winter Quarter 1993   8 students (4 new, one graduated)
- Spring Quarter 1993   12 students (5 new, one graduated)

We are running the project class component of the masters degree for the first time during academic year 1992-3. As with the other software engineering masters courses, the project course is being taught as a graduate-level elective for the MS and Ph.D. programs. The enrollment statistics for the graduate lab are:

- Winter Quarter 1993 (first offering)   6 students
- Spring Quarter 1993   6 students (two new, two withdrew)

Because of scheduling conflicts, the first offering has been a two quarter series, not the planned three. Also, we are relaxing our prerequisites. Because the software engineering core courses are new, we have accepted students who have not taken the prerequisites. This has caused problems because many students know less about fundamental software engineering techniques than we anticipated. To some extent these gaps in knowledge can be remedied by reading and special classes (see Section 6). Several students were taking the requirements and prototyping course while they were developing the requirements for the system. The following quarter, four of the six students took the software design course while they were working on the design for the system.

The level of turnover we have experienced in both programs is consistent with typical industrial turnover rates by phase of project. The remaining students have to be able to explain their progress before the newcomers joined the project and provide background information about the application and justifications for design decisions. This has proved invaluable. Not only do the new students benefit directly; the existing team members are forced to step back and reflect on their progress and technical decisions.

3.   STUDENT ROLES

3.1.   Undergraduate Level

The first task a new undergraduate participant accomplishes is to write a resume and fill out a job application. This exercise has several benefits:

(a) The student is required to use Real World Lab tools and resources, allowing the student to learn the lab's standard document processor and to become familiar with the lab itself;

(b) Experienced students act as mentors. This helps the new students become integrated into the lab and gives the mentors leadership and teaching experience.

(c) Students are placed onto projects that complement their experience and learning goals.

To overcome the frequent problems with leadership in student projects and to mimic standard industry practice, our students progress through a set of "job levels." They are "promoted" as they become more experienced or display aptitude.

Entry level - The first quarter that students participate in the Lab, we treat them as individual contributors. They receive instruction on the Lab's computing environment, process model, and the standards that have been established. They receive explicit directions and close supervision, with instructors and senior students providing guidance, goal setting, and progress tracking. The Entry Level student is responsible for a small task, perhaps sharing that task with a more senior student. We choose tasks that use students' experience.

Associate Level - Students are typically promoted to Associate Level in their second quarter, but outstanding Entry Level students or students with considerable industry experience can reach this level in their first quarter. Associate level students are familiar with the Lab environment and practices. They are expected to contribute with less direction, set their own schedules, and may be responsible for leading a small subproject. Students are encouraged to identify their strengths and weaknesses when they enter the lab. We use this information when assigning the second quarter tasks. Entry level students get tasks for which they have the skills; associate level students get tasks that stretch them in new directions.

Principal Level - A Principal Level student is responsible for customer contact, scheduling and tracking an entire project, and managing the other members of a team (up to 7 students).

The Lab instructor decides when to promote students by considering quality of work, adherence to schedules, and understanding of required technique. Organizational needs are also considered. For example, competent Entry Level students have been promoted to Associate Level when a new subproject developed that required a new team leader. The Instructor also allocates students to the different projects, depending on the predicted needs submitted by the project leaders.

3.2. Masters Level

Students will be accepted to the master's program only with an appropriate undergraduate degree and at least two full-time years of software development experience. As the students enter the program with differing amounts of work experience it would be inappropriate to put such a formal process in place as in the undergraduate practicum. All students must be prepared to accept responsibility for subprojects from the start (equivalent to the undergraduate Associate Level).

Students need not work on the project in contiguous quarters. It is feasible for a student to participate for one quarter, sit out a quarter and then participate in the third. This student would still, of course, need to participate in one more quarter in the following year to graduate with an MSE. It is unlikely that student turnover from quarter to quarter will be a major problem in the software engineering graduate sequence, however, because it is scheduled toward the end of their degree.

3.3. Early Experiences

We have found that the promotion structure generates incentive and motivation for the students to remain in the Lab program for the full three quarters. In fact, one student who graduated decided to remain in the lab sequence for the experience of being a project leader while he interviewed for jobs in industry. In the first quarters of our Lab offering, there were no Principal Level students and the instructor managed the project. Two students were promoted in the middle of the quarter to Associate Level so that they could serve as subproject leaders. In the second quarter, two more were promoted to Associate level and one was promoted to Principal Level. Currently , in the third quarter, all three projects have Principal Level students as team leaders.

We have also found that the promotion structure does enhance the role of student leader. The newer students respect the experience and knowledge of the more senior students, and therefore do not seem to resent being managed by them. The new students also see a path for greater accomplishment and responsibility when their peers are promoted, and it gives them a goal to work toward. We have had far fewer complaints about team leadership from the Real World Lab class, whose leaders "earn" their position, than from the introductory classes, whose leaders are chosen arbitrarily. The teams seem to function and communicate better, with less conflict and "power struggle" problems.

4. PROJECT MANAGEMENT

4.1. Undergraduate Level

The Lab gives students experience in many facets of software development, including project management. Therefore the students are encouraged to take responsibility for managing their own teams, including coordinating schedules, decomposing and allocating tasks to team members, and leading discussions and meetings. However, it is also important for the instructors to help lead the teams and show management skills to students. Undergraduates are not expected to be completely autonomous. They should take management responsibilities, but only under the guidance of the instructor.

Each student is required to write a weekly status report for their own progress, and if the student is a team leader, for the progress of their team. Team leaders are responsible for collecting the status reports of their team and consolidating them into one cohesive report. Status meetings for the entire group occur weekly. Students are allowed to relate their experiences, their successes, their problems, and their frustrations to the group. Status reporting is important, because it teaches students to record their commitments and accomplishments. It also provides a record of progress on each task, which can be useful data for the research component of the Lab. At the end of each quarter, the student writes a performance review to enumerate individual goals and accomplishments for that quarter. The student also completes a self-evaluation, and identifies areas and goals for his or her technical growth. This gives the student more control over their "career" in the Lab, allowing them to meet their own educational goals as well as the goals of their team and Lab.

4.2. Masters Level

Because we expect graduate students to be more autonomous to start with, project management at the graduate level is the responsibility of the project group. The instructor selects one student who wishes to learn or hone some project management skills and assigns that student as the group coordinator or project manager. (The graduate lab is smaller than the undergraduate lab, so there is less need to promote individual contributors to management positions in new projects.) A student manager is responsible for setting project milestones and coordinating collaborative activities.

4.3. Early Experiences

There have been cases where group progress has been hindered by the lack of commitment of a single student. This is a common observation in industry, of course, but in an academic environment two further factors exacerbate the delays that a single person can cause. One is that management responsibility and authority cannot be vested in the same person. The instructor may give the student manager responsibility, but cannot give the student very much authority. The ultimate sanction against a student who is not pulling his or her weight is to award a lower course grade. (This sanction is 'ultimate' in the sense that it comes into play only if peer pressure - that other great influence on student behavior - proves ineffective.) This sanction, of course, is not available to the student manager. At a less extreme level, many students are uncomfortable at admonishing their peers. It is a lesson that supervisors and managers must learn, but it is difficult nonetheless, and in an educational setting is even more of a sensitive issue.

Another problem is that the students are working on the project only part-time. The undergraduate and graduate courses both count for three credit hours - which translates into an average of nine hours of expected additional work per week. Students have other classes to attend and some of them have jobs that make it difficult to schedule group meetings at short notice at times other than the published class times. If a student misses a meeting or fails to produce a promised deliverable, it may not be possible to recover quickly and the schedule may slip a whole week.

5. DELIVERABLES

We require undergraduates to produce at least one written and one oral presentation per quarter during their design project. Each quarter, practicum students write at least one document and give at least one presentation appropriate to the life cycle phase of their project. For example, during its first quarter one project performed a requirements analysis, produced a requirements specification, a market analysis, and a requirements review presentation for their customer.

The graduate lab is less artificially structured, in the expectation that graduate students will produce the documentation and verbal presentations consistent with their project responsibilities. So far, this has happened.

6. PEDAGOGY

6.1. On-the-job Education

In an ideal world, students would have obtained from the prerequisite courses all the background knowledge they need for their projects. In reality, however, student projects are no different from industrial projects in their requirements for "on-the-job" training. At the undergraduate level, we accomplish his by introducing occasional lectures into the project schedule. At the masters level, we envisage this being less common. We expect graduate students to assimilate method-related information without having to arrange special lectures for them. By having taken the prerequisites, they are starting the project course with a higher level of specialization in software engineering techniques.

We try to keep our Lab's processes operating in the state of the art by constantly bringing in new technology. We draw on faculty expertise to expose students to new techniques and methods that they can apply in their projects. Applying the new techniques to real projects also creates case study data that could aid our research.

Other members of the software engineering faculty often give short lectures about their areas of expertise. For example, when a project group was preparing to perform a requirements analysis, a faculty member whose research expertise is in requirements analysis led a class on requirements definition and elaboration techniques.

Interestingly, however, we have not seen clear evidence that the students used the knowledge gained in these classes. The requirements class is a good case in point. It was a lively discussion, informed by examples from the application the students were working on. When it came time to produce a requirements document, however, the students did not seem to know where to begin. The message we take from this is that it is not enough to bring in a faculty 'consultant' for an afternoon. The faculty member must work with the group for a short, sustained period. (There is a powerful meta-lesson here that our students probably have not yet grasped concerning the role of consultants in industry!)

Both the undergraduate and graduate labs supplement taught courses that introduce students to design methods. We have no interest in promulgating a single method; one of our objectives - especially at the graduate level - is to educate students in making methodological decisions for themselves.

We guide the undergraduates in using methods they have been taught in their introductory courses, such as SASD and Object Oriented design techniques. In this respect, as in most others, we expect graduate students to show more initiative. At the instructor's encouragement, the graduate students are using a mixture of object-oriented analysis and design techniques taken from Rubin and Goldberg [5] and Lorenz's book [6]. The Rubin and Goldberg paper contains a detailed set of recommendations on scenario-based object identification and class and interface documentation. Lorenz contains an action-oriented combination of object-oriented design techniques and established management practices. The students are using the substantial appendices in the book as a source of project standards.

We encourage the students to fill the gaps in their knowledge by reading and by teaching each other [7] techniques that they have learned in previous courses or in work experience. For example, the graduate project is developing a system in C++. Only one of the six students has substantial experience in C++, although one other has experience in C and several have taken a course in object-oriented programming. Four are taking a course in software design that uses Rumbaugh [8] as the set text. Thus as a group, the students have a fair amount of expertise to bring to bear on the problem if they help each other.

6.2. Reflection in action

Our commitment to training reflective practitioners requires that we not only have the students 'do' the project, but also reflect on what they have learned and how they might have done things differently. This reflection takes the form of periodic project reviews and a debriefing session at the end of each quarter.

Our experience is that the experience of working on a sustained project stimulates students to reflect on what they have done. This is in contrast to our experience with the project component of the undergraduate and masters level introductory software engineering courses, in which we frequently encounter a 'split brain' phenomenon. The name stems from the observation that many students seem to partition their software engineering knowledge into two independent compartments: one comes from class and is reproduced and used in discussion and test conditions; the other seems to be tacit knowledge of barely disciplined practices picked up during previous projects or work experience and is used whenever the students have to make design decisions. For these students, reflecting and doing are quite separate activities.

Although, in our experience, 'split brains' are less common in the labs than in classroom courses (at least, after the first quarter) we do need to question the assumption that prerequisite courses or "on-the-job" training classes automatically equip students with what it takes to use the taught skill.

An opposing but equally incapacitating tendency can also occur. This we call 'reflection inaction'. It is characterized by a willingness to plan and to talk about what the project has accomplished but not to do anything. An especially reflective student temporarily stalled one of the four projects, and another project lost time from over-reviewing a requirements document.

6.3. Educational Coordination

The undergraduate lab and the masters' program are both spearheaded by committees, currently consisting of the Software Engineering faculty. These committees have the responsibilities of evaluating and accepting projects from industry and other academic units, planning the computing environment for the lab, prioritizing research ideas and experiments, and obtaining financial support for the Lab. Individual instructors control the day-to-day operation of the lab projects. But it is the steering committee, acting as a governing body, which decides the future direction and activities of the Lab, and ensures that the Lab maintains its value to the curriculum and as a source of research.

One instructor currently coordinates each project class. A three quarter sequence amounts to much of a faculty member's annual teaching load. As it is in the interests of the faculty to teach a variety of subjects in a variety of ways, we are considering ways to involve the faculty panel more broadly.

6.4. Student Assessment

Evaluating performance in a team project setting is always difficult [9]. Institute regulations require that individual students each earn their own grade, although in a project course, the grades are affected by the performance of the whole team. In both the undergraduate and graduate labs we evaluate individual performance by adopting a performance review. Students receive a grade that reflects the quality of their deliverables, adherence to schedule, responsibility, participation, and cooperation. We grade the tangible outputs of each task for quality, completeness, conformity with standards, and delivery on schedule. In the undergraduate practicum, the project leader and colleagues of a team member evaluate his or her participation. Individuals are accountable for different parts of the project, and their performance is reflected in their grade. At the end of each quarter, the instructor reviews the students' self-evaluations and progress reports, and holds an individual meeting with each student to discuss their progress, problems, and goals for further participation in the Lab.

7. PROJECT SELECTION

The success of the Lab experience can be influenced by the nature of the projects selected. We seek projects with these characteristics:

(a) An expected duration of between two quarters and two years. It is important that projects last longer than a single quarter so that there will be turnover and realistic within-project communication demands.

(b) Can be easily partitioned into subtasks. This allows us to manage risk and gives some basis for individual assessment.

(c) Moderate complexity. We request - especially at undergraduate level - that the project not be too domain-specific, requiring extensive knowledge of a specific field or technology.

(d) Interactive systems, rather than embedded systems. Embedded systems require specialized engineering knowledge and equipment.

(e) Either can be implemented on lab platforms (Unix), or on equipment and software that the sponsor is willing to provide.

(f) Meets a real, continuing need.

(g) Does not have firm deadlines. The Lab students set goals and deadlines of their own, but we do not want our sponsors to suffer if the students fail in their objectives.

Sponsoring organizations receive all results. In return they are expected to make time available for meetings with the students. These interactions include requirements gathering, design validation and reviews, and management and milestone setting. Sponsors also may provide training, marketing, or beta testing of products.

We have received project proposals from local industry, from our Office of Information Technology (computing support for the campus), and from other educational units on campus, such as the Materials Handling Research Center (MHRC) and Georgia Tech Research Institute (GTRI). Currently, to avoid complicated legal issues, we have accepted proposals for projects from on-campus groups. As we investigate and resolve legal problems, we will accept proposals from local industry groups as well. Sponsors contribute projects that fall within a set of specific guidelines that we have established to improve the chances of projects being suitable for the Lab.

7.1. Current Projects

Because we are still working out the legal issues involved with industry sponsors, we have initially accepted projects from on-campus organizations. The undergraduate Real World Lab currently has three ongoing projects:

Email Project - For the Office of Information Technology (OIT), the students are enhancing existing public domain main programs on three different platforms (MacIntosh, IBM PC, and Unix workstation) to provide a "return receipts" capability that will work across all platforms and mailers. This group has completed requirements and design, and is currently in the implementation stage.

Distributed Calendaring and Scheduling (DISCS) - Also sponsored by OIT, this project is tasked with developing a group scheduling tool to replace an older one that became obsolete. This group is currently completing an extensive market survey and requirements definition process.

Infrastructure Project - This project is sponsored by the College itself to provide software support for the Real World Lab. It includes project and personnel databases, configuration management, and project tracking tools. This project is new this quarter, and the students are currently in the requirements analysis phase.

The graduate program currently has one project:

MHRC Order Pick System - The sponsors for this project are industrial engineers from the Materials Handling Research Center who have implemented a rough prototype decision support system for order pick system design and optimization. (Order pick systems are systems of storage and retrieval equipment and strategies.) The project has raised many standard industrial issues of application domain unfamiliarity, incomplete and ill-understood requirements, evolution of an existing implementation, platform implementation constraints, etc.

8. DISCUSSION

8.1. Student Evaluations

As part of an institute-wide policy to promote teaching effectiveness, students are asked to complete an anonymous course evaluation survey at the end of each quarter. Response from small classes such as the lab are evaluated by means of open-ended surveys.

Below, we give a representative sample of student comments on the labs. Responses from undergraduates and graduates are included. We report specific comments that address our three hypotheses: that students can cope better with size and complexity, are more autonomous, and can cope better with the unexpected.

Overall, the students felt they got a lot out of the labs. Even when progress was frustratingly slow, they felt that the intangible lessons they had learned were valuable to them.

(a) Coping with Size and Complexity. Most students appreciated the size, complexity and ill-definedness of the problems with which they were faced. Typical comments were:

The project was well chosen and when needed, the instructor provided full information.

[Instructor] found an excellent problem for us to attack.

Some students, however, wanted more direction, especially early in the project:

Due to the project objective per se, the first stage of the class was in a difficult situation where to go.

At the beginning, I could not understand the whole system and what we are going to do.

If [Instructor] gave us the overview of the system and our plan in early time, I could learn and do more.

(b) Autonomy. It was by providing opportunities for autonomy and responsibility that the labs really satisfied the students. One student described the lab this way:

Not really much like a class, more like a part-time job with very flexible hours.

The structure of the undergraduate lab was definitely necessary.

I found this structure (project leaders, etc.) to be helpful in order to understand leadership roles.

Organizing students into a company chart was a good idea and it allowed for more effective/efficient goal assignment, planning, etc.

Most students felt that instructors should get everyone to participate in the project. When students do not pull their weight, it is the instructor's responsibility, not the student's peers, to take action:

[Instructor] managed to get everyone to participate -- even the most shy and reserved members of the class.

Class participation is highly encouraged, since it is most of the grade.

[Instructor] failed to make students accountable for failing to attend meetings. A few people failed to attend many meetings and this hurt morale.

Students claimed that they needed guidance from the instructor. At times, the instructor should be the real project manager, setting goals and direction; at others he or she should become a fly on the wall, intervening to instruct and help, but not to direct the project:

[Instructor] was an active participant in the project.

[Instructor] was a great assistant in keeping us on track throughout the project and providing organization.

[Instructor] guided us well and we could achieve satisfactory result finally.

The course was well prepared and presented -- [Instructor] led us in technical areas that we lacked experience in. He didn't help too much, though -- he provided just the right amount of guidance and support without being obtrusive.

Inevitably, however, there are students who are uncomfortable with the autonomy they are given:

I expected more lectures.

This response came from the same student who complained that the direction of the project was not set by the instructor at the beginning of the first quarter. We probably have not developed adequate strategies to acculturate such students into the lab environment.

(c) Coping with the Unexpected. Few of the students commented on their ability to cope with surprises. However, most students appreciated the realism - and therefore unpredictability - of the project. The following comment is typical.

Couldn't have been much closer to real world situations (i.e. no machines - had to find 'em, no money, real design issues were discussed and/or solved as would be in the real world.)

(d) Assessment. Our students also think about grades a lot. As mentioned above, grading group project work is difficult. Most students understand this:

There is no real way to have grades, so I understand that this is a problem.

However, they do have some constructive suggestions:

It might be helpful to tell a student how he/she is doing at midterms.

Self-evaluation and individual meetings with instructor are the best ways to evaluate.

Free-form comments are subjective and cannot always be taken entirely at face value. What students find memorable about a course may not predict their subsequent abilities. Nevertheless, we are encouraged by the student's responses. They certainly feel better able to deal with real projects after the lab experience.

8.2. Issues

To close, we raise several issues that our first year of experience has not resolved.

(a) Ownership of Output. To date, all four projects have been for users on campus. We would like to work with local companies too, but need to resolve issues concerning the ownership of the resulting products and the legal rights of the sponsors and the University. State funding cannot be used to subsidize for-profit organizations. We have experience, however, with corporate sponsorship for class projects, having drafted special licenses in return for corporate support [Rugaber92].

(b) Assessing Individual -v- Group contribution. In many of our courses, we are introducing cooperative learning practices and small group projects. The undergraduate and graduate software engineering labs, however, remain the largest and most sustained group projects in our curriculum. By the time they take these courses, most students have had some group project experience. (At the masters level the students certainly should have had some group experience because of their work experience.) However, our curriculum still carries the vestiges of a system that encouraged students to compete with each other and jealously guard their potential grades.

We are torn between two tendencies: to reward individuals only or largely according to the performance of their group and to grade individuals according to their individual contribution, irrespective of their group's performance. We are conscious that students listen to what we do, not what we say. If we talk about cooperation, but grade students for their individual contributions only, we encourage them to shine as individuals and eclipse their peers. If, on the other hand, we grade the group as a unit, we are unable to reward individual initiative where it has been hidden by lack of group progress.

(c) Educational objectives -v- Project objectives. While one can make an educational virtue out of a real project not being under control, the unpredictability of project events can undermine the instructor's educational objectives. It is sometimes necessary to step in and artificially impose project goals for the sake of preserving the educational value of the project experience. This can happen, for example, if the requirements turn out to be unexpectedly vague, thus making the requirements ill-defined and fuzzy. We are excited at the prospect of our students catching a glimpse of such pitfalls, but we try to lead them back from the brink. In such a situation, we force the issue by setting artificially constrained goals.

Our students are very bright and mature. They already know that life is unpredictable, so they do not need to take a two or three-quarter lab sequence to find that out. Nevertheless, by so restricting the project, we run the risk that the resulting product will not be useful to the customer, and we therefore contravene one of our principles: that the lab experience should not be just another group project with a well-defined, but unreal problem concocted by the instructor for the benefit of no one else. When to step in and how narrowly to constrain a project are difficult judgments.

(d) The university timetable. Most students are part-time. They have less commitment to and less time for a group project than they would have for a full-time job. Furthermore, they work to a quarter system, so that the project is punctuated by artificial gaps. It is during these gaps that personnel turnover occurs, not continuously as in industry. At certain times of the quarter (typically halfway through during the midterm tests and at the end just before finals) everyone is busy with other courses. Thus, external "noise" activities are much more intense than in industry and tend to peak synchronously for all members of the group. There are conflicting responses: to expect students to contribute constantly throughout the quarter and pick up where they left off, and to accept that students are part-timers with other obligations that come and go. The first response makes the project more realistic but places a burden on the students from time to time. The other may seem more humane but leads to project management and scheduling decisions that reflect the educational setting.

(e) Instructor -v- Manager. A smooth running project often requires the instructor to step in as temporary project manager. This is especially necessary when a student is having difficulties or is obstructing progress either by not completing deliverables or disruptive discussion in design meetings. If the instructor steps in too soon, the student manager's perceived authority is undermined, but if the instructor waits too long, the student manager lacks the authority and experience to redress the situation. Knowing when to act requires delicate judgment. One compromise that we intend to experiment with is to have graduate students manage undergraduates.

(f) Learning experience -v- Research experiment. A student project group provides the software engineering researcher with an easily accessible and manipulable experimental device. The issue here is how much educational value the students can get from experimenting with untried techniques (bearing in mind that innovations often fail and that it requires experiments to find out). The pro-research argument is that being in a research university and in the forefront of research inspires students in many intangible ways. The pro-teaching position argues that it is unjustifiable to use student projects as research experiments unless students can learn something much more tangible from the experience. We are undecided. Both points of view have merit.

8.3. Plans.

We intend to track our students as best we can to assess the correlation of lab membership with the ability to cope with size and complexity, exhibit autonomy, and cope with unpredictability. This will include keeping in contact with students who have graduated and gone to industry, to see how their Lab experience affected their employment.

9. REFERENCES

[1]   Denning, Peter J. "Educating a New Engineer", Communications of the ACM. Vol. 35, No. 12, December 1992.

[2]   Schon, D.A. The Reflective Practitioner: How Professionals Think in Action, Basic Books, 1983.

[3]   Shaw, M. and J.E. Tomayko, Models for Undergraduate Project Courses in Software Engineering, SEI Tech. Report, CMU/SEI-91-TR-10, 1991.

[4]   Georgia Institute of Technology, College of Computing. An Undergraduate Curriculum in Computing, September 21, 1992.

[5]   Rubin, K.S. and A. Goldberg, Object-Behavior Analysis,' Comm. ACM, 35(9):48-62, 1992.

164

[6]   Lorenz, M. Object-Oriented Software Development - A Practical Guide, Prentice Hall Object-
        Oriented Series, 1993.

[7]   Smith, K., R.T. Johnson and D.W. Johnson, Cooperative Learning: Increasing College Faculty
        Instructional Productivity, ASHE-ERIC Higher Education Report #4, 1991.

[8]   Rumbaugh, J. et al., Object-Oriented Modeling and Design, Prentice-Hall, 1991.

[9]   Sigwart, Charles D. and Van Meer, Gretchen L., "Evaluation of Group Projects in a Software
        Engineering Course", SIGCSE Bulletin, Vol. 17, Number 2, June 1985.

A "Just in Time" Course Framework:
Project-Oriented Courses

Edward C. Epp

Department of Mathematics and Computer Science
The University of Portland
Portland, OR 97203

Abstract. Typically, a course's framework is built around a set of topics. Elementary concepts are followed by more advanced topics which build on ideas previously presented. Projects are often added to computer science courses to illustrate and reinforce these concepts. This paper looks at an alternative framework in which the course is built around a project and topics are introduced to support that project. The paper begins by justifying this approach, looking at an example course, comparing it with standard curriculum, addressing some of the issues encountered, and documenting the results of students.

1 Introduction

Undergraduate courses and texts are typically organized by topic. For example, a Programming II[1] course may be organized by elementary data structures such as lists, stacks, queues, trees, graphs, etc.[2]. Material is carefully arranged to support each newly emerging topic. Software engineering discussions are often inserted as appropriate to support projects that are sprinkled throughout the course. Although this careful sequencing of material makes pedagogical sense, experience indicates that it does not work for many students. No matter how enthusiastically and carefully concepts are emphasized and practiced through exercises and quizzes, it is always surprising that many students are unable to apply these concepts to new problems in projects and on tests. James Hoburg[3] at Carnegie Mellon University states:

> My students and I have forced ourselves through a distasteful process of pounding in material they find mysterious and useless and I find beautiful and important.

Projects for undergraduate courses often appear contrived. It is difficult to choose projects which represent an interesting real-world problem while demonstrating the current topic and being solvable by beginning students. Because students are unmotivated to master algorithms which do not represent real-world problems, projects are often sloppily done and thrown away as soon as they are graded.

In a project-oriented approach, the sequence of topics is dictated by the project, i.e., topics are introduced in an order necessary to keep a project on track. This "just in time." strategy is what Leonard[4] calls this the "software engineering approach." In comparison studies he has concluded that "a software engineering approach can produce significantly better student performance than a more traditional approach."

2 Justification for Project Oriented Courses

The project-oriented approach is being used in the engineering programs at Carnegie Mellon University and Worcester Polytechnic Institute[5,6]. One justification for this approach, as observed by one Carnegie Mellon Professor, is that current students are not the "tinkerers" that previous generations of students have been. As a result, students do not arrive with the same intuitive understanding of working systems. These universities hope to build this intuition by beginning, in the freshman year, projects which may be carried through to the senior year.

Additional justification for the project-oriented approach comes from employers of computer science graduates. A recurring theme is that students need to understand how to work in teams on large projects. Employers are particularly concerned that students are able to place a problem in the context of a complete system. A common complaint is that new graduates' views are too microscopic. For example, students do not understand that a change may have a ripple affect through an entire product or an entire organization. In addition to coding, employers want graduates to be able to define problems, design solutions, understand the impact on the entire system, test for correctness, and disseminate changes.

Lastly, in our experience when semester long projects have been used in some of our topic organized courses, there seemed to be a correlation between timing of the presentation of topics (in relation to the status of the project) and student retention, i.e., the closer project status and lecture topics coincided, the better the retention. For example, data representation information (addresses, storage, and number bases) was presented early in one course with the goal of laying a foundation for pointers. However, students had forgotten this information by the time they needed to apply it. When the topic was reviewed within the context of its application, (as would be the case in a project-oriented course) retention was much higher.

Based on these observations, it was decided to organize our sophomore courses around a project. On the surface this sounded easy to do. The plan was to teach the same material, only present it when needed for the project. In practice the process is more complex. What follows is the organization for an actual course and a summary of some of the issues that were faced.

3 Example Organization of a Project Oriented Course

A rule-based expert system shell was chosen as a project. As a framework for a project-oriented course, it has the following advantages: a bare bones version can be easily implemented, it can be decomposed into representative data structures, can be enhanced incrementally, can benefit from a graphical user interface, and has some interesting applications. What follows is a course summary. Several of the topics associated with Curriculum 91[7] were integrated into this project, specifically, since the project formed the backbone of the course, topics in software methodology and engineering formed a natural outline for the course.

3.1 Project Requirement

The course began with a brief overview of artificial intelligence (AI). This overview was designed to place expert systems in its appropriate AI context. As a result, this project presented an opportunity to introduce students to AI.

The first step in the project was a requirements document. Students were required to describe the expert system from a user's perspective. In addition to helping the student differentiate the user's perspective from the implementation, it also presented an opportunity to help students with writing. (Other documents also require writing skill: design document, testing report, user's manual, and project report.) Students made several drafts of their document. Each was returned for revision. This process also introduce the students to the process of submitting their work, having it critiqued, and then resubmitting it with revisions. Too often students turn assignments in with the hope of never seeing them again. This processes of critiquing and resubmission was continued through the project.

The following is an example project that would be described in a requirements document: Rule-based systems are built around a list of rules. Each rule has an antecedent (condition) and a consequent (action). The following three rules are examples of rules that may be found in a rule-based system designed to help students choose a restaurant for a date.

```
if       important date and          rule 1
         have money
then     expensive and
         atmosphere

if       important date and          rule 2
         little money
then     inexpensive
         atmosphere

if       atmosphere and              rule 3
         inexpensive
then     Perry's
```

The antecedent in rule 1 is "important date and have money" and the consequent is "expensive and atmosphere." Antecedents and consequents are further decomposed into clauses, each separated by an "and", e.g., "important date." A rule-based expert system has a set of rules and a context. The context contains a set of facts that are initially known or deduced from rules. For example, when the restaurant expert system starts executing, the context may consist of the following two known facts: "important date and little money." The expert system will find a match between the clauses in the antecedent of rule 2 and the facts in the context. Rule 2 will fire, placing the clauses of its consequence into the context. The context will now contain "important date and little money and inexpensive and atmosphere." The next rule to fire will be rule 3, resulting in "Perry's" (a local restaurant) being added to the context. Thus, the expert system is suggesting Perry's as a suitable choice. More detailed explanations and examples of rule-based systems can be found in Wintson[8] and The Handbook of Artificial Intelligence[9].

3.2 Project Design

Students were introduced to the major components of an expert system shell (context and rule-base) during the requirements analysis. The object-oriented (OO) design methodology was chosen for the design phase of the project. Focusing on one design methodology enabled students to know one method well enough to apply it successfully. Other design methodologies where also introduced in class in an effort to place OO design in a context, but detailed coverage was reserved for later courses. Teaching OO design was easier than expected.

Effort focused on formalizing objects in terms of their state and operations. Example operations on a rule-base are initialize, insert, delete, and find. Each object was defined in terms of other objects. A simplified view of the overall design is shown below. For example, a rule-base is a list of one or more rules, rules have antecedents and consequences, and antecedents have one or more clauses. The students had less problem than expected following this decomposition. The process of building higher level abstraction on lower level abstractions matched students' intuition. As a result, it was easy to motivate OO language features and syntax.

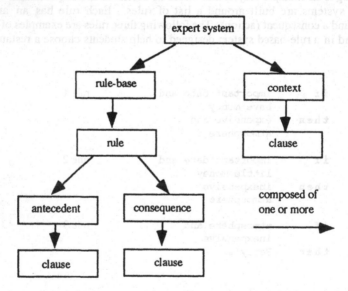

3.3 Project Implementation

Much of the implementation phase was spent presenting algorithms and data structures. Antecedents were represented as lists of clauses which were implemented with arrays. Rule-bases were represented as lists of rules which were implemented as linked lists. Stacks and queues were presented as special cases of lists (though they were not needed by the project and therefore not implemented by the students.)

During this implementation process, students were introduced to a new language (C++). Many language features were illustrated in closed laboratories using a debugging tool (dbx) to illustrate data representation and control flow. Introducing students to a debugger early, and using it consistently through labs, improved their intuitive understanding of program execution and gave them a tool to find program faults. After this brief introduction to C++, students were assigned the task of implementing and testing the "clause" object class. All member functions were documented with assertions that include pre- and post- conditions. This afforded an opportunity to introduce testing strategies and test data selection to validate these assertions. There was also an opportunity to introduce loop invariance and informal program verification.

Attention was also given to software development tools that make the implementation process easier. These tools included make, rcs, dbx, and shell scripts. Make was introduced when the number of classes grew and it became obvious to students that a make tool would be helpful. rcs was introduced when team members started to clobber each other's modifications.

3.4 Project Maintenance

Once a prototype of the system was running, the expert system shell could be enhanced to improve functionality, performance, and ease of use. Analysis of algorithms became an important tool to explore possible performance enhancements. Hashing strings to integers became one option for improving string comparisons. Various searching techniques (i.e. search trees) were introduced to improve search performance for facts within a context.

3.5 User Interface

The user interface was improved by using the Guide interface generator for X-Window systems. This provided an opportunity to introduce human-computer communication. Developing windowing interfaces was also a great student motivator.

3.6 Final Project

On the last day of class students where expected to turn in a complete project. It consisted of the final versions of requirements, design, and testing documents in addition to a user's manual and code listing. They also wrote a project report that evaluated what they had learned, problems they had encountered, project cost (charged at $35 an hour), and an evaluation of each group member's performance.

4 Relationship to Standard Curriculum

Currently our students in the standard curriculum take an introduction to Pascal course and a discrete structures course during their Freshman year. This is followed by a data structures and breadth first survey of computer science during their sophomore year. (The order of this sequence is likely to change over the next year). This gives coverage of the topics in Curriculum 91. The project-oriented approach is seen as one way to implement Curriculum 91 recommendations. The role of the project is to emphasize the software engineering content of this curriculum. In addition we have laboratories that support all areas of a student's first two years of course work.

5 Issues Faced in Designing a Project Oriented Course

5.1 Goals

The first issue we faced was the resolution of student, institutional, departmental, and course goals. While many of our students are finding their way into engineering jobs[10], our curriculum focuses on "classical" computer science with an emphasis on underlying theory and concepts. We are looking at two different potential markets for our students: one for pure research and another for industry. In reality, most of our students are going into industry. It was important for our department to determine how to meet the needs of these students. It was determined that underlying theory and concept remain important to our students while we look at ways of organizing our curriculum to teach our students applied skills.

5.2 Project

The choice of a project was critical. It should demonstrate important concepts, have some utility (this helps motivation), be large enough to be partitioned into components, and be small enough to accomplish. The expert system shell lent itself to a trivial solution (one that can be easily accomplished in a few weeks) and also allowed endless enhancements. This allowed students an opportunity to get a project prototyped early, thus increasing student morale. Through the process of prototyping and enhancement, students were introduced to project maintenance, good design, analysis of algorithms, and testing.

5.3 Sequencing

One of the hardest and most important decisions was to determine how to get the project started. There is much a student needed to know at the start of the project. The project may have been delayed while students were introduced to all the fundamentals. For example, before a student can work on requirements, they must be familiar with the problem space. Before a student can work on design, they must know about objects, data flow, or data structures. Before a student can implement the design, they must know the computer language, the operating system, software development tools such as make, debuggers, and configuration tools. Before a student can test, they need to know about test data selection.

It turned out that students did not need to know everything before they started. Some parts of the project were begun without complete knowledge. This resulted in some parts of the implementation being thrown out as better techniques were learned. However, re-implementation was a positive experience because it illustrated the importance of good design (i.e., information hiding) and demonstrated incremental development[11].

Careful planning was required. Material presented too early was often forgotten and material presented too late halted progress and created unnecessary frustration.

5.4 Code generality

We had to determine how general the implementation should be. The more general the implementation was at the beginning, the less coding was needed later. However, some general features were initially too complicated for beginning students to implement. They required more advanced language features, such as generics (templates or macros) or inheritance and unfamiliar data structures. For example, initially the "clause" class was designed to allow output to both standard output and file output. The code necessary to do this, even though small, was a road-block for some students. This delayed project implementation. It took forethought to determine the appropriate level of generality. As new concepts and language features were introduced to make a class more general, subsequent re-implementation was a good learning experience.

5.5 Lecture generality

There was a depth versus breadth trade-off in this course. It was necessary to determine how general to make the lectures. For example, the project required lists but not queues or stacks. Queues, stacks, and their applications were introduced, but in less detail than in former courses. It was decided not to teach everything in the same depth as in previous courses.

5.6 Student Skill Levels

The expert system shell worked for students with a wide range of programming ability, it was a challenge to the strong students without being impossible for weaker students. Typically, students have a difficult time determining what they can accomplish. They may perceive projects as whole with no granularity not knowing how to create reasonable milestones. Students often attempt to implement all features at once and do not know how to test incrementally. They seem to have difficulty setting limits on their expectations. We addressed this problem by partitioning the project together during class. Implementation and testing of a single class formed a natural milestone. Since object classes were built on lower level classes, students gained a sense of building abstractions. They also saw the project take shape gradually as test drivers evolved into a working prototype. In addition, each assignment stated how many points were to be awarded for each operation (feature) completed. This allowed students to determine how much effort they would place into the project. Students with less coding expertise turned in working projects with less functionality. Overall, compared to past courses, students turned in fewer programs which attempted to "do everything" but were plagued by syntax or logic errors.

Although all features were not required for completion of the project, all students tried to get as much done as they could. It was interesting to note that the students with the best results spent 5 to 10 hours per week, while the students with poorer results spent more than 20 hours per week on the project. This supports Brooks'[12] observation that there is substantial difference between programmers.

5.7 Compromises

One semester is too short to do all of this well, resulting in many compromises. This was particularly evident during the concentrated summer term for a 3 credit version of a 4 credit course. Some documents were not critiqued and modified enough times. The testing document was rather ad hoc. During the summer there was not enough time to write a user's manual. Possible modifications were often talked about, but not implemented. During the most recent school year the project spanned two semesters to allow sufficient time to work on all phases of the project.

6 Student Results

6.1 Test Scores

Adding large projects into the sophomore year has been a gradual process. It began with the second semester course when a project that spanned half a semester was introduced in the 1989 school year. This was expanded to a semester-long project during the second semester course of the 1990 and 1991 school year. Finally, during the 1992 school year, it was further expanded into a full year project. This approach appears to be successful. In comparison with topic-driven courses, students did between 5 and 10 percent better on the tests, while test content remained about the same (see Figure 1.) This occurred in spite of the fact that students were still required to understand algorithms that were not reinforced by the projects. For example, even though sorting was not used in the rule shell, students were expected to know the algorithms for tests.

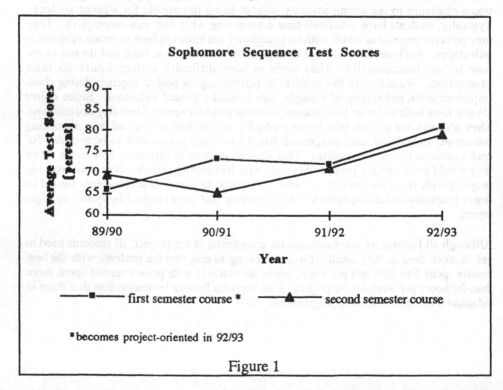

Figure 1

Since our class sizes are small (10 to 20 students), and because of a university policy which prohibits the use of students as test subjects, it is difficult to carry out controlled experiments that evaluate curriculum modifications. As a result, there are many independent variables that have not been held constant. For example, classroom teaching may have improved independently of course organization. Although test content has not changed, the tests may have been better written. A laboratory component has been added to the courses with new equipment and space. In addition, the student body is dynamic.

6.2 Project quality

During the project-oriented courses, students spent more effort creating functional projects with attractive support documents. As a result, project quality and project scores have substantially increased (see Figure 2.) Due to the lack of controls, it is difficult to attribute cause and effect.

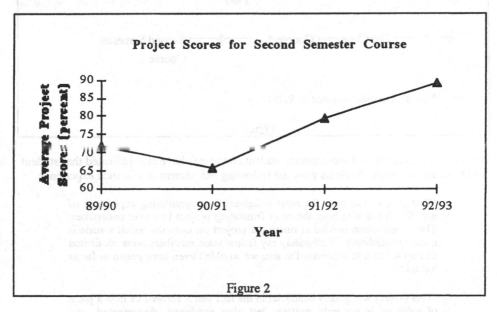

Figure 2

Student enthusiasm was also higher. The clearest support for this observation has been students' willingness to work outside class. In an end of semester evaluation, students have reported hours spent outside of class. Since these times were estimates, their absolute values are in question, however, they do show that students felt they have been putting in more time (see Figure 3.) More specific evidence comes from the 1992/93 school year when students were required to keep weekly logs of time spent on the project. Results showed that each group (of three students) logged on average 394 hours or 9.4 student hours per week, despite the fact that they may turn in a project of less functionality if they so choose. An interesting subnote is that the best projects had fewer hours associated with them.

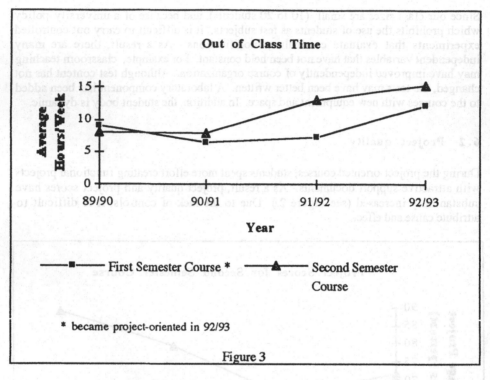

Figure 3

Semester evaluations and spontaneous student comments have also indicated that student enthusiasm has risen. Students gave the following assessment of one such experience:

> "This project has been the most enlightening programming experience of my life. It has also been the most frustrating project I've ever undertaken. The coordination needed in running a project on even this small a scale is quite extraordinary. Fortunately my fellow team members were motivated and up to the task otherwise I'm sure we wouldn't even have gotten as far as we did."

> "This project was greatly beneficial in the fact that it showed us how a piece of software is not only written, but also produced, documented, and contracted. ... This project greatly expanded and solidified our knowledge of computer programming and software development."

6.3 Related Comments

Response from industry has been positive. Informal discussions with industry representatives has leant support, at least on a philosophical level, to this approach which theoretically will give students a much better understanding of how a complete system is maintained over its life-time.

Organizing computer courses around a project may also help retain women in computer science. Daniell Bernstein, associate professor of computer science at Kean College, states that "while men may be passionate about computers, women use computers as tools for solving problems. When women do not see computers as efficient tools, they lose interest, but when both sexes see computers as tools, they perform equally well."[13] Informal discussions with women students have also indicated that beginning the project by writing requirements and design documents has buoyed their self confidence and subsequent ability to move comfortably through the project.

7 Conclusions

This approach to teaching is unique because it focuses on the complete project life-cycle early in the curriculum. In addition, the project (rather than topics) is used to drive course organization. This approach appears to be successful. In comparison to topic-driven courses, students did better on the tests, indicating that they are learning more even if some of the material is covered in less depth. Student enthusiasm is also being transferred to other courses, leading to a better experience in school. Student hacking has increased, but with a more disciplined and intelligent form. Students are asking for permission to continue work on projects when the term ends. They spent substantial effort making their documents attractive through the use of graphics and binding. In addition, most students, no matter how well their project turned out, made additional copies of their project for future reference.

This approach has received high marks from the software firms. In general they feel it easier to turn graduates into productive employees if, as students, they developed a more global view and receive more experience with the software development process. They also feel that a good foundation in underlying theory and concepts is essential for long term viability. It is important that a project approach enhances the understanding of fundamentals.

Our approach has been conservative. We have made an effort to remain in the main stream of computing curriculum while making small evolutionary changes to improve instruction. Much more effort needs to be focused on goal setting, planning, and evaluation before we apply the project approach more broadly. Certainly this approach could be and is being applied to many other courses, i.e., compiler design.

References

1   Richard H. Austing, Bruce H. Barnes, Della T. Bonnette, Gerald L. Engel, Gordon Stokes, Curriculum 78, Communications of the ACM, vol. 22, no. 3, (March 1979), pp 147-166.

2   Robert L. Kruse, Bruce P. Leung, and Clovis L. Tondo, Data Structures and Program Design in C, Prentice Hall, 1991.

3   Donald Christiansen, Spectral lines, IEEE Spectrum, vol. 29, no. 6, (June 1992), p 19.

4   James Leonard, Using A Software Engineering Approach To CS1: A Comparative Study Of Student Performance, SIGCSE Bulletin, vol. 23, no. 4, (December 1991), pp. 23-26.

5   Donald Christiansen, Spectral lines, IEEE Spectrum, vol. 29, no. 6, (June 1992), p 19.

6   Donald Christiansen, Spectral lines, IEEE Spectrum, vol. 29, no. 7, (June 1992), p 25.

7   Allen B. Tucker, et. el., Computing Curricula 1991, ACM Press, 1991.

8   Patrick Henry Winston, Artificial Intelligence, Addison Wesley, 1984, p 166.

9   Avron Barr and Edward A. Feigenbaum, The Handbook of Artificial Intelligence: volume 1, William Kaufmann, Inc., 1981, p 190.

10   David L. Parnas. Education for Computing Professionals, IEEE Computer, vol. 23, no. 1 (January 1990), 17-22.

11   Frederick P. Brooks, Jr., No Silver Bullet, IEEE Computer, vol. 20, no. 4, (April 1987), pp. 10-20.

12   Frederick P. Brooks, Jr., The Mythical Man-month, Addison Wesley, 1979.

13   Karen A. Frenkel, Women & Computing, Communications of the ACM, vol.33, no. 11 (November 1990), pp. 34-46.

Project Courses at the NTH:
20 Years of Experience

R. Andersen, R. Conradi, J. Krogstie, G. Sindre, A. Sølvberg

Department of Electrical Engineering and Computer Science
Norwegian Institute of Technology, N-7034 Trondheim

Abstract

Project courses are a cornerstone in the information systems and software engineering education offered at the NTH (Norges Tekniske Høgskole = Norwegian Institute of Technology). In this paper we present our two main project courses, one taught in the 2nd year and one in the 4th year.

We focus most on the 4th year project course, which is the most special, in that there are real, external clients. The course is compared to other project courses which have been reported on. A major distinction between our 4th year course and other courses is that our students are provided with problems which are only very loosely defined at the outset of the project. Advantages and disadvantages of this approach are discussed. This course has been very well received both by students and clients.

Keywords: project courses, teamwork, software engineering

1 Introduction

1.1 The problems of teaching project courses

As observed by several educators, many of the engineering principles which are essential in large-scale industrial software development are hard to illustrate without projects of considerable size [1, 6]. The problem of project courses is to make something which is small enough in terms of student effort, and yet realistic enough to convey at least some of the most important engineering principles. For instance, a fully realistic project should address problems such as:

- literature study of relevant material

- feasibility study

- planning, limited budgets, choice of methods and tools

- requirements engineering, analysis — and to be realistic, the problem should be wicked [7], i.e. requirements evolving during the course of the project and the customer being uncertain about what, exactly, he wants or needs

- design, coding

- quality assurance, configuration management

- reuse of existing modules, adaptation, integration

- documentation (both for use and maintenance)

- installation, training of users, operation, maintenance

As can be seen from this list, which is not even supposed to be comprehensive, the development of a system of realistic complexity from preliminary study to maintenance, requires far too much time to fit into a one term — or even a full year — course. On the other hand, going for a project of a more agreeable size, some of the issues above cannot be covered — not only because there is not enough time, but also because the issue may be impossible to illustrate with systems of too little complexity — for instance, it may be difficult to make the point for configuration management, reuse, or integration problems with a small assignment.

1.2 Various approaches to project courses

There are many possible approaches to the above problem. Two major alternatives are:

1. to reduce the complexity of the system to be developed, which might make it possible to go through all the development phases, or

2. to leave out some phases or engineering issues (e.g. feasibility study, quality assurance, maintenance), which might make it possible to have a rather complex problem assignment.

Usually, a course will do both these things, but still a distinction can be found between courses which have rather big systems but cover few phases, and courses which cover many phases but with smaller systems.

There are also several other dimensions by which project courses can be distinguished, for instance

- *product vs. process:* is the emphasis mostly on the product, or mostly on the process (for instance concerning the documentation to be written)?

- *methodological generality:* does the course prescribe particular methods (and possibly tools) for the students to use, or is it more general, leaving the choice of methods/tools to the students?

Previous discussions of project courses exhibit various ways of dealing with these issues. For instance,

Shepard and Hoffman [8] report on a course on the Rational Design Process (or actually two courses, one undergraduate and one graduate). Students are supposed to develop a working piece of software within the real-time system domain, going through six steps from requirements specification to testing. To make the projects small enough, the steps of the prescribed process have been simplified. Most simplification has been made in the requirements specification phase. Undergraduates are given a finished requirements specification as a starting point and only have to read it. There seems to be no interaction with end-users.

Bruegge [3, 2] reports on a course with a real, external client, where groups of 12–30 students have successfully delivered systems of 15–27 KLOC for one semester, going through phases from requirements analysis to acceptance test. For the spring 92 course, technical writers were also included in the course.

Offutt and Untch [6] report on a course where aspects of maintenance and reuse has been included in the project course, together with a strong emphasis on system integration. This is achieved by making a project template which can be instantiated in various ways, i.e. the students can be asked to make some subsystems from scratch and reuse/modify other subsystems. The project goes from requirements specification to system integration (including test). The instructor and previous students play the parts of users of the system. Students are provided with an architectural design and divided in groups of 4–5. One group responsible for the total interface and one for the integration. The rest are responsible for one subsystem each.

Kantipudi et al. [5] report on a course where groups of 5–6 students develop some sort of software engineering tool, normally 7–10 KLOC, the instructor serving as a customer. Teams are selected by the instructor based on student abilities.

Grau and Wilde [4] report on a course using an Individual Exchange Project Model. Students work in small teams building miniature programs, intermediate documents being exchanged among team members.

1.3 Project courses at the NTH

At the NTH we have also had to make some reductions of complexity to make our project courses fit into one semester. We have two main project courses, one in the second year and one in the 4th year, and we have tried to make these rather complementary.

The second year course fits into the time frame mainly by a reduction of problem size, yielding systems which are small enough that a finished implementation can be expected during the course (2–4 KLOC). A relatively fixed requirements specification is provided at the outset of the project. The students go through the phases of analysis, design and coding, probably with most emphasis on the latter two.

The fourth year course has a quite different approach — also differing from the courses listed in section 1.2 — in that the problems are usually so complex that a finished system cannot be developed during the course. The students deliver a requirements specification and an architectural design for the whole system, but the detailed design and particularly the coding may be done only for parts of the system. Thus, there is relatively more focus on the requirements engineering phase, which is not dealt with in the second year project.

The rest of the paper is structured as follows: in section 2 we discuss the second year course on programming methods, and in 3 we discuss the fourth year course. We spend most time on the latter, both since this is the course which we have most experience with, and since this course is the one which is most different from the mainstream of project courses to be found.

2 Programming methods

2.1 Course description

Programming Methods is taught in the spring term of the 2nd year at the NTH and is compulsory for all computer science and cybernetics students, which means that there are about 200 students each year. Before this course the students have had only two relevant courses: the introductory course in programming (Pascal), plus a course in algorithms and data structures. However, many of the students have had programming experience before entering the university, and 30% have their own PC.

The course starts with six lectures presenting theory on object-orientation, C++, object-oriented design and the software life-cycle, but the main focus is on a programming project done in teams of 4 students, put together arbitrarily. The teamwork is done in a cycle of four large exercises:

1. Requirements and design specification.

2. Evaluation of 1.

3. Implementation and demonstration.

4. Evaluation of 1-3.

Evaluations (specification and code reviews) are done by exchanging deliverables between groups. The instructors also assist in this evaluation. The exercises count for 60% of the students' marks in the course, the theory exam only for 40% . Accordingly, roughly 60 hours (of a total 100) that each student is supposed to spend on the course, are allocated to the teamwork project, which means that the total man-hour budget for each team is close to 250 hours.

There are new assignments from year to year, but each year all the teams are given the same programming task, to make evaluation and guidance easier. The requirements to be met by the program are fixed, so that the students do not have to talk to any users. Coding is done in C++, usually 2-4 KLOC per 4 person team. Students are encouraged to make use of provided module and class libraries.

2.2 Course goals and evaluation

The course has several goals:

- to teach the students the use of ADTs, object-orientation and C++ (about 2/3 of the effort).

- to teach the students about the software life-cycle, design, and testing (about 1/3 of the effort)

Moreover, it is considered a useful practical experience in teamwork Although not very big, the program is significantly larger than what normal students have been developing on their own, e.g. in the 1st year introductory course in programming.

One of the observations made at the course evaluation is that the course may be too ambitious compared to its size (in terms of student effort). The students, who previously have little but individual programming experience with toy examples, are exposed to the problems of cooperation, and to the software life-cycle. At the same time a new programming language is introduced, as well as the principles of object-orientation. Students generally spend more time on the project than demanded, and make more sophisticated solutions than demanded, especially when it comes to user interfaces. Groups are often dominated by the most ambitious students, usually those with own PCs and lots of programming experience, and these tend to put pressure on the others. Although there is more to the project than coding, this polarization of student abilities is a serious problem.

3 The 4th year project course

The second large project course being part of the computer science education at IDT NTH, is performed in the autumn of the 4. year. Formally, there are two parallel courses: one for students with a specialization in information systems, and one for students with a specialization in software systems. These are very similar, the main distinction being that the assignments in the latter course are somewhat more technical than the former — for the information systems students, the client is typically a user of software, whereas for the software systems students the client is a producer of software. In all other respects, the two courses use the same approach, so to simplify the discussion, we will talk about the two courses as one.

3.1 Course description

Each year, between 60 and 80 students participate in the project course, working in teams of 6–8 persons. The project course is compulsory for the information and software systems students within our department. Also other students, sometimes from other faculties, apply to follow the course and are allowed to attend if the number of assignments permits it. The projects last for 13 weeks, and each student is supposed to spend 19 hours per week, which yields 250 hours per student and a total budget, roughly, of one man-year per team.

Before entering the course, the students have been through the basic computer science subjects, as well as an introductory course in system engineering and a course in database systems, and are supposed to use the techniques learnt in these courses on real-life problems.

The course was first given in 1974, but then with internal staff playing the client roles. Since 1987, the teams have mostly been given external clients (one per team) with real problems to be solved. According to the number of students enlisted for the course, a sufficient amount of problems are negotiated with potential clients during the summer. After running the course for some years now, this is usually not a big problem, since we have certain recurring customers, which are satisfied with previous results and want a similar treatment of new problems. We also have good contacts with many of the major Norwegian producers and users of software.

The problems are different for each group, highly varying in nature, complexity and scope, and new in the sense that they have usually not been addressed in any detail by the company before, even in the cases of the recurring clients. To demonstrate the variety, a couple of examples of assignments given in the last 2–3 years are given below.

182

- Defining the need for electronic message passing within the regional hospital in Trondheim (employing 3200 people), and investigating to what extent the need is covered by existing standards such as EDIMED and EDIFACT and how these would be applied at the hospital. This is one of several tasks being done for the hospital during the last years. Others that can be mentioned, are the development of a data model for the hospital and the visualization of medical processes.

- Tracking of salmon transport: This assignment was originally given by an institute of the department of Marine Technology at NTH some years ago, and has later spawned several follow-up projects.

- Case processing system for a large Norwegian insurance company. This project appeared as a subproject on larger cooperation between NTH, the insurance company and other companies within case processing.

- A system for a local cleaning company to help follow up their present and potential customer arrangement.

- A map system for the Norwegian Telecom.

- An object-oriented database interface to the repository of a 4GL/CASE-tool by a Norwegian producer.

There is normally one main contact-person in the client company, who is the team's primary source of domain knowledge, but many groups find it necessary to get in touch with several of the client's personnel. For instance, the group with the hospital assignment conducted interviews with approximately 20 persons from all main departments of the hospital in addition to contacting most other major hospitals in Norway to investigate how they had solved similar problems. The client's contact will usually also be a major provider of technical knowledge — however, the computing expertise of the contact person may vary highly from project to project. For technical information, staff instructors may also contribute. And of course, the teams can also gather information from existing written material, both on technical issues and on the problem domain.

Each team is supposed to deliver a project plan, a preliminary study and problem statement, a requirements specification, a design specification, and implementation and users' guide, and a project evaluation report. Obviously, with the scope of some of the tasks given and the time frame for the project, it is not feasible to come up with a complete system, and the main emphasis in this project is on the earlier phases of system development, especially problem specification, requirements specification and the architectural design. An average distribution of effort would be:

Initial summary, project plan	5%
Preliminary study, problem statement	25%
Requirements specification	25%
Design specification	20%
Implementation, users' guide	15%
Evaluation report	5%
Oral presentation & demo	5%

However, this distribution is just meant as a guideline to the team. Depending on the nature of the problem and the wishes of the client, the team is free to adjust the effort, e.g. if the problem is rather simple and the client is interested in a prototype of some size, the effort on implementation can be somewhat increased, and if the problem is complex and the client is most interested in clarifying the system requirements, the efforts in this phase can be increased, for instance reducing design or implementation. The relative importance of various deliverables in the evaluation of a team will be adapted to such effort adjustments.

Anyway, all teams have to implement a limited prototype of the solution — it is not allowed to skip any of the deliverables listed above. At the end of the project there is an oral presentation of the problem and the team's solution, including a demonstration of the prototype. This presentation is supposed to show the feasibility of the ideas and convince the client that the ideas should be carried through. And many clients wish to do so, for instance by hiring the students for summer or evening jobs.

3.2 Course organization

The teams are put together arbitrarily (except for some bias concerning the allocation of females and other minority groups[1]). [5] recommends that student abilities should be taken into account here. However, NTH being a German style polytechnic university, all our students have been through the same computer science subjects before they enter the project course, and although abilities vary, students are rather homogeneous. At the outset of the course, each team is provided with one page of information about their client and task, including personalia of the contact person at the client site. Moreover, each group is given a student supervisor (5th year or doctoral) who has participated in a similar project relatively recently. This supervisor will take part in the teams' initial meetings with the client to assure that a productive working-relationship is established, and generally serve as a resource person for the group. The student supervisor also participates in the weekly meetings which the group has with the main supervisor of the project (prof. or ass.prof.), who usually has several years of experience with the course. At these meetings the group will deliver a progress-report and get feedback on the material being prepared so far. The project management part is emphasized, especially that man-hour budgets are not overrun. The first task of each team is to develop a project plan taking into account their resources and goals. They also have to organize the group, and delegate responsibility of tasks. No direct guidelines are given on how a team should

---

[1] Females, unfortunately, must be considered a minority in our department, roughly 10% of the students

be organized, but students get some pointers to reference material and reports from previous years' projects. Obviously, due to the variety of tasks, they cannot reuse this information blindly.

There are no requirements concerning what development methods or tools should be used — the teams are free to choose what they feel most suitable, in negotiation with their client. Most of the projects end up using a fairly traditional waterfall approach with structured development techniques, but there are also examples of groups who have used object-oriented techniques or prototyping through several iterations. When it comes to the implementation environment and other technology support, the students are free to use whatever is available that suits their and the client's needs. If possible, the usual choice will be to implement on the same kind of environment as the one found in the client organization.

3.3 Course Goal

The project course has several goals, in addition to integrating the technical and theoretical knowledge from the first three years of study:

- Exposure to big, partly undefined problems. Most other project courses (as the ones referenced above) either use smaller problems or at least problems which are more strictly defined at the outset. For instance, the course described in [2] starts with providing the students with a problem statement containing functional and global requirements to the system, and in the course reported in [6] the students are provided with an architectural design. Our teams are exposed to problems to which neither the clients nor the course organizers know the solution in advance. In other projects, the instructors often have a rather detailed idea of a correct solution in advance; thus, if a team gets into trouble, they may ask a supervisor who can help them get into track quite easily. As everyone knows, this situation rarely occurs when you get into a system development job. Even if someone might have performed something similar, each new project is a new experience involving new people and new problems. This aspect also make the project a challenging task for the supervisors.

- Dealing with customers who have limited technical knowledge and often limited knowledge of how they want their final system to behave. In projects where a professor gives the same assignment year after year, or even if the assignment is new for each year, this factor of system development is not covered very well. Especially the problems that arise in communicating with people with a completely different background and terminology is important to experience.

- Project administration: An important lesson we try to teach the students is the design to cost principle. Systems development problems have no right or wrong solution, they can always be solved better. Typically in the projects, the scope is very wide during problem description, whereas it has to be narrowed as the projects approach implementation. This means that they have to continuously take into account what they should use their time on, in cooperation with the customers who obviously wants to get as much as possible done since their costs in connection with the project are pretty stable anyway.

- Teamwork: System development is almost without exception performed in teams of varying size. To be able to be efficient this obviously necessitate coordination, collaboration and good communication within the groups, which is one of the problems that are most clearly felt in the groups in the earlier phases of the project. Group-cohesion is encouraged throughout the project, and about midway through the project, the groups have usually developed a strong group-identity.

- Documentation of the process and the product is highly emphasized, and is the main basis for the evaluation of the project (i.e. the reports delivered count for much more than the final running prototype). The students deliver several milestone documents during the project, such as project plan, problem statement, requirements specification, design specification, implementation specification, and a limited users' manual. One project team will produce something between 200 and 500 report pages.

In other evaluations of project courses (e.g. [2, 5]) the success of the course seems to be viewed as almost synonymous with the quality of the developed software. We rather tend to evaluate our course from a purely educational point of view. After all, the software delivered is only a limited prototype. The main lessons to be learnt are the wickedness of real-world problems, the need to integrate knowledge from previous courses — as well as gathering new knowledge — to find a solution, the constraint of working within a narrow time frame and a limited budget, and the problems of working tightly together within a group. Wickedness, as such, will usually be contradictory to a strong focus on success from the project point of view (at least in terms of working code), and we feel it is important for people to experience the uncertainty that faces most real projects. Almost all our project teams go through moments of crises, usually during requirements specification, and they are followed closely during this period. Still, almost all projects come through this phase landing on their feet. It is usually after such incidents that the group develops its group-identity which helps them through the rest of the project. In our opinion, this experience of crisis is a very important lesson to learn, and if a team in fact should succeed to make a finished implementation of the whole system, it might be questioned if the problem has been too simple.

The relatively low focus on the implementation phase, and the frequent occurrence of crises, do not mean that the groups deliver inferior results. Some indicators of success in our view is:

- Most previous students say in retrospect that the project course was the most generally useful lesson they learnt at the NTH.

- Graduates from our department are generally well received in industry - their teamwork abilities being mentioned as one of their major pros compared to candidates of other educating institutions.

- External clients in the project course are generally satisfied with the job done by the students — which is probably why we still have no problems with finding willing clients in a small country like Norway (4 million inhabitants). After all, the client organization spends resources on the project in terms of man-hours and sometimes also traveling expenses (in cases where clients have been based outside Trondheim — in particular, we have had some clients in Oslo who have been flying to Trondheim once a week during the semester to meet with the team).

- Often, the results have uses beyond the intended customer. The usual project censor[2] wrote in his evaluation of the system for the cleaning-firm mentioned above: "Since the problem has several things in common with a large set of problems within administrative information systems, it would be fruitful to use the solution as part of the education". This advice has partly been followed.

- The censor, who works in large industry, has also remarked that the quality of the documents delivered is usually better than most industrial documentation.

Some problems that we have encountered with the project are:

- Even if the budget is emphasized, the students tend to overrun their budgets with 10–30% . Earlier, the overruns could in certain cases be even worse, but we have decided not to punish this very hard, since that might result in indecent budgeting, which we would not like to teach the students.

- Since the project takes quite some time, the students have less time for other courses that semester. Generally the impression is that even if they have to work hard with the project, they feel that it is worth it.

It might be suspected that we would also have large problems due to lack of control — both of the external clients (who might, for instance, lose interest in the project at an early stage, or who might give the students tasks unfit for the educational goals of the course), and of the students (who are free to organize and plan their work almost any way they want, as long as they provide the required deliverables — and who might destroy the school's reputation with clients in case their work is of little value). However, we have not experienced any problems in this direction so far. The problem that some odd students do not contribute their full share of work to the team *has* been observed. This is not usual in our course, but difficult to avoid. Although a team can do fine with a sleeping passenger, students are naturally somewhat dissatisfied when such things happen, and if a group should be so unlucky as to have two members who do not contribute, this will be noticeable in the quality of the work.

4 Conclusion

4.1 Contribution and comparison

We have presented the two project courses offered in the software engineering education at the Norwegian Institute of Technology. We have two such courses, one in the 2nd year and one in the fourth year. These are complementary, in that the former

---

[2]= the person responsible for marking the projects. Just as for ordinary exams delivered at Norwegian universities, each project report requires an *external* person (i.e. not employed at that university) to evaluate it. Marks are decided by the censor and teacher in common.

focusses most on design and coding aspects, whereas the latter has a stronger focus on the early phases of development, including problem statement and requirements engineering.

Most of the discussion in this paper has been focussed on the 4th year course, which is rather special. First of all, each team is assigned a real, external client. This is also done in the course reported in [2]. However, our course is different from this and many other courses in that

- there is no lecturing within the project course itself, apart from an initial one hour briefing for all the teams together, just informing about the nature of the course and introducing the teams to their customers and internal advisors.

- the problem is much more loosely defined. Clients often uses the course as an opportunity for exploratory development, not knowing in advance exactly what they want. Students are not provided with an architectural design by the instructors, not even with a problem statement — this must be developed after negotiation with the client.

- no particular development methods or tools are selected — each team is free to choose what they feel most fit to their problem. The choice of one particular method would be problematic, since the assignments vary highly in nature. In some cases, the client may already have a tool which he prefers be used — if the solution is supposed to be an extension to some existing software.

- although both a student and a senior instructor are provided to each team, these play a rather laid-back role compared to what we have heard from other projects, not tutoring students to any extent on what to do and how to do it, but mainly reviewing the deliverables provided, checking the progress of the work and interfering more strongly only in case of real trouble.

The use of an external client with a loosely defined problem, as well as the fact that students are free to organize the group the way they want and choose whatever development method they want, means that it is much more difficult to control the projects. Thus, it is also impossible to assure the quality of the produced systems. However, this does not imply a lowering of the *educational* potential of the course. Students may learn just as much (or more?) from failures and crises. If our students had generally been able to deliver working code covering the whole problem, we would have thought that the problems given were too simple to convey the wickedness found in real world problems.

4.2 Further work

Although we are rather satisfied with our project courses, there is still room for improvement, especially in the 2nd year course (which is not as well received by the students as the 4th year course). Our courses do not include aspects such as maintenance and reuse, and it could be an idea to improve the 2nd year course in this respect, using the project template idea of [6]. The problem that the 2nd year course is somewhat dominated by hackers, could be diminished by adopting a stricter process, such as the Rational Design Process used in [8]. Another problem of the 2nd year course is that there is too much to learn in too little time. Either, the time allocated to the course should be increased, or the burden of topics should be reduced. For instance, if students could learn about C, C++ and object-orientation already in the 1st year, the theory in the project course could focus more on life-cycle and design principles.

For the 4th year project, we intend to focus even more on the group process for the next semester, hiring people from the department of economy and administration to give a lecture on group dynamics midway in the project. The interaction between software developers and technical writers, presented in [2], could also have been interesting for the 4th year course. However, the problem in this respect is that our university does not offer a proper education in technical writing, which makes such an extension of the course impossible in the short term.

An alternative to trying to incorporate maintenance and reuse issues in any of the existing projects, would be to introduce another project to deal with this in the third year. However, it is hard to get accept for new project courses, since many teachers also feel that there is too little time for various theoretical subjects.

References

[1] A. T. Berztiss. Engineering principles and software engineering. In *Proc. 6th Intl Conf. on Software Engineering Education, San Diego, 5–7 Oct.* Springer Verlag, 1992.

[2] B. Bruegge. Teaching an industry oriented software engineering course. In *Proc. 6th Intl Conf. on Software Engineering Education, San Diego, 5–7 Oct.* Springer Verlag, 1992.

[3] B. Bruegge et al. A software engineering course with a real client. Technical Report TR CMU-SEI-91-EM-4, Carnegie Mellon University, July 1991.

[4] J. K. Grau and N. Wilde. Use of the individual exchange project model in an undergraduate software engineering laboratory. In *Proc. 6th Intl Conf. on Software Engineering Education, San Diego, 5–7 Oct.* Springer Verlag, 1992.

[5] M. Kantipudi et al. Software engineering course projects: failures and recommendations. In *Proc. 6th Intl Conf. on Software Engineering Education, San Diego, 5–7 Oct.* Springer Verlag, 1992.

[6] A. J. Offutt and R. H. Untch. Integrating research, reuse, and integration into software engineering courses. In *Proc. 6th Intl Conf. on Software Engineering Education, San Diego, 5–7 Oct.* Springer Verlag, 1992.

[7] H. Rittel. On the planning crisis: Systems analysis of the first and second generations. *Bedriftsøkonomen*, (8), 1972.

[8] T. Shepard and D. Hoffman. On teaching the rational design process. In *Proc. 6th Intl Conf. on Software Engineering Education, San Diego, 5–7 Oct.* Springer Verlag, 1992.

Session 4:
Process Issues

An Adventure in Software Process Improvement
Laurie Honour Werth, The University of Texas at Austin, Austin, Texas

Process Self-Assessment in an Educational Context
Pierre N. Robillard, École Polytechnique de Montréal, Montréal, Quebec, Canada, Jean Mayrand and Jean-Normand Drouin, Bell Canada, Longueuil, Quebec, Canada

Teaching Software Project Management by Simulation—Experiences with a Comprehensive Model
Marcus Deininger and Kurt Schneider, University of Stuttgart, Stuttgart, Germany

An Adventure in Software Process Improvement

Laurie Honour Werth
Department of Computer Sciences
The University of Texas at Austin
Austin, TX 78712
lwerth@cs.utexas.edu

Abstract

Software process improvement concepts, applied in an effort to increase productivity and quality in industry, are also needed in the academic environment. By teaching process improvement we can prepare students for the future and simultaneously improve our own understanding and teaching of the software engineering .

In this paper, the Software Engineering Institute's Capability Maturity Model and the ISO9000 standard are introduced. Our Software Engineering class is described, including two different team organizations which were tried. Technical and process job descriptions are given, together with our experience teaching team skills. The lessons learned are given in the conclusion.

Applying software process concepts gives students a meta-model to understand and help manage project complexity. Having explicit technical and process roles improves students' learning and, while difficult to quantify, seems to effect the quality of the end-products in a substantive way. Teaching and applying quality improvement ideas is a vital part of preparing students for modern software technology.

Introduction

Earlier efforts by the author to incorporate software engineering techniques into software engineering courses at the University of Texas at Austin have been previously described [Werth88-92]. Over the years, using higher level software such as MacApp, HyperCard and Oracle in a Macintosh II laboratory, we developed software engineering tools to provide support for various aspects for our class projects such as testing, costing, version control, analysis and design, software process assessment, and defect tracking. A successful collaboration with a local company provided valuable experience for students using industry-strength CASE tools. Recently, we explored the area of software process improvement, both by teaching the foundations and by applying it directly to the class project.

Our reasoning was, if attention to software process improves the commercial software development environment, then the application of software process techniques should also strengthen the classroom environment. Two positive effects could be expected. First, successful experience with the techniques on the class project would result in students even better prepared to meet the challenges of modern software technology. Second, the use of quality improvement techniques, applied to the software engineering project as currently taught, would be a step in the direction of improving academic education as suggested, for example, by Peter Denning in "Educating the New Engineer" [Denning92].

Software Process

While great strides have been made in developing software engineering methodologies and techniques, companies have been largely unable to consistently produce high quality software. Stories of software problems appear on a regular basis, for example [Neumann92]. Large amounts of money have been spent on projects that have produced little usable software, as illustrated graphically in the results of a General Accounting Office (GAO) survey shown in Figure 1.

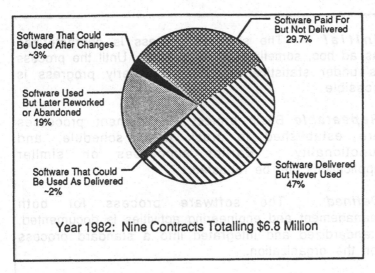

Figure 1. Results of GAO survey of software contracts

Humphrey [89] has observed that successful projects have been largely based on individual or dedicated team effort rather than on software development methods. We have come to understand that benefits of better methods and tools cannot be realized in undisciplined projects. In the typical "firefighting" mode in which immature software development organizations function, software quality is compromised to meet unrealistic schedules.

Process improvement ideas for software are similar to current business practices based on Total Quality Management (TQM). These ideas were popularized, beginning ten years ago, by books such as *Quality is Free*. [Crosby79] and *In Search of Excellence* [Peters82]. Many of the process management and quality improvement concepts have been adapted from the work in statistical process control done by W. Edwards Deming and Joseph Juran [Deming86, Juran89].

Based on work done at IBM, Watts Humphrey introduces early software process concepts in his book *Managing the Software Process* [Humphrey89]. Humphrey's work became the foundation of the Software Engineering Institute's (SEI) software process improvement program. The SEI adapted this model, providing five *maturity levels* called the Capability Maturity Model (CMM), shown in Figure 2, which define an effective, staged, progression toward a statistically controlled software process. In more detail, the five maturity levels of SEI's CMM are:

1. *Initial*   The software process is characterized as ad hoc, sometimes even chaotic. Until the process is under statistical control, no orderly progress is possible.

2. *Repeatable* Basic project management processes are established to track cost, schedule, and functionality.   Earlier successes on similar applications can be repeated.

3. *Defined*   The software process for both management and engineering activities is documented, standardized and integrated into a standard process for the organization.

4. *Managed*   Detailed measures of process and product quality are collected, understood and controlled.

5. *Optimizing* Continuous process improvement is enabled by quantitative feedback from the process and from piloting innovative ideas and technologies.

As an organization increases in maturity, the difference between targeted and actual results decreases across the project. Development time and cost decrease, while productivity and quality increase.   With an objective basis for measuring quality and setting improvement priorities, time and costs become more predictable as rework and errors are removed from the system [Humphrey89].

Paulk [93], describes in detail the series of five stages or levels through which a company must move in order to improve process and resulting product quality.   Each level of the model, shown in Figure 2, is the foundation for the next, so it is important not to try to move too quickly or to skip levels.

Cost savings resulting from the use of the CMM, illustrated in Figure 3, have been substantiatial, resulting in cost savings in the range of 5 to 10 times the cost of making the process improvements.

However, companies report that improvements in work environment and motivation have turned out to be an even greater benefit than the cost saving [Dion92, Henry92, Humphreys91, Mays90]. In a mature organization, everyone knows the processes and their own responsibilities. Workers become empowered by helping to develop the process descriptions and by the ability to update processes as needed.

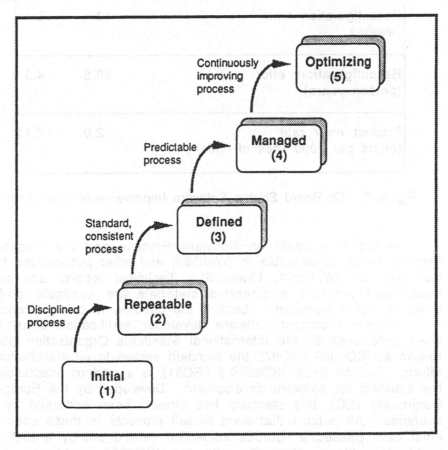

Figure 2. Five levels of software process maturity [Weber91]

Project internal processes become more visible. Managers know current project status and can monitor quality and customer satisfaction. SEI efforts to assess and help companies improve their software process has recently extended from military contractors to include commercial software developers as well.

NASA	1982	1985
Early error detection (% errors found)	48	80
Reconfiguration time (weeks)	11	5
Reconfiguration effort (person-years)	10.5	4.5
Product error rate (errors per 1000 lines of code)	2.0	0.11

Figure 3.   On-Board Shuttle Software Improvements [Humphrey91]

Additional material on Software Process and the Capability Maturity Model is available in [Werth93] and other publications from SEI such as [Weber91, Florac92].   Technical reports and other educational software engineering materials are available on-line using ftp: ftp.sei@cmu.edu.   Look in the directory /pubs/documents.

Another important software developer certification effort has been undertaken by the International Standards Organization (ISO). Known as ISO9000 [ISO87], the standard applies to all manufacturing efforts.   Section three, ISO9000-3 [ISO91], is a modern adaptation of the standard for software development.   Developed by the European Community (EC), this standard has already been endorsed by 57 countries.   All nations that want to sell products in these countries must have passed a rigorous inspection carried out by a ISO9000 certified auditor.   Products with the ISO9000 certification are already beginning to appear in the marketplace.

The ISO9000 audit process is similar to the way SEI's Software Process Assessment (SPA) using their Maturity Questionnaire is carried out.   Using a methodology reminiscent of accreditation for academic departments, a questionnaire, describing the use of software engineering principles at the installation, is completed. After analyzing the results, a trained team visits the site for a more detailed discussions and analysis. Finally, a report is prepared and presented. The major difference between the two assessments is that SEI's CMM includes a suggested ordering of the implementation of key process areas for overall process improvement, while the ISO9000-3 does not.

Software Process in the Classroom
Software process issues become even more important in the classroom, working with inexperienced students. Using the CMM role definitions and job descriptions in classes can ease students' transition to working as a cohesive software engineering team in a professional environment. They have a better appreciation of why software development can be so difficult and it gives students a high-level model for reducing this complexity.

The transfer of knowledge from university to industry should begin to include process material in software engineering classes. Even if they do not apply the ideas on a class project, students can gain a clearer idea of the complications inherent in developing large software products and how they can be managed.

Course Description

CS373 is a standard undergraduate software engineering senior project course. The class project for the past two semesters has been a metrics tool, specified by the Software Engineering Institute [SEI91], to collect and analyze software defect reports. The class adopted the name Inferno Engineering and our product was called Dante's Defect Tracker, or DDT.

Class Project
A significant part of software quality improvement is careful monitoring and controlling of defects. The life cycle of a defect, taken from the User's Manual [DDT92] is shown below in Figure 4. DDT provides a systematic way to enter, track and analyze defects.

The defect report screen, in Figure 5, shows the progress of a defect as it moves through the five phases in its life cycle:

Origination: A defect has been found and submitted to the central database.

Evaluation: The report is being reviewed for validity. If valid, it is assigned to a team for repair.

Resolution: The defect is being investigated.

Verification: A repair has been made, and it is being tested.

Closure: The repair has been tested and it has been shown to be successful.

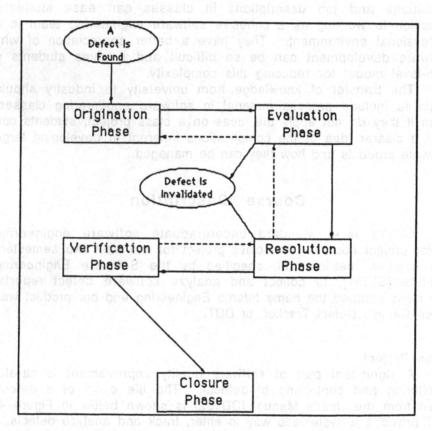

Figure 4.   Life Cycle of a Defect [DDT92]

The DDT system is made up of two separate software products: a *server* which maintains the database and oversees tracking of the defects from a single location, and a *reporter* application which is used to originate defect reports from any of several reporter sites.

In addition to the defect report shown in Figure 5, DDT provides logon security and three editors for entering system administrator(s), projects and their associated team members. Each team member can be given privileges to modify information at any or all of the defect phases and everyone is provided with password protection. A Defect Browser window provides statistical data, the ability to view defect information according to selected viewing criteria, or to sort defects by priority, date, age, status, class and team. Five trend graphs, in any of three formats, are also available for viewing summary statistics.

Defect Report Screen

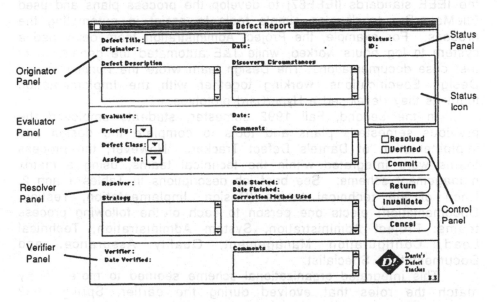

Figure 5.   Defect Report Screen [DDT92]

The textbook by Rakos [90], motivated the students, but did not provide sufficient detail for them to accomplish their work. Humphrey's [89] text was also used, as it includes detailed information about the software process in general and defect tracking in particular.

Team Organization

Team organization and scheduling are essential parts of the software process for class projects. A new textbook on team management [Scholtes88] has proved extremely helpful to students in organizing their team meetings and reports.

Students request their team roles by submitting a cover letter with their resume. Most get their first choice. Students are often correct in assessing their job skills, but without some small adjustments, there is likely to be an imbalance in the relative strengths of the teams.

Tomayko's [87] model Software Engineering course was the basis for the first, Spring 1992, semester. Class organization was based on disjoint subteams for design, implementation, testing and evaluation (T&E), documentation, configuration management (CM), quality assurance (QA) and project administration (PA).

Students worked from Tomayko's example documents as well s the IEEE standards [IEEE87] to develop the process plans and used FileMakerPro to develop simple tools to assist in automating the process. For example, the Project Administration team developed a system to log hours worked, while T&E automated the generation of test case documentation. The Design team wrote the Functional and Design Specifications, working together with the Implementation team as they developed a HyperCard prototype.

In the second, Fall 1992 semester, students employed the previous semester's plans and tools to complete the design and implementation of Dante's Defect Tracker. However, the process teams were integrated within the technical teams, using a matrix management scheme. See brief job descriptions in Tables 1 and 2. Each of the technical teams (Design, Implementation, Testing, Documentation) elects one person to each of the following process teams: Project Administration, System Administration, Technical Lead, Configuration Management, Quality Assurance, and Documentation Specialist.

This integrated organizational scheme seemed to more closely match the roles that evolved during the earlier, Spring 1992 semester's effort, as well as incorporating natural liaison and communication of process procedures within the technical teams. Because of lack of experience, undergraduates seem to find it easier to monitor and impose control when they are a member of the process teams, rather than acting as an outsider "interfering" with the technical team's efforts.

Technical Team Activities

Technical teams met and developed documents appropriate to their role: Functional and Design Specifications by the Design team; software with Programmer's Manual by the Implementation team; Test Plans, Cases, Results and Reports by Test and Evaluation team; and an interactive, HyperCard User's Manual by the Documentation team. For more details, see Table 1, adapted from Tomayko [87].

Technical Team Job Descriptions Table 1.

Design - primary responsibility is developing aspects of the design as specified by the Systems or User Requirements document. During the pre-design stage, this team could assist in a literature search to explore similar product or problem areas. Primary products are the Requirements or Functional Specification and the Design Specification.

Implementor/Prototyper - primary responsibility is to implement the individual modules of the design and serve as the technical specialist for a particular language and operating system. During the requirements specification and design stages, the implementors could experiment with new software and prototyping tools expected to be needed in the product and to develop tools. They are also responsible for developing and maintaining programmer or system documentation.

Testing - responsible for testing and evaluating prototype, individual modules and subsystems, and for preparing the appropriate test plans. Test results are reported and the item returned to the proper person for changes. Responsible for the creation and execution of test plans to verify and validate the software as it develops.

Documentation - responsible for the creation of user manuals and documentation standards. Other documents might include tutorials/training materials, reference manuals, etc.

The Fall '92 Design team's understanding of the problem had been greatly enhanced by the earlier Spring '92 team's efforts on the Specifications and Prototype. They were able to work very efficiently on the detail needed to completely specify the user interface, once they comprehended the original high-level design.

While the Design team worked, the Implementation team learned the Oracle database and HyperCard interface software. While everyone had been assigned a simple Oracle exercise early in the semester, the product is sufficiently complicated that more time was needed to comprehend it. The second semester team had a relatively easy transition since they had working code from which to learn.

The coding process is so all consuming that it is difficult for students to stand back and take the tester's point of view about their own code. We have had more success with testing in classes where the testing project was different from the earlier analysis and design projects or where the project was to modify an earlier project effort. Where the code to be tested already exists, the students are able to concentrate on their test cases and on managing their results and summary reports, without getting bogged down in the details of the design and/or coding.

Test teams also have trouble getting started early enough. Somehow, it is hard to convince students that test cases can be written before working code is developed. Our students have such heavy schedules that it is easy for them to procrastinate, despite project milestones. Also, there do not appear to be good testing tools available for the Macintosh. Improved methods and materials for teaching testing clearly need additional study.

The original, interactive User's Manual was not as polished as we have come to expect, though one student developed an innovative, animated tutorial to explain the phases of defect tracking using DDT. The second semester, the Documentation team was extremely professional and produced an impressive User's Manual, complete with artwork by two students in the class.

Developing and enforcing internal documentation standards requires concentrated effort. Using software such as PageMaker helps with the standardization, but at the usual cost of a large learning curve. Even when a knowledgeable student sets up PageMaker templates, it still takes time and training to get other students to use them consistently. A powerful word processor such as Word, can provide sufficient support for high quality documentation, if standards are strongly enforced. We have been more successful in later semesters where the students needed only to modify existing PageMaker documents.

Process Team Activities

During the first semester, the process teams spent most of their time developing planning documents based on the IEEE standards [IEEE87] and Tomayko's [87] student examples. The Project Administrator(s) designed schedules and contract costs using software tools such as MacProject. The Configuration Management team developed the CM Plan, the Quality Assurance team created a QA Plan, while the Documentation Specialists evolved internal documentation standards. An excellent student developed and implemented a comprehensive System Administrator's Plan for the Mac II Software Engineering lab. System Administration continues to be difficult problem both because student needs and Mac skills vary widely, and because the equipment is aging rapidly.

The second semester process teams enhanced the existing plans to better describe their process function. We added a subteam Technical Lead and (optional) Copilot who wrote the Project Management Plan and formed the basis of the Configuration Control Board (CCB) membership. Like the original teams, all wrote insightful project legacies to pass along their increased understanding of their process role(s) for future teams.

One of the biggest problems this semester seemed to be keeping students from re-inventing the wheel and starting over from the beginning. Some took the attitude that the inherited process plan was impossibly complex. They couldn't possible need all that. Students changed their mind during the semester as they came to appreciate the need for a complete and detailed plan. Process plans will continued to be passed along from semester to semester and modified as needed.

Students with work experience in the larger companies that require these processes, understand the need for the plans better than the students who haven't worked yet. Similarly, experienced students can provide models of weekly progress reports and other project activities for the less experienced students. The process organization actually varies somewhat each semester as a function of the experience, skills and motivation of the students in the class.

The configuration control board (CCB) consisted of each team's configuration management representative, together with the head of quality assurance, the external auditor (the teaching assistant) and CEO (the instructor). Overall project management and coordination

Process Team Job Descriptions   Table 2.

Technical Lead/Copilot - responsible for the creation of the software document or product. Primary responsibilities include coordinating the document/code development, advising and supervising product development and maintenance.

Project Administrator - responsible for resource allocation and tracking. Primary responsibilities are cost analysis and control, computer and human resource acquisition and supervision. Collects data and issues weekly cost/person reports and the final report.

System Administration - responsible for maintaining the hardware/software configuration for the team or class. Includes monitoring hardware problems, assisting team members with software problems, selecting utilities and other support material.

Configuration Management - responsible for change control. Responsibilities include writing the configuration management plan, calling/conducting change control board meetings, archiving, and preparing product releases.

Quality Assurance Management - responsible for the overall quality of the released product. The customer's representative on the project, oversees all phases. Primary responsibilities include preparing the quality assurance plan, calling and conducting reviews and code inspections, evaluating documents and test plans/results. Acts as a member of the independent group. Primary users of a defect tracking tool such as DDT.

Documentation Specialist - responsible for the appearance, consistency and clarity (not necessarily entering) of the technical documentation for the team of which they are a member.

gravitated to the CCB meetings, held in the lab before class. Since other teams' members were often working in the lab during this time and all teams were represented on the CCB, many questions and issues were resolved quickly and easily. Results were announced or further discussion took place immediately after the CCB meeting during class. The turn-around time for change requests must be kept short and this arrangement seems effective at expediting defect tracking, a bottleneck on an academic schedule.

The second semester we assigned the Technical Lead as the CCB representative, figuring that the Configuration Management person was already busy maintaining backups and controlling versions. The head of the QA process team is automatically a member of the CCB, as is anyone whose advice is need on a regular basis. Change requests are liberally used to resolve ambiguities and to establish needed standards, so the CCB meetings become the central clearinghouse for settling conflicts. All meetings and walkthroughs are open to any student that wants to attend.

QA sets up walkthroughs and inspections and is in charge of keeping notes on the meetings. The QA representatives, like the CM and other process teams, form their own group which maintains standards appropriate to their process responsibility. In particular, the Documentation Specialists develop general documentation standards and monitor documents for compliance.

Team and Meeting Skills
The Team Handbook: How to Use Teams to Improve Quality [Scholtes88], provided the single most important increase in team skills. The text provides information on quality improvement generally, but the two chapters on team skills are the primary ones used. Chapter Four provides guidelines for productive meetings, keeping meeting records and forms to be used for agendas, meeting reports and meeting evaluations. Chapter Six discusses team dynamics: forming, storming, norming and performing, together with a discussion of necessary team skills and an extensive discussion of handling team problems. Knowing that everyone is nervous about their first team project and that all teams go through a certain amount of thrashing at the beginning, helps students feel more confident and eases transition to smoothly functioning teams. The ability to run effective meetings, with an agenda, minutes and action items, is a very valuable skill for students.

More motivation to get students started early is needed. The team skills, project roles, standards, and documents must be well-understood early in the semester. Additional time must be devoted to these aspects, despite the tendency to emphasize the technical aspects at the beginning of the course. The process plans, textbooks and student legacies help, but unless required, process will be overlooked in the rush to work on the technical parts with which students are more comfortable.

Team Schedules

We coordinated team efforts though status meetings held each Friday and via walkthroughs of the emerging design which were attended by appropriate representatives of the various teams. The project really began to jell when the Configuration Management Board (CCB) began meeting to discuss change requests. Making the development process visible had a strong, positive effect on the class project. The level of effort rose rapidly, as students began to understand the process and became actively involved in improving the quality of the emerging software product.

At the status meetings, held during class each Friday, one technical team presented their work, while other teams made announcements, asked questions and reported their progress. Everyone in the class acted as either the status meeting moderator or recorder at some point during the course. Agendas and minutes were sent by e-mail to class members. Status meetings worked very well, greatly improving communication and student process learning, as well as reducing the instructor workload. Our industry "users," Herb Krasner and Jim Terrel, attended these meetings as their schedules permitted.

Walkthroughs or reviews were held during the week, often after class on Monday or Wednesday, in preparation for the Friday presentation. Attendees include the presenting team and appropriate representatives from related technical and process teams.

Conclusions

Student learning included the usual lessons such as the discovery of the complexity of software development, the need for communication and teamwork, and the importance of configuration management. However, understanding of these issues was considerably deeper than in past semesters with the new course organization.

Even in a class with little work experience, significant learning took place due to the improved process structure. Scholtes'

Team Handbook [88] provides excellent information, but additional class time needs to be used to practice team techniques such as walkthroughs. Meeting notes, progress reports and other process documentation must be required. The students themselves suggested assignments, quizzes or other means to insure that everyone learn team skills, roles and process descriptions early in the semester. Further work on improving written job descriptions and process plans should help as well.

Software process techniques lead naturally to an analysis of the educational environment itself. When processes work smoothly, the underlying environment and infrastructure weaknesses become more apparent. Process improvement applied to the students' working environment identifies bottlenecks. In a time of limited resources, this is especially helpful for guiding instructors in directing their course organization efforts.

One of the greatest benefits arose from the empowerment of the students, an integral part of the quality improvement process. Students take more responsibility, while at the same time, the instructor is able to dedicate more energy to improving the course as a whole. As the process experts promised, the development process became more "visible". We didn't always like what we saw, but we had a much clearer understanding of the things that were and were not working on the project.

It is important that the instructor genuinely gives control to the students and does not simply hide the rule book and expect students to guess the instructor's intended agenda. With grade-conscious students such as ours, empowerment may require encouragement for some, but most students relish the opportunity to act in a more professional and creative way than the usual classroom organization permits. Students are have been enthusiastic about the course in the past, but many have complained about the large amount of work involved. Now, however, students work smarter and complain less.

Peer pressure is far more effective than instructor exhortations. Team meeting reports are professional and there are fewer complaints about team members who don't contribute equally to the team effort. It is especially heartening to see a shy student taking the initiative on some part of the project or to watch an "average" student confidently leading the class status meeting. The level of professionalism has risen, as have the student course evaluations.

Class legacies show remarkable wisdom and insight into team and individual personality problems, not to mention considerable creativity and wit. Reading each other's legacies has helped some students to see where they may have contributed to the very problems they had been complaining about. Students' level of awareness of the power of teamwork and commitment to quality makes teaching the class especially rewarding.

As usual, the instructor learned more than the students during the semester. Technical analysis, design, and testing techniques are important, but the empowerment, shared learning and more stable environment provided by quality improvement efforts seem to increase learning in the software engineering project course. As the students frequently observed, the sum of the parts is indeed greater than the whole. Learning and applying software process concepts gives students a meta-model to understand and help to manage the complexities of a large software development project. Teaching and applying software process is a vital part of increasing the timeliness of technology transferred as students move from the classroom to industry.

Acknowledgments

This work would not have been possible with the dedication of our users, Herb Krasner and Jim Terrel; Teaching Assistants, Tommy McQuire and Vicki Almstrum, and of course, the Inferno Engineering teams:

Spring 1992   Project Manager: Karen Mustard; Principal Architect: David Snider; Design: Randy Clarke, Peter Kraemer; Configuration Management: Stan Stone; Quality Assurance: Steve Moore, Mathew Colquhoun; Validation and Verification: Scott Boland, James Morris; Documentation: Gray Mack, Teshin Lin, Eric Brown.; Project Administration: Chris Owan, Lee Murray, Shinta Tijo.

Fall, 1992   Design: Paul Dedeyan, Jon Sligh, Adriane McFetridge, Roger Thompson, Charlie Wood; Implementation: Christoph Borst, Chris Chenault, Robert Dennett, Nick Lauland, Minh Tran, Chris Traynor, Joe Warrington, Jr.; Testing and Evaluation: Scott Boland, Gray Mack, Paul Lewis, John Scalo, Javier Seen; Documentation: W. Perry Copus, Jr., Belinda Easley, Alan Soong.

References

Crosby79   Crosby, P. B. *Quality Is Free*. New York: McGraw-Hill, 1979.

DDT92   *Dante's Defect Tracker Reference Manual*. Inferno Engineering, The University of Texas at Austin, CS378 Software Engineering Project, Fall 1992.

Deming86   Deming, W. E. *Out of the Crisis*. Cambridge, Mass.: MIT Center for Advanced Engineering Study, 1986.

Denning92   Denning, P. J. "Educating a New Engineer." *Comm. ACM 35*, 12 (Dec. 1992), 83-97.

Dion92   Dion, R. "Elements of a Process-Improvement Program." *IEEE Software* (July 1992), 83-85.

Florac92   Florac, W. *Software Quality Measurement: A Framework for Counting Problems and Defects*. Tech. Rep. CMU/SEI-92-TR-22, Software Engineering Institute, Carnegie Mellon University, Pittsburgh, PA, Sept. 1992.

Henry92   Henry, J. and B. Blasewitz. "Process Definition: Theory and Reality." *IEEE Software* (Nov. 1992).

Humphrey89 Humphrey, W. S. *Managing the Software Process*. Reading, Mass.: Addison Wesley, 1989.

Humphrey91 Humphrey, W., T. Snyder, and R. Willis. "Software Process Improvement at Hughes Aircraft." *IEEE Software* (July 1991).

IEEE87   *Software Engineering Standards*. IEEE Press, 1987.

ISO 9000.87 *Quality Management and Quality Assurance Standards— Guidelines for Selection and Use*. 1987. Available from Global Engineering Document, Irvine, Calif. and

ISO91   Quality managment and quality assurance standards - Part 3; Guidelines for the application of ISO 9001 to the development, supply and maintenance of software. Available from: American Society for Quality Control, Customer Service Department, P.O. Box 3066, Milwalkee, Wisconsin 53201. 1-800-248-1946, Fax Order to: 1-414-272-1734.

Juran89   Juran, J. M. *Juran on Leadership for Quality*. New York: The Free Press, 1989.

Mays88   Mays, R., E. Jones, G. Holloway, and D. Studinski. "Experiences With Defect Prevention." *IBM Systems Journal 29*, 1 (1988), 4-32.

Paulk93   Paulk, M. C., B. Curtis, M. B. Chrissis, and C. V. Weber.
               Capability Maturity Model for Software, version 1.1.
               Tech. Rep. CMU/SEI-93-TR-24, Software Engineering
               Institute, Carnegie Mellon University, Pittsburgh, Pa.,
               Feb. 1993.
Peters82   Peters, T. J. and R. H. Waterman, Jr. *In Search of*
               Excellence: Lessons from America's Best-Run
               Companies. Harper & Row, 1982.
Rakos90   Rakos, J. *Software Project Managment for Small to*
               Medium Sized Projects. Prentice-Hall, 1990.
SEI91   *Measuring Software Quality Using a Problem*
               Management System, Draft for Review.   Quality
               Subgroup of the Software Metrics Definition Working
               Group, August, 1991.
Scholtes88   Scholtes, P. *The Team Handbook: How to Use Teams to*
               Improve Quality. Madison,Wis. Joiner Associates,1988.
Tomayko87   Tomayko, J. E. *Teaching a Project-Intensive*
               Introduction to Software Engineering. Tech. Rep.
               CMU/SEI-87-TR-20,ADA200603, Software Engineering
               Institute, Carnegie Mellon University, Pittsburgh, Pa.,
               1987.
Weber91   Weber, C. V., M. C. Paulk, C. J. Wise, and J. V. Withey.
               Key Practices of the Capability Maturity Model. Tech.
               Rep. CMU/SEI-91-TR-25, ADA240604, Software
               Engineering Institute, Carnegie Mellon University,
               Pittsburgh, Pa., Aug. 1991.
Werth88   Werth, L. H.   "Software Tools at the University: Why,
               What and How." *Software Engineering Education*, Ford,
               G., ed. New York: Springer-Verlag, Apr. 1988,169-186.
Werth89   Werth, L. H. "Preparing Students for Programming-in-
               the-Large." *Proc. 20th SIGCSE Tech. Symp. Computer*
               Science Education, Barrett, R. A. and M. J. Mansfield,
               eds. New York: ACM, Feb. 1989, 37-41.
Werth90   Werth, L. H. "Object Oriented Programming and Design
               Class Projects." *J. Object Oriented Programming*
               (Nov./Dec. 1990).
Werth91   Werth, L. H.   "Industrial-Strength CASE Tools for
               Software Engineering Classes." *Software Engineering*
               Education, Tomayko, J. E., ed. New York: Springer-
               Verlag, Oct. 1991, 245-256.
Werth93   Werth, L. H. *Lectures in Software Process.* Tech. Rep.
               CMU/SEI/EM8 Software Engineering Institute,
               Carnegie Mellon University, Pittsburgh, Pa., Feb. 1993.

Process Self-Assessment in an Educational Context

Pierre N. Robillard*, Jean Mayrand**, Jean-Normand Drouin**

* Department of Electrical and Computer Engineering
École Polytechnique de Montréal
C.P. 6079, Station A, Montréal Qc, CANADA, H3C 3A7
Tel.(514) 340-4238   Fax(514) 340-3240
robillard@rgl.polymtl.ca

** Bell Canada, Acquisitions Technical Services
2265 Roland Therrien, Suite 226
Longueuil, Qc., Canada, J4N 1C5
Tel.(514) 468-5549   Fax(514) 647-3163
jmayrand@qc.bell.ca
jndrouin@qc.bell.ca

Abstract. This paper describes a studio in software engineering based on the delivery of a product within the framework of a defined process. The studio is a 3-credit fourth year elective course in computer engineering. Students have to compromise between the effort expended on the product and that expended on the process. The process based on the SEI CMM has been used in professional research labs and was supported by commercial CASE tools. The use of the process is formally assessed by a professional evaluator. A working product was obtained by the team that invested the least effort and were the more liberal regarding the process. They were prototype-oriented. The team that was truly process-oriented expended much more effort than expected and did not deliver an integrated product. The team with a mixed approach followed the proper process and delivered an integrated product, but expended a tremendous amount of effort. The students were unanimous in acclaiming the learning benefits of having the process formally assessed.

1 Introduction

This paper relates an experience with a software engineering studio where the objective is for the students to understand the importance of the software process while developing a real product. A novel aspect of this project was a formal evaluation of the students' involvement in the process.

Students develop software within a real software environment process. They have to deliver a working software product and the corresponding internal documentation within fixed time schedules. They must compromise between product-related activities like coding and deskchecking, and process activities like documentation, inspection and validation. The ultimate goal is to learn through experience that a good process guarantees good product.

A prior course in software engineering that is mandatory for all the students enrolled into the studio teaches the basics of software engineering [1]. This course offers six laboratory sessions that introduce each of the CASE tools to be used in the process.

The process used in the studio was designed and used by professional engineers at the Laboratoire de Recherche en Génie Logiciel (Software Engineering Research Lab.). The students were initiated to the SEI Capability Maturity Model [2] and the Bell Canada 's Trillium Model [3]. The Trillium Model has been adapted to the course environment. A Trillium evaluator from Bell Canada did a formal process maturity evaluation of each team. These evaluations were considered professional services to the students and the results were not marked. The process-related documentation, however, was marked.

The project involved the design and implementation of a restructuring module based on existing software tools. The module's input and output tools were running. The students had to close an existing product. The complexity and size (25 KLOC) of the module to be implemented prevented any student from solving it on his or her own and required rigorous analysis. We also expected students to compromise on delivering functionalities. Formal acceptance tests were conducted at delivery time. Students were given production tests prior to the acceptance tests. Special care was taken to reduce failure factors [4]

The studio is structured as follows: students work in teams of six, called companies (A, B, C). Each team (company A, for example) is divided into three departments with two students each. (A1, A2, A3). Course enrolment is elective and limited to 18 students. The schedules for delivering the documents and the product are fixed and firm. In this case, students had a weekly one hour meeting with a professional instructor knowledgeable in the problem domain and a full afternoon lab period with an instructor knowledgeable in the CASE and process domains. Students were free to take extra time if they wished. They were often reminded that this project is a regular 3-credit course and that they should budget their time accordingly, and it was emphasized that instructors are receptive to planned and documented compromises on the product and the process.

The studio outcomes yield interesting results. We were surprised to learn, for example, that students are reluctant to compromise. Some expended much more effort than they had planned to and they all agreed that this was the toughest course they had ever had, but the most rewarding. All the students understood the importance of the process in terms of the quality of the software. It was also interesting that the best product was not the result of the best process, and that the best process did not produce a good product. Of course, these results cannot be generalized yet. In our concluding remarks, we try to explain this behavior.

2 Studio in Software Engineering

The studio in software engineering is a one-semester 3-credit course offered in the fourth year of the computer engineering program at the Ecole Polytechnique de Montreal. A prerequisite in software engineering given the semester before presents the concepts, and includes six projects that serve as an introduction to the commercial software tools used in the studio (see Table 1). The SEI Capability Maturity Model is presented in the software engineering course, while the Trillium model (Bell Canada) is presented in the studio (more on the Trillium model in a next section).

The studio is based on the realization of a software project through all the phases of its life cycle. Students are grouped into teams. Each team applies a defined process based on systematic reviews at each stage of the software development process. This process integrates the tools listed in Table 1. The students received training in technical reviews, programming standards and quality assessment. [5] [6]

Table 1. Software Tools

Tool Name	Purpose
Costar	Cost estimation
Microsoft Project Manager	Project planning & tracking
Software Through Pictures	Design
HP Softbench	Tools integration environnement
SCHEMACODE	Schematic pseudocode editor
Compiler	C compiling
Debugger	C debugging
DATRIX	Quality assessment

The companies compete for the same product. A formal competition with acceptance tests is held on the last day of the course. The best company is the winner. The results of the competition count for only for 20% of the student's total mark. The remaining 80% of the marks are obtained through successive evaluations of the documentation released during the project.

This project was designed to minimize the causes of failure [4]. Three categories of major reasons for failure were discussed: technical issues, personal issues and management issues.

The technical issues category includes 8 factors. Of these, *programming experience with a given language/environment* was minimized by selecting students with the same prerequisites. They included courses on: programming language C, databases, operating systems and software engineering. *Last minute coding effort* was taken into account by defining fixed milestones and phase schedules. Students were provided with a *programming guide*. Conformity with the guide was validated through formal inspection by the peers and the instructors. *Last minute integration effort* was minimized by means of the scheduled milestones. The *fantasy factor* was the most difficult to control.

Instructors set up weekly meetings to negotiate any compromises regarding the project or the process. Students were reluctant to compromise. This happens because of the inability of the students to anticipate the workload involved. We believe this to be the major technical cause of project failure. *Having attitude of learning on the project* did not cause any problem since we have full control over which students enter the course. The students experienced difficulty with the *version controls or management policy change factor*, and last-minute changes account for some project failures. We set a *strict review process* that seems to have contributed to the project's success.

The personal issues consist of 4 factors. *Attitude that B is a good enough grade* was not an issue. Selected students were highly motivated and would not settle for less than an A. *Very heavy work load for some team members* was a major issue. Some students neglected other courses to work on the project. The results section shows the distribution of time spent for each team. Students were regularly reminded to consider product or process compromises instead of overtime resources. We still do not know how to reduce this risk factor. Worse, results show that the best performances took the least time. *Not being able to admit having a problem until the end, when it is too late* is an important factor. We believe it is related to the fantasy factor and their inability to estimate task effort or their lack of experience in doing so. *Very strong opinions on the way things are done* was an important factor for one team and led to team breakdown two weeks before the end of the project. This could be reduced by improving team building. It is necessary for the course instructor to guide the team through the various stages of team development: forming (awareness), storming (conflict), norming (cooperation) and performing (accomplishing) [7].

Management issues were governed by six factors. *Poor team selection* was not an issue since the students were selected for their motivation and their performance in the previous software engineering course. This studio was elective. *Lack of team growth* was simulated by having a competition on the best team product at the end based on acceptance tests, formal inspection and process assessment. *Poor coordination of group meetings* was identified as an issue. No formal project organization structure is followed although a team leader normally emerge in each team. We strongly support [8] the concept of self-managed work teams. In this strategy, management determines what is to be done and the team decides how it will be done. Students commented that they were not ready for this type of management structure and they asked for formal sessions on team management. To make improvements in this area, we could ask for the minutes of team meetings. *Team members wanting to take control* is a factor related to the personal factor of a strong opinion on the way things are done, and the same remarks apply. *Poor communication* was not a factor since they had all the facilities for supporting team communications. A classroom was available during lab hours for team meetings. Each student had access to a SUN workstation and electronic mail to communicate with other team members or instructors. *Ego* as a feeling of, I am right, was reduced by the fact that each department (two people) was changing job, at every task.

3 Project Description

The project was to restructure the control flow graph of a function containing breaches of structure and to transform this structured flow graph into pseudocode. The students were given all the necessary theoretical information on restructuring using the Oulsnam approach [9]. A control graph generator and a pseudocode viewer were provided for the students [10].

This project was divided into 3 sections, one for each department, as follows:
- a)   Load and reduce the structured part of the flow graph.
- b)   Detect and repair the unstructuredness.
- c)   Produce the pseudocode from the flow graph and the source code.

Within each company, the departments worked alternately on each section, as shown in the Table 2 where the numbers represent the 3 departments. For example, department A1 of company A does the planning for the Load section, while department A2 does the planning for the Repair section and department A3 does the Pseudocode planning. The analysis of the Load section is then performed by department A3, while the Repair section is analyzed by department A1 and the Pseudocode section is analyzed by department A2, and so on. This approach proved to be useful in reducing ego programming and justifying the need for proper documentation at every phase.

Table 2. Work alternation

Phase/sub-project	Load	Repair	Pseudocode
Planning	1	2	3
Analysis	3	1	2
Realization	2	3	1
QA & integration	1	2	3

4 Software Process

Figure 1 presents the graphical notation use to describe the software process [11], including the activities, documents and tools used to develop the software.

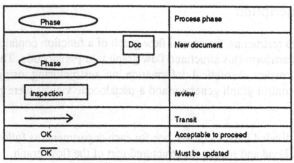

Figure 1. Graphical notation

Table 3 defines the documents produced and the corresponding software tool used in each phase. Figure 2 defines the process and the corresponding document according to Table 3 definitions. This iterative process flows from the specification activity to the integration activity.

Table 3. Process elements

Phase	Abr.	Document	Tool
Specification	SP	Specification	Text editor
	SW	Specification walkthrough	Text editor
Planning	PT	Task description	Text editor
	PE	Project planning	Microsoft Project 3.0
	PW	Planning walkthrough	Text editor
Analysis	AT	Task detailed analysis	Text editor
	AF	Task data flow	Software Through Pictures
	AS	Task data structure	Software Through Pictures
	AH	Task hierarchical diagram	Software Through Pictures
	AW	Analysis walkthrough	Text editor
Realization	RT	Task report	Text editor
	RP	Schematic pseudocode	SCHEMACODE
	RD	Quality assessment	DATRIX
	TC	Unit level test case	Text editor
	RW	Realization walkthrough	Text editor
Integration	IT	Task integration	Text editor
	IM	Integration walkthrough	Text editor

The information contained in each textual and review document is based on IEEE software engineering standards [12]. The strict and rigorous application of this software process can be very costly. The students had to suit the process and its documentations to the resouces available.

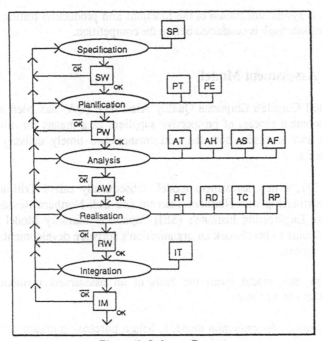

Figure 2. Software Process

The specification (SP) document contains the project functionalities and the theoretical background. It has been written and reviewed by professional software engineers. Students run the Specification Walkthrough (SW) to make sure they understand it.

The students produce a set of task descriptions (PT) in the planning phase. Schedules (PE) are set up according to the resources available and the established milestones. The specification and Planning phases are caried out at the project level. The following phases are carried out for each of the three project sections (Load, Repair, Pseudocode).

The students use Software Through Pictures during the analysis phase to produce the data flow (AF), the data structures (AS) and the hierarchical diagrams (AH). They use the structure-based editor SCHEMACODE to describe the function algorithms (AT).

The realization phase includes detailed design, coding, quality assessment and unit testing. The detailed design is completed with SCHEMACODE, which generates C source code from the schematic pseudocode (RP) [13]. Schematic pseudocode is an efficient code inspection (RW) tool.

Test cases (TC) are generated on the functions' source code. DATRIX processes the source code to ensure that it conforms with the company's metrics profile. Each function outside the profile had to be explained or rewritten (RD) [14].

The last phase is system integration of the functions and production testing (IT) [15]. A final product walkthrough is conducted before the competition.

5 Trillium Assessment Model

Since 1982, Bell Canada's Corporate Quality Assurance (QA) has been assessing the software development process of prospective suppliers as a means for minimizing the risks involved and to ensure both the performance and timely delivery of software systems purchased.

Since April 1991, a new assessment model, subsequently called Trillium, has been developed in partnership with Northern Telecom and Bell Northern Research. Inspired by the Software Engineering Institute's (SEI) Capability Maturity Model (CMM), the Trillium model aims to benchmark an organization's software development capability in a commercial context.

Like the CMM, this model forms the basis of an assessment methodology and a questionnaire that can be used:

- in *capability determination* mode, to help a purchasing organization determine the capability of a potential software supplier,

- in *process improvement* mode, to help a development organization improve its own software development process,

- in *self-assessment* mode, to help an organization determine its ability to implement a new project.

All key practices defined in the CMM have been included in Trillium, although at different levels in some cases.

The Trillium model has been developed from a strong user and customer perspective, as perceived in a competitive commercial environment. This implies that an adequate assessment model must:

- cover as much of the development life-cycle as possible,
- cover all the software development capability issues,
- cover technological maturity,
- incorporate performance benchmarks.

The practices in the Trillium model have been organized into *road maps*. A road map is a sequence of practices that spans many levels, according to their degree of difficulty.

The Trillium model groups the practices into *Capability Areas*, as may be seen in Figure 3. Some capability areas have only one road map (i.e. themselves), while other have several. The model also covers the following development topics:

-Quality Management	-Technological Maturity	-Development Environment
-Process Performance	-Reliability Engineering	-System Engineering
-Usability Engineering	-Customer Support/Partnership	-Concurrent Engineering

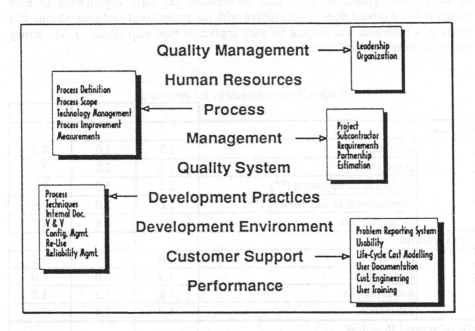

Figure 3. Trillium capability areas

The Trillium model was applied in self-assessment mode and downsized to fit the needs of the software engineering studio. The following 5 capability areas of the Trillium model were inapplicable and the 'subcontractor manager' key practice was removed since none of the companies was authorized to subcontract any part of their work.

- Quality Management	- Human Resources	- Quality System
- Customer Support	- Performance	

Of the 316 questions that composed the Trillium evaluation model, 185 are being used for the assessment in the academic environment.

6 Trillium Evaluation

The self-assessment was done when the course was two-third (2/3) completed. By that time, the students had enough experience on the project and with the process to critically evaluate their level of maturity. The evaluation started with a 3-hour presentation of the Trillium model by a BELL CANADA professional evaluator. This presentation outlined the relationship between the SEI Capability Maturity Model and the Trillium model. The following week, each company department performed a self-assessment. The departments were not authorized to communicate or exchange information on their views of the process application. After data compilation, the three departments of each company had a private three-hours meeting with the professional evaluator. During this meeting, a consensus was reached for each applicable road map (Table 4). The strong and weak areas were highlighted.

Table 4. Results obtained by the three teams.

Process		A	B	C
	Definition (**)	2.7	2.0	2.2
	Scope (**)	2.0	2.0	3.0
	Technical Management (**)	2.5	3.0	3.0
	Improvement & Engineering (**)	2.0	2.0	2.0
	Measurements	1.3	1.8	1.5
Management				
	Project	1.0	1.7	1.2
	Partnership	1.3	2.0	1.0
	Requirements	1.6	1.3	1.3
	Estimation	1.0	1.5	1.0
Development Practices				
	Development Process (**)	2.6	3.0	2.8
	Development Techniques	3.0	2.8	2.8
	Internal Documentation	2.7	1.7	1.7
	V&V	1.3	1.3	1.7
	Configuration Management	1.0	1.0	1.0
	Re-Use	1.0	2.5	1.0
	Reliability Management	1.0	1.0	1.0
Development Environment		1.3	1.7	1.7

The ** indicates that the road maps start at level 2. The meanings of the Trillium levels are as shown in Table 5.

Table 5. Meanings of the Trillium levels

Level	Meaning
1	Unstructured
2	Repeatable and project-oriented
3	Defined and process-oriented
4	Managed and integrated
5	Fully integrated

7 Results

One of the goals of the application of the self-assessment methodology to 3 teams working on the same project was to evaluate the capability or sensitivity of the Trillium questionnaire. We expected the same score for each team.

We found that the 3 groups were applying the process differently, although the software, hardware, milestones, project and background were the same. They struggled to attain two different goals. One was to apply and learn a software process. The other was to deliver a working system on April 15, 1993. Only 10 % of the final mark was directly attributed to the product meeting full acceptance tests.

We suspect that the variation between the companies' evaluation scores is related to the priority given to each goal. Company A had a mixed priority scheme, the process and the product were equally important. Company B was devoted entirely to the application of the process. Company C was devoted entirely to the product, even skipping the mandatory alternation between departments, so that the students who designed a task also realized it.

At self-assessment time, the overall evaluation of company B was slightly higher than those of the other two companies. Their progress report was well-structured and complete. At this point of the project, they seemed to be the team that was most in control of their project.

Each company officially had 810 hrs to spend on the project. The time spent by each individual on the project was recorded. Exceptionally, one extra student was admitted to company A. The human resource budget adds up to 945 hrs for this company. Table 6 presents students' workload in terms of total recorded hours spent on the project. The total project time was 1161 hrs, that is, 216 hours of overtime. Even with the extra student, they had a 22% overrun to do the same project. This is equivalent to having 8.6 students on the project instead of 7. Company A's product was integrated, but failed all the acceptance tests.

Company B spent 1087 hrs with 277 hrs of overtime. They achieved the equivalent of 8 person-resources. The project did not achieve product integration at competition time. We were unable to predict such a failure since all the progress reports were excellent and since they had the highest score in the Trillium evaluation. The distribution of effort as shown in Figure 4 stresses the 'burst' operating mode of this company. They made a special effort before reaching each milestone, including the assessment interview to provide the necessary material. Although this approach enabled them to present all the required documentation, they were not able to achieve product integration. Members of this company had a major communications problem, which was only reported the day before the competition.

Company C had a 7.2% overrun. They achieved the equivalent of 6.4 person-resources. This company was truly product-oriented. The Trillium evaluator perceived this company as applying the process because they were forced to do so. The progress reports were satisfactory. From the interviews, we found that communications among the members was very good. The groups had invested at lot of time in analyzing the specifications and found some shortcuts to the proposed approach. This good communication and the amount of work done at the specification level led them to rapidly obtain an integrated prototype. From this prototype, they iterated to obtain a fully functional product at the end of the project. In the competition, they passed 90% of the acceptance tests. The missing 10% was caused by a last-minute error in the configuration management product.

Table 6. Team resource distributions vs product and process status.

Company	A	B	C
Total hours	1161	1087	869
Overrun	216	277	59
Persons (real)	7	6	6
Person (effective)	8.6	8	6.4
% overrun	22%	34%	7%
Product status	good	bad	very good
Process status	good	very good	fair

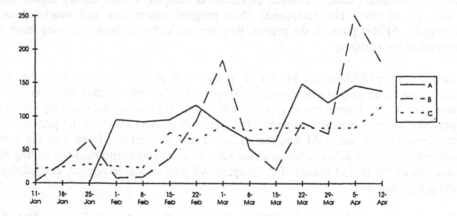

Figure 4. Weekly logs of time spent on the project for each company.

8 Concluding remarks

The aims of the studio in software engineering are to introduce the students to the design and implementation of a real project using a defined process. The product, based on a re-engineering engine, was formally evaluated from acceptance tests. The process, based on six commercial CASE tools, was formally evaluated from self-assessment questionnaires and meetings with professional evaluators. The time spent by the students on the project was recorded. Students were very receptive and enthusiastic.

An independent course evaluation was conducted by the Ecole's pedagogical services. The overall course evaluation rates high. Students like it and unanimously give maximum score to process self-assessment and interviews. Students find the project too difficult. They confirm that the prerequisite is required. They find the CASE tools useful and efficient. They require more training on team management and formal inspection. They feel that an even better defined process will help. They are looking for recipes. They all spend more time than required.

We are surprised by the outcomes of the process assessment. A good process is not a guaranty of a good product (We said the opposite in the introduction). We were lured by the ability of the students to deliver process oriented documentation. It seems that team cohesion and communications is better than process rules to obtain a good product. These results are partial and restricted to a specific experimental set-up. They could not be generalized.

Capability models are excellent to stress the importance of the process. We find that the Trillium or SEI model are manager-oriented, that they cannot be easily downsized and that software engineers are not comfortable with most of the questions.

We find lots of variability in the student understanding of the self assessment questionnaires. This variability is due to various factors, which are the lack of experience of the students, the question formulation, and the evaluator interpretation. The same evaluator performed the three assessments. His understanding and interpretation of the answers provided by the students evolved with the number of meetings. Part of the team variability is due to evaluator perception. Formal evaluations were done once a week for three weeks in a row. The last team assessed had more process experience than the first team.

This course will be repeated next year with an easier project and a new revised version of a capability model.

Acknowledgments

We thank members of our group who have worked on this research project, and offer special thanks to Jean-Sébastien Neveu, Frédérick Chouinard, Martin Leclerc and Denis Pomerleau. We are grateful to the 19 students enrolled into the studio. Their collaborations make this course and unforgettable experience.

Support for this work was provided in part by BELL CANADA, Schemacode International Inc., the National Science and Engineering Research Council of Canada under grant # A0141 and and National Research Council PARI-M program under grant 11443Q.

References

1. Schach S., "Software Engineering", Irwin, 1990

2. Key Practices of the Capability Maturity Model CMU/SEI-91-tr-25, August 1991.

3. Trillium - Telecom Software Product Development Capability Assessment Model, Bell Canada, Draft 2.2, 1992, This version of TRILLIUM (draft 2.2) has been submitted to the ISO/IEC JTC1/SC7 working group (WG) 10 responsible to develop a new standard on Software Process Assessment. The number WG10/N015 that appears on the cover page has been assigned in Dublin on January 18th, 1993.

4. Kantipudi M., Collier K.W., Collofewllo J.S., Medeiros S., Software engineering Course Project: Failures and Recommandations, Software Reengineering education, SEI Conf. San Diego Oct., 1992, Springer Berlag, pp 324-338.

5. Freedman, D.P., Weinberg, G.N., Handbook of Walkthroughs, Inspections, and Technical Reviews, Third Edition, Dorset House, N.Y. 1990.

6. Oualine, S, C Elements of Style: the Programmers Guide to Developing Well-Written C and C++, M&T Books, 1992

7. Strokes Jr., S.L., Building Effective project teams, The Journal of information Systems Management, vol 7, no 3, Summer 1990, pp38-45, 1990.

8. Owens, T. The Self-Managing Work team, Small business reports, Vol. 16, no 2, Feb. 1991.

9. Oulsnam, G., Unravelling Unstructured Programs. the computer journal, Vol. 25, No 3, pp. 379-387 1982

10. Robillard P. N., Simoncau M., "Iconic Control Graph Representation", Software-Practice and Experience, Vol. 23(2), 223-234, Feb., 1993.

11. Schulmeyer G. Gordon,"Zero Defect Software", McGraw-Hill, 1990

12. IEEE Software Engineering Standards collection, Spring Edition, N.Y. 1991.

13. Robillard P. N., "Schematic Pseudocode for program constructs and its computer automation by SCHEMACODE", *Communications of the ACM*, Nov. 1986, Vol. 29, no 11, pp. 1072-1089.

14. Robillard, P.N, Coupal D. and Coallier F., "Profiling Software through the Use of Metrics", *Software - Practice and Experience*, 21(5), pp. 507-518, May 1991.

15. Poston R. M., "What is Wrong with Testing from Code", The Letter T, vol. 6, no 4, dec., 1992

DATRIX™ is a registered trademark of Bell Canada.

SCHEMACODE™ is a registered trademark of Schemacode International Inc.

Softbench™ is a registered trademark of Hewlett-Packard Company.

Software Through Pictures™ is a registered trademark of Interactive Development Environments

Teaching Software Project Management by Simulation
– Experiences with a Comprehensive Model

Marcus Deininger, Kurt Schneider

Software Engineering Group, Dept. of Computer Science, University of Stuttgart
Breitwiesenstr. 20-22, D-70565 Stuttgart, Germany

e-mail: sesam@informatik.uni-stuttgart.de

Abstract. Students of software engineering very rarely have the opportunity to gather experience in leading projects. This not only restricts their management skills, but also prevents them from learning about the project manager's point of view. We consider this lack of experience a major flaw of software engineering education. In this paper, we describe an approach to educate software engineers by simulating a software project. Students became project leaders of our simulated project and had to finish this given project successfully. To reduce biases and obtain reproducible effects, we decided to use a simple, but quantitative mathematical model. This simple model turned out to be sufficient to an amazing extent: Many effects well-known from real projects arose during the simulation. The project managers made many characteristic errors which led to plausible project distortions. The evolution of the simulated projects provided valuable feedback to teachers and students. This model is one result of our long-term project SESAM.

Introduction

In software engineering education we face a problem: Students are taught the basic principles of software project management, but have almost no opportunity to apply this knowledge to a real software project. First, they very rarely go through a software project during their studies. Second, if they do, they participate as programmers but don't have the opportunity to control the project. Thus, they never apply their software management knowledge actively.

In this paper we describe our experiences in teaching software project management by simulation. This approach allowed us to communicate project leading experiences within the restrictions of a university environment. Instead of a real project, students were assigned to a simulated software project which they had to finish successfully. The underlying simulation model was kept simple but nevertheless comprehensive covering the whole software development process. This allowed us to reduce biases and gain reproducible effects.

The model performed much better than originally expected, provoking many characteristic situations and effects project leaders experience in real life. During the simulation, students gained valuable insights in the job of a project manager, while the advisers gained experiences in simulating software development projects.

The simplicity of our model makes it feasible to use our approach in software engineering education of classroom projects, even if run manually. Within our long-term project SESAM, we develop a model building and simulation environment. It allows larger and more complicated models to be run automatically in an adventure game fashion.

1 Software Engineering Education

Software engineering education at the University of Stuttgart aims at teaching the skills needed to manage and participate successfully in an average software development project. Initially, we took a conventional approach to reach this aim: Based on the textbooks of Fairley (1986) and Sommerville (1989) we offer a software engineering course which lays the theoretical foundation of software engineering. In this course, we first discuss the overall principles of software engineering, such as project management, life-cycle concepts, software quality assurance, and software metrics. In the second part of the course, we step through the single phases of the waterfall-model discussing the results of each phase, as well as the basic methods and notations. At the end, students know about the basic concepts and techniques of software engineering.

This course is complemented by exercises. In these exercises, the methods and notations acquired earlier are applied to case-studies and examples. As these exercises only highlight some isolated topics, but cannot offer real project management experience, we introduced the following practical courses:

- **Practical course of software development.** In a team, students perform a small, but complete software development project. They get an initial assignment of a six-month-project. A member of the software engineering department is the "manager" of this team. Students should get aware of several problems arising during a project, and experience working in a team.

Course	Participants	Students' effort
Software engineering course	120 students	15 weeks, 4 hours each week
Exercises to the software engineering course	120 students	parallel to the software engineering course, every 2 weeks, 2 hours each week
Practical course of software development	about 10 groups of 3-4 students each	26 weeks, about 4 hours each week
Practical course of software development and project management	about 6 groups of 3 students each	12 weeks, about 8 hours each week
Practical course of project management	about 5 groups of 2 students each	12 weeks, about 8 hours each week

Table 1. Overview of our software engineering education activities.

- **Practical course of software development and project management.** In the abovementioned course, students experience a project from the programmers' point of view. In this course, students get a time schedule defining the project phases and major milestones. However, they are responsible for keeping the schedule and doing all other management tasks, such as organizing reviews, producing clean interfaces and so on. To stress these topics, the project itself is kept rather simple, but the artifacts are shifted between groups after each main milestone. This shifting provides the experience to work with requirements, designs and other artifacts they have not produced themselves. Depending on them, students pay far more attention to the quality of these documents. At the end of the project, students have experienced a series of problems a software developer and project leader will encounter: Slipping schedules, the effect of weak specifications or designs, dirty interfaces and so on.

- **Practical course of project management.** The main flaw of the previous practical course (as seen from our department's view) was its two-fold goal: First, experience the life as a developer (something already known after the practical course of software development) and second, experiencing the problems of a project manager (something never experienced before). To allow both kinds of experiences, the project had to be kept rather small. In such a small project, however, some effects could not arise, simply for lack of project complexity. Therefore, we decided to create a new type of course concentrating fully on *project management*, dropping the *actual* development activities for the sake of accommodating bigger-scale projects. Consequently, we had to simulate all dropped activities. Below, we describe the goals, models, and experiences we developed for this last and very promising type of software engineering education.

2 Goals of the Course

2.1 Goals

The main goal of the project management course was to give the students a "pure" project leader experience, not drained by any kind of other activity. They should get aware of the following topics:

- Planning is crucial! Working without a phased life-cycle plan will lead to poor product and process quality. Learn to make plans, estimates and adapt according to the feedback of your project's behaviour.

- Quantity isn't quality; if you continue working on a document, quantity will rise - but quality will not necessarily rise as well. Quality will only be improved if you perform explicit quality assurance activities. Working without quality assurance will lead to inconsistencies between documents (analysis specification, requirements, design, code).

- The most effective way to assure quality (especially in the early phases) is to perform reviews. Reviews have to be well-prepared to be effective. Findings in a review often are an indication for a well-done review and not for a development disaster.

- Take care of your customer - try to do what *the customer* really wants, not what you would want in the customer's place. Take care of your team - don't expect miracles from them.

- *You* are responsible for the project success (and the disaster) and no one else.

And as a global goal: Try to get as much feedback as possible from the project, and reflect about the roots of software-management problems to improve your process gradually.

2.2 Framework of the Course

The course took place within one term, i.e. twelve weeks. Maximum load of work was about one day per week for each student. The interaction with the course advisers was planned to be once in a week.

The students themselves should not perform the actual development activities of their project, but concentrate on the project manager's tasks:

- All participating students should gain management experience; no one was interested in yet another small-scale project to gain further hacking experience.

- Project leaders should get to the interesting problems within twelve weeks: If a real project can be carried out in twelve weeks, it is too small to get to the real problems. If the project is too big, students won't get beyond the early phases.

Many real difficulties, however, only occur at the end when the schedule runs short due to early mistakes and low quality.

Therefore, no real project could be used for the course:

- In a real project, someone has to do the real developing activities.

- Real projects are far too time and effort consuming to let students "crash" them merely as an exercise.

- A real project would be beyond our control and, thus, not permit enough feedback.

- In twelve weeks, students could only have led a very small real project or only a section of a bigger project.

To operate within this framework, we had to simulate a software project. This simulation covered all aspects of a software project.

3 Organisation of the Course

3.1 The Simulated Project

All project leaders were assigned to instances of the same project independently. They had to develop a cheque accountancy program for an external customer. At the beginning, the players received an initial analysis document of this project. The analysis document was four pages long and described the main functional requirements of the product being developed.

This analysis stemmed from Knöll (1990), a textbook on cost-rating methods. It was a real world project example to demonstrate the Function Point method. The Function Point method yielded 234 Function Points, an expected effort of 17 man-months and an expected duration of 7 months. Of course, this information wasn't given to the players.

The players got a slightly tighter schedule: The time frame was six months, the cost frame was a fixed price of DM 400.000,- and a planned budget of DM 250.000,-. This frame was set by an anonymous "management". Both time and budget were a bit too tight to keep; this reflected realistic shortage of resources and provoked compromises.

3.2 Layout of the Simulation and Interaction

The simulation had to be performed within twelve weeks, students making one move per week. A move consisted of:

- A list of actions to be performed in the project, including their duration in days,

- further explanations of details and reasons for these actions,

- a list of expected results and consequences,

- all project management related documents which a real project manager would have to provide, such as project plan, a rating of the team members, etc.

In turn, the project "managers" received the simulation results two days later. The results consisted of all the information, feedback and documents a real project manager would get in this situation, including remarks by his simulated team members.

We had not determined a list of "possible actions": Whatever a real project manager could do was a possible action in our simulation, too. Forbidden were only miraculous actions like "I'll hire a project manager assistant who will do all the work for me." Despite this unrestricted range of possible actions, only the following set of actions was actually used:

- Assign a task to one or several project members. The tasks performed were:
  - write a systems requirements document
  - write a system design document
  - write a module design document
  - code
  - perform module tests
  - perform integration tests
  - perform system tests
  - write handbooks
  - prepare a review
  - review a document
  - correct the errors found in a review.

- Involve the customer in some action (like review, social event).

- Call for information about training courses (on languages, tools, testing).

- Send projects members to such a course.

- Ask for information about software tools.

- Buy a tool.

- See a consultant.

- Announce a job opening.

- Hire a job applicant or fire a project member.

- Negotiate with management or customer about a higher budget or shift of the project end.

- A set of social events, reaching from project dinner invitation to a weekend-trip. These efforts improved the team's motivation.

The following information about the state of the projects was returned:

- All the tasks resulted in a quantitative reaction. That is, the players were informed about the number of pages or lines of code their team had written, the numbers of errors found during a review, etc. They did *not* get any full real document (except for the initial analysis presented at the beginning). So, they had to base their decisions solely on the quanitative data.

- Players could get ads for training courses: COBOL, Ada, Testing, Structured Programming, Structured Design and Project Calculating. The ads were only sent if a player asked for corresponding information. If a project member was sent to a course, his capability doing a related task would rise.

- Some software tools were offered upon demand: three different CASE tools, a testing facility, a standard database, an Ada -, and a COBOL Compiler. As with training, the tool would raise the efficiency of an associated activity - of course, after some time spent for learning.

- In a personal consultation, the project managers could get some advice themselves (all training courses were only offered for simulated personnel). Consultants were impersonated by us - they did cost a high amount of (simulated) money.

- Letters of possible new project members.
- Hired personnel was assigned to the project.
- Students were informed about all prices and costs, but not about the money spent in the move - they had to keep track of their budgets themselves!

All this information was embedded in full sentences of natural language to give the simulation a more lively feel.

4   The Simulation Model

How did we produce these results? We decided to use a mathematical model as backbone. This model is sketched below. The model was run manually, only supported by a spread-sheet program. Such a model allowed reproducible events and consistent, unbiased quantitative reactions to all projects. We tried to keep the model as simple as possible. Only such a model would ensure traceable effects which are a precondition for validation, understandable feedback and avoidance of too many computational errors. We started by defining criteria for a successful software project:

- Perform the project within the given time.
- Perform the project within the given budget.
- Deliver a product of satisfying quality.
- Finish the project with a satisfied customer and motivated project members.

4.1   The Static Model

To cover all these goals and their interactions in compromise, the simulator had to be able to keep track of them.

Time and Budget

As all costs of all actions were previously defined, time and money spent simply had to be added up.

Motivation and Satisfaction

All actions had an impact on the satisfaction of the simulated project members or the customer. The motivation was counted by so-called "motivation-scores". Each project member and the customer had a motivation-point account, were the scores were added or removed.

Product Quality

While the simulation of time, money and motivation was relatively easy, the simulation of the product quality was a big problem. As we didn't want to create real documents, the contents of the documents had to be modelled.

All metrics which measure documents only count the *size* or the *errors* of the document in some way: COCOMO (Boehm 1981) rates the delivered source instructions, Albrecht (1983) counts the Function Points of the requirements specification. Cyclomatic complexity (McCabe 1976) counts the branches of the source code. The metrics suggested in IEEE Standard 1045 (IEEE 1993) count the number of pages or ratio of graphics in any non-formal documents. The error-metrics proposed in IEEE Standard 982.1 (IEEE 1988) count the number of errors according to their introduction but give no hint on the nature of the errors.

It is crucial for a software project to transfer the initial requirements from the customer via a specification, and a design to a final software product. This transfer must not loose requirements, nor add obsolete functionality. Obsolete functionality causes as much effort as required one. Missing functionality or missing non-functional requirements cause customer dissatisfaction. This concept allows us to simulate quality, as well as the quantitative evolution of documents:

- A document consists of a set of elementary requirements; these requirements are measured by Albrechts Function Point measure which can be applied to any software.

- When a document is written, the elementary functions of the base document have to be transmitted into the actual document. E.g., if a designer writes the system design he has to cover all the functions stated in the requirements, nothing more and nothing less.

- All transmission activities result in some loss: Some of the original requirements are not met or transferred (missed by the writer), some additional functions are introduced (due to the biasing of the writers).

- As a consequence, at the end of each writing activity there are differences between the original document and the new document.

- The function modelling this transfer is described in the next subsection.

4.2 The Dynamic Model

Figure 1 shows the evolution of documents in terms of Function Points against effort.

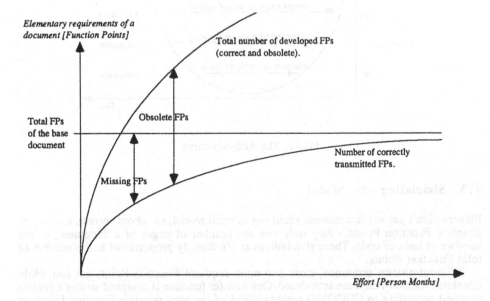

Fig. 1. Mapping effort to correctly transmitted, totally developed, missing, and obsolete Function Points in a document.

The number of correctly transmitted Function Points, of course, is limited by the contents of the previous document. This previous document is the reference for the actual document. The transfer function takes the form of a negative exponential function over the effort spent to produce the subsequent document. Together with the correct Function Points, obsolete Function Points are introduced. Obsolete Function Points are defined as the difference between total Function Points and correct Function Points. The total Function Points are calculated with the help of COCOMO (Boehm 1981). The missing Function Points are defined as the difference between the total number of Function Points of the predecessor and the correctly transferred Function Points.

Note that the total number of Function Points doesn't separate required from obsolete Function Points. Both kinds lead to the same amount of effort to be implemented. From the perspective of all subsequent documents there is no difference between them: What was obsolete in the design, seems to be mandatory to the coder. A consequence of this effect is described by the bath-tub curve which is shown in Figure 2: Errors (the obsolete and missing Function Points in our model) can only be detected when checked against a previous document. This means: in the phase in which they were introduced or in the respective test phase, but not in any development phase between! So, the amorphous set of total Function Points forms the base for the next development phase.

A simple model of coding errors was also introduced: coding errors were assumed proportional to the size of the source code. In contrast to missing or obsolete Function Points, this kind of errors was defined not to have any ripple effects. They simply represented syntax or presentation weaknesses, or evident typing errors.

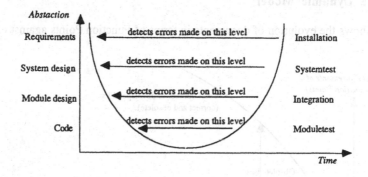

Fig. 2. The bath-tub-curve.

4.3 Simulating the Model

Players didn't get any information about our internal model, i.e. about correct, missing or obsolete Function Points - they only saw the number of pages of a document, or the number of lines of code. These size indicators are directly proportional to the number of total Function Points.

Without quality assurance, more and more required Function Points get lost while obsolete Function Points are introduced. Our transfer function is designed so that a project planned according to COCOMO catches 80%[1] of the total possible Function Points in every activity (i.e. of the previous document). So, in a nominal COCOMO project, *without* quality assurance 80% of the original user requirements were transformed into the

---

[1]   We assumed the Pareto distribution holds here.

specification. 64% (that are 80% of 80%) were transformed from the requirements into the system design. 51% (80% of 64%) were transformed from the system design to the module design. Finally, only 41% (80% of 51%) reached the code. This means: the code contains 41% of the original user requirements. Despite this dramatic loss, the code may have the initially assessed size: Many obsolete Function Points silently took the place of the dropped required ones.

How could the players do better than that? First, by spending more effort - although this increases not only the number of correct Function Points, but also the number of total Function Points. Then the player would have to develop much bigger subsequent documents to transfer all total Function Points. Such a policy would result in a gigantic, late product, as the documents size would rise and rise with each new activity. The second policy is to perform quality assurance. In our model that were reviews of the documents. A well-prepared review yielded 60% of the errors, assumed to be 60% of the obsolete Function Points and 60% of the missing Function Points. The detected obsolete Function Points were removed without effort, the missing Function Points had to be developed during rework.

5 An Example Move

This chapter shows an example move to demonstrate the capabilities of our model and to give an impression of the simulation in general.

The move is an excerpt from the seventh (out of twelve) move of group 2 (the wining team).

5.1 Project History

The project started June 1, 1992. The current date is September 7, 1992. The project has an overall budget of DM 250 000,- from which DM 123 830,- are spent so far.

The project manager has assigened three persons to the project: Mrs. Lovelace, Mr. Curtis, and Mrs. Smith.

Some informations on training were received, among others MENTOR-5, a course on software testing.

The requirements analysis took 18 person days and is finished now. The requirements specification contains 225 (of 234 possible) correct Function Points and 10 obsolete Function Points. 68 of these 225 correct Function Points had been gained during two extensive reviews.

System and module design are in progress. The system design took 36 person days so far, yielding a 143 pages document containing 187 correct and 3 obsolete Function Points. The module design lasted for 20 person days, yielding a 112 pages document containing 70 correct and 4 obsolete Function Points.

In the last move a review of the system design had been conducted, yielding 31 medium errors (i.e. missing or obsolete Function Points) and 37 light errors (i.e. spelling errors), thus accepting the design with some rework.

As explained earlier, only part of this information was available to the players.

5.2 An Actual Move

The move consists of the following actions, shown in table 2.

No.	Action	Participants	Start/Duration
1	We give the managment an overview of the general project situation. Because of the estimated project development we apply for an increase of the budget of DM 60.000,-.	Project Manager Management	September 7/ 1 Day
2	We negotiate with customer about a shift of the project end to December 19, 1992.	Project Manager Customer	September 8/ 1 Day
3	Correct the errors found during the system design review.	Mr. Curtis	September 7/ 5 Days
4	Continue work on module design.	Mrs. Lovelace Mrs. Smith	September 7/ 5 Days
5	Continue work on module design.	Mrs. Lovelace Mrs. Smith	September 14/ 3 Days
6	Birthday greetings to Mrs. Lovelace, a bouquet and a snack for all.	all project members	September 14/ 30 Minutes
7	Attend MENTOR-5 training course	Mr. Curtis	September 14/ 3 Days
8	Preparation for the module design review.	Mrs. Lovelace Mrs. Smith Mr. Curtis	September 18/ 2 Days
9	*several other actions*	...	...

Table 2: Excerpts from a move.

Included was a detailed description of the work packages to be done in the move as well as a revised project plan.

5.3 Reactions to the Move

Group 2 received the following results:

"The Management is very concerned about the slippage of your schedule. You are asked how you will get through the remaining project and even hold the new scheduled end of December 19. The increase in the budget is not accepted at the moment, a final decission will be made next month.

The customer is not glad shifting the schedule but accepts it under the condition that no further slippage will take place.

Mr. Curtis corrects the design review, Mrs. Lovelace and Mrs. Smith work on the module design which has a size of 177 pages now.

Mrs. Lovelace is very pleased by the bouquet (DM 60.-). The snack costs you DM 40.-.

Mr. Curtis returns highly motivated and full of new ideas from the MENTOR-5 training course.

..."

These results had the following internal consequences:

- Budget will be raised in the next move to DM 310.000,-.
- Scheduled project end date will be shifted to December 19, 1992.
- Motivation of the Customer falls by one motivation point.
- The System design now contains 219 correct and 2 obsolete Function Points.
- The module design now contains 142 correct and 14 obsolete Function Points.
- Motivation of Mrs. Lovelace rises by one unit after her birthday.
- Testing capabilities[2] of Mr. Curtis rises one unit after the training course.
- Motivation of Mr. Curtis rises one unit after the training course.
- ...
- Salaries (with all taxes and insurance costs) for the last four weeks were:
  ° Project Manager: DM 16.000,-
  ° Mrs. Lovelace: DM 12.000,-
  ° Mr. Curtis: DM 12.000,-
  ° Mrs. Smith: DM 8.000,-
- Other costs:
  ° MENTOR-5 training: DM 1.470,-
  ° Bouquet and snacks: DM 100,-
- New project date is October 5, 1992.
- Total costs so far are DM 173.400,-

6 The Development of the Projects

The course started in October 1992 with 5 groups of two students each. Each two-person team played together, impersonating one project manager. It was finished in February 1993. All groups participated successfully (in terms of the course, not of the simulated project!) and delivered a "complete system" within twelve moves. No group needed less than twelve moves.

6.1 Overall Results

All groups performed according to the waterfall model, stepping from requirements specification to integration, though this was not required. During the project all groups made a real project plan. All used some COCOMO knowledge for project planning, one group performed a successful Function-Point-Analysis but couldn't cope with the results.

Groups concentrating on early quality assurance performed better than groups with late or no quality assurance at all. All groups became very close attached to their simulation projects, resulting in true personal crises when some of the projects experienced problems.

---

[2] Capabilities were modelled with the help of the COCOMO effort multipliers described in Boehm (1981).

6.2 Determining the Winner

To determine the winner, we rated the group results by table 3. Table 3 also provides a weighting function to determine a best compromise between conflicting project goals.

Category	very good	good	medium	weak	Weight
Project end	Dec. 4, 1992 or earlier	Dec. 12, 1992	Dec. 26, 1992	Jan. 8, 1993 or later	5
Budget (DM)	280.000,- or less	320.000,-	360.000,-	400.000,- or more	5
missing FPs compared to the original analysis (containing 234 FPs).	5 or less	10	15	20 or more	Requirements: 3 System design: 3 Module design: 3 Code: 5
obsolete FPs compared to the original analysis.	5 or less	10	20	40 or more	Requirements: 3 System design: 3 Module design: 3 Code: 5
Coding errors	3 or less	6	10	15 or more	5
Average motivation of the project members	2 or more	1	0	-1 or less	1
Motivation of the customer	2 or more	1	0	-1 or less	1
Score	4 Points	3 Points	2 Points	1 Points	

Table 3. Weighting function to calculate the final results.

6.3 Individual Results

Group 1 didn't care too much for quality assurance and produced a rather straight-forward system. In the end, they finished almost within schedule and budget, but developed a product which differs significantly from the original requirements.

Groups 2 and 5 thought about buying a standard database for solving the task. Finally, they didn't purchase it because it was too expensive.

Groups 3 and 5 spent too much development effort without enough reviewing and testing afterwards. This resulted in giant products, low quality, time and budget slippage. Interestingly, both groups decided to cut off a part of their product at the end of the development, finally gaining relatively small products. The decision of which part to keep and which to drop was made in a rather unplanned, uncontrolled way, loosing a lot of so far collected correct Function Points. Both groups showed an obvious lack of planning and low ability to stick to their plans.

Group 4 stopped all activities too early, i.e. before they reached the required functionality and required quality. This resulted in a rather small system without many obsolete Function Points, and good time and budget figures. This made them win the second place.

Group 2 didn't show too exciting results in any single phase, but delivered a full 15 pages (!) project plan which was permanently updated. The secret of their success was a sensible, pretty regular plan to which they would stick over the whole project. As the score tells, this group was the winner.

Table 4 gives an overview of the five groups' individual results and the corresponding scores. After the simulation was over, we held two plenary sessions with all players to review their performance and results. Many sources of problems were identified. Students also criticized our model.

Group	1	2	3	4	5
Project end (all projects started at June 1, 1992)	Dec. 4, 1992	Dec. 21, 1992	Dec. 27, 1992	Dec. 11, 1992	Jan. 29, 1993
Budget (DM)	276.660,-	310.596,-	398.616,-	303.615,-	391.508,-
Correct Function Points (cFPs), missing FPs (mFPs), and obsolete FPs (oFPs) in the *requirements specification* compared to the original analysis.	215 cFPs 29 mFPs 15 oFPs	225 cFPs 9 mFPs 10 oFPs	228 cFPs 6 mFPs 50 oFPs	214 cFPs 20 mFPs 23 oFPs	213 cFPs 21 mFPs 8 oFPs
Correct FPs, missing FPs, and obsolete FPs in the *system design* compared to the original analysis.	198 cFPs 36 mFPs 51 oFPs	210 cFPs 24 mFPs 11 oFPs	217 cFPs 17 mFPs 70 oFPs	214 cFPs 20 mFPs 34 oFPs	202 cFPs 32 mFPs 24 oFPs
Correct FPs, missing FPs, and obsolete FPs in the *module design* compared to the original analysis.	166 cFPs 68 mFPs 48 oFPs	200 cFPs 34 mFPs 15 oFPs	164 cFPs 70 mFPs 63 oFPs	198 cFPs 36 mFPs 39 oFPs	202 cFPs 32 mFPs 24 oFPs
Correct FPs, missing FPs, and obsolete FPs in the *final system* compared to the original analysis.	186 cFPs 48 mFPs 66 oFPs	215 cFPs 19 mFPs 19 oFPs	180 cFPs 54 mFPs 58 oFPs	212 cFPs 22 mFPs 24 oFPs	212 cFPs 22 mFPs 25 oFPs
Code errors	44 Errors	0 Errors	3 Errors	10 Errors	1 Error
Average motivation of the project members	0,75	3,3	0,2	0,75	2,8
Motivation of the customer	-3	-1	0	-2	-1
Score	48	95	48	66	54

Table 4. Overview of the result of the projects.

7 Lessons Learned

We found the course very successful:

- we could simulate plausible project behavior reacting to different actions of five "project managers";

- we used a relatively simple quantitative model of the development process. The model stood unchanged over the whole simulation;

- students reported about real excitement, real panic and real confusion similar to the one experienced in practical courses, resulting from the same lack of planning and quality assurance;

- post-mortem feedback was much stronger than it could be in real projects, leading to much more insights;

- effort for simulation was high, but could be afforded due to the simple model;

- simulation did not distort the behavior too much: No one had the impression of non-plausible effects.

7.1 Lessons Learned for Further Simulations and Education

A crucial factor of the simulation success is a lively presentation. As soon as the students can identify themselves with the project managers, they behave accordingly, with no less effort or seriousness.

Most players criticized that they had gotten no real documents and no informative answers from their project members:

- "If I could see the document, I knew if it met the customer needs and if it is well-written." The blind flight was a negative experience - but this is a thing they have to cope with in a real project frequently.

- "In reality, people are more active, they tell more about their work." No, they don't! This uncovered, however, how important it is to let the simulated project members act more lively. Embedding the raw numbers coming from the quanitative model into full sentences manually is a good way, but must even be evolved further.

- "There must be work-breakdown structures for specification, design, code. You can't review a complete document within one review-session." This is true and is definitely a flaw of our model.

What can stay unchanged:

- The simple model was quite satisfactory. Currently we are developing a better simulation aid to allow more complicated dependencies. This will also reduce the danger of miscalculating simulation results.

- Granularity of the moves of one day was fine enough. It prevented players from getting lost in details.

- The foreseen set of actions turned out to be sufficient, and so did the prepared set of simulated programmers, training courses, and tools.

8 Integration of this Course

8.1 Related Work

Simulating software projects is not a new idea. Abdel-Hamid (1991) describes a simulation model for the software development process which is based on System Dynamics. Unlike our model this is a "closed loop simulation", i.e., project managers are simulated too. The user of the simulation only watches the evolution and is not intended to interact with the system. At the beginning of a run he supplies the starting situation, then the simulator will calculate the project development which can be inspected at the end of the run. In contrast, we do have an "open loop simulation": in a simulated environment, players interactively make management decisions.

McKeeman (1989) reports a tutoring program for the training of software developers. Using the program, developers learn how to conduct a review. This program has the nature of a game, much like our project simulation course, but looks only at a small part of the software development process.

A step further, but in an entirely different problem domain, went Vester (1987). He developed a game called "Ökolopoly" which puts the player into the role of the president of a fictional country. The player has to solve the economical and ecological problems of this country within a restricted set of decisions and moves. Again, the dependencies are based on System Dynamics. The basic principle, i.e., opening the loop and putting in the player, is the same as ours.

8.2 The SESAM Project

The course described in this paper was part of our long-term project SESAM (Software Engineering Simulation by Animated Models). Its goals are to

- develop animatable dynamic models of the software development process;

- develop graphical editors to enter, modify and store such models. Models must be highly changeable to reflect different situations and integrate new software engineering research results;

- provide simulation tools tailored for the SESAM dynamic models and

- offer a graphical interactive adventure game interface to allow students using the system without an adviser.

We reported on SESAM in Ludewig et al. (1992), Schneider (1993) and Schneider (1993a).

We will continue to work on all of these topics. After three prototypes investigating critical questions, we now have a basis for automated model editing and simulation support. We have realized our simple model in this simulation tool and will now add some feedback loops and additional dependencies which were too complicated to keep track of manually.

For the purpose of a classroom project, however, we think that the simple model presented above is sufficient to bridge a gap in software engineering education: It provides an opportunity for many students to act as project managers and gain real experiences within a simulated environment. Due to the simplicity of the model we are sure that it can be used manually in other education institutions interested in software engineering, too.

Acknowledgements

Many of the original ideas used within this course were developed by Thomas Bassler, former member of our departement.

References

Abdel-Hamid, T. K. (1991): **Software Project Dynamics - An Integrated Approach.** Prentice Hall, Englewood Cliffs, New Jersey.

Albrecht, A. J., J. E. Gaffney (1983): Software Function, Source Lines of Code, and Development Effort Prediction: A Software Science Validation. **IEEE Transactions on Software Engineering, SE-9,** Nov. 83, 639-648.

Boehm, B. W. (1981): **Software Engineering Economics.** Prentice Hall, Englewood Cliffs, New Jersey.

Fairley, R. (1985): **Software Engineering Concepts.** McGraw-Hill, New York.

IEEE (1989): **Standard Dictionary of Measures to Produce Reliable Software.** IEEE Std 982.1-1988.

IEEE (1993): **Standard for Software Productivity Metrics.** IEEE Std. 1045.

Knöll, H.-D., J. Busse (1991): **Aufwandsschätzung von Software-Projekten in der Praxis: Methoden, Werkzeugeinsatz, Fallbeispiele.** (Reihe Angewandte Informatik Bd. 8), BI-Wissenschaftsverlag, Mannheim, Wien, Zürich.

Ludewig, J., Th. Bassler, M. Deininger, K. Schneider, J. Schwille (1992): **SESAM - Simulating Software Projects.** Proceedings of the Software Engineering and Knowledge Engineering (SEKE) Conference, Capri, Italy.

McCabe, T. J. (1976): A Complexity Measure. **IEEE Transactions on Software Engineering, SE-2,** pp. 308-320.

McKeeman, W. M. (1989): Graduation Talk at Wang Institute. **IEEE Computer, Vol. 22,** No. 5, pp. 78-80.

Schneider, K. (1993): **Object-Oriented Simulation of the Software Development Process in SESAM.** Proceedings of the Object-Oriented Simulation Conference (OOS '93), part of the Western Simulation Multiconference, San Diego, January 1993.

Schneider, K. (1993a): **SESAM-Zwischen Planspiel und Adventure Game.** "Informatik und Schule '93", Koblenz, Germany, October 11-13, 1993.

Sommerville, I. (1989): **Software Engineering.** 3rd Edition, Addison Wessley, Workingham, England.

Vester, F. (1987): **Ökolopoly - Ein kybernetisches Umweltspiel.** Otto Maier Verlag, Ravensburg, Germany.

Session 5:
Implications of Practitioners

Awareness Week at Texas Instruments: An Alternative Approach to Instructor-Led Delivery
Barbara J. Weinberger, Texas Instruments, Plano, Texas

Implication of Practitioners in a Post-graduate Curriculum, a Successful Collaboration
Jacques Guyard, Jean-Pierre Jacquot, Université de Nancy, Vandœuvre-lès-Nancy, France, and Bernard Amar, Yves Benoit, CEGELEC, Clamart, France

Reducing the Gap Between Academic Theory and Professional Practice in Software Engineering Education
Gunnar Hartvigsen, University of Tromsø, Tromsø, Norway

Awareness Week at Texas Instruments:
An Alternative Approach to Instructor-Led Delivery

Barbara J. Weinberger

Texas Instruments
Plano, TX 75086

1 Introduction

For the past few years, the Information Systems and Services (IS&S) group at Texas Instruments (TI) has been focused on the use of the Software Engineering Institute's (SEI) Capability Maturity Model (CMM) as a roadmap for software process improvement. This focus on process improvement has created a huge demand for courses on software process improvement concepts and techniques. After attending numerous required classes, however, students have quickly become jaded and unenthusiastic. Since the need for software process courses continues to grow, our challenge as a training organization is to identify a training approach that will maintain student interest in the midst of this flood of information.

2 The Target Audience

The IS&S organization consists of roughly 1500 software and hardware professionals who support the various businesses of Texas Instruments. Most IS&S personnel are located in Plano, Texas, but a non-trivial number of IS&Sers work at various TI sites throughout the United States, Europe, and the Far East. In terms of background and attitude, the population can be divided into three categories: the Newly Arrived, the Veteran Hopefuls, and the Veteran Cynics.

The Newly Arrived tend to be the most open to new approaches to process improvement. If this is their first job out of college, they tend to appreciate the structure of a pre-existing software process and are eager to learn. Those who had previous jobs and are Newly Arrived from the job market are also eager to learn because, as one student explained to me, "We're just happy to have a job." This is perhaps not the most positive motive for buying into process improvement, but it is a genuine motive nonetheless.

The Veteran Hopefuls are those who have been with the company for some period of time, have been involved in some process improvement activities, and are now seeing benefits they can believe in. This group still questions and challenges each new process improvement activity, but it does so in the spirit of continuous improvement.

The Veteran Cynics pose the greatest challenge. These are IS&Sers who have been with the company for a while and have maintained a closed mind to the process improvement thrust. The reasons vary, but the most common examples are (1) highly technical people who despise writing documentation and see the process improvement thrust as a lot of red tape, (2) developers who resent the implication that their process was "wrong" in the past, and (3) people who resent upper management telling them what to do and see it as a threat to empowerment.

3 Broad-Scale Delivery: Our First Approach

At the beginning of the process improvement thrust, IS&S management decided the best way to ensure thorough deployment of process improvement concepts was to require the same training of all IS&Sers, with additional required courses for project managers and Software Quality Assurance (SQA) analysts. Within the space of one year, over 2500 students had attended seven required courses.

This broad-scale delivery of required training had certain advantages. It was easy to track metrics for deployment of process improvement training. The courses were designed as stand-up lectures, so the information delivered was consistent from class to class.

The question of effectiveness, however, still remained. Were students who attended the required classes getting anything from them? There was some evidence to indicate they were not. The ratings for these required courses were lower than any other courses offered by the training organization. When I began to teach these required courses myself, I noticed so much resistance and cynicism among the students that I included a "resistance to change" activity at the beginning of each class. We were certainly successful at ensuring that all IS&Sers heard the same information, but was it falling on deaf ears?

4 The Birth of the Awareness Week Concept

In the fall of 1992, we created a roadmap for new process improvement training to be developed in 1993. The greatest and most immediate need was for SEI Level 3 Awareness Training, making the organization aware of the challenges we would face as we worked for continuous improvement against the CMM. Three of us met to discuss the approach, and we all quickly agreed that another required stand-up lecture class was not the answer. What if instead we could get the entire organization to focus on software process improvement for one week and explore SEI Level 3 Key Process Areas through a variety of activities, such as skits, demonstrations, and displays? The idea of an Awareness Week was born.

4.1 Training Project Organization

The original project team consisted of two people, one from the IS&S software engineering process group and one from the Education Center. (A second person from the Education Center was added to the project later on.) We began with a review of preliminary requirements. The first and most important requirement was that the week be fun. At the same time, we had to convince IS&S management that we could control the training objectives in a less structured setting than a classroom. The Education Center had already begun to experiment with a more rigorous training development methodology by taking the IS&S software development methodology and applying it to training projects. We decided to use this same approach for planning the Awareness Week.

4.2 Management Commitment

We documented the proposed approach, the alternatives we considered (traditional instructor-led course, developed either in-house or by a vendor), and the basic project plan in an Approach Document that was reviewed by the IS&S management team. Their support for the plan was critical to assuring widespread participation across the organization. We received their approval to proceed with little difficulty. They too had heard complaints from their departments about the required courses, and they were ready to try something new. The use of a structured methodology to develop the week gave the Awareness Week project credibility as a legitimate training effort and not just a week of "fun and games."

4.3 Managing the Training Project

With the approval of the IS&S management team, we were ready to proceed. We formed a customer team to provide direction and began documenting requirements, learning objectives, and course outlines. We wrote a Test Plan (including peer reviews of all written materials and dry runs of all presentations) and an Implementation and Support Plan to cover the logistics of materials and room preparation and the movement of as many as 180 students at a time in an efficient manner. We established attendance metrics and goals and designed a method to track actuals against the goals.

5 Structure and Content

The Awareness Week itself consisted of two primary pieces: an on-going display in a central hallway with new information appearing each day, and a series of hour-long sessions with speakers, skits, and demonstrations on various topics. To meet the needs of IS&Sers at other TI sites, all sessions were video-taped for future viewing.

DAY	MORNING SESSIONS	AFTERNOON SESSIONS
Monday	Level 3 Overview	IS&S Software Status
Tuesday	Intergroup Coordination	Inspections
Wednesday	Inspections	Level 3 Overview
Thursday	SQA	Metrics
Thursday		IS&S Software Status
Friday	Tailoring	Level 3 Overview
Friday	IS&S Software Status	

5.1 The Learning Objectives

Since the purpose of the Awareness Week was to distribute information, the learning objectives for each session were based on recall and recognition of the information in the session, not on demonstration of a specific job skill:

Level 3 Overview. Describe the general requirements the organization must meet to achieve SEI Level 3.

IS&S Software Status. Describe the organization's current process maturity and the actions planned to achieve SEI Level 3.

Intergroup Coordination. Identify functional groups within the organization that are available to support software development project teams.

Inspections. Explain the purpose, benefits, and basic characteristics of software inspections as a form of Peer Review.

Software Quality Assurance. Describe the SQA role and activities in the organization.

Metrics. Describe common barriers to successful collection, reporting, and analysis of organization and project metrics.

Tailoring. Describe one structured method for tailoring the organization's standard software process.

5.2 A Variety of Activities

Each session was an hour long and was scheduled for three time-slots in the morning (8:30 am, 10:00 am, and 11:30 am) or afternoon (1:00 pm, 2:30 pm, and 4:00 pm.) Some sessions, such as the Level 3 Overview, were offered on more than one day, so students had as many as nine different times from which to choose. In each session, students received a set of handouts and exercises to use as reference material on the job. These same handouts and exercises were also distributed at the central hallway display, along with popcorn and candy. Small giveaway items were distributed in the sessions (embossed with the IS&S Software Process Improvement theme), and prize drawings were held at the end of each session. The goal was to create a sense of excitement and interest through constant activity.

The sessions had many different formats. The Level 3 Overview and IS&S Software Status sessions were both stand-up lectures. The Intergroup Coordination session included a series of four short presentations from different functional areas within IS&S. The Inspections and Tailoring sessions consisted of skits designed to demonstrate techniques. The Metrics session was a panel discussion, and the SQA session revolved around an exercise the students filled out to test their SQA knowledge.

Over forty IS&S employees helped prepare for and present at the various sessions throughout the week. Since the project team that planned and coordinated the Awareness Week consisted of only three people, the participation of these other IS&Sers was critical to creating an interesting and varied set of presentations.

6 The Outcome

Was the Awareness Week a success? We think so. We exceeded all of our attendance goals, and the vast majority of those who attended said the week of activities was more effective than a traditional classroom setting. Individual session ratings indicated that nearly all students felt session objectives were met.

6.1 Lessons Learned: Success Factors

We certainly learned a great deal from the experience. We believe our success was due to three critical factors: strong support from upper management, a rigorous methodology that ensured traceability of all activities and content to the learning objectives, and an emphasis on variety and fun throughout the week.

6.2 Lessons Learned: Opportunities to Improve

We also learned what to do differently next time. The session evaluation forms indicated the students often did not know what the session objectives were before attending. They either had not received the listing of session objectives or they had received it and had not read it. During the Awareness Week, every session began with a discussion of the session objectives but at that point it was too late to effectively manage student expectations.

For the two required sessions, we were overly concerned with ensuring consistency of content and as a result we chose a traditional stand-up lecture approach. This was especially unfortunate since these two sessions kicked off the week of activities, leaving students with the impression that all sessions would be just as dry. The required sessions did not conform to one of our fundamental requirements, to have fun!

Last but certainly not least of the lessons learned relates to the planning and management of a project of this scope and nature. We greatly underestimated the effort required to plan and execute this project. Having collected actual data on effort expended this time, we will be better prepared next time.

7 The Future

Will there be a next time? With results this promising we can't resist! Awareness Week 1994 is already in the Planning phase and has all the signs of a tradition in progress.

Implication of Practitioners in a Post-Graduate Curriculum, a Successful Collaboration

B. Amar and Y. Benoit
CEGELEC/RED
5 av. Newton
F-92142 Clamart, FRANCE

J. Guyard and J.-P. Jacquot
Université de Nancy 1 – ESIAL – CRIN
Campus V. Grignard — BP 239
F-54506 Vandœuvre-lès-Nancy, FRANCE

abstract

A collaboration between academics and practitioners is successfully running in the context of the *DESS en génie logiciel* at the University of Nancy. This paper reports on this collaboration. In addition to presenting our experience, we also propose an analysis of pedagogical collaboration between industry and university. We discuss the difficulties with and the benefits of such collaborations and the forms they may take. By analyzing our current collaboration along those three axes, we try to understand why it is effective, how we can make it last, and how we could reproduce it with other partners or in other contexts.

1 Introduction

"Academic education must be professionalized; so let's introduce professionals[1] into the curricula." This idea is now an integral part of folklore: i.e., it is blindly trusted, but nobody can explain where it comes from! We are firmly convinced that practitioners must take part in the education of engineers, but we believe that there are specific factors which may improve the effectiveness of such collaborations

During the last few years, the authors have slowly built up a fruitful collaboration. The process we have followed has been mostly informal, including intuition and bits of luck. However, we now think establishing effective collaborations could be made more rational. In this paper, we want to analyze the general problem of collaboration between academics and practitioners in a graduate level curriculum in software engineering. Our aim is to address the important question: "What are the most effective ways to integrate the interventions of practitioners ."

The paper is organized as follows. We first discuss the difficulties raised by pedagogical collaboration between industry and university. Next, we analyze the expected benefits of

---

[1]It is well known that teaching is not a profession, but an occupation.

collaboration. The subsequent section presents a list of possible forms of collaboration. Then, we discuss the actual collaboration between the Software Engineering Department of CEGELEC, a big company working in process controls and commands, and the Computer Science Department of the University of Nancy. We conclude with some afterthoughts on the reasons for practitioners to involve themselves in educational activities.

2 Do we need to bother with practitioners?

This question is posed somewhat whimsically, but nonetheless a fact remains: introducing people-of-the-trade inside an academic curriculum is difficult. From the opposite point of view, coping with academy is not easy. Let us have a look at the difficulties.

The first problem concerns the costs. Two kinds of cost must be considered: money and time. On strictly economic grounds, universities cannot afford to pay companies the true cost of their involvement in educational activities. At best, universities can cover direct expenditures, such as travel and accommodation; they may also pay lecturers on the standard academic hourly basis. The time and salary of a lecturer are gifts. In itself, this situation is rather healthy, but its consequences are not. In particular, few companies can afford gifts of several days (a short module of 30 hours in front of students represents 5 days, or 1 week); companies may be tempted to send "cheap" collaborators (the less experienced, hence the less interesting from a pedagogical point of view); and other things may take precedence over educational activities. Every teacher knows only too well what a one hour lecture costs in preparation time; practitioners are discouraged to learn that at their first lecture. As a consequence, finding conscientious practitioners who agree to invest in educational activities is not easy.

The second problem concerns the quality of the practitioners' interventions. Students know their time is short and rightfully they insist on learning something from all organized activities. So, practitioners must have some knowledge to transmit. But they must also know *how* to transmit it to students. In contrast to practitioners, students lack knowledge of real-life problems and precise objectives (apart from getting grades). Speaking to a classroom is an exercise for which practitioners are often not prepared.

The third problem concerns pedagogic management. Two facets of this problem are to be considered. First, there are many practical difficulties in integrating interventions of practitioners in the pedagogic progression. The right person at the wrong time is only marginally better than nothing! It took us three years to find an adequate timing for CEGELEC's interventions, and we were very lucky that CEGELEC's constraints were compatible with the pedagogic organization. Second, grading students is always difficult when practitioners are involved. On the one hand, practitioners are not used to academic grading criteria, while on the other hand, universities are responsible for the value of diplomas which is mostly expressed through grades.

The last problem concerns the justifications. This is in fact a consequence of the preceding difficulties. Hierarchies, both academic and industrial, require that we justify the costs (money, time, administration, ...) implied by the collaborations. A sensible response would be to balance the costs against the benefits. Unfortunately, we have no means of quantifying those benefits. We are condemned to live with the permanent threat of collaborations being suddenly broken.

Successful education involves managing several schedules: students', lecturers', and that of the curriculum. Students' time must be highly structured, lecturers' time is a costly resource, and a curriculum spans several years to become thoroughly effective. The common characteristics of these time factors is the crucial need of *stability*. The problems discussed above are indeed related to this need. The best way to overcome them is to consider collaboration between industry and university as a *strategic action* on both sides. The rest of the paper analyzes this point of view.

3 Expected benefits

In this section, we list the potential benefits of collaboration between a company and a university. We restrict our discussion to collaboration in educational activities. Research or technology transfer are driven by different rationales, outside the scope of this paper. We consider three points of view: the university's, the students' and the company's. It is important to remember that any collaboration can only last if all parties get their fair share of benefits.

3.1 Benefits for the university

Universities, as institutions, cannot expect to gain much from pedagogical collaborations. In fact, they may even loose on financial terms if companies make their live-participation a part of their donations to universities.

The most interesting result of collaborations is to keep informal networks of relations alive. A rich network will help to initiate more formal research or transfer activity. This is particularly important in the current European context where many pre-competitive research programmes based on consortia involving academic and industrial institutions have been launched (ESPRIT, ESF, EUREKA, ...). Knowing people beforehand makes it easier to write such proposals.

Although not really important in France, where universities do not compete against each other, strong and rich relations with industry are a good means of attracting top students.

3.2 Benefits for the students

Benefits for students should obviously be the primary concern of university and industry collaboration. In a professionally oriented curriculum, like the *DESS (Diplôme d'Etudes Scientifiques Supérieures) en Génie Logiciel*, it seems quite natural to have interventions by professionals. But we need to examine why. We have already advocated [JGB90] that a *DESS* should have two aims:

- to teach students state-of-the-art techniques and tools
- to help students to pass smoothly from the academic to the industrial world.

The second aim does not mean that we want students to be productive from their first day of employment, but rather that we want students to be able to transfer their fresh knowledge into their industrial environment quickly.

In the software engineering field, except for very few leading-edge companies, most practices are several years behind the concepts and techniques taught in university. So, practitioners are not better than academics in teaching such matters. However, practitioners can be invaluable in helping learn the techniques: they can convince students of the necessity of these techniques in real-life situations. Our experience shows the importance of motivating students. It also shows that it is not so simple. Students lack experience and are generally more impressed than enriched by horror stories and funny anecdotes. That kind of lecture requires a careful pedagogical treatment.

Although universities are founts of knowledge, some domains lie outside their reach. We see two such domains in the software engineering field: transferring new theories into actual use in industry, and managing highly uncertain environments. With respect to our second aim, these domains must be taught. Without this teaching, there is a very serious risk of inducing in students a manichaean view: a dream world in academia, and a dirty real world in industry, and of course, two such worlds cannot communicate. This view is well rooted in French society; it is our actual duty to show it is false.

It seems obvious that engineering students should learn what the industrial world consists of. From our point of view, this topic does not require lectures by practitioners. Teachers are indeed as qualified as practitioners to lecture about theories in economics, management, communications, and so on. The most important practical lessons about the world of industrial software are learned during the training courses. This requires only that companies be convinced of the educational importance of these training courses.

3.3 Benefits for the companies

In a pedagogical collaboration, the benefits expected by companies will vary greatly, according to the company's size, involvement, and aims.

A first benefit is to get a low cost workforce. It is legitimate from the company's point of view, but, as a rule, we think it best to avoid collaborations motivated solely by this benefit. It tends to emphasize quantity over quality of work and to lead to the assignment of purely technical tasks.

Keeping a live relational network is a benefit arising from pedagogical collaborations. This is more important to companies than to universities, since it is a means of performing technological surveys and of updating in-house training strategies.

In long-lasting collaborations, practitioners get a good knowledge of students and can then use them as *experimental material*. This kind of collaboration objective is legitimate so long as the pedagogic team agrees with it and judges that it will not work to the detriment of students. Experiments can be *passive*: observing how students react to lectures or analyzing students' behavior during a project for instance. They can also be *active*: suggesting a team structure or a way to tackle a problem for instance. Many problems in the software engineering industry are human problems: continuous education, team management, programmers' psychology, and so on. Universities provide a reasonably safe place to assess tentative improvements in this domain.

In the tense market of software specialists, companies are obviously interested in viewing students as potential collaborators. Pedagogic collaborations have three direct benefits in this context. First, they are a form of *corporate advertising*. Students will remember the companies which have participated in their education. Second, companies have better criteria to judge applicants whom they have known as students. The collaboration between CEGELEC and the University of Nancy has lead to several highly praised recruitments (and even to some disappointment when some students did *not* choose CEGELEC...) Third, well known people are easier to integrate into the company. Collaborating companies are aware of what the students know and also who they are.

A last benefit of collaboration lies in the possibility of making constructive criticism about the curricula. Practitioners involved in academic education have a better understanding of its rationale; they can make effective practical proposals. Such proposals are precise and pragmatic; they are a good complement to recommendations issued by commissions which work at a higher level [Mis91].

4 Some forms of collaboration

In this section, we want to discuss the main forms of collaboration, their advantages and their drawbacks with respect to pedagogical aspects.

The simplest form of collaboration to initiate and manage is a collection of seminars where practitioners present aspects of their actual work and activity. Strictly speaking, such seminars are not a teaching activity: students gain little knowledge and no "know-how." Presentations play rather the important role of exploding myths about the professional world. So, they help prepare students to leave the academic world. Seminars are best when they illustrate a course, hence motivating students to learn certain topics. For instance, a seminar by a team manager can improve attention to lectures about project management; presentation of a tool can do the same for lectures on software environments. The main difficulty is to get these seminars synchronized with the courses. Seminars aimed at "selling" a company or a product should be avoided.

Practitioners can make interventions inside a course module, or can even be given responsibility for a whole module. Such collaborations are most enriching for both parties. The main difficulty is to find the right practitioner: who accepts investing time and who likes teaching activities. If we except the, unfortunately, rare practitioners who take on teaching on their own time, the most adequate people are found in training departments of companies. Such practitioners are used to teach and have already some pedagogic material (slides, case studies, ...) They will nevertheless need to adapt their lecture style to a very different attendance. It is not uncommon to find alumni or alumnae, who feel a kind of "nostalgia" from university, willing to collaborate in this way.

Industrial projects are another form of collaboration. These projects are proposed by companies. They are realized by small groups, 2 to 4, of students. Compared to *internal* projects, their primary advantage is to induce a more active and responsible student behavior: i.e., a professional behavior. Students must take positions on the proposed subjects; sometimes, they must even actively participate in the search for and in the definition of projects. Another advantage lies in the students' integration into the professional world. The theme of projects and quantity of work have a very wide spectrum. Depending on the time allotted and the students' qualifications, projects can range from evaluation of a simple tool to the complete industrialization of a piece of software. Obviously, the depth and quality of the integration vary in the same ratio. Two main difficulties are associated with this form of collaboration. The first one is to get projects with a good balance between quality and quantity of work: students should have time to learn during their project. The second one lies in the practical management of the projects: getting a sufficient number of proposals on time, elaborating formal conventions between university and companies, supervising students, guaranteeing good working conditions, and so on. Trivial problems, as well as unapproachable ones, arise from this management. [Kno91] provides a good discussion of this form of collaboration. From our point of view, challenges and competitions sponsored by companies, most notably by computer manufacturers, can be classified in the category of industrial projects. Such collaborations have the additional advantage of allowing the comparison and evaluation of different universities and curricula.

A classical, but nonetheless essential, form of collaboration is the *training course*. Firms actually participate in students' education by integrating them as collaborators for several months. For our DESS students, the training course lasts from April to July. They are generally extended until September, particularly when considered as a pre-recruitment. Through this form of collaboration, which is the only one we have with a majority of companies, a dense network is maintained. This network is very important to make curriculum evolve: the analysis of proposals shows us the actual trends in industry, and the evaluation of training courses by practitioners gives us feed-back on the general quality of the training. Although students must be granted a great deal of autonomy in looking for training courses and for choosing among proposals, teachers must filter proposals very strictly. In the software industry, engineers with a very wide and ill-defined range of competence are used—perhaps more than in traditional engineering fields.— We always fear to see a student used only for purely technical tasks (typically restricted to programming) in a poor human and material environment. It can be noted that industrial projects and training courses have a lot in common. Practically, they can be designed to be chained: the industrial project is begun at the university and completed during the training course.

Consulting is a traditional form of collaboration. It should be noted that it can work both ways: an academic consultant to a company project, or an industrial consultant to an academic project. In the first type of consulting, the academic person is used mostly to help the transfer of technology. In the second type, the industrial consultant must help students to work more professionally and to be more pragmatic. Although the principle of this second kind of collaboration is very simple, it is not easy to put it into practice. The main problem is to find a practitioner willing to play his or her real role with students.

Cooperative programmes are generally advocated as a very effective means of education. They are not well developed in France (mostly for structural reasons). In our social system, workers have the possibility of getting a sabbatical year to follow a professional curriculum. Every year, several professionals enter the DESS. They are very interesting students who improve the spirit of the classroom by introducing new points of view. Unfortunately for potential collaborations, nearly all of these students use their new diploma to find a new job, thus cutting the link which could be established between the university and their former company. The idea of cooperative systems can be extended to cover the continuous education needs of big firms. [SS90] presents a very interesting cooperation where a company and a university share their resources to develop a curriculum, to deliver the lectures, and to train practitioners.

To be exhaustive, we must also consider the lectures delivered by academic people to practitioner audiences in commercial seminars. Such courses address new techniques, such as specification languages, formal verification, advanced data-base systems, methodology, and so on. Paradoxically in France, these courses are generally managed by companies specialized in professional training (often subsidiaries of big software companies). They have a great success, but their real impact has never been assessed. Their main advantage is to allow people from different fields and companies to meet together.

Pedagogical collaborations between university and industry can take a lot of different forms. The preceding analysis indicates the main lines along which a general collaboration strategy can be elaborated. It also gives a framework in which an actual and effective collaboration may be instantiated. The following section presents the successful instantiation between the *DESS Informatique* in Nancy and CEGELEC.

5 Our experience

Our collaboration started in 1985. Since then, it has greatly evolved in its operation and in the people involved; it reached a stable state in 1990. We present this current state.

5.1 The teamwork project

Practitioners from CEGELEC are involved in several pedagogic activities with Nancy students. They regularly give seminars and they are advisers during training courses. But the most interesting collaboration occurs during the *teamwork project*. We have already presented this original project, [JGD90]; in this section we discuss the pedagogical organization.

The teamwork project is built as a scale model of real software projects. An important parameter is the teaching staff which models human resources external to the project. It is composed of four persons: two clients/executive managers (academics), a technical consultant (academic), and a project management consultant (practitioner). The three roles are clearly distinguished and we avoid interference between them as much as possible.

The role of the technical consultant is to advise students about technical difficulties in the specification, design, and realization of the pieces of software. He or she is also responsible for the technical evaluation of the product at the end of the project. We have chosen to give this role to an academic for practical reasons. The most important one is his or her "availability:" students can consult him or her at any time.

The role of the clients/managers is to control how the project runs. They meet the project manager weekly, who must report about the state of the project (work done, work scheduled, team structure, members' activities,. . .) Although they take no decision about the project, they are responsible for the final acceptance of the required documents. They must also accept the students' decisions about the project, such as the final requirements, the schedules (and re-schedules), the team re-organizations, the production tools used, and so on. Students issue proposals which are argued during the weekly meetings. We have chosen two academics to fulfil this role for several reason. First, as it is a hierarchical role, it fits well with traditional academic relations; in particular, students know and accept that their clients/managers will be the most important judges of the project. Second, the time is structured mainly by the weekly meetings, this requires an important "availability." Last, and most important, the teamwork project is a central piece of the software engineering curriculum. This induces the necessity of a strong pedagogical management of the project itself, but also of its interference in and relationship with other courses.

The role of the project management consultant is to help students to organize their project. He or she must suggest solutions to management problems and practical techniques and tools to use. This role is fulfilled by a practitioner for three main reasons. First, he or she introduces a real-life flavor into the project, which induces a professional behavior among students. Second, he or she introduces actual tools, techniques, and methods used in industry. Doing so, he or she prepares students for their future professional life by providing a strong link between topics taught in university and their use in industry. Last, he or she offers students the opportunity to discuss their problems, feelings, and even resentments, outside the academic circle. This last point is very important since the teamwork project pushes students to their limits.

The project management consultant is also responsible of the lectures about software construction. The evolution of this course during the last few years is very interesting. Three organizations have been tested. First, course followed by project. The basic idea was that students would apply the course material to the project. Next, project followed by course. The idea was to let students experience problems so that they would get a better understanding of the course. Now, the course is totally integrated into the project. Although the first two organizations were not failures, the third one proves to be the most effective. The consultant comes approximately every three weeks; he or she stays one day. One half of the day is devoted to a lecture whose topic is synchronized with the state of the project, the second half is devoted to discussion of the actual project problems. With this structure, students get immediate hints about solutions. They can also apply their new knowledge directly and get very quick feed-back during the next visit. Although the lectures are slightly less formal and are more difficult to prepare (due to the necessary synchronization), we think the benefits of this organization far outweigh those minor drawbacks.

As a whole, we consider the current teamwork project as a real success which benefits all parties: students, academics, and practitioners.

5.2 Analysis of the success

Noting the success is a pleasure, but understanding it seems more important. Here are some elements which, from our point of view, provide the main explanations of the situation.

The first element is the mere existence of a collaboration between academics and practitioners. The quality of this collaboration is due to the good balance we have drawn: the university provides the framework while industry provides the spirit. Without practitioners, the teamwork project would not have taken off; it is not clear that a course combining in an effective way training and education (as does the teamwork project) could be established outside the university.

The second reason lies in the benefits. Students are absolutely positive about the teamwork project: they really feel they are learning software engineering. The best proof is their investment: over 25 hours of work on the project per week per student, while they continue to follow lectures and to work on other assignments! Academics have learned a lot from the project. Besides a lot of numerous details about project management, group dynamics, and the like, academics get very significant feed-back on their teaching during the project. Since students must use materials from nearly all their courses, we can assess how they have received them. In fact, the project has fired a reflection on the "informatics" curricula at the University of Nancy, particularly on the way to introduce software engineering principles and practices earlier.

Our collaboration requires an important investment from CEGELEC. It is paid back in two ways. The first way concerns the recruitment of top-level students. Nearly all our students are favorably inclined to work at CEGELEC, and CEGELEC can screen the best students on objective criteria. In fact, several DESS alumni work at CEGELEC. Their integration has always been very easy and quick. The second way, quite unexpected, has been to provide us with some feed-back on our practices. The project management consultant of the teamwork project has a very good perspective of the project. In particular, there is no stress, no pressure, and no conflict between team and consultant as is generally the case in an actual project. Moreover, the academic framework is less formal than the industrial one; so students explain their problems and difficulties freely. In this manner, numerous insights have been gained about "team life." The design of the teamwork project allows us to change parameters. It has been possible to suggest some changes to students in order to observe the effect of new ideas. This long lasting collaboration has allowed the same persons to participate to several projects. The observed differences between students' behavior in different years also provided very insightful comparisons.

The key reason for the success is the fact that practitioners do not act a part, but really do their actual job. The practitioners involved in the teamwork project come from the methodology department of CEGELEC. This department maintains the in-house method (MODAL), organizes courses for CEGELEC engineers, and provides consultants on project management and quality insurance to CEGELEC development teams. The advantages of this situation are numerous. First, the teaching material already exists (slides, case-studies, lecture plans,...), so the time to be invested in preparing a lecture is reasonable. Second, practitioners knows how to manage a classroom, although student and professional attendances require different treatment, the basic techniques and tricks are the same. Third, the experience in consulting makes it possible to anticipate the needs of students: lectures can be delivered at the right time and consulting actions can be prepared (anticipation of problems). Fourth, students trust practitioners. Last, practitioners have less constraints, particularly on their calendar. It can be argued that people more involved in developments may present a more precise view of the reality of a project to students. This is probably true, but we want our students to learn and experience a lot of things in a short span of time. In particular, we want them to learn *concepts* beyond crude techniques. For this aim, we think that professional educators are best qualified.

Although it may seem presumptuous to speak for ourselves, we think that the qualities of all people involved in the collaboration account for a part of the success. Two main qualities must be cited: involvement and mutual trust. The involvement comprises the quantity of work (maximal for students, but also important for the pedagogical staff) and the share of objectives. The mutual trust between students, academics, and practitioners has never been broken. As a net result, we have a very motivating and enriching climate which allows high-quality work.

5.3 The future of the collaboration

The collaboration between the University of Nancy and CEGELEC is exemplary. Can it be continued? Can it be reproduced with other partners?

The answer to the first question stands unfortunately outside our reach. Conjuncture, as well as industrial strategy, may change quite unexpectedly. We have shown the benefits gained through the collaboration, but since they can hardly be put into figures (in contrast to the costs), it is not easy to justify it in front of decision-makers. A possible answer would be to sign a formal contract between CEGELEC and the DESS. Although it may seem safe, we do not support this idea. We have succeeded because of the faith and involvement of people who are deeply convinced of the utility of their work. Bringing in people who would feel the job as an imposed burden would probably break the spirit, and hence lower the quality, of the current work.

Answering the second is difficult. The history shows that the collaboration has been started up with a practitioner who felt interested in teaching in Nancy's curriculum. He or she adopted the idea of the teamwork project and accepted to work in its definition. He or she also convinced the CEGELEC methodology department of the interest of the work, which quickly supported it. So, personal relations were at the root of the project and we have had the good fortune that the person was the right one (professionally speaking). At present, the approach we would follow to bring about a collaboration with other partners would be the following:

1. to define precisely the pedagogical project and the expected roles of participants

2. to find the "right" persons in our informal network of relations

3. to experiment with the project

4. to involve the management hierarchy in the company and other colleagues at Nancy.

6 Do we still need the universities?

As a conclusion, we would like to give some personal feelings. Participation in educational actions requires an important investment, particularly in time. So, what reasons motivate practitioners, who have generally more than enough work in their shop, to come and teach in a university?

Despite some stupid statements about "the university's ivory tower" or "universities ignoring real-life," lecturing students has maintained a real prestige. Adding a few lines in a *curriculum vitae* may be interesting to some, but the main motivation is a kind of challenge: being able to communicate one's knowledge and experience to a critical audience.

Preparing students to jump into the real world is a form of social duty. Working in a group one has not chosen, feeling well, professionally and personally, in a rough environment, communicating efficiently, or feeling responsible for oneself and the whole group, are difficult. Students know, and fear, that. It is probably not possible to teach such matters formally, but one can show how, by considering a project as a group adventure, a useful and simple life can be achieved. Smoothing the transition from university to industry and keeping young practitioners from the difficulties experienced by their older colleagues will benefit everybody, company included.

The role of a practitioner is to be a link. He or she will initiate students to a new world where work is judged less on elegance than on economic criteria, where people should not only be bright but well integrated, or where people must be active and not passive. This role is difficult. The practitioner must be fully integrated into the academic team while appearing neutral to the students. She or he has to explain the role and utility of academics in a professional education.

All the efforts are forgotten when, at the end of the teamwork project, students explain what they have understood: the respective use of specification and design, the necessity of imposing rules at the beginning of a project, the difficulty of allotting a task to someone, or the relation between trust and work quality. After that, one feels rather proud to have participated in the education of people who will not only know some theories, but also how to apply them in real life.

Acknowledgments

We wish to address our most grateful thanks to Peter King and especially one of the anonymous referees who have greatly contributed to bring the text to a readable state.

References

[JGB90] J.-P. Jacquot, J. Guyard, and L. Boidot. Modeling teamwork in an academic environment. In L.E. Deimel, editor, *Proc. Software Engineering Education*, pages 110–122, Pittsburgh, PA, April 1990. SEI, Springer-Verlag.

[Kno91] P.J. Knoke. Medium size project model: Variations on a theme. In J.E. Tomayko, editor, *Proc. Software Engineering Education*, pages 5–24, Pittsburgh, PA, October 1991. SEI, Springer-Verlag.

[Mis91] J. Misselis. Recommandations pour l'adaptation des formations supérieures aux métiers de l'informatique. in Bulletin Spécif N. 18, November 1991.

[SS90] G. Sanders and G. Smith. Establishing motorola-university relationships: A software engineering training perspective. In L.E. Deimel, editor, *Proc. Software Engineering Education*, pages 2–12, Pittsburgh, PA, April 1990. SEI, Springer-Verlag.

Reducing the Gap Between Academic Theory and Professional Practice in Software Engineering Education

Gunnar Hartvigsen

Department of Computer Science, University of Tromsø,
N-9037 Tromsø, Norway
gunnar@cs.uit.no

Abstract. Software engineering is a core area in computer science. This observation has to be considered when developing a curriculum for the area. At the Department of Computer Science, University of Tromsø, we have identified four basic elements as the key to a modern curriculum in software engineering: textbooks covering both academic and industrial issues, realistic software projects with professional employers, modern hardware and software, and understanding of underlying scientific theory. The paper discusses how these elements are fulfilled to meet the upcoming challenges in the computing field.

1 Introduction

As one of the research paradigms in computing, formal education in software engineering (or design) is an essential part of a computer science curriculum. In addition, knowledge of software engineering is fundamental for professional software practice. Denning et al. [8, 9] define "software methodology and engineering" as one of nine subject areas in computing. Since the 1983 IEEE-CS curriculum report [16], we have experienced an increased attention to the integration of laboratory work with classroom lectures. The area of software engineering has faced a rapid development within user interfaces, real-time systems, distributed systems, interoperable systems, etc., due to the hardware advances. The rapid development in hardware has, e.g., increased the focus on large-scale software engineering. NRC [11] recommends continuing efforts across a broad front to understand large-scale software engineering.

At the Department of Computer Science, University of Tromsø, the research concentrates on distributed systems, including large distributed applications. Most of the research projects are laboratory intensive. The curriculum integrates laboratory work in all courses. In software engineering, the department offer one fundamental course (one course corresponds to five credits or 1/4 year of full-time studies). This course is especially constructed for the graduate civil engineer[1] students. The knowledge of software engineering is refined in subsequent courses and theses. Most students do individual semester theses (five credits) involving both theoretical and laboratory work as a preparation to their final thesis.

The Department of Computer Science has since the mid 1970'ies been given courses in software engineering. The courses were until 1988 characterized by an academic approach, focusing on textbooks and constructed student projects (exercises). The problems identified with the former courses in software engineering were:

---

1. At the University of Tromsø students may graduate with the following computer science degrees; B.Sc. (after min. 3.5 years), graduate civil engineer (after 4.5 years), M.Sc. (after min. 5 years) and D.Sc. The graduate civil engineer ("sivilingeniør") program comprises 4 years of courses followed by 0.5 year of thesis work. The main differences between the graduate civil engineer and the M.Sc. are the length and volume of the thesis. In addition, the engineers need to follow a fixed curriculum.

- The courses were too theoretical.
- The lack of real-life laboratory project–no industrial anchor existed.
- Little or no industrial contact.
- Missing connection between the software engineering in the research projects, the curriculum, and the industry.

Since 1987, these problems have been thoroughly addressed at the department.

The problem we faced in the development of a new curriculum for our software engineering education can be rephrased into the following problem definition: "How *can we meet the need for an industrial foundation without losing the academic and scientific approach?*"

The paper discusses the curriculum elements in software engineering, gives an overview of the software engineering course(s) talked at the University of Tromsø, and addresses the basic elements in the reviewed curriculum for software engineering.

2 Curriculum Elements in Software Engineering

Denning [7] argues that institutions and businesses are facing a drastic revision of the basic assumptions in which our practices and world views are rooted. He claims that these roots are visible in the traditional answers to the six basic questions underlying engineering education and research:

1. What is a profession?
2. What is a university?
3. What is an education?
4. What is research?
5. What is work?
6. What is innovation?

Denning stresses that "finding new answers to these questions is a task of special urgency." Denning's paper suggests new answers to all six questions. Although the software engineering courses in a computing curriculum haven't to face all six questions, emphasis should be put into question 1, 4 and 5. The courses should assure that:

1. textbooks used are rooted in reality.
2. project work is done and the problem with this kind of work is discovered.
3. laboratory work is done with the use of modern software engineering tools.
4. scientific methods and their relation to software engineering are understood.

These points are addressed in the following sections.

2.1 Textbooks

The ACM/IEEE joint curriculum task force [38] recommended the following core material in "software methodology and engineering":

- Fundamental problem-solving concepts (SE1)
- The software development process (SE2)
- Software requirements and specifications (SE3)
- Software design and implementation (SE4)

- Verification and validation (SE5)

Beyond the core curricula, advanced material that covers methods and tools that increase the quality and decrease the cost of constructing and maintaining advanced software systems, should be addressed in the textbook(s) used.

We have three categories of textbooks:

1. *Academic* (theoretical); e.g., [35]

2. *Industrial* (practical); e.g., [1]

3. *Both academic and industrial*; e.g., [25]

Supplementary textbooks covering user interface design, specialized books on the different stages in the software development model and methods suitable on the different levels, software testing, etc., can be included or recommended.

2.2 Project Work and the Software Team

Whatever software model, the question of infrastructure organization and methods for specific tasks will be raised. The team organization in software development and the upcoming problems and solutions need to be experienced by the students. The project should be as realistic as possible. A project with a professional external employer who demands deliveries and gives response is strongly recommended. The challenge is to find an adequate balance between the tight interaction with the external employer and shortcuts and assumptions (partly) made by the teaching assistants.

2.3 Laboratory Work

Tucker et al. [38] argue that "theory, abstraction, and design are included throughout the common requirements, and are reinforced by the integration of laboratory work with subject matter in a principled and thorough way." Denning et al. [8] suggest that principles should be separated from technology in a way that maintain the coherence between them. According to Denning et al., the laboratories serve three purposes. They should

1. demonstrate how principles covered in the lectures apply to the construction of hardware and software systems.

2. emphasize processes leading to good computing know-how.

3. provide an introduction to experimental methods.

The work in the laboratory should be motivated against teaching the students correct laboratory working rules, i.e., how to "behave" in the laboratory. This includes tool instruction, software (and hardware) testing and experimenting, etc. Experiences from the University of Tromsø suggest that the software testing has to be carefully taught. To our knowledge, the value of this part seems underestimated–few textbooks exist (e.g., [14, 17, 29, 30]) and experienced test engineers with deep knowledge on test techniques are rare. E.Yourdon writes that "testing has been part of the culture of programmers and software engineers since the first binary-code machine language program was written–but only recently has it begun to enter the consciousness of the general public, which depends on proper functioning software more and more each day." (In the foreword of [29]).

2.4 Scientific Methods

Although scientific methods are compulsory and obvious elements of a study in mathematical and physical sciences, this has not been the case within the field of computer science.

Denning et al. [8, 9] describe three research paradigms in computing, theory, abstraction and design, where design is rooted in engineering and consists of four steps followed in the construction of a system to solve a given problem.

Being a young research area with roots from mathematics, science and engineering, also implies the lack of a scientific tradition. This means that extra attention needs to be taken to ensure that the engineering paradigm is clearly understood and controlled in the software engineering education.

3 "Software Engineering and Project Work"

The Department of Computer Science, University of Tromsø, offers each spring semester (January to June) the course D211 "software engineering and project work." The average number of students following the lectures of this course over the last five years has been about twenty. The following excerpt from the "Handbook of Studies" at the University of Tromsø, 1993, states the contents and purpose of the course:

> "The course gives a theoretical and practical base for development of large-scale software systems. (...) The lectures cover models, methods, techniques and approaches to software development, software development environments, documentation, software quality and managing software development. The laboratory work includes compulsory exercises."

D211 contains sixty lecture hours and sixty hours guided exercises and laboratory work. The students use the following software tools:

- HP C++/Softbench 3.0

- HP Encapsulator

- HP Interface Architect

- FrameMaker

Recently, the department has bought CynerVision and ChangeVision. We plan to buy Software Through Pictures (STP) within this year. The tools run on HP 9000/720 and 735 workstations (thirty-six workstations with 32-64 Mbyte RAM, 1280x1024 color display, etc. are at the undergraduates disposal).

The software engineering knowledge is further developed in succeeding courses in distributed system, computer networks, databases, computer graphics, which all includes laboratory intensive project work and large compulsory exercises. In addition, most graduate civil engineer students write individual semester theses (five credits) comprising both theoretical and laboratory work as a qualification to their final thesis (equals to ten credits).

Figure 1 illustrates the course calendar for the 1993 spring semester. The lectures/exercises, the seminars and the project start in January. In 1993 five seminars with external participants were arranged. The project groups had three major deliveries with plenum presentations, and several smaller presentations to the employer. The results from the student groups have been taken further by students on summer jobs for NIT. In addition, graduate civil engineer thesis proposals have been extracted from the student projects.

4 Meeting the Industrial and Educational Challenges

As initially referred, until 1988, the software engineering education at the Department of Computer Science, University of Tromsø, was characterized by being to theoretical, solving artificial paper problems, far away from the real world, and isolated from the research activity at the department.

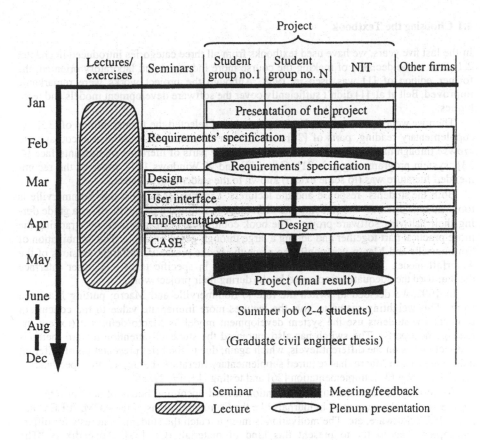

Fig. 1. Course calendar Spring 1993.

Along with the establishment of the graduate civil engineer program in the mid 1980'ies, especially the engineering part of the curriculum had to be redesigned. To meet the industrial and education challenges, based on the experiences with the software engineering education both nationally and internationally, we focused at four basic elements:

1. The textbook and classroom teaching

2. Software project work with professional employees

3. Use modern hardware (workstations) equipped with state-of-the-art software engineering tools.

4. Improve the students' understanding of the relationship between software engineering and computer science research.

The decision made and experiences from the department with respect to the four elements are discussed in the following sections.

268

4.1 Choosing the Textbook

In the last five years, we have used textbooks from all three categories introduced in chapter 2.1. Due to the decision of making the course more industrial and laboratory oriented, the former edition of [1] was used in 1988. Although the project works were remarkable improved, Bell et al. [1] didn't sufficiently cover the software development models and techniques.

Then we went for a more academic approach and selected the former edition of [35]. As supplementary reading, parts of [25] were chosen. The students were also encouraged to *browse* through historical stuff as [3], with necessary parts of literature on user interface [4, 33], system programming [13, 21], C++ [37] and X Windows [19]. Most of the recommended literature was (to some extent) known to the students in advance.

Both the students' response and the lecturers' experiences suggest that Sommerville is too academic oriented–the students had difficulties in following the textbook as a guide during their half-year software project. The book could have been improved by wrapping the more practical part together and adding a large through-going example. The combination of Sommerville and Macro was confusing since the books presented different versions of the waterfall model. The students who were involved in specific tasks, e.g., user interface design, used the adequate recommend books during their project work.

In 1992, we decided to switch the role to Sommerville and Macro, putting Macro in front. This weighting seems to give the lectures more immediate value to the concurrent project. The students use the system development model as Macro defines it (except the management parts). The switch has also increased the students' attention toward methods and techniques on the different levels, which again, due to the brief presentation of different methods given in Macro, has required supplementary literature. Examples are; specification [20, 34], design [36], implementation [26] and testing [14, 17, 29, 30].

We also try to draw the students attention toward upcoming books of special interests, e.g., [39], and relevant papers in journals like the Communications of the ACM, IEEE Computer, IEEE Software, etc. The motivation is more to catch the students' interests for different topics, than to try to present this kind of material. (Cf. [39], Appendix B "The Programmer's Bookshelf".)

The software development model chosen has from the beginning been the "traditional" waterfall model (today, as it is defined by [25]). Other models as object-orient models (e.g., [2, 5, 6, 27, 28]), information engineering (e.g., [10]), etc., are briefly addressed in the lectures.

To create an industrial environment, parts of the lectures are held as 1/2 to 1 day seminar with participants from local and regional industry at their locations. The seminars are practical oriented with a strong focus on methods and techniques. In 1993, the seminars covered specification (1 day), design (1 day), user interface design (1 day), CASE (1 day) and implementation (software development tools) (1/2 day). The lecturers in the different topics were partly recruited from industry, i.e., persons with special experiences in the topic they covered.

4.2 The Search for an Optimal Student Software Development Project

Since 1988, the thoroughgoing software development project has been given full attention. The students are divided into chief programmer teams (6-8 students), and where all teams develop the same software. The projects have been related to the industrial participants (coordinated through the company Norwegian Information Technology (NIT)) in the Storm-Cast-project [18] at the department. The student teams have acted as part of the R&D department at NIT constructing prototypes of (potentially) new products. The projects have mainly worked with distributed applications for meteorological and environmental monitoring.

A side-effect of the project is that the students get the opportunity to expose themselves to a potential employer and possibly establish personal contacts. In addition, they get inside information of the work in a large software firm, i.e., what they can expect when the graduate from the university.

In 1993 the students constructed an application wanted by the Norwegian Institute for Air Research (NILU) in cooperation with Norwegian Information Technology (NIT), the largest Norwegian owned software firm. The application receives different air pollution parameters continuously monitored by air pollution centrals in the Olympic campus and displays them in different formats on different locations in the campus. The system will be used during the 1994 Winter Olympic Games at Lillehammer, Norway.

Active participation in the project is mandatory. Students are on an individual basis controlled, and students that don't participate are expelled from the course.

4.3 Laboratory Work

In our software engineering course, more attention has been put on the laboratory work, in particular, the laboratory attitude. The students have partly been guided through controlled experiments, enforced to employ the tools thoroughly, etc. The focus on laboratory work presupposes the existence of an adequate hardware and software infrastructure. At the department, the project teams have access to HP workstations nearly twenty-four hours a day. The teams have a dedicated project laboratory at their disposal.

The use of HP C++/Softbench 3.0 is mandatory. The project teams have to use all the tools in SoftBench. Special attention is put on the version control rcs (in the development manager), the program debugger and the static analyzer. The laboratory work is partly supervised by teaching assistants. In addition, the teaching assistants take care of the quality inspection.

4.4 A Thing Called Science

The general goal in the laboratory work has been to introduce the students to the design paradigm–to get them to understand software engineering as a scientific paradigm. Students need to learn the scientific approach to software engineering. This activity of course must be put into the right perspective of the discipline computer science encompassing far more than "programming."

In our software engineering course, the students are very briefly introduced to reports as "Computing as a discipline" [8, 9], "Computing the future" [11], etc., with classical philosophy of science materials (e.g., [22, 23, 31]). These aspects are in later semesters elaborated (in connection to the preparation of the thesis).

The research paradigms are covered in the beginning to the course, and repeated during the course. In the software testing lectures, emphasis is put on the difference between the software testing as a way of assuring compliance and modifiability, and software testing as a scientific approach to make reproducible results. The pedagogical goal is to give the students an understanding of the connection with and distance between software engineering as a scientific and a productional paradigm.

4.5 Supporting Activities

A major goal in the course planning has been to integrate the student project in StormCast, a research project at the department. The objective of the StormCast project is: (1) to investigate the prospects of distributed computing in the weather and environmental domains, (2) to construct distributed applications in a controlled manner, and, (3) to evaluate current operating system services for construction of new services. The StormCast project also aims at increasing the potential for distributed computing by building realistic distributed applications. The weather and environment domains have been chosen for this project. Currently, the StormCast project has resulted in several versions of a distributed application that monitor and use weather data. StormCast runs in both local area and wide area networking environments [12, 18].

Figure 2 illustrates the integration of student projects into the StormCast project. The axes show the applicability (x), the complexity (y) and the activity scale (z).

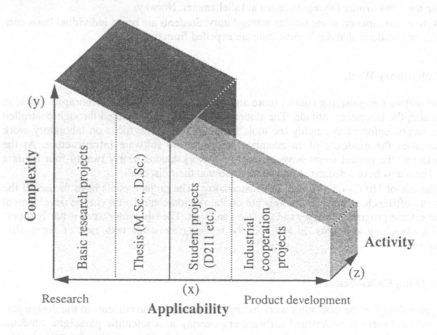

Fig. 2. The Software engineering courses' relations to the StormCast project.

The continuous contact and cooperation in the StormCast project between the department and research institutes and industrial partners have been of great value for the preparation of the software development projects in the course D211.

5 Discussion and Open Problems

The response from former students, industrial participants and partners has confirmed the realism and pedagogical goals in the development of a new curriculum for software engineering education. The students graduated have been productive for their employers from the beginning and their knowledge on software methodology has been absorbed by the other staff members.

The seminars held at company locations with industrial participants have been the kick-off and catalyst for a continuing internal debate on methods and techniques. The seminars themselves have for the industrial participants worked as further education in software engineering. One of the firms, e.g., has introduced object-oriented methods in their software life cycle as a direct result of presentations and discussions in the seminars. In the future, the seminars will form the basis of a local forum for software engineering.

Based on the experiences and feedbacks from the software engineering education at University of Tromsø, teaching a course in software engineering without simultaneously presenting the theoretical foundation for software construction and addressing the major themes in realistic laboratory work, are not recommendable. This observation also demands a textbook, or more realistic, a set of textbooks, which enable such an approach.

An important outcome of the course is the students understanding of the awareness and continuing need for software engineering literature. During the course the students are strongly encouraged to join the ACM, the IEEE Computer Society and the Norwegian Computer Society. As argued by Yourdon [39, p. 313]:

> "There are three important things for you to realize if you're going to avoid getting left behind in the software industry: (1) it is vital to read important books and journals and attend key professional conferences, (2) it's an ongoing process since the information you read today will be obsolete within three to five years, and (3) the company you work for will probably provide limited support at best and no support at worst."

In the last three years, the majority of the students have during the software engineering course joined one ore more professional societies.

As of 1993, there are still some problems that have to be solved before the software engineering education has found an acceptable form:

- the part on test methods and techniques has to be enhanced. This includes a presentation of testing tools (cf. [15, 32]).

- the presentations of software management have to be more directed toward the actual problems the student teams face.

- during the team work students browse through many textbooks on various topics. Their experiences with these books should be given attention at the end of the course.

Other ideas that are being discussed are:

- to offer a one day software engineering "brush up" seminar to students graduated from the department.

- to give the students access to mobile computing equipment during the course, e.g, let the students have their personal laptops with portable communication and necessary software.

The organization of the software engineering education fits well into what we mean is the correct relationship between a university and the industry - a university witch train students to become innovative for the industry, i.e., students that could act as catalysts to the transferring of new methods and ideas. The opposite to this model is a university that stumbles behind the industrial R&D.

6 Concluding Remarks

Software engineering is a core area in computer science. This observation has to be considered when developing a curriculum for the area. At the Department of Computer Science, University of Tromsø, we have identified four basic elements as the key to a modern curriculum in software engineering: textbooks covering both academic and industrial issues, realistic software projects with professional employers, modern hardware and software, and understanding of underlying scientific theory.

The contacts with local and national industry, the link between research projects at the university and R&D activity in industry, and the interplay between theory and practice, meet to some extent the recommendations in "Computing the Future" [11].

Acknowledgment

Numerous people have contributed to the development of the software engineering education at my department and to the StormCast project. Especially, Dag Johansen has a vital role in both activities.

References

1.   D. Bell, I. Morrey, J. Pugh: *Software Engineering. A Practical Approach. Second Edition.* Englewood Cliffs, New Jersey: Prentice-Hall 1992

2.   G. Booch: *Object Oriented Design.with Applications.* Redwood City, California: Benjamin/Cummings 1991

3.   F.P. Brooks: *The Mythical Man-Month: Essays on Software Engineering.* Reading, Massachusetts: Addison-Wesley 1975

4.   J.R. Brown, S. Cunningham: *Programming the User Interface.* Principles and Examples. New York: Wiley 1989

5.   P. Coad, E. Yourdon: *Object-Oriented Analysis.* Englewood Cliffs, New Jersey: Prentice-Hall 1991a

6.   P. Coad, E. Yourdon: *Object-Oriented Design.* Englewood Cliffs, New Jersey: Prentice-Hall 1991b

7.   P.J. Denning: Educating a new engineer. *Communications of the ACM 35* (12 December), 82-97 (1992)

8.   P.J. Denning, D.E. Comer, D. Gries, M.C. Mulder, A. Tucker, A.J. Turner, P.R. Young: Report of the ACM Task Force on the Core of Computer Science. New York: Association for Computing Machinery 1988

9.   P.J. Denning, D.E. Comer, D. Gries, M.C. Mulder, A. Tucker, A.J. Turner, P.R. Young: Computing as a discipline. *Communications of the ACM 32* (1 January), 9-23 (1989)

10.   C. Finkelstein: *An Introduction to Information Engineering.* Sydney, Australia: Addison-Wesley 1989

11.   J. Hartmanis, H. Lin (eds.): *Computing the Future: A Broader Agenda for Computer Science and Engineering.* Washington, D.C.: National Academy Press 1992

12.   G. Hartvigsen, D. Johansen: Co-operation in a Distributed Artificial Intelligence Environment–the StormCast Application. Journal of *Engineering Applications of Artificial Intelligence 3* (3 September), 229-237 (1990)

13.   K. Haviland, B. Salama: *UNIX System Programming.* Wokingham, England: Addison-Wesley 1987

14.   W. Hetzel: *The Complete Guide to Software Testing. 2nd Edition.* Wellesley, MA: QED Information Sciences 1988

15.   J.R. Horgan, A.P. Mathur: Assessing Testing Tools in Research and Education. *IEEE Software 9* (3 May), 61-69 (1992)

16.   IEEE: The 1983 model program in computer science and engineering. (Educational Activities Board), Technical Report 932, IEEE Computer Society, December 1983

17.   R. Jain: *The Art of Computer Systems Performance Analysis.* New York: Wiley 1991

18.   D. Johansen, G. Hartvigsen: StormCast–A Distributed Application. In: Proceedings of the Autumn 1991 EurOpen Conference (Budapest, Hungary, 16-20 September, 1991). Buntingford, Hertfordshire, U.K.: European Forum for Open Systems 1991, pp. 273-286

19. O. Jones: *Introduction to the X Window System.* Englewood Cliffs, New Jersey: Prentice-Hall 1989

20. K.E. Kendall, J.E. Kendall: *System Analysis and Design.* Englewood Cliffs, New Jersey: Prentice-Hall 1992

21. B.W. Kernighan, R. Pike: *The UNIX Programming Environment.* Englewood Cliffs, New Jersey: Prentice-Hall 1984

22. T. Kuhn: *The Structure of Scientific Revolutions.* Chicago: University of Chicago Press 1962

23. I. Lakatos: Falsification and the Methodology of Scientific Research Programmers. In: I. Lakatos, A. Musgrave (eds.): *Criticism and the Growth of Knowledge.* London: Cambridge University Press 1974

24. B. Laurel: *Computers as Theatre.* Reading, Massachusetts: Addison-Wesley 1990

25. A. Macro: *Software Engineering: Concepts and Management.* New York: Prentice-Hall 1990

26. M. Marcotty: *Software Implementation.* New York: Prentice-Hall 1991

27. J. Martin, J.J. Odell: *Object-Oriented Analysis and Design.* Englewood Cliffs, New Jersey: Prentice-Hall 1992

28. B. Meyer: *Object-oriented Software Construction.* New York: Prentice-Hall 1988

29. D.J. Mosley: *The Handbook of MIS Application Software Testing.* Englewood Cliffs, New Jersey: Yourdon Press 1993

30. G.J. Myers: *The Art of Software Testing.* New York: Wiley 1978

31. K.R. Popper: *Conjectures and Refutations.* London: Routledge and Kegan Paul 1963

32. R.M. Poston, M.P. Sexton: Evaluating and Selecting Testing Tools. *IEEE Software 9* (3 May), 33-53 (1992)

33. B. Shneiderman: *Designing the user interface: strategies for effective human-computer interaction. Second Edition.* Reading, Massachusetts: Addison-Wesley 1992

34. K.C. Shumate, M.M. Keller: *Software Specification and Design: a Disciplined Approach for Real-time Systems.* New York: Wiley 1992

35. I. Sommerville: *Software Engineering. Fourth Edition.* Wokingham, England: Addison-Wesley 1992

36. W. Stevens: *Software Design.* New York: Prentice-Hall 1991

37. B. Stroustrup: *The C++ Programming Language. Second Edition.* Reading, Massachusetts: Addison-Wesley 1991

38. A.B. Tucker, B.H. Barnes, R.M. Aiken, K. Barker, K.B. Bruce, J.T. Cain, S.E. Conry, G.L. Engel, R.G. Epstein, D.K. Lidtke, M. Mulder, J.B. Rogers, E.H. Spafford, A.J. Turner: *Computing Curricula 1991. Report of the ACM/IEEE-CS Joint Curriculum Task Force.* ACM Press & IEEE Computer Society Press 1991

39. E. Yourdon: *Decline & Fall of the American Programmer.* Englewood Cliffs, New Jersey: Yourdon Press 1992

Session 6:
Panel Discussion

Bridging the Gaps
Panel Moderator: J. Fernando Naveda, Rochester Institute of Technology, Rochester, New York

Panelists:
John Beidler, University of Scranton, Scranton, Pennsylvania

James E. Cardow, Air Force Institute of Technology, Wright-Patterson Air Force Base, Ohio

Everald Mills, Seattle University, Seattle, Washington

Frances Van Scoy, West Virginia University, Morgantown, West Virginia

Bridging the Gaps

J. Fernando Naveda, Rochester Institute of Technology (panel moderator)
John Beidler, University of Scranton
James E. Cardow, Air Force Institute of Technology
Everald Mills, Seattle University
Frances Van Scoy, West Virginia University

1 Introduction

A problem frequently faced in reviewing students for a graduate program in software engineering is a "gap" between the desired level of knowledge of incoming students and their actual backgrounds. Different departments have identified different gaps depending upon a variety of factors like school's geographical location, market, etc. Gaps range from weak academic computer science background, to strong continuous mathematics background but weak discrete mathematics background, to lack of practical experience but good academic computer science background, etc. Typical problems that are faced are:

1. Prospective students do not have an undergraduate education in the computing sciences, but have substantial relevant experience. Typically these are Mathematics or Electrical (Electronics) Engineering undergraduates with reasonably strong science backgrounds, but with a few gaps in their backgrounds.

2. Prospective students are good students who attended schools with weak undergraduate computing programs. They have good work experiences, but, much like the students mentioned in item 1, there are gaps in their backgrounds.

3. Prospective students have been through a good undergraduate program and have good work experiences, but the years since they have graduated places in question the student's formal education.

4. Prospective students have no formal computer science or engineering backgrounds but have been software practitioners for a good many years. Typically, these students have business or economics backgrounds and over the years have learned the intricacies of software development, software maintenance, and software project management.

Different institutions have found interesting ways of addressing these gaps without jeopardizing the quality of their graduate programs. Methods range from the presentation of various preparatory courses designed to fill these gaps, to recommending selected undergraduate courses, to the integration of materials designed to overcome the typical problems due to gaps in students' backgrounds into the first several courses in the program.

An institution's admission standards are affected by a variety of parameters: geographical location, the institution's statement of mission, school politics, economics, etc. It is therefore important to realize that no single recommendation for pre-MSE preparation can possibly satisfy all institutions. Nevertheless, it is compelling to note that although a variety of MSE programs have been put in place across the Nation, little is known about how these programs are coping with what program administrators perceive as their candidates' academic weaknesses. Little is also known about the *reasons* behind the pre-requisite structures put in place and the positive or negative impacts that they may be having on their respective programs.

This panel presents a cross section of various approaches that have been taken in overcoming the various gaps in students' backgrounds. The panelists will describe the cause/effect relationships that led them to the approach taken at their institution, the regional and political considerations and an evaluation of the effectiveness of the approach.

2 Participants

J. Fernando Naveda (Panel moderator). *Biographical sketch.* Dr. Naveda is currently an assistant professor with the department of Computer Science at Rochester Institute of Technology, Rochester, NY. Before joining RIT, he was an assistant professor with the department of Computing Sciences at the University of Scranton. From 1989 to 1991 he directed that department's Master's on Software Engineering where he taught Mathematics for Software Engineering and Requirements Analysis and Software Specification. Professor Naveda received his Bachelor Degree in Computing Systems Engineering in 1975 from the *Instituto Tecnológico y de Estudios Superiores de Monterrey*, Mexico and his Ph.D. in Computer and Information Sciences from the University of Minnesota, Twin Cities, in 1986. He has been a member of the Naval Postgraduate School's Computer Aided Prototyping System's (CAPS) development team since 1989. His research interests include software engineering education, software engineering, software prototyping, formal methodologies for software development, and software integration.

John Beidler. *Bibliographical sketch.* Dr. Beidler received his Ph.D. in Computer Science from the Pennsylvania State University. He was responsible for the development of the undergraduate program in Computer Science at the University of Scranton, where he served as Department Chair for eighteen years. The department offers three degree programs, undergraduate degrees in Computer Science and in Information Systems, and a graduate program in Software Engineering. In 1989 he stepped down as chair to concentrate on his research interests and assist in the development of the graduate program. His current research interests are in formal methods and software reuse.

Position statement: We recognized two areas of concern, the formal mathematics background of students and a lack of experience with modern software development issues. Mathematics issues are addressed in the first year through a pair of courses that address these shortcomings while leading to Formal Specifications using "Z". Since the majority of our graduate students work in very traditional software development environments, we decided to address the upgrading of weaknesses in modern software development techniques by teaching a traditional introductory software engineering course with a few interesting twists that force the students to reassess the approaches they use to software development.

James E Cardow. *Bibliographical sketch.* Captain James E. Cardow is currently an Instructor in Software Engineering at the Air Force Institute of Technology. He is currently the director for the Software Professional Development Program's courses in Software Generation and Maintenance and Software Verification & Validation. Captain Cardow received his Bachelor of Computer Science Degree from Texas Tech University in 1982 and his Master of Science Degree in Computer Science from Wright State University in 1989. During his twenty year Air Force career he has served as computer technician, chief of software quality, chief of software maintenance, staff officer, and finally instructor.

Position Statement: If software engineering is going to gain status as a discipline there must be formal education for software engineers. This has been implemented at the Master's Degree level, and is starting to be initiated at the Bachelor's Degree level. Degrees at the Master's level must be targeted to both, students with strong computer science background and students with other backgrounds such as mathematics and electrical engineering. Virtually all Master's degrees being offered today, assume that potential students must have practical on-the-job experience in software development. Preparing otherwise qualified students for a successful completion of a Master's degree on Software Engineering is addressed through so-called bridge courses.

Software Engineering bridge courses should present information relevant to the domain of software engineering from computer science, mathematics, and management, without attempting to teach a macro-level scans of the topics.

Everald Mills. *Biographical sketch.* Dr. Mills received his Ph.D. in Computer Science from Washington State University. After serving as a member of the Computer Science faculty at Wichita State University for twelve years, in 1983 he accepted an appointment as Chair of the Computer Science Department at Seattle University. He was instrumental in establishing the graduate program in Software Engineering at Seattle and has published several articles describing the philosophy behind the graduate program in Software Engineering. His current research interest is in Software Metrics.

Position statement: Given the extensive experience we have at the graduate level, Seattle has attempted to address this issue using a variety of methods with a desire to address the gaps in student backgrounds without compromising the quality of the graduate program. Over the decade our program has existed, our philosophy regarding bridge courses has evolved. This evolution should be of interest to other institutions that are in the early stages of developing a graduate program in software engineering.

Frances Van Scoy. *Biographical sketch.* Dr. Van Scoy is an associate professor with the department of Statistics and Computer Science at West Virginia University, Morgantown, WV where she has taught a wide variety of graduate and undergraduate courses in computer science and software engineering. Among the courses most recently taught by professor Van Scoy are formal methods in software engineering, verification and validation, development of parallel software, and concurrent Ada. She was also a visiting scientist at the Software Engineering Institute in 1982-83, 1988, and 1989. Professor Van Scoy received her Bachelor of Science in mathematics from the Michigan State University in 1970 and her Ph.D. in Computer Science from the University of Virginia in 1980. Her research interests include software engineering, software engineering education, artificial intelligence, parallel programming, CASE tools, and software development in Ada.

Position Statement: A variety of Master's on Software Engineering (MSE) programs across the Nation have evolved about the premise that the great majority of the students joining such programs are a) experienced practitioners in the field and b) graduates from a variety of disciplines other than newer computer science programs. Although the great majority of these potential students make prime candidates for competent software engineers, their weak computer science and mathematics backgrounds get in the way. However, a solidi MSE program stems from solid mathematics and computer science backgrounds. There is a contradiction between expectations and practice.

Bridge courses have been implemented to both prepare new MSE students for successful completion of the degree, and to maintain a level of credibility of the MSE itself. Disagreements exist as to what these bridge courses should consist of and how such material should be delivered. It is well known that formal computer science and discrete mathematics tend to discourage otherwise qualified students from pursuing the degree. To the practitioner, a great percentage of the material presented in these courses is perceived as both irrelevant and difficult. The challenge is then to deliver these courses effectively from both an academic point of view and from a consumer stand point.

A proposed solution to this challenge is the development of bridge courses based on problems which have an applied flavor but which require the use of some formal concepts to produce good solutions. For example, a problem might be the generation of test cases. If a set of test cases satisfying data flow coverage criteria (as in Weyuker's work), then students will need to apply some concepts from compiler optimization (data flow analysis). If the test cases are to satisfy Cleanroom criteria, then they must apply formal grammars and probability. By careful choice of applied problems whose solution is aided by formal concepts the instructor can motivate the students to appreciate the need for formal concepts.

Session 7:
Industry Influence in Software Engineering Education

Experiences with CCB-Directed Projects in the Classroom
James M. Purtilo, University of Maryland, College Park, Maryland and Stan Siegel, Science Applications International Corporation, Arlington, Virginia

Putting into Practice Advanced Software Engineering Techniques Through Students Project
Naji Habra and Eric Dubois, Facultés Universitaires Notre-Dame de la Paix, Namur, Belgium

Cachesim: A Graphical Software Environment to Support the Teaching of Computer Systems with Cache Memories
Cosimo Antonio Prete, Università di Pisa, Pisa, Italy

Suggested Scenarios of Software Maintenance Education
Frank W. Calliss and Debra Trantina Calliss, Arizona State University,Tempe, Arizona

Experiences with CCB-Directed Projects in the Classroom

James Purtilo
Computer Science Department
University of Maryland
College Park, MD 20742

Stan Siegel
Science Applications International Corp
200 N. Glebe Road, Suite 300
Arlington, VA 22203

Abstract. Success in a software effort often depends upon communication skills of the developers, whether reading and writing specifications, or cooperating with one another to solve problems. Unfortunately, most undergraduate education places emphasis upon individual achievement that does not challenge students to refine necessary communication skills; and even when teams are formed, communication among participants is rarely organized. This paper describes our experience with a classroom approach to organizing communication activities in software engineering education. A single class project of large scale is initiated, with each team in the class assuming responsibility for a distinct task. During the project, responsibilities are rotated, so that students must operate on software artifacts that they themselves did not write. Central to the success of this approach is that technical decisions are coordinated by a configuration control board (CCB), run by the class.

1 Introduction

How does one teach software system development? This paper describes our experience in giving students a firsthand feel for the complexities of real-world software systems development in a senior and graduate level projects course. Based upon our experience in four iterations of the course at the University of Maryland at College Park, we are able to report that the concept of a configuration control board (CCB) is central to achieving our educational objectives.

In addition to exposing students to the usual broad array of concepts in software design and development, our approach is intended to cultivate a deeper appreciation for the benefits of rigorous process than can be easily communicated via small projects. These intents are realized by running a single class project of large scale, with a strong focus on teaching skills in requirements reading and writing — challenging students to examine how artifacts appear to others, something that is frequently not introduced to undergraduates.

We first describe our course organization, beginning with a summary of the course prior to our modifications, and concluding with the four iterations of our course. Next, we describe the CCB role and principles as they are taught and applied in the course. Finally, we conclude with a list of some lessons we have learned in this approach, expressed as maxims for someone seeking to duplicate our success.

2 Course Organization

This section first characterizes the state of the course at the university prior to our revisions, and as such provides motivation for why we made certain changes. It then describes our laboratory approach, and gives details of our experiences (called *iterations*) with each of the four semesters we used this organization at the university.

2.1 Previous Approach to the Course

In contrast to our process-oriented approach, the course prior to our involvement was narrowly focused upon design issues. Instructors typically approached software engineering through the study of relatively small and individual projects. The class was run without input from independent practitioners, and students generally only dealt with software artifacts which they themselves had a direct hand in creating.

Students in the CS program at this university are considered to be 'software savvy,' in spite of having generally been taught (as with so many curricula) that software artifacts are created in a vacuum, transferred to a solitary 'customer' (the instructor) for evaluation, and then simply dropped once a grade has been issued. That is, they throw it over the wall, and need not deal with the consequences of their decisions. Even if done subliminally, this approach to instruction emphasizes that software is disposable, and that dramatically simplifying assumptions are a way of life.

The course had been offered in this manner for at least ten years, and was not thought of as a failure — it met its stated objective of dealing with design. But the first author felt that the traditional approach completely bypassed most of the challenges faced by developers, and therefore set out to devise an approach that also incorporated the communication aspects of large scale software development. This approach is embodied by three key principles, which we refer to as ones of **realism**, **independent feedback**, and substantial utilization of another's artifact (which we will call simply **artifact study** for short), respectively.

- **Realism.** Students need to learn how to solve problems even when they are not free to negotiate away the tougher constraints. Therefore, a requirement of any revised approach is that projects selected should be real applications; it must be clear to students up front that they will have real users of the product — so the software is not disposable. Dramatically simplifying the assumptions or conditions is not acceptable.

- **Independent feedback.** Students need not only concrete feedback on their creative efforts, but also incentive to truly study that feedback. Therefore, a requirement of our revised approach must be to find some 'forcing function,' that will help students compare serious evaluations with their work product in detail. The absence of such a mechanism allows a student to just accept the grade and move on to other studies, leaving unrecognized the gems of detailed evaluation.

- **Artifact study.** As with students who study other creative engineering fields, students of software engineering need to study software artifacts from a variety of stages of a typical project development. Moreover, they must do so to a level of understanding which is sufficient for them to manipulate and extend the artifact. Instructors typically arrange for students to work to this level of mastery either by having them operate upon their own artifacts, or by having them work upon another student's version of the same artifact. This pedagogic approach all too often denies students the full benefit of artifact study: when faced with a design specification with which the student has experiences, then it is all too easy for him to implement what is "in the head" rather than on paper. In this way, the study of communication issues is diluted. Therefore, a requirement of our revised laboratory approach must be that students should read *for comprehension* artifacts that they themselves have had no experience in writing.

2.2 Our Approach to the Course

The requirements listed above are met by running a single, collaborative project in which all students play some (but not necessarily the same) role. Initially the class is given a top-level requirements specification for a system to be built. Decisions concerning initial system level problem decomposition are made by the entire class (which also affords the instructor the opportunity to quickly illustrate a problem solving cycle in its entirety, along with a few examples of how to run technical problem solving meetings). The class then is divided into teams of approximately four students, each having an initial, unique task responsibility.[1]

The development life cycle is essentially four stages (with some iteration) — requirements definition, design, coding and system integration. Several intermediate checkpoints are built into the schedule as well, to keep the class on track, but they are not graded. Outside, industrial evaluators are used to provide comment and feedback at each of the major deliverable points; these engineers are to be different from those who may be acting as customers, depending on how the project is chosen.

By choosing a project of large scale, with all students collaborating to solve it, we address our requirement for realism, and the involvement of volunteers from industry meets our requirement for independent feedback. Our third key requirement is met by how the tasks are reassigned throughout the term. Each team deals with a unique task throughout the term, but they will trade these tasks at the end of each of the first three stages. A team will be given responsibility for requirements definition on one task item, then pass the specification to another team for design; in its place, the team will be given the requirements from another task to design; in the same way, they will later receive someone else's design for implementation (i.e., coding). This overall concept for the course is illustrated in Figure 1. Each team will need

---

[1] The instructor needs some lead time before the term to select a project based upon the predicted class size, in order for the partitioning to work out. At this early stage, it is generally possible to lead the class to 'discover' the desired decomposition of tasks.

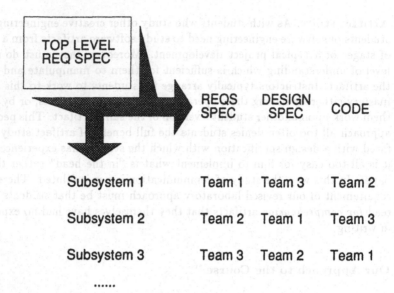

Figure 1: Organization of teams in course.

to manipulate *in substantive ways* software artifacts that they themselves did not create. Moreover, while all students will have a common 'system culture,' none will even have the luxury of having created artifacts similar to what they are given, even though they are responsible for later maintaining that document — keeping it in line with the evolving decisions of the class effort. Finally, students will not be taught that their efforts are in some sense "disposable" since they will be responsible to their classmates who subsequently use their work product.

The last phase is system integration, and is generally where the lessons come home most effectively. Each team must nominate a representative to the committee responsible for assuring that system requirements are met. The final deliverable from the class is a consistent set of detailed system requirements, designs, implementation, and system test data.

Our first attempt at teaching software engineering according to a version of this approach was in the fall term of 1989. From each of the subsequent classes we gained feedback, and have converged upon the approach just described. What emerged from these experiences, and one of the major points of this paper, is the importance of the CCB to the success of our laboratory approach. A class-run CCB evolved into the hub around which most of the separate team activities revolved.

A CCB is used as the primary vehicle for effecting decision making regarding specification and code development. Minutes of the CCB meetings are taken to give visibility to the decision-making process and to establish accountability; and when minutes are poorly captured, students get to experience firsthand all the problems which can result from lack of visibility in decisions. The CCB mechanism impresses upon the students that real-world software engineering problems do not have unique solutions. The operation of the CCB impresses upon the students that software systems development is an exercise in mutual maturation of understanding between the developer and customer. Each student is expected at some time in the course to handle a solo (delegated) task and report to the CCB — such as preparation of a system integration plan or presentation of a risk assessment regarding alternative design approaches. This approach serves to focus CCB activity so that decisions are not being made in real time by the committee.

The remainder of this section gives details of each of our classes; details concerning the message we communicated to the class concerning the CCB in general are provided in the subsequent section. All classes were approximately size 25.

2.3 Iteration One: Fall 1989

The first iteration in this sequence departed from traditional organization of this course at the university, in its focus on process and the laboratory study of engineering principles. From the initial problem statement:

> "Our company has a computing network comprised of many workstations that are linked by an ethernet. We would like a reliable mailing system to support user communication between users who work in this environment. This document is intended to present an initial description of what we desire for this distributed mailing system. . . . "

The organization of the class was as presented in the preceding section; however, because of its distance from us now with respect to time, many details that affect success in this approach make this look least like what we now advocate. This was the 'least real' of the projects, in the sense of making the most simplifying assumptions concerning the context of use of the product. As a result of the moderate project size, the class had enough teams that we performed two concurrent efforts on the same problem. The hope was that there should be interchangeability between components products.

Several concessions to simplicity were made, at what we now know was a cost to pedagogy. We had the coarsest granularity of deliverable points, and, unfortunately, the due date for teams to produce a working implementation coincided with the last day of class. A successful integration was achieved during finals week, by both the instructor and volunteers from each team, but most of the best lessons were lost to the students due to the rush of the end of the term. On the positive side, the involvement of the second author (along with other volunteers from industry) to red-team software artifacts was a resounding success. The introduction of a CCB was made at the urging of the second author.

We concluded from this initial experience that the fundamental approach was sound; the CCB could have assumed greater roles than we initially assigned; the complexity of the problem should have been greater to meet our realism requirement; and we belatedly discovered how rich were the lessons (concerning choice and organization of requirements) taught by system integration.

2.4 Iteration Two: Fall 1991

From the original problem statement:

> "The computer science department at the U runs a facility containing many Unix workstations interconnected by a LAN. Within the facility is a great deal of information — source programs, professional papers and so forth — that we would like to make generally available to our colleagues on the many national networks to which we are connected. Ideally, information that is to be made available for network access could be distributed via regular bulletin board systems or FTP services. The problem is that not everyone has direct network access to our information servers. But a great number of information consumers do have email access. Therefore, we want to automate the task of dispensing information via existing mail systems."

> "We would like a reliable mail-based communication system to support users who work in this type of environment. Called BBOARD, this resource is a cross between a mailing system and a network bulletin board. Users should be able to send electronic mail to a known host at our site; in the body of the message should be a request. BBOARD should automatically respond to the request by sending back, by return mail, the desired text. Ideally, BBOARD will provide a means for reliably transmitting *any* type of file in the system. . . ."

Based upon our prior experience, we knew to choose a 'real' problem (and in fact ended up with a product having greater functionality than a later software product called LISTSERV, now widely available.) We kept three main deliverable deadlines (for requirements, designs and code), but allowed two weeks at the end of the semester for the class to perform system integration as a group. These were clearly the right steps to take, and we learned we could have gone further in this direction.

System integration was a frantic activity, due to inconsistencies in the interfaces that remained undiscovered; this was the one semester when we had the least involvement from industrial volunteers, and even our 'best efforts' by only loosely-involved on-campus personnel was not sufficient for independent review. Also, integration by group, though entertaining, was not efficient; and the deadlines could have been compressed even further.

Nevertheless, the BBOARD mechanism succeeded, and is now in use at the first author's site, for example, serving the Internet information on collected research abstracts provided by several government research agencies (at their request).

2.5 Iteration Three: Spring 1992

From the original problem statement:

> "Techniques and tools for automatically analyzing computer programs are be-
> coming increasingly important. Often, information concerning control flow,
> symbols and type of data can be extracted from the text' of a source pro-
> gram so that developers can study it for correctness. Similarly, programs can
> be altered into versions of the source that are pretty-printed, or perhaps in-
> strumented with profiling instructions and debugging hooks. Unfortunately,
> operating directly on source programs in these ways can be very tedious and
> error prone for programmers proceeding without assistance, yet it is costly
> for the programmers to build custom tools for these tasks themselves. . .
> ." "Our objective is to develop an environment that will simplify the task of
> building analysis tools for programmers, even across across programs written
> in different languages."

> "We will develop an environment that allows input of source programs written
> in multiple source languages; analysis and storage of those programs; and
> output of transformed versions of those source programs. Initially, our output
> routines should act as *interface extraction* tools, although the overall design
> should support extension so that other analysis operations can be performed
> easily in the future."

In this iteration, system interface requirements definition, along with CCB responsibilities, were handled by students who had completed the previous semester's course
and were intent on a followup course via independent study. This group, consisting
of both graduate and undergraduate students, had eight members. We built in an
extra week for systems integration, and increased the oversight responsibilities of the
CCB; the project was a resounding success. The result of this project was a system
called SANE, for *Software Analysis Environment*. The tool is now an integral part of
the software interconnection environment and research program; as such, it has been
shipped to several industrial partners for use in their product organizations. SANE
is a basis for interface extraction and domain engineering for C and Ada artifacts;
and also the basis for some amount of work in data flow analysis of C programs.

2.6 Iteration Four: Spring 1993

The most recent iteration was completed in May of 1993. A complete example
of the initial problem statement appears in Appendix A, and in Section 3 is our
characterization of the CCB as was given to the students in this most recent iteration.
We did not have the benefit of prior SE students to run the CCB, and so returned to

intra-class role. The fine-tuning performed in this class consisted of: (1) allocating one class day per week, throughout the entire term, for the exclusive use of the class CCB; this was done to increase availability of the CCB to teams, and was done in response to feedback from the class about how much they needed a time to reliably meet. (2) Building in intermediate checkpoints into the schedule; before official requirements were due, a non-graded draft was to be delivered, giving students a better basis for reaching consensus and resolving inconsistencies. (3) Responsibility to build some test data for the system was built in as a first-class task, right from the start.

Because of finer-grain checkpoints, and an increased emphasis on asking each student to take responsibility for individual quality assurance tasks during the semester, we knew early in the term that preliminary system integration had succeeded. The most important of demonstration problems required for the project came up and met the requirements specification. The product as of the end of the term was deemed by the class to be generally unsatisfying to use, due to performance questions, which in fact were not present in the early requirements; nevertheless, a subsequent refinement of the product (an event-based programming environment) is a suitable basis for several new experiments run by PhD students within our department.

3 CCB Role and Principles

The preceding sections of the paper repeatedly cited the CCB as an integral course element and described the operation of the CCB throughout the course. This section describes the CCB role and principles underlying the course approach as given to the students; the classroom presentation, in turn, was derived from one of the textbooks used in the course.[2]

To ensure that candidate software changes are processed in a visible and traceable manner, a controlling mechanism that channels these candidate changes to the appropriate project participants is needed. This controlling mechanism is called the *configuration control board* (CCB). In the course, this concept is likened to a control tower that controls the movement of software from stage to stage in whatever life cycle is defined for the project. (The concept of software is defined to encompass specification documentation—such as requirements and design specifications—as well as computer code.) As indicated in Section 2, the development life cycle in the course consists essentially of requirements definition, design, coding and system integration. The students are told that the CCB concept is used in the real world in life cycles with different numbers and types of stages. The CCB concept can be applied to any life cycle model.

The life cycle is viewed as a game board consisting of a sequence of stages (wherein product development is accomplished—e.g., requirements specification) surrounding an area marked "Review." At the "end" of each stage is a gate that descends and

---

[2] W. Bryan and S. Siegel. **Software Product Assurance: Techniques for Reducing Software Risk**, Prentice-Hall, 1988.

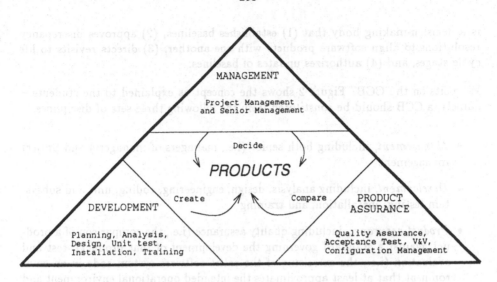

Figure 2: The CCB coordinates product effort.

forces project activity into the review area of the game board. This review area embodies the product review activities.[3] Central to these activities is the CCB control tower, which is also envisioned as occupying the review area of the game board.

As we proceed through whatever life cycle has been defined for a project, the need arises to consider one or more candidate changes to the software product under development (or to previously developed products). To address this need (which may occur at any point within a life cycle stage), we symbolically close a gate, as noted above, that diverts us from the outer loop of the life cycle game board into the area marked "Review." In the review area, we assess these candidate changes, determine their impact on the software system development effort, and make appropriate decisions. These decisions include specifying what to do with the candidate changes (e.g., implement them, reject them, or hold them in abeyance), which software products to modify (e.g., none, the one currently under development, products developed in previously visited life cycle stages), and what revisits, if any, to make to other life cycle stages.

Readers who have some background in configuration management will immediately recognize the CCB as the control organization historically used by the configuration management (CM) process to control modifications and enhancements to a system. On some projects, the CCB may also control changes to the computer code). In the course, it is stressed that the CCB extends beyond this classical CM role. In fact, the CCB performs the broader function of managing *all* change on a software system development project during *all* stages of the life cycle. In this capacity, the CCB

[3]Ibid. Page 362, figure 4.3.

is a decision-making body that (1) establishes baselines, (2) approves discrepancy resolutions to align software products with one another, (3) directs revisits to life cycle stages, and (4) authorizes updates of baselines.

Who sits on the CCB? Figure 2 shows the concept as explained to the students—namely, a CCB should be constituted from the following three sets of disciplines:

- *Management*, including both senior (i.e., managers of managers) and project management

- *Development*, including analysis, design, engineering, coding, unit and subsystem testing, installation, and training

- *Product assurance*, including quality assurance (i.e., the comparison of a product against a standard governing the development of that product), test and evaluation (i.e., the exercising of the entire software system code in an environment that at least approximates the intended operational environment and assessment of its operation using written test plans and procedures based on requirements and design specifications), verification and validation (i.e., the process of assessing traceability and congruence of software products with predecessor documents and requirements), and configuration management (i.e., the management discipline of visibly, traceably, and formally controlling software evolution through baseline management).

In explaining the CCB concept to the students, they are given the following rationale for constituting CCBs from the above three sets of disciplines:

> Experience in the software industry shows that the synergistic efforts of these three disciplines are needed to achieve software products with integrity (i.e., products that do what they are supposed to do, whose evolution can be easily and completely traced, and that are delivered on time and within budget). The CCB is the forum that is central to the product assurance function of change control (as discussed above). It therefore seems reasonable that the CCB should have representatives from all three disciplines in its membership—that is, the CCB should have representatives on it from management, from the developers, and from the product assurance practitioners.

Unfortunately, it has not been possible in any of the iterations of the course to date to set up an independent product assurance function on the classroom project. Consequently, the CCB concept as used in the classroom is a truncated version of the concept described above. In future versions of the course, it is planned to use students who have previously gone through the course in the role of (independent) product assurance agents. These students will participate in CCBs by, for example, presenting the results of product assurance audits they perform on specifications produced by the students currently taking the course. They will, if time permits, serve as acceptance testers by (1) producing test plans and procedures from the requirements and design specifications produced by the students currently taking the course, (2) executing these test procedures using the coded system produced by these students, (3) writing test incident reports (TIRs) based on this execution that documents discrepancies between what the test procedures said they should observe and what they actually observe, and (4) presenting these TIRs at a CCB for resolution. In this manner, students will be able to experience firsthand the checking-and-balancing role product assurance plays on a software system development project. They will also be able to experience how product assurance can act as a forcing function on the development process. In particular, through the interaction of the testers and the developers while the testers are writing their procedures and the developers are developing their designs, the students will be able to experience firsthand how questions asked by testers naturally uncover design (and requirements) issues that might otherwise not be brought to the fore until somewhere during coding (or post deployment).

In the four iterations of the course accomplished to date, the product assurance function has been modeled to a limited extent by the instructor. This modeling has been accomplished primarily through questions raised such as, "Have you considered the testability of this statement?" In the first iteration of the course, the second author, together with another associate from industry, served in a limited product assurance capacity by auditing the initial versions of requirements specifications turned out by the students. The comments provided gave the students insight into how others might interpret their specifications. To say the least, it was an eye-opening experience for the students. To give the students some additional insight into how product assurance is performed in industry, the second author presented a one-hour lecture on acceptance testing during the first, third, and fourth iterations of the course.

As indicated in Figure 2, the CCB offers the opportunity to teach management techniques. At the outset of the course, the instructor primarily plays the management role at the CCB. As the students become more comfortable with the CCB concept, more of the management role is shifted to them. Instead of having the instructor head a CCB, the students take responsibility for the direction of CCB activities. The value of the CCB in helping to teach software management techniques cannot be over-emphasized. Putting a student in charge of a CCB meeting and giving him or her the responsibility for making decisions (in the presence of his/her peers) regarding how the project should proceed, drive home software management principles that, in our opinion, no amount of lecturing on these principles can even approach.

The students are informed that a CCB need not be, and generally is not, permanently staffed with a representative from each subfunction constituting each discipline mentioned above, for example, with a coding representative and a training representative, among others. Many CCB meetings, it is pointed out, will be concerned with neither coding nor training. It is stressed that the CCB should be permanently staffed with at least one representative from management, from development, and from product assurance, with additional representation provided according to the subject matter under consideration at any particular meeting. The students are continually re-

minded that the CCB is a forum for the exchange of information, whose purpose is to make change control decisions. It is essential for this purpose to have representatives from and interaction among all concerned parties relative to whatever matter is under consideration.

We evolved to a scheme where most CCB meetings are held during regular class time to simplify scheduling for the team members. Minutes of each meeting meeting are recorded (this recording is a course requirement), with particular attention given to documenting the decisions reached. However, it is important to note students hold frequent meetings outside the classroom. It turns out that the students apply many of the CCB principles to these other meetings (including the taking of minutes), which provides striking positive confirmation of the teaching approach (this is not to say that students do not short cut some of the things they might otherwise do during the classroom meetings under the watchful eye of the instructor, such as recording what takes place at the meetings—they do).

There are, of course, a multiplicity of CCB principles and related issues other than those discussed above. The exigencies of a 15-week course impose limitations on what can be examined. Mention is made of some of these principles and issues during lectures, but the principles are not applied on the classroom project. Thus, for example, when discussing who should participate on a CCB, the subject of user, buyer, and/or seller CCBs is mentioned. It is indicated to the students that they are software sellers in the sense that they are attempting to develop and "sell" a software system to a customer (or buyer/user), who is the instructor. The business nuances of these perspectives are not explored in general, nor are they explored within the CCB context. Thus, for example, the students are not sensitized to the fact that it may be prudent to have an internal (seller) CCB to iron out issues before having a CCB with the customer (i.e, seller/buyer CCB). Time also does not permit examination of the issues associated with establishing a CCB hierarchy on a project (e.g., system-level CCB, subsystem-level CCB, hardware CCB, software CCB, internal interface CCB, intersubsystem CCB, and system external interfaces CCB).

To summarize this section, the course presents CCB principles and provides an environment for the students to apply these principles. The CCB is the focal point of the change control process. This most important organization is the control activity for the entire change process throughout the project lifetime. The role defined for the CCB is broader in scope than is generally granted to it, particularly within the confines of classical configuration management. The students come to experience firsthand through active participation in the CCB—both as managers and supporting participants—how the CCB controls the change process in a disciplined, visible, and traceable manner.

4 Lessons Learned

We express these lessons as a sequence of maxims for those who may wish to pattern a laboratory environment after ours; we also call out some of the known limitations to this approach, based upon our experiences.

Use tools ... but judiciously. Heavy use of commercial CASE tools has been tried on campus in the past; we know anecdotally that imposing tool use forces students to spend too much of their time learning the mechanics of the tool, rather than understanding just what it is as engineers they should want to communicate using the tool. On the other hand, on-line discussion aids, such as email and bulletin board systems, have proven to be invaluable to the class CCB in keeping key issues visible for discussion. Selection of common document processing languages and tools is essential, for the CCB to integrate task deliverables.

Build time for the CCB into the class time proper. One of the key, recurring observations from students is the need for opportunities to interact.

Use at least four students per group. Three is actually manageable for them; but let students learn the fun of reaching consensus. This size also has the effect of minimizing the impact on system success of a small number of less motivated students; our experience has been that students are much less forgiving of late or poor deliverables than are the faculty.

Let students form their own teams. Many off-line meetings are enabled when the students already know each other and have compatible schedules. But prior friendships are no guarantee of good communication or technical success, so allowing students to pair up as they want helps deflect against rationalizations such as "We'd have done better if only we'd been allowed to work with people we already knew." Some effective lessons in management can be made when the top performing students are allowed to team together. Though at first this may appear to create some potentially unfair disparity, we have found that the best students are also fairly aggressive and the most likely to act as individuals, rather than in the team interests. Excellent 'teachable moments' arise when such a team is clearly surpassed by a group that knew how to pitch in an solve problems as a unit.

Do not discuss much about intra-team organization early on — let the teams explore how to organize themselves. Sharing experiences on how teams organized and reached consensus is a marvelous class discussion late in the course.

Lead by example. Take responsibility for control of the configuration in the first few weeks, and run meetings according to the principles of a CCB to illustrate the effectiveness. Gradually pass responsibility to the class, and allow students to rotate responsibility for directing the CCB.

Don't give large examples to work from early in the term. This may be controversial, but our experience is that if you show students a concrete previous example, then students spend their time 'pattern matching,' mechanically looking for ways to express their requirements or design decisions in terms of the example format. We have found it much more valuable to challenge students to think about how they would establish their own document organization, based upon the description of desirable characteristics expressed in such documents as IEEE 830.

Don't shortchange the system integration period at the end of the course! This is where we see most of the lessons being driven home.

Build in non-graded intermediate checkpoints. They act as forcing functions and also allow students to discover needs for interaction before those needs become critical. The students can have a dry run with handing in their deliverable, and practice the completion strategy for their team. Most important, they can get concrete feedback on their progress *from their peers*. We were surprised to learn how important this maxim is for purposes of breaking down taboos erected from other classes on campus: most students still have vestigial reservations about collaboration on campus. They are still used to a reward structure based upon individual achievement instead of group achievement. Hence, the concept of passing around reports well ahead of the official due date is titillating at least; but we find that exposing the best efforts early tends to drive marginal teams to produce a much better report at the time of the hard deliverable.

Select projects to complement existing and prominent resources in your own environment. In our case we have been successful in choosing projects to go along with emerging research systems which are already in use at the undergraduate level. Students generally feel excited about becoming part of a larger project, with some permanence to their creative efforts.

Ensure everyone becomes involved with the CCB at some point, whether on the board or making a pitch in front of it. Our initial organization of the CCB was based upon requiring each team to provide a representative; but without input from the instructor, it is very easy for aggressive students to dominate meetings.

Overlap a second term course with the first. When two terms of SE education are available, then its better to run the student through the whole life cycle twice (once per term) in different roles, than to run through once on a larger project. Product assurance activities are of much more utility once the student has been through the process once in the trenches.

No preparation – no meeting. As with any organization, arranging time for team members to meet is difficult, and the time is best spent only when there are concrete materials prepared and distributed ahead of time. Assigning individuals responsibility to prepare these materials gives the instructor an opportunity to grade solo efforts (as often required by the institution); perhaps more important, it also helps the instructor to reach and involve students who would otherwise hang back and not participate.

Be sure to build class ego, not just team ego. As organized, system integration at the end of the term is performed by representatives of each team. This is a point where the last remaining barriers between teams must be overcome for the system to succeed. But end of term pressures also make it tempting for a team to focus on meeting the acceptance criteria for their component, and eschew system concerns. A whole-class ego must be at stake for the integration to get as much attention as did components. One crude but effective way to ensure this is simply to base a portion of each student's final grade upon the success of the system, not just parts.

Its worth noting what we have found are some limitations of our approach, primarily imposed by pedagogy. First, limited availability – whether of instructor or team-mates – can make little problems into bigger ones too quickly. As one student (who, like several of our students, had prior industrial experiences) commented, "When I have a question at company, I know just what door to go pound on. But here I have to wait." Second, there are only a limited number of hours per week that are reason-able to demand from a student, even if in a laboratory course. Third, the campus format fixes the size of the overall effort, and requires it to be constant throughout the term. This constraint is fairly artificial, whereas in a realistic project the size of a group would vary depending upon the stage of the effort. This constraint is a challenge to pedagogy, especially early in the product life cycle when smaller groups would normally be responsible for system level decisions.

5   Conclusion

We have described an approach to running a laboratory-oriented software engineer-ing course targeting college seniors and graduate students. As we have attempted to document, basing project activities on top of a strong CCB has been essential to al-lowing students opportunity to explore real-world engineering issues, and to impress upon them that the problems do not have unique solutions. This fact of software system development life is difficult if not impossible to convey only in a lecture, even one sprinkled with a multitude of war stories. It is indeed a rich experience for the instructor to watch and help students (primarily through the CCB) wrestle and resolve the multitude of vexing issues that arise as their projects evolve.

Our performance in the course can be measured only anecdotally, but nevertheless the results are suggestive of success. In the short run, being able to ship working products, especially in conjunction with research products from our campus, is one objective testimony to the effectiveness of this process. As mentors, however, a much more satisfying measure is in the success our students subsequently find in their careers. As our students have moved into marketplace, local industry now calls and specifically asks for access to our SE students, for purposes of recruiting. (Some companies, having discovered the nature of projects completed in the course, have contacted us for access to the products themselves too.) And all graduates seeking advanced degrees in software engineering areas have had uniform success in placing at top universities in the country.

APPENDIX A: EXAMPLE PROJECT ASSIGNMENT

USER-PROGRAMMABLE EVENT MANAGEMENT ENVIRONMENT
REQUIREMENTS OVERVIEW, VERSION 1.0 OF 22 JANUARY 1993

The purpose of this [appendix] is to describe the initial set of requirements for a programming system to be built by the CMSC 435 (software engineering.) From this initial description, and with discussion and guidance in-class, the class will refine and expand this description, then create a system level design sufficient for us to distribute work tasks to the four-person teams. These teams will be responsible for establishing a set of clear, unambiguous, complete, consistent, and testable requirements for their respective components or subsystems. Subsequently, teams will evaluate the requirements; derive detailed designs for the sub-systems; implement the sub-systems; perform component tests as appropriate; integrate the components according to the system level design; and perform system test and installation.

MOTIVATION AND INITIAL DESCRIPTION

Event-based program execution refers to a convention whereby programs are activated based upon some independent condition from elsewhere in the environment. When some agent — whether an operating system or application program — detects such a condition (or *event*), then it runs a program; the choice of program run by this agent or *dispatcher* may depend upon the nature of that event. One characteristic of this paradigm is that application programs which generate events usually do *not* know which programs their event will cause to be activated. Potentially, there might be *many* programs activated based upon a single event; and in other cases there may be no programs activated (that is, the event is simply ignored.)

There are many examples of event-based execution in today's computing environments. In our Unix machines, rwho daemons continuously check who is logged in on their machines, and announce those names (that is, *broadcast* them) to the network; this broadcast is, in effect, and event, and other rwho programs are activated when those messages arrive on other machines. The activated programs receive the message, and then store it in a system file, where it can be displayed for the users who then run their own rwho program — revealing who is logged in and active throughout the local computing network.

Another example, which is more personal to individual users, is the biff family of programs — programs which are activated based upon the event of mail arriving in the user's system mail box. When this happens, they may 'beep' the user, or display a 'mail' icon in the user's window environment, or play a 'sound file' (often to the annoyance of other users in the same room.)

Dispatchers are typically built to recognize only certain types of events, and they are equally likely to only have a fixed set of possible responses to those events. In the past, dispatchers have been set up by the systems managers for a facility (as is the case for our rwho example, for security and uniformity reasons), or, with limited flexibility, by individual users in their environment (as is the case with our biff example ... users can really only have the sound or icon programs run which the biff designer built in.)

The purpose of this project is to create a more general Unix-based, event management system, which will enable programmers to define their own class of events to be handled, simplify their task of getting these events into the network environment, and allow them to build custom tools to interpret what is to happen in the event of their personal ... err ... events.

1. Programmers must be able to write, perhaps in a simple and new high level language, a definition of what abstract events they wish to handle in a network (or possibly only on one local host, at their choice). Their definition should identify how many agents are necessary, name the events they wish to handle, and show how those events are to be either distributed or immediately handled. We will call this entire definition an *event specification*.

2. Programmers need some way to transform their event specification into a form which, when executed, causes the agent or agents to start up and begin operation on behalf of the user's new event protocol.

3. Programmers need an easy way to write ordinary programs (say, in C on Unix hosts) so that they can either be invoked by agents upon demand, and hence participate in this general environment; or so that their programs can be initiated by the user. In the latter case, there must be some way so that the program can be introduced to a given agent in a given running session. Once connected, the user program should be free to receive events from the agent, and also generate events. Because events are relatively abstract (in a sense, they are 'typed'), we must ensure that the agents and application programs treat their interfaces to one another consistently. Hence, it is possible that the event specification may be used as one of the inputs to the user's development of an application program. But because of the abstraction, different users are free to build their own application programs to interpret events differently, once the event specification has been established. We must therefore account for a level of indirection between programs named in event specifications and what actually gets invoked by the agent on a personal workstation in the network.

4. We need to provide for communication between agents in a running session. The class is strongly encouraged to use the Polylith programming system for this purpose — it deals with all the yukky socket code and protocols so you don't have to. For a manual, use anonymous ftp to retrieve a compressed postscript image from `flubber.cs.umd.edu`. If you are interested in software bus organization, then there are other files in that directory which you might want to access and print as well.

5. The system must neither exploit nor expose security holes in the underlying Unix systems for which the project must work (defined to be "any workstation in the CS department's laboratory.") Reasonable care must be taken so that agents do not open our systems up to attack.

6. One of the most common anticipated uses of this system is to display image or sound files when events such as 'mail arrived' or 'the prof logged in' occur. But we must assume that in general, there may *not* necessarily be a common network file system uniting all the hosts which participate in a session. Therefore, an important part of our project will be to provide a 'persistent object base' access by agents in the run time environment. This database may be viewed as a 'special agent' to be named in event specifications, and should allow storage of heterogeneous, non-textual data structures, which can then be transmitted between agents and made available as a parameter in an event being delivered.

7. No such programmable system as this would be complete without having a collection of both inter- and intra-user environment demo programs, to illustrate that, indeed, our graduates can make 'way cool' projects. One of the demos should illustrate how a single user may wish to start up a custom session, having program development tools set up to graphically display the state of his or her running session via the event system. Another demo should illustrate how multiple users can benefit from this user-tailorable event system. In particular, it should show how individual users can allow personalized application programs to interpret events on the named session. At least one spiffy demo of the distributed nature of this project is required as well ... for example, one might want to have an image of the 'Eveready rabbit' march from window system to window system of users participating in a session.

THE FINE PRINT

An immediate objective is to reach consensus on an initial system level decomposition of tasks, sufficient for distribution among class teams. We will have three major checkpoints during the semester: one at the end of detailed requirements capture; one at the end of detailed design; and one at the end of implementation and unit testing. Each of these points will signal the redistribution of task responsibilities between teams (and also be points where team deliverables are handed in for grading.) The final task will be system integration and system testing, which will be performed by representatives from all teams. To assist in the smooth adherence to schedule, an informal checkpoint will be scheduled for approximately one week prior to the official checkpoints; the teams should divulge a draft of their deliverable for CCB comment, so that they will be able to later hand in a deliverable reflecting updates and class consensus.

This is a whole-class effort, and not only our programs but our documents must be well integrated. *latex* will be used as the document paste-up system of choice. The CCB will be responsible for maintaining the set of files from each team so that, once handed in, the reports can be processed and printed a single document with consistent and uniform appearance. Each deliverable must include a log of team activities and progress; it must include an assessment of the quality of all materials which formed input to the team at the given stage; and it must log when changes to input documents are authorized, when, by whom, and why. Keep good, scientific notes about what you do right from the start.

Putting into Practice
Advanced Software Engineering Techniques
through
Students Project

Naji HABRA and Eric DUBOIS

Institut d'Informatique,
Facultés Universitaires Notre-Dame de la Paix,
Institut d'Informatique
21 rue Grandgagnage, B-5000 Namur (Belgium)
Email: nha@info.fundp.ac.be, edu@info.fundp.ac.be

Abstract. The paper describes an experience of software engineering
education concerning the guidance of students project during about ten
years. The project aims mainly at putting into practice the concepts,
methods and techniques taught in a software engineering course through
the development –by teams of students– of an actual, practical, real-
size case. The concerned course involves several advanced topics, e.g.,
semi-formal requirements, formal specifications, transformational development process, Object-Oriented design,... which are sometimes considered as *purely academic* topics. Therefore, the main feature of the students project is to illustrate the applicability of these topics in a *realistic*
project and thus to achieve an *integration* of modern techniques with
more classical ones.

1 Introduction : Context of the Students Project

Our Computer Science department has a dominant orientation towards Information Systems design. Our curriculum prepares students to a M.Sc. degree in five
years. The main goal of this curriculum is to turn out computer professionals for
public and business companies (banks, insurance companies, trade companies,
administration,...). And it is worth saying that this professional environment in
Belgium remains conservative; well-established languages (e.g., Cobol) and tools
are still the most widely used.

The Software Engineering course is addressed to the fourth year students,
it represents the first and main course where "in the large" aspects of software
design are covered. One of the specific goal of the course is to teach modern SE
concepts and principles (e.g., formal specification languages, transformational
paradigm), even though they are not already supported by common tools which
are widely used in the organizations. The idea is that today's concepts will
underlie tomorrow's tools and techniques.

Taking into account the professional environment constraints on the one
hand, and the course advanced topics on the other hand, the strategy of the

project is a real challenge. In fact, the project is organized so as to integrate modern topics within a realistic environment. Our ambition is to achieve a dual objective: preparing students to be operational in *present* professional environment and training them to put into practice *future* SE concepts. An extra advantage of this approach is to allow students to acquire a critical judgment about the applicability of theoretical concepts.

The project and the course are interlaced, they both span over one semester: 30 hours (1 module) for the course and 120 hours (4 modules) for the project. They both follow –more or less– the phases of software life-cycle. The project is carried out by teams of 6 students each. Groups start with structured and semi-formal requirements specifications and undertake the whole life-cycle of the same case study. The case study used for several years is a medium-size application concerning a Hospital Information System (HIS).

In short, the considered Information System involves information concerning the hospital structure (e.g., the different services, rooms and beds); information about the medication (e,g., the different medical acts and medicaments prescribable by doctors, their full prices, the part of prices supported by the public health insurance) and information about doctors and nurses (e.g., their respective responsibilities and prerogatives). The required functionalities of the HIS includes patients management (e.g., functions like patient admittance, patient change of room, patient departure) medical functions (e.g., medical acts prescription, execution and cancellation) and general management functions (e.g., invoices preparation and statistics). Different terminals are located in the different services, each can issue a subset of the available functionalities which corresponds to its location: a medical service, the reception, the emergency service,...

The rest of the paper is organized as follows: Section 2 outlines and justifies the adopted life-cycle; Section 3 outlines the framework (viz. the models and languages) in which students are asked to carry out their project; Section 4 describes how the project takes place in practice and points out some interesting experiences; the team-management aspects are described in Section 5; and finally, Section 6 gives some conclusions.

2 Adopted Life-cycle

Our aim is to be as close as possible to a "real world" life-cycle. We use the constraints implied by the academic environment (e.g., the constrains about phases duration, the necessity of checkpoints for evaluation,...) in order to simulate "production world" constraints.

Since the classical *waterfall* model [8] is now judged highly controversial, we have decided to adopt an alternative software life-cycle. Our choice adheres to a software life-cycle based on the *transformational* paradigm where correctness-preserving transformations are applied to convert formal specifications into programs, and where maintenance is performed on specifications [4, 2, 5, 3]. This life-cycle was preferred to a *prototyping* approach since, in our case study, we make the hypotheses that (i) the requirements document for the business I.S.

is complete and (ii) the nature of man-machines interfaces is not complex (and thereby do not need be prototyped).

In a *transformational* life-cycle, the key issue relies upon the nature of the *design decisions* taken by software engineers all along the transformational process. In order to cope with the complexity and the number of design decisions, we have proposed to group them into four different groups and, thereby, to delineate four basic *phases* to be performed by software engineers: *specification*, *static design*, *dynamic design* and *implementation*.

Each *phase* is characterized by one *formal product* having to be correctly built and maintained. We distinguish: the *functional specification*, the *static architecture*, the *dynamic architecture* and the *code*.

Phases should not be confused with the concept of *activities* used in the classical *waterfall* model. *Phases* are viewed under an organizational point of view (homogeneous nature of the design decisions) as well as a succession of fixed periods of work. In addition to the activity that consists in producing the main formal product, each phase involves several other activities. Thus, activities like validation and documentation are made all along the different phases. This is also the case of the *maintenance* activity needed in case of requirements evolutions where a *replay* of design decisions has to occurred.

In terms of organization for our students, each phase is characterized by evaluation meetings defined at fixed dates but, within the interval, students are left free to organize their work as they want. In practice, since the nature of the *phases* and of the *products* are new for them, backtracking is often necessary to adjust some former design decisions.

3 Proposed Models and Languages

This section details the transformational life-cycle proposed to the students. Subsection 3.1 outlines the nature of the different *phases* introduced in the previous section. Subsection 3.2 presents the nature of the languages used for for describing the different *formal products*. Subsection 3.3 emphasizes the nature of the major *design decisions* taken in the different phases. Finally, subsection 3.4 briefly describes the nature of tools made available to the students.

3.1 The Different Phases

Requirements Analysis The very early stages of the requirements analysis phase (viz. the acquisition of the requirements and their first formulation) are not actually covered by the project. The reasons are the limited time allocated to the project (one semester) on the one hand, and the fact that those phases are covered by another course of the preceding year, on the other hand. So, students receive a requirements document written in a structured semi-formal language studied by them before. Deliberately, the requirements document includes incompleteness, contradictions and ambiguities.

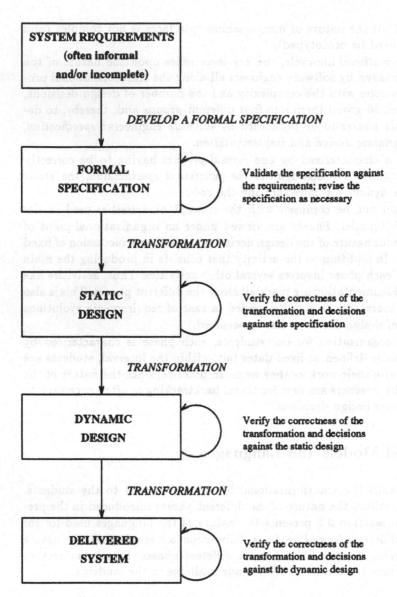

Fig. 1. Transformational life-cycle

Specification Starting with a structured semi-formal requirements document describing the Information System (viz the software system and its environment made of manual procedures), students are asked to produce a complete and rigorous functional specification of the software part of the I.S. To this end, from the requirements document, they have to (i) isolate the different functionalities required for the application and (ii) provide for each of them a formal characterization in terms of inputs/outputs relationships and state's changes. In parallel, we also propose to them to discover a certain number of usually called non-functional requirements (performances, space memory, properties of the HMI, etc) in the requirements document. These non-functional requirements remain informally described but are important to be isolated since they will influence design decisions taken during the next phases to be performed.

Static Design Starting from the specification document describing the *what*, students have then to move towards the identification of the static design describing the *how*. At this level, students have to take decisions about (i) the nature of operations and data required by the specification, (ii) the way interactions will take place between the software and its users, (iii) how persistent data will be stored (as in files or in databases), and (iv) how possible errors are handled.

At this level, an important point to be mentioned (and motivating the use of the word *static design*) is that we make the hypothesis that the developed software is a *single user* system. This hypothesis makes it possible to avoid, at this level, problems related with the distributed aspects of a software and requiring the introduction of concepts dealing with *synchronization, concurrency*, etc.

The static design phase results in the production of a global architecture. This architecture consists in a collection of modules having well-defined relationships with each others. In this architecture, each module is viewed as a collections of "services" described in an abstract and static way.

Dynamic Design The detailed design phase consists of a refinement of the static architecture where is taken into account software *distribution* aspects. In our Hospital Information System case study, the requirements document describes the existence of terminals at several locations of the hospital. Thereby, strategies have to be imagined in terms of the granularity of parallelism that can be incorporated in the developed software.

The dynamic design phase results in the production of new global architecture where modules are now structured as a collection of *concurrent processes*. This architecture takes into account elements related to resources allocation scheduling, concurrent transactions on databases, monitors and semaphores, etc.

Implementation Static design and dynamic design are both describing executable solutions to the problem formulated in the specification. However, these solutions are only operational on a *virtual* computer. At the implementation phase, the objective is to transform the dynamic design into an implemented software written in an adequate programming language and interfacing specific databases, user interface management tools as well as the operating system. It should be noted that, in some cases, the resulting *physical* architecture may differ from the *logical* dynamic architecture. In this case, it is asked to students to keep of a *trace* of the transformations applied for deriving the physical architecture.

All long the different phases of the development process, students are asked to use an informal but rigorous *transformational* approach. More precisely, they should be able to trace how each specification element evolves all along the development process through the different phases. However, we do not ask them to exhibit a formal proof of each transformation. Without adequate tools, this works would be too cumbersome for students. A posteriori, keeping track of this trace is very important for the students since, at the end of the project, we propose some evolutions in the requirements document and ask to the students to implement them.

3.2 The Proposed Languages

Although we know that the use of formal languages is very limited in the industrial practice, our basic objective is however to familiarize students with them and (hopefully) promote their use.

At the level of the choice of a formal language, a first possibility would be to use a wide-spectrum language (like VDM or RAISE [6, 15, 12]) that can be used in all phases of the software development. However, we have declined this idea in absence of a common general agreement on a *standard* wide-spectrum language. Moreover, it is not sure that an adequate wide-spectrum language exists for covering all aspects of the development of a large Information Systems (for example, at the level of databases aspects);

Thereby, our choice is to propose a set of formal languages (one for each phase), each language being characterized by the usefulness of the notations it proposes with respect to the description phases having to be done in the concerned phase.

Hereafter, we briefly characterise the different languages used.

- At the requirements analysis level, the requirements document provided to the student is written in a semi-formal language based on MERISE [20, 24] and SSADM [16] (two popular methods used in Europe). In such formalisms, data aspects are covered by using an entity-relationship [7] formalism while processing phases are described in terms of state's changes diagrams.
- The specification of the software is written using Z [13, 23]. This mathematical formalism based on simple concepts like *sets* and *relations* was proved adequate for expressing specifications in a declarative way. In Z, persistent data are modelled in terms of a collection of *states* (each state being characterized by a structure of data and some possible invariants) and functionalities are modelled in terms of *operations* (each operation being characterized as a mathematical relation between inputs and outputs, together with its effect on states).
- The static design is expressed in terms of number of modules. Each module is described in terms of a dialect of the RSL language [12]. RSL is an extension of VDM based on a model-oriented specification; modules are characterized in terms of the services that they provide to the outside, together with the

services they are using from other modules (in the sense of the *use* relationship introduced in [19, 18]). Within this framework, two kinds of modules can be identified:

- *function-oriented* modules where a module groups together services around a *function*. Such modules implement a *procedural* abstraction;
- *data-oriented* modules where a module groups together services around a shared *data structure*. Such modules implement a *data* abstraction. In the RSL language, abstract data modules can be described either in an algebraic way or in a model-oriented way.

On top of the *use* relation among provided services, modules are also structured according to *inheritance* and *genericity* structuring relationships.

- The dynamic design is also expressed in terms of a number of modules offering services. Each module is described in terms of the OBLOG[1] formal language [22, 21] making it possible to describe the software in terms of a collection of *communicating processes* [14]. In such a language, modules correspond to so-called *objects* which are identified on basis of *function-oriented* or *data-oriented* strategy. The structure of an OBLOG description can be summarized as follows:
  - an object encapsulates a state structure represented by the attributes of that objects,
  - the state of an object may only change by actions within the object, extended Petri-nets are used for defining the possible and admissible orderings of actions,
  - objects communicate with each other via action calls.

It should be noted that the *use* relationship of the *static design* is now replaced by *send* and *receive* action calls.

- The classical implementation is carried out in the programming language Cobol with the Data Base Management System SQL and the User Interface Management System DecForm[2].

3.3 The Proposed Methodological Guidelines

We believe that the design phases (viz. the static and dynamic architectures) are the most creative activities in the development process. Therefore, we aim at giving students a large freedom to create their own architecture and thereby to acquire a practical creative experience. Only few methodological guidelines are suggested, viz. guidelines to decompose system into modules and guidelines to deal with temporal aspects.

Decomposition Criteria. Basic ideas are learned to students about the quality of a "good" architecture: (i) the decomposition into well-defined units called

---

[1] OBLOG is a Trademark of ESDI Portugal
[2] DecForm is a Trademark of Digital Equipment Corporation

"modules" related by well defined relationships; (ii) the desired qualities of modules (cohesion, information hiding, encapsulation,...) and (iii) the wished qualities of relationships (hierarchy, weak-coupling,...) [19, 18].

We also outline different specific methodological approaches to elaborate good architectures: functional and O.O decompositions [9]; classical top-down, bottom-up and also outside-in [26, 27] approaches. Finally, in the SE theoretical *course*, a complete example of an IS design is developed. This example suggests the blueprint of a general architecture based on a hierarchy of modules presented at different abstraction levels [25]:

- at the level 4, we found modules which are directly derived from the functionalities described in the specification document;
- at the level 3, we found modules dealing with input/output services. In particular, we found the modules in charge of the man-machine interface;
- at the level 2, we found modules dealing with accesses to persistent data of the Information System;
- at the level 1, we found modules offering services provided by the *middleware* infrastructure (Database Management System, Dialogue Services, etc);
- at the level 0, we found modules offering services provided by the *operating system.*

In the project, students are not required to stick to a fixed rigid methodological rule. They are free to use any mixed approach providing they produce a "good" architecture in the general sense of the course and they can *justify* their choices.

In practice, the most of the produced architectures present certain similarities since they are trying to stick to the blueprint presented above. In Section 4, we discuss some properties of basic architectures defined by students.

Dealing with Time. In order to deal with distribution aspects and concurrency, the general guideline that we suggested to students is to design a static architecture first before to envisage a dynamic architecture.

More precisely, the hypothesis made in the static design is to consider the system as *single-user* and to consider all the functions as *timeless*. As a consequence, functionalities are specified as mathematical "functions" between their results and their arguments (and not considered as *procedures*). Thereby, services offered by modules are considered as instantaneous and no concurrent.

Concurrency is introduced in the dynamic design phase when the architecture is refined to become closer to the implementation: more algorithmic, more physical and also more dynamic. In this phase, the timeless and non-concurrent hypotheses are discarded. As a consequence, the detailed architecture should involve new modules (or new services) to deal with concurrency. Typically, Hoare's monitors or resources schedulers are identified at this level.

The rationale behind the choice of delaying temporal aspects until the dynamic design is twofold: on the one hand temporal aspects description appears to be closer to the implementation (in terms of physical resources) than to the abstract specification; and on the other hand we observe that concurrency in classical IS is not the key feature that determines the architecture choice - in contrast to real-time systems for example.

3.4 The Proposed Pools

It is well recognized that, by now, formal methods are poorly supported by adequate and efficient tools. Thereby, for the moment, by lack of time and of computer resources, adequate tools are only proposed at the dynamic architecture and implementation phases.

During the dynamic architecture phase, students have the opportunity to use the prototype of the OBLOG workbench (which will be pre-commercialized in the beginning of 1994). This workbench is an *IPSE* centered around a central repository of OBLOG descriptions and offers the following facilities:

- a session manager;
- a graphical editor (the formal OBLOG language has a complete graphical syntax);
- syntactic and semantic checkers;
- a C-code generator (100% of the code can be generated, including the interfaces and the databases accesses);

Besides this experimentational CASE tool and its powerful facilities for generating code, we also propose to our students to perform the implementation activity by hand, viz. by using very traditional and non-integrated tools: COBOL + SQL + DecForm. The objectives of that are :

- to provide students with some expertise in such classical tools which will be more likely analogous to their working environment in the first years of their careers. This allows them to experiment the real difficulties of using non-integrated tools and also the strong distinction that may exist between *logical* and *physical* architectures (see above). In particular, the use of COBOL obliges them to strongly revised the possibility of communication between modules;
- to demonstrate the potential benefits of using formal languages and thereby to take profit of the semi-automatic correct code generation facilities.

4 Process in Work: Practice and Experience

It is interesting now to observe how the methodological rules sketched above are used in practice and what experience could be retained.

4.1 Static Architectures

As mentioned above, the most of the produced architectures present in practice certain similarities; they are inspired -more or less- by the blueprint architecture of the example developed during the theoretical course. Thus, architectures seem to respect a kind of "generic model" produced following a "generic process". At the end of the project, the different processes actually used are discussed and compared.

Let us now outline the typical architecture models. In fact, typical architectures are organized as a hierarchy of modules. They involve different kind of modules: "functional" modules appearing in one or several layers on the top of the hierarchy, "object" modules appearing in one or several intermediate layers and "persistent data" modules appearing in the bottom.

- Modules of the functional level(s) correspond to the basic "functionalities" appearing in the requirements specification document which are decomposed and/or grouped according to certain criteria (e.g., similarity, organizational constraints, menu-driven, ...).
- Modules of the data level consist of either one big module encapsulating the whole system database or several modules encapsulating each a part (or a view) of the database.
- Modules of the intermediate level(s) are "objects" which encapsulate each a collection of "services" (e.g., input/output services, general purpose services, ...). Services of an object module can be used by functional modules and/or by other higher-level object modules which play the role of "clients". Services are grouped according to classical O.O. criteria (e.g., [9]) and the objects specifications are close to abstract data types specifications.

Monitoring students during the elaboration of their architectures and following their progress step-by-step allows us to derive the outline of the process underlying the elaboration of their their typical architectures. This process could be roughly described as the following stages:

- A *top-down function-driven* and/or *menu-driven* analysis stage which starts with the functions appearing in the requirements document to produce a first draft of the higher layers; and in parallel a *bottom-up data-driven* analysis stage to produce the lower layer module(s) encapsulating the permanent data, together with their corresponding access methods.
- A subsequent stage that corresponds to an *object-oriented* analysis by which some useful and reusable object modules arise in one or several intermediate layers.
- A refinement stage including several backtrackings to the former decisions in order to improve the architecture according to the general modularization criteria (information hiding, weak-coupling, esthetic,...).

Obviously, some groups produce architectures which differ from the above typical schema, e.g., full object-oriented or full function-oriented architectures. Thus, at the end of the project we organize a comparison session in which the relative merits and demerits of the different architectures are discussed.

At the comparative session, we can observe for example how sticking to full O.O. decomposition could lead to some artificial "object" modules which correspond more naturally to functions than to objects of the considered universe.

We see also how sticking to a full functional decomposition could lead to miss the opportunity of finding very general and reusable "object" modules.

4.2 Dynamic Architectures

As mentioned above, the guideline suggested to the students in order to deal with temporal aspects is to delay them until the detailed design. The hypothesis made in the global design is to consider that all functions are timeless. Concurrency is introduced only in the detailed design when this hypothesis is discarded

Practically, the dynamical architecture modules are produced by refinement from the static architecture modules. And, in the HIS case study, only few functions involves concurrent aspects (actually this is also the case in most of classical IS systems). Thus in the dynamical architecture, either few modules are extended to describe concurrent aspects or some new specialized modules are added to deal with this concurrency.

As an example, in our HIS case study, different external functions (e.g., patient admittance, changing patient service, patient departure,...) can change the allocation of beds to patients. In the *static architecture*, under the fixed hypothesis, those functions can specified by preconditions and postconditions that determine the desired properties before and after the function activation (e.g., a new bed is allocated or deallocated), together with invariant properties (e.g., one patient at most in each bed). In the dynamic architecture, the concurrent activation of several functions from several terminals should now be considered. A possible solution is then to insert an new module which manages all the concurrent allocation requests. The role of that module is to satisfy the different requests to allocate and deallocate beds issued by the different functions. It should fulfill the pre/post/invariant conditions of the static design, and in addition it should fulfill the dynamic constraints given informally in the requirements document (e.g., the respective priorities,...). Obviously, the description of that module involves more operational aspects like waiting queues, semaphores and flags; those aspects have their right place in the detailed architecture.

From the pedagogical point of view, this methodological rule allows to make a clear distinction between static and dynamical aspects. By consequent, static modularization criteria (based on relations like "uses" or on the "client-server" paradigm) can be experimented independently of the dynamical modularization criteria (based on relations like "calls" or "triggers off").

4.3 Architectures under the Maintenance Proof

In order to familiarize students with the maintenance *activity*, a slight but realistic requirements change is proposed at the end of the first implementation. Students are then asked to adapt their design in order to respond to the modification. They are asked to trace the impact of this change all along the different products: the specification, the static architecture, the dynamic architecture and the code.

It is interesting to observe how much the difficulty of such maintenance task is dependent on the quality of the design. For some groups having appropriate architectures, the suggested modification involves the extension of only one module or the insertion of one new module. For other groups having less proper architectures, the modification could involve deep changes in several modules.

5 Teamwork Management

The curriculum of our faculty includes different courses that cover managerial topics like the "teamwork management" and the "social and psychological aspects of Information Systems". Meanwhile, the SE project remains the main field of application for those courses.

Students work as "chief programmer teams" (see [1]). They are not asked to fix their roles in the team (e.g., as coordinator, documentation responsible,...) all along the project but to take turns to achieve these roles.

Periodically, at least once at the end of every major phase, each group have a review meeting with two staff members: one responsible of the technical aspects and one responsible of the managerial aspects. These meetings involve thus two kinds of discussions. Technical discussions involve topics like the choices made by the group during the concerned period and the possible alternatives; while managerial discussions involve topics like the followed planning and the teamwork problems. The goal of those meetings is to make a complete evaluation of the achieved work and to fix a detailed planning for the work to be done. Outside those meetings, students can ask to meet one (or more) of the staff members to have precise technical advises.

Staff members, in turn, organize themselves in a kind of "team" with different fixed roles: a coordinator, a specification consultant, a teamwork consultant, a tool consultant,... They also have periodical meetings to ensure a reasonable coherence of the evaluation.

6 Conclusions

The paper described an experience of a software engineering project achieved in our university. Different original characteristics of the project have been discussed. The key motivation behind all those topics is to train our students to practice modern SE principles within the limitations of different constraints. Those constraints are due to our academic environment, on the one hand, and to the future working environment of our students, on the other hand. The feedback we have from our former students for ten years —working at present in different public and private organizations— confirms us in the choices made.

Obviously the SE project described in this paper has been evolved deeply during the last years; and probably it will continue to evolve in parallel to the SE field in general and to the spreading languages and tools.

References

1. F. Baker. Chief programming team management of production programming. *IBM Journal*, 11(1):58, 1972.
2. R. Balzer. Transformational Implementation: an Example. *IEEE Transactions on Software Engineering*, 7(1):3–14, 1981.
3. R. Balzer, D. Cohen, M.S. Feather, N. Goldman, W. Swartout, and D. Wile. Operational Specification as the Basis for Specification Validation. In D. Ferrari, M. Bolognani, and J. Goguen, editors, *Theory and Practice of Software Technology*, pages 21–49. North-Holland, 1983.
4. R. Balzer, N. Goldman, and D. Wile. On the Transformational Implementation Approach to Programming. In *Proc. Second IEEE International Conference on Software Engineering*, pages 337–349, San Francisco, CA, USA, October 1976. The CS IEEE Press.
5. R. Balzer, N. Goldman, and D. Wile. Operational Specification as the Basis for Rapid Prototyping. *ACM Sigsoft Software Engineering Notes*, 7(5):3–16, 1982.
6. D. Bjørner and C.B. Jones. *The Vienna Development Method. The metalanguage*, volume 61 of *LNCS*. Springer-Verlag, 1978.
7. F. Bodart and Y. Pigneur. *Conception assistée des applications informatiques. Première partie: Etude d'opportunité et analyse conceptuelle*. Masson, Paris, 1983.
8. B. Boehm. Software engineering. *IEEE Transactions on Computers*, 25(12), 1976.
9. G. Booch. *Object Oriented Design with Applications*. The Benjamin Cunnings Publishing Company, 1991.
10. Richard E. Fairley. *Software Engineering Concepts*. Mc Graw-Hill, 1984.
11. C. Ghezzi. *Fundamentals of Software Engineering*. Prentice Hall, 1991.
12. Raise Language Group. *The RAISE Specification Language*. BCS Practitioner Series. Prentice-Hall, 1992.
13. Ian Hayes. *Specification case studies*. Prentice-Hall International, 1987.
14. M.A. Jackson. *System Development*. Prentice-Hall, 1983.
15. C.B. Jones. *Systematic Software Development Using VDM*. Prentice-Hall Series in Computer Science. Prentice-Hall, 1986.
16. G. Longworth and D. Nicholls. SSADM manual. Technical report, National Computing Center, UK, 1987.
17. T. De Marco. *Structured Analysis and System Specification*. Prentice Hall, Englewood Cliffs, N.J., 1981.
18. D.L. Parnas. On the criteria to be used in decomposing systems into modules. *Commuications of the ACM*, 15(12), 1972.
19. D.L. Parnas. A technique for software module specification with examples. *Commuications of the ACM*, 15(5), 1972.
20. A. Rochfeld and H. Tardieu. MERISE: an information system design and development methodology. *Information & Management*, 6(3):143–159, June 1983.
21. A. Sernadas, C. Sernadas, and H.-D. Ehrich. Abstract object types: a temporal perspective. In B. Banieqbal, H. Barringer, and A. Pnueli, editors, *Proc. of the colloquium on temporal logic and specification*, pages 324–350. LNCS 398, Springer-Verlag, 1989.
22. Amílcar Sernadas, Cristina Sernadas, and Hans-Dieter Ehrich. Object-oriented specification of databases: an algebraic approach. In Peter Hammersley, editor, *Proceedings of the 13th international conference on very large data bases*, pages 107–116, Brighton (UK), September 1-4, 1987.

23. J.M. Spivey. *The Z notation – a reference manual.* Prentice-Hall International, 1989.
24. H. Tardieu, A. Rochfeld, R. Coletti, G. Panet, and G. Vahee. *La méthode MERISE vol 1 and 2.* Editions Hommes et Techniques, Paris, 1985.
25. A. van Lamsweerde. Cadre général pour un modèle de cycle de vie d'un projet informatique. Technical report, University of Namur, Namur (Belgium), 1985.
26. A.I. Wasserman, P.A. Pircher, and D.T. Shewmake. Building reliable interactive information systems. *IEEE Transactions on Software Engineering*, 12(1), 1986.
27. A.I. Wasserman, P.A. Pircher, D.T. Shewmake, and M.L. Kersten. Developing interactive information systems with the user software engineering methodologie. *IEEE Transactions on Software Engineering*, 12(2), 1986.

Cachesim: A Graphical Software Environment to Support the Teaching of Computer Systems with Cache Memories

Cosimo Antonio Prete

Dipartimento di Ingegneria dell'Informazione: Elettronica, Informatica, Telecomunicazioni,
Facoltà di Ingegneria, Università di Pisa,
Via Diotisalvi, 2 - 56126 PISA (Italy)

Abstract. We present an educational software package (Cachesim) used as a teaching tool for studying and analysing computers with cache memories. Cachesim allows students to execute a program step-by-step, to observe the cache activity needed for a memory operation, to evaluate system performance by varying the program and/or the cache parameters and, finally, to analyse program behaviour by means of the memory references. The user interface is fully graphic: architectural modules of the simulated computer are managed as graphical objects and the main actions on them can be made by mouse clicks. The environment is based on Personal Computer and can be used on both MS-DOS and Microsoft Windows platforms. This paper describes this software package and the simulated computer features by examining a student's exercise.

1 Introduction

Sometimes, lessons based on physical systems do not produce good results as these systems do give no or give little useful information as far as understanding the system operating is concerned. More information can be obtained by supplying the system with ad-hoc hardware which builds trace files for recording the events and the actions of the system. Moreover, this technique is not always applicable as in certain systems it is not possible to detect all the events. The main raisons that prevent detection of the events are: i) the large number and high frequency of these events may require a too expensive acquisition system; and ii) several events happening inside the chips.

For these reasons, in basic and advanced courses of Computer and Electronics Engineering at Pisa University (Italy), the teachers continue to use simulation environments as learning tools in computer science [1-3, 6]. Simulators offer a number of advantages compared to experimenting on a physical system. In the teaching of Computer Architecture, a simulator allows us to observe and trace actions and events that usually could not be observed in a physical system. The observation of such actions and events, in several cases, facilitates learning about the functional and design aspects of a computer system [4, 9]. Simulators offer other advantages, such as: i) the possibility of having several computer architectures and of comparing them in various application areas; ii) the possibility of evaluating new solutions in a short time; and iii) the low cost of a virtual laboratory.

In this paper, as an example of teaching techniques based on simulation tools, we present a simulation environment of a computer with a cache memory [7-8, 10]. The simulator (called Cachesim) allows the student to observe the CPU and the cache activities during the execution of a read or a write memory operation, to evaluate system performance and to analyse the reference locality [5] and the distribution of memory accesses due to execution of the program. A student organises an exercise in three phases: configuration, simulation and analysis. In the first, students write a program in assembly language (like the Assembly Intel 8086) and then configure the system. For a cache memory (see Appendix A) the student chooses: i) the cache capacity, ii) the placement policy (direct, full or set associative mappings), iii) the cache block size, iv) the degree of set associative (in the case of set mapping), v) the main memory update policy (write-through or copy-back) and, finally, vi) the block replacement policy (FIFO, random or LRU). For I/O devices, the student specifies the I/O type (monitor, keyboard or general purpose), the synchronisation scheme (none or handshake), the interrupt scheme (none, vectored interrupt or non vectored interrupt) and the addresses of the relevant device registers. Finally, the student indicates the main memory size.

At the end of the configuration phase, students start the simulation on the execution of a memory operation or of a program. The simulator however illustrates, by drawings, i) the action sequence the computer needs to perform the required memory operation and ii) cache and main memory events. At the end of simulation, Cachesim produces certain statistical results about the cache and processor activities. Finally, in the analysis phase, students can see how their solution performs, analyse cache use and the memory location distribution accessed by the program and the program locality.

The program is in C language and may be executed by a Personal Computer with MS-DOS or Windows. The assembler (see Appendix B) and the disassembler are made using Lex and Yacc tools. In the following Sections we shall explain Cachesim by means of an example.

2 The configuration phase

The simulator starts with the command "CACHESIM": after the presentation screen (see Figure 1), the user can choose the cache memory structure, the main memory size, the kind of microprocessor (at present, only an Intel 8086-like microprocessor is available), the

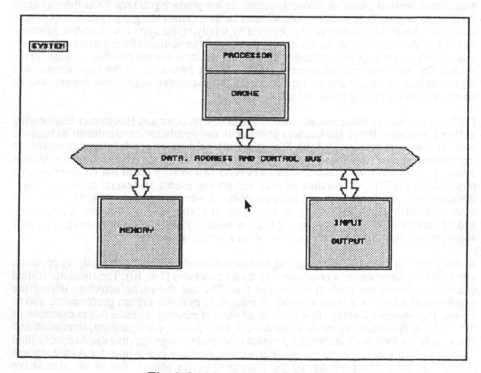

Fig. 1. Initial window of Cachesim.

parameters of simulated I/O devices and, finally, the source program. In Figure 2 we can see a number of choices made for our example: a 64-kbyte main memory and a 8-kbyte two-way set associative cache, a 16-byte block, Least Recently Used (LRU) as the replacement policy and copy-back as the main memory update policy.

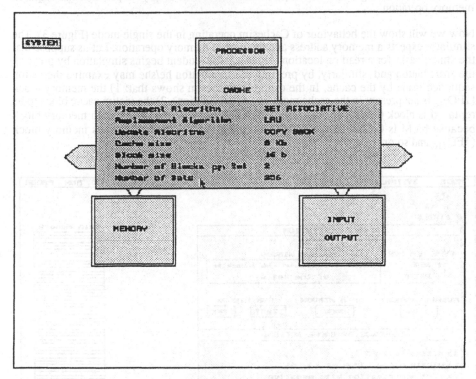

Fig. 2. Configuration of the cache memory.

Now, the student can go ahead with the simulation phase and Cachesim draws icons representing the main memory and the cache. The contents of the data field, the tag field, the valid bit and the modified bit (for copy-back caches) of any cache block can be examined by clicking on the cache the icon and then on icon of a particular cache block. The processor registers can be examined and changed by the "PROCESSOR_INFO" sub-menu.

3 The simulation and analysis phases

In simulation, Cachesim can work in one of the following three modes:

single: the student can ask for the execution of a memory operation by specifying the memory address and the type of operation.

trace: the student can execute a program step by step, a memory operation or an instruction at a time.

exe: the student can ask for the execution of a program.

3.1 The single mode

Cachesim executes a single memory operation and shows the cache and main memory events by means of drawings, and the sequence of actions necessary to perform the required memory operation.

Now we will show the behaviour of Cachesim operating in the single mode (Figure 3). The simulator expects a memory address and the type of memory operation. Let us suppose that the student asks for a read on location $(1FD4)_{16}$. The student begins simulation by pressing the *start* button and, similarly, by pressing the *step* button he/she may examine the action sequence made by the cache. In the example, cachesim shows that: 1) the memory block $(1FD)_{16}$ is not present in the cache memory (miss condition), 2) the victim cache block to be replaced is block 0 in set $(FD)_{16}$; 3) it is not necessary to update the main memory block because bit M is 0 (that is, the copy is not modified); 4) the cache loads memory block $(1FD)_{16}$ and so on.

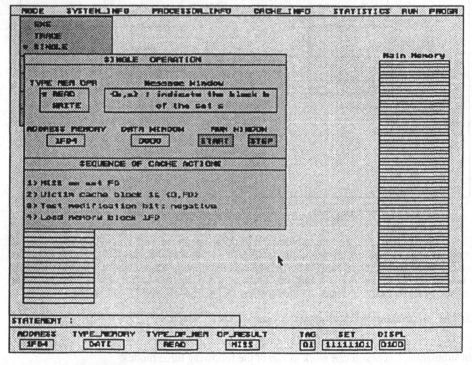

Fig. 3. Example of Cachesim operating in the single mode.

In the bottom of the picture, Cachesim summarises the operation information and shows how the cache uses the memory address. In our example, the address $(1FD4)_{16}$ is split into $(01)_2$ used as the tag field (that the cache compares with the tag field of both blocks of set $(FD)_{16}$); into $(11111101)_2$ as the set field (that the cache uses as the set address) and, finally into $(0100)_{16}$ as the word offset in the block. To understand the cache structure and how it operates, the student can open a window representing the logical scheme of the cache and the relevant use of the above address field.

3.2 The trace and exe mode

Both in the trace and the exe mode, Cachesim executes a program. If Cachesim operates in the trace mode, it executes one instruction or one memory operation at a time and shows the trace information.

In case of memory trace, it executes the program and, for each memory operation, shows: i) the memory address, ii) the cache access result (hit or miss) and iii) the tag field, the valid bit and the modified bit (in the copy-back mode) of the cache block involved in the operation. In the case of instruction trace, it provides: i) the next instruction, ii) the fetch address, iii) the actual memory address and the operation type, iv) the tag, the set and the displ fields of the address (Figure 4).

In any case, Cachesim also shows the cache and the main memory icons by highlighting the cache and memory blocks involved in the operation.

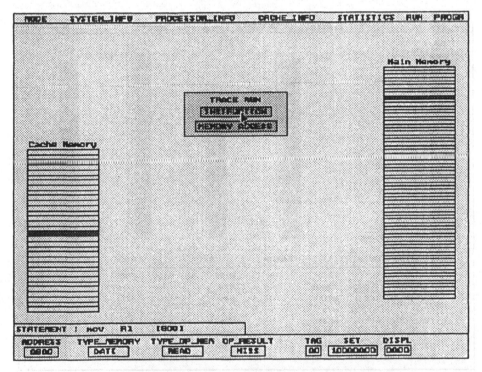

Fig. 4. Cachesim operating in a trace mode. Using the mouse, the student can choose between instruction trace and memory access trace.

At the end of the simulation, both in trace and exe mode, it proposes three recapitulating windows. The first one shows the following percentages (as a bar chart): i) the hit and miss conditions; ii) the hit and miss conditions occurred during fetch, data and stack operations; and iii) the read and write operations. The window also summarises the numbers both of block read and write operations performed in main memory. Figure 5 shows the above percentages belonging to the following sorting program.

```
PROG                                EXCHANGE PUSH R3
CODE     SECTION                             PUSH R4
BEGIN    MOV  R1,#100                        MOV  R3,VETT[R1]
         SUB  R1,#1                          MOV  R4,VETT[R2]
         MOV  R2,R1                          MOV  VETT[R1],R4
         SUB  R2,#1                          MOV  VETT[R2],R3
A        MOV  R3,VETT[R1]                    POP  R4
         CMP  R3,VETT[R2]                    POP  R3
         JNE  B                              RET
         CALL EXCHANGE           ENDC BEGIN
B        SUB  R2,#1
         JGE  A                  DATA SECTION
         SUB  R1,#1                   STACK 20
         JL   C                 ENDS
         MOV  R2,R1             DATA SECTION
         SUB  R2,#1             VETT DATA 100 (15 6 8 .... 5 78)
         JMP  A                 ENDS
C        STOP                   ENDP
```

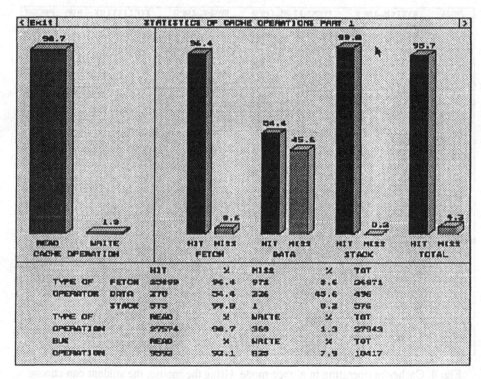

Fig. 5. Statistics of cache operations.

The second window shows 7 diagrams: memory accesses, misses, hits, reads, writes, data accesses and fetches versus cache blocks are charted. The zoom of a specific diagram is obtained by clicking on the relevant diagram icon.

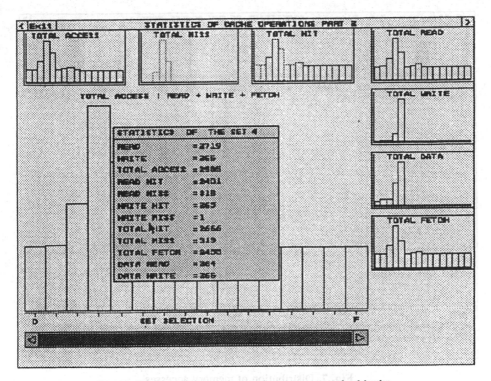

Fig. 6. Statistics of cache operations versus cache blocks.

In Figure 6, the student has zoomed on the total access diagram and has opened a window to find out the statistics of set number 4.

The third window summarises the main statistics by specifying total accesses and the accesses for fetch, data and stack operations. In any case, the accesses are also specified in terms of read operations, write operations, hit conditions and miss conditions. The number of memory blocks transferred into the cache, blocks write back in memory (only for copy-back caches) and bytes transferred on the bus on write operations (only for write-through caches) are also displayed.

Finally, Cachesim records the address sequence produced by execution of the program. The analysis of this sequence produces two windows. The first shows the frequency distribution (versus the memory address) of the addresses for write, data and fetch accesses. In figure 7, the student analyses the address distribution of the data accesses from $(420)_{16}$ until $(45E)_{16}$.

As from the address sequence:

$$a_0, a_1, a_2, ..., a_{i-1}, a_i, ..., a_{n-1}, a_n$$

Cachesim calculates the following sequence:

$$a_1 - a_0, a_2 - a_1, ..., a_i - a_{i-1}, ..., a_n - a_{n-1}$$

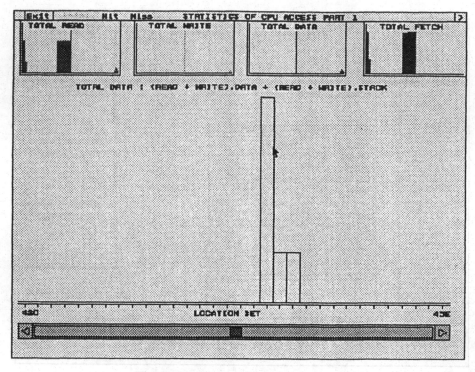

Fig. 7. Distribution of memory accesses.

The distribution of the number sequences produced by the data and fetch accesses are presented in a window (Figure 8). These distributions give the idea of the program locally both in the data and the code areas. In particular, Figure 8 shows that the locality in code area is more marked that in the data area.

4. Conclusions

Teaching tools based on the simulator are able to show and analyse the features and the problems of a complex system. As an example, we have shown a teaching tool which simulates a standard computer system.

The package was written in C programming language and it could be used on a Personal Computer with MS-DOS or Windows operating systems. The user interface is fully graphic. Now we are working to expand this environment by giving full details of the other computer modules and by also considering multiprocessor architecture [6-8, 10] and memory management units.

Acknowledgements

This work has been supported by the Italian Ministry for the University and Scientific and Technological Research. Many people contributed to the design of Cachesim; the author wishes to thank S. Cinquini for his help in the design phase, and M. Giusti, R. Storti and F.

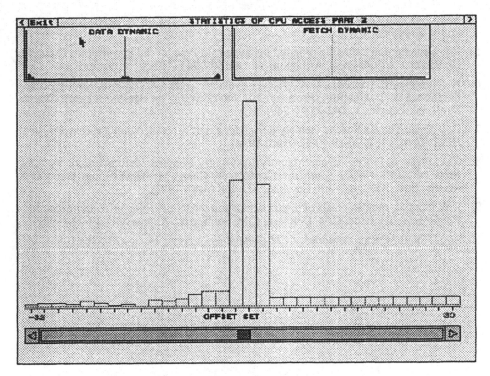

Fig. 8. Examination of the program locality in the data area.

Vernia for their contribution to the code phase. The author would also like to thank the students for their comments on the improvement of the man-machine interface and for their contribution to testing of the program.

References

1. S. Cinquini, C.A.Prete: An Interactive Software Environment to Help in the Teaching of Cache Memories, Proc. of Third biennial meeting on Microcomputers and their applications, Education and Application of Computer Technology, Community of Mediterranean Universities, M. De Blasi, E. Luque, E. Scerri (eds.), Spain, 295-306 (1990) .

2. S. Cinquini, C.A. Prete: Teaching in Computer Architecture based on simulation environments, *Proc. of First World Conference on Parallel Computing: In Engineering and Engineering Education*, UNESCO, Paris, 39-43 (1990).

3. P. Corsini, C.A. Prete: SYNCONET: A Tutor for the Synthesis of Combinational Networks via Karnaugh Maps and Prime Implicant Charts, *Proc. of Second biennial meeting on Microcomputers and their applications, Education and Application of Computer Technology*, Community of Mediterranean Universities, M. De Blasi, J. Donio, E. Luque, E. Scerri (eds.), Malta, 687-692 (1988).

4. M. De Blasi, F. Tangorra: A Prolog Simulator for the Teaching of Computer Architecture, *Proc. of Second biennial meeting on Microcomputers and their applications, Education and Application of Computer Technology*, Community of

Mediterranean Universities, M. De Blasi, J. Donio, E. Luque, E. Scerri (eds.), Malta, 263-278 (1988).

5. P.J. Denning: On modeling program behaviour. In Proc. of the Spring Joint Computer *Conference*. AFIPS Press, Arlington, Va., 40, 937-944 (1972).

6. A. Domenici, B. Lazzerini, C.A. Prete: A Synthetic Trace Generator for Multiprocessor Performance Evaluation, *Proc. of 3rd Inter. Symp. on Multiprocessor System*, Stralsund, G.D.R., 1, 242-253 (1989).

7. C.A .Prete: The RST cache memory design for a tightly coupled multiprocessor system, *IEEE Micro*, 11, 2, 16-19 40-52 (April 1991).

8. C.A. Prete: A Process Cache Memory for Tightly Coupled Multiprocessor Systems, *Proc. of 30-th Annual Southeast Conference*, Cherri M. Pancake and Douglas S. Reeves, Eds., Raleigh, North Carolina, 131-138 (April 1992).

9. J. W .Shmidt: Fundamentals of digital simulation modeling, *Proc. of Winter Simulation Conference*, T.I. Oren, C.M. Delfosse, C.M. Shub (eds.) Atlanta, GE, 13-21 (1981) .

10. A.J. Smith: Cache memories, *ACM Computing Surveys*, 14, 3, 473-530 (1982).

Appendix A: the memory cache

A cache memory is a high-speed buffer, placed between the processor and the main memory, that temporarily holds the data and the instructions which have been used most recently. Its success has been explained in relation to the property of the locality. Generally, programs spend most of their time repeatedly executing a few tight loops of code; read access to that code and to the relevant data is faster if the code and the data are held in cache memory. Write accesses are more complex, because the cache must update its copy of data and the one in the main memory. There are two main memory update policies: *write-through* and *copy-back*. In the first case, during a write operation the data are copied both in cache and in main memory. Therefore, the cache and main memory are always consistent. In the copy-back policy, the data are copied only in the cache, and the main memory is updated only when the cached copy that has been modified must be overwritten by another copy.

A cache memory is made up of a set of blocks (called *cache blocks* or *cache lines*), each of them able to store the copy of the contents of a *memory block* (i.e., a sequence of memory locations). A copy can be stored in a cache on the basis of a placement function (direct addressing, set associative and full associative). The structure, the management and the performance of the cache itself depend on this function. In the case of direct addressing, a specific memory block can be stored in only one cache block; in the case of set associative cache it can be stored in a cache block of only one set. Every set can contain 2, 4 or 8 blocks and the cache is defined as two-way, four-way and eight-way set associative, respectively. In the fully associative cache, a memory block can be placed anywhere in the cache. In the case of miss conditions, set and full associative caches chose a victim block to replace it. The most used replacement policies are: Least Recently Used (LRU), First In First Out (FIFO) and Random. In the miss condition for direct addressing ones, the cache does not have the problem of victim block selection because only one cache block can store the copy.

Appendix b: The features of the processor and the instruction set

The features of the processor simulated by CACHESIM are the following: the processor can operate on a 64-Kbyte main memory, each memory operation involves a 16-bit word, and the processor includes a program counter and a stack pointer (PC and SP), a flag register and four 16-bit general registers R1, R2, R3 and R4. The general registers are directly accessible, the flag register is used only by some "jump on condition" instructions and contains the number of flags needed to code the following conditions: less than 0; greater than 0 and equal to 0 (the overflow condition is not considered).

The instruction set is a simplified version of the Intel 8086 set. As far as the teaching goal of the project is concerns, the instruction set includes the minimum number of instructions that are needed to write any program. The addressing modes are: immediate, register, direct and index. In two-operand instructions, one of them is a general purpose register. The language includes a set of directives to: i) indicate the program entry point; and ii) declare the stack and data area. Table 1 summarises the instructions and their formats.

INSTRUCTIONS			
MOV *dst src*	ADD *dst src*	SUB *dst src*	MUL *src*
DIV *src*	CMP *dst src*	NOT *dst*	AND *dst src*
OR *dst src*	XOR *dst src*	PUSH *src*	POP *dst*
JMP *label*	JE *label*	JZ *label*	JNE *label*
JNZ *label*	JL *label*	JLE *label*	JG *label*
JGE *label*	CALL *label*	RET	IN *dst*
OUT *src*	NOP	STOP	

Tab. 1. The instruction set.

Suggested Scenarios of Software Maintenance Education

Frank W. Calliss and Debra Trantina Calliss

Department of Computer Science and Engineering
College of Engineering and Applied Sciences
Arizona State University
Box 875406
Tempe, AZ 85287–5406, U.S.A.

Abstract. To improve the quality of software maintenance work and to reduce the time taken to perform maintenance tasks, programmers need to be educated on how to maintain programs. Despite the complexity of software maintenance and the need for informed maintainers, there are few training programs or academic courses aimed at developing the skills that are required of maintenance programmers. In this paper we will look at four different scenarios for teaching software maintenance. These scenarios will be suitable for industrial training as well as university or college courses and are based on courses on software maintenance that the authors have given in industry and academia.

1 Introduction

The inclusive definition of software maintenance is that collection of activities that are performed on a program after it is installed at a customer's site or approved for general release. The maintenance process is complicated and prone to errors, yet this process is important as a large portion of many programs' lifetime will be spent in maintenance and a great deal of money will be spent on and resources dedicated to the maintenance of these programs. To improve the quality of software maintenance work and to reduce the time taken to perform maintenance tasks, programmers need to be educated on how to maintain programs. Despite the complexity of software maintenance and the need for informed maintainers, there are few training programs or academic courses aimed at developing the skills that are required of maintenance programmers.

With the recognition that we need to train people in maintenance comes a second problem; how do we educate people about software maintenance? Software maintenance is often ignored or belittled as a discipline and these prejudices are carried out in the information and educational support available on the subject. One problem that an instructor will encounter is a lack of choice in a adequate text. There are very few texts that address software maintenance specifically. An alternative to using a text book is to use a collection of papers from the literature. These papers introduce many key concepts as well as provide a description for particular tools or strategies. Additional support for planning a software maintenance course can be found from the Software Engineering Institute (SEI) which has a collection of curriculum modules that outline the material that should be covered when teaching some software engineering topics. Some of these curriculum modules apply to software maintenance, e.g., Wilde's curriculum module on understanding program dependencies [19], or Collofello's curriculum modules on walkthrough and inspections, or validation and verification [6]. Unfortunately, the SEI does not have a curriculum module on software maintenance, so the initial course outline must still be developed unaided by the instructor .

In this paper we will look at four different scenarios for teaching software maintenance. These scenarios will be suitable for industrial training as well as university or college courses and are based on courses on software maintenance that the authors have given in industry and academia. For each scenario, we will look at the material that needs to be covered and the type of exercises that can be given to support and supplement the material covered in the classroom.

2 The Layered Scenarios

It is not possible to define a single course in software maintenance as software maintenance education will have varying emphases, goals, durations and settings, e.g., a one day industrial training course, a two or three week section as part of a general software engineering course at a university, or in a one semester university course. Each course type will cover software maintenance in varying degrees of detail, and will require different course work to supplement the material presented. For the sake of generality, a four level scenario for software maintenance eduction is presented. Each level corresponds to a particular need for a software maintenance course. The material covered at each level will consist of the material in the previous level with some additions or refinements to the material, with level 1 being the lowest level course. The levels are defined below and then discussed in depth in the following sections.

Level 1 The first level corresponds to a one day industrial training course or a one to two week segment of a university course (5 - 6 hours). With this form of course students can only be introduced to the topic of software maintenance. However students leaving this kind of course must leave with an appreciation for the problems that confront people working in software maintenance. The students would be given simple exercises on trivial programs.

Level 2 This course typically would be either a two or three day industrial training course or a four to five week segment in a university course. The longer length provides for a more detailed introduction to software maintenance and allows for larger, more complex exercises with fairly trivial programs.

Level 3 At this level, a course would be a three week industrial training course, or at a University, either a 10 week segment in a semester course or a quarter course. A more detailed description of the maintenance process would be given and the students would be expected to perform maintenance tasks on a program consisting of 4000–10000 lines of code. This size of a program allows the students to work on software of a non-trivial length, but which is small enough to allow meaningful maintenance exercises.

Level 4 The last level is the more involved and would be a one semester course dedicated to software maintenance. An equivalent industrial training course would be extensive and extended. The workload for this course includes performing several different maintenance tasks on the non-trivial software.

3 Level 1 Scenario

The goal of a level 1 software maintenance class is to present to the students key aspects of software maintenance. Suggested participants in this course would be software managers and other technical staff members that would need an overview of the material. Students taking this form of the course should gain an appreciation for what software maintenance is, what problems confront programmers who are maintaining software and what some possible solutions to these problems are. A suggested source for this material is Schneidewind [16] who identifies some of the problems that beset software maintenance). The techniques of maintenance would be introduced in the course, but the course is not technical in nature.

3.1 Content

Below are the main topics that need to be covered in a level 1 course.

Software Maintenance Software maintenance needs to be introduced to students so that they appreciate that maintenance is an interesting and challenging area. Students, at universities or colleges need to know that when they go into industry they are likely to spend a large amount of their time on maintenance related tasks, and the people in industry need to know that what they are learning will be of value to them in their work.

Forms of Maintenance With software maintenance being defined as post delivery activities, it is common for people to equate maintenance with error detection and correction. It is important therefore, to get the students to broaden their view of software maintenance. A common breakdown of maintenance activities is to classify the maintenance work as being one of the following: corrective, adaptive, perfective and preventive.

Corrective maintenance is failure driven maintenance. This is the form of maintenance that students have most familiarity as it encompasses error detection and correction. However, this is not the only form of coding failure that can occur. It is very common for companies (or languages) to have a coding style; failure to adhere to this coding standard is also an error. Maintenance activities aimed at addressing this problem are also corrective maintenance.

Adaptive maintenance refers to the changes made to a program as a result of changes to the environment, e.g., a new operating system, or new hardware. Students need to understand that the environment in which a program operates will not remain static: new hardware will be added or used to replace old hardware, the operating system of the computer will be upgraded, or the language in which the program is written will be revised by a language standardization committee. Not all of these changes to the environment will be transparent to the program, e.g., languages changes may not be upwardly compatible, e.g., Fortran 90 is not upwardly compatible with Fortran 77, or changes to an operating system may result in some of the old commands being modified that can affect the program.

Students also need to be made aware that programs that get written are not "old news." Software represents an investment by both the company that selling the program and the company purchasing it. Both groups want the existing system to evolve to meet new market requirements and user needs. Perfective maintenance is the term used to denote this form of program evolution.

Preventive maintenance refers to the changes of a program to help extend the lifetime of the program by improving the quality of the code is preventive maintenance. This form of maintenance is different from the first three as it is not done as part of an explicit change request. It is can be done as a separate task or as part of another maintenance work. By introducing this form of maintenance, the students appreciate that there is more to software maintenance that making "noticeable" changes to a program. An analogy that has been useful in getting students to appreciate the need for this form of maintenance is having you car check regularly. The mechanic will make adjustments to the car, maybe replace some worn out item with an identical new item. All of this is done to extend the life of the car. With software, we call check the complexity of the code and data structures in the program, and reorganize the code if it is too complex. Sometimes it is necessary to rewrite completely a procedure or function because the old version was beyond fixing by merely restructuring.

The results of the Leintz and Swanson maintenance survey [13] should be presented to the students as it reveals a characteristic about the maintenance process that many students will find surprising. The only exposure to maintenance that many students will have had will have been debugging their own programs, so the discovery that this is not the major form of maintenance will give them a new perspective on the material.

Reverse Engineering Reverse engineering is the process of analyzing a program to identify the program's components and their interrelationships and possibly create a representation at a higher level of abstraction [5]. The value of reverse engineering to software maintenance should be emphasized. As an example reverse engineering strategy, student should be told about how a call graph can be used in software maintenance, as it show the architecture of a program, and it reveals the functional dependencies that exist in a program.

3.2 Exercises

The exercises in this type of course should be short so that they can either be done in one hour in an industrial training course, or be work that would be equivalent to a short homework assignment in a university course. Although the duration is short, it is important that this exercise emphasize the point that software maintenance is not an easy activity. The following are some example exercises.

Exercise 1 Seed an error into a small program and require that the students locate the error and fix it. This exercise emphasizes the detective skills that are required when working on a program that you did not write.

Exercise 2 For a small program with several subprograms, the students can recover the design or reverse engineer the call graph for the program. If the program has redundant routines in it, then one of the action items for the students would be to identify these routines. If this activity is first attempted without using reverse engineering techniques and then attempted using reverse engineering, the students will grasp the importance of reverse engineering in software maintenance.

4 Level 2 Scenario

As in the level 1 course, this is a short course that must introduce the area of software maintenance to the attendants. The extended length of this course allows for some new material to be introduced, and for some analysis of different software maintenance topics to be performed. Again this course would be suitable for non-maintenance management or technical staff that needed to have an understanding of maintenance activities.

4.1 Content

As the different scenarios are layered, the material from the level 1 course will be built upon in this level. The sections below correspond to new material that needs to be addressed.

Software Evolution The need for software to evolve and the problems associated with this evolution need to be presented to the students. Lehman's [12] first two laws on software evolution form a good base on which to teach the importance of software evolution. The first law is the *Law of Continuing Change* which states that a system needs to change in order to remain useful. The changes, that can be a reaction to some environment change or new requirement, or can be proactive where a vendor is anticipating the new needs of a customer, need to be appreciated by the students. Failure to change a program to meet the new needs of a customer can result in the loss of that customer and failure to change an existing system to meet new user needs before the customer request the service can result in the system being less competitive in the marketplace. The second law is the *Law of Increasing Complexity* which highlights the phenomenon that the structure of a program degrades as it evolves. This degradation is due to many factors if which the students need to be aware. Firstly, when revisions to a program are requested rarely do the customers place restrictions on the complexity of the code, hence the complexity of the software does not appear to be as important as implementing the required change on time as without errors. Secondly, the complexity of the code degrades over time because of sloppy programming practices by both programmers and project managers. The programmers should be more careful about the quality of the code that they produce, and the managers need to be more conscious of the effect that current coding practice has on the complexity of code. A consequence of the second law is that unless care is taken when maintaining a program, the structure of the code will continue to degrade until it becomes more cost effective to rewrite the program. The second law highlights how a program can be "maintained to death."

Reengineering Reengineering is the process of renovating a program by transforming the structure of the program and making the program conform to the current best practice in software engineering. One form of reengineering is restructuring. Restructuring can involve low level transformation as with the work based on low level control flow [20], or high level transformations that modify the architectural structure of a program [2]. A comparison of the values of reengineering and reverse engineering can be examined. In particular, students should be made to consider when is reverse engineering better as a maintenance activity than reengineering and what are the costs and advantages of reengineering.

4.2 Exercises

As with the level 1 course, the exercises should be small so that they can either be completed in 1 hour in an industrial training course or as a short homework. The exercises given for the level 1 course are also suitable for the level 2 course, but additional exercises should be given which require the students to analyze key aspects of software maintenance. Some example exercises are given below.

Exercise 1 The students should develop the criteria to be used in determining when to reengineer a program rather than to reverse engineer a program. This exercise can be given as a half hour exercise in an industrial training course either individually or in small groups, or as a one day homework assignment in a university course. The goal of the assignment is to stimulate the students into thinking about the relative merits of reverse engineering and reengineering. After this assignment has been completed, the instructor can lead a discussion on comparing reverse engineering and reengineering.

Exercise 2 Give the students a small program and require that a new function be required of the program. This exercise requires that the students become aware of the many skills that are required to enhance software: design the new feature, find the section of code that need to be modified to add the new feature, and regression testing.

5 Level 3 Scenario

This is a much more detailed view of software maintenance than can be obtained from the level 1 or level 2 courses. As a result, much more emphasis can be placed on the maintenance process. In this course, we are able to add discussion on the personnel involved in the maintenance process, and add sections to describe how software maintenance can actually be performed.

5.1 Content

Software Maintenance Myths There are many misconceptions about what software maintenance is, and the skills and resources needed to perform effectively software maintenance. Schwartz [15] discusses some of these misconceptions as eight myths about software maintenance. These myths range from views such as "maintenance cannot be anticipated and does not take up much time anyway" or "any programmer can maintain any program." Using this paper as a discussion piece, many important aspects of software maintenance can be addressed. For example, the need for skilled and motivated programmers, the need for control over the maintenance process and the need for suitable tool support for the maintenance process.

Maintenance Models In order to be able to control the way that we perform software maintenance, it is important to be able to model that process. Several models of the maintenance process have been proposed. These models fall into two families: process oriented, and organizational or business oriented. These two families of models provide different yet complimentary view of the maintenance process. By combining the two models, the students can see the order of events that need to be performed and the people involved at each phase of servicing a maintenance request. This enhances their ability to understand the maintenance process and how software maintenance is performed.

Process Oriented Models The process oriented model views the maintenance process in terms of the activities that are performed and the order that these activities are performed. Many form of process models have been published, e.g., Boehm [1], Chapin [4] and Yau and Collofello [21].

Organizational Oriented Models The organizational oriented model views the maintenance process in terms of the activities that are performed and the flow of information between the processes. There is no explicit ordering imposed with these models. Another important feature of these models is that they show the organizations or people involved at the various stages of the software maintenance process. Published versions of this form of model include [9, 14]. This form of maintenance model is important as it shows the channels of communication between the different organizations and people involved in the maintenance process.

Maintenance Personnel The important attributes and roles of the personnel involved in software maintenance needs to be explored, together with strategies on how they are to perform their work.

Maintenance Programmers Maintenance programmers are required to have skills that are not expected of development programmers. For example, a maintenance programmer has to be a detective when trying to locate the cause of a program error. Problem solving strategies need to be taught that assist programmers with this error detection. Kepner and Trogoe [11] present a systematic problem solving strategy that is well suited to locating the cause of errors. Code reading skills are essential for maintenance programmers. How programmers read and understand code has been the subject of much research. Weiser [18] introduces the concept of a slice, and gives empirical evidence to show that programmers use slices when debugging programs. Program plans are another program understanding idea. Soloway [17] has given much empirical evidence that programmers use plans when understanding programs. The concept of a programs plans need to be introduce to the students.

Maintenance Management The importance of good management is critical to the success of a maintenance project so the roles of the maintenance managers and tool support for managers need to be examined. As a project leader, the manager is responsible for ensuring that the maintenance work is done on time, within budget, and with as few errors as possible being introduced. This requires that a manager be able to monitor and control the work that is being performed. How software metrics can be used to monitor the work in progress should be examined [10]. Metrics can record the degradation in the complexity of a system, but the students need to be aware of the problems in trusting blindly the value of existing software metrics. The use of configuration management systems in controlling maintenance tasks also should to be examined.

5.2 Exercises

Because of the extended time, more detailed work assignments can be given with this form of class. Several different forms of projects have been proposed to assist the teaching of software maintenance. Two of this are briefly described below

Exercise 1 The Documented Ada Style Checker (DASC) is a 10,000 line Ada program that is used with the SEI's Education Materials CMU/SEI-89-EM1 [8]. This curriculum module consists of a discussion of the software and several maintenance exercises. One suggested organization of the class is to model an industrial maintenance environment where change requests are processed, approved, etc. by a change control board. The exercises can also be done on an individual or small group basis. The maintenance exercises consist of various changes of varying complexity to the documentation and code that reflect requests for porting the software, error correction, and capability enhancements. The students gain experience several different activities on a large, non-trivial program.

Exercise 2 A different form of a project was developed that had different students making modifications to the same source code [3]. The software in this project is 4,000 line Pascal program. This project emphasized the need for management of the maintenance process, and also showed the importance of using version control with the maintenance process. Several changes are made to the software. The class can be organized into teams or the work can be done individually.

6 Level 4 Scenario

At this level course, a business perspective of software maintenance added to the material from the previous levels. With the perspective, many of the aspects of maintenance that were first encountered in the level 1–3 scenarios will have to be reconsidered.

6.1 Content

Leman's first three laws address software evolution from the context of a organization. Although they are not widely accepted, they do serve as a good starting point to discuss how do businesses consider software maintenance work. The role of the project leader as a liaison with senior management needs to be introduced.

Software Evolution Lehman's [12] first two laws on software evolution describe characteristics that are widely believed about software evolution. Lehman's last three laws are not so widely accepted, but they serve to introduce software evolution in a business setting. The third law is the *Fundamental Law of Large Program Evolution*. which states that the changes that occur to a program reflect ongoing decisions rather than a spontaneous decision. This means that by recording histories of maintenance changes it should be possible to predict the nature of future enhancement to a program. The fourth and fifth laws are probably the most controversial of all the laws. These laws imply that the rate of change to a program or the productivity of the programmers is relatively constant during the life of a program. The reason for this stems from organizational inertia. To require a major improvement in productivity would require that an organization be prepared to change the structure of the organizational model of the maintenance process. This is a major overhaul of working practices and so is rarely ever done.

Maintenance Management Another important role of a project manager is to raise the profile of software maintenance into a favorable light with senior management. This is necessary in part to tackle some of the myths that Schwartz highlights. In order for maintenance to be seen favorably by senior management, it is important that maintenance projects be delivered on time and within budget. To do this a manager needs to be able to accurately estimate the man power and delivery time for a given maintenance task. The use of estimators such as COCOMO should be examined.

6.2 Exercises

The same exercises that are used for the level 3 course can be used here. With this course being of a longer duration, it is possible to have students make several modification to the code. This way the students get experience on how the documentation for a system can easily become out of date, and how it eventually becomes useless unless a continuous effort is made to keep the documentation current.

References

1. B.W. Boehm, "Software Engineering," *IEEE Transactions on Computers*, vol. C-25, no. 12, pp. 25–32, December 1976.
2. F.W. Calliss and B.J. Cornelius, "Two Module Factoring Techniques," *The Journal of Software Maintenance — Research and Practice*, vol. 1, no. 2, pp. 81–89, December 1989.
3. F.W. Calliss and D.L. Trantina, "A Controlled Software Maintenance Project," *Software Engineering Education* (SEI Conference), Springer-Verlag, Lecture Notes in Computer Science 536, pp. 25–32, October 1991.
4. N. Chapin, "The Job of Software Maintenance," in *Proceedings of the Conference on Software Maintenance - 1987*, IEEE Computer Society Press, pp. 4–12, 1987.
5. E.J. Chikofsky and J.H. Cross II, "Reverse Engineering and Design Recovery: A Taxonomy," *IEEE Software*, vol. 7, no. 1, pp. 13–17, January 1990.
6. J.S. Collofello, *The Software Technical Review Process*, SEI Curriculum Module SEI–CM–3–1.5, June 1988.
7. J.S. Collofello and S.N. Woodfield, "Evaluating the Effectiveness of Reliability-Assurance Techniques," *Journal of Systems and Software*, pp. 191–195, 1989.
8. C.B. Engle, G. Ford and T. Korson, *Software Maintenance Exercises for a Software Engineering Project Course*, SEI Curriculum Module CMU/SEI–89–EM1, February 1989.
9. S.A. Gamalel-Din and L.J. Osterweil, "New Perspectives on Software Maintenance Processes," in *Proceedings of the Conference on Software Maintenance - 1988*, IEEE Computer Society Press, pp. 14–22, 1988.
10. W. Harrison, K. Magel, R. Kluczny, and A. DeKock, "Applying Software Complexity Metrics to Program Maintenance," *Computer*, pp. 65–79, September 1982.
11. C.H. Kepner and B.B. Trogoe, *The New Rational Manager*, Princeton Research Press, New Jersey, 1981.
12. M.M. Lehman, "On Understanding Laws, Evolution, and Conservation in the Large-Program Life Cycle," *The Journal of Systems and Software*, vol. 1, pp. 213–221, 1980.

13. B.P. Lientz and E.B. Swanson, *Software Maintenance Management*, Addison-Wesley, Reading, Massachusetts, 1980.
14. R.S. Pressman, *Software Engineering: A Practitioners Approach*, McGraw-Hill, 1992.
15. B. Schwartz, "Eight Myths about Software Maintenance," *Datamation*, August 1982.
16. N.F. Schneidewind, "The State of Software Maintenance," *IEEE Transactions on Software Engineering*, vol. SE-13, no. 3, pp. 303–310, March 1987.
17. E.Soloway and K.Ehrlich, "Empirical Studies of Programming Knowledge," *IEEE Transactions on Software Engineering*, vol. SE-10, no. 5, pp. 595–609, March 1984.
18. M. Weiser, "Programmers use Slices When Debugging," *Communications of the ACM*, vol. 25, no. 7, pp. 446–452, July 1982.
19. N. Wilde, *Understanding Program Dependencies*, SEI Curriculum Module SEI-CM-26, August 1990.
20. M.H. Williams and H.L. Ossher, "Conversion of Unstructured Flow Diagrams to Structured Form," *The Computer Journal*, vol. 21, no. 2, pp. 161–167, May 1978.
21. S.S. Yau and J.S. Collofello, "Some Stability Measures for Software Maintenance," *IEEE Transactions on Software Engineering*, vol. SE-6, no. 6, pp. 545–552, November 1980.

Session 8:
Tutorial Presentation

Software Design Methods for Concurrent
and Real-Time Systems

Hassan Gomaa
George Mason University
Fairfax, Virginia

Abstract. This tutorial surveys the state of the art in software design methods for concurrent and real-time systems. The important concepts of concurrent tasking, fundamental to the design of this class of system, information hiding, fundamental to the design of modifiable and reusable components, finite state machines, for addressing the behavioral aspects of a system, and object-oriented concepts, for the systematic adaptation of components, are introduced. Several design methods for concurrent and real-time systems are presented and compared. The design of distributed applications will also be addressed. The tutorial is illustrated by means of several examples. The tutorial will also discuss the industrial and academic courses that can be given based on this material.

Session 9:
Experiences in Academic Education

Building on Experience: An Undergraduate Course with Two Year-Long Projects
Lorraine Johnston and Philip Dart, The University of Melbourne, Parkville, Victoria, Australia

Software Engineering Beginning in the First Computer Science Course
Jane C. Prey, James P. Cohoon, and Greg Fife, University of Virginia, Charlottesville, Virginia

Non-Functional Requirements in the Design of Software
Alfs T. Berztiss, University of Pittsburgh, Pittsburgh, Pennsylvania

Building on Experience: An Undergraduate Course with Two Year-Long Projects

Lorraine Johnston and Philip Dart

The University of Melbourne, Parkville, Victoria, Australia, 3052.

Abstract. The University of Melbourne recently introduced a new four year engineering degree course in software engineering. This degree course includes two project subjects, each running for the duration of our academic year. Educating students through project work invariably results in tradeoffs. Exposing students to two team projects in successive years builds on the students' experience and provides a much greater opportunity to address the relevant issues than is possible with a single project. This paper examines some of the problems we have experienced in running software engineering projects and how we address these problems in our course by including a project component with two distinct parts. We also examine the overheads and other issues that arise from student projects, especially where external clients are involved. The paper is based on our experience of over one hundred different student projects with external clients over several years.

1 Introduction

Solving software problems, like solving mathematical problems, is a practical skill that is acquired by imitation and practice. The teacher might therefore discuss the rules explicitly in small parts of a lecture or two, but the student learns them only as they are applied in solving interesting problems. The teacher should unobtrusively help the student not too much and not too little, ... — Jon Bentley [3]

In 1990, the University of Melbourne introduced a new four year course specifically to educate software engineers. The first group of students will finish this course in 1993, graduating with a degree in engineering. The software engineering course shares both structure and subjects with its sibling computer engineering and electrical engineering degree courses. Software engineering students are required to undertake team software projects in both their third and fourth years. Both of these projects run throughout the entire academic year.

Like many other tertiary institutions, this university has for many years been offering subjects in software engineering as part of a three year computer science course. One of these subjects involved a full year team project. The design of our current software engineering project subjects is based on our experience of over one hundred different student team projects with external clients* over a

---

* We have a fixed set of criteria for selecting projects and have had projects from private industry, government departments, other universities, and staff of this university.

period of five years.

Good teachers know that the 'right amount' of information needs to be offered at the 'right time' to optimise learning. They also know that the lessons learned by 'doing' are far more likely to result in long-term benefit than those learned by 'listening'. While the running of project subjects is resource intensive (and, at times, stressful!) we believe it to be crucial that students experience for themselves as much as possible of the software engineering process. While many of our students have a high degree of technical competence, many have little experience—or indeed knowledge—of communicating and managing. While we wish to present the students with situations where they confront many of the issues in engineering quality software, it is possible to overload them so that the only outcome is a negative one. Therefore our course is designed so that the project work in the third year is relatively structured. The project work in the fourth year offers experiences different from, but building on, those gained in the third year.

This paper examines the problems we have experienced in running software engineering projects and how we address these problems in our course by including a project component with two distinct parts. The overheads and other issues arising from these projects are examined, with particular focus on the involvement of external clients. Section 2 gives some background information on our software engineering course to give context to the project subjects. Section 3 examines student software engineering projects from the perspective of the different participants, specifically: student, teacher, client, and coordinator. We present some of the problems that have arisen, discuss some of the solutions we have tried, and describe the current state of evolution of our projects.

2 A Software Engineering Degree Course

A number of Australian institutions have introduced courses specifically to educate software engineers [2, 4, 10, 12]. At the University of Melbourne, the School of Electrical Engineering and Computer Science offers engineering students the choice of specialising in electrical, computer or software engineering. All three streams share a common first year, after which they begin to diverge. It is possible for students to delay choosing their specialty until the start of third year. All engineering students must undertake a minimum of twelve weeks of approved (relevant) vacation work experience as part of their degree requirements.

By the time software engineering students reach third year, they should have a solid grounding in computer science, be competent programmers and users of system utilities, and have a basic understanding of software engineering. For the third and fourth years of their course, these students study specialist software engineering subjects for approximately half of their load, most of the remainder being selected from a range of computer science and electrical engineering subjects. A typical student would select subjects such as *Data Management, Networks and Communications, Computer Design, Graphics, Operating Systems* and *Digital Electronics and Computer Systems*. It is also recommended that they study a management-oriented subject in their third year, for example, *Human Resource Management*, and the non-technical subject *Professional Issues in Computing* in their fourth year.

The specialist software engineering subjects include project subjects, one in each of the final two years, and a range of lecture subjects. The formal lectures cover topics such as project management, quality assurance and standards, as well as more technical topics such as formal specification, reliability modelling and performance analysis. Projects are effectively laboratory subjects in which students have the opportunity to experience some of the lecture material for themselves.

The coordinators of our project subjects need to do a large amount of preparation before the start of each academic year. In particular, they need to generate a set of new projects with external clients. These issues are discussed further in Sections 3.3 and 3.4.

2.1 Third Year Project

The third year project is done by students from both the software engineering course and the computer science course. Through the first project, students can gain first-hand knowledge of the software engineering process and its associated techniques and tools. Most also become familiar with the problems that arise from poor project management and team dynamics. The projects themselves at this level are reminiscent of those described by Knoke [6] as being *medium sized projects*.

For this subject, the students divide themselves into teams of four. Each team must then submit a list of preferences from the project list, and will subsequently be allocated a project. Then each team either has a project manager allocated to it from the pool of fourth year software engineering students (see Section 2.2) or selects one of its members as project manager. Each team is also allocated a staff member as supervisor. (See Figure 1).

All participants in the project are given a copy of a project manual [1], based on IEEE software engineering standards [8] and developed specifically for this project subject. The manual defines the roles and responsibilities of the participants, outlines a framework for the software process that students are expected to follow, and describes the products that students are expected to produce in each phase of the process.

The purpose of the manual is to give some structure to the subject, as well as to emphasise the importance of project management and documentation. In general we expect the students to use a variant of the waterfall model as outlined in the manual. Any departure from this must be approved by the project coordinator. The manual also gives a list of milestones, each with the set of required project deliverables and a default submission deadline. Teams are permitted to negotiate new deadlines with their supervisors.

In following the prescribed process model, we expect the students to undertake appropriate reviews of their material before submission, get the client to

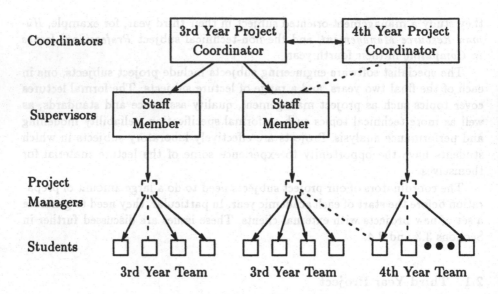

Fig. 1. Project Management Structure

sign off relevant documents, and ensure that deficiencies detected in project documents are corrected. Their submissions are assessed by the staff for feedback, but no actual marks are allocated until the end of the academic year. We believe that formal assessment and teaching should not be carried out at the same time, and we encourage the students to improve on their earlier submissions. A side effect of requiring the students to use a version control system is that we have the benefit of being able to use the logging facilities to check that documents from earlier phases have been kept up-to-date. It also enables us to check on the individual contributions of team members.

While a product that 'works' is usually seen by students and clients as the end-point of the project, our emphasis is on the process, not the product. The project assessment is designed to add weight to this, and is discussed further in Section 3.2.

2.2 Fourth Year Project

The fourth year project is specifically aimed at the final year software engineering students. Through this second, larger project, the students can make use of their experience to take control of the process used in their project, address the problems they experienced on the first project, and focus on the issues of management, communication and quality. While our first class of fourth year students has only seven members, we are using a *large project team model* similar to that described by Shaw and Tomayko [13]. The whole class works as a team on a project for an external client. In time we expect the class size will grow to about twenty, but if numbers increase much beyond that it may become necessary to consider splitting the class.

For this subject, the class selects one of its members as project manager. In contrast to the third year project, the subject coordinator allocates a project to the team without their input. This project is much more challenging than those offered to the third year students, even considering the greater number of team members. The coordinator also acts as supervisor for the team. (See Figure 1).

While the fourth year students can draw on the guidance of the third year project manual, they are expected to tailor their process to fit their project. They refer directly to the relevant standards to do this and are expected to apply a much higher standard of quality assurance. External reviewers are made available to the fourth year team to assist with formal reviews.

As well as playing a role as team member on the fourth year project, each fourth year software engineering student acts as project manager for a third year project. Clearly these students have no real authority over their team. We therefore emphasise to them the importance of good project documentation when resolving problems that arise in project management. The fourth year students are told that, while they can and should provide advice to their third year teams, they should *not* get involved doing work for the team such as design or coding. Assessment of this project management role contributes to the student's final mark in the fourth year project subject. (See Section 3.2).

3 Projects — A Range of Perspectives

3.1 The Student's Perspective

> *Quality has much in common with sex. Everybody is for it. (Under certain conditions of course.) Everyone feels they understand it. (Even though they wouldn't want to explain it.) Everyone thinks execution is only a matter of following natural inclinations. (After all, we do get along somehow.)* Crosby [9, quoted on page 549])

This succinctly describes the reaction of most of our students to the issue of quality. They are not sufficiently mature and have inadequate 'life experience' to have much understanding of how quality may be perceived by clients and users, or indeed by maintainers. Without this understanding, it is difficult for them to comprehend the role the software process has to play in achieving quality.

The calibre of our incoming students is very high. They have high tertiary entry scores and many are the top students in their high schools. While this means that they have the intellectual skills to be able to cope with the more theoretical issues involved, it does not usually give any indication of the level of their social maturity. Many of our students are highly competent programmers but despite our best efforts in lectures, these students are initially unconvinced of the need for software engineering. They still believe that their current methods of programming can be scaled up to produce large systems.

In the computing subjects done prior to the software engineering subjects, projects are designed to reinforce a concept being presented in lectures. Students work to produce programs that correctly calculate the required result for a relatively limited set of test data. By fixing the formatting and adding comments 'as instructed', they can achieve a high mark. In this way, from early in the course, students are constantly being reinforced in their 'it works!' perception of good practice. Further, for an extended period of time from the start of their course, students *program* solutions to relatively small problems. The better the programmer, the larger the problem required before issues of scalability arise. In doing their team projects, the students therefore perceive that the overheads of team dynamics and project management invariably outweigh the benefits.

One solution would be to offer students projects of such a size that scalability becomes an issue and that the extra costs of team work are justified. However, experience has shown us that constraints on the students' time and on our departmental resources prevent us from giving large enough projects. Therefore we have had to design our project courses with the aim of convincing students to do what would be necessary for any large software project.

The Department of Computer Science is aware of this problem and is attempting to tackle it in two ways. First, we are lessening the emphasis on *coding* and strengthening *problem solving* as the central theme of the introductory computer science subjects. Second, a new subject *Software Development* is being introduced at the second year level where there will be a much greater emphasis on the techniques and tools used for the development of software.

Our observations on the difficulties of dealing with students at this age and level of experience are borne out by Richardson [11], who compared graduate and undergraduate software engineering courses. He found that the immaturity of the undergraduates added additional layers of complication, and identified three main factors: (a) the lack of computer science experience, (b) the lack of academic maturity to be able to cope with ambiguity, and conflicts between reality and theory, and (c) the lack of interpersonal skills. On the other hand, software engineers must be able to communicate with clients to determine requirements, and must also be able to set aside their ego to work for the good of the whole. To quote Richardson, *This is a very difficult concept to explain to anyone who has insufficient social maturity to reach beyond the* me.

Shaw and Tomayko [13] observed that *Software engineering ... has long stretches of tedium associated with it*. We found some years ago that students tended to become bored with the year-long projects they were doing. At this time, we dealt only with projects thought up by one of the staff members from our department. Some students were so bored they dropped the subject completely. Our answer to this was to advertise for projects from people requiring a software solution to a real problem. Since offering such projects, we have noticed a marked improvement in the enthusiasm of the students. They feel someone really cares about the outcome, and that they are getting experience that will put them in a good employment position after leaving the education system. We have observed also that using different clients and projects gives an opportunity for students to learn from the struggles of other teams. The resulting cross-fertilisation of ideas means that their experience is essentially broadened.

In contrast to the situation in many other institutions (for example see [5, 6, 7]), each of our project subjects spans two semesters. We have also run a one-semester project subject, of a similar nature to our third year project subject, for the last five years. The classes involved have all consisted of graduates in a field other than computing. Our finding was that one semester is insufficient time to learn enough of the development process. When a premium is placed on time, the students focus on the end-product and neglect critical parts of the process such as design and testing. This subject is being discontinued.

At the third year level, we protect our students from some of the issues involved in large-scale software development, but allow them to take control of their projects and learn from their mistakes. It is our contention that they learn far more by experiencing what can go wrong than by being tightly constrained to a specific development method. We expect to see them come to grips with the basic *process* of software development, and also experience for themselves the importance of good management on even a relatively small project. Informal feedback from our students over the last few years supports this. To quote one student, *This is an awful lot of work, but I've learnt far more from it than from anything else.*

We expect the fourth year students to build on their third year experience. They work on a more challenging project in a larger team, and are required to be more formal in their methodology and techniques. Our belief is that learning to manage projects and to communicate with other people is critical to becoming a successful software engineer. This is reflected in our requirement that the fourth year students act as a project manager for one of the third year teams.

We feel that combining the experience of the two projects in this way gives our students the greatest possible opportunity to learn about software engineering.

3.2 The Teacher's Perspective

Our approach is that the students in a team should *own* their project and manage their own work, to allow them to learn from their mistakes. As teachers in a university environment, we see ourselves as educators, not trainers. It is our concern that students learn about the software development process and do not just develop one software system under close instruction.

At the commencement of the project students are told of our expectation that by participating in the subject, they will learn something of:

- the need for good communication skills;
- the difficulty of eliciting the client's requirements;
- the advantage of careful project design;
- the benefits of being resourceful and using initiative;
- the volume of work remaining after coding;
- the effort required to produce suitable documentation; and
- *the necessity for consistent project management.*

Failure to understand this latter factor sufficiently early seems to be the main cause of difficulties for the students.

Project management is very much a part of the learning experience, and a student project manager has the responsibility to see that work is shared equitably amongst the team members. It is the role of the teacher to check that unequal contributions are being handled properly. Where there are perceived or reported problems the supervisor will step in to try to sort out the situation. Often, all that is necessary is for the team to sit down with their supervisor and talk sensibly about their problem. If they are confronted with each other's point of view, more often than not they are able to resolve the issues. Such situations also allow the opportunity to discuss topics such as team goals and ego-less programming. The biggest problem for the teacher is to identify those situations where conflict is arising.

Team project supervision is time-consuming and can often be quite stressful. Knoke [6] indicated that he had found 'team teaching' was more difficult than having only the one person involved. We agree with this, but in our situation we have no alternative to using several staff members. For example, in 1992 we had 21 separate teams doing different projects. With numbers of this size it is necessary to appoint a staff member to coordinate the work, with other staff each taking responsibility for a subset of the teams.

Assessment At the end of the year, it is necessary to assess both the product and the process. Our approach has been to set the assessment criteria to reinforce what we are trying to teach. For example, while a team may end up with a product that performs well and is easy to use, they may have been able to 'design in retrospect'. That is, the project may be small enough for the team to be able to code the system successfully (at least in some sense) and then produce design documents to match. Therefore they would be penalised for not carrying out the process as they were requested.

Assessment is designed to reflect our emphasis. At the third year level, the process is allocated 75% and the product 25%. For the fourth year students, the figures are 55% and 20% respectively, with the remaining 25% of their mark allocated for the way they manage their third year team. At both the third and fourth year levels, students are reminded that they are to learn about the software engineering *process*, and that achieving a product which satisfies the client is therefore not the only criterion for success in the subject. Similarly, the fourth year students are reminded that a third year project which succeeds *despite* their poor project management will earn them a low mark.

Feedback from the client is important in determining whether the student teams have met their specifications, but there are many facets of the project about which the client has no information. Their judgment of success is only one view of the situation, and others need to be considered. Knoke's assessment [6] was based strongly on feedback from clients, but he has commented on the difficulty of giving grades which do not match a client's perception. We have experienced the same situation, and have altered the assessment criteria accordingly, making sure we inform the clients of these criteria in the initial interviews. Our concern is that students learn about the process—a 'successful' final product is an added bonus. Even so, our observation has been that insisting students are careful about the process has positive results in terms of the final product.

3.3 The Client's Perspective

We regard the interaction with a real client on a real project to be an important part of our course. Having a client who really wants the end-product means that students are sensitised to the difficulties of assessing accurately the needs of the user. This is an experience they would probably not get in any other way.

Finding suitable student software engineering projects is a time-consuming and delicate task. We ask clients (or their proxy) to give up many hours of their time to participate in requirements elicitation and reviews, to read documents produced by students, to attend demonstrations and to provide feedback. External clients are motivated to offer projects for a variety of reasons ranging from the altruistic ("I'm performing a community service") to the selfish ("I'll get something for nothing"). Clients also see their involvement with students as an opportunity to have input into the education system, to make students and staff aware of their organisation, and to 'try out' potential recruits.

Whether the client's motivation is selfish or altruistic, it is necessary to emphasise to the client that the major aim of these projects is the education of the students. Clients must be told that we cannot guarantee that a usable product will result from a project, even though experience tells us that clients get a satisfactory or better result in most cases. Many clients are not conversant with the vagaries of the academic year and need to be reminded that the students' time is not dedicated to their project. On the other hand, after observing that the team working on their project fails to communicate well, produces rough documents and misses deadlines, some clients become concerned that 'their' team is not up to standard and may fail the subject. It must be made clear to clients that *they* are not responsible for the students' progress. The client may be unaware that what they are seeing is the 'normal' behaviour of students attempting to practise software engineering for the first time. This problem can be magnified where a second-time client had a better-than-average team working on their first project. These clients are usually pleasantly surprised when the students come up with a usable final product after all.

Another issue of concern to clients, that of intellectual property, is discussed in Section 3.4.

It is apparent that we need to deal carefully with these concerns and help clients understand what we expect students to gain from the experience of a team project.

3.4 The Coordinator's Perspective

Project subjects tend to be resource intensive. We have found it necessary to tailor our offerings to students with the very real limits of our resources in mind.

These resources include both hardware and software, supporting documentation, and teaching and technical staff. Responsibility for 'making ends meet' lies with the subject coordinators.

The coordinators also have responsibility for finding projects. In particular, they need to advertise and contact past clients for new projects, discuss projects with potential clients and examine the projects closely to determine their viability. Whether a project is viable will depend on issues such as resource availability (for example, platforms, software packages and languages), client availability (will the client or suitable proxy be available for reasonable access by project team members?) and scale (is it reasonable to expect a team of students with other commitments to complete this project within the permitted timescale?).

Our policy with respect to student teams being assigned to projects differs in third and fourth year. In third year, we believe the students have so many lessons to learn in such a short time that helping them feel comfortable with the environment of the project optimises the outcome. We therefore allow them to form their own teams, and offer them a choice of projects. In the fourth year, the entire class works together on one much larger project, which must be chosen with greater care. For this project, the coordinator is seen more in the light of a (benevolent) dictator, and no choice is offered—a situation much more in keeping with life outside of academia.

When accepting projects from clients, it is necessary to ensure that the platforms on which the students are able to work are compatible with the needs of client. Even when platforms are compatible, we cannot assume that the supporting software is installed on our university computers. Occasionally students use the client's facilities, but usually the client's machines are too much in demand for them to be happy about a team of students adding an extra load.

While a finished piece of software may not need a large amount of memory or a fast machine, development of that software requires sufficient computational power for the process not to be frustrating. Similarly software development tools either make or break the process. The availability of an adequate supply of manuals and other documentation is another factor to be considered as it is often difficult to obtain extra copies of the required documentation. Before accepting projects it has been necessary to consider whether particular projects can be supported with respect to these factors.

In the past, clients have agreed to provide particular software packages for the students, but this has more often than not caused problems. The client often supplies only one copy, or limited documentation—in short, they do not look at licensing issues in the same light as we do. This causes problems, not only of a productivity nature, but raises issues of equity across the whole class. We have reached the situation where we have chosen a limited number of tools and platforms, and we will no longer consider projects that require other facilities. Specifically, we prefer projects on UNIX systems, and have invested in industrial strength CASE tools to support projects in the UNIX environment. However, we must also accept projects on Macintoshes and MS-DOS machines, where we have the requisite software, in order to have a sufficient supply of clients and projects.

The human resources involved in running project subjects are critical to the success of the work. Both teaching and technical support is required. One lecturer cannot sensibly keep in touch with more than a few projects, so where there are many teams, there needs to be an adequate number of staff allocated to supervising them. Where project teams are being supervised by different staff members, the coordinator needs to take on the task of ensuring that assessment is done consistently.

Technical support is needed for setting up accounts, installing any required software (new or upgraded) and ensuring that the system is set up correctly. Invariably problems occur during the year which the students do not have the experience or, perhaps, the permission to fix. Some of the problems are obscure and students find it helpful to discuss them with an experienced technical person.

Legal Issues One of the important issues needing further work is that of intellectual property (IP) rights. In our experience, a view frequently held by prospective clients is they should own the product of their project. Similarly, a view frequently held by students is that there is potential for the team to make money if their product is good enough. These differing views can come into conflict long before anything of value is produced as a result of a student project.

We have had discussions with our university solicitors over a period of years, with the intention of producing a standard 'contract', so that we could define where the IP rights lie at the start of any project. The law with respect to IP is still rather grey, and more time is required to produce a suitable document.

The major difficulty lies in the number of variables to consider. The people with potential IP rights are the client, the students, their supervisor and, sometimes, the subject coordinator. The client may be from a university department, or from an external organisation. They may have already had some form of program, but the program may need replacing or upgrading. In other cases, the client knows they want software to do a particular job, but the only contribution they make is in identifying the requirements — perhaps no trivial task in itself. The projects undertaken are so varied that the relevant IP issues need to be thought through carefully right from the start.

4 Conclusions

Our experience with running project subjects has strengthened our belief that team projects are a critical part of any course in software engineering. However, our experience has also been that presenting students with a single attempt at a team project forces us to compromise on important issues. Our current course structure provides for a first project that emphasises the software process while constraining its form. This is followed by a second, larger project that allows more flexibility in the software process but demands a greater degree of project management. By providing two successive project subjects, we enable students to build on their experience and fill many of the gaps that are left in their knowledge of the software process after their first attempt.

Our four year engineering degree course in software engineering is very new and will not stabilise for some years. In the meantime, we are carefully monitoring the progress of our students through our standard assessment procedures, as well as through day-to-day contact, staff-student meetings, and student and client surveys. We will have evidence for the success of our approach when our students have demonstrated a thorough understanding of the software process, and have applied it successfully to produce a quality product for their client.

Acknowledgements

We are grateful for the assistance of Liz Sonenberg, Zoltan Somogyi and Margaret Hassall in reading and discussing this paper.

References

1. Tim Arnold, Lorraine Johnston, and Philip Dart. Software engineering project manual. Department of Computer Science, The University of Melbourne, 1993.
2. Paul A. Bailes, Eric J. Salzman, and Andreas Rosel. A proposal for a Bachelor's degree program in software engineering. *Proceedings of the Third SEI Conference on Software Engineering Education, LNCS 376*, pages 90–108, 1989.
3. Jon Bentley. Teaching the tricks of the trade. *Proceedings of the Second SEI Conference on Software Engineering Education, LNCS 327*, pages 1–8, 1988.
4. Douglas D. Grant and Ross Smith. Undergraduate software engineering – an innovative degree at Swinburne. *The Australian Computer Journal*, pages 106–113, 1991.
5. Manmahesh Kantipudi, Ken W. Collier, James S. Collofello, and Scott Medeiros. Software engineering course projects: Failures and recommendations. *Proceedings of the Sixth SEI Conference on Software Engineering Education, LNCS 640*, pages 324–338, 1992.
6. Peter J. Knoke. Medium size project model: Variations on a theme. *Proceedings of the Fifth SEI Conference on Software Engineering Education, LNCS 536*, pages 5–24, 1991.
7. William M. Lively and Mark Lease. Undergraduate software engineering laboratory at Texas A&M University. *Proceedings of the Sixth SEI Conference on Software Engineering Education, LNCS 640*, pages 315–323, 1992.
8. Institute of Electrical and Electronic Engineers. *IEEE Software Engineering Standards Collection*. 1991.
9. R. S. Pressman. *Software Engineering: A Practitioner's Approach, 3rd edition*. McGraw-Hill Inc., 1992.
10. K. Reed and T. S. Dillon. An undergraduate software engineering major embedded in a computer systems engineering degree. *Proceedings of the Fourth SEI Conference on Software Engineering Education, LNCS 423*, pages 49–66, 1990.
11. William E. Richardson. Undergraduate software engineering education. *Proceedings of the Second SEI Conference on Software Engineering Education, LNCS 327*, pages 121–144, 1988.

12. Terence P. Rout. Quality, culture and education in software engineering. *The Australian Computer Journal*, pages 86–91, 1991.
13. Mary Shaw and James E. Tomayko. Models for undergraduate project courses in software engineering. *Proceedings of the Fifth SEI Conference on Software Engineering Education, LNCS 536*, pages 33–71, 1991.

Software Engineering
Beginning in
the First Computer Science Course[1]

Jane C. Prey   James P. Cohoon   Greg Fife

Department of Computer Science
School of Engineering and Applied Sciences
University of Virginia
Charlottesville, VA 22903

Abstract. The demand for computing and computing power is increasing at a rapid pace. With this demand, the ability to develop, enhance and maintain software is a top priority. Educating students to do competent work in software development, enhancement and maintenance has become a complex problem. Software engineering concepts are typically not introduced in beginning computer science courses. Students do not see software engineering until the third or fourth year of the curriculum. We do not believe students can acquire an adequate software engineering foundation with the present approach. We believe an emphasis on software engineering should begin in the very first course and continue throughout the curriculum. We are redesigning our curriculum to reflect this. The first course of the new curriculum is complete. This article focuses on two of the laboratory activities we have developed which deal with specific software engineering concepts.

Introduction

Computer science has changed rapidly in its brief history. What we once considered necessary subject areas, skill and knowledge levels are now inadequate. Today's computer professional must have an extensive set of skills and detailed knowledge in many different technical areas. Similarly, the individual entering the research community needs a thorough grounding in many diverse areas.

The Department of Computer Science at the University of Virginia is part of the School of Engineering and Applied Sciences. From this vantage point, we have embraced a strong commitment to the engineering aspects of computer science. We seek to educate computer scientists with a clear understanding of, an appreciation for, and skills that support the engineering and comprehension of large software systems, reengineering of existing systems, use of modern tools and environments, and application of innovative techniques such as software reuse.

Problem Statement

The demand for computing and computing power keeps on increasing. "Indeed, computing and increasingly powerful computers are the driving force behind the movement of society into the information age, affecting transportation, finance, health care, and most other aspects of modern life; computing technology and related services account for about 5% of the gross national product". [1] With the demand for software becoming a larger and more significant portion of the GNP, the ability to develop, enhance and maintain the software is a top priority.

Educating students to do competent work in software development, enhancement and maintenance has become a complex problem. We are not presently providing students with the skills, knowledge or experience to successfully handle the new challenges found in today's software.

Traditionally, computer science curriculum emphasizes:

- the construction of relatively small programs, at most a few hundred lines;
- the use of a programming language that is rarely used outside of undergraduate courses;
- development of programs "afresh" for each assignment or course;
- a development environment lacking modern tools;

[1] The work detailed in this paper was supported in part by NSF grant CS-NSF-5239-92.

- programming in isolation or in small groups at best;
- the belief that if a program "works" it is acceptable;
- informal development approach rather than one which is rigorous and exercises analytic skills.

Software engineering concepts are not introduced in beginning computer science courses. Students do not see software engineering until the third or fourth year of the curriculum. Students take courses in algorithms or syntax and semantics of a particular programming language as prerequisites, but these courses are not true software engineering. Software engineering is left to one course which must squeeze both its theory and practice into one semester, and this theory and practice is not reinforced by use in subsequent courses.

Why Change?

We do not believe that students can acquire an adequate software engineering foundation with the present curriculum approach. "The problem is a serious mismatch between what is taught, how it is taught, and the emphasis it receives on one hand, and what the consumers of the education actually need on the other." [2]

Comparing the content of the curriculum with the situation in the real world, we see a considerable contrast. Practicing computer scientists and software engineers deal with the antithesis of what we teach:

- software systems that are often thousands or even millions of source lines long;
- tasks that involve modifying such systems rather than developing them;
- existing systems that might be very old but remain important and have to be maintained;
- tool-rich working environments;
- development efforts that are undertaken by large teams;
- the realism of cost/performance trade-offs in business contexts;
- system development according to mandated processes and standards;
- expenditure of considerable effort on tasks other than source-code development.

We believe there must be a shift of emphasis in the computer science curriculum to meet these needs. Our new curriculum is driven by the desire to provide the education needed for competent computer and software engineering professionals. These changes necessitate a complete revision of the content, approach, and resources used in the undergraduate program.

We believe that an emphasis on software engineering must begin in the very first course and continue throughout the entire curriculum in order to provide the foundation necessary.

Approach

The Computer Science Department at the University of Virginia has undertaken a shift of emphasis in the undergraduate computer science curriculum to meet the needs outlined above.

This approach emphasizes:

- a philosophy of engineering incorporated into all of the core courses;
- an emphasis on software engineering beginning in the very first course and continuing throughout the curriculum;
- a high degree of mathematical rigor especially in discrete mathematics included in the form of (a) new mathematics courses and (b) increased use of mathematics in other courses;
- a strong prerequisite structure which emphasizes the interdependence of the material;
- hands-on artifacts included to the extent possible in assignments and projects;
- inter-personal and engineering skills developed through laboratory and other projects;
- emphasis on use of knowledge and skills as they are acquired.

What Is The Impact Of These Changes?

The incorporation of these ideas into our teaching program has lead to a need for an entirely new undergraduate curriculum - courses designed to be more mathematically rigorous, more practice-oriented, more software engineering concepts and practice, more closely related to the real-world environment. This has necessitated a number of substantial changes to our program, specifically:

- extensive revision of many existing courses. All of the core courses containing elements of programming, data structures, machine representation, etc. will undergo extensive revision.

- development of several new course, especially in discrete mathematics and computation theory.

- the replacement of the programming language used for teaching purposes. C++ was selected as the new programming language and although not ideal, it has the benefits of supporting object-oriented programming and increasing industrial acceptance.

- a belief in the importance of reuse of courseware. We intend to make our artifacts available to other universities that choose to adopt elements of our curriculum.

- the development of the "closed laboratory" facility to support closed-laboratory exercises. The facility is being expanded to include devices such as motorized vehicles and other elements that simulate realistic applications.

What We Want To Share In This Paper

We offered the first course of our new curriculum (Introduction to Computer Science - 1CS) for the first time in Fall, 1992 and again in Spring, 1993. This first course has been enthusiastically accepted by our students.

What follows are some of our experiences and ideas about including software engineering concepts and activities in a closed laboratory setting as part of an introductory computer science course.

The course content and laboratory activities were developed under the guidance of Dr. James P. Cohoon. The laboratory activities were written by Dr. Cohoon, Messrs. Scott Briercheck, Dan Werbel, and Greg Fife.

How Can Software Engineering Happen In 1CS

What makes our first course (especially the laboratory component) of the curriculum revision different from other introductory Computer Science courses is our commitment to software engineering starting in the introductory courses. We have designed laboratory activities which deal with specific software engineering concepts and practices.

There are many aspects to software engineering. Techniques and procedures for developing, maintaining and improving software products are not easily learned nor easily adapted to one's existing working approach. Many of these techniques and procedures can only be learned and understood by repeated expose and progressively more in-depth work.

Students should be made aware early on that "real" software products can be hundreds of thousands or even millions of lines long. They should have some exposure to what "real" software is - how it happened, what makes it good (or bad), why it's important to have standards, how programmers and users interact with it, etc. We believe students can have meaningful software engineering experiences in introductory Computer Science courses.

There are many software engineering techniques and procedures students need to be exposed to and have experience with before they can develop a true sense of the discipline. To begin building this framework, we have included one laboratory activity which has students doing a code walkthrough, and another laboratory activity which has the students work with a large software system.

Both of these laboratory activities are discussed in more detail below. The exact text for each can be found in the appendix. Also included in the discussion below are some comments by students from evaluations of each laboratory activity. Although the comments are anecdotal, they give a sense of the attitude the students have for the laboratory experience and for the course.

Code walkthrough

Code walkthrough is a process described in every software engineering text. This technical review of some aspect of the software system can occur at any time during the development process. The focus of a code walkthrough is to review the material to date. "During the walkthrough the reviewee 'walks through' the material while the reviewers look for errors, request clarifications, and explore problem areas in the material under review." [3]

A simple text editor (miniroff) was written to demonstrate a code walkthrough. The idea of a code walkthrough was first introduced in lecture. Its concept and rationale are described in general terms. In the following laboratory sections, the TAs review the purpose of a code walkthrough, this time in relation to miniroff. The students also saw an overview of the function and organization of miniroff.

Groups of 2-4 students were formed and assigned a particular section of the program. Two weeks later, the groups were to make a presentation to the entire laboratory section on their portion of the code. A set of general guidelines on what information should be presented was included with the laboratory activity handout.

On the day of the presentations, the students are given a set of questions to answer - one question for each function (or section) of the code. These questions could all be answered if the student listens to the presentation and discussion. The TAs also have a list of questions (for reference) to help direct the discussion following each presentation.

The students believed this was a good experience. Their comments repeatedly stated working with their group was extremely helpful in understanding the code and that understanding and learning happened more quickly and easily. They did ask for more guidance with respect to the actual presentation and made several good suggestions which we will incorporate next semester.

When students were asked if they found working in groups useful in understand the code, they responded:

"Yes, it definitely helped because even if you get the basic idea of what the function is trying to do, someone else might pick something up that makes it that much clearer to you."

"Yes, because the more you talk about the code the easier it is to understand it."

"Yes! The items that I don't understand immediately are given other viewpoints, such that the code is considered in more than one way, it will be easier to understand the programmers's purpose."

Large software systems

Once our students were exposed to the idea of a code walkthrough, we wanted them to have an opportunity to examine a large piece of software. Students do not have a realistic idea of just what large software system are. They can use them, but they have no concept how difficult it is to track through large amounts of code. They need to experience just how complicated and tricky working within large software systems can be.

We used a large software system called Fractint written by Messrs. Bert Tyler, Tim Wegner, Mark Peterson and Pieter Branderhorst. Fractint is freeware and the copyright is retained by the Stone Soup Group. Fractint calculates fractals and displays the results graphically. At 60,000 lines, Fractint is only about one-tenth as large as a typical inventory control system, but it is large enough to demonstrate some of the issues of software complexity.

Before the students came to lab, they were asked to respond to questions about their ideas on large software systems. The questions raised important issues about large software systems. For example, students were asked to respond to statements such as:

The most important attribute of a program is correctness. As long as a program runs properly, nothing else really matters.

As long as a program is properly commented, there is no need to create any other documentation concerning its[sic] design and internal organization.

In the lab, student groups of 2-3 first played with the software and executed its various options. They then picked one of three problems which forced them into the code.

They were not expected to be able to solve the problem. In fact, the objective was for the students to realize how complex large software systems are and how difficult it is to work within these systems even with other people helping.

Once the students seemed frustrated enough, the TAs lead them in a discussion on what factors made the problem(s) difficult and what might help make the problem(s) more solvable. The TAs were given a set of questions (for reference) which could help to get the students involved in the discussion and notes identifying important points of information.

When the students were asked to make a general comment on this laboratory activity, they responded:

"It was nice to do something that could help us realize situations in the 'real world'."

"Good intro to large program management."

"Made a point."

"Very helpful in understanding importance of good programming organization before the actual code is written. Also, the importance of communication."

What's Next?

We are in the development phase of the second course of the new curriculum - Software Development Methods under the direction of Dr. John C. Knight. It will be offered for the first time in Fall, 1993. It will continue with an emphasis on software engineering concepts and ideas.

We also plan to offer a third/fourth year course which will focus in much more depth on software engineering. This course will begin development in the Summer, 1994 and will be offered in Spring, 1995.

Summary & Conclusions

We have recognized the need for software engineering to become an integral part of a professional computer scientist's skill and knowledge. One course in software engineering taken late in one's academic career will not provide the needed foundation and experience. With the development of the closed laboratory activities and the emphasis of software engineering throughout our new curriculum, we believe we are providing students with the necessary software engineering education to build, enhance and maintain quality software products for the multitude of modern computer applications.

The response and support of our students tells us we are on the right track.

Appendix

Bibliography

1. Communications of the ACM, v35, n11, November, 1992, p. 32.

2. Knight, John C., "International Perspectives in Software Engineering," The Rocky Mountain Institute of Software Engineering, Boulder, CO, Q1, 1993.

3. Fairley, Richard E., Software Engineering Concepts, McGraw-Hill Book Company, 1985, p. 186.

Curriculum Committee Members

Dr. Wm A. Wulf   Dr. James P. Cohoon

Dr. John Knight   Dr. Worthy N. Martin

Dr. Randy Pausch   Dr. Jane C. Prey

Mr. Greg Fife   Mr. Rob Deline*

Ms. Sally McKee*

*Student representatives

CS 186 Laboratory IX — Preparation
Miniroff Code Walk-through

Description

For an upcoming lab you will be doing something a little different. It is called a code walk-through. A code walk-through for our lab implies that you will read the provided source code to gain an understanding of what the code does. When you are done with your reading and preparations, you should be able to intelligently discuss what a section of the code does with the rest of the lab members.

The program you will be analyzing is called `miniroff`. It is a simple document preparation program. Your lab manual contains a listing of `miniroff.cpp`. A sample input for `miniroff` and the resulting output are also provided. The sample `miniroff` input is actually a `miniroff` User's Guide. The name of the file is `miniroff.in`.

`miniroff` reads from standard input. The suggested form of execution is below. The file `miniroff.in` is the input file with text and `miniroff` commands. The output is directed to the file `miniroff.out`. That file can then be viewed or printed as you see fit.

```
miniroff < miniroff.in > miniroff.out
```

Come to the code walk-through lab fully prepared to explain your functions to the class. Be ready to run through your functions line by line, and be ready to answer the following:

- What jobs does the function perform?

- What input and output parameters does it use and why?

- Why there are global variables (if any) used in your function?

- How does your function fit into the program as a whole?

In addition, you will be asked one or two questions about the workings of the function which the causal observer might not catch simply by reading the `miniroff` comments.

As you read the `miniroff` source listing, you might want to pay special attention to the following:

- Lines 20-46 contain constants that are used by the various `miniroff` functions.

- Line 49 contains a `typedef` to give a new name to an array of characters. `miniroff` will use this name for the type of its input and output buffers.

- Lines 55-78 contain global variables. These variables are defined outside the scope of any specific function, and they can be accessed by any function in `miniroff.cpp`. (Uncontrolled use of global variables is, in general, a *Very Bad Thing*. When you get to classes and objects later in the course, you will see a much better approach to program design).

- Lines 79-184 contain *function prototypes* for each `miniroff` function. A function prototype is a declaration for a function—it indicates the return type of a function, the number of parameters that the function takes, and the types of the parameters. Because of these prototypes, `miniroff` functions can be called in lines of the program that appear before the actual function definition.

- Lines 185-827 contain definitions for the various functions that perform the text input, text rearrangement, state variable maintenance, buffer manipulation, and text display.

No bugs or defects have been deliberately placed in `miniroff`. However, should you find any, be sure to discuss them next week.

Function overviews

The first several functions are concerned with input manipulation.

- *readline ()* reads one line of text into the input buffer. It tests if the first character is a period, and it passes the input buffer to *readtext ()* or *directive ()* as needed.

- *readtext ()* passes a line of normal text character-by-character into the output buffer. Multiple spaces between words are discarded here.

The next several functions manipulate the output buffer

- *bufferchar ()* is called by *readtext ()* to store characters in the output buffer. If the output buffer fills up, indicating that we are ready to write one complete line out output, *bufferchar ()* calls *flush_buffer ()*.

- *flush_buffer ()* passes the line down to *format_line ()* for the actual formatting, and then it resets the output buffer to start collecting the next output line.

- *start_paragraph ()* and *set_parms ()* are called by the functions that handle directives. They make changes to the output buffer as needed to execute directives.

The next several functions format the output buffer and produce the output to standard output.

- *format_line ()* inserts spaces in between words in the output buffer and prints a line of output.
- *new_line ()* starts a new line of output.

The last group of functions process the *miniroff* directives.

- *directive ()* is called from *readline ()* to interpret and execute a directive. *directive ()* examines the next two characters after the period (elements 1 and 2 of the array), and it calls the appropriate function to execute the directive.

- A number of *miniroff* directives adjust global *miniroff* values. For example, *.lm* sets or changes the left margin. The *dir_adjust ()* function calculates the new value needed for directives such as these.

- After *dir_adjust ()* calculates a new value and *directive ()* stores the new value in a global variable, the *adjust_globals ()* function will be used to update other global values based upon the change just made.

- *dir_br ()*, *dir_sp ()*, and *dir_pp ()* handle the three directives that cause explicit breaks between output lines.

- *read_integer ()* interprets the number which follows a "value adjust" directive.

- *check_end ()* insures that the user has not put extra garbage characters at the end of a legal *miniroff* directive. If such characters are found, *check_end ()* prints a warning.

- *abend ()* prints an error message and aborts *miniroff*.

Code Walkthrough Questions

main ()

Q: Explain how the while loop terminates.

A: Once the last line of the input stream has been read, readline will return a 0 (false) rather than a true.

readline()

Q: What would happen if a pre-increment were used rather than a post-increment in line 242?

A: Note that chars_seen is initialized to 0 in line 220. If the variable is incremented and then referenced, then the first character will go in position 1, the 2nd character will go in 2, and so on. The first character in the array will be garbage, and a full line will extend past then end of the array.

readtext()

Q: There is only a single = sign on line 288, not a ==. Is this an error, and if not, why not?

A: Not an error. The assignment in the while loop has a value equal to the value assigned into the variable. When we reach the end of the buffer, a 0 is assigned into char_read, the value of the loop expression is false, and the loop stops.

buffer_char()

Q: What is the reason for the assignment on line 326?

A: The output buffer will most likely contain a partial last word when we reach the line limit. We do not want to print these characters when we flush the buffer. The word_pos variable gives us the boundary of the last complete word, which is also the position where we want to stop formatting the output buffer.

flush_buffer()

Q: Under what conditions would we execute lines 361 and 362?

A: If flush_buffer is called as a result of a .pp, .sp, or .br directive, the number of chars_buffered will not yet have reached the line_limit. This will cause a partial output line to be flushed. Note that flush_buffer is called by buffer_char if and only if chars_buffered is equal to the line_limit (line 39), and that call to flush_buffer will always decrease chars_buffered. Thus, if chars_buffered is less than the line limit, the call must have come as a result of a directive.

start_paragraph()

Q: If we adjust the line_limit explicitly on line 401, why do we also keep a first_line flag?

A: In lines 351-356, in flush_buffer, we use the first_line flag to decide whether or not to add a paragraph indentation to the "left margin" of the current output line.

set_parms()

Q: What is the difference between the line_limit variable and the line_width variable?

A: The line_limit variable is the number of characters that can be stored in the output buffer for the specific output line now being printed. The line_width variable is the number of characters left after the left and right margins are subtracted from the physical page width. The two will be different if a paragraph indentation creates an extra amount left margin for a specific line.

directiv()

Q: How would the behavior of the program change if we removed lines 449-451?

A: It wouldn't. If either of the first two characters is 0, then none of the if statements in lines 455-477 will be true, and we will print the same error message at line 480.

dir_adjust()

Q: Does the call to flush_buffer (line 505) belong in dir_adjust?

A: No, it doesn't. Since the intention of this function is merely to calculate a value based upon a command, the actual processing of the command and use of the value belongs elsewhere. This confusion of the purpose of dir_adust is an example of poor software design.

adjust_globals()

Q: What's wrong with line 544?

A: The message "Underflow" isn't particularly descriptive. The user of the program would have a much easier time if he were told that his margins were wider than his page.

dir_br(), dir_sp(), dir_pp()

Q: The call to check_end in line 567 only contains a single parameter, but the the definition of check_end on line 678 contains two parameters. What's going on?

A: The function prototype on line 171 provides a default value for the 2nd parameter.

read_integer()

Q: What would happen if we removed line 626?

A: If no + or - is present in the input buffer, leading will contain random garbage. If this random garbage happens to be a + or a -, then the program will act incorrectly. Tracking down this particular error could be painful.

check_end()

Q: What would happen if we removed line 690?

A: The loop would continue after an illegal character had been detected. No error message would be printed, and the program would process the illegal line.

format_line()

Q: All the other functions in MINIROFF that accept `charbuffer` parameters use a 0 in the array to mark the end of the buffer. `format_line` uses a 2nd parameter, `nchars`, to indicate where the buffer actually ends. Why the change?

A: There may be a few letters at the end of the output buffer that form a partial word. We do not want to include these in the current output line because we do not want to break a word across lines, so we want `format_line` to ignore them.

new_line()

Q: This is a 1 line function. Why bother?

A: If we change the way that we start a new line in the output stream, then we could make that change here, in 1 place, rather than in all the places that call `new_line`. In particular, if we wanted to count the number of lines printed and start a new page at some point, this would be the place to maintain the counter variable.

abend()

Q: The call to `exit` on line 826 stops the program after it sees the first error. Is this necessary?

A: For some types of errors, like the imminent overflow of a buffer, if we do not stop the program immediately, we need to take some other action to prevent random writes to memory at the end of the array. For other types of errors, like syntax errors, it would be easy to ignore the line with the error and continue processing. A better design for MINIROFF would be to continue processing to give the user a list of errors rather than just the first error in the input.

CS 186 Laboratory IX — Post Laboratory Exercises

Please perform the following activities. You are allowed to talk with others, but your work must be your own. They are due at the start of next week's laboratory.

Exercises

(1) *MINIROFF*'s most obvious functional deficiency is a lack of control over vertical spacing. There are no top or bottom margins, and there is no way to specify that text is to be "double-spaced."

Suppose that the following five directives were to be added to *MINIROFF*:

- *.tm* - set or adjust the top margin (default number of lines is six);

- *.bm* - set or adjust the bottom margin (default number of lines is six);

- *.pl* - set or adjust the page length (default number of lines per page is sixty-six);

- *.ls* - set or adjust the line spacing (default number of line spacing is one for single-spacing);

- *.bp* - break page. skip to the top of the next page.

Briefly describe the changes that you would make to *MINIROFF* to implement these directives. Identify the functions you would change, and identify any new variables or functions that you would add. Where possible, be specific about the line number where your changes would be made.

Assume that the document is being printed out on a continuous sheet of paper, with perforations that separate pages occurring every "so many" lines. "so many" is set by the *.pl* directive, and this value is 66 for most printers. For an example of this type of printer, see the Stacks or the Epson printers in Olsson 018.

CS 186 Laboratory XI
Large Software Systems

Reboot your computer before the start of this lab. Make sure that you use a Revision B boot disk - the Revision A disk will not leave you with enough memory to complete this lab.

You will not need to copy any files to your floppy disk to complete this lab.

Objective

To date, the largest program we have worked with is only 800 lines long. A real software system can easily contain tens of thousands, hundreds of thousand, or millions of lines of code. In this lab, we will examine a program of moderate size and consider some of the practical issues involved in dealing with the design, implementation, and maintenance of a large software system.

The program we will examine is called fractint. It is a program that calculates and draws fractals on IBM PC graphics hardware. At 60,000 lines, fractint is only about a tenth as big as a typical inventory control system, but it is large enough to demonstrate some of the issues of software complexity.

1. Playing With Fractals

Before we examine the source code to *fractint*, we will want to see what the program does and how it runs.

- Type *g:* and *cd g:\fractint* to go to the directory that contains the *fractint* program and files.

- Type *fractint* to start the program,

- You should now see a credits screen. Note the number of programmers that worked on the *fractint* program, and then hit enter to go to the main program

- You should now be looking at the main menu. Note that the maroon highlight bar is on *Select Video Mode*. If the bar is not on that option, move it with the arrow keys. Hit enter.

- You should now be looking at the *Select Video Mode* menu. Hit the down arrow key to put the maroon highlight on *F4 IBM 16-Color VGA* and hit enter.

- The program will now draw a Mandelbrot set in 16-color graphics. The program will beep when it completes the calculation. Hit the *Esc* key to go back to the main menu.

- On the main menu, move the maroon highlight bar to the *Select Fractal Type* (under *New Image*) and hit enter. On the *Fractal Type* menu, move the maroon highlight bar from *Mandel* to *Plasma* and hit enter.

- You should now see an options menu for the *Plasma Fractal*. Hit enter. The program will generate a pseudo-random plasma fractal in 16 colors.

- When the image completes, hit *Esc* to go back to the main menu. Go to the *Select Video Mode* option and hit enter.

- On the video mode menu, hit the up-arrow key to move the maroon highlight bar to *F3 IBM 256-Color VGA/MCGA* and hit enter. *fractint* will generate a pseudorandom Plasma Fractal in 256 colors. At first, this fractal will look like it only contains 3 colors - red, green, and blue. However, if you look closely, you will note that it contains colors that form a gradual shading between the three primaries.

- Hit the + key. What is happening? You can control the speed of this change with the number keys. When you are done, hit *Esc* a couple times, and type *y* when you see the *Exit fractint?* message.

2. Building `fractint`

Now that we have seen *fractint* run, we will compile the 60,000 lines of *fractint* source. These lines of code are divided into a number of separate source files - a single source file with 60,000 lines would be unmanageable. These source files are *held together* with a *Project File* called `fractint.prj`. Basically, `fractint.prj` is a list of all the source files that must be compiled in order to build `fractint.exe`.

Your floppy disk is to small and to slow to compile *fractint*, so we will use the hard disk.

- Change to the `c:\fractint` directory on your hard disk and clean up any files from the previous lab section with `DEL *.*`. If this directory does not exist, create it with the `mkdir` command.

- Copy the source files and the project file from the file server: `copy g:\classdir\cs186\fractsrc\*.*`.

- Type `tc` to enter Turbo C++. Turbo C++ will automatically open the `fractint.prj` project file and show you the list of source files that it needs to compile. Select the `Make` option from the `Compile` menu to start your build.

- Notice that the compiler is going through *fractint* file-by-file. A separate `.obj` file is created for each `.c` file that is compiled. The last step you will see is the linker, that will combine all the `.obj` files into a single `fractint.exe`.

- Quit Turbo C++ and type the command `hc /a`. This command is needed by *fractint* to build in the help system.

- Demonstrate your working `fractint.exe` to your TA.✔

3. Working with the `fractint` Source

Now, we'll take a closer look at the *fractint* source. Your current line number in a source file can be found in the lower left corner of the Turbo C++ edit window.

- Form groups of 3 or 4.

- Choose one of the following problems:

  — Suppose that one of the author's names was misspelled on the credits screen. Where in the *fractint* source would you correct the error? Function `main()` starts at line 235 of `fractint.c`.✔

  — Find the statements that move the maroon highlight box to the left when you hit the left arrow key. You might want to start with function `get_fracttype()` at line 762 of `prompts.c`. You might also need to consult the source fle `reados.c`.✔

  — Find the global variable `fudge`, which is defined in `fractint.c`. Determine the purpose of this variable. You might get some useful information from the DOS command `grep fudge *.c *.h`. This command will search all source files for the string `fudge`. To find `fudge` within a file, you might try the Turbo C++ search facility available from the `Search` menu. ✔

- When you are done with the *fractint* source, clean out all the files on the hard disk with `del *.*`

4. Lab Discussion: Large Software Systems

Now that we've had a chance to work with a large program, the teaching assistants will lead a discussion on our activities. In this discussion, you might want to consider any problems you had answering the *fractint* questions, and you might try to suggest what might have been done differently in *fractint* to make your job easier. If you can think of any documentation that might have helped you, or if you can think of any tools that could have made your job easier, identify them in the discussion. Also, you might consider your answers to the pre-lab survey in the light of your *fractint* experience.

5. Taking *fractint* Home

All the files you need to run *fractint* are in *frain17.zip*. This *.zip* file can be obtained by ftp from the */pub/msdos/graphics* directory of *oak.oakland.edu*.

If you need help in retrieving or unpacking this file, see the instructions in Lab 6. These instructions will work from ACC microcomputers as well as from Olsson 001.

CS 186 Laboratory XI — Pre Laboratory Exercises

For each of the statements which follow, indicate whether you strongly agree, agree, disagree, or strongly disagree. You will not be asked to hand in this survey, but you should be ready to discuss your answers in next week's lab.

(1) The most important attribute of a program is correctness. As long as a program runs properly, nothing else really matters.

       Strongly Agree   Agree   Disagree   Strongly Disagree

(2) Software maintenance (correcting bugs and adding new features) must be considered when a program is designed and written.

       Strongly Agree   Agree   Disagree   Strongly Disagree

(3) A professional programmer's single most important skill is his or her ability to communicate and work effectively in groups. His or her ability to write code is less important.

       Strongly Agree   Agree   Disagree   Strongly Disagree

(4) It is unnecessary and unrealistic to expect a CS 186 student to work in a group if he or she is capable of doing the entire lab on his or her own.

       Strongly Agree   Agree   Disagree   Strongly Disagree

(5) The only difference between a 100 line program and a 60,000 line program is that a 60,000 line program takes 600 times longer to write. If a single programmer can complete a 100 line program in 2 hours, then he or she can complete a 60,000 line program in 1200 hours, or 30 working weeks.

       Strongly Agree   Agree   Disagree   Strongly Disagree

(6) Preliminary and detailed designs are a waste of my time, because the actual program is the only important part of a CS 186 assignment.

       Strongly Agree   Agree   Disagree   Strongly Disagree

(7) As long as a program is properly commented, there is no need to create any other documentation concerning it's design and internal organization.

       Strongly Agree   Agree   Disagree   Strongly Disagree

(8) It is vital that a program's instructions be broken up into functions of manageable size.

       Strongly Agree   Agree   Disagree   Strongly Disagree

CS 186 Laboratory XI — Post Laboratory Exercise

Please perform the following activity. Hand in a written copy at the start of Laboratory XII. You are encouraged to talk with others, but your work must be your own.

Exercise

Review your answers to the pre-lab. Has your exposure to the *fractint* source or the lab discussion changed any of your answers? If so, pick one of the pre-lab questions, and in two or three paragraphs explain the issue and the reason for your change. If you have not changed your opinion on any of these issues, pick one of the pre-lab questions, and in two or three paragraphs explain your position.

Non-Functional Requirements
in the Design of Software

Alfs T. Berztiss

Department of Computer Science, University of Pittsburgh
Pittsburgh, PA 15260, USA (alpha@cs.pitt.edu)

and

SYSLAB, University of Stockholm, Sweden

Abstract. We argue for greater emphasis on design in software engineering courses, and for design under consideration of non-functional requirements. In particular we show that it is sometimes quite easy to determine early whether a design satisfies performance and reliability requirements. This is done by means of examples we have used in our courses. Performance and reliability analyses, which acquire particular importance with embedded real-time systems, require familiarity with probability and queueing theory. We recommend a special course on these topics.

1 Introduction

It has been rightly noted that the transformation of a craft into a professional engineering discipline is characterized by the infusion of relevant scientific theory [1]. It should be further noted that a major shift of emphasis occurs when theoretical foundations become established – theoretical foundations allow a design to be evaluated without actual construction. Our main purpose is to point out that much of software engineering has acquired sound theoretical foundations. This implies that in software engineering education more emphasis can be put on system design rather than system implementation. For example, because theoretical foundations allow a design to be evaluated without actual construction, a design can legitimately be the end product of a project course. This is the practice in other areas of engineering – mechanical engineering students design machinery; they rarely build machinery.

In software engineering projects, however, we continue to insist that students produce code. The time constraints that this practice imposes have several negative consequences. First, alternative designs are hardly ever explored. Yet the presentation of alternative designs is standard practice in traditional engineering (see, e.g., [2]). Second, the single design that is developed is rarely adequately polished before implementation begins. Third, the requirements statement given to students typically relates to functionality alone, with no mention of non-functional requirements. We shall concentrate on specification of non-functional requirements, and indicate how some non-functional requirements can be validated at the design stage.

We do not wish to imply that code is unimportant; only the laborious translation of design into code has limited didactic value. Software engineering students must be exposed to modern code validation practices such as Cleanroom [3], but this can be achieved by making available code that has already been written, similarly to what is suggested in [4]. Also, students should be exposed to iterative determination of user requirements based on a prototype, but the initial prototype can be supplied to them. We fully agree that in practice requirements gathering, design, prototype construction, prototype iteration, and final implementation have to be closely intertwined [5, 6], particularly under concurrent engineering [7, 8]. However, in software engineering education we can and should isolate components of the software process, and study these components on their own. Specifically, in teaching design, it helps to assume that the requirements from which students are to work will not change during the design phase. As a final note, we do require coding in one of our own undergraduate software engineering courses. A team of students implements a software system from a design that has been developed by another group in another course. But our purpose is not just coding practice; rather, students are to experience the frustration generated by design incompleteness and poor documentation, and thus learn in a telling way the importance of good design.

The organization of the rest of the paper is as follows. In Section 2 we examine how theory allows us to predict the behavior of a system before the system has been built. Section 3 introduces some non-functional software attributes. In Sections 4 and 5 we discuss, respectively, the place of performance engineering and reliability engineering in software design. Our conclusions and recommendations in Section 6 include the outline of a course on applied probability and statistics that is to provide the required background for performance and reliability engineering.

2 The Predictive Role of Theory

Scientific theories express in compact form the knowledge embodied in large numbers of empirical observations, which enables the theories to make predictions about the behavior of individual objects or systems. Typically, the effect of a particular cause can be established. For example, Charles' law allows quantitative estimation of the increase in pressure of a gas in a closed container as temperature is increased. Further, applied elasticity and materials engineering enable us to determine the pressure at which the container is likely to rupture. Next we can show that the rupture is likely to be explosive, and estimate the force of the explosion. A qualitative "law" tells the likely consequences of the explosion to people who happen to be in the vicinity of the container at the time of explosion.

All of these cause-effect relations involve physical objects, but software engineering deals with abstractions rather than physical objects. The non-materialistic basis of software engineering has led to the view that software engineering cannot really become a legitimate branch of engineering [9], and a rebuttal based on the observation that what software engineers do is not much different from what any other engineer does [10]. The discussion of whether software engineering is or is not a legitimate engineering discipline is rather irrelevant to us here. What matters is whether we can make accurate predictions about the behavior of software, and, if not, what is to be done to improve the situation.

Before doing so, let us discuss validation in general terms. To begin with, we make no distinction between validation and verification. Boehm [11, p.37] has defined validation as relating to the question "Are we building the right product?" and verification as relating to "Are we building the product right?" Now, if the product has not been built right then it is not the right product either, so that a distinction between the two terms is somewhat arbitrary. We shall give preference to *validation* here. Validation is normally undertaken by program proofs or program tests. If specifications can be adequately formalized, a program can be validated by logical proof, i.e., a proof in which each step is rigorously justified by reference to the inference rule used. An alternative is to use an informal mathematical argument, and then we have a mathematical proof. Testing, if done in a systematic manner, is proof by statistics, and about this we shall have more to say in Section 5. In short, we have a progression from statistical to mathematical and finally to logical validation.

Traditional engineering is not known to make use of logical validation, and mathematical calculations are often invalidated by material imperfections, so that validation in traditional engineering is primarily by testing. Disasters are, hopefully, averted by hefty safety factors. In this sense software engineering is, in principle, more advanced than traditional engineering. Operations of the more basic data types can be logically validated, and functional correctness of most other software can be established by mathematical reasoning. The problem is not a lack of validation techniques, but a reluctance to make proper use of them. Once again, the fixation on coded products at end-of-term deadlines for student projects simulates the worst aspect of software production in some software shops – deadline-induced disregard of software quality.

Formal foundations can be established in various ways. As an example, let us consider three axioms that constitute a mathematical theory of greatest common divisors (GCDs):

$$gcd(x, x, 0);$$ (2.1)

$$gcd(g, x, y) = gcd(g, x+y, y);$$ (2.2)

$$gcd(g, x, y) = gcd(g, y, x).$$ (2.3)

From these axioms, together with

$$x = y \times div(x, y) + rem(x, y)$$ (2.4)

and some other properties of multiplication and division, the following predicative specification can be derived:

$$y > 0 \longrightarrow gcd(g, x, y) = gcd(g, y, rem(x, y))).$$ (2.5)

After (2.5) has been derived, with each step of the derivation fully justified, it can be regarded as a theorem in a theory defined by the axioms. But (2.5) can serve as a basis for an implementation of a function that computes the GCD of x and y. We have a cause-effect relationship just as with physical phenomena: remaindering applied to positive integers produces smaller integers that have the same GCD as the original integers.

Next we should reason that repeated remaindering ultimately has to reduce one of the two integers to zero, at which point Axiom (2.1) tells us that the other integer is the GCD of the two original integers. Expression (2.5) represents a design, and validating this design is as far as we need to go. The actual writing of a program for the GCD is just "busy work".

The validation referred to above relates to the functional correctness of a design for a program that is to compute the GCD, and validation is the proof that the design has a particular property. In our case the property is that repeated application of (2.5) to the righthand side of itself ultimately produces (2.1). The proof of this property could be by means of mathematical reasoning. For more on the benefits of a formal approach to software development see, for example, [12] and [13].

The theory of (2.1)–(2.3) is a formal mathematical theory of GCDs. Because the world of GCDs is a world of abstract mathematical entities, validation in this world can be carried out with full rigor. Then we are not dealing with prediction, but with predetermined certainty. Engineering theories, on the other hand, because they are dealing with concrete objects, have to leave room for uncertainty. We shall see that validation of non-functional requirements is also subject to uncertainty, which puts it in close agreement with practices of traditional engineering. Indeed, the methods for validating software performance and reliability properties derive from traditional engineering.

3 Non-Functional Requirements

Non-functional requirements can be partitioned into technical and managerial requirements. Managerial requirements have to do with costs and risks. In defining technical requirements the goal is to arrive at systems that satisfy the managerial requirements, but we shall not discuss managerial requirements here. For this there are several reasons. First, these requirements have to be considered within the context of total enterprise management. Second, most software engineering students lack the practical experience to be properly motivated for meaningful cost-benefit and risk-benefit analyses. Third, the same remark applies to most software engineering instructors. Fourth, if anything in software engineering is still at a craft stage, then it is cost and risk estimation. Although we have a few techniques that can help, such as COCOMO [11] and Critical Success Factor analysis [14], the estimates they help provide are at best qualitative – COCOMO does give numerical estimates, but they are of little value if the input parameters are as uncertain as they usually are in organizations without fairly long histories of extensive record-keeping.

Some technical non-functional requirements can be expressed in quantitative terms. With others we are still at a qualitative stage, but a lot of effort is going into the search for ways of expressing qualitative requirements in a verifiable form. One approach is to define benchmarks, and the system is required to pass a benchmark test. Thus, a maintainability test can be defined as follows: when the requirements for a system are formulated, a change to the requirements is also drawn up, but not shown to the designers; the system designers carry out the initial design; then they are given the change and asked to transform the design to take this change into account. The time it takes to modify the design is a measure of the maintainability of the initial design; a maintainability requirement sets a limit on this time.

An example: The requirements for an elevator system assume an elevator subsystem and a dispatcher subsystem, calls for service go to the dispatcher, and the dispatcher determines which elevator is to respond to a call for service. Under the modification a call for service puts the floor from which the call originates on the agenda of every elevator. After an elevator has responded to the call, the dispatcher removes the floor from the agenda of every other elevator, unless the floor has been added to the agenda of the elevator by passengers within the elevator as well. The task is to redesign the elevator subsystem. (This and the other examples introduced further down are all selected from examples we have used in our software engineering courses.)

We shall look in some detail at a benchmark for measuring user-friendliness. Instead of just stating that a system be user-friendly, which is a statement that cannot be validated, objective criteria that relate to learning time and operational use are formulated. They encompass [15]:

1. *The learning effort.* It has been found that an effective learning strategy is to present the material in small segments, each presentation being followed by a test relating to the segment presented. System designers have to define the segments, determine an appropriate learning period for each segment of the material, and decide what the test is to measure. It is customary to measure the time to perform a given task, and to count the errors made by the subject.

2. *Operational use.* On the day after the learning session the subjects are to perform a benchmark task that is to range over the entire functionality of the software system, hopefully in proportion to the expected operational profile.

3. *Retention.* One week after the learning session the subjects are to perform the same task they performed six days earlier.

The user-friendliness requirement should specify the learning period, and levels of proficiency to be attained in the three kinds of tests. For example, the requirements may state that in a test with 10 users, after a total training time of three hours, (a) the average total time for the segment tests is to be 20 minutes, with the average total number of errors not to exceed 4.0; (b) the average total time for the benchmark test is to be 20 min after one day and 30 min after seven days, and the average error rate for these tests is not to exceed 1.5 and 2.0, respectively.

Now, most benchmarks relate to implementations rather than designs, but designers should be aware that benchmark tests will ultimately be performed, which should stimulate them to make their designs as simple as possible. One way of achieving simplicity is to have a well-designed collection of modules. In our design projects we encourage students to follow the classic advice by Parnas [16]: identify modules with data types or with processes constructed from operations of these data types.

4 Performance Engineering

In the early days of computing nearly everything else was sacrificed in the interests of performance. Then, as the cost of computing power began its downward slide, performance came to be neglected. This was partly due to the misconception that performance concerns cannot co-exist with clear, well-structured, elegant code, that performance improvements require tricky code that nobody understands afterwards. Software developers were advised to work on functionality and hope for adequate performance. If the hopes were misplaced, one could supposedly "fix it later". The fix could be faster hardware or fine tuning of the software. Unfortunately there are limits on hardware speeds, the more serious performance shortfalls are too gross for fine tuning, and, where fine tuning would work, it can easily destroy good structure, elegance, and clarity.

Performance relates to time. The objective is to get the most done in the shortest time. Actually these are two objectives – *throughput*, which relates to dealing with a specified workload in a given amount of time, and *responsiveness*, which relates to getting a particular task done within a time limit. In the past emphasis was primarily on throughput, but, with the current widespread use of very powerful workstations, performance in this sense is no longer as important. Today we are more concerned with system responsiveness: the user of an information system wants a fast response to a query; a control system must respond to its inputs with a control action within a strict time limit.

The purpose of software performance engineering is to emphasize that responsiveness requirements are as important as functional requirements, that both are to be introduced at the same time, and that compliance to both is to be monitored throughout the evolution of an application system. It can well happen that a prototype built to satisfy functional requirements alone underperforms by a factor of 50 or more. It is unlikely that this kind of problem can be solved with a "fix"; its correction may require costly redesign and reimplementation of the entire system, possibly even a realignment of the hardware-software boundary. It is therefore essential to establish early that one's favorite design can satisfy responsiveness requirements. If it does not, redesign has to take place, which, at the design stage of the software development process should not be too costly. In the worst case it has to be admitted that the project is too ambitious. New performance requirements can then be negotiated, or the project abandoned before too much effort has been expended on it.

During design the aim is to avoid serious mismatch between goals and expected performance. The estimate of performance of a software system is determined from three inputs. They are the system workload, the execution patterns by which the system is to deal with the workload, and the characteristics of the environment in which the system will be operating. On the effort that has to go into the estimation of a workload see, for example, [18].

The workload estimate specifies, for each type of process, the frequency with which the process is invoked by the system. If there are special patterns in the use of the processes, these patterns should be noted. The workload estimation is complicated by a nonuniform workload distribution in time. In a university library, return activities peak in the morning, borrowing activities in the afternoon. Returns peak also at the end of term. Let us assume an average workload in our example. We shall consider a large library that holds 3,000,000 copies, with 1% of the holdings out on loan. The average duration of a loan is 7 days. The library is open 100 hours in the week. It is accessed by 50,000 persons, each making an average of 0.5 catalog searches in a week. Catalog updates are of two types. The status of a copy is updated after each borrowing or return event, and an entry is added to or deleted from the catalog. The status updates will be considered part of the borrowing or return activities. Since catalog additions and deletions can be made outside the opening hours of the library, we shall disregard them. We then have 250 catalog search events an hour, 300 borrowing events, and 300 return events.

Next we have to determine the sequence of more primitive actions that defines each of the activities. We assume that a catalog search requires on the average 6 accesses to the data base. Borrowing and return activities also require access to the catalog, to update the status of the copy. The scenario for a borrowing event:

> Input of borrower and copy identifiers
> Copy identifier is used to access copy status entry
> Status is changed to: On loan to x till date y
> Updated status is stored
> Borrower identifier is used to access borrower information
> Borrower information is updated
> Updated borrower information is stored

The scenario for the return of a copy is similar.

Let us now turn to the characterization of the environment in which the library system is used. First consider the CPU. Suppose it executes 2,000,000 machine level instructions in a second. The average total number of activities in an hour is 850. Since there are 3,600 seconds in an hour, we can allocate close to 8,500,000 instructions to each of our activities. The actual requirements will be measured in thousands rather than millions of instructions executed. Hence we have a safety factor of three orders of magnitude, and contention for CPU access will not be a problem. It can also be shown that interface management has very little effect on the use of either CPU or I/O facilities.

Our only real concern is then the number of I/O operations in the accessing of the data base. We shall assume that each I/O operation in our application requires 100 msec. Let us translate the data base activities into counts of I/O operations. Assume that each read from the borrower data base requires 2 operations, and each read from the catalog requires 3 operations. In both cases assume that the address of the data is saved as part of the read, so that the corresponding write requires just a single I/O operation. Then the total number of I/O operations in an hour is

$$250 \times 6 + 300 \times (3 + 1 + 2 + 1) + 300 \times (3 + 1 + 2 + 1) = 5,700.$$

The total time is 570 seconds. Considering that there are 3,600 seconds in an hour, we are safe as regards throughput.

In queueing theory terms the 5,700 requests for I/O service in an hour are "customers", and service time is 100 msec. With all times measured in seconds, the customer arrival rate is $5,700/3,600 = 1.58$, the service time is 0.1, the service rate is 10, and server utilization is 0.158. Our concern is the mean waiting time, which for the queueing discipline appropriate for our application (an $M/D/1$ system) is 0.009. This is only 9% of the service time, and hence a satisfactory result.

However, a sensitivity study should be undertaken on our result. The data about which we are uncertain relate to the catalog searches. First, we do not know that six I/O operations per catalog search is a reliable estimate. Second, the number of searches could greatly increase when the library users realize how useful the catalog can be. Third, the number of searches can be expected to show a high degree of variability from hour to hour, and from day to day. We therefore check the effect of a *tenfold* increase in the number of catalog searches. The mean waiting time now becomes 0.057, which is still acceptable.

Our results justify continuing with the project. If, at a later time, we were to find that our study had grossly underestimating actual loads, there is a way out. Instead of considering the entire data base as a single entity, we can split off the index to the catalog, and even duplicate the index if need be. Then we have two (or more) data bases – the initial I/O operations of a catalog search can be confined to an index; only the final operation of a search sequence accesses the actual catalog itself.

Queueing theory can also be used to determine the amount of equipment needed. Suppose there is a proposal to provide k public terminals for catalog searches. What is k to be? We estimate that an average catalog search takes 2 minutes, which puts the hourly service rate at 30. Further assume a peak average hourly arrival rate of 540 customers (about twice the over-all average). Then, the minimum number of servers (terminals) is $540/30 = 18$. Assuming $k = 20$, and an appropriate queue discipline ($M/M/k$ here), we can show that the average time spent in the queue is 0.6 min, and that the 90th and 95th percentile values are 1.7 min and 2.4 min, respectively.

5 Reliability Engineering

For the most part non-functional requirements are constraints imposed on functional requirements. Reliability is different – it relaxes functional requirements by admitting that systems can fail. Ideal software quality is achieved when the software is free of defects: zero-defect software satisfies its requirements perfectly. Unfortunately the interactions of components of a large system are often too complex for human comprehension, which means that ideal quality not only is not, but cannot be achieved – people who write that ideal quality can be achieved, should count the typos in their own books. The next best position is to accept this limitation, but to make sure that deviations from the ideal are measurable and under strict control. The control is provided by reliability engineering. A typical requirement is that software reliability be better than 0.95 for a 40-hour period.

Reliability theory was developed for predicting mechanical failure of lightbulbs, electronic circuits, aircraft components, and suchlike. Knowing the reliability of individual components, which is established by testing, the reliability of an entire system can be estimated, and arbitrarily high reliability can in principle be achieved by duplication of components. For example, the required mean time between failures of a telephone hardware system can be stated as 20 years.

The adaptation of the theory to software has met with considerable skepticism, which was justified at first because there are major differences between hardware and software. One difference is that hardware failures are due to imperfections in physical objects, but software failures result from human errors. Another relates to duplication of components. Whereas hardware components tend to fail independently, software exhibits common-cause failure: given two independently designed and coded versions of a procedure, both can fail together for some inputs [20, 21]. However, the skepticism is no longer justified. The outstanding work by Musa's group at Bell Labs and by other researchers in developing a dependable software reliability theory has made this theory a very useful tool for software developers. The main results are available as a book [22]. There remain just two difficulties. First, it is not always clear what statistical distribution should be applied to failure data during system tests. However, continuing research is improving the situation [23]. The other problem is more serious: validation of ultra-high reliability requirements (a 10-hour reliability requirement of 0.99999990) is not feasible [24], at least not until we learn how to account properly for common-cause failures in n-version software.

Reliability estimation serves two purposes. First, failure history during testing allows determination of the reliability of the released system. Testing can stop when an acceptable level of reliability has been reached, say at time t. This time t can be estimated from early test data, which permits early estimation of the cost of system tests. Second, given an overall system reliability requirement, minimal reliability levels for individual components can be determined, and reliability goals for the components adjusted within these limits so as to minimize costs. Only the second purpose relates to design. It is particularly interesting to consider software reuse in this context. We can assume that the reliability of reusable components is known (at least it should be). Then, given an overall software reliability requirement, the reliability requirement for the new software components can be determined.

Consider a simple example, which has been adapted from Case Study 4.1 of [22]. A supermarket is to install an inventory and sales system. Input from points-of-sale, inventory counters, and a terminal located at the unloading dock enters a data collecting computer. After preprocessing, these data are sent into a transaction processing computer.

The supermarket is open every day from 07:00 till 23:00. The reliability of the inventory/sales system, which includes the data collector and the transaction processing subsystem, but not the input devices, is to be 0.95 for the 16 hours of operation on one day. We shall look at two hardware configurations: the data collector (DC) feeding into a single transaction processor (TP), and the DC feeding into two TPs. The hardware reliability of every system component is the same, namely 0.99 for the 16 hours, and the software reliability of the DC is 0.96. The DC is to be in operation (being utilized) the full 16 hours, but the transaction processing component (one TP or two TPs) is to be in use for only half this time. The problem: find the lowest reliability value for the TP software that will ensure a reliability of 0.95 for the entire inventory/sales system.

Note that the two hardware configurations allow us to define three system models: (A) DC and a single TP; (B) DC and two TPs, where each TP has its own version of the software, each transaction is processed by both TPs, and the common-cause failure phenomenon has to be taken into consideration; (C) DC and two TPs, where the TPs have identical software and a shared load strategy is followed – the DC assigns a transaction to just one of the TPs.

Using the approaches of [22] it can be established in a reasonably straightforward way that the required reliability of TP software is the impossible 1.01 for Design A, 0.989 for Design B (but under the unrealistic assumption that there are no common-cause failures), and 0.9998 for Design C. Seeing that the software reliability for DC is only 0.96, it seems unreasonable to require significantly higher reliability for TP. These results have been obtained before the transaction processing subsystem has been built, and at this stage it should not be too difficult to renegotiate the system reliability requirement. With the overall requirement reduced to 0.90, the reliability requirements for the TP software become 0.956 for A, a value in the range 0.777–0.947 for B, depending on the magnitude of the common-cause effect, and 0.973 for C. An analysis of costs is likely to lead to selection of Design A.

Let us return now to what we called proof by statistics in Section 2. Given a test suite that reflects the anticipated operational usage for the system. Given also a failure distribution function that is appropriate for the software under consideration [23]. The system is exercised with the test suite, failure times are registered as cumulative execution times since testing began, and fault removal is undertaken after each failure. The failure times permit estimation of the reliability at the present moment, as well as of confidence limits on the reliability value. After the reliability estimate has risen to the value stated in the requirements, we can say that we have performed statistical validation of the reliability requirement.

6 Conclusions and Recommendations

We have shown that some properties of a software system can be predicted during design of the system, which implies that in software engineering curricula more emphasis can be put on design. In one example we looked at a system that was to be composed of an existing component with known reliability, and a new component. We showed that the initial overall reliability requirement for the total system was unrealistic because it imposed unattainable reliability requirements on the new component. In another example we demonstrated that the responsiveness of a proposed library system was acceptable. In both cases we merely presented the final results of fairly lengthy calculations. We suspect that even if we had shown the calculations, some readers would have had difficulty in following the calculations because their professional experience has not required them to make much use of applied probability theory and statistics.

As greater emphasis is being put on highly reliable embedded real-time systems, we have to make sure that the students graduating from our programs can cope with the new challenges. Although, in principle, advanced operating system courses should have dealt with performance, they have not always done so. Reliability has been almost totally neglected. This has been partly due to the lack of adequate preparation in probability and statistics.

We found that the texts on which we have based the introduction of reliability and performance engineering into our curriculum have assumed a much more extensive background in the foundations than our students possess: [22] has a review of probability, stochastic processes, and statistics as an appendix, but that is precisely what the appendix is – no more than a review; [17] does not deal with queueing theory concepts to the depth required to permit students to solve responsiveness problems on their own. In our software engineering courses we have introduced the statistical techniques as needed, but time constraints have made our treatment necessarily shallow. A separate course that supports reliability and performance engineering is needed. In outline, the course should deal with four main topics:

Probabilities, and distributions of random variables
Poisson and Markov processes
Queueing theory and some queueing disciplines
Estimation of parameters

All these topics are covered in [19]. The examples in this text deal mostly with computer systems. Some of the examples relate to rather dated computer technology, but this has to be overlooked – [19] is to our knowledge the only text with the broad coverage needed to support both reliability and performance engineering. Additional and more modern examples can be found in [25-27].

Concentration on design in our curricula is not to imply total neglect of code, and preparations need to be made for dealing with important software engineering topics that relate to code, such as requirements elicitation and validation by means of prototypes, validation of implemented systems, instrumentation of code for performance measurement of released systems, and maintenance. Students have to be supplied with the relevant code so that they can practice using the techniques appropriate for these tasks. At the research level, more work needs to be done on benchmarks for validating systems with respect to non-functional requirements, on reliability estimation when there are common-cause failures, and on reliability as it relates to non-functional requirements – for example, performance failures are in general due to defective overall system design, but sporadic failures may be caused by localized code defects.

References

1. M. Shaw: Prospects for an engineering discipline of software. IEEE Software 7, 6, 15-24 (Nov. 1990).

2. A. Spector, D. Gifford: A computer science perspective on bridge design. Comm. ACM 29, 268-283 (1986).

3. M. Dyer: The Cleanroom Approach to Quality Software Development. New York: Wiley 1992.

4. A. J. Offutt, R. H. Untch: Integrating research, reuse, and integration into software engineering courses. Proc. SEI Conference 1992 on Software Engineering Education (Springer-Verlag LNCS 640), 88-98.

5. W. Swartout, R. Balzer: On the inevitable intertwining of specification and implementation. Comm. ACM 25, 438-440 (1982).

6. R. Balzer, T. E. Cheatham, C. Green: Software technology in the 1990's: using a new paradigm. Computer 16, 11, 39-45 (Nov. 1983).

7. R. T. Yeh: Notes on concurrent engineering. IEEE Trans. Knowledge and Data Eng. 4, 407-414 (1992).

8. P. Dewan, J. Riedl: Toward computer-supported concurrent software engineering. Computer 26, 1, 17-27 (Jan. 1993).

9. R. Kerr: A materialistic view of the software "engineering" analogy. ACM SIG-PLAN Notices 22, 3, 123-125 (Mar. 1987).

10. A. T. Berztiss: Engineering principles and software engineering. Proc. SEI Conference 1992 on Software Engineering Education (Springer-Verlag LNCS 640), 437-451.

11. B. W. Boehm: Software Engineering Economics. Englewood Cliffs, NJ: Prentice-Hall 1981.

12. C. A. R. Hoare: An overview of some formal methods for program design. Computer 20, 9, 85-91 (Sept. 1987).

13. A. Hall: Seven myths of formal methods. IEEE Software 7, 5, 11-19 (Sept. 1990).

14. J. F. Rockart: Critical success factors. Harvard Business Review 57, 2, 81-91 (March-April 1979).

15. B. M. E. De Waal, G. H. van der Heiden: The evaluation of user-friendliness in the design process of user interfaces. In Human Factors in Information Systems Analysis and Design, A. Finkelstein, M. J. Tauber, R. Traunmueller, Eds., 93-103. Amsterdam: North-Holland 1990.

16. D. L. Parnas: On the criteria to be used in decomposing systems into modules. Comm. ACM 15, 1053-1058 (1972).

17. C. U. Smith: Performance Engineering of Software Systems. Reading, MA: Addison-Wesley 1990.

18. R. G. G. Cattell, J. Skeen: Object operations benchmark. ACM Trans. Database Systems 17, 1-31 (1992).

19. A. O. Allen: Probability, Statistics, and Queueing Theory with Computer Science Applications. New York: Academic Press 1978.

20. J. C. Knight, N. G. Leveson: An experimental evaluation of the assumption of independence in multiversion programming. IEEE Trans. Software Eng. SE-12, 96-109 (1986).

21. R. K. Scott, J. W. Gault, D. F. McAllister: Fault-tolerant software reliability modeling. IEEE Trans. Software Eng. SE-13, 582-592 (1987).

22. J. D. Musa, A. Iannino, K. Okumoto: Software Reliability – Measurement, Prediction, Application. New York: McGraw-Hill 1987.

23. S. Brocklehurst, B. Littlewood: New ways to get accurate reliability measures. IEEE Software 9, 4, 34-42 (July 1992).

24. R. W. Butler, G. B. Finelli: The infeasibility of experimental quantification of life-critical software reliability. Proc. ACM SIGSOFT '91 Conf. Software for Critical Systems (Software Engineering Notes 16, 5 (Dec. 1991)), 66-76. [Reprinted: IEEE Trans. Software Eng. 19, 3-12 (1993).]

25. S. V. Hoover, R. F. Perry: Simulation, a Problem-Solving Approach. Reading, MA: Addison-Wesley 1989.

26. R. Jain: The Art of Computer Systems Performance Analysis. New York: Wiley 1991.

27. K. Kant: Introduction to Computer System Performance Evaluation. New York: McGraw-Hill 1992.

Session 10:
Teaching Techniques

Teaching Formal Extensions of Informal-Based Object-Oriented Analysis Methodologies
Thomas C. Hartrum and Paul D. Bailor, Air Force Institute of Technology, Wright-Patterson Air Force Base, Ohio

Teaching Iterative and Collaborative Design: Lessons and Directions
Bernd Bruegge and Robert F. Coyne, Carnegie Mellon University, Pittsburgh, Pennsylvania

The Use of Computer Ethics Scenarios in Software Engineering Education: The Case of the Killer Robot
Richard G. Epstein, West Chester University of Pennsylvania, West Chester, Pennsylvania

Computer Productivity Initiative
Kurt J. Maly, Dennis E. Ray, J. Christian Wild, Irwin B. Levinstein, Stephan Olariu, C. Michael Overstreet, Tijen Ireland, George Kantsios, Old Dominion University, Norfolk, Virginia and Nageswara S.V. Rao, Oak Ridge National Laboratory, Oak Ridge, Tennessee

Teaching Formal Extensions of Informal-Based Object-Oriented Analysis Methodologies

Thomas C. Hartrum and Paul D. Bailor

Department of Electrical and Computer Engineering
Air Force Institute of Technology
Wright-Patterson Air Force Base, Ohio 45433-7765

Abstract. Teaching formal methods of software specification is often difficult. This is in part due to the lack of well defined methodologies for applying formal methods to large software system specifications. We have integrated formal specification with a more informal object-oriented modeling methodology. This allows the students to follow an established modeling approach and still generate formal specifications. We find that the students learn the formalism much easier with this approach than with our prior technique of teaching formal methods as a separate block of instruction. However, the lack of good computer-aided tools for some formal specification languages can prevent the students from directly seeing all of the benefits of using formalism. This paper describes our use of Z *schemas* to add formalism to the object-oriented modeling methodology of Rumbaugh, et.al. [RBP+91], describes the introductory software engineering course in which it is taught, and discusses our experience.

1 Introduction

Formal methods have evolved over recent years to the point of being supported by specific languages. At one end of the spectrum there exist mathematically-based, non-executable languages such as Z [PST91] [Inc88] [Spi89] [Hay87]. At the other end of the spectrum there exist mathematically-based, wide-spectrum languages such as Refine^{TM} [RS90] which are also executable. However, we have found the teaching of formal methods to be difficult. Part of the problem is the abstractness of the formal-based languages, which is a problem that can be easily overcome by simply doing a better job of teaching applied discrete mathematics at the undergraduate level. A more substantial problem to overcome is the lack of well defined methodologies for applying formal methods to real problems. While progress is certainly being made in this area, much still needs to be accomplished.

In our software engineering curriculum, we have developed an introductory approach that integrates well-established informal methods with formal methods. The first course in our software engineering curriculum covers object-oriented system modeling and is based on the book by Rumbaugh, et.al. [RBP+91]. We extend this approach by using the Z formal specification language to produce a formal-based, object-oriented specification. Our modeling language is an extension of the object-oriented model to include formal specification of its basic constructs, and our methodology builds on that already evolving for object-oriented modeling. The result is a process that is easy to understand and apply, while resulting in a formal specification.

Given that we admit formal-based methodologies are still incomplete, a valid question to ask is "why do this?" To some extent this was addressed by the speakers at the Sixth Conference on Software Engineering Education [Sle92]. One of the more detailed presentations was that by Garlan [Gar92] which presented four course models and the advantages/disadvantages of each. We find the in-depth Master's level course to be extremely effective as well, and we would like to add a few more reasons for teaching formal methods.

1. The development of formal specifications forces students to apply the discrete mathematics learned in lower level computer science courses. This not only gives them more experience at being mathematically precise as other engineering disciplines are required to be, but it also provides an environment in which proof obligations on the specification can be conducted.

2. Formal specifications tend to be much more loosely coupled than the specifications produced by informal methods. Thus, they really do serve to specify classes of possible behaviors as opposed to very specific behavior which leads to very specific solutions.

3. Formal specifications more clearly show the benefits of reuse at higher levels of abstraction. As stated above, they more clearly specify classes of possible behaviors which means they can be more readily reused. Additionally, their mathematical basis lends them to be more easily combined by mathematical means in order to compose higher level behaviors. This capability is especially important if we are ever to realize the benefits of domain analysis and domain modeling.

4. The formality of the specification languages shows students how greatly increased automated capabilities can be obtained over current generation CASE tools. In general, this is true from both an analysis of properties perspective and a generation/synthesis of lower level code perspective.

5. Having students learn and apply these techniques does not affect their ability to use other, less formal techniques. Quite the contrary, it makes them all the more aware of their shortcomings!

Another important consideration in teaching formal methods is the question of executable versus non-executable specification languages. Both types have their merits. In our case, we chose the non-executable language Z for the introductory course described in this paper. Specifically, we like Z because it *forces* the student to think more abstractly by removing the all too familiar programming level terms from their use. When using executable, wide spectrum languages like that provided with the Software Refinery environment [RS90], the students can still rely on these lower-level concepts. However, one should not get the impression that Z is completely a "pencil and paper" language. We do have simple tools for syntax checking, type checking, and pretty-printing the Z specifications, and we have found these tools to be sufficient for an introductory course. While more sophisticated tools for Z are under development, the only other tool we would like to have for such an introductory course is a general-purpose theorem prover. For our advanced course in formal methods, a more significant capability is required, and we use the Software Refinery environment and associated applications tools to treat more advanced topics like software synthesis from specifications.

The remaining sections of this paper describe our approach for integrating informal-based object-oriented analysis methodologies with formal-based specification. Specifically, Section 2 defines the informal model that is the basis for our approach, and Section 3 defines our formal extensions. Section 4 describes our work on extending the approach to also cover object-oriented design and implementation. Section 5 presents the course structure. Lastly, we conclude this paper with a discussion of the results of using this approach in four course offerings over the last two years.

2 The Informal OOA Model

The informal object oriented analysis model used for the basis of our approach is that of Rumbaugh [RBP+91]. This specific model was chosen largely because the text was already being used in our object oriented modeling course; however, the formal extensions presented here could as easily be used with the approach of Coad and Yourdan [CY91] or that of Shlaer and Mellor [SM88]. (Extensions to Booch's work have not been explicitly considered [Boo91]). This section briefly reviews the basic Rumbaugh model; for more detail, especially diagram syntax, the interested reader is referred to [RBP+91].

Rumbaugh's model consists of three parts: the *object model*, which captures the structural properties of objects and their relationships to each other; the *dynamic model*, which captures the control aspects of the object which change over time; and the *functional model*, which captures the transformation of data values within a system of objects. In each part, the model consists of a graphical representation, augmented by a *data dictionary* to provide a more detailed natural language description of the system. Our approach uses Z schemas to add formality to both.

2.1 The OOA Object Model

The object model captures the static structural properties of objects, and their relationships to each other. The object model is represented graphically by the *object diagram*, essentially a traditional Entity-Relationship (E-R) diagram [KS86].

Objects Each *object class* is defined by a set of *attributes*, the values of which define the state of the object. Each definition is a template that represents any actual *instances* of that class. Objects are represented on the object (E-R) diagram by a rectangle containing the object class's name.

Associations Relationships are modeled as *associations* between objects. An association, similar to an object class, represents a group of possible relationships between object instances. Most associations are binary and appear on the object diagram as a line between the two object rectangles. Associations are named, with the name written next to the line, and can have attributes themselves.

Multiplicity defines how many instances of a class are associated with a single instance of the other class, and can be 1:1, 1:n, or m:n. *Membership* of an object instance in an association may be "required," indicating that all instances of that object class must participate in an instance of the association, or "optional," indicating that the object instances may or may not participate. Such factors are represented on the object diagram by a system of special symbols at each end of the line.

There are two special types of association. *Aggregation* ("part-of") allows explicit modeling of one object that is composed of other objects. A diamond is added to the end of the line connected to the parent. *Inheritance* ("is-a") allows subclasses to be defined which inherit all of the properties of their superclass. This is represented on Rumbaugh's object diagrams by adding a triangle to the association line, with the apex pointing to the superclass.

2.2 The OOA Dynamic Model

The dynamic model captures those aspects of an object and its associations that change over time. It is graphically represented by a traditional state transition diagram.

States Rumbaugh's dynamic model represents a partitioning of an object into *states*, where each state represents unique behavior with respect to the other states. States are named, and represented on a state transition diagram by ovals. States can be hierarchically decomposed into substates to help overcome the problem of state explosion.

Events Directed arcs between the state ovals represent allowable *transitions* between states. *Events* cause the transition between states, and are written as labels on the corresponding transition arcs. An event can carry *parameters*, and can be constrained by Boolean *guard conditions*.

Since an object can only be in one state at a time, transitions out of a state must be mutually exclusive. The same event can appear on more than one transition arc, making the state entered dependent on both the event and on the state in which the event occurred.

Activities and Actions A state can be viewed as an object's response to an event. Behavior associated with a state is defined as an *activity*. An *action* is associated with a transition. Although Mealy and Moore machines are generally considered alternate modeling approaches [Dav90], both activities and actions are allowed in the same Rumbaugh dynamic model, providing a rich set of modeling possibilities.

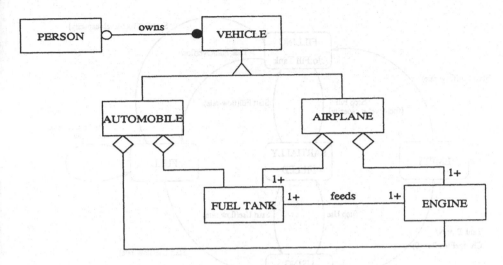

Figure 1: Informal Model Example.

2.3 The OOA Functional Model

The functional model consists of traditional data flow diagrams (DFDs) used for the classical purpose of diagramming the flow of data between processes. The functional model for an object complements the dynamic model by capturing the functional spec-ification of the object's behavior in the sense of what calculations are to be performed, along with the sources and destinations of the input and output data of each calcu-lation. Process descriptions are developed for the lowest level, or *leaf* processes only. Data exchanges with other objects are handled in two ways. To simply read or write another object's attribute values, that object is represented by a data store. To send or receive data as a parameter of an event, the sending or receiving object is shown as an actor (terminator). If data is to be stored or retrieved from an association, then the association is shown as a data store.

2.4 Example

Consider a system of vehicles and owners. A person can own zero or many vehicles, but each vehicle can only be owned by zero or one person. There are two subclasses of vehicle, automobiles and airplanes. An automobile has one engine and one fuel tank. An airplane has many fuel tanks and many engines, and an association between them indicating which tank feeds fuel to which engine. (Although the automobile's fuel tank also feeds its engine, the one to one mapping makes an association unnecessary). The graphical representation of the object model is shown in Figure 1.

Consider the state transition diagram for the fuel tank, shown in Figure 2. This is based on a discrete-event simulation model that includes filling the tank and using fuel from the tank. Along with the graphical representation, consider the following three state descriptions.

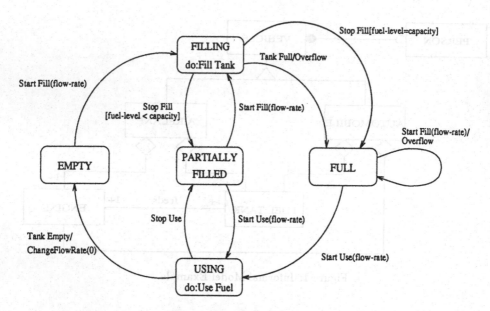

Figure 2: Fuel Tank State Transition Diagram.

Full State In this state the tank is filled to capacity with fuel. It represents a stable condition, with no input or output flow of fuel. There are no actions or activities in this state.

Filling State In this state the tank is being filled. There is no output flow of fuel. Upon entering this state the fuel tank determines when it will be full, and schedules a Tank Full event for that time. When leaving this state the fuel tank updates its fuel level. There are no other actions or activities while in this state.

Empty State In this state the tank is empty, and no fuel is flowing in or out. There are no actions or activities in this state.

Finally, consider the data flow diagrams for the fuel tank's Fill Tank activity in Figure 3. The corresponding leaf-level process descriptions are as follows.

Determine Interval Determines the (simulation) time increment between the current simulation time and the time that the attribute values were valid.

Calculate Filled Level Calculates the new level to which the tank has been filled.

Predict Overflow Time Calculates the simulation time at which the tank will overflow. This is needed to schedule the overflow event.

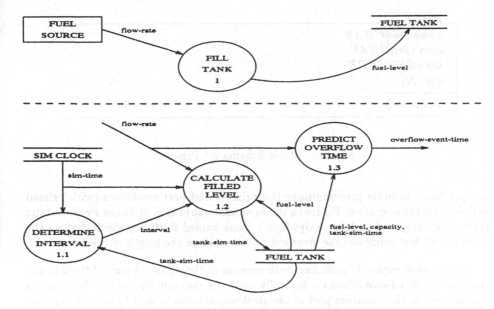

Figure 3: Fuel Tank DFD for Fill Tank.

3 Formal Extensions

Our approach is to use formal specifications to define the informal elements of the model. To do this we have chosen the language Z [PST91] [Inc88] [Spi89] [Hay87]. This was chosen since several references were available, it is a well-defined language that has been used in several real developments, it is in a form similar to the discrete mathematics that the students are familiar with, and unlike Refine, it does not include procedural statements, forcing the students to think in terms of the predicate calculus representation.

In Z both objects and operations are represented as *schemas*. As shown in Figure 4, a schema consists of a *schema name* and two parts separated by a short horizontal line. Set-theoretic variables are declared in the *signature* part which represents the union of the individual declarations. General sets are defined using all upper case letters and are not defined in any further detail. The *predicate* part is used to make statements about relationships between the variables, and while not explicitly shown, the predicate part represents the conjunction of all the statements. Figure 4 is a *static* schema, representing an entity's state space in the signature, along with invariant statements about the variables in the predicate.

A *dynamic* schema represents an operation that changes some or all of the entity's state variables. In Z the state variables are not traditional "programming" variables which represent storage locations that can have new values assigned to them. Rather they are *logical* variables. Thus change is represented by including both a "before" (unprimed) and an "after" (primed) version of the variables. To define the operation,

$$
\begin{array}{|l|}
\hline
\textit{Person} \underline{\hspace{6cm}} \\
name : \text{seq} \, CHAR \\
ssan : \text{seq} \, CHAR \\
sex : SEXTYPE \\
age : \mathcal{N}_1 \\
\hline
\#ssan = 9 \\
\hline
\end{array}
$$

Figure 4: Static Schema for Person.

the predicate includes pre-conditions (no primes) and post-conditions (with primed variables) of the operation. Figure 5a shows an example of this. Here the *Person* static schema is being used to define a dynamic schema named *Birthday* which changes the age variable but maintains the invariant relationship on the length of the *ssan*.

Rather than explicitly including both versions in the signature part of the schema, the concept of a *Delta* schema is typically used. As shown in Figure 5b, the notation "$\Delta Person$" in the signature part of the *Birthday* schema is used to implicitly represent both the "before" (unprimed) and "after" (primed) version of the variables *and* predicates of the *Person* schema. Additionally, the signature of dynamic schemas can include input variables (decorated with a "?") and output variables (decorated with a "!").

Schemas can themselves be used as types for declaring variables. We use this fact heavily in our approach. Schemas can be combined through the use of *schema inclusion*. One schema is "included" in another by simply stating the first schema's name in the signature of the second. This has the effect of unioning both schema's signatures and conjuncting their predicates. In fact, the $\Delta Person$ schema (which itself "includes" *Person* and *Person'*) is "included in" the *Birthday* schema in Figure 5.

In our approach, we utilize static and dynamic Z schemas to formalize the specification of all three parts of Rumbaugh's model, the *object model*, the *dynamic model*, and the *functional model*. We describe how this is done in the following sections.

3.1 Extended Objects

The object model is formalized by defining a Z static schema for each object class. The signature portion of the schema defines each attribute by its name and a set-theoretic type over which it is defined. The *predicate* portion of the schema contains Boolean predicates that represent *invariants* for the object; that is, assertions that must be true at all times. Predicates can also be used to specify *derived attributes*, that is, attributes that can be derived from other attributes of the object. The *Person* schema in Figure 4 specifies the *person* object of Figure 1. Consider the model of the *Vehicle* class in Figure 6.

```
┌─ Birthday ─────────────────────────────
│  name : seq CHAR
│  ssan : seq CHAR
│  sex : SEXTYPE
│  age : N₁
│  name' : seq CHAR
│  ssan' : seq CHAR
│  sex' : SEXTYPE
│  age' : N₁
├─────────────────────────────────────────
│  #ssan = 9
│  #ssan' = 9
│  age' = age + 1
└─────────────────────────────────────────
```

a. Expanded Dynamic Schema.

```
┌─ Birthday ─────────────────────────────
│  ΔPerson
├─────────────────────────────────────────
│  age' = age + 1
└─────────────────────────────────────────
```

b. Abbreviated Dynamic Schema.

Figure 5: Dynamic Schema for a Person's Birthday.

```
┌─ Vehicle ──────────────────────────────
│  model_type : MODELS
│  model_year : YEAR
│  weight : N₁
│  max_speed : N₁
└─────────────────────────────────────────
```

Figure 6: Static Schema for Vehicle Class.

Note that this schema has no predicate. If logically combined with another schema, the value of this predicate is taken as "true." Similarly the schemas for the fuel tank and engine objects of Figure 1 are shown in Figures 7 and 8, respectively.

```
┌─ FuelTank ──────────────────────────────
│ input_flow_rate : R
│ output_flow_rate : R
│ fuel_level : R
│ capacity : R
├──────────────────────────────────────────
│ fuel_level ≤ capacity
└──────────────────────────────────────────
```

Figure 7: Static Schema for Fuel Tank Object.

```
┌─ Engine ────────────────────────────────
│ model_num : MODEL_TYPE
│ engine_weight : R
│ engine_fuel_flow_rate : R
├──────────────────────────────────────────
│ engine_weight > 0
│ engine_fuel_flow_rate ≥ 0
└──────────────────────────────────────────
```

Figure 8: Static Schema for Engine Object.

3.2 Extended Associations

Each association is represented by a Z static schema. The set theoretic types used in the schema are the static schemas defining the object types that are related. The signature includes a form of mathematical relation (relation, function, injection, etc.) that, in most cases, captures both the multiplicity and the membership (required or optional participation) of the association.

Consider the "owns" association in Figure 1. This is 1:n and can be represented as shown in Figure 9. Here the symbol ↠ indicates a partial function, which captures the membership and multiplicity requirements that every owned vehicle has one owner, but not all vehicles have to be owned. The Z syntax includes functions to cover all other cases of multiplicity and membership. These are summarized in Table 1. The association "feeds" in Figure 1 is a special circumstance, and is explained later.

Associations can have attributes themselves. We treat all such cases as *associative objects* and define a separate schema for the associative object. Suppose in the example

```
┌─Owns─────────────────────────────────────────────────────
│ owns : Vehicle ↠ Person
│
```

Figure 9: Static Schema for "owns" Association.

Table 1: Multiplicity Representation

Multiplicity	Domain Membership	Range Membership	Formal Specification	Symbol
m:n	either	either	Relation w/ predicates	↔
n:1	optional	optional	Partial Function	↠
n:1	required	optional	Total Function	→
n:1	optional	required	Partial Surjection	↠
n:1	required	required	Total Surjection	↠
1:1	optional	optional	Partial Injection	>↠
1:1	required	optional	Total Injection	>→
1:1	required	required	Bijection	>↠
1:1	optional	required	Partial Bijection	None

of each vehicle being owned by a single person that such an association is characterized by a "registration number" and "registration date." These are attributes of the association, not of the person or the vehicle alone. Using Z this would be expressed as shown in Figure 10.

```
┌─Registration─────────────────────────────────────────────
│ reg_number : seq CHAR
│ reg_date : DATE
│
```

and

```
┌─Registered───────────────────────────────────────────────
│ registered : (Vehicle ↠ Person) → Registration
│
```

Figure 10: Schemas for an Association with Attributes.

Inheritance Inheritance is a special type of association and is treated differently. We first define the superclass schema, then *include* it in the subclass schema. Consider the automobile and airplane of Figure 1. Using the *Vehicle* schema already defined, we could specify the subclasses (exclusive of their components) as shown in Figure 11. Multiple inheritance can also be specified in a similar manner.

```
┌─ Automobile0 ──────────────────────────────────────────────
│  Vehicle
│  serial_number : seq CHAR
│  color : COLORS
│
└────────────────────────────────────────────────────────────
```

```
┌─ Airplane0 ────────────────────────────────────────────────
│  Vehicle
│  tail_number : seq CHAR
│  power : {JET, PROP, ROTOR, GLIDER}
│
└────────────────────────────────────────────────────────────
```

Figure 11: Schemas for Subclasses of Vehicle.

```
┌─ Automobile ───────────────────────────────────────────────
│  Vehicle
│  serial_number : seq CHAR
│  color : COLORS
│  tank : FuelTank
│  engine : Engine
├────────────────────────────────────────────────────────────
│  engine.engine_fuel_flow_rate = tank.output_flow_rate
└────────────────────────────────────────────────────────────
```

Figure 12: Schema for Automobile Subclass of Vehicle.

Aggregation Since aggregation is a special type of association, we find it convenient to adopt a slightly different approach. The aggregate association is represented as a variable or set declared over the appropriate schema. The predicate of the aggregate object is used to "connect" the parts. Continuing the example of Figure 1, the automobile would be better represented by the schema in Figure 12.

Since an aggregate object represents an object in and of itself, we find it useful to embed associations between its component objects in the schema definition of the aggregate. Consider the "feeds" association in Figure 1. Rather than use a stand alone schema, our approach is to define it within the "airplane" schema, as shown in Figure 13.

This has several advantages. First, the "feeds" association only has meaning within the context of an airplane. Second, "feeds" can now be declared over only the fuel tanks and engines that are part of an airplane, allowing the additional predicates that specify that all tanks and all engines must participate in the association. Third, this perspective clarifies the ambiguous interpretation of Figure 1 that the associated fuel tanks and engines might be part of different airplanes.

```
┌─ Airplane ──────────────────────────────────────────────────────
│ Vehicle
│ tail_number : seq CHAR
│ power : {JET, PROP, ROTOR, GLIDER}
│ tanks : ℙ FuelTank
│ engines : ℙ Engine
│ feeds : tanks ↔ engines
├─────────────────────────────────────────────────────────────────
│ power ≠ GLIDER ⇒ #engines > 0
│ power ≠ GLIDER ⇒ #tanks > 0
│ dom feeds = tanks
│ ran feeds = engines
│ ∀ e : engines; t : tanks • (t, e) ∈ feeds ⇒
│           e.engine_fuel_flow_rate = t.output_flow_rate
└─────────────────────────────────────────────────────────────────
```

Figure 13: Schema for Airplane Including "feeds."

3.3 Extended States

An object's state space is defined by: (1) the allowable values of all of its attributes, (2) its membership (or lack of) in those associations in which it can participate, and (3) the link attribute values of such associations. The object's state space can be partitioned into areas that represent unique behavior with respect to the other partitions. In the dynamic model, each of these partitions of the state space is referred to as a *state*, and is represented by a bubble on the state transition diagram. In our extended model each state is given a name, and a corresponding Z schema is defined. However, a basic static schema is inappropriate, because predicates there define invariants for all members of the class that hold for all time, while different instances of an object can be in different states. Thus for a state schema we *declare* an object of the specified type in the signature portion of the schema and *include* any involved associations. In the predicate portion, the partition of state variables that define this state is expressed as a predicate over the state variables of the declared variable using tuple notation (object.attribute) and/or membership of the input variable in the appropriate associations. These reflect invariants of that state.

A *transition* represents the change from one specific state to another. A transition is caused by an external (to the object) *event*, which may carry parameters. Parameters need to be formally declared as set-theoretic types. The transition may be conditional on some *guard condition*, a Boolean predicate expressed over the object's state variables and the event's parameter values. The transition can cause the execution of an *action*, often the sending of an event to some other object. Thus a transition can be completely characterized by an initial state, an external event, optional parameters, an optional guard condition, a target state, and an optional action.

We find the most effective way of capturing this aspect of the specification formally is through the use of an *event transition table*, in which we group the rows by "Current State." Although a dynamic schema could be defined for each row in the table, such a presentation is not as clear due to the disjoint nature of the schemas and the amount of information that each schema must carry.

Note that if an action consists of sending an event to another object, the event name is shown in the *Action* column and must appear in the *Event* column of at least one other object's table. If the action involves more, an' action name appears in the *Action* column and a corresponding dynamic schema is defined as part of the functional model.

An *automatic transition* occurs when an object has finished its specified task in a state and transitions to another state without waiting for an external event. This is shown on the state transition diagram as an unlabeled transition arrow (although it *may* have a guard condition and/or an action), and appears in the state transition table with no entry in the "Event" column. Note that this should be used to model an internal transition between two states in which the object's behavior differs, and not used to break up a state's activity into sequential steps.

As an example of using static schemas, consider the three states for the fuel tank example. The schema defining the Empty state is in Figure 14, that for the Full state is in Figure 15, and the Filling state is shown in Figure 16. The state transition table for the fuel tank is shown in Table 2.

Empty

$t : FuelTank$

$t.fuel\_level = 0$
$t.input\_flow\_rate = 0$
$t.output\_flow\_rate = 0$

Figure 14: Static Schema for *Empty* State.

Full

$t : FuelTank$

$t.fuel\_level = t.capacity$
$t.input\_flow\_rate = 0$
$t.output\_flow\_rate = 0$

Figure 15: Static Schema for *Full* State.

```
┌─Filling──────────────────────────────────────────────────
│ t : FuelTank
├──────────────────────────
│ t.fuel_level ≥ 0
│ t.fuel_level ≤ t.capacity
│ t.input_flow_rate > 0
│ t.output_flow_rate = 0
└──────────────────────────────────────────────────────────
```

Figure 16: Static Schema for *Filling* State.

Table 2: The Fuel Tank State Transition Table

Current State	Event	(Parameters)[Guard]	Next State	Action
Empty	StartFill	(flow_rate: $\mathcal{R}$)	Filling	
Filling	StopFill	[fuel_level = capacity]	Full	
Filling	StopFill	[fuel_level < capacity]	PartiallyFilled	
Filling	TankFull		Full	Overflow
Full	StartFill	(flow_rate: $\mathcal{R}$)	Full	Overflow
Full	StartUse	(flow_rate: $\mathcal{R}$)	Using	
Using	TankEmpty		Empty	
Using	StopUse		PartiallyFilled	ChangeFlowRate
PartiallyFilled	StartFill	(flow_rate: $\mathcal{R}$)	Filling	
PartiallyFilled	StartUse	(flow_rate: $\mathcal{R}$)	Using	

3.4 The Extended Functional Model

The extended functional model uses data flow diagrams (DFDs) in the manner specified in Section 2.3. We define a top level process bubble for each state activity or transition action. These are then decomposed as appropriate. For each leaf bubble, a Z dynamic schema is defined. It *includes* either the corresponding object's Δschema, in the case that the object's attribute values are modified by the operation, or the object's Ξschema, in the case that the object's attribute values are *not* modified by the operation. (Note that Ξ schemas also define both sets of unprimed and primed variables with the added constraint that their values must be equal.) Inputs that come from other active objects are defined by Z decorated input variables, while outputs that go to other active objects are defined by Z decorated output variables. Access to attributes of other passive objects should be handled by including either the Δ or Ξ schema of the corresponding object. The dynamic schemas for the DFDs of Figure 3 are in Figure 17.

$$
\begin{array}{l}
\underline{\;DetermineInterval\;}\rule{5cm}{0pt}\\
\Xi FuelTank\\
\Xi SimClock\\
interval!: SIMTIME\\
\rule{6cm}{0.4pt}\\
interval! = sim\_time - tank\_sim\_time\\
\end{array}
$$

$$
\begin{array}{l}
\underline{\;CalcFilledLevel\;}\rule{4cm}{0pt}\\
\Delta FuelTank\\
\Xi SimClock\\
input\_flow\_rate?: \mathcal{R}\\
interval?: SIMTIME\\
\rule{6cm}{0.4pt}\\
fuel\_level' = fuel\_level + (interval?)(input\_flow\_rate?)\\
tank\_sim\_time' = sim\_time\\
\end{array}
$$

$$
\begin{array}{l}
\underline{\;PredictOverflow\;}\rule{4cm}{0pt}\\
\Xi FuelTank\\
input\_flow\_rate?: \mathcal{R}\\
overflow\_event\_time!: SIMTIME\\
\rule{6cm}{0.4pt}\\
overflow\_event\_time! = tank\_sim\_time+\\
\quad (capacity - fuel\_level)/input\_flow\_rate?\\
\end{array}
$$

Figure 17: Dynamic Schemas for Fill Tank.

4 Design Transformations

We have begun work in defining a set of transformations that can be applied to the Z *schemas* from the analysis phase that will properly map the specification into a design. Our design representation is also object-oriented, using Classic Ada^{TM} to define the appropriate objects and encapsulated methods.

The first step in our approach is to define new data types as appropriate to capture the set-theoretic types specified in the schema signatures. Then each object is transformed by mapping its static schema into a class declaration. Each signature variable becomes an attribute (instance variable), and a *set_attribute*, *get_attribute* pair of methods is defined for each. Invariants from the predicate are mapped to validation checks in the appropriate *set_attribute* methods. Associations involving attributes are handled in a similar manner, with two additional attributes that point to the associated object instances.

Methods are defined by first re-grouping the object's state transition table on

Event, then defining a method for each external event. The event parameters, if any, become input parameters for the method. Each row of the state transition table for this event type becomes a *case* in a case statement for the method. Determination of the proper case is done by conjuncting the *From State*'s schema predicate with any *Guard Condition*.

For each case three things must be done. (1) The *Current State* and *Next State* static schemas are compared, and those state variables that differ are updated. This is done by invoking the appropriate *set_attribute* methods in order to assure that any constraints are met. (2) Any *Actions*, including sending events to other objects, must be specified. For other than sending events, this is handled by a procedure call in the method, to a procedure that is developed subsequently. (3) Any *Activities* defined in the *Next State* description must be specified. This, too, is handled by a procedure call at this point. This procedure will also be called by any other events that lead to the same *Next State*.

Finally, for each procedure called as a result of the actions and activities, there should be a corresponding *Z* dynamic schema in the analysis model. From this *Z* dynamic schema, a procedure is defined, using "pseudo-code" based on Classic Ada syntax. Note that the procedure definition must be based on the pre- and post-conditions contained in the dynamic schema and these should be included as code comments (similar to the notion of annotations in Annotated Ada).

At this point, the resulting design specification can be checked for syntax and consistency errors by the compiler, and in some cases the design specification is executable. All that remains for a completed Classic Ada implementation is the final definition of the operations from the design level specification.

5   Course Structure

CSCE 594 Software Analysis and Design is a one quarter, 4 credit hour graduate level class that meets for four lectures and one problem session each week. Prerequisites consist of an introduction to discrete mathematics (note that this is sufficient for this course, but not formal methods in general), and an introduction to data structures and program design. The course examines the object-oriented paradigm and the formal specification of software. Topics include object-oriented analysis (to include context analysis, problem analysis, and specification), object-oriented design (to include architectural and detailed design), and formal specification (to include model-based specifications, set theory, and predicate calculus). Hands-on experience is emphasized through the use of homework and class projects, through the use of formal/informal specification and design languages, and through the use of computer-based software development tools, where available. Specifically, the course objectives are as follows.

- To comprehend the distinction between system and software engineering.

- To comprehend and be able to apply discrete mathematics to the formal specification of software systems.

- To be introduced to the terms *domain analysis* and *software architectures* and comprehend their role in software development.

- To comprehend and be able to apply object-oriented approaches to software analysis and design.

- To be able to determine when to choose a functional or object-oriented approach to software design.

- To comprehend the issues associated with selecting analysis and design representations and their impact on the remaining phases of software development.

- To comprehend the importance of computer-assisted tools to software product engineering in terms of the generation and evaluation of various specification and design artifacts.

The following topic areas are covered in this course. It should be noted that a specific ordering is not being implied here. Some of the areas can and should be presented in an integrated manner.

1. Introduction

    (a) Lecture Hours: 3

    (b) Learning Objective: Knowledge

    (c) Topic Components: Overview of systems modeling, Overview of domain analysis, System versus software engineering, and Overview of the object-oriented approach.

2. Object-Oriented System and Software Analysis

    (a) Lecture Hours: 19

    (b) Learning Objective: Comprehension/Application

    (c) Topic Components: Mathematics for formal specification, Z formal specification language, Information/Object Model, Dynamic Model, Functional Model, Pre/Post conditions, System Specification, Domain Analysis, Domain Modeling, and Verification/Validation of system/software specifications.

3. Formal Specification of Software

    (a) Lecture Hours: 5

    (b) Learning Objective: Comprehension/Application

    (c) Topic Components: State-based model of computation, Z formal specification language, Introduction to proof obligations and theories, and Methodology of formal specification.

4. Object-Oriented Design

   (a) Lecture Hours: 8

   (b) Learning Objective: Comprehension/Application

   (c) Topic Components: System Design, Design Foundations (Design qualities, Design assessment, Design representation, and Verification/Validation of system/software designs), Architectural design (Object design, Association design, and Software architectures and domain models), Detailed design (Design operations and methods).

5. Languages for Software Analysis and Design Representation

   (a) Lecture Hours: 2

   (b) Learning Objective: Knowledge

   (c) Components: Implications of language choice and Analysis of alternatives.

6. Classical Methods of Software Design

   (a) Lecture Hours: 3

   (b) Learning Objective: Comprehension/Application

   (c) Components: Functional decomposition, Transform analysis, and Transaction analysis.

In addition, there are a set of projects involving individual and team exercises applying modeling tools and languages appropriate to each of the topic areas. Examples of projects we have used are home heating systems, library systems, cruise control systems, elevator systems, and models of rockets.

6 Discussion

One of the things we would like to emphasize is the need to integrate informal methods with formal methods in an introductory course such as this. In the first two course offerings, we taught informal object-oriented modeling for the first seven weeks of the quarter, then introduced formal methods during the last three, loosely coupling the two using objects as the basis for the Z schemas. Students tended to treat this as a change in topic, and found the three week formal portion somewhat difficult to understand as a stand-alone topic. Also, although all had taken or (mostly) waived an undergraduate class in discrete mathematics, most lacked any practical experience at applying set theory, function definition, and predicate calculus which added to the difficulty of the three week block. By introducing the mathematics and Z formalism at the beginning of the quarter, there is more time to "relearn" the mathematics over the space of the quarter, and integrating the formalism as a way to document the informal model in the data dictionary adds to the sense of purpose of the formalism.

However, some of the students still "just don't get it." They don't see the usefulness of the formal extensions. These students express the perception that "you've added unnecessary complexity and difficulty to an existing methodology." Part of this is due to the lack of an executable formal language and a general lack of automated tools for Z that build on the formal specification. Much of the work in performing Z data and operation refinement as well as the final mapping to some implementation language must be done manually. Another problem is cultural in nature. While it is improving with each new class, many of our students have seen nothing concerning the use of formal methods other than possibly proof of correctness techniques (which provided an extremely negative impression).

Note that the course described in this paper is a required course for all our graduate computer students (approximately 50 per year). Therefore, we have exposed a substantial number of students to the use of formal methods for system development. In addition to this course, we also require all of our software engineering students (approximately 15 per year) to take an additional course entitled *Formal-Based Methods in Software Engineering*. This course uses the Software Refinery environment which contains a mathematically-based, wide-spectrum formal specification language called Refine which is also executable. Refine integrates set theory, logic, objects, a formal object base, transformation rules, and pattern matching [RS90]. Additionally, the Software Refinery environment includes a parser generator and X11 interface toolkit. Essentially, Software Refinery can be used to build program transformation systems [LM91] in which high level formal specifications are used as the basis for synthesizing lower level implementations in languages like C and Ada. With the basis provided by our introductory course CSCE 594, the software engineering students are now in a position to build object model transformation systems. In particular, it is shown how object-based domain models can be used to develop domain-specific languages and how these languages can be transformed in a behavior-preserving way using object model to object model transformations. Thus, the elements of how to build a specification to code level transformation system are not only discussed in class, but practical experience with constructing and using such systems is obtained.

Overall, we feel this course has been very successful at simultaneously introducing students to formal methods and object-oriented modeling. While some problems still remain in terms of computer-aided tools for supporting the Z formal specification language, we feel the overall benefits greatly overcome this specific deficiency. Additionally, this course coupled with our advanced course in formal-based methods, where we do have more sophisticated tool support, produces a very enlightened set of software engineers.

References

[Boo91] Grady Booch. *Object Oriented Design with Applications*. Benjamin/Cummings Publishing Company Inc., Redwood City, CA, 1991.

[CY91]   Peter Coad and Edward Yourdan. *Object-Oriented Analysis, 2nd Ed.* Your-
           dan Press, Englewood Cliffs, NJ, 1991.

[Dav90]   Alan M. Davis. *Software Requirements, Analysis and Specification.*
           Prentice-Hall, Inc., Englewood Cliffs, New Jersey, 1990.

[Gar92]   David Garlan. Formal Methods for Software Engineers: Tradeoffs in Cur-
           riculum Design. In *Proceedings of the Sixth SEI Conference on Software
           Engineering Education*, pages 131–140, San Diego, CA, Oct 1992.

[Hay87]   Ian Hayes. *Specification Case Studies.* Prentice Hall International (UK)
           Ltd, Hertfordshire, 1987.

[Inc88]   D. C. Ince. *An Introduction to Discrete Mathematics and Formal System
           Specification.* Oxford University Press, New York, 1988.

[KS86]   Henry F. Korth and Abraham Silberschatz. *Database System Concepts.*
           McGraw-Hill, New York, 1986.

[LM91]   Michael R. Lowry and Robert D. McCartney. *Automating Software Design.*
           MIT and AAAI Press, Menlo Park, California, 1991.

[PST91]   Ben Potter, Jane Sinclair, and David Till. *An Introduction to Formal
           Specification and Z.* Prentice Hall, New York, 1991.

[RBP+91]   James Rumbaugh, M. Blaha, W. Premerlani, F. Eddy, and W. Lorensen.
           Object-Oriented Modeling and Design. Prentice-Hall, Inc., Englewood
           Cliffs, New Jersey, 1991.

[RS90]   Inc. Reasoning Systems. *Refine User's Guide.* 3260 Hillview Avenue, Palo
           Alto, CA 94304, 1990.

[Sle92]   Carol Sledge, editor. *Proceedings of the Sixth Software Engineering Edu-
           cation Conference.* Springer-Verlag, New York, New York, 1992.

[SM88]   Sally Shlaer and Stephen J. Mellor. *Object-Oriented Systems Analysis.*
           Yourdan Press, Englewood Cliffs, NJ, 1988.

[Spi89]   J. M. Spivey. *The Z Notation, A Reference Manual.* Prentice Hall Inter-
           national (UK) Ltd, Hertfordshire, 1989.

Teaching Iterative and Collaborative Design: Lessons and Directions

Bernd Bruegge
School of Computer Science
Carnegie Mellon University
Pittsburgh, PA 15213

Robert F. Coyne
Engineering Design Research Center
Carnegie Mellon University
Pittsburgh, PA 15213

Abstract

We describe the motivation for an ongoing series of experiments to enhance a team-based object-oriented software engineering course with a collaborative design tool. The course, which is taught in a single semester to senior undergraduates has achieved success in several dimensions, in particular in its application of object-oriented methods for analysis and design to the associated course project. We have recently started to increase the realism of the course by involving the students increasingly in iterative development, in particular on the system design level. We analyze some of the problems emerging from this decision and identify the key issues that must be addressed to allow for iteration in a single project course. A specific prototype information modeling environment supporting collaborative design is described and its applicability in the classroom is illustrated based on actual material from a recent version of the course[1].

1 Introduction

Software engineering has been recognized as a collaborative social design process requiring the adaptation of methods and tools to the needs of cooperation and incremental teamwork. Important aspects of this collaborative view of software production are the creation of a "theory" or shared understanding of the software artifact under development, and the dynamic coordination of the development process[10][21]. A comprehensive approach to software engineering must address the integration of software technologies with software development processes and practice encompassing social, organizational, communication and information issues and structures [25]. However, the research and teaching (which typically mirrors the state of research in the field more closely than practice) of software engineering have tended to focus almost exclusively on technical issues such as tools and processes revolving around the description of the software artifact at its various levels of abstraction and development. This is in spite of the fact that it is also known that multiple teams of people are typically required for most projects of any significant scale and therefore productive teamwork and effective collaborative work processes are central concerns. No one person can be expected to have all the requisite knowledge and skills, and the sheer magnitude of software systems commonly puts analysis and design beyond the abilities of even the most brilliant and multi-talented of individuals.

Arguably, one of the most important contributions to software engineering is object technology [2] [8] [16] [23] [31] including all levels of its application in terms of modeling - from busi-

---

1. This research was sponsored in part by the National Science Foundation under grant number USE-92511836.

ness or strategic modeling, through analysis, design, construction, testing, support and maintenance. Recently, with the widespread adoption of object-oriented development more emphasis has been placed on the importance of teamwork and collaboration. This is partially due to the fact that the exploratory modeling and iterative prototyping approaches, so commonly used in object-oriented development, are more conducive to group processes involving the free exchange of ideas and the negotiation of diverse and distinct viewpoints[7] [17] [22]. These approaches are reinforced by general trends toward iterative process models for software development[1].

Educators have picked up on the potential of combining object-oriented software engineering with a team-based project course in order to give students the desired experience of "real" software engineering practice on systems of sufficient scale and complexity while coping with the organization and management issues that such scale brings. We support and have experienced success with this trend as reported elsewhere[5], but have also identified certain limitations with respect to a combination of the scale of systems, the number of students and teams involved, and the ability to teach realistic system development -- especially in enabling students to participate in the engineering of the requirements and system decomposition and in allowing modifications to these through an iterative analysis, design and implementation process. We feel that it is important, with respect to pedagogical goals and management of project courses, to find ways to provide these experiences to students who will be the new practitioners in the field and who will encounter these concerns regularly in any commercial or industrial software engineering context.

Building on our experience with a team-based software engineering project course [3] [4] we believe we know how to continue developing the course to enhance students involvement with an increasingly comprehensive and realistic software engineering experience. This new direction of course development, involving a pedagogical shift in the dimensions of software engineering issues that students are directly involved with, comes directly from our understanding of important lessons we learned from the course. These lessons indicate our need to better understand and support the dynamic communication and negotiation processes that lead to shared meaning and decision making in software development. In this paper, we discuss experiments and plans that we have already initiated in that direction based on the incorporation of technology that supports team-based information management for design.

In Section 2 we describe our experiences with our team-based software engineering project course, summarize the strengths of the approach and its current status, and relate some particular examples of problems and difficulties that have occurred that are indicative of deeper issues. We also describe the problems in communication and understanding that can be caused by changes due to evolving requirements, system decompositions, organizational and communication structures, and task assignments. We discuss these sources and their interrelationships in order to identify key components within the development infrastructure that we believe must be more adequately supported in future courses. By far the most important of these components is maintaining a shared understanding of the state of a project, in its multiple information dimensions, by all participants (who are typically from multiple disciplines and backgrounds.)

We observe, in Section 3, that the need for maintaining a "shared memory" (as the term is used in the context of teamwork and concurrent engineering) in software engineering shares much in common with all intellectual problem solving activities involving multiple participants, and most in common with other engineering design processes and practices. We describe research in these broader areas of collaborative work that indicates that a shared understanding requires maintenance of an explicit shared memory. A specific prototype information modeling environment to support shared memory is described and its applicability illustrated --based on actual material from a recent version of the course -- as a suitable candidate "technology" with which to experiment in providing computational support for shared memory in collaborative object-oriented software engineering.

In Section 4, we present an outline of our plans to the course structure by introducing a series of incremental and evolutionary experiments to better support collaborative system design -- including iterative cycles of analysis, system decomposition and construction. The expected impact of this research on students, teachers and future software engineering related curricula is also envisioned.

2 Experiences with an object-oriented project course

We have offered a single project course since 1989 and in this time the course has grown significantly in terms of complexity and numbers of students. In general we have not exposed the students to some of the harder issues in software development, namely requirements engineering, requirements analysis in the context of ill-defined or missing functional requirements and design decomposition. We avoided these topics so far, because an important pragmatic constraint in the selection of the project was to expose the students to those problems that could be solved with a high chance of success within a single semester.

The rapid change in our field over the last few years, however, has relaxed our constraints along several dimensions, the most important ones being the need for well-definedness of the initial system description and the number of students that we admit to the project. A primary characteristic of the process in developing a system with ill-defined requirements is the iteration through one or more development phases before the requirements or the design are clarified. By exposing students to the problem of revising and iterating a larger scale system design through several levels of the software lifecycle, we are able to give them better exposure to actual software engineering practice.

In fact, even in moderate scale systems development problems emerge if the developers are unable to revise and iterate throughout the lifecycle. There is an additional reason why we are looking at larger scale systems. Software development is not only the (iterative) creation of artifacts such as requirements analysis documents or system designs. What we also want to teach the students is how to negotiate these artifacts and how to arrive at a solution while keeping track of the design alternatives. When dealing with small and medium scale system development, the design history is very simple, because the "right" decomposition is usually found quite early in the project as was the case in our earlier courses. Tracking the history of a design becomes a real problem when several designs need to be evaluated against each other. This is typically more the case in a larger scale system that requires iterative development of the system decomposition.

2.1 Emerging problems and issues

Given our extensive experience with single project courses [3] [5] [26] [29] and based on our reasoning mentioned above, we have begun to expose our students to the development of larger and more complex systems. The current culmination of this trend is our 1992 Fall semester course, in which we offered a single project to 45 students dealing with the emergency management of accidents. Involving a large number of students causes several problems to appear.

One of the issues that arises is whether a project course should be taught in a single semester. There are many arguments for a two semester course[12], in particular if the instructor is in the position to define a multiyear strategy[19].

We believe there is one advantage in teaching a single project course in one semester. In a course organized around a project, students can instantiate concepts taught in class almost immediately in the project and the project experience in turn can be used to illustrate problems taught in class. In our undergraduate course, this means we have to deal with students who are not experienced in analysis and design. We therefore teach the course in a very ambitious time scale, dovetailing the discussion of the software development activity concepts with the need for using them in the project phases.

As a consequence we have always employed a water-fall lifecycle throughout the semester. From a pedagogical point of view, the waterfall model works quite well, because the students are incrementally exposed to the lifecycle terminology and can immediately apply it in the corresponding project phase. However, the waterfall model places heavy constraints on the process and as it is quite well known, it does not support realistic software development of problems that require iteration. We applied some modifications to the basic waterfall model to deal with incomplete requirements. For example, we asked for the delivery of a prototype about half way through the semester. However, we observed that beginners asked to deliver a prototype will concentrate immediately on coding and delivery issues and tend to avoid high level analysis and dialog needed to investigate the requirements.

Another assumption we made was that ill-defined requirements can be dealt with by simply iterating several times through the requirements analysis and design phases. One of the claims of object-oriented methodologies is that this is easy because the developer has to deal more or less with a single representation of the problem. OMT[23], for example, allows the developer to use the same notation for object models in the requirements analysis and in the object design phase. However, the real problem is that ill-defined requirements cannot be always be solved by iteration on the system model alone. Sometimes the clarification of a requirements leads to a redecomposition of the system, which in turns demands a change in the communication structure and the task assignments. And moving to larger projects means without question moving to incomplete requirements and designs requiring several redecompositions during the project. Thus our fixed communication and task assignment structures have become an obstacle for teaching effective software engineering of large-scale systems.

We have been exposed to the need for redecomposition in our course before, but have in general been quite inflexible to these needs. For example, in the 1989 project course the instructor's top-level design was based on functional decomposition. Early in the semester the students proposed a set of processes collaborating with each other via messages. Not prepared to deal with such a design change, we "convinced" the students to continue with the original design.

In the Fall 92 project course we once more experienced the need for a system redecomposition but this time we made a different decision and the following discussion illustrates the problems encountered. The requirements in the problem statement asked for access to a multitude of information stored in a set of geographically distributed databases by so-called first responders. The top-level design allowed for a dynamic connection between first responders and databases and this connection was to be provided by a separate communication subsystem. The (simplified) top-level design in Figure 1a shows a first responder module accessing a database via a communication subsystem.

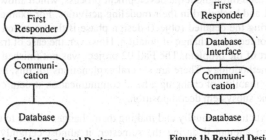

Figure 1a Initial Top-level Design　　　　　**Figure 1b Revised Design**

Each of these modules had to be implemented by a group of students called EMOC, DBASE and COMM, respectively. These groups had to communicate with each other to analyze and design the system. For intragroup communication, we established two primary mechanisms: group-specific bulletin boards and project meetings. The group-specific bulletin boards were set up for discussing module-specific problems and the weekly project meetings where held for each group to discuss progress, ideas, and plans. For intergroup communication, a separate bulletin board--discuss--was created for the "discussion of project-related issues."

The intention behind the top-level design was a reduction in the overall communication. The communication structure derived from the top-level design was such that the EMOC group and the DBASE group had to communicate with members from the COMM group, but EMOC members did not have to talk to DBASE group members. However the design had a flaw. An important design goal of the system was the provision of location-transparent access to the databases. To deal with this design goal, a new module Database Interface (see Figure 1b) was proposed by the students and the DBASE group volunteered for its implementation. This change in the design involved a change in the task assignments as well as a change in the communication structure, because EMOC members now had to talk to members from the DBASE group as well.

How did we deal with this design change? Making this change explicit with respect to the project structure would have involved the creation of a sub-group or another group, the installation of a new bulletin board, a change in the task assignment description in the project management plan, a change in the group meetings and various other changes. Looking at the expected organizational overhead we hesitated to implement any of these changes in the middle of the semester. Instead we told the students to go ahead with the redecomposition, but within the context of the original group and communication structure. Looking back at the communication traffic on the bulletin boards we could see that this clearly caused a problem. Several questions concerning the database interface posted by EMOC members to the discuss bulletin board were not answered, possibly because nobody felt responsible to answer these questions. In fact, these questions were not even answered when EMOC members cross-posted their questions to the DBASE bboard.

Fixed communication structures and the task assignments have a deep impact on the size and complexity of the project that can be attempted within the classroom. Large-scale systems are rarely well-specified and many insights gained late in the development process change early decisions[1]. In fact, object-oriented development methodologies emphasize the need for iteration and incremental development. One of the strengths of the OMT methodology is that it provides a small set of notations used throughout the development process, which allows the software developer to move forward and backward in their modeling activities. For example, requirements can easier be changed during the detailed (object) design phase if the transition back to the requirements analysis does not require a change of notation. However, the ease of traversing object models is only a small part of the problem. The Fall 92 project was not finished successfully despite the use of the OMT methodology. There are several explanations for this, but the main explanation, we believe, is the inability of changing a fixed communication structure and task assignment to reflect changes in the subsystem decomposition.

Changing these structures manually and making their changes visible to the students is a time consuming task. When attempted during the semester, it almost certainly leads to problems, because the change cannot effectively be communicated to all of the project members in a short time to effectively set it into place. The instructors, who set up the communication structure at the beginning of the semester, do not have the time during the semester to effect the change, because they are busy with the lectures and with managing the project. And teaching assistants generally don't have enough project management experience to communicate this change.

Our reasoning is that we can actually resolve the problems by opening the project course even further to the students and engage them in redecomposition as well. In fact, we believe this is not just to expose students to more complicated design issues, it is a matter of practicality; in software engineering, it is simply not possible to predetermine the structure of the system, task assignments and system decomposition at the beginning of system development, in particular if the requirements are not pre-specifiable. This is exactly, what people in the rapid prototyping and in the object-oriented community have observed for quite some time.

The main problem is that we don't have a mechanism that can communicate a change without intervention by the teacher. What we really need, is a tool that can broadcast changes such as a redecomposition to all the project members within a "reasonable update cycle".

Several collaborative design tools have recently appeared which promise to improve the situation. Their existence has prompted us already to add a lecture in the course covering the occurrence of communication and negotiation problems and how they could be minimized by a collaborative design tool. Section 3 illustrates the use of such a tool, n-dim[20], in the Fall 92 course. In a homework at the end of the semester we asked the student to describe the communication and negotiation problems that emerged during the development of the project, their reaction to n-dim and how such a course might benefit from this tool (The homework is described at the end of this paper). The responses of the students were quite interesting. While a few students see such a tool as unnecessary overhead to an already overburdened project, many of the students could see the need for such a tool to improve the visibility of a project structure exposed to change.

3 Supporting team-based iterative development

System design generally entails articulation of a set of modules, and this system configuration must be mapped onto the staff in terms of division of labor. When any of these get out of sync, they must be renegotiated - the infrastructure must support negotiation of these during development [25].

Problematic situations regularly arise in software engineering due to changes in a multitude of factors. This is so because software engineering occurs within a dense web of social, technical and economic factors. We have described problems that occurred in our project course when a more complex system was attempted that required an iterative development process. These kinds of problematic situations are unavoidable, and cannot be viewed as negative phenomena but as an inherent part of the dynamic decision making processes (including evaluation of progress, reassessment and reallocation of resources, etc.) involved in iterative development. However, these mismatches cannot be well handled by strictly centralized project management and imposition of structures and order between project components. The resolution of these situations depends on the ability of the students to regularly negotiate issues and agreements and to maintain a mutual shared understanding or *shared memory* of the state of the project [18] [25]. If the students get too far or remain to long out of sync in their shared understanding, wasted work, frustration and loss of commitment will result and the chances for success in a project are compromised.

Constantine[7] notes the fundamental importance of maintaining a shared memory to support teamwork in object-oriented system development, in which it is preferred to engage in iterative processes and decision making. Among several critical roles he identifies for team members to play, that of "information manager" is deemed most important and central.

Constantine and others [32] advocate a primarily organizational approach to support the dynamic negotiation and decision making processes. However, organizational approaches alone suffer certain drawbacks in maintaining a shared memory within a project or across projects -- key personnel, who are the carriers of shared memory may leave a project or an organization. Therefore, a complementary approach to supporting shared memory is needed that integrates organizational approaches with technical capabilities and infrastructure for creation of an explicit external record of shared memory composed of structured information from multiple media [18] [27] [28].

Currently, there are a variety of efforts, growing out of concerns with teamwork in software engineering and other design activities, that can be loosely classified as intending to support collaborative teamwork through the integration of organizational approaches with *computational support for shared memory* [9][19][20]. Though these efforts are not yet mature, each is attempting to understand and articulate the requirements for the computational support for shared memory and to build a prototype environment to test and elaborate these requirements. At a general level there is common agreement regarding the following kinds of requirements.

Coordination and management of group activities and work-flow requires that information be made available in a meaningful form at the appropriate time. It is the creation of and access to meaningful information with the seamless integration of these varieties of information created and used during the design of the product, that is called information modeling and management.

The support environment should enable design and design management to be carried out within the same uniform information modeling environment. Facilities should be built into the environment that will enable designers to create shared structures of information (text, object models, source code, sketches, pictures). The environment should also permit asynchronous group activity. Finally, facilities are required to enable retrieval of information by designers with diverse views of that information.

3.1 n-dimensional information modeling (n-dim)

... my first premise, based on what I have observed, is that designing is a social process....

[the design] exists only in a collective sense. Its state is not in the possession of any one individual to describe or completely define, although participants have their own individual views, their own images and thoughts, their own sketches, lists, diagrams, analyses, precedents, pieces of hardware, and now spreadsheets which they construe as the design[6].

n-dim is a software environment implementing an information modeling infrastructure that addresses the issues involved in communication between multiple participants in design activities. We consider *n*-dim to be the best and most comprehensive tool currently available for creating and maintaining shared memory in software engineering design and development. The philosophy, current structure, and development history of *n*-dim are documented in a series of papers [18][20][27][28]. The following brief description is drawn directly from those sources and focuses on the essential features of *n*-dim for supporting collaborative work and its suitability as a core infrastructure for team-based software engineering.

The space of objects in *n*-dim is conceptually flat; that is, objects do not, in any physical sense, contain other objects. Instead, multiple structures can be imposed on this flat space by means of *models,* which are comprised of *links,* or relationships between objects (models themselves being objects). In this way, the same object may participate in many models.

A model is a set of links. The value of a link object is a 3-tuple, *<source, target, type>,* where *type* is merely a label for the link; link types are given their meaning(s) by the modeling language(s) in which they occur. All objects, are constructed using another model as their *modeling language.* Typically, modeling languages specify what objects can be in a model and what relations they can have to one another.

There are three unique features of *n*-dim which taken together distinguish it from other approaches and form a foundation for computational support for shared memory:

1. *Flat Space.* This feature captures the fact that an individual object can be situated in multiple contexts. There is a special link called a *part* link, which is canonically represented as a box inside of a box; part links denote objects "inside" models. All other links are shown as directed and labeled lines. Due to this flat space in *n*-dim, a model does not (in any physical sense) contain objects that appear inside it. Also, things can be found in the context(s) in which they are used (referred to, referenced by, placed in relationship to other things, etc.)

2. *Generalized modeling.* This feature allows people to operate on things and kinds of things interchangeably, and move freely from one level of abstraction to the other. Every unpublished model is mutable, and can have operations and attributes defined on it without affecting any other model. This means that models (information structures) can serve as *prototypes* of other models; any model can serve as the starting point for another model, in the sense that it can be copied and the copy modified in ways independent of the original. Models can also serve as *modeling languages.* Modeling languages are represented as models themselves (another level of things to be designed, negotiated, etc.).

3. *Published.* Using the library as a metaphor, this feature is a mechanism for making models formally exchangeable and persistent. Hence, traces of the evolution of information and its structure over time can be found in the growing repository of published objects.

These three features of n-dim support the following capabilities which we believe are essential to supporting collaborative teamwork activities: Incremental creation and/or reuse of models (structuring of information); (selective) sharing of models with others in a shared information space (shared memory); and recording and preserving of all project models for future reference (with no additional overhead, but as a side effect of current project activities).

3.2 Illustration of an information modeling infrastructure

In Section 2 we described certain problems that arose in our object-oriented project course taught in the fall of 1992. Now that the course, its problems and the specific tool for computational support for shared memory, n-dim, have been introduced we give a concrete example of some specific models that illustrate how various diverse pieces of information in the development process can be related to one another. This is a rational reconstruction based on actual information materials from the project, but was done post mortem and not during the course of the work. Also, the figures shown are actual screendumps of models created in a prototype version of n-dim available at that time; subsequent versions of n-dim have improved many features including the interface[2]. However, these models (roughly) illustrate a structure for a web of information that could also be generated and maintained during the course of development -- and which, we hypothesize, would help to resolve some of the problems that arose. Each of the Figures 2-6 which follow, shows a cascade of opened models within n-dim that are part of the **Workspace** of user **coyne** (this workspace is shown in the upper left of Figure 2).

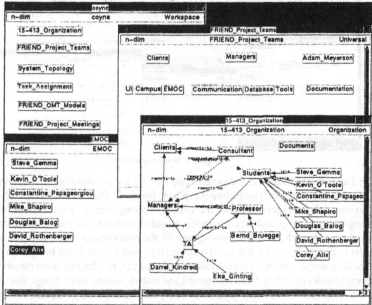

Figure 2 Organization into Teams

---

2. For the planned experiments we discuss in section 5, a robust, customized version of n-dim adapted for teaching object-oriented software engineering will be prepared and tested before it is deployed in the course.

420

Each of the labelled boxes in the workspace, or within any other model, is an "icon" of a model which may be opened by selecting it and choosing open from a menu, or double-clicking on the model. The name for an opened model appears in the top center of the model and is the exact same text-object as the label in its icon (and in the following figures this label is repeated by the window manager in the title for the window in which the model is presented). As described above the same model may be referenced from many other models (indicating interrelationships and multiple indexing of the same information from different contexts); for instance, the model[3] named **EMOC** (Emergency Management Operation Center) shown within the opened model named **FRIEND_Project_Teams** in Figure 2 is itself shown opened in that figure, and it appears in the model named **Task_Assignment** in Figure 3.

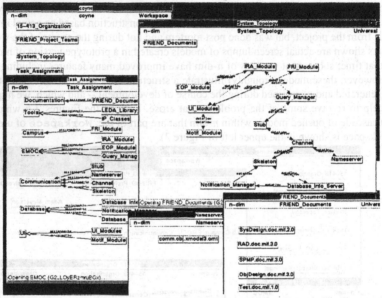

Figure 3 Task Assignments

Figure 2 also shows models of the organization for the project development within the course ("**15-413 Organization**") including the people involved, their roles and their (current) allocation to various teams. Figure 3 shows the (initial) decomposition of the system into modules and the assignment of responsibility for those modules to respective teams. Note that one can determine who is on each team by opening any of the team models as illustrated by the open **EMOC** model in Figure 2; in turn, the models for each person a team might be opened to get information regarding access, contact, specialization, assignments, etc. for that team member. Also, the **Nameserver** model in Figure 3 can be opened and shows, among other things, that it references the OMT object model for the communication subsystem (**comm.obj.xmodel3.omt**), which is shown in Figure 4.

3. Hereafter, when it is clear in context to which we are referring, we do not distinguish the "icon" of a model from the model itself, or its presentation when opened.

In this example, the OMT model (actually a pointer to it) has been included in another model and annotated with a textual object. This action may be broadcast through messages in various appropriate mediums depending on time, circumstance and people or teams that may need the updated information, e.g., e-mail, bboard posts, phone, postit notes, memo, conversation, etc., or (as illustrated in Figure 5) to all currently active *n*-dim users via the *n*-dim talk window[4]. With

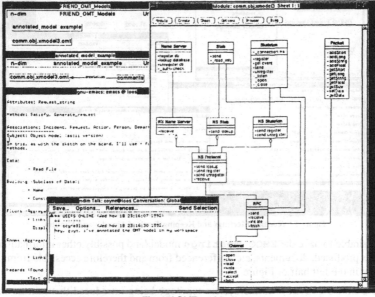

Figure 4 OMT model

only minimal effort expended on the creation of the script that runs OMT, a large improvement in the ability to communicate (and negotiate about) structures created in this external tool can be gained. For instance, in the window `annotated_model_example` in Figure 4, an OMT model has been pointed to and annotated inside of an *n*-dim model, and other developers have been told that such an annotation exists. We conjecture[5] that this capability goes a long way towards alleviating communication breakdowns and errors that can occur. For instance, we observed that our students attempting to describe object models outside OMTool[24] resorted to drawing ASCII version of parts of OMT models (see the `gnu-emacs:emacs@loos` window in Figure 5) within computer bulletin board and e-mail traffic, resulting in large, ungainly and hard to interpret messages. The ability to simply pass reference within a uniform information and communication environment for development can be quite a powerful tool in itself.

Figure 5 shows a possible structure for recording various meetings and keeping track of associated agenda, minutes, comments, follow-up, etc. Even though it is not shown in this illustration,

4. The talk window is a very early experimental prototype of possible real-time communication facilities in *n*-dim; it is currently very limited, and allows for simple textual messages and references to published object to be passed around by all active users of the system.

5. We plan to test this hypothesis and others by actually using *n*-dim experimentally with the software engineering course; see section 4.

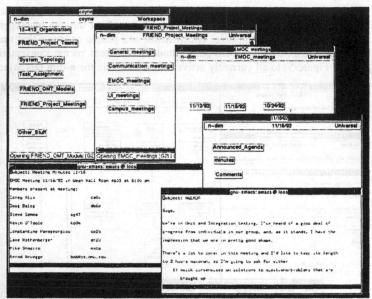

Figure 5 Recording Meetings and Keeping Track of Agendas and Minutes

it may be desirable to have the `EMOC_meetings` model (and possibly other information, such as OMT models produced, documents, etc.) referenced from and therefore accessible from the `EMOC` model shown in the left half of Figure 2.

Figure 6 shows a revision to the system topology being introduced that mirrors the design change discussed in Section 2.2. The original topology model `System_Topology` (in the upper left of the figure) was copied and is being updated as `System_Topology_V2` (lower right of the figure), while the original model remains as part of the design tracking and history of the project. *N*-dim can also, in case this may be desirable, include both models in another model along with annotations as to why the change is being introduced. And it is possible to cross-index this change back to other models which refer to topology models, for instance the `Task_Assignment` model in Figure 3.

4 Plans for experimentation and expected impact

The main challenge in a larger scale project course is the provision of a mechanism that deals with change in the project structure, namely the communication structure, the task assignments and the documents used to describe the system artifacts.

Even more important, this mechanism has to make the change visible to the members of the project within a reasonable update time. While we strongly believe that this can be done with collaborative design tools, the introduction of these tools imposes a high learning curve for the teacher as well as the student. A major issue therefore is how to introduce collaborative design in our software engineering curriculum. We believe it is possible to gradually introduce the tool in several phases.

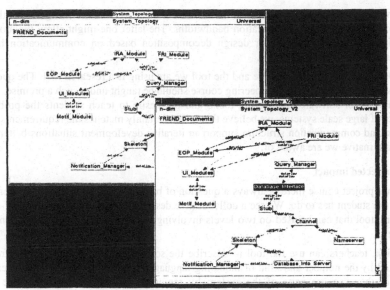

Figure 6 Revised Topology

In the first phase the instructor alone uses *n*-dim on a descriptive level to analyze the project structure (communication structure, artifacts and task assignments). This structure is made visible to the students, for example at the end of the project. In this phase, *n*-dim is not used during the course, neither by the students nor by the instructor. The goal of phase 1 is make the instructor familiar with *n*-dim as a descriptive post-mortem tool. For example, in the figures shown above, we used the tool as a postmortem tool, extracting the project structure from the FRIEND system and presenting it to the students. The project structure was derived from the bulletin boards and interviews with the students and teaching assistants.

In phase 2, the teacher uses *n*-dim as a tracking tool, that is, the tool is involved in setting up the project structure and tracking the evolvement of the project during the course. In our course, this next phase is planned for the Spring 94. We plan to introduce a set of interrelated models of the tasks, organization and artifacts and have a certain convention for using and consulting it on a daily basis. Tools like OMTool and other artifact modeling tools will be able to run out of the *n*-dim environment. If redecomposition or regrouping occurs, the instructors will modify the description and make the change visible to the students.

Having gone through phase 1 and 2, we can assume that the teacher is now familiar enough with the tool to teach it to students at the beginning of the course, for example by presenting the initial project structure in *n*-dim. In phase 3, the tool is placed in the hand of the students. Similar to phase 1 for the instructor, their task is to track any changes in the project structure that is, to use *n*-dim as a descriptive tool.

In phase 4 which we plan to introduce in an advanced software engineering course involving a smaller group of students the students will actively engage in the information structure modeling process, using the tool to influence the discussion but with fixed modeling languages.

In phase 5, n-dim becomes an active assistant for quality control, convergence of the design, recognition of unusual communication bandwidths. The latter one might allow the tool to come up with possible suggestions for design decomposition based on communication bandwidth between people or subjects topics.

Our plan is based a conjecture and the tool we are using is a research tool. The question can be raised whether a software engineering course should be taught under such a premise. Given the current state of software engineering tools, and our desire to teach students the problems and aspects of large scale systems, we believe that n-dim certainly matches the requirements for information and communication structure support in iterative development situations better than any other alternative we are aware of.

4.1 Expected impact

In a project course there is always a question of balance on how much the teacher and how much the student has to do. We see a collaborative design tool such as n-dim as a self-contained teaching tool that can be used on two levels involving a wide spectrum of software engineering courses.

First, teachers can use the tool to describe the software-engineering process infrastructure reflected by the number and kind of modeling languages and their relationship with each other. Second, they can use parts of the system by removing a component. The course we have described in this paper is currently taught as a senior level undergraduate course. Depending on the complexity of the removed component the system could be used in lower levels and other courses. For example, the street database developed in the Interactive Pittsburgh project[5] has already been used in a graph algorithm class. Such a system could also be used in a data structure and algorithm course with an algorithm or a component selectively removed[11]. The advantage of this approach is that we can expose students to system issues quite early in their career. By introducing system issues in lower courses, we would be following other curricula in other areas. The MIT robotics course, for example, involves the design of a robot in a freshman course. System design issues in electrical engineering at Carnegie Mellon University are also now routinely taught on the freshman level.

The introduction of a collaborative design tool as we have suggested in this paper does not diminish the challenges on how to grade students. This issue has to be addressed by *any* software engineering course. Because we believe that team-based courses draw a lot of energy from the fact that students are working together, we have not followed a traditional grading policy. In fact, we tell the students at the beginning of the project course, that they cheat if they do not acknowledge the contributions made by others. As a result, this course is a radical departure from competition and throw-away homeworks. Students who are used to work against a normalized grading curve are now expected to collaborate instead of competing against each other. This makes it sometimes difficult to recognize the contributions made by individual students. We believe with an information management structure like n-dim and its indexing capabilities it will be easier to identify the individual contributions of students in a team project.

5 Conclusion

In this paper we have outlined an advanced curriculum for teaching software engineering that integrates teamwork, model-based software engineering and collaborative design in a state-of-the-art distributed design modeling environment supported by the advanced technology of n-dim.

Our goals are twofold: 1) to teach a broad range of students more effectively the complex issues involved in team-based software design processes and give them explicit experience with negotiation processes and the creation and structure of a shared design history, 2) to test, evaluate and improve tools that support team-based software design.

With an information structures described in this paper we consider it possible to teach software engineering to a larger number of students. In addition to increasing the scale of systems for course projects, we see another way teachers will benefit. Within the near future, we envision an methodology and supporting technology that makes teaching team-based system design in the context of software engineering more realistic, predictable and repeatable.

Our long term vision is the creation of templates for larger scale systems for software engineering courses which can be reused from course to course and distributed to other teachers as self-contained teaching platforms. Such platforms could be used in a wide spectrum of classes, enabling us to teach students software engineering issues right from the beginning of their education.

6 Acknowledgments

This paper would not be possible without the contributions of many people. First and foremost, we would like to acknowledge the contributions of several generations of students and teaching assistants of the software engineering course at Carnegie Mellon University. Without the enthusiasm of these students and their eagerness to learn more about team-based software engineering this course would not exist. We also wish to acknowledge the n-dim group for their pioneering work in collaborative team-based design work and for providing us with the n-dim prototype described in this paper. We especially thank Eswaran Subrahmanian and Sean Levy for discussions about the relationship of n-dim to software engineering, and Sean Levy for his help in prototyping and presenting to students the illustration of adapting n-dim to support object-oriented software engineering by means of interrelated models for the artifact, the process and organization.

7 Appendix

At the end of the semester we asked the students of our Fall 92 project course to reflect on the system development process of the system using the homework shown below. The collected answers[15] are available from the authors.

15-413 Software Engineering Carnegie Mellon University School of Computer Science
Homework 4
For this assignment, please work in teams of up to three people, preferably from different project teams.

What kinds of communication and negotiation problems have emerged in the development (analysis, system design, object design, implementation, unit testing, system testing and delivery) of the FRIEND system?

Given your experience with the FRIEND system development process, what kind of team communication structure is good for collaborative analysis design? Speculate on what kind of information structure is needed for team-based design in conjunction with object-oriented software engineering methodologies. For example, do you think an issue database as presented in class will solve these problems? What would be the problems? How could the issue database be linked to resulting OMT models? In your discussion you may use the above questions as a starting point, but we encourage to discuss other issues from your own experience as well. What other comments do you have about the FRIEND project concerning

- the life cycle used in the project
- the project management
- the documentation process?

The homework should not be longer than 4-5 pages (Illustrations such as sequences of OMT models or examples from the bulletin boards can be added as an appendix).

8 Bibliography

[1] B. Boehm, A Spiral Model of Software Development and Enhancement, in Software Engineering Project Management, R. Thayer (ed), IEEE Computer Society Press, pp. 128-144, 1987.

[2] G. Booch, Object-Oriented Design with Applications, Benjamin Cummings, 1991.

[3] B. Bruegge, J. Cheng and M. Shaw, A Software Engineering Course with a Real Client, Carnegie Mellon University, Technical Report CMU-SEI- 91-EM-4, July 1991.

[4] B. Bruegge, Teaching an Industry-oriented Software Engineering Course, C. Sledge (ed), Software Engineering Education, Lecture Notes in Computer Science, Vol 640, pp. 65-87, Springer Verlag, 1992.

[5] B. Bruegge, J. Blythe, J. Jackson and J. Shufelt, Object-Oriented System Modeling with OMT, Conference on Object-Oriented Programming Systems, Languages and Applications (OOPSLA '92), Vancouver, October 1992.

[6] L. Bucciarelli, An Ethnographic Perspective on Engineering Design, Design Studies, Vol 9, p. 160, 1988.

[7] L. Constantine, Teamwork Paradigms and the Structured Open Team, Proceedings: Embedded Systems Conference, San Francisco, Miller Freeman, 1989.

[8] P. Coad and E. Yourdon, Object-Oriented Analysis, Prentice Hall, 1991.

[9] J.C. Ferrans, D. W. Hurst, M.A. Sennett, B.M. Covnot, W. Ji, P. Kajka and W. Ouyand, Hyperweb: A Framework for Hypermedia-based Environments, In Software Engineering Notes, Vol 17, pp. 1-10, December 1992.

[10] F. Floyd, F. Feisin and G. Schmidt, STEPS to Software Development with Users, 2nd European Software Engineering Conference, pp. 48-64, 1989.

[11] A. J. Offutt and R. H. Untch, Integrating Research, Reuse, and Integration into Software Engineering Courses, C. Sledge (ed), Software Engineering Education, Lecture Notes in Computer Science, Vol 640, pp. 88-98, Springer Verlag, 1992.

[12] C. Ghezzi, M. Jazyeri and D. Mandrioli, Fundamentals of Software Engineering, Prentice Hall, 1991.

[13] I. Graham, Object Oriented Methods, Addison-Wesley, 1991.

[14] First Responder Interactive Navigational Database. 15-413 Software Engineering, Documentation submitted by the students, Carnegie Mellon University, December 1992.

[15] 15-413 Software Engineering, Reflections on the FRIEND project, submitted by the students, Carnegie Mellon University, December 1992.

[16] I. Jacobson, M. Christerson, P. Jonsson and G. Overgaard, Object-Oriented Software Engineering: A Use Case Driven Approach, Addison-Wesley, NY, 1992.

[17] J. Jacquot, J. Guyard and L. Boidot, Modeling Teamwork in an Academic Environment, in Software Engineering Education, J.E. Tomayko (ed.), Lecture Notes in Computer Science, Springer Verlag, pp. 110-122, 1990.

[18] S. Konda, I. Monarch, P. Sargent and E. Subrahmanian, Shared Memory in Design: A Unifying Theme for Research and Practice, Research in Engineering Design, Vol 4, pp 23-42, 1992.

[19] B. Meyer, Toward an Object-Oriented Curriculum, Journal of Object-Oriented Programming, pp. 76-81, May 1993.

[20] G. Toye, M. Cutkosky, L. Leifer, J. Tenenbaum and J. Glicksman, *SHARE: A Methodology and Environment for Collaborative Product Development*, Technical Report 0420, Center for Design Research, Stanford University, 1993.

[21] S. Levy, E. Subrahmanian, S. Konda, R. Coyne, A. Westerberg, Y. Reich, An Overview of the n-dim Environment, Technical Report, EDRC-05-65-93, Carnegie Mellon University, January 1993.

[22] P. Naur, *Computing: A Human Activity*, ACM Press, Addison-Wesley, NY, 1992.

[23] M. Rettig, The Practical Programmer: Software Teams, Communications of the ACM, 33 (10), October 1990.

[24] J. Rumbaugh, M. Blaha, W. Premerlani, F. Eddy and W. Lorenson. Object-Oriented Modeling and Design, Prentice Hall, Englewood Cliffs, NJ, 1991.

[25] J. Rumbaugh, P. Halverson, C. Hansen, S. Masline, T. Topka, C. Roffler, Object Modeling tool (OMTool) User's Manual, GE Corporate Research and Development, Schenectady, NY, August 1991.

[26] W. Scacchi, Managing Software Engineering Projects: A Social Analysis, IEEE Transactions on Software Engineering, 10 (1), pp. 45-59, January 1984.

[27] M. Shaw and J. Tomayko, Models for Undergraduate Project Courses in Software Engineering, in Software Engineering Education, J.E. Tomayko (ed.), Lecture Notes in Computer Science, Springer Verlag, pp. 33-71, 1991.

[28] E. Subrahmanian, S. Konda, S. Levy, I. Monarch, Y. Reich, A. Westerberg, Computational Support for Shared Memory in Design, To appear in: Automation-Based Creative Design: Issues in Computers and Architectures, edited by I. White and A. Tzonis, Elsevier, 1993.

[29] E. Subrahmanian, R. Coyne, S. Konda, S. Levy, R. Martin, I. Monarch, Y. Reich, A. Westerberg, Support System for Different-Time Different Place Collaboration for Concurrent engineering to appear in: WET-ICE (Workshop on Enabling Technologies In Concurrent Engineering), CERC, West Virginia, USA, 1993.

[30] J. Tomayko, Teaching a Project-Intensive Introduction to Software Engineering, Software Engineering Institute, Carnegie Mellon University, Technical Report CMU-SEI-91-EM-6, July 1991.

[31] R. Winant, The Search for Order (Focus on Managing Object Projects), Object Magazine, 2(4), pp. 79-81, Nov-Dec 1992.

[32] R. Wirfs-Brock, B. Wilkerson and L. Wiener, Designing Object-Oriented Software, Prentice Hall, Englewood Cliffs, NJ 1990.

[33] J. Wood and D. Sover, Joint Application Design, Wiley and Sons, New York, 1989.

The Use of Computer Ethics Scenarios in Software Engineering Education: The Case of the Killer Robot

Richard G. Epstein

Department of Mathematics and Computer Science
West Chester University of Pennsylvania
West Chester, PA 19383

Abstract: Computing Curricula '91 stipulates that undergraduate programs in computing should introduce students to the subject of computer ethics. This paper discusses a novel way of introducing computer ethics into the curriculum: the use of *detailed* computer ethics scenarios that *introduce important technical issues* as well as issues in computer ethics. This paper describes a computer ethics scenario that the author uses as a point of departure for an undergraduate software engineering course. The novel element here is the use of computer ethics scenarios to teach *both* computer ethics *and* to introduce significant concepts in software engineering and user interfaces (viewed as an aspect of software engineering). This paper describes the philosophy behind the design of such computer ethics scenarios and suggests how they can be used in other courses in the undergraduate curriculum.

1. Introduction

In recent years, computer science educators have been paying increasing attention to the subject of computer ethics. *Computing Curricula '91* [1] recommended that all undergraduates majors in computing should be given some instruction in computer ethics. The curriculum report presented a specification for the design of undergraduate curricula in computing. That specification included a core curriculum that consisted of a collection of "knowledge units" in ten subject areas. Nine of these subject areas derived from the report of the ACM Task Force on the Core of Computer Science, *Computing as a Discipline* [2]. The Joint Curriculum Task Force added a tenth subject area, "Social, Ethical and Professional Issues". This subject area was represented in the core curriculum by four knowledge units that were entitled: (1) Historical and Social Context of Computing, (2) Responsibilities of the Computing Professional, (3) Risks and Liabilities and (4) Intellectual Property. The curriculum report did not specify how this material and additional materials relating to computer ethics would be covered. Most of the example curricula included in an appendix at the end of the curriculum report integrated the computer ethics material into technical courses (such as software engineering and database management systems).

This paper reports one approach that has been used to introduce computer ethics issues into an undergraduate course in software engineering. This approach involves using a detailed computer ethics scenario in order to introduce significant topics in software engineering at the very beginning of the course. In other words, the computer ethics scenario is used both to introduce the subject of software engineering and to introduce some of the ethical issues inherent in software engineering. The computer ethics scenario is called "the case of the killer robot" and it introduces in very concrete terms software engineering concepts that are discussed in greater detail later in the course. These software engineering topics include:

1. Software engineering paradigms: the lifecycle model and the prototyping model,
2.. Programmer psychology and group dynamics,
3. The mythical man-month [3] and its implications,
4. The role of a requirements document, functional and non-functional specifications,
5. The user interface (Shneiderman's eight golden rules [4]).

In addition, the scenario is a computer ethics scenario and it discusses the responsibilities of computing professionals, the risks and costs of failure and the issue of who is ultimately responsible when software fails.

2. Computer ethics scenarios and the undergraduate curriculum

The author views the case of the killer robot as a model for a new sort of computer ethics scenario that could be used in a variety of courses in the undergraduate curriculum, not just software engineering. Thus, in addition to presenting details of the killer robot scenario itself (this is done in Section 4), the author wishes to explain in some detail the philosophy behind its design and how this technique might be extended to other courses in the undergraduate curriculum. These issues are explored in this and the following section.

The case of the killer robot is *broadly* based upon two computer–related disasters that have been reported in the literature:

1. An assembly line robot killed its operator in Japan during the 1980s (as reported in Forrester and Morrison [5]).

2. An early Mariner space probe had to be destroyed upon launch because a programmer mistook a derivative for an average in a physics formula (as reported in ACM Sigsoft's *Software Engineering Notes* [6]).

Except for borrowing these basic facts, there is no other relationship between the fictitious killer robot scenario and these factual disasters.

Three characteristics of the case of the killer robot distinguish it from the sort of computer ethics scenarios that is commonly employed in teaching courses in computer ethics (for example, the scenarios found at the end of each chapter in Forrester and Morrison [5] and used in other computer ethics texts or that have been used to discuss computer ethics in periodicals such as the *Communications of the ACM* [7,8]). These are:

1. The killer robot scenario is intended to introduce basic concepts of software engineering (including user interface design) at the beginning of an undergraduate course in software engineering,

2. The killer robot scenario is a detailed scenario that is a full book chapter in length.

3. The computer ethics scenario is not primarily intended for use in a course on computer ethics (although it could be used in such a course); rather, it is intended for use in any course that discusses large software systems.

The possibility and efficacy of integrating technical subject matter with issues in computer ethics by means of detailed (say, book chapter length) computer ethics scenarios is the main point of this paper. We are suggesting that the idea of a computer ethics scenario can be expanded to include technical computer science content. This has the advantage that the ethical concerns of computing professionals are viewed as central to the discipline (especially, the engineering aspects of the discipline) and not as peripheral.

The case of the killer robot touches upon the following knowledge units from the core curriculum given in *Computing Curricula '91*:

> *SP: Social, Ethical and Professional Issues*:
> > SP1: Historical and Social Context of Computing
> > SP2: Responsibilities of the Computing Professional
> > SP3: Risks and liabilities

SE: Software Methodology and Engineering
SE2: The Software Development Process
SE3: Software Requirements and Specifications
SE4: Verification and Validation

HU: Human–Computer Communication
HU1: User Interfaces

In the context of an undergraduate course in software engineering, the case of the killer robot was used as a primary vehicle for introducing students to the subject of software engineering. The author could see such a detailed scenario with appropriate annotations serving as an introductory chapter in an undergraduate software engineering text. Annotations would be important, because the author expanded upon the scenario considerably in lecture, providing additional details on the technical topics (e.g., the software engineering paradigms and the role of requirements specifications). Invariably, over the years, student response to this scenario has been very positive, and in fact, the most positive response seems to have come from students who were already working in industry and who recognized the situations being portrayed in the scenario (e.g., the "prima donna" programmer who was not open to criticism).

The author believes that the killer robot scenario represents a promising new strategy for integrating computer ethics issues into the undergraduate curriculum, whether at the introductory level or in more advanced courses. A collection of such scenarios could be integrated throughout the curriculum so that the computer ethics topics could be introduced in conjunction with the relevant technical material. One concern among those interested in computer ethics education is whether professors will take the time to discuss ethical issues in technical courses that have associated ethical issues (e.g., databases, user interfaces, artificial intelligence, operating systems, networks and data communications). The author's belief is that the availability of suitable ethics scenarios for such courses would increase the likelihood that professors will discuss the ethical dimensions of their subjects.

3. Design goals for computer ethics scenarios

Figure 1 summarizes the four basic design goals that guided the development of the case of the killer robot. These are presented as general goals for the creation of future computer ethics scenarios of this type. The figure assumes that the purpose of the computer ethics scenario is to integrate the discussion of computer ethics with traditional technical issues in computer science and engineering (e.g., artificial intelligence, databases, software engineering, user interfaces). This section expands upon the four basic design goals given in Figure 1.

Figure 1: Basic design goals for computer ethics scenarios

1. To introduce one or more issues in computer ethics.

2. To introduce technical material relating to one or more subject areas of the discipline of computing.

3. To present this material in a manner that is made concrete by the use of fictitious characters.

4. To paint a portrait of one or more computing science and engineering professionals in a network of relationships.

Goal 1: To introduce one or more issues in computer ethics.

The first design goal in creating a computer ethics scenario is to cover one or more issues in computer ethics. In the case of the killer robot, the issues are software reliability and the responsibilities and liabilities of computing professionals. Just about any topic in computer ethics can be explored using such a scenario.

Goal 2: To introduce technical material relating to one or more subject areas of the discipline of computing (beyond computer ethics).

The second design goal is to use the computer ethics scenario as a device for exploring technical issues in computer science and engineering. As noted above, the case of the killer robot introduced students to issues in software engineering and user interfaces. Many technical subjects would seem to be amenable to this kind of treatment. For example, a scenario dealing with hacking and / or viruses could be used to introduce technical issues relating to operating systems and telecommunications. A scenario dealing with data privacy could be used to introduce security issues in operating systems and in database management systems. There seems to be no limit to the actual scenarios that could be constructed in this manner. What is important is that the scenario render both *concrete* and *vivid* technical issues that have some interface with the ethical dimension of computing.

Goal 3: To present computer ethics in a manner that is made more concrete by the use of fictitious characters.

The computer ethics scenario should be written in a manner that is both informative and engaging. The fictitious characters in the ethics scenario can help bring these issues to life for the students. The essential goal, as mentioned above, is to render the dilemma or dilemmas both concrete and vivid in the students' minds. The ethical dilemmas can be presented in a variety of formats. For example, the case of the killer robot employs five newspaper articles and one journal article to present its scenario. The newspaper articles were completely fictitious (in terms of the characters involved) and the journal article was written by a fictitious expert on user interfaces. The newspaper articles presented issues in software engineering and the journal article presented issues in user interface design.

The killer robot articles were written to be fun to read. In fact, when the killer robot scenario was first used in a software engineering course (in the liberal arts software engineering course described in [9]), the articles were being generated about one per week. The idea was that students would read the new article as homework in order to discuss the issues raised at the next class. The author discovered that he could not distribute the new killer robot materials at the beginning of the class, because if he did, the students would become so involved in reading the newest developments in the case, that they would not pay attention to the lecture.

Goal 4: To paint a portrait of one or more computer science professionals in a network of relationships.

One of the primary goals in the killer robot case was to focus on one computing professional (Randy Samuels, one of the programmers in the robot project) and to portray that professional as existing at the center of an ever widening network of relationships. It is not that Randy Samuels' network of relationships grew as the scenario unfolded, rather the student's awareness of that network grows with each new article in the scenario. In this way, the case of the killer robot attempts to capture a profound truth concerning the life of a professional computer scientist or engineer; namely, that he or she does not work in isolation, but rather in a very complex web of relationships and that professionalism involves, in part, becoming aware of that network of relationships and one's role in it.

It would seem that computer ethics is fundamentally about this issue (the computing professional and / or the computer user in a network of relationships) and thus that all computer ethics scenarios must make an attempt to portray that network is some manner. This is especially important because most of our students work in relative isolation through most of their undergraduate careers. When they think of a computing professional in the real world, unless they have had some exposure to what it means to be a computing professional, they think of someone like themselves working in relative isolation on the "real world" analogy of "the homework assignment."

The next section presents an overview of the case of the killer robot, as an example of the sort of computer ethics scenario that the author is propounding. It is useful to bear in mind, however, that in the largest sense, this sequence of articles is all about increasing the student's awareness of the complex network of relationships alluded to above. The first article in the series announces the indictment of the programmer in the killer robot case on the charge of manslaughter. This article is intentionally written focus upon the programmer in the narrowest of contexts, a context not unlike the academic situation of being given a homework assignment and then either succeeding or failing at that assignment. Each subsequent article introduces new characters and forces in the programmer's professional life. Slowly, the student gets an opportunity to understand how different the work–world situation is from the normal academic setting.

4. Synopsis of the killer robot scenario

This section presents a synopsis of the killer robot scenario, article by article. This summary emphasizes how technical material relating to software engineering and user interfaces is integrated into the scenario. The first five articles (summarized in sections 4.1 – 4.5) were written as newspaper articles (for a fictitious newspaper, *The Silicon Valley Sentinel–Observer*. The last article was written as a journal article (for a fictitious journal, *Robotics World*). In addition to the six articles, students were given supplementary lecture materials that served as a commentary on the issues being raised. These lecture materials pointed out the and expanded upon the software engineering and user interface issues being raised in each article and provided students with references on these topics in the literature. Of course, these lectures were accompanied by lively classroom discussions of the ethical issues and controversies inherent in the scenario.

It should be mentioned that all characters and organizations used in the scenario are purely fictitious. "Silicon Valley" was used as a symbol of high technology, and there is no relationship (for example) between Silicon Valley University and any actual university, or between the businesses that are mentioned and any actual companies or corporations.

4.1 Silicon Valley Programmer Indicted for Manslaughter

This article announces the indictment of Randy Samuels, a programmer for Silicon Robotics, for manslaughter. This article informs the students that Randy Samuels misinterpreted a physical dynamics formula and this caused a Robbie CX30 robot to oscillate wildly and to kill its operator.

At this point, the student, who has done some programming, might agree with the prosecutor that Randy Samuels is responsible, morally, if not legally, for the robot operator's death. After all, his misinterpretation of the robot dynamics formula was a form of negligence on his part. Most students (except those who have had some exposure to the realities of the workplace) are unaware of the vast network of professional relationships that might have been contributory factors to the accident. It is the goal of the subsequent articles to slowly reveal that complex network of relationships.

4.2 Developers of 'Killer Robot' Worked Under Enormous Stress

This newspaper article initiates the process of portraying the network of relationships surrounding the indicted programmer, Randy Samuels. The student learns that the project was late and that management made a decision to hire more programmers so as to expedite the production of the robot software. The article points out that these new hires were never fully integrated into the project and only made the project fall further behind schedule. The commentary that accompanies the article refers the students to Brooks' influential book, *The Mythical Man–Month* [3]. which first introduced the idea that adding people to a late software project only makes that project later.

In this article, the student also learns that Ray Johnson, the project leader, expounded the "Ivory Snow Theory" of software design and development. The newspaper article explains the Ivory Snow Theory in this way: *"The gist of* [Ray Johnson's] *'Ivory Snow Theory' is simply that Ivory Snow is 99 and 44/100 per cent pure and there is no reason why robotics software had to be purer than that"*. This leads the students to consider the implications of failure. When are the costs of failure so great that the Ivory Snow Theory should not apply? Does the Ivory Snow Theory ever make sense? Clearly, not all systems can tolerate failure to the same degree. Certainly, tolerance for failure is much less in a "life critical" application.

Another of Ray Johnson's software design and development principles is that "Perfection is the enemy of the good". The commentary that accompanies the newspaper article explains that this is one of four basic human engineering principles enunciated by Rubenstein and Hirsh [10] in their book on user interface design. The students are asked to ponder whether this principle, arguably applicable to the design of user interfaces, applies to the construction of software systems such as the Robbie CX30 robot.

4.3 'Killer Robot' Programmer was Prima Donna, Co–Workers Claim

This article introduces the student to the subject of programmer psychology, a subject introduced by Weinberg in his influential book, *The Psychology of Computer Programmers* [11]. Indeed, the commentary that accompanies this article refers to Weinberg's text and its advocacy of "egoless programming". This article also draws heavily upon Ledgard's discussion of programming teams and group dynamics [12].

The fictitious software psychologist, Sharon Skinner, a faculty member at Silicon Valley University, is used as a device to introduce this material on programmer psychology and group dynamics. The student is introduced to three basic programmer personality types (self–oriented, task–oriented and interaction–oriented) and is told that empirical research suggests that heterogeneous teams perform better than homogeneous teams (homogeneous meaning that all team members have the same personality type). Professor Skinner then discusses various problems that programming teams encounter, including talent overload and responsibility drift, the latter being a major symptom of team fragmentation (according to Ledgard). As the title suggests, Professor Skinner voices the opinion that Randy Samuels, the killer robot programmer, was a "prima donna", a person who did not take criticism very well, and the students are confronted with the possibility that this personality flaw might have played a role in the killer robot accident.

4.4 'Killer Robot' Project Mired in Controversy Right from Start

This article introduces the students to two basic software process models (or, software engineering paradigms): the waterfall model and the prototyping model. This article also raises issues concerning personal and institutional commitments to existing technologies and resistance to change.

After presenting a brief description of the waterfall model and the prototyping model, the article goes on to describe a conflict between management, who wanted to use the waterfall model, and members of the programming team, who preferred the prototyping model. Students are introduced to the idea that the prototyping model might be better for a project in which the user interface is bound to play a significant role (i.e., the robot operator user interface). Management wins not because the waterfall model was better suited to the problem at hand, but because of institutional inertia.

4.5 Silicon Robotics Promised to Deliver a Safe Robot

This article introduces the students to the concept of a requirements document. The nature of a requirements document is discussed and the difference between functional and non-functional requirements is introduced. The student is then told that Silicon Robotics was obligated, by specifically cited paragraphs in the requirements document, both to deliver a safe robot and to provide the customer (Cybernetics, Inc.) with adequate operator training.

This article introduces the student to the idea that a requirements document serves as a business contract between developers and customers. In addition, the student learns that a requirements document might include specific requirements in terms of product safety and operator training. In the case of the killer robot, the significance of the user interface as well as the significance of operator training was not well appreciated by either party to this business contract – the robot developer and the robot customer.

4.6 The 'Killer Robot' Interface

This item takes the form of a journal article published in a fictitious journal, *Robotics World*. The article includes an abstract, suitable references and all of the pompous self–confidence of a fictional world–class computer expert. That expert is Dr. Horace Gritty, who naturally enough serves on the faculty of the fictitious Silicon Valley University.

The following excerpt from the abstract summarizes Dr. Gritty's perspective on the killer robot case:

> " ... This paper propounds the theory that it was the operator–robot interface designer
> who should be on trial in this case. The Robbie CX30 robot violates nearly every rule
> of the interface design. This paper focuses on how the Robbie CX30 interface violated
> every one of Shneiderman's 'Eight Golden Rules'."

Dr. Gritty goes on to present a detailed analysis of the robot console user interface, introducing and explaining in some detail Shneiderman's "Eight Golden Rules" [4]. These are:

1. Strive for consistency
2. Enable frequent users to use shortcuts
3. Offer informative feedback
4. Design dialogues to yield closure
5. Offer simple error handling
6. Permit easy reversal of actions
7. Support internal locus of control
8. Reduce short–term memory load.

By introducing the rules first abstractly and then concretely in terms of the robot console user interface, Dr. Gritty's article serves as a rather complete tutorial on Shneiderman's rules for interface design.

The Appendix includes the text of one of the killer robot articles and some example questions that could be used in a classroom discussion of the ethical and technical issues.

5. Further discussion

In the author's opinion, computer ethics scenarios represent an interesting technique for communicating information about the discipline of computing. As suggested earlier, there would seem to be almost no limit to the scenarios that could be constructed. Certainly, the scenarios need not take the form of newspaper and journal articles. For example, they could simply be presented as technological short stories.

The author believes that computer ethics scenarios of this type (that is, extensive scenarios with considerable technical content) may provide an excellent means of communicating to students the nature of the complex web of relationships that surround the computing professional and which are the very source of all ethical dilemmas. In the case of the killer robot, the articles systematically expand the student's awareness of the complex web of relationships that surrounded the programmer, Randy Samuels. By extension, the student can envision himself or herself in a professional setting that includes a similar complex network of relationships.

The following is an extended quote from an early draft of an essay on software reliability that was intended for Volume II of *Fundamentals of Computing* [13]. This is the second volume of a four volume breadth-first introduction to computing that is being developed by Allen Tucker, this author and educators at various institutions. This quote appears in the published text, but in an abbreviated form. This quote serves as a good summary of what the case of the killer robot is ultimately attempting to communicate:

> " ... [T]he computing professional sits in a complex web of relationships. It is important
> for the computing professional to become aware of those relationships in order to per-

form his or her tasks in an effective and ethical manner. For example, imagine yourself newly employed at a software firm that is developing an off–the–shelf income tax system for home use that will be used by millions of people. Your work places you in an enormous network of relationships that will slowly make its presence felt as you progress in your career. At first you may only be aware of your immediate co–workers and your supervisor, but as you progress you will slowly come to realize the 'big picture'.

"That big picture includes the larger picture at your company: the corporate battles and strategies, the conflicting personalities and interests. It includes the sort of raw human emotions that are not usually a part of your education as a computer scientist. It includes your company's customers and their financial health. It includes your company's competitors and, if those competitors are overseas, global economic relationships and the possibility that your country will lose jobs to your competitor's country. It includes the broader social impact of the product that you are developing — upon tax accountants and lawyers, for example. Thus, working on a software project is not a small matter at all.

"Imagine, now, the enormity of the 'big picture' if you are working on software that will be used in a life–critical medical application (e.g., administering radiation dosages to cancer patients) or software that will be used to control the flight dynamics of an airplane. Then, your network of relationships includes the lives of the potential patients and their families (in the case of the medical application) and the lives of their airplane crews, passengers and their families (in the case of the flight control application). Computing professionals have enormous power and influence on the lives of others in part because their artifacts are so easily reproduced and disseminated. Computing professionals like other professionals need to understand the network of relationships in which they work."

Ironically, several months after the above paragraphs were written, a software reliability case involving one of the largest vendors of personal computer income tax software captured national headlines (this was the winter of 1992). The vendor in question became aware of the fact that their software was giving wrong advice on business deductions, but the vendor chose not to make their knowledge public out of fear that it might impact negatively on their sales. The news broke when the IRS announced that they were flagging returns produced by this software package for auditing. Evidently, the IRS came to the conclusion that this software package was contributing to the already ballooning federal budget deficit.

6. Summary

This paper described the design philosophy behind and the use of a detailed computer ethics scenario in an undergraduate software engineering course. This paper suggests that such scenarios could be used through the undergraduate curriculum in computing. Such scenarios are intended to: (1) Introduce an issue in computer ethics, (2) Introduce technical materials from various subject areas of computing in a concrete manner and (3) provide some insight into the complex network of relationships within which the computing professional works. We believe that the use of such scenarios can help realize some of the goals of *Computing Curricula '91* insofar as the teaching of computer ethics is concerned. In particular, we see the possibility of meaningfully integrating computer ethics into the technical courses rather than relegating computer ethics to a separate course.

7. References

1. Tucker, A. (ed.), Barnes, B., Aiken, R., Barker, K., Bruce K., Cain, J., Conry, S., Engel, G., Epstein, R., Lidtke, D., Mulder, M., Rogers, J., Spafford, E., and Turner, A., *Computing Curricula 1991*, Report of the ACM / IEEE CS Joint Curriculum Task Force, ACM and IEEE CS Press, New York, 1991.

2. Denning, P., Comer, D., Gries, D., Mulder, M., Tucker, A., Turner, A. and Young, P., "Computing as a Discipline", *Report of the ACM Task Force on the Core of Computer Science*, ACM, New York, 1988.

3. Brooks, Frederick P., *The Mythical Man-Month: Essays on Software Engineering*, Addison-Wesley, Reading, MA 1975.

4. Shneiderman, Ben, *Designing the User Interface*, Addison-Wesley, Reading, MA, 1986.

5. Forrester, T. and Morrison, P., *Computer Ethics: Cautionary Tales and Ethical Dilemnas in Computing*, MIT Press, Cambridge, MA, 1990.

6. *SOFTWARE ENGINEERING NOTES*, publication of ACM Special Interest Group on Software Engineering.

7. Weiss, Eric A., "The XXII Self-Assessment: The Ethics of Computing", Communications of the ACM, 33(11), November 1990, pp. 110–132.

8. Anderson, Ronald et al., "Using the New ACM Code of Ethics in Decision Making", Communications of the ACM, 36(2), February 1993, pp. 98–107.

9. Epstein, R., "A Liberal Arts Software Engineering Course", *Computer Science Education*, 2(2), Summer 1992.

10. Rubenstein and Hirsch, *The Human Factor*, Digital Press, Bedford, MA, 1984.

11. Weinberg, Gerald, *The Psychology of Computer Programming*, Van Nostrand Reinhold, New York, 1971.

12. Ledgard, Henry, *Professional Software*, Volume I, Addison-Wesley, Reading, MA, 1987.

13. Tucker, A., Bradley, J., Cupper, R., and Epstein, R., *Fundamentals of Computing*, Volume II, McGraw-Hill, New York, 1993.

Appendix

This appendix presents the third of the killer robot articles in order to illustrate the way in which technical material (in this case, programmer psychology and group dynamics) was integrated into the computer ethics scenario. Please bear in mind that this article only served as a point of departure for a more detailed discussion of programmer psychology and group dynamics. That more detailed discussion took the form of formal lecture materials plus classroom discussion of the technical and ethical issues being raised.

438

'Killer Robot' Programmer
Was Prima Donna
Co-workers Claim

Special to the SILICON VALLEY SENTINEL-OBSERVER
Silicon Valley, USA

by Mabel Muckraker

Randy Samuels, the former Silicon Robotics programmer who was indicted for writing the software that was responsible for the gruesome "killer robot" incident last May, was apparently a 'prima donna' who found it very difficult to accept criticism, several of his co–workers claimed today.

In a free-wheeling interview with several of Samuel's co-workers on the 'killer robot' project, the Sentinel-Observer was able to gain important insights into the psyche of the man who may have been criminally responsible for the death of Bart Matthews, robot operator and father of three small children.

With the permission of those interviewed, the Sentinel-Observer allowed Professor Sharon Skinner of the Department of Software Psychology at Silicon Valley University to listen to a recording of the interview. Professor Skinner studies the psychology of programmers and other psychological factors that might impact upon the software development process.

"I would agree with the woman who called him a 'prima donna' ", Professor Skinner explained. "This is a term used to refer to a programmer who just cannot accept criticism, or more accurately, cannot accept his or her own fallibility".

"Randy Samuels has what we software psychologists call a task-oriented personality, bordering on self-oriented. He likes to get things done, but his ego is heavily involved in his work. In the programming world this is considered a 'no–no' ", Professor Skinner added in her book-lined office.

Professor Skinner went on to explain some additional facts about programming teams and programmer personalities. "Basically, we have found that a good programming team requires a mixture of personality types, including a person who is interaction-oriented, who derives a lot of satisfaction from working with other people, someone who can help keep the peace and keep things moving in a positive direction. Most programmers are task-oriented, and this can be a problem if one has a team in which everyone is task-oriented."

Samuels' co–workers were very reluctant to lay the blame for the robot disaster at his feet, but when pressed to comment on Samuels' personality and work habits, several important facts emerged. Samuels worked on a team consisting of about a dozen analysts, programmers and software testers. (This does not include the twenty programmers who were later hired and who never became actively involved in the development of the robotics software.) Although individual team members had definite specialties, almost all were involved in the software process from beginning to end.

"Sam Reynolds has a background in data processing. He's managed several software projects of that nature", one of the team members said, referring to the manager of the Robbie CX30 project. "But, his role in the project was mostly managerial. He attended all important meetings and he kept Ray [Ray Johnson, the Robotics Division Chief] off our backs as much as possible."

Sam Reynolds, as was reported in yesterday's Sentinel-Observer, was under severe pressure to deliver a working Robbie CX30 robot by January 1 of this year. Sam Reynolds could not be reached for comment either about his role in the incident or about Samuels and his work habits.

"We were a democratic team, except for the managerial guidance provided by Sam [Reynolds]", another team member observed. In the world of software development, a democratic team is a team in which all team members have an equal say in the decision–making process. "Unfortunately, we were a team of very ambitious, very talented – if I must say so myself – and very opinionated individualists. Randy [Samuels] was just the worst of the lot. I mean we have two guys and one gal with masters degrees from CMU who weren't as arrogant as Randy."

CMU refers to Carnegie–Mellon University, a national leader in software engineering education.

One co-worker told of an incident in which Samuels stormed out of a quality assurance meeting. This meeting involved Samuels and three 'readers' of a software module which he had designed and implemented. Such a meeting is called a code review. One of the readers mentioned that Samuels had used a very inefficient algorithm (program) for achieving a certain result and Samuels "turned beet red". He yelled a stream of obscenities and then left the meeting. He never returned.

"We sent him a memo about the faster algorithm and he eventually did use the more efficient algorithm in his module", the co–worker added.

The software module in the quality assurance incident was the very one which was found to be at fault in the robot operator 'murder'. However, this co–worker was quick to point out that the efficiency of the algorithm was not an issue in the malfunctioning of the robot.

"It's just that Randy made it very difficult for people to communicate their concerns to him. He took everything very personally. He graduate tops in his class at college and later graduated with honors in software engineering from Purdue. He's definitely very bright."

"Randy had this big computer-generated banner on his wall", this co-worker continued. "It said, 'YOU GIVE ME THE SPECIFICATION AND I'LL GIVE YOU THE COMPUTATION'. That's the kind of arrogance he had and it also shows that he had little patience for developing and checking the specifications. He loved the problem-solving aspect, the programming itself".

"It doesn't seem that Randy Samuels caught on to the spirit of 'egoless programming'", Professor Skinner observed upon hearing this part of the interview with Samuels' co-workers. "The idea of egoless programming is that a software product belongs to the team and not to the individual programmers. The idea is to be open to criticism and to be less attached to one's work. Code reviews are certainly consistent with this philosophy."

A female co–worker spoke of another aspect of Samuels' personality – his helpfulness. "Randy hated meetings, but he was pretty good one on one. He was always eager to help. I remember one time when I ran into a serious roadblock and instead of just pointing me in the right direction, he took over the problem and solved it himself. He spent nearly five entire days on my problem".

"Of course, in retrospect, it might have been better for poor Mr. Matthews and his family if Randy had stuck to his own business", she added after a long pause.

Some Questions for Classroom Discussion

1. List ways in which you believe the "real–world" of computing differs from your experience at school thus far. In particular, how was the environment in which Randy Samuels worked different from the environment for doing programming assignments here at school?

2. The three basic personality types are task-oriented, self-oriented and interaction-oriented. Why do you think it is a bad idea to have a team that consists solely of task-oriented individuals such as was the case with the killer robot team?

3. Randy Samuels is identified as a "prima donna". Compare the implications of such a personality for academic work versus work in a business setting where the emphasis is on team work.

4. Ledgard, a software engineer, has written about fundamental problems that confront programming teams (he calls them "groups" unless they are truly a team working in the cooperative spirit of "ego-less

programming"). One of these problems is "responsibility drift", in which tasks that have been assigned to one person are taken over by another person or persons. Why do you think that this might be an indication of a team in trouble? Or, do you think it is a good idea to let responsibilities drift?

5. Does the concept of "egoless programming" that was originally introduced by Weinberg have any relevance to an academic setting? How might we foster egoless programming in our curriculum? Do you believe that egoless programming is essential in a professional setting or is it just some sort of abstract, philosophical concept?

6. Do you think that management was negligent in allowing Randy Samuels to behave in the manner in which he did? What could management have done to improve the group dynamics on the Robbie CX30 robot team?

Computer Productivity Initiative

Kurt J. Maly[1], Dennis E. Ray[1], J. Christian Wild[1], Irwin B. Levinstein[1],
Stephan Olariu[1], C. Michael Overstreet[1], Nageswara S. V. Rao[2], Tijen
Ireland[1] and George Kantsios[1]

[1] Department of Computer Science, Old Dominion University
Norfolk, VA 23529-0162, email: cpi@cs.odu.edu
[2] Intelligent Systems Section, Center for Engineering Systems Advanced Research,
Oak Ridge National Laboratory, Oak Ridge, TN 37831-6364

Abstract. Over the last three decades computer science has evolved
into a mature and experimentally oriented discipline with a well defined
curriculum. Only recently have we come to realize that as a discipline
computer science must reach beyond its own subject area to applications
in other disciplines in order to stay relevant. Most computer science curricula teach principles and programming skills in isolation from an application perspective, provide limited laboratory experience, and introduce
inadequate integration with non-CS components. The Computer Productivity Initiative, described in this paper, proposes to alleviate these problems by integrating a multi-year project into the curriculum. The project
involves courses normally taken in three different years of the curriculum.
It includes hardware and software issues and also addresses engineering,
business, and other non-CS issues. The initiative uses prototyping and
simulations in the development of specifications for an integrated television communication and display computer system. The students apply
principles of productivity and make extensive use of leading-edge technologies both in the process of the project development and the product
being developed. They hone essential career-oriented skills in the areas
of management, formal presentations, and group problem solving. This
paper is a report of work in progress. It emphasizes the implementation
issues we are facing and the integration of evaluation into our curriculum development. It describes our preparation for the dissemination of
a model curriculum when we are able to demonstrate that the approach
is adaptable to CS departments across the country.

1 Introduction

The Computer Productivity Initiative (CPI) is a concerted effort designed to
modify the traditional computer science curriculum to better prepare new computer professionals for the careers awaiting them. Its formal birth came in response to a singular complaint echoed by many fronts concerning the quality
and preparation of the newly graduated students. Several deficiencies have been
identified, in part, by many studies and papers. In particular, reports by the
ACM/IEEE Joint Curriculum Task Force [2] and NSF Computer Science Education Workshop Report (Foley *et al.* [9]), British Computer Society and Institution of Electrical Engineers [1], and articles by Denning [10], Parnas [18], Shaw

[22] and Wulf [25] discuss several aspects of computer science education. The CPI innovation evolved during various departmental faculty meetings and was subsequently supported by the Old Dominion University. This support led to the commitment of combined financial resources by the National Science Foundation and Old Dominion University to develop this complex project over several years.

The continuing discussion of what higher education institutions should be teaching the new computer scientist is documented in several studies, and is a focal point of educational professionals (Parnas [18], Shaw [22]). Their evaluations call for changes in the current educational curriculum to meet the needs of year 2000 and beyond (see the report of the Commonwealth of Virginia's Commission on The University of the 21st Century [3]). Locally, the notion that shifting needs require curricular changes has been diagnosed from several symptoms uncovered in annual departmental self-assessment activities. During interviews with graduating computer science majors over the past few years, students have reported difficulties in describing, during job and graduate school entrance interviews, how their background meets the emerging requirements of computer scientists. Graduates who have been practicing professionals for one to five years report that their initial work experience was devoted to several months of company training programs before being allowed to take on active company responsibilities. Discussions with business and industry leaders as well as government and military representatives, including those on our advisory board, have revealed that employers have the same impression of recent graduates. This picture, when brought into focus, displays a curriculum which develops graduates who are less than prepared for immediate productive efforts in entry level positions. They are often found to be functionally incapable of productive work without significant training beyond their university education.

Interestingly enough, the same newly graduated professionals, although considered inept and incapable of productive efforts, are perceived by the same employers as having a sound education and a great promise of potentially significant productive efforts in the future. They are perceived as certified computer scientists who, generally, do not possess the skill to apply their scientific education in the fields where they are needed. Their capabilities are strong but fall just short of societal, business, and industry expectations.

In this paper we describe the CPI effort currently in progress. As we shall explain, the current project, Logically Integrated Family Entertainment System (LIFE), involves designing a modular interface unit to a picture-on-picture television system that extends the functional use of the television to incorporate typical household functions. Three basic modules were described by students: home safety and security, message data base and television directory, and remote telephone access and operation. All modules interact with the family television either as the primary or secondary window of the family's picture-on-picture television.

The remainder of this paper is organized as follows. In Section 2 we identify some of the shortcomings we have found in our computer science undergraduate program. We have incorporated a multi-year project into the computer science curriculum; a brief outline of our approach is described in Section 3. Our plan and its execution is based on a design described in Section 4. Section 5 describes our evaluation approach to ensure the soundness of the model curriculum we are planning to disseminate. We report the current status of the implementation cycle and future work in Sections 6 and 7 respectively.

2 Limitations of Current Curricula

In recent years, the discipline of computer science is increasingly perceived as a laboratory science. Some of its concepts are best illustrated by a repetitive application of a sequence of investigative actions: analysis, proposed solution, experimentation, observation, and new analysis. As history has taught us, the availability of technology is not enough, we must also learn to make productive use of that technology.

The traditional computer science curriculum is successful in addressing the fundamental concepts of the field, as described in several ACM/IEEE reports on the contents of the CS curriculum. In particular, the ACM/IEEE curriculum achieves the objectives for which it is designed [2]. Students are carefully guided through the development of problem solving methodologies and programming skills. Typically the students are exposed to theoretical concepts which underlie computer science. These theoretical concepts are illustrated using well understood and well structured applications such as compilers, operating systems and databases. These illustrations generally include clear specifications of a problem to be solved (as do most laboratory assignments) and so students are rarely exposed in classes or laboratories to the system development process which precedes these clear specifications. Some enhancements to the conventional curriculum could provide a significant exposure to that process, beginning with a broad, unstructured problem and aiming at a structured solution which improves productivity of the process for which the project is carried out. These enhancements will enable the students to go beyond the following limitations associated with traditional undergraduate computer science curricula:

1. *Teaching principles and programming skills in isolation from application perspective:* The material from several courses is rarely integrated in a way to illustrate its applicability to practical projects.

2. *Limited laboratory experience:* Conventional instructional methods based on lecturing in the class and leaving the students to themselves to perform the implementation work do not provide students with adequate laboratory experience.

3. *Restricted comprehensive framework that does not provide for enough integration with non-CS components:* Typical industrial projects are not restricted to contain only modules that are exclusively CS-related; often integration of hardware/software modules that require knowledge of engineering, etc., are required to complete the project. But few traditional curricula attempt to integrate solutions from outside of the CS domain.

4. *Inadequate emphasis on life-long skills:* Students are virtually unexposed to life-long skills, such as justification presentations of a project or its subsystems to groups, project planning, and cost estimation. Also, group interaction and cooperation skills are not formally developed in the curriculum, yet the students are expected to possess such skills as soon as they enter graduate school or work environments.

Some of these limitations have been identified in the past by several educators. Various universities have efforts underway to address these problems. For example, the initiative at University of Virginia [5] addresses the issues of limited laboratory experience. The Software Engineering Institute addresses several issues of solving large scale real-life problems in the domain of software engineering [6].

3 The CPI Solution:

The primary objective of this initiative is to increase the effectiveness of the undergraduate learning experience. This objective will be achieved by applying a multi-year, real-life project with a coordinated infrastructure of formal laboratories. The effect of the proposed initiative will be the education of computer scientists who have a thorough understanding of fundatmental CS principles, and who can apply this knowledge to enhance the productivity of an application process.

The principle features of this initiative can be summarized by presenting them as foci of coordinated effort.

Focus 1: *Multi-year project experience:* Students will have the opportunity to solve well-specified problems in the regular course work and also to apply these principles in a less structured environment of a project. The hands-on experience in the laboratories provides both motivation and application of the principles. The following topics will be emphasized:

(a) planning, specification and development; design, implementation, evaluation and improvements;

(b) use of material from different courses; and

(c) management skills, presentation skills, and group problem solving and coordination

Focus 2: *Experience beyond computer science:* By the choice of a real-life project, the students will be exposed to various issues such as engineering, societal and economic impact, and other similar concerns that are not covered in mainstream CS curricula. Of a particular interest is the impact of non-traditional subjects such as security, human to system interfaces, available technology and its acceptance by society on the solution to the project.

Focus 3: *Exposure to leading-edge technologies:* While the main emphasis of this initiative is to develop graduates who are capable of increasing the productivity of the users of computing technology, students will learn to increase their own effectiveness, both as individuals and as teams, through the use of computer technology, e.g. multimedia, hyper-case, and software engineering tools.

Focus 4. *Principles of productivity:* Students will be exposed to concepts to improve productivity using computers and measure the productivity gains in the context of a concrete project.

Focus 5. *Portable Curriculum:* As a tangible output, we expect to produce a portable curriculum package so that CS departments at other universities can implement CPI without incurring all of the initial development costs. The proposed package consists of the following items:

(a) Instructional Material: course folders, instructors manual, curriculum modifications, video tapes, and textbooks.

(b) Organizational Material: manpower and resources analysis, facilities, and equipment.

(c) Software: Our evaluation approach is based on evaluating the decisions in the development process, and adapting our model curriculum to other environments by using only those portions which are appropriate and developing individualized components for the remainder.

The major innovations of this initiative are:

1. The fundamental characteristic of our effort is to provide students with general problem-solving methods which relate to the use of computers to improve productivity.
2. An infrastructure which integrates a coordinated set of formal laboratories into the curriculum.
3. Exposing and teaching students life-long skills to develop coherent and persuasive application development plans.
4. Teaching students effective scientific methods for experimentation.
5. Effective utilization of computer technology emphasizing the problem-solving process.

In developing this solution we considered alternative solutions including the senior projects found in many existing curricula. We decided instead on a broader approach. First, the project pervades the entire curriculum: students are exposed to parts of the project early in their curriculum and will carry it out in its entirety at the senior level. Secondly, this project is done by the class as a group, where different solutions are proposed, presented and discussed to arrive at a final solution. In particular, our approach is different from the method used at the University of Virginia [5] and Clemson University (Turner [23]) in that a single larger scale project carried out by groups is a unifying factor in the laboratories of various courses. This integrating factor introduces software engineering principles that are presently being investigated for incorporation into the undergraduate education. A need for exposure to such principles in undergraduate education has been recognized universally; (see [1, 4]). An alternative we did not consider was a separate undergraduate program in software engineering [6, 12]; instead our approach is based on integrating software engineering methods into the existing curriculum at a larger scale. Thus, our approach is also different from those that attempt to incorporate software engineering principles into individual courses Bruegge [7], Kantioudi *et al.* [13], Lively and Lease [14], and Offutt and Untch [15].

Finally, although our approach is laboratory-based, it goes beyond adding formal laboratories to an existing set of courses, since the laboratories are integrated to bring material from various courses to bear on the solution of a single focussed project. Efforts that introduce closed laboratories into individual courses are described in Epp [8], Olson [16], Penny and Ashton [19], Prather *et al.* [11], Ray [20], Roberge and Suriano [21].

4 Implementation

Overcoming the limitations outlined in Section 2 requires changes to the curriculum. The fundamental CPI approach is to coordinate student activities (e.g., laboratory assignments, class projects, course papers, class presentations) such that each activity always achieves two or more educational requirements simultaneously. One of these achievements is always a CPI issue.

To incorporate the five foci of Section 3 into the curriculum required us to define the details of how to coordinate the various courses in the program. Our implementation adapts the existing curriculum so that a large scale real-life project is developed by students in several courses during several semesters. We recognize that the typical industrial project has many factors such as: the development of functional requirements and system specifications, the selling of the proposal to higher management, the construction of a development plan with schedules, budgets, and personnel requirements, the recognition and resolution of perceived risks, and the development of detailed system specifications which have gone through a cycle of evaluation and refinement.

In choosing a method for implementing the foci, we had to overcome an apparent contradiction. In a typical large-scale development project that has software as a component, the software is developed over several years by various professionals devoting their full time effort to the project. Students, even as a team, are at best available for two semesters (mostly one) and are just part timers (they take other courses). We needed a method which allowed seniors to do the planning but which permitted freshmen, sophomores and juniors to have the experience of participation in a large project at a level that is consistent with their knowledge and skills. The pieces of the large project must as well conform to the individual course concepts and required materials. The large project must be sufficient to allow the lower class explorations and significant enough to require major efforts by the design and specification courses. The logical connectivity for these efforts is the laboratory associated with the courses.

The coordination of the laboratories, the CPI project, and the overall program is administered by the CPI committee. The committee is composed of seven full time faculty and two graduate research assistants. One faculty member serves as the coordinator of project elements. Others function not only in an advisory capacity but individually as course coordinators for each of the courses associated with the project. The committee meets weekly to analyze outstanding problems and develop solutions. The members of the committee are augmented by an advisory board composed of seven members from diverse organizations or activities (education, research, production, system design, or development). The advisory board and committee meet three to four times a year to further define the function and operation of CPI.

With the concurrence of the advisory board, the committee chose to include two lower level courses along with the senior level Computer Based Productivity laboratory courses (CS 400 and 401) for the initial implementation year of CPI. CS 250 (Problem Solving and Programming) was selected as the sophomore level course primarily because of its long standing use of a formal laboratory and its fundamental problem solving course concept. CS 300U (Computers in Society) was selected as the junior level course because of its two laboratory like activities (paper and class presentations) and for its source of critical non-CS resource information for support of CS 400 and CS 401 laboratories. Additional courses, such as Data Structures, Graphics, and Software Engineering, may be incorporated into the CPI concept but as informal, non-participating courses for evaluation purposes.

4.1 Support Courses

The fundamental modifications of CS 250 include the specific use of the CPI project as the theme for programming assignments and course examples all at the sophomore level. Prototypes will be given to the class to use in performing experiments with the experiment results reported to the senior courses. The critical difficulties expected with these modifications is the availability of problem definition from the senior level productivity laboratories early enough for use in the sophomore course. The CPI coordinator will function as the expediter to insure sufficient statement definitions are described in CS 400 and 401 suitable for CS 250 use. While the flow of information from CS 400 is critical for the achievement of CS 250 course requirements, the reverse flow of product definition is expected to provide direct support to the CS 400 laboratory efforts.

CS 300U currently requires two major forms of student class activities: a formal course paper and student presentations of topics in a forum environment. To utilize this course and the student presentations in the large CPI project, the topics of both the paper and the forum issues will be focused on such critical factors as:

Personal security	Energy sources	Expected life span	Occupations
Education	Personal Privacy	Food supply and type	Government
Transportation	Health and medicine	Economics	Labor supply
General tools	Communication	Business finances	

The subject requirements are products of the ongoing CS 400 and CS 401 courses. The CPI coordinator will function as the expediter to insure that the required topics and issues are identified and provided in a timely fashion suitable for use in CS 300U. The results of these taskings are critical components of the senior level courses. The flow of information with the junior level courses is critical in both directions for the success of the CPI project.

The CPI modifications to the lower level courses (i.e. CS 250 and CS 300U) do not alter the course structures nor the theory or skill development of the courses. The modifications affect the subjects and general theme of the student activities that are assigned during the normal concept-learning within each of the courses. This is viewed as a critical factor in that curriculum-evaluating bodies must not see substantive changes in these core courses that may affect certification decisions as result of CPI incorporation. Fundamentally, we believe that the installation of CPI must not adversely impact the scope of theory, concepts, and knowledge of existing courses.

4.2   Senior Courses

The senior level laboratory courses are the vehicles for ensuring that the primary CPI objectives are achieved. The sequence of CPI senior level laboratories provides students with a clear view of applying the many theories and concepts illustrated and learned in previous courses. It is at this level that all of these knowledge-based skills are applied. Students are faced with new problems that did not appear in their previous courses. They are tasked to develop a solution to a typical problem of increasing the productivity of a system. The problem is the CPI project and is presented as a non-structured requirement. The students must develop the problem solution taking all product-related concerns into account in their decision-making process. In this context, the students participate as leaders of small groups, managers of a larger group, and support technicians and professionals. They function essentially as project managers, defining the problem, developing solutions, and evaluating alternatives for feasible solutions. They must present formal documents for project continuation and produce specifications suitable to be used for production development.

The senior level laboratory students will task lower level courses with software programming requirements, prototype experimentation, impact studies, problem solution plans and implementation algorithms. They will evaluate the products from the lower level courses and use the information to support their ongoing efforts in developing problem solution specifications. The laboratory course material provides students with a guided set of methods to meet the course requirements. It is in the application of these methods that students will likely develop the major productivity improvements. Their laboratory requirements will largely be similar to the requirements of productive computer scientists in their first few years after graduation. Their laboratory experiences will virtually qualify them as assistant project managers who are knowledgeable in most of the facets of applying the technical computer science knowledge to actual problems either in industry or in advanced graduate studies. They will have explored the fields of planning and scheduling, resource allocation and budgeting, to the incorporation of computer hardware and software systems to produce the specifications for a tangible product that society needs and will buy.

4.3 Project Execution

The selected CPI project is carried out over the period of one year (or more years if the problem is sufficiently large) in various courses. Two main courses at senior level deal with the generation of a solution to the project; this step involves many issues not traditionally considered in software development for university course projects. The goal of this initiative is not to develop commercially acceptable systems but rather to develop system specifications that solve a problem. The specifications include a detailed design description, the expected functional performance, cost budget analysis, and a production plan based on analyses, simulations, and prototyping. The project selected as the CPI project will require a solution that consists of not just computer software or hardware, but requires the design of a system where a computer is only one solution factor albeit an important one. The initial selection of the expansion of using the family television as an interface for other family activities as the CPI project meets these requirements. The LIFE system as described by the initial 10 students of CS 400 is a challenging project that defines the hardware and software modules that support many aspects of family life using the family television as a graphic display and communication device.

Since the CPI project theme will have been used in several supporting courses, computer science students will have the sense of participating in a computer productivity project for several years. By the time the student is presented with the entire task of the project, the majority of the basic computer science material has been seen in various courses. The senior students will then be able to readily integrate material of previous core courses into a single project solution at the senior level. It is the early piecemeal introduction of the CPI project that provides an increased productivity for the senior students, an efficient design and description of the problem solution that is the gathering of many of the pieces the students have seen in previous courses.

For most students, their project experiences will involve the same basic project. Developing an entirely new project each year imposes an excessive burden on the faculty. Therefore it is essential that projects be reusable. Reuse of projects can take two forms: the same project is repeated from year to year, as is often the case in engineering senior projects; or the original project is refined, revised, and improved from one year to the next. Our method combines the two approaches because we wanted every student to have the initial "blue sky" development experience when presented with an open ended problem area, but we wished to incorporate the best of the previous classes' work. The seniors will initially approach the problem area in a blue-sky fashion, but the instructor will introduce worthy materials to supplement their work after they have achieved a definition of their project goals.

We are convinced that the single theme project introduced and incorporated in courses throughout the curriculum will enhance the student's ability to rapidly grasp the concepts of the new course. At the senior level laboratories the students will see the total picture of the CPI project. Because of their previous knowledge of the project theme, they will not require the "learning curve" time to begin active project prosecution and specification development. They will also likely reflect on tasks they received at the lower level courses and use that knowledge in generating similar requirements to support their laboratory requirements. This integrated and coordinated project theme across the course boundaries is the CPI innovative concept that we believe will solve many of the problems with our curriculum of today.

5 Documentation and Evaluation

We are using a locally developed software-engineering tool, D-Hyper-Case, to document a decision-based history of the project and to help us determine ways to evaluate the project's effectiveness. Details of D-Hyper-Case can be found in Wild, Maly and Liu [24]. D-Hyper-Case takes its inspiration from Parnas' suggestion [17] that each program module encapsulate one design decision. The tool permits each decision to be described in terms of the problem to be addressed, the alternatives considered, the decisions made, and the relations (links) of the decision to other problems and decisions. The result is a directed acyclic graph with a decision at each node. The graph nodes depict solved problems which likely generate new problems. Solutions links are then established in both directions. Each decision node may be linked to the code and documentation that implements the decision.

We have used this tool to record the history of the project in a problem-oriented fashion. A sketch of part of the decision tree may be seen in Fig. 1. A sample node is shown in Fig. 2. The initial decision to revise our curriculum is progressively refined as we move toward the bottom of the decision tree. Each node lists the alternatives we considered in making the decision and each decision is given one or more justifications which explain why a particular alternative was chosen or rejected.

These justifications, which we call "prejustifications," represent our best judgment at the time of making the decision: they are a pre-evaluation of a number of what-if states, but they may not provide evidence that the decision made was actually the best one. To evaluate the actual course taken, i.e., to "post-justify," requires that we collect data on the project with an eye toward determining whether our decisions were good ones and to provide useful information to other computer science departments which might wish to use our project as a model for curricular revision of their own.

If all of the alternatives could have been simultaneously chosen, then we could use the alternatives as control groups and collect data with an eye toward establishing whether the favored alternative was indeed the correct one. In general, such a course is far from feasible. Nevertheless, we decided to consider at each node what sort of data could be used to validate our implementation relative to the other alternatives. Such data, if collected, would serve several purposes.

(1) In some cases we can find somewhat comparative data. If, for example, we considered doing nothing or requiring our students to take courses in other

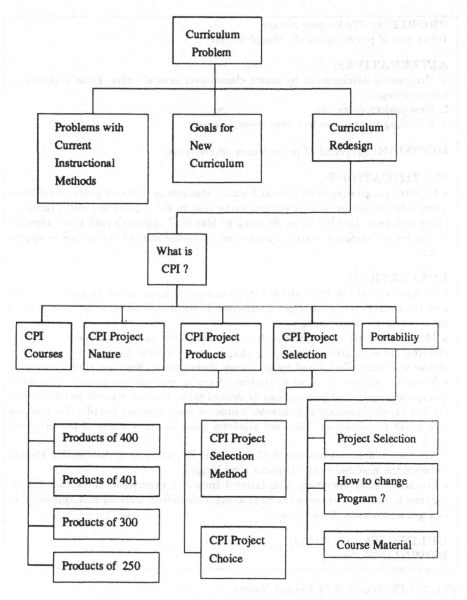

Fig. 1. Decision Tree

departments, we could gather similar data on our current students or those of them who choose to take such courses.

(2) The data gathered displays what was done, even if there is no comparison with other possible alternatives. We could demonstrate significant improvement in student oral presentation skills or show that major elements of the curriculum had been used in a course without gathering comparative data.

(3) The data would often be useful to others considering curricular changes of

PROBLEM: CPI-Project-Nature
What sort of project schedule should we use?

ALTERNATIVES:
1. Progressive development by senior classes over several years. From planning to full prototype.
2. New project every year.
3. Recycling of same project over several years.

DECISION: Recycling of project over several years.

JUSTIFICATIONS:
• Rejected progressive development because students in different years would learn quite different things. A new project every year would require too much ramp up effort each year. Decided to recyle using a "blue sky" approach each time, allowing instructor to introduce material generated by earlier runs of the course as appropriate.

EVALUATIONS:
• To some extent the alternatives can be compared from our own experience. The first time course is offered is like alternative 2 except that we must factor out ramp up costs for the whole program.
• Measures: hours spent by directors and assistants on project specific matters (leaving out e.g., getting facility in shape, overall course design.) Second run of course will show effort saved by not using alternative 2. Requires time logging.
• What are differences in what students learn in first run vs. second? Measures: Comparative pre- and post-ratings of desired skills; can use student portfolios (including taped presentations), director's observations, advisory board's observations of student presentations. Also ask students what use they made of predecessors' work.
• Are there differences in student efforts, either in total time or distribution thereof between the first two runs. Requires time logging.
• Cannot directly document alternative 1 from own experience. If another CS department, or even a department from another discipline, pursues this approach we can get information from them.

UPLINK: What-is-CPI? (5)
DOWNLINK: (none)

Fig. 2. CPI: Node 7: CPI-Project-Nature

their own. Our course of action may be one of the alternatives they reject. Then our data would serve, to some extent, as a control on their own.

The question of what data to gather begins with relatively high level descriptions near the root of the tree. Those descriptions are refined as we move toward the leaves until we have concrete descriptions of what we want to measure.

6 Current Status

After much discussion about feasible projects, appropriate course contents, delivery approaches, and evaluation mechanisms, we realized that we needed a test offering of courses that included as many CPI features as possible. Tables 1 and 2 are simple summations of a large number of hours of debate over the project to be used. We would use a test class experience as a mechanism to better identify successful techniques and administrative procedures, validate implementation concepts, and provide tangible data to be used to further define the initiative. While we expected to gain valuable knowledge as to what would be successful and what would not and the degrees of each, we also anticipated the identification of new issues. Although the implementation of CS 400 required a large expenditure of resources, the results have exceeded our expectations. The data gained has served to crystallize the CPI approach and served to guide creation of clearer solutions to the myriad of problems to be solved before the first offering of the two senior courses beginning in the Fall of 1993. Of particular importance has been the experiences and data the courses have yielded to support further decisions on several complex CPI issues. The more important of these are discussed here.

Abbreviation	Project Description
Naval Charts	Automatically update and disseminate that change frequently
Library	Build a computerized library card catalog
HITTCom	Integrate TV, telephone and computer to allow people to control lighting, security, temperature, appliances
Toll Booth	Automate toll booth collection on highways
VIT	Loading and unloading of ship containers using cranes
Radar	Analysis, design, specification and emulation of a radar interface
Filled Landmass	High performance filled landmass capability using the world vector shoreline
Teaching Project	Programs to teach math and science to teach junior high school students
Student Database	Expansion of university databases to include photographs
Re-Engineering	Writing programs to convert different source codes to standard source code, e.g., from COBOL to Ada

Table 1. Project descriptions

Problem-Solving in the curriculum, a critical challenge: This issue of expanding fundamental problem solving is one of the central concerns not only to CPI but as well to all CS curricula. CS 400 students were initially tasked to describe potential enhancements to the family television. They had to take this completely unstructured open-ended problem scenario and identify potential solutions to the problem. The descriptions of their selected enhancements, along with their reasons for the selections formed the basis for the eventual CPI project description. Essentially, the students defined a set of application solutions to a real-world problem. Some of their findings were used in CS 300 as topics in both oral and written presentations.

Multi-year project: While the full complexity of introducing a multi-year project was only partially evaluated in this test, several of the complex timing issues previously anticipated were demonstrated. The decision of selecting the specific content of each course that mutually supports the multi-year approach has been narrowed somewhat. The original expectations of significant support for the senior courses from the lower level courses may be too great without larger modifications to the lower level courses. These lower level courses will require additional course material, with associated course changes, to provide the required level of support.

Advisory Board use as student evaluators: One of the roles initially defined for the Advisory Board was to become a board of directors for the students. The students were tasked to present to this board the description of their product along with their plans to develop and produce the product. They were challenged to view this board as the decision panel for the continuance of their project. Thus, they were required to justify and support each of their decisions. These students had never been faced with a critical review board presentation. They met the challenge and made the presentation. The advisory board provided critical comments on both the technical quality of the proposed project and the quality of the presentation. The results of this first test case were enlightening to the students, generally supportive of CPI, and also highlighted additional considerations of the process. The new considerations include issues of: how do we ensure success by the students in this critical presentation, how do we ensure the students do not embarrass the university in front of the advisory board, and how do we ensure the board provides the necessary feedback to the students and the CPI faculty?

Value of using speakers in class: The CS 400 test course arranged for a guest speaker on a topic that was critical to one of the course's presentations. The use of guest speakers was viewed as a method of expanding the course content with relevant and current topics. The speaker was a recognized industry professional who provided current business data. Scheduling considerations prevented additional speakers from also participating in the course. The students appeared to readily accept the ideas of the speaker easier than the same ideas from the instructor. Again, new issues were identified as a result of the outside speaker's presentation. Coordination of timing is more difficult than expected. For maximum effect, students must actively participate in the presentation. How to insure this participation is of significance.

Incorporation of leading-edge technology: The early offering of the CS 400 course brought with it a sense of incompleteness of the course preparation. Students initially expressed concern with the promises of equipment and facilities. The students were initially excited about using multimedia equipment and facilities to support them in the generation of their course requirements. However, because of the piecemeal delivery of the multimedia hardware and software, students were faced with rapid introduction and use of new technology without a prolonged training period. While this seemed a shortcoming, in retrospect it caused students to "make do" with what they have available in keeping with typical real-world problem solutions. It is clear however, that adequate training on new multimedia systems will be required to fully use the technology to support course requirements. Either a tutorial or synthesized set of documentation or both may be required.

Criteria for project selection	Explanation
Lifelong skills	skills such as design processes, writing, communication, presentation, managing groups, developing mission statements, budgets for projects, work for clients
Productivity gain	Productivity gained by the user of the system
Relevance to local industry and government agencies	Partnership in education
Application orientation (non-CS)	Amount of non-CS knowledge
Time investment of the buyer	Amount of time needed for the students to complete the project, by an outside
Time investment of builders	party, members of CPI board, faculty, industrial employees, students
Time investment of domain experts	and other experts or clients
Relevance to society	Benefits of the project to society

Table 2. Criteria for project selection.

Interoperability between senior and support courses: The CPI faculty has described several critical and largely unresolved issues in the orderly installation and administration of the project throughout all courses. The test offering, although restricted in this sense, indicated that the complexities of the coordination problem are indeed as difficult as currently expected. The generation of requirements at the senior courses cannot be delayed; nor can the generation of the supportive results be delayed from the lower level courses. The content of the task must be sufficiently clear to be prosecuted by the support course. The results must be of the required quality to be useful at the senior level courses. The issue that remains is: how do we insure these minimums are met or what is the alternative if one or more timely requirements is not met.

Class trips to project installation sites: Early expectations included the necessity of field trips to view and experience the installation and use of similar components of the chosen CPI project. The trip to the "Smart House" in Baltimore, Maryland, was one of the more enlightening aspects of the CS 400 test course. Students were exposed to the myriad of hurdles that seemingly simple problem solutions can generate. They saw actual installation decisions that had cost, efficiency, and functional factors mitigating the easy technical problem solution. The use of this trip was effective but required significant scheduling efforts. Other projects will likely not easily find host implementation sites that are available for student viewing.

While the use of the test courses provided significant assistance in solving many of the outstanding CPI issues, they also added new issues. The prototype CS 400 course has provided the faculty a functional testbed for many aspects of the project. Without this prototype and partially supportive courses, it is expected that valuable time and effort would have been lost in following arbitrary decisions. The data provided has only partially been digested. The end of the Spring semester will begin the full evaluation and design phase of the project.

7 Summary and Future Plans

While the project is on schedule, we are in the middle of the effort and much remains to be done. Much of the remaining work is routine though nontrivial such as the additional course development for CS 401, and handling the "ripple effect" of these courses into existing computer science courses, particularly our two undergraduate software engineering courses. These topics are not discussed further here. Instead we focus on two issues which we perceive as key risks to the success of the project: resource requirements and effectiveness.

From anecdotal evidence (both personal experiences and discussion with colleagues) it appears that many believe that project-focused curricula are beneficial but too time-consuming for faculty and hence perhaps undoable given typical university funding, staffing, and reward structures. This may be, and our experience thus far does not contradict this. Obviously, accurate assessment of the additional efforts required is confounded by the work resulting from any new curriculum development. We are keeping time records to document both faculty and student time. The lack of a model of how to achieve the goals we have in mind increases the development time significantly. The lack of support materials (for example textbooks, workbooks, or even sample multi-class projects) obviously increases instructor preparation time.

We will address the issue of additional effort in two ways: by record keeping (to estimate the additional time required) and by developing curriculum support materials so that others can use this approach more efficiently. After a course is repeated at Old Dominion University, comparison of instructor times for the first and second offerings (and also with existing project-oriented classes) will provide an initial indication of the additional time required. The key to reducing any increased overhead with this approach is in providing adequate support material. This material will include standard curricular material (lecture outlines and notes, syllabi, suggested readings) and sample schedules, sample project descriptions, practitioner guidebooks, guidelines to students for conducting group meetings, presentations, and evaluations, sample documents produced by students, video tapes of some required student activities (interviews with clients, student presentations, board evaluations). Low cost dissemination techniques will be put in place (such as use of FTP to allow retrieval of documents) to share these materials. We will also develop and report effort measures from our experiences; we will make available a variety of materials which others can use for similar courses. If other schools choose to participate, we can provide a repository for related materials developed elsewhere.

We will continue to work on mechanisms for measuring the costs versus the benefits of this curriculum. Many cost metrics are obvious (such as measuring instructors' preparation time) and in general, costs are more easily quantified, but the benefits to computer science students over the course of their careers is more difficult to measure. Most of our students are employed by business and government immediately upon graduation. For these students, some benefits are immediately evident. For example during our initial offering CS 400 we saw dramatic improvements in students' oral presentations (and these students had already taken a required speech class). Many other benefits are less tangible but measurable. For example, we will track the students who have taken these courses so that we can compare them with earlier graduates who did not take these courses. Still the development of reliable and inexpensive metrics requires additional work.

However, many important benefits are difficult to quantify. For one example, we perceive several types of benefits in involving an external board made up of major business and government employers in the area: bringing these people onto campus to discuss how undergraduate computer science education should be conducted benefits them and us; having board members interact directly with our students has benefits (and some risks). As a second example, many of our students go on for M.S. and Ph.D. degrees. This exposure to many of the "real" difficulties in providing automated solutions to real-life problems should give them an improved perspective of computer science, but we see no inexpensive measures to validate this expectation.

We will provide documentation of the costs associated with this approach (equipment, space, supplies, travel). This is relatively easy. We will also continue to struggle with effective evaluation mechanisms; some procedures are in place to collect required data. We have in place (using D-Hyper-Case) a mechanism for recording our decisions along with their justifications and anticipated effects. We will measure some effects for the choices we have made and compare them with the anticipated results. Additional metrics must be defined and evaluation procedures developed to provide them.

For the Old Dominion University faculty participating in this project, many of our discussions focused on four questions: 1) what should we do, 2) how should we do it, 3) what will it take to do it, and 4) how will we know if it works? At this point, we have reached agreement (with some details left to resolve) on the first 2 though as we offer the courses, ideas about 1 and 2 will be revised. We are collecting data on 3, and have some initial mechanisms in place to deal with 4. But evaluation and dissemination techniques will continue to be a topic of our committee meetings. We feel that our initial offering of CS 400 has demonstrated many aspects of the feasibility and some of the benefits of what we propose; other aspects remain to be demonstrated.

8 Acknowledgments

This work is funded by the National Science Foundation under grant #CDA-9214930 and Old Dominion University.

References

1. A report on undergraduate curricula for software engineeing. British Computer Society and Institution of Electrical Engineers, 1989.
2. ACM/IEEE-CS Joint Curriculum Task Force, 1991. Computing Curricula 1991.
3. The Case for Change. Commonwealth of Virginia, Commision on The University of The 21st Century, Richmond, Virginia, 1992.
4. Discipline review of computer studies and information sciences education, 1992.
5. Computer science curriculum. Department of Computer Science, University of Virginia, Charlettsville, Virginia, 1993.
6. P. A. Bailes and E. J. Salzman. A proposal for a bachelor's degree program in software engineering. In N. E. Gibbs, editor, *Software Engineering Education; SEI Conference 1989*. Springer-Verlag, New York, 1989.
7. B. Bruegge. Teaching an industry-oriented software engineering course. In C. A. Sledge, editor, *Software Engineering Education; SEI Conference 1992*. Springer-Verlag, New York, 1992. 65-87.
8. E. Epp. An experimental computer science laboratory. *SIGCSE Bulletin*, 23(1), 1991.
9. J. Foley et al. Report of the NSF Computer Science Education Workshop. *SIGCSE Bulletin*, 20(3), 1988.
10. P. Denning et al. Computing as a discipline. *Communications of the ACM*, 1, 1989.
11. R. E. Prather et al. A lecture/laboratory approach to the first course in computing. *SIGCSE Bulletin*, 10(1), 1978.
12. N. E. Gibbs. Software engineering and computer science: the impending split? *Education and Computing*, 7:111–117, 1991.
13. M. Kantioudi, J. S. Collofello, K. W. Collier, and S. Medeiros. Teaching an industry-oriented software engineering course. In C. A. Sledge, editor, *Software Engineering Education; SEI Conference 1992*. Springer-Verlag, New York, 1992. 323-338.
14. W. M. Lively and M. Lease. Undergraduate software engineering laboratory at Texas A & M university. In C. A. Sledge, editor, *Software Engineering Education; SEI Conference 1992*. Springer-Verlag, New York, 1992. 315-323.
15. A. J. Offutt and R. H. Untch. Integrating research, reuse, and integration into software engineering courses. In C. A. Sledge, editor, *Software Engineering Education; SEI Conference 1992*. Springer-Verlag, New York, 1992. 88-98.
16. L. J. Olson. A lab approach for introductory programming. In *Proceedings of the 14th SIGCSE Symposium on Computer Education*, Orlando, Florida, 1983.
17. D. L. Parnas. On the criteria to be used in decomposing systems into modules. *Communications of the ACM*, 15(2), 1972.
18. D. L. Parnas. Education for computing professionals. *IEEE Computer*, 23(1):17–22, 1990.
19. J. P. Penny and P. J. Ashton. Laboratory-style teaching of computer science. *SIGCSE Bulletin*, 22, 1990.

20. D. E. Ray. Course syllabus: CS250- Problem Solving and Programming. Department of Computer Science, Old Dominion University, Norfolk, Virginia, 1988.

21. J. Roberge and C. Suriano. Embedding laboratories in the computer science curriculum. *SIGCSE Bulletin*, 23(1), 1991.

22. M. Shaw. We can improve the way we teach CS students. *Computing Research News*, 4(1):2–3, 1992. letter to the editor.

23. J. Turner. private communication. Clemson University, 1993.

24. C. Wild, K. Maly, and L. Liu. Decision-based software development. *Software Maintenanace: Research and Practice*, 3:17–43, 1991.

25. W. A. Wulf. SE programs won't solve our problems. *Computing Research News*, 3(5):2, 1991. letter to the editor.

Session 11:
Perspective on Software Engineering Education

Alternative Assessment for Software Engineering Education
Jody Paul, University of Colorado at Denver, Denver, Colorado

A Five Year Perspective on Software Engineering Graduate Programs at George Mason University
Paul Ammann, Hassan Gomaa, Jeff Offutt, David Rine, and Bo Sanden, George Mason Univeristy, Fairfax, Virginia

Falling Down is Part of Growing Up; the Study of Failure and the Software Engineering Community
Darren Dalcher, South Bank University, London, England

Alternative Assessment for Software Engineering Education

DR. JODY PAUL

Department of Computer Science and Engineering
University of Colorado at Denver, Campus Box 109
Denver, Colorado 80217-3364

Voice: (303)556-8425 • Fax: (303)556-8369
Internet: jody@cudnvr.denver.colorado.edu

Abstract. In this paper we present a new architecture for assessment that involves the integration of hypermedia with key requirements for advancing students' education. The result is an interactive system for assessing student competence that fosters individualized progress through a given software engineering curriculum and provides instructors and administrators with quantitative, standardized assessments of confidence, states of knowledge, and problem-solving ability. We present preliminary results of our prototype development effort and describe an architecture and rationale for such systems.

1 Introduction

Assessment methods can enhance the educational experience when used as techniques for evaluation and as guides for instructors and administrators in curriculum design and teaching methods.[1] Standardized assessment methods typically fail to indicate the degree of students' confidence in their answers, to discriminate between finer-grained states of knowledge, and to reflect the ability of students to *apply* what they've learned in problem-solving contexts. In addition, instruction is significantly influenced by the expected assessment instrument. Therefore, to better address the goals of improving students' problem-solving and thinking abilities, alternative assessment methods are needed. However, attempting to apply such methods on a large scale, such as state- or nation-wide, using traditional technology may prove infeasible due to high costs of providing adequate, standardized materials and controlled, responsive environments.

The availability of hypermedia-capable interactive computer systems suggests a means to achieve these goals in a cost-effective way. Such systems can present exercises (simulating a task-environment if necessary), accept and evaluate student responses, and provide customized feedback in real time.

In the following sections, a brief presentation of the prototype built to test the proposed new architecture is followed by a discussion of the architecture itself and the rationale behind developing alternative assessment methods.

2 Concept Feasibility Prototype

Our initial prototype addresses university-level software engineering education, focused on life-cycle models and requirements engineering. Our motivations include achieving the necessary degree of control and consistency, in a resource-limited environment, to accomplish standardized testing that (a) provides discrimination between students' knowledge states, and (b) reflects the ability of students to apply what they have learned in a real-world problem-solving context.

The prototype uses both textual and multimedia vehicles to present problem context and feedback that includes corrective and directive suggestions. It primarily employs a general model for assessment based on confidence-measuring procedures and multipolar testing, and includes a task-performance assessment exemplar. The prototype was implemented on the Macintosh™ platform using HyperCard™ as the integration substrate and QuickTime™ for real-time audio-visual presentation.

2.1 Mixed-initiative Interactive Exam Construction

Setting up a new examination and entering new problems is simplified by allowing instructors to engage in an interactive dialog with the system. A full spectrum of levels of initiative-sharing between the system and instructor is available. This supports instructors who desire complete flexibility in problem design, presentation, scoring, and feedback, while also supporting those who prefer to accept standardized templates and to be prompted for the necessary information.

2.2 Training Phase

A hypermedia-based training phase is provided to prepare students for the actual assessment process. During this phase, students are tutored in the use of the system and become acquainted with the multipolar confidence-measuring method. They practice using the system and gain understanding of the implications of their responses.

2.3 Confidence-Measuring Assessment

The basic assessment model centers on the use of 3-way multiple choice questions and a 16-region response template (see Figure 1). Proximity to a vertex roughly corresponds to the degree of belief that the answer indicated by that vertex's letter is correct. The regions are colored for easy identification and, as the student moves the pointer over different regions, text provides feedback as to the interpretation of that region (note the "hand" pointer and textual description towards the bottom of Figure 2).

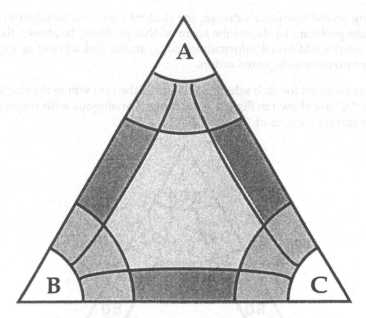

Figure 1. Confidence-measuring response template

Figure 2 shows a simplified layout of a sample question-response presentation (actual presentations use color, shading, sound and action sequences as appropriate). Once a region has been selected, a "commit" button appears. At this point the student can still change the selection. When the student commits to the selection, that response is locked in.

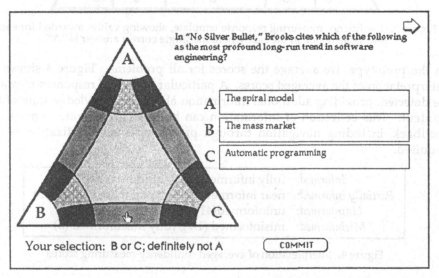

In "No Silver Bullet," Brooks cites which of the following as the most profound long-run trend in software engineering?

A	The spiral model
B	The mass market
C	Automatic programming

Your selection: B or C; definitely not A   (COMMIT)

Figure 2. Sample question-response presentation.

Depending on the instructor's design, the student may now be taken to the next appropriate problem; be shown the score on this problem; be shown the correct answer; receive additional information, suggestions and advice; or experience any other instructor-designated action.

The values awarded for each selectable region in the case where the single correct answer is "A" are shown in Figure 3. (Scoring is analogous with respect to each vertex for correct answers of "B" or "C".)

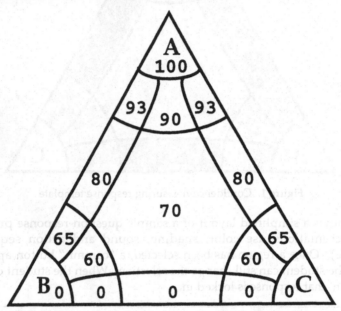

Figure 3. Confidence measuring response template, showing values awarded for each selectable region in the case where the single correct answer is "A".

In the prototype, we average the scores for all problems. Figure 4 shows an interpretation of the averaged scores. A particular pattern of responses may also be detected, providing additional information about the knowledge state of the student. This collection of information can be used to generate appropriate feedback, including navigation through problems if standardization is not required.

Informed:	fully informed (100); informed (92-99)
Partially informed:	near informed (86-91); part informed (77-85)
Uninformed:	uninformed(41-76); random (8-40)
Misinformed:	misinformed (1-7); fully misinformed (0)

Figure 4. Interpretation of averaged confidence-measuring scores

2.4 Task-Performance Assessment

The prototype also includes basic task-performance assessment. Figure 5 shows a snapshot of a task-performance display and interaction. Here, the student has observed a customer explaining his concerns, and is in the process of developing a top-level data-flow-diagram (DFD), the context diagram, using the palette of available objects and diagramming tools.

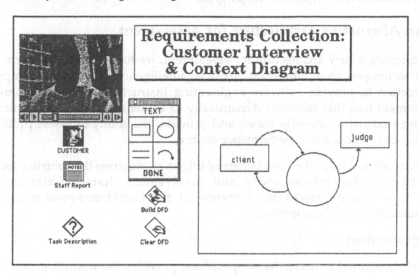

Figure 5. Sample task-performance environment.

Initially, the only items displayed are the heading (shown at the top) and a brief description of the task the student is to perform. When the student has acknowledged understanding the nature of the task, the customer's dialog is shown as a video sequence in the upper left corner of the display. After viewing the sequence, four buttons become visible: CUSTOMER, Staff Report, Task Description, and Build DFD. The student may replay the sequence by clicking the CUSTOMER button. In this particular video clip, the customer indicates the availability of a report produced by the customer's staff. That report is available for the student's perusal by clicking the Staff Report button. The description of the task the student is to perform may be recalled by clicking the Task Description button.

The remainder of the display concerns the task to be carried out by the student. When the student clicks the Build DFD button, a palette of DFD tools appears just above the button and a blank drawing space appears to the right. Using the tools from the palette, the student constructs a top-level data-flow diagram in the drawing space. During this time, the student is free to refer to the staff report, customer interview, and task description as often as desired.

A key issue that arises when attempting to assess the task-performance of a student concerns *what to measure*. We could choose to look only at the result achieved, but that information may not be sufficient. For example, it may be possible to achieve the result by inappropriate means, such as using quicksort when a binary sort is requested. Alternatively, we could look at the specific command sequence issued by the student. In this case, there may be an infinite variety of functionally equivalent sequences. Our approach, instead, is to look at intermediate-goal satisfaction, which presumes a set of necessary sub-goals that must be satisfied to achieve the major goal.

3 An Alternative Architecture for Assessment

In designing a new architecture for assessment, we have blended hypermedia with techniques from education, artificial intelligence and human-computer interaction to provide software engineering instructors with an automated assessment tool that responds dynamically to students' actions, discriminates among students' knowledge states, and provides the ability to assess problem-solving behavior in a task-performance context.

We now acknowledge the foundations of this work, describe the contributions of the hypermedia, interactivivity and involvement characteristics of this architecture, and present an overview of the confidence-measuring and performance-assessment methods.

3.1 Foundations

A well-integrated hypermedia support-base provides the desired multimedia capability coupled with the ability to link and navigate through domain and pedagogical information. Hypermedia techniques facilitate students' use of the system, enhance the presentation of a problem's context, and support the human-interface to the simulated environment used for performance assessment.

The predominant contributions from the field of education are the essentials of assessment, principles leading to the design of beneficial feedback, and the basic notions concerning performance testing.[1-8] Notions of discourse and discourse-modeling from natural-language processing are incorporated to enhance student–system interaction.[9-11] Our design is also influenced by the student-modeling work done in the field of intelligent tutoring systems (ITS).[12-14] A significant, fundamental distinction between this and general work in ITS is our objective of student assessment, not of teaching a curriculum. Assessment is a key factor in influencing the nature of instruction, in particular, in stimulating a shift toward teaching and fostering higher-level cognitive abilities. (Assessment systems such as these may prove to be useful components of an ITS or a tool for ITS researchers to evaluate the effectiveness of their systems.)

3.2 Characteristics of the Architecture

Hypermedia. Hypermedia, the organization of a multiply-connected set of text, sound, graphics and animation (dynamically-evolving images), offers unique advantages for advancing students' education. The subject-specific collection of multimedia elements permits nonsequential processing of knowledge by specifying connections between the component parts of the medium.[15] This aspect extends the involvement of the student (e.g., by bringing additional senses into play and employing both "left-" and "right-brain" faculties), expands the set of applicable domains (e.g., including both software engineering and music appreciation), and provides a unique opportunity for practicable performance-testing.

Interactivity. The interactive nature of such a system makes it a participatory, rather than static, assessment tool. We can provide timely feedback, unlike conventional examinations where the student reads questions and writes answers which are later evaluated and, even later, the results presented to the student. (We note that providing immediate feedback is not always the best pedagogical choice. As such, our architecture is flexible with respect to the immediacy or latency of feedback.) The feedback may include explanations specifically tailored to the performance of the student.

Increased Involvement. Along with the use of the computer to provide timely, customized feedback, we seek to increase student involvement by using multiple media, including tactile (e.g., keyboard and mouse), aural (e.g., voice and non-voice sounds), and visual (e.g., text, diagrams, and animation) modes. Involvement may be further enhanced by discourse knowledge that enables the system to respond to the particular student in the active context.

3.3 Assessment Methods

Confidence Measurement. We have extended work in multipolar-testing and confidence-measuring assessment to discover students' states of knowledge (e.g., *informed, partially informed, misinformed, uninformed*) and enable the system to provide corrective and directive advice that addresses typical misunderstandings associated with a student's particular pattern of responses.[16] For example, if a student's responses form a pattern consistent with an "uninformed" state, remedial support may be indicated. A student whose pattern indicates "partially informed" may simply require some conceptual fine-tuning.

Performance Assessment. We have added a new dimension to automated assessment by providing the ability to do performance assessment, in which the student is given a task to perform in a "virtual world" provided by the system. For example, where physical observables must be simulated (e.g., an interview with an end-user) a video sequence may be displayed. The use of such simulation is indicated when actual performance tests are impractical due to cost, danger, the serious consequences of mistakes, or the impossibility of arranging actual performance situations. By simulating performance conditions the system controls most of the variables in the testing situation and we can standardize the assessment across students and administrations.[5]

4 Why a New Approach to Assessment?

Significant concern has been raised about the nature of assessment methods currently in use: in particular, whether they currently hamper or support the goal of fostering "intellectual development and educational success."[17] Resnick and Resnick report that the nature of standardized tests now widely used for accountability is "fundamentally incompatible" with the goal of improving students' higher-order abilities (i.e., problem solving and thinking) and that alternative assessment methods are needed.[18]   There is a widely recognized need for a "reformulation of assessment to help not hinder the effort to teach thinking."[19]

Potential contributions to the educational experience of individual students come from both the assessment process itself and the resulting feedback. The more involving the assessment process is and more appropriate the response delay, the more effective is the exercise.[7]   A review that includes explanations of why answers were incorrect and likely sources of incorrect reasoning is more useful than simply a final score or "correct/incorrect" indicators.   A method particularly appropriate for software engineering education is *performance testing* which evaluates a student's ability to solve problems that require the performance of particular tasks or procedures.[1, 2, 5]

Difficulties with achieving the involvement, feedback, and performance-testing goals are the prohibitive resource requirements of standard assessment tools and environments.   Achieving immediate, customized feedback requires an impractical student-instructor ratio.   Providing all students with complete, controlled task environments is often costly or otherwise infeasible.

Thus we see the need for alternative assessment methods that foster intellectual development and favor the goals of improving thinking and problem-solving skills. Such methods should be more responsive and involving, reveal students' confidence, discriminate between finer-grained states of knowledge, and reflect the ability of students to apply what they've learned in problem-solving contexts. However, accomplishing these objectives using traditional technology is generally impractical due to resource constraints.

5 Conclusions and Work in Progress

We have presented an alternative architecture for assessment suited to the goals and characteristics of software engineering education. Blending hypermedia with techniques from education, artificial intelligence and human-computer interaction, the architecture provides instructors with an automated assessment tool that responds dynamically to students' actions, indicates students' confidence in their answers, discriminates among students' knowledge states, and provides the ability to assess problem-solving behavior in a task-performance context.

Although we have focused on the particular needs for software engineering education, we believe that the methods and techniques developed for and employed in the prototype are in no way confined to this domain of application, and we are currently investigating application to high-school chemistry curriculum. Such flexibility allows the same machines to be used for several different educational areas at different times. Coupled with the simulated task-environment aspect of the architecture, this provides the potential for institutions to realize significant savings in an era where cost-effectiveness has become increasingly important.

We are currently developing a more substantial system that extends the performance-testing aspect and improves the student and discourse models. In our initial design, we incorporated skeletal, generic student-models.[3, 14] As we assimilate the results of field trials, our models will be extended to include the identification and tracking of students' styles, goals, and plans.

References

1. P. W. Airasian, *Classroom Assessment*. New York: McGraw-Hill, 1991.

2. R. W. Sweezey, *Individual Performance Assessment: An Approach to Criterion-Referenced Test Development*. Reston: Reston Publishing Company, Inc., 1981.

3. R. Freedle, ed. *Artificial Intelligence and the Future of Testing*. Hillsdale: Lawrence Erlbaum Associates, 1990.

4. B. R. Gifford and M. C. O'Connor, eds. *Changing Assessments: Alternative Views of Aptitude, Achievement and Instruction*. Boston: Kluwer Academic Publishers, 1992.

5. M. Priestley, *Performance Assessment in Education and Training: Alternative Techniques*. Englewood Cliffs: Educational Technology Publications, 1982.

6. T. Kellaghan, G. F. Madaus, and P. W. Airasian, *The Effects of Standardized Testing*. Boston: Kluwer-Nijhoff Publishing, 1982.

7. A. Dworkin and N. Dworkin, *Problem Solving Assessment*. Novato: Academic Therapy Publications, 1988.

8. R. J. Sternberg, "CAT: A Program of Comprehensive Abilities Testing," in *Changing Assessments: Alternative Views of Aptitude, Achievement and Instruction*, B. R. Gifford and M. C. O'Connor, eds. Boston: Kluwer Academic Publishers, 1992. p. 213-274.

9. K. McKeown. *User-Oriented Explanation for Expert Systems*. Department of Computer Science, Columbia University, CUCS-85-83, 1983.

10. K. R. McKeown, M. Wish, and K. Mathews. *Tailoring Explanations for the User*. Department of Computer Science, Columbia University, COCS-172-85, 1985.

11. B. J. Grosz, "Discourse Analysis," in *Understanding Spoken Language*, D. E. Walker, eds. Elsevier North-Holland, 1978. p. 235-268.

12. P. H. Wood and P. D. Holt, *Intelligent Tutoring Systems: An Annotated Bibliography*. SIGART Bulletin, 1990. 1(1): p. 21-42.

13. H. S. Nwana, *Intelligent Tutoring Systems: An Overview*. Artificial Intelligence Review, 1990. 4(4): p. 251-277.

14. T. Murray and B. P. Woolf, *A Knowledge Acquisition Tool for Intelligent Computer Tutors*. SIGART Bulletin, 1991. 2(2): p. 9-21.

15. J. A. Jensen and T. Nissen, *Paedagogik, Psykologi, Hypermedier: Hypermediers paedagogiske potentiale i erkendelsesteoretisk og kognitionsteoretisk perspektiv*. Psyke and Logos, 1988. 9(2): p. 419-442.

16. J. Paul, "Hypermedia-based Interactive Student-Assessment System (HISAS): Concept and Architecture," in *Educational Multimedia and Hypermedia Annual, 1993*, H. Maurer, ed. Charlottesville: Association for the Advancement of Computing in Education, 1993. p. 415-421.

17. M. C. O'Connor, "Rethinking Aptitude, Achievement and Instruction: Cognitive Science Research and the Framing of Assessment Policy," in *Changing Assessments: Alternative Views of Aptitude, Achievement and Instruction*, B. R. Gifford and M. C. O'Connor, eds. Boston: Kluwer Academic Publishers, 1992. p. 9-35.

18. L. B. Resnick and D. P. Resnick, "Assessing the Thinking Curriculum: New Tools for Educational Reform," in *Changing Assessments: Alternative Views of Aptitude, Achievement and Instruction*, B. R. Gifford and M. C. O'Connor, eds. Boston: Kluwer Academic Publishers, 1992. p. 37-75.

19. L. A. Shepard, "What Policy Makers Who Mandate Tests Should Know About the New Psychology of Intellectual Ability and Learning," in *Changing Assessments: Alternative Views of Aptitude, Achievement and Instruction*, B. R. Gifford and M. C. O'Connor, eds. Boston: Kluwer Academic Publishers, 1992. p. 301-328.

Acknowledgments

Special thanks to Allen Klinger (UCLA) for contributions to the work on confidence-measuring, to Patricia Supon (University of Colorado at Denver) for contributions to this effort in the area of performance-assessment, and to Tammy Kilgore (University of Southern California) for most helpful critical reviews.

A Five Year Perspective on Software Engineering Graduate Programs at George Mason University

Paul Ammann, Hassan Gomaa, Jeff Offutt, David Rine, and Bo Sanden

Department of Information and Software Systems Engineering, George Mason University, Fairfax, VA 22030-4444. phone: 703-993-1640 email: hgomaa@isse.gmu.edu

Abstract. This paper describes the experience obtained at George Mason University while developing a Master of Science program in software engineering. To date, the program has graduated over 45 students, with a current production rate of 10 to 15 a year. The paper also describes experience with a certificate program in software engineering, which is a software engineering specialization taken by Masters students in related disciplines, and the software engineering specialization within the PhD program in Information Technology. We discuss our courses, students, the successes that we have had, and the problems that we have faced.

1   INTRODUCTION

George Mason University (GMU), which is situated in suburban Washington D.C., has more than 21,000 students, including 5,500 master's students, 1,100 doctoral students and 2,000 post-baccalaureate extended studies students. Of a total of 1,400 faculty, 643 are full-time. GMU offers 35 master's programs, 12 doctoral programs and 8 certificate programs.

The School of Information Technology and Engineering (SITE), established in 1985, houses the departments of Computer Science (CS), Information and Software Systems Engineering (ISSE), Systems Engineering (SE), Electrical and Computer Engineering (ECE), Operations Research and Engineering (ORE), and Applied and Engineering Statistics (AES). The emphasis is on graduate education; whereas four BS programs produce a total of 220 graduates yearly, primarily CS and ECE, seven MS programs – CS, ECE, Information Systems (IS), Operations Research, Software Systems Engineering (SWSE), Statistical Science, and Systems Engineering (SE) – graduate 250 students annually. A school-wide doctoral program in Information Technology and Engineering graduated 13 PhDs in academic year 1992, and 20 in 1993.

Part of GMU's unique mission is to serve the Metropolitan Washington and Northern Virginia area. The Master of Science program in Software Systems Engineering (MS-SWSE) was established at George Mason University in an attempt to respond to the needs of high technology industries in the area. The discipline of software engineering is concerned with technical and managerial issues related to developing and modifying complex, large scale computer software systems. The purpose of the program is to train students in the theory and practice of software engineering.

One important aspect of GMU's location, impacting our program in many and diverse ways, is that the majority of our students are part-time students who work for high technology companies, research laboratories, consulting firms, and federal government agencies located in the Metropolitan Washington area. The most obvious result of this is that all of our courses meet once a week, in the late afternoon or early evening. Additionally, many of our students have their tuition paid by their employers.

2 THE SOFTWARE SYSTEMS ENGINEERING MASTER'S PROGRAM

The Master of Science program in Software Systems Engineering (MS-SWSE) was established at George Mason University in the fall of 1989, a year after the introduction of the Certificate program in Software Systems Engineering. Planning for the MS and certificate programs started in the fall of 1987 when three of the faculty of the Wang Institute of Graduate Studies moved to George Mason after the Wang Institute closed down in the summer of 1987. A three year $2.4 million grant from the Virginia Center of Innovative Technology was instrumental in providing the funding basis for establishing a software engineering group at George Mason University.

The masters and certificate programs are housed in the Department of Information and Software Systems Engineering (ISSE) and supported by the ISSE and CS departments. ISSE also offers a related MS program in Information Systems. Many of the software engineering courses are cross-listed with the Computer Science Department, which often provides faculty to help teach the courses.

To receive the Masters degree in Software Systems Engineering, students must complete 30 semester hours of graduate work. Students have a choice of a professional track of six core courses and four electives, or a research track of six core courses, two electives, and a six hour Masters thesis. The core courses are:

- Software Construction
- Software Requirements and Prototyping
- Software Design
- Formal Methods and Models
- Software Project Management
- Software Project Lab

We are currently considering expanding the core to include Software Testing and Quality Assurance.

Students may choose either software engineering electives or electives from related disciplines. Software engineering electives include Software Engineering Economics, Object-Oriented Software Development, User Interface Design and Development, Software Testing and Quality Assurance, Advanced Software Requirements, Advanced Software Design Methods, Special Topics in Software Engineering, and Directed Readings in Software Engineering. A wide range of electives is also available in the areas of computer science, electrical and computer engineering, systems engineering, etc.

GMU's current program represents an evolution from the Wang Institute Master of Software Engineering program [2, 6, 1, 7]. The Formal Methods and Models, Software Project Management, and Software Project Lab all existed at the Wang Institute. Software Construction replaces the Wang Institute course on Programming Methodology.

The Wang Institute course in Software Engineering Methods, which emphasized requirements and design, evolved into a Software Requirements, Prototyping and Design course at GMU. However, it was soon found that there was insufficient time to do justice to both requirements and design in one course, and so the course was split into the two courses now being offered: Software Requirements and Prototyping, and Software Design. Each of these courses has a substantial group project component. The Software Project Lab course represents the culmination of the program, where students, working in teams, apply the technical and project management skills from the courses to the development of a software system. The project lab is intended to simulate industrial conditions and is discussed in more detail by McKeeman [13].

To be accepted into the SWSE program, students must have satisfactory GPA and GRE scores, preferably at least one year's industrial experience, and undergraduate courses or equivalent knowledge in block-structured programming, data structures and algorithms, computer organization, and discrete mathematics.

3   THE INFORMATION TECHNOLOGY PHD PROGRAM

Our PhD program is administered through the Dean's office of SITE. The students obtain a PhD in Information Technology (INFT) by taking six MS-level breadth courses from at least three of the departments in SITE, six depth INFT PhD-level courses, other supporting coursework and seminars, and writing a PhD dissertation. There are currently over 300 students in this program. The ISSE and CS faculty contribute to the PhD program by teaching several INFT courses and by advising and serving on committees of PhD students.

The following software engineering courses have been offered as part of the PhD program: Software Engineering Seminar, Software Productivity, Topics in Software Requirements, Experimental Methods in Software Engineering, Software Maintenance and Reuse, Software for Critical Systems, Software Analysis and Design of Real-time Systems, Concurrent Object-oriented Systems, and Software Reuse.

Software engineering has become one of the major focus areas in our PhD program, with 8 of the last 21 PhDs awarded being in the software area. The topics have primarily been in the areas of requirements engineering, prototyping and domain analysis. Plans are currently underway to formalize this interest by creating several tracks within the program, one of which would be software engineering.

4   INTEGRATION WITH OTHER GRADUATE PROGRAMS

The Software Sysetms Engineering program at George Mason University is closely integrated with three other degree programs: the masters degree programs in Computer Science, Information Systems, and Systems Engineering. Together, the programs allow students to select a focus of study from a spectrum that ranges from traditional computer science topics through the technical engineering issues of constructing software systems to the business, management, and use of information systems.

4.1 The Certificate in Software Systems Engineering

One aspect of the integration between the four programs is the Certificate in Software Systems Engineering. The certificate program was created to provide software engineering education to MS students in related disciplines. It is mostly pursued by students in the computer science, systems engineering or information systems masters programs who take five SWSE courses, consisting of the MS-SWSE core courses with the exception of the project laboratory, in addition to the core of their masters program and in place of other electives. Partially to make it easier for students to complete the certificate as well as their own requirements, the Computer Science Department has several of the SWSE courses cross-listed as their own courses. The certificate may also be pursued by students who already have an MS degree in a related discipline.

4.2 The Foundation Courses

We are currently considering standardizing foundation requirements for the Software Systems Engineering, Computer Science, and Information Systems programs. Although there are undergraduate courses that can satisfy a student's need for missing foundation courses, such courses are not a good fit for our typical students, many of whom return for graduate school after an extended experience in the workplace. Problems with undergraduate foundation courses include the ability of graduate students to cover foundation work at a faster pace than undergraduates, a lack of tailoring of the material to the specific needs of our program, an inability of employer-sponsored students to obtain support and tuition-reimbursement for courses that are not offered at the graduate level, and the fact that most of our students need to take courses at night so they can work during the day. To meet the needs of students who are deficient in one or more foundation courses, graduate level foundation courses either exist or are planned for each of the prerequisite subjects: block structured programming languages, data structures and algorithms, computer organization, and discrete math.

5 SOFTWARE SYSTEMS ENGINEERING COURSES

Our masters curriculum has six core courses, and we offer several electives. Each of these courses is described below, with emphasis on what we actually teach in the courses, rather than the formal catalog descriptions.

5.1 The Core Courses

SWSE 619: Software Construction. This course presents the concepts of information hiding, data abstraction, concurrency, and object-oriented software construction, as well as general issues relating to the software lifecycle. The course focuses on reactive software, and uses sequence diagrams and state diagrams (including some basic concepts of automata theory) to describe software. We have typically used Ada as a vehicle to present the concepts, and the course usually includes several Ada programming projects. The class uses Sanden's text [19], and presents design and implementation issues at the small to moderate level.

SWSE 620: Software Requirements and Prototype. This course presents an in-depth study of the methods, tools, notations and validation techniques for the analysis and specification of software requirements. It includes a group project. SWSE 620 has been taught with an emphasis on prototyping and with an emphasis on object-oriented analysis according to Rumbaugh's OMT [16]. The main requirements text is Davis's [5]. A variety of prototyping tools are used including PC Access, Oracle/C, Hypercard, Toolbook and Expert Problem Solving System (EPSS).

SWSE 621: Software Design. This is a course in concepts and methods for the architectural design of software systems of sufficient size and complexity to require the effort of several people for many months. We introduce fundamental design concepts and design notations. Several design methods are presented and compared, with examples of their use. The course text is by Gomaa [10]. Students undertake a term project working in small groups to design a relatively complex software system using one design method.

SWSE 623: Formal Methods and Models in Software Engineering. SWSE 623 covers formal mechanisms for specifying, validating, and verifying software systems. The course presents program verification using Hoare's method and Dijkstra's weakest preconditions (based on Gries's text [11]). Formal specification is taught through algebraic specifications and, to a larger extent, abstract model specifications. The treatment of algebraic specifications is based on the approach of Liskov and Guttag [12]. The treatment of abstract model specifications currently employs the specification language Z (using Potter, Sinclair and Tills' text [15]) and covers both initial specifications and refinement towards implementation. The course addresses the integration of formal methods with existing programming languages such as Eiffel and Ada, the application of formal methods to a variety of topics such as requirements analysis, testing, safety analysis, and object-oriented approaches, and arguments for using formal methods, including appropriate conditions for their application and trade-offs with less formal techniques. The course presently includes the formal specification of a simple file system as an exercise designed to show how formal methods can disambiguate informal specifications and separate genuine requirements from implementation decisions.

SWSE 625: Software Project Management. SWSE 625 covers lifecycle and process models, process metrics, and planning for software projects. It includes mechanisms for monitoring and controlling schedule, budget, quality and productivity, as well as leadership, motivation, and team building. The course emphasizes computer-based tools to support software project management.

SWSE 626: Software Project Laboratory. In this course, students are involved in the analysis, design, implementation and management of a software system project. They work in teams to develop or modify a software product, applying sound software engineering principles. Although the project varies each semester, the purpose of the project has usually been to develop a software system either according to ADARTS [10] or Entity-life Modeling [19]. SWSE 626 is taken almost exclusively by MS-SWSE students. One section is offered each semester with enrollments from 7 to 25. Occasionally, students may work on the same project in SWSE 621 and SWSE 626. While this is desirable, we cannot systematically rely on multi-semester projects since the students do not progress through the program as one class.

The project laboratory is ideally suited for students entering graduate school immediately from college and for junior software engineers with little previous opportunity to follow a project through several development phases. It is also popular among students who manage to put a good team together and produce a software product that far exceeds course requirements.

The two core courses on software construction and design plus the project lab permit us to address fairly advanced design issues. In particular, the project lab has made it necessary for us to introduce a common programming language. We have selected Ada, which has been a good choice particularly in a geographical area where many students have a background in systems development for government and defense [18].

5.2   Elective Courses

SWSE 630: Software Engineering Economics. SWSE 630 covers quantitative models of the software lifecycle and cost-effectiveness analysis in software engineering. Some of the specific topics are multiple-goal analysis, uncertainty and risk analysis, software cost estimation, software engineering metrics, and quantitative lifecycle management techniques.

SWSE 631: Object-Oriented Software Development. SWSE 631 covers principles of object-oriented design, development, and programming in Eiffel, based on Meyer's text [14]. It includes relationships between object-oriented design concepts and software engineering principles, techniques of object-oriented design and programming, and applications of object-oriented techniques. It also includes emphasis on design, evolution and reuse through supplemental readings.

SWSE 632: User Interface Design and Development. This design course studies the role of the human in the design and implementation of software, and prepares students to design and evaluate the quality of interfaces between computer software and human users. The course presents theories of human-computer interaction, including human cognitive limitations, syntactic versus semantic knowledge, transitionality, and the "outside-in" design approach. It also presents guidelines for designing various types of computer interfaces, including command interfaces, menus, desktop views, and graphic interfaces. The course currently uses Shneiderman's text [20], with supplemental material derived from Brown and Cunningham [4], and recent literature. Students evaluate several user interfaces, and either write a paper covering an interface topic or design and implement a user interface.

This course has appealed to SWSE students, CS students, and students from a variety of disciplines, including education and visual information technology (from the Arts department). Part of the challenge of this course is to balance the interdisciplinary nature of the subject with the technical aspects of software engineering, which are often quite difficult for students in less technical majors.

SWSE 635: Software Testing and Quality Assurance. SWSE 635 covers software testing and quality assurance techniques at the module, subsystem, and system levels. Topics include control and data flow coverage, mutation analysis, fault-based testing, symbolic evaluation, test specifications, test generation, category-partition testing, inspections, requirements-based testing, statistical testing, and reliability assessment. The course uses Beizer's book [3], heavily supplemented with research papers from the recent literature. Students plan for and carry out the testing of an example software system. The course has a technical focus, and many of the management-oriented concerns are deferred to SWSE 625.

SWSE 720: Advanced Software Requirements. This course covers the current research and the current applications of requirements engineering. It focuses on critical problems in software engineering and discusses how their resolution might enhance the quality and productivity of real software and system developments in industry.

SWSE 721: Advanced Software Design Methods. This course studies advanced software design methods for large-scale software systems, including concurrent, real-time, and distributed systems. Students apply one or more of the methods to the design of a relatively complex software system. This course complements

SWSE 621 for students particularly interested in software design. With SWSE 621 focusing on DARTS and ADARTS, SWSE 721 has been based on entity-life modeling (ELM) according to Sanden [19].

5.3 Physical Laboratories

The Software Systems Program has access to computer facilities provided by the University and the School, as well as a laboratory of networked Sun workstations provided by the Center for Software Systems Engineering. These suns are currently connected to the ISSE department file server, with the internet subdomain of isse.gmu.edu. The University provides DEC machines running both Unix and VMS for general use. SITE provides a networked lab of HP X-terminals that we have used in courses, particularly for the Ada programming projects in SWSE 619. A surprising result of our mix of students is that university-provided equipment is in less demand than at more traditional universities. The majority of our students are working full-time and do not come to campus every day, so they prefer to use their own equipment at home or at work when possible.

6 CURRENT STATUS AND STATISTICS

Student enrollment in the two programs has grown rapidly. Approximately 83 students are currently enrolled in the Masters program. The fact that many of these students are working professionals in the field has impacted many aspects of our program, both positively and negatively. As compared to traditional master's students at other universities, most of our students are older and, because of the extra burdens of completing an advanced degree with the responsibilities of jobs and often families, are more determined to succeed. They are also more cognizant of the value of an education and aware of the difficulties. From a technical perspective, the students tend to be better writers (a result of their experience and maturity), but because their undergraduate degrees are often 5 to 15 years old, our students are often less prepared technically than more recent graduates. Some of the material that is currently being taught in data structures courses, such as data abstraction, information-hiding, and data structures and algorithms for advanced graph and tree structures is known to only a fraction of our incoming students. In spite of these problems, we are constantly impressed by their hard work, dedication and enthusiasm.

The software engineering courses also attract many students from other Master's programs, in particular Computer Science and Information Systems, who take the courses as electives counting towards their degrees. Some students switch to the Masters program in Software Systems Engineering. Many of the students from related disciplines take the Software Systems Engineering certificate.

6.1 Enrollment Statistics

The intentions of the many students in software engineering courses can be derived only in part from enrollment data, and so we conducted a survey of students taking software engineering courses during the Spring 1993 semester. The survey results reflect school-wide interest in the software engineering curriculum. A total of 248 questionnaires were returned (some duplicate entries were rejected and are not counted in the 248 replies). The results were tabulated by the type of degree being pursued and by whether or not students intended to pursue a Software Systems Engineering Certificate. The results are summarized in Table 1 below.

Degree Being Sought	Number of Students
Masters in Software Systems Engineering	83
SWSE Certificate Students	
SWSE Certificate Only	10
CS Masters and SWSE Certificate	18
IS Masters and SWSE Certificate	16
Other Masters and SWSE Certificate	4
Total SWSE Certificate Students	48
Other Students	
CS Masters only	64
IS Masters only	22
Other Masters only	20
Other responses	11
Total Other Students	117
Total	248

Table 1: Majors of Students Enrolled in SWSE Courses in Spring 1993.

The table shows that about one third of the students enrolled in SWSE courses are pursuing a Masters in Software Systems Engineering. In addition, about a fifth of the respondents are pursuing a certificate in some form or other. Putting the previous two observations together, we see that just over half of the students in software engineering courses are pursuing a Certificate or Masters in Software Systems Engineering. Correspondingly, the remaining students find software engineering courses interesting as electives, even though such students do not plan either a Certificate or a Masters in Software Systems Engineering.

6.2 Course Offerings

Up to and including the Fall 1992 semester, each of the core courses was offered in both the Fall and Spring semesters, and the electives were offered once a year, with typical course enrollments of between 35 and 50 students. However, a sudden growth in enrollments was experienced last fall, forcing us to accept over 60 students in some classes. Consequently, in the Spring '93 semester, two sections were offered for three of the core courses. In Fall '93, two sections will be offered for four of the five courses that compose both the software engineering core and the software engineering certificate. The courses in Spring '93 were capped at 40, and with two sections offered in several cases, it was thought that this would more than compensate for student demand. To our surprise, most of the sections were filled to maximum capacity.

SWSE 619 has become a very popular course with students in various majors; for example, over half of the students taking SWSE 619 in Spring 1993 were computer science majors. We are offering an additional section of 619 in the summer.

The first graduates of the Certificate program were in Spring 1989, while the first graduates of the MS program were in Spring 1990. Up through May 1993, 45 Master's students have graduated in Software Systems Engineering.

7   DISCUSSION

The teaching faculty consists of four full time professors in the ISSE department and one professor who has a joint appointment with the CS and ISSE departments, assisted by one or two research professors (funded primarily by research contracts) and several adjunct professors. The department is fortunate to have a pool of dedicated, experienced and highly capable adjunct professors, without whom the SWSE program would be compromised. In addition to the core courses, there are usually two or three electives taught each semester.

Several of the software engineering courses offered in the Masters and PhD programs have resulted in text books being written by GMU faculty. These include books on Software Systems Engineering [17], Software Construction [19], and Software Design [10].

The Masters and Certificate programs in software engineering have grown rapidly over the last five years, even though budget cutbacks due to the difficult economic climate in the state of Virginia has actually resulted in two less faculty than originally planned. Because of budgetary constraints and because there are comparatively few full-time students, the pool of potential graduate teaching assistants (GTAs) is small. In addition, because of the fact that the group projects in Software Requirements, Software Design, Software Project Management, and Software Project Lab require considerable software engineering expertise to manage, the contribution that can be made by GTAs is limited. Thus, teaching an effective software engineering program is particularly demanding on the faculty, requiring considerable faculty time for meetings with students and grading project deliverables in addition to a regular lecturing schedule.

The ISSE department recently proposed an undergraduate program in Information and Software Systems Engineering, combining the product (software systems) and process (software engineering) perspectives of large scale software system development. Unfortunately there are no resources available for such a program in the foreseeable future, as the department is already understaffed in both masters programs it offers.

8 CONCLUSIONS

The Master of Science program in Software Systems Engineering is now in its fifth year at George Mason University. There has been rapid growth in student enrollment in software engineering courses, by MS students in software engineering as well as graduate students enrolled in other programs. The Certificate program has proved to be an effective vehicle for channeling students in other degree programs into a specialization in software engineering. There is also considerable interest in software engineering at the PhD level.

Our program specifically meets the 7 criteria listed by Freeman [8], originally from Freeman et al. [9]:

1. Be based on the five content areas of computer science, management, communication, problem solving, and design.
2. Be flexible so that they can change easily and be adapted to substantive developments in the field.
3. Be based on computer science and be viewed as "applied computer science".
4. Prepare students to push forward the boundaries of knowledge and techniques, not just apply what is already known.
5. Include a large amount of realism and practical work.
6. Provide for multiple implementations, dependent upon career objectives and backgrounds of students and upon the academic home of the program.
7. Build on existing curricula to the extent possible.

These criteria were appropriate when originally proposed in 1976, and still apply today. In one form or another, these criteria help determine all the decisions we make about our program.

One of the most challenging aspects of our curriculum is the unusual mix of students that we teach. The fact that most of our students are experienced professionals is an element that is likely to be common to future software engineering programs. Although our location exacerbates the challenges, software engineering educational programs will continue to be populated, and should be populated, by part-time professionals with experience. We have found that this results in a large number of unusual situations, from students who are more dedicated to their education and appreciative of the principles we teach, to students who, because of professional obligations, must resort to submitting assignments and even exams by fax. It is our belief that the traditional educational systems are undergoing drastic changes, and the non-traditional educational choices that we have made in our program provide models for appropriate advanced education into the next century.

9 ACKNOWLEDGEMENTS

Our program was initiated through a proposal by Richard Fairley to the Commonwealth of Virginia, and we gratefully acknowledge his groundbreaking efforts, as well as the efforts of Peggy Brouse, Al Davis, Carolyn Davis, Peter Freeman, Jorge Díaz-Herrera, Ken Nidiffer, Larry Kerschberg, Gene Norris, Jim Palmer, and Andy Sage, who have all contributed to the program's success.

References

1. P. Ammann, A. Davis, R. Fairley, H. Gomaa, and B. Sanden. Graduate programs in Software Engineering at George Mason University. In *Proceedings of the 1991 SEI Software Engineering Education Workshop*, Austin TX, May 1991.
2. M. Ardis. The evolution of Wang Institute's Master of Software Engineering program. *IEEE Transactions on Software Engineering*, SE-13(11):1149–1157, November 1987.
3. B. Beizer. *Software Testing Techniques*. Van Nostrand Reinhold, New York NY, 2nd edition, 1990.
4. J. Brown and S. Cunningham. *Programming the User Interface*. John Wiley & Sons, New York NY, 1989.
5. A. Davis. *Software Requirements: Objects, Functions, and States*. Prentice-Hall, Englewood Cliffs, NJ, 1993.
6. R. Fairley. Post-mortem analysis of software engineering at Wang Institute. *ACM SIGSOFT Notes*, 13(2):41–47, April 1988.
7. R. Fairley. The software engineering programs at George Mason University. In *Proceedings of the SEI Conference on Software Engineering Education*, Fairfax VA, April 1988. IEEE Computer Society Press.
8. P. Freeman. Essential elements of software engineering education revisited. *IEEE Transactions on Software Engineering*, SE-13(11):1143–1148, November 1987.
9. P. Freeman, A. I. Wasserman, and R. E. Fairley. Essential elements of software engineering education. In *Proceedings of the 2nd International Conference on Software Engineering*, pages 116–122. IEEE Computer Society Press, 1976.
10. H. Gomaa. *Software Design Methods for Concurrent and Real-Time Systems*. Addison-Wesley, Reading MA, 1993.
11. D. Gries. *The Science of Programming*. Springer-Verlag, New York, 1981.
12. B. Liskov and J. Guttag. *Abstraction and Specification in Program Development*. The MIT Press, Cambridge, MA, 1986.
13. W. M. McKeeman. Experience with a software engineering project course. *IEEE Transactions on Software Engineering*, SE-13(11):1182–1191, November 1987.
14. B. Meyer. *Object-Oriented Software Construction*. Prentice-Hall International, Englewood Cliffs, NJ, 1988.
15. B. Potter, J. Sinclair, and D. Till. *An Introduction to Formal Specification and Z*. Prentice Hall, New York, 1991.
16. J. Rumbaugh, M. Blaha, W. Premerlani, F. Eddy, and W. Lorensen. *Object-oriented Modeling and Design*. Prentice-Hall, Englewood Cliffs, NJ, 1991.
17. A. P. Sage and J. D. Palmer. *Software Systems Engineering*. John Wiley & Sons, New York NY, 1990.

18. B. Sanden. An Ada-based, graduate software-engineering curriculum at GMU. In *Proceedings of the 7th Annual ASEET Symposium*, pages 119–124, Monterey CA, January 1993.

19. B. Sanden. *Software Systems Construction with Examples in Ada*. Prentice-Hall, Englewood Cliffs, NJ, 1993.

20. B. Shneiderman. *Designing the User Interface*. Addison-Wesley, Reading MA, 2nd edition, 1992.

Falling Down is Part of Growing Up; the Study of Failure and the Software Engineering Community

Darren Dalcher

School of Computing, South Bank University
103 Borough road, London SE1 0AA, ENGLAND

Software development efforts are characterised by; project failures, runaway projects and integration and communication problems. Analysing why some projects finish on target while others lose track of their original objectives, constraints and milestones, can only be viewed as a long term investment. The study of failures is a sensible approach for utilising past experience and advancing to the next level of maturity. This paper introduces the discipline of Forensic Engineering and frames it within the software development environment. The value of failure analysis is discussed from a number of viewpoints and the educational implications explored. Finally the paper calls for a new attitude towards failure, where in order to maximise potential learning, acceptance of failure is the new order of the day.

1 Introduction

Software Engineering is a relatively new discipline ready to celebrate a mere quarter of a century of existence. A person of similar age may still be classified as a recent graduate -- endeavouring to acquire the necessary skills to become a seasoned professional.

The traditional engineering professions have accumulated a significant body of knowledge about building bridges, aeroplanes, structures and cars. Many of the facts constituting this body of knowledge were highlighted by glorious disasters. As the need for those artefacts persisted, lessons from failures were taken on board and incorporated into new designs. The results of these failures were improved products as well as an enhanced understanding of how to develop then.

Given time and the required attitude, Software Engineering, too, will mature to the extent that it can institutionalise a process of learning from its failures.

2 Background

The management of software developments projects is gradually becoming synonymous with late delivery, exceeded budgets, reduced functionality and questioned quality. A 1985 survey for the UK Department of Trade and Industry (DTI) investigating 42,000 software projects, revealed that 66% had overrun time scales, 55% were over budget and 58% experienced major unexpected problems [1]. The Software Engineering Institute at Carnegie Mellon University, rates about 85% of projects in the chaotic level of the process maturity framework. Another DTI study, questioning board-level executives of more than 400 UK users (including many of Britain's biggest firms), reveals that when measuring actual against expected benefits in more than 50% of their projects, only 11% of surveyed organisations were successful !

The commander of the US Air Force Systems command, Air Force General Bernard P. Randolph, conceded that software is a large problem that runs industry-wide. " *We have a perfect record on software schedules - we have never made one on time yet, and we are always looking for excuses* " [3].

There is a 30-70% chance that estimates will be wrong [4, 9]. Failure outweighs success by a factor of at least 5 [4].

A Management Consultancies Association recent survey suggested that poor project management is costing the UK at least £1 billion per annum (about $1.5 billion at time of writing). The final figures come from a recent survey looking at 400 UK firms, reviewing all projects in excess of one million dollars, undertaken over the last 10 years. In total these firms lost a grand total of 1 billion dollars in abandoned projects alone!

20% of all projects were abandoned,
60% were late,
90% exceeded their budgets,
While a staggering 98% had changed specification to lower the required functionality.

3 Falling down is part of Growing up

The idea of failure has often been cited as central to the understanding of engineering.

" *... Engineering has at its first and foremost objective the obviation of failure ... but lessons learned from disasters can do more to advance engineering knowledge than all the successful machines and structures in the world* " [11].

Engineering is about trial and error. Effective knowledge emerges from the process of probing the environment, which is an essential pre-requisite for both learning and fostering additional variety (i.e. surviving). Creative responses evolve through a straight-forward series of conscious steps. If each step on this evolutionary path were successful then complete and total repetition would ensue, with no changes whatsoever. This would lead to stagnation, false optimism and ultimately to failure!

Obviously failure is an inevitable part of life especially in the wake of prolonged success, which encourages lower margins of safety. Success may be grand, but it cannot be sustained. Disappointment can teach us more - as engineers discover what not to do, what cannot work and the need to keep trying.

" *The history of engineering may be told by its failures as well as its triumphs* " [11]

Forensic project engineering is the science investigating the history of Information Technology failures.

4 Forensic Engineering

Forensic is derived from the Latin 'Forensis', meaning making public. Forensic Science is the applied use of a body of knowledge or practice in determining the cause of death. Nowadays extended to include any skilled investigation into how a crime was perpetrated.

Forensic systems engineering is the post-mortem analysis and study of project disasters. The work involves a detailed investigation of the project, the environment, decisions taken, politics, human errors and the relationship between subsystems. The work draws upon a multidisciplinary body of knowledge and assesses the project from several directions and viewpoints. The concept of systems is a central tool for understanding the delicate relationships and their implications in the overall project environment.

The aim of the study is to improve our understanding of failures; their background and how they come about. The long-term objectives are improving the state-of-the-practice and generating new insights into methods of managing complex projects. The knowledge generated is then fed-back into the process via a double loop learning system in order to improve the internal (organisational) or external (disciplinary) body of knowledge. In the best tradition of TQM, this approach leads to continuous improvement to the process of managing projects, thus enabling the organisation to advance to the next level of maturity. The work may also highlight the direction required to advance the entire discipline to the next plateau of excellence [6]. Some of the research resulting form this work has already yielded promising results in the areas of risk management, decision making, project management and the application of chaos and complexity theories to diagnosis, prediction and dynamic management practices.

5 Forensics and Computer Based Systems Engineering

CBSE - the engineering of computer based systems is emerging as a new discipline linking systems engineering with software engineering to provide a holistic view of problems, issues and the environment. This new inter-disciplinary branch of engineering provides a coherent and comprehensive discipline dealing with complex systems. The IEEE has formed an international task force to define and promote the discipline.

The task force has been active for three years and is making some progress at the international level. The state of the practice working group has recently reported that,
" *Generally engineers do not analyse detailed data from programs to understand cause and effect* " [13].

More recently forensic engineering has been identified as the central theme and the main justification for the existence of the task force. As a result we are now in the process of setting up a new working group dedicated to forensic engineering, while the theme for the next workshop has been identified as forensic CBSE.

6 Planning Failure

Researchers in management theory instil the virtues of intelligent and modest failure as a tool for strategic organisational learning and growth . The long-term benefits of knowledge, translated into organisational resilience, clearly outweigh the short-term offerings of success. The liabilities of success were identified as: complacency, restricted search, low levels of attention, risk aversion, missed opportunities and homogeneity [12]. These can be overcome by gently probing the environment in a trial and error fashion.

In the software development environment, cases of failures abound. Knowledge - if made available can be utilised to improve the state-of-the-art, practice, education and training.

" *With the increased scale of systems, the risks increase more than proportionally* " [5].

The stakes are getting higher, our failures more spectacular.

Tom Peters sums it up, " *do it badly, do it quickly, make it better, and then say you planned it* " [10].

7 The Value of Failure

Educators

The primary value of the study of failures, is in feeding knowledge back into the engineering schools. Utilising the case study method to highlight failed approaches or the importance of central topics enables educators to make full use of detailed analyses and the resultant knowledge. Cases can serve as a departure point for discussions and comments about the state-of-the-practice especially when Used in conjunction with comparisons of good and bad practices. New knowledge in the form of a statistical resource may be used to frame encountered problems, and to suggest how these problems can/cannot be overcome.

Detailed analysis of failures pinpoints areas for future research, which are essential rather than accidental, as they result from observed shortcomings of contemporary approaches. The forensic experience injects a dose of reality into our courses. It is also an attractive way of instilling a balanced and informed understanding of the topics while using examples the students are likely to remember - we all like to read about a good disaster.

Practitioners

The main benefit to practitioners is in reframing our body of knowledge. Highlighting the state-of-the-practice and identifying core problems will lead to more pertinent research. The acquired knowledge can also be used as a historical baseline within the organisation to improve assessments and estimates. This will result in better tuned processes and enhanced confidence.

Forensics highlights the central role of Risk Management and Decision Making, leading to a new perception of their importance in the development of sound and reliable software systems. In the long-run the field of forensics will help us understand what it is we are doing as software engineers before we can start learning (or teaching) how to do it [2].

Continuous Improvement

Continuous improvement is concerned with feeding knowledge back into the organisation. The knowledge from forensic analysis can be used as a reference for planning, estimating, scheduling, budgeting and resource allocation. While detailed historical knowledge would be used to calibrate existing methods and models, the feedback can also be used to improve the methods themselves, by making them more relevant and ensuring they address the right problems.

Forensics can also teach us how to improve feasibility assessments by incorporating risk considerations and provide a more reliable risk management technique for observing risky patterns. These will range from simple generic/ organisation-specific/ methodology-specific/ application domain-specific checklists based on past projects to sophisticated forensic knowledge based systems. Forensic KBS's will have the ability to record current decision rationale, relate past decisions to failures, retrieve similar decision situations and aid in making new decisions

In addition to being the new basis for decision making and trade-off criteria, forensic analysis could provide a knowledge resource for training aspiring project managers in chaotic reality conditions. Forensic analysis is a real eye opener.

Organisational Resource
The view of knowledge as an organisational resource requires recognition of software development as a growing asset for the organisation. This strategic resource improves organisational ability to survive. Process improvement which is clearly the key to organisational growth, utilises double loop learning to ensure the right aspects of the process are being addressed. This enables the organisation to consciously sample the environment and regain the vitality and variation needed to survive and excel, while constantly learning and hence, improving its strategic posture.

Improved risk assessment capacity which is tailored to organisational parameters will enhance the ability to deal with uncertainty. Allocation of resources within the organisation will be optimised, partly due to the improved knowledge, but also due to the lifting of the physical and mental stress and the lack of distortion in the use of resources. These resources can then be better invested in sampling the environment to discover new avenues for growth. This results in a positive feedback loop striving for improvement.

In summary, we can expect improved decision making, optimal strategy selection and the ability to evolve and survive changes and major interruptions.

8   Educational Structure and Objectives

The ideal structure for maximising benefits in an educational setting is an MBA style approach emphasising a practical and relevant component. a forensic course should boast heavy emphasis on flight simulation of real case studies of both success and failures, combined with an extensive theoretical basis, labs. and practical projects.

This will enable students to analyse past projects and relate them to the taught theory, while learning to utilise more effective approaches and testing them out.

The forensic course may be taken within any current software engineering/ computer science framework [7]. As well as teaching students project management, software engineering or systems engineering, the course aims to teach students how to carry out forensic analysis, how to benefit from the results, and how to improve future performance. It is therefore related to quality, TQM, measurement, metrics and strategic management modules.

Educational Objectives:
on completion of the course graduates should:

* Gain a holistic view of development
* Appreciate the strengths and weaknesses of development
  approaches in realistic setting
* Cultivate the special attitude required in a rapidly evolving
  environment
* Approach confidently and gain full benefits from
  uncertainty and risk
* Be able to identify new areas with potential for growth
* Understand the essential role of failure
* Improve ability to make decisions and frame situations
* Appreciate the value of Total system approaches and
  continuous improvement
* Learn how to learn and benefit from failure

9 Results and Products

The emphasis on holistic analysis will result in graduates who understand disciplinary fundamentals and barriers and know how to derive more information and test different approaches. The experience of post-mortem analysis, will ensure that students are skilled at synthesising and integrating different forms of knowledge and are able to handle and solve inter-disciplinary problems.

The use of real cases results in understanding and appreciation of the value modern technology, current industrial practice and prevailing perceptions. As analysis and discussion are subject to group interaction, students gain experience of multifunctional teams with people of differing abilities and different levels of experience. The value of effective communication is clearly demonstrated in the analysed cases.

The emphasis on risk management, continuous improvement and learning from failures can easily be applied at the personal level by the more discerning and brave students. Some of our group formation exercises are currently applying risk management and failure analysis techniques to group dynamics. This however can be done in a more private setting.

10 Summary

A new attitude is called for in order to succeed - actively looking for risks This attitude resembles the testing phase where a successful test, is the one uncovering a bug. A successful risk assessment would highlight the potential harms and bring them to the surface. There is a stigma attached to risks, suggesting they are negative. In reality risks are a set of potential consequences, and acknowledging their existence does not endanger your health. Another, more optimistic way of colouring risks is as a set of opportunities.

This kind of attitude needs to be extended to failures. While it is unrealistic to expect developers to actively seek risks in order to gain experience, we can hope that developers can gain experience when risks are discovered, and even assess their relevance in failures and disasters [8].

What next ?

Currently industry standard solutions to disasters are:

Solution 1   search for the guilty
Solution 2   punish the innocent
Solution 3   promote the uninvolved
Solution 4   all of the above

Instead we are offering another solution;

Solution 5   acknowledge the failure

This would entail studying the failure, retaining the knowledge and utilising it in the future to improve performance.

Adjusting to this worldview will take getting used to, but we can always remind ourselves of the success paradox;

**" If at first you (always) succeed
  Failure is ultimately guaranteed "**   [8]

References

1. Anon: Benefits of software engineering methods and tools, A study for the Department of Trade and Industry. London, UK: PA Computers and Communication 1985

2. B. R. Blum: Software Engineering a holistic view. New York: Oxford University Press 1992

3. R. N. Charette: Software Engineering Risk Analysis and Management. New York:Mcgraw-Hill 1989

4. R. N. Charette: Application Strategies for Risk Analysis. New York: Mcgraw-Hill 1990

5. W. W. Cotterman, J. A. Senn: Challenges and Strategies for Research in Systems Development. New York:John Wiley & Sons. 1992

6. D. Dalcher: Total Project Management. To appear in: Proceedings of the 1993 PMI Annual Seminar/ Symposium. Virginia: PMI Press

7. D. Dalcher: Forensic Engineering in practice. To appear in : Proceedings of the IEEE CBSE Task Force Proceedings. Kansas 1993

8. D. Dalcher: Dynamic Software Project Management. Maidenhead, England: McGraw-Hill . To appear 1994

9. J. Hihn & H. Habib-agahi: Cost Estimation of Software Intensive Projects: a Survey of Current Practices. in: Proceedings of the 13th International Conference on Software Engineering, May 13- 17 1991. Austin, Texas: IEEE Press

10. T. Peters: Thriving on Chaos, a Handbook for Management Revolution. New york: Alfred A. Knopf 1987

11. H. Petroski: To Engineer is Human. New York: St. Martin's Press 1982

12. S. Sitkin: Learning Through Failure; the strategy of Small Losses: Unpublished report. University of Texas 1990

13. S. White et al.: Improving the Practice in CBSE: State of Practice Working Group Special Report: IEEE Computer Society CBSE Task Force

14. A. Wildavsky: Searching for Safety. New Brunswick: Transaction publishers 1988

Session 12:
Software Reuse Education

Guided Reuse for Programmers
Pei Hsia, Richard H.S. Wang, and Dave Chenho Kung,
The University of Texas at Arlington, Arlington, Texas

A Practical Approach to Teaching Software Reuse
James E. Cardow, Air Force Institute of Technology,
Wright-Patterson Air Force Base, Ohio and
William D. Watson, Jr., The Charles Stark Draper
Laboratory, Inc., Cambridge, Massachusetts

Introducing a Software Reuse Culture in Practice
Thomas Grechenig and Stefan Biffl, Vienna University
of Technology,Vienna, Austria

Guided Reuse for Programmers

Pei Hsia, Richard H.S. Wang and Dave Chenho Kung

Computer Science Engineering Department
The University of Texas at Arlington
Arlington, TX 76019-0015

Abstract. This paper attempts to achieve one primary goal: to teach students the concept of reuse and thereby instill a reuse culture in them. We believe that teaching students the reuse concept in their first programming courses and encourage them to use it throughout their entire programming training will increase their productivity. The practice of reuse will then become second nature to them. A controlled experiment is designed and executed to measure the relative effects of a non-reuse paradigm and a reuse paradigm in terms of the Pascal programming course. It also explains how to use the pedagogical laboratories to help students acquire the reuse concept. Conclusions from the analysis of the collected data are presented and the complete experiment is reviewed. Finally we summarize the results of the experiment and present further research and direction in software reuse.

1 Introduction

Reuse is a concept that has been in existence since the beginning of programming [12, 20, 24] and has many advantages. However, the top management directed software reuse has not resulted in any significant improvement in productivity gains in the past ten years. There are several reasons, both technical and managerial, that prevent reuse from reaching its full potential [1]. For example, the representation technology [10, 21], lack of a clear and obvious direction [7], not invented here syndrome [15], performance concern [15], and high initial capitalization [4, 23], etc. all exert negative forces in practicing reuse. The lack of a reuse culture in the software engineering community is the main contributing factor. "Our real stumbling block is educational ... It is the major reason that we are not progressing aggressively in this direction" [12]. For example, in any programming course, students are seldom taught to accomplish their tasks by reuse. Many are even penalize for reuse, especially of others' work in academic environments.

We believe that this situation can be greatly improved if we teach students the reuse concept in their programming courses, and continue to emphasize the concept throughout their entire training. The concept of reuse will become second nature to them. An experiment was therefore designed to examine this hypothesis.

In the experiment, students were taught how to reuse software and to practice different levels of reuse in their programming laboratories. The motivation of the experiment was to instill a reuse culture in students. The goal was to teach students to perform code reuse, design reuse, and specification reuse. Our null hypothesis is that software reuse would not affect the software productivity. Here we define productivity as the inverse of the effort expended to produce a specific software product [16].

Section 2 presents the design of the experiment and introduces the subjects and the specifications of the tasks performed. Section 3 defines the measurements of the collected data. Section 4, 5 and 6 give the experimental results of questionnaires and tasks. The overall conclusions appear in Section 7.

2 Experimental Method

The experiment was conducted in a novice-level programming language course CSE 2303 "Introduction to Pascal" given by the Computer Science and Engineering Department in fall, 1992 at the University of Texas at Arlington (UTA). For the start of the experiment, subjects were asked to complete a pre-experimental questionnaire on their knowledge about reuse. Subjects were then given a computer menu containing information about the rules of doing their task. The task contained six different labs. All subjects were supposed to do the same lab at the same time, in the same order. Subjects' data collected from the task were analyzed by using the Statistical Analysis System (SAS). A post-experimental questionnaire was finally given and used to check the validity of the collected data. Appendix A gives the course schedule and grading policy. We will describe subjects, tasks and questionnaires below.

2.1 Subjects

Two classes with different section numbers were selected for the experiment.
1. Class A (2303-002): non-CSE major students (around 20 subjects).
2. Class B (2303-001): non-CSE major students (around 20 subjects).

There were two instructors, one for each class. It is assumed that all the other experiment factors of the class were the same since both instructors were using the same textbook and they followed the same syllabus with the same basic schedule for the chapter assignments.

Class A and class B were considered as group A and group B, respectively. Each student was an independent subject. Group A was the control group and the group subjects were informed that there was a reusable library. Group B was the experimental group and the group subjects were informed there was a reusable library, too. In addition, group B was encouraged to reuse existing codes and given detailed explanations of reuse.

Subjects in group B were given a handout with text and figures explaining reuse. Both group A and group B were informed that there was a reusable library that they could use to do their labs, but only subjects in group B were encouraged to use the reusable library. No subject was told about the experiment at all.

To accurately determine influential factors, the experimental subjects must perform all of the tasks according to the following rules:
1. Subjects must work their labs by themselves on the class designed computer facility only.
2. Subjects must use their own accounts.
3. Subjects must not modify the previous labs after they begin the current one.
4. Subjects must not work on the next lab before they finish or stop working on the current one.

2.2 Tasks

The six labs are all based on card games. They are strongly related; many functions in each lab are similar and portable to the other for software reuse purposes. There are three different levels of reuse here: code reuse, design reuse, and specification reuse. Each model was explained with text and figures to help students understand the idea of software reuse.

A software library was constructed that contains functions for students to use in their programs. If necessary functions cannot be reused from the previous labs, then they shall be found in the software library. Since these existing functions do not exactly match the requirements, individuals must understand these functions before reusing them. Thus, it provides practice for individuals with the three steps of reusing code, which are understanding, modifying, and integrating[4]. The following is the explanation of the goals that are supposed to be achieved in each lab:

Lab 1 is a coin-flipping game, used as a warm-up project. The program will randomly generate a number that will be used to indicate the status of the coin. Then the player inputs his/her guess and the program will verify if the guess is correct or not. Students are supposed to reuse the existing random-number-generator-code in the reuse library. It gives them the practice of statement reuse. This is the simplest approach to code reuse. Students need to know simple input/output and arithmetic functions for this lab which will probably take them four hours to finish a twenty-line program.

Lab 2 is a number-guessing game. The program will generate a random number within a range (e.g., 0 to 100) and the player has to find it in 10 or less guesses. Each time after receiving the player's guess, the program has to report if the guess is larger than, equal to, or smaller than the answer. The program has to display the comparing result to help the player to make the next guess. This lab is designed to reuse the random-number-generator-code for code Students need to know structured programming and modular design for this lab which will probably take them six hours to finish a twenty-five-line program.

Lab 3 is a blackjack game. The program will give as many cards as the player wants before the sum of ranks is over twenty-one. Students can reuse the formats of program heading and footing, and modify the random-number-generator-code from lab 1. This is an improved code reuse practice and it also introduces design reuse. Students need to know control structure and simple procedure for this lab which will probably take them ten hours to finish a fifty-line program.

Lab 4 is a collection of two games which are the coin-flipping and number-guessing games. These games are the same as lab 1 and lab 2. A text-file-access procedure to read and write a text file will be provided. Subjects need to modify the procedure to fit their need. Therefore, besides code-reuse, it also gives them the practice of design-reuse. Students need to know nested control structure and text file processing for this lab which will probably take them ten hours to finish a seventy-line program.

Lab 5 has the same requirements as for lab 3 except the program should be constructed in a totally different data structure (one-dimensional array). Subjects can reuse the code and design from lab 3 to display the output. Also they will practice the specification reuse while implementing this lab using the logic structure and the display-card procedure from lab 3. Students need to know one-dimensional array handling for this lab which will probably take them six hours to finish an eighty-line program.

Lab 6 has the same requirements as for lab 5 except the program should be constructed in another data structure (two-dimensional array). More requirements (allow more players for one game) have been put into lab 6 than lab 5. Subjects can again practice the code reuse, design reuse, and specification reuse from lab 5 by reusing the display-card procedure. Students need to know multi-dimensional array handling for this lab which will probably take them six hours to finish a ninety-line program.

2.3 Questionnaires

The pre-experiment questionnaire was given to subjects at the beginning of the experiment. This questionnaire assessed subjects' knowledge about reuse. Their expectations and learning motivations about reuse were evaluated. After subjects had finished all their task, the post-experiment questionnaire on their programming experience was given to them. This questionnaire assessed the validity of the computer usage data and prior programming experience of the subjects. They were asked if they had used other computer systems to do their assignments. Several questions were designed to measure the subjects overall Grade Point Average (G.P.A.) , their Computer Science G.P.A., the number of programming languages they know, and their impressions of the lab assignments. These two questionnaires are listed in Section 4 and 5 respectively.

3 Experimental Criteria and Measurements

All the data collected during the experiment were used to measure a subject's effort in completing the assignment. The measurements of productivity, their abbreviations and definition are included in the following list:

1. Main productivity measures
   .Comp.: the number of compilations made during task development and testing.
   .CTime: CPU time (in seconds)
   .LTime: Login time (in minutes)
   .IR: incomplete ratio. the ratio of incomplete labs to the total possible labs
2. Secondary productivity measures
   .Edit: the number of edit sessions performed during system development and testing.
   .Login: the number of logins made to system.
   .Run: the number of runs made during system development and testing.
   .TLine: total number of executable source code lines
   "A subject with a high value for a given measure is considered less productive than a subject with a low value. Multiple productivity measures are used to obtain a more complete picture of the development process" [16].

To assure the data validity, all the computer usage records were automatically collected by the Academic Computing Services (ACS) at UTA. The usage reports were coded such that no subject name was ever revealed nor connected to any particular data. An analysis of variance test was performed on each of the evaluating factors using group and task as two variables. Since two groups' mean values of evaluations factors are to be compared, the t-distribution [6] was used to test hypothesis. If the p-value for the test was less than 5% ($p<0.05$) then the difference in means was considered significant .The statistical analysis of the subject data is described first, followed by the analysis of the lab data.

4 Pre-experimental Questionnaire Results

There were twenty-eight subjects (ten from group A and eighteen from group B) who turned in the questionnaire. The results are listed in Table 1.

Pre-Eperiment Questionnaire

This is a questionnaire designed to help provide background concerning you and might be used to improve the CSE 2303 course. Your name will not be associated with these data and the values themselves will have no bearing on your course evaluation. For the following questions, please choose only one answer.

Q1. The main reason for taking the course is:
1. required for a degree
2. interested in programming
3. to get a certificate
4. used as a foundation to obtain a job
5. other

Q2. Your industry/academic background is:
1. have degree in another field (not CSE related)
2. have job or work experience with computer
3. have taken four or more computer courses
4. have taken not more than four computer courses
5. have job plus academic (computer courses) experience
6. other

Q3. How much do you like to work with computers or computer technology?
1. very much
2. much
3. fair
4. not much
5. not at all
6. other

Q4. How much do you know software reuse?
1. very well
2. well
3. fair
4. not much
5. not at all
6. other

Q5. Do you think software reuse is:
1. money saving
2. time saving
3. ineffective
4. possible
5. impossible
6. other

Q6. What is the benefit you will expect from software reuse?
1. time saving
2. money saving
3. reliability
4. both time and money saving
5. other

Q7. How much would you like to know software reuse?
1. very much
2. much
3. fair
4. not much
5. not at all
6. other

Q8. Under what situation would you be interested in software reuse?
1. required for a course
2. interested in programming
3. to get a certificate
4. used as a foundation to obtain a job
5. other

Q9. Which topic are you most interested in?
1. reusable data
2. reusable architecture
3. reusable designs
4. reusable programs and common systems
5. reusable modules
6. other

Table 1   Answers of pre-experimental questionnaire

Question 5   How much do you know software reuse?

	answer1	answer2	answer3	answer4	answer6	Total Subjects
Group A	0 ·	1	2	4	0	10
Group B	0	1	3	5	0	18

Question 8   How much would you like to know software reuse?

	answer1	answer2	answer3	answer4	answer6	Total Subjects
Group A	4	3	2	1	0	10
Group B	7	5	5	0	1	18

Question 9   Under what situation would you learn reuse?

	answer1	answer2	answer3	answer4	answer6	Total Subjects
Group A	1	5	0	2	0	10
Group B	7	4	1	2	0	18

Concerning question 5 ("How much do you know software reuse?"), 7% of subjects answered "much", 18% answered "fair" and other 75% answered "not much" or "not at all". Therefore it is assumed that most of the subjects did not know software reuse before taking this class.

Concerning question 8 ("How much would you like to know software reuse?"), 39% of subjects answered "very much", 29% answered "much", 25% answered "fair", 7% answered "not much" or "other." More than half of them seemed to have a strong desire to learn software reuse.

Concerning question 9 ("Under what situation would you be interested in software reuse?"), 29% of subjects answered "required for a course", 32% answered "interest in programming", 18% answered "to get a certificate" or "used as a foundation to obtain a job", and other 21% chose "other". To subjects, it seems that the major motivation of learning software reuse comes from their degree requirement or personal interest.

5 Task Evaluation Results

Table 2 shows the numbers of complete labs, incomplete labs, missing labs and total subjects for each lab assignment of both groups. All the results but lab 1, which was considered a warm-up lab, are analyzed by using the t-test later.

Table 2 Lab assignments

		Lab 2	Lab 3	Lab 4	Lab 5	Lab 6
Complete Labs	Group A	7	3	6	4	5
	Group B	9	9	13	8	11
Incomplete Labs	Group A	5	6	7	5	4
	Group B	6	3	0	6	1
Missing Labs	Group A	10	13	5	6	6
	Group B	0	3	2	0	1
Total Subjects	Group A	22	22	18	15	15
	Group B	15	15	15	14	14

Appendix B gives the results of the t-test for lab 2 through lab 6. In lab 2 (Fig. 1), the login time, the CPU time, edit sessions, and the number of compilations are significantly different between these two groups.

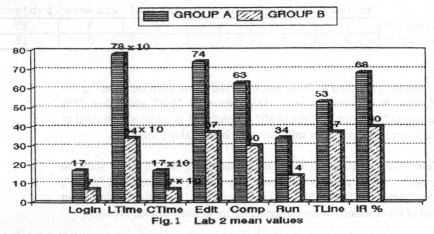

Fig. 1   Lab 2 mean values

In lab 3 (Fig. 2), the login time and the number of compilations are significantly different. There were only three subjects in group A that had finished the lab assignment completely. (They possibly were the top three students in group A and their proficiency might overcome any lack of advantage from the reuse concept.)

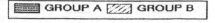

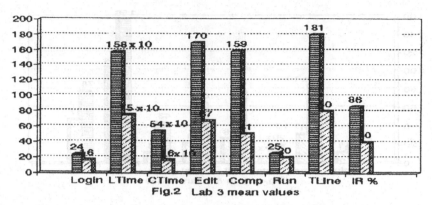

Fig.2   Lab 3 mean values

In lab 4 (Fig. 3), the number of logins, the login time, the CPU time, edit sessions, and the number of compilations are significantly different.

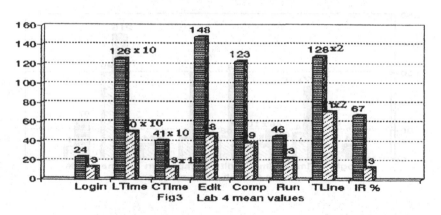

Fig3   Lab 4 mean values

In lab 5 (Fig. 4), the login time, edit sessions, and the number of compilations are significantly different.

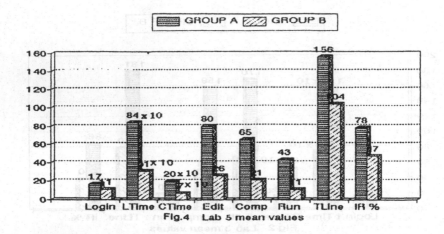

Fig.4 Lab 5 mean values

In lab 6 (Fig. 5), the login time, edit sessions, the number of compilations, and the total executable lines are significantly different.

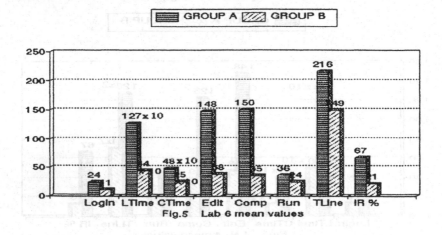

Fig.5 Lab 6 mean values

The code reuse percentage of each lab is listed in Table 3. It shows that group B reused code from previous labs at least 10% more than group A did. Table 4 gives the productivity increase percentage of group B, compared to group A. The results also prove that group B has significantly higher productivity than group A.

Table 3   Code reuse percentage from previous labs

	Lab 2 %	Lab 3 %	Lab 4 %	Lab 5 %	Lab 6 %	Average %
Group A	25	32	64	54	60	47
Group B	48	48	74	72	71	63

Table 4   Productivity increase of group B over Group A

	Lab 2 %	Lab 3 %	Lab 4 %	Lab 5 %	Lab 6 %	Average %
Login	143	50	85*	55	118	90
LTime	129*	111*	152*	171*	187*	150
CTime	143*	238	215*	186	92	175
Edit	100*	154	208*	208*	289*	192
Comp	110*	212*	215*	210*	329*	177
Run	143	25	100	291	50	122
TLine	43	126	80	50	45*	69

* Significant at 0.05 level or less

6 POST-EXPERIMENT QUESTIONNAIRE RESULTS

There were twenty subjects (nine from group A and eleven from group B) who turned in the questionnaire. The results are listed in table 5. Some of them did not give their G.P.A., so there was no way to check the significant value of subjects by using their G.P.A. Therefore we reviewed their programming experience to check if the selection of subjects was biased.

POST-EXPERIMENT QUESTIONNAIRE

This is a questionnaire designed to determine background information to allow us to improve the CSE 2303 course. Your name will not be associated with this data and the values themselves will have no bearing on your course evaluation. You do not have to answer every question, but your help will be greatly appreciated. Thank you.

SECTION 1 : YOUR BACKGROUND

1. Did you know how to program in the following languages before you enrolled in the CSE 2303 class?
   __ BASIC __ FORTRAN __ ASSEMBLY __ COBOL __ DBASE3
   __ C __ LISP __ SMALLTALK __ PASCAL
   __ NONE OF THE ABOVE __ OTHERS _____(PLEASE SPECIFY)

SECTION 2 : GVAX and LABS
1. Before you enrolled in the CSE 2303, how much did you know about using the GVAX system?
   __ NOT AT ALL __ A LITTLE __ FAIR __ FAMILIAR __ VERY FAMILIAR

2. Besides the CSE 2303 course, are you taking any other programming language course this semester?
   __ NO __ YES (Please specify) _____

3. How many hours do you spend using the GVAX for your lab every week?
__3 or less __4 to 6 __7 to 9 __10 to 12 __13 to 15 __16 or more

4. Have you ever used PC Pascal (e.g., Turbo Pascal) for your labs?
__ NO __ YES (Please specify labs) _____

Table 5   Answers of post-experimental questionnaire

Question 1.1   Did you know any of these languages ...?

	BASIC or FORTRAN	C or Pascal	None	Total
Group A	4	4	1	9
Group B	5	1	5	11

Question 2.4   Have you ever used PC Pascal for labs?

	Lab 2	Lab 3	Lab 4	Lab 5	Lab 6	Not used
Group A	0	0	0	1	1	7
Group B	1	2	0	0	1	7

In group A, eight subjects knew the Pascal or BASIC or FORTRAN programming language before taking the CSE 2303 course. Their computer usage records would still be used for analysis since we needed all the subjects for the t-test.

In group B, one subject knew the C programming language and his record was not used for analysis. Five subjects knew BASIC or FORTRAN before taking the class and their data were still used for the t-test. There were some subjects that used PC-Pascal for lab assignments, so their records were not used for analysis.

It would seem that group A had an advantage as several of the subjects already knew the Pascal programming language before they took the CSE 2303 course. However, the analysis results show that group A had a lower overall performance than group B.

7 Conclusions

The experimental results show that all the evaluation mean values of group B are lower than those of group A. The login time and the number of compilations are significantly different between these two groups through lab 2 to lab 6. Obviously group B has better performance than group A in all the productivity measurements. According to the significant results from the analysis of lab assignments, we rejected the hypothesis that software reuse will not affect software productivity. We have to conclude that teaching software reuse and encouraging students to do it can improve software productivity measurably.

After reviewing the experiment process, we plan to continue the same experiment by using the same instructor for both sections. Therefore the different impact on subjects caused by different instructors will be minimized. An alternative way is to divide a class into both group A and group B according to subjects' G.P.A. or prior programming experience. It must be handled very carefully to cluster students, so the selection of subjects will not be biased. By doing this, the different impact on subjects, caused by different schedules, will disappear. Concerning the future work, some further examination will be conducted to find the proper way to encourage students to learn software reuse. There are four groups to be defined according to different encouragement levels, such as, forced to reuse, encouraged to reuse, and may or may not reuse. Another investigation is a longitudinal study by following students to their next computer science courses and compare their performances. Furthermore, this experiment should be performed and verified in other universities to check if the experiment results are reproducible in different environments.

We believe that teaching students the reuse concept early will increase their programming performance. It also can be applied to different subjects, say employees, to help them to improve their software productivity. Continual emphasis of the concept throughout their entire programming training will instill the reuse culture and make it second nature to them.

Appendix A

Course Schedule

Week	Topics Covered	Chapters Assigned	Lab Assigned
1	Introduction	1	
	Representations		
2	Algorithms	2	
	Data Types		
	Arithmetic		
	* Give pre-experimental questionaire		
3	Assignment	3	1
	Simple I/O		
	Syntax and Semantics		
4	Sequential Structure	4	2
	Booleans		
	* EXAM 1 : Chapters 1, 2, & 3		
5	Selection - IF	4	
	Repetition - WHILE		
	Procedures		
6	Selection - CASE	5	
	Repetition - REPEAT		
	Repetition - FOR		
	Functions		
7	Scope Rules	6	3
	Top Down Design		
	Recursion		
8	Input & Output	7	
	* EXAM 2 : Chapters 4, 5, & 6		
9	Text Files	8	4
	Enumerated Types		
	Subranges		
10	Arrays	9	5
	Sorting & Searching		
11	Strings	10	
	* EXAM 3 : Chapters 7, 8, & 9		
12	String Processing	11	6
	Multidimensional		
13	Array Processing	12	
	Records & Fields		
14	Record Processing	13	
	Variant Records		
	* Give post-experimental questionaire		
15	Review		
16	FINAL EXAM		

Grading Policy

Exam 1	10%
Exam 2	10%
Exam 3	10%
Final	20%
Homework	20%
Lab1	3%
Lab2	3%
Lab3	4%
Lab4	6%
Lab5	6%
Lab6	8%

Appendix B

Lab 2 mean values of evaluation factors

	MEAN of GROUP A	MEAN of GROUP B	T-VALUE	PROB>|T|	
Login	17	7	1.7984	0.1191	
LTime	780	340	4.7026	0.0005	*SIGNIFICANT
CTime	170	70	3.0048	0.0182	*SIGNIFICANT
Edit	74	37	2.6801	0.0200	*SIGNIFICANT
Comp	63	30	2.5221	0.0268	*SIGNIFICANT
Run	34	14	1.8918	0.0829	
TLine	53	37	1.9001	0.1031	
IR %	68	40			

Lab 3 mean values of evaluation factors

	MEAN of GROUP A	MEAN of GROUP B	T-VALUE	PROB>|T|	
Login	24	16	1.0405	0.3285	
LTime	1580	750	2.4276	0.0414	*SIGNIFICANT
CTime	540	160	1.9024	0.1890	
Edit	170	67	2.1414	0.0646	
Comp	159	51	2.3488	0.0468	*SIGNIFICANT
Run	25	20	0.3667	0.7223	
TLine	181	80	3.0919	0.0882	
IR %	86	40			

Lab 4 mean values of evaluation factors

	MEAN of GROUP A	MEAN of GORUP B	T-VALUE	PROB>|T|	
Login	24	13	2.1694	0.0478	*SIGNIFICANT
LTime	1260	500	3.4054	0.0137	*SIGNIFICANT
CTime	410	130	3.5622	0.0110	*SIGNIFICANT
Edit	148	48	4.1456	0.0010	*SIGNIFICANT
Comp	123	39	4.3980	0.0006	*SIGNIFICANT
Run	46	23	1.6868	0.1138	
TLine	128	71	2.3977	0.0610	
IR %	67	13			

Lab 5 mean values of evaluation factors

	MEAN of GROUP A	MEAN of GROUP B	T-VALUE	PROB>|T|	
Login	17	11	0.9932	0.3466	
LTime	840	310	3.9203	0.0035	*SIGNIFICANT
CTime	200	70	2.4341	0.1283	
Edit	80	26	3.4103	0.0077	*SIGNIFICANT
Comp	65	21	3.9493	0.0034	*SIGNIFICANT
Run	43	11	2.6381	0.1110	
TLine	156	104	2.3220	0.1415	
IR %	73	43			

Lab 6 mean values of evaluation factors

	MEAN of GROUP A	MEAN of GROUP B	T-VALUE	PROB>|T|	
Login	24	11	1.9879	0.0701	
LTime	1270	440	3.9082	0.0021	*SIGNIFICANT
CTime	480	250	1.3367	0.2061	
Edit	148	38	7.7126	0.0001	*SIGNIFICANT
Comp	150	35	3.6405	0.0322	*SIGNIFICANT
Run	36	24	0.9532	0.3593	
TLine	216	149	2.9341	0.0125	*SIGNIFICANT
IR %	67	21			

References

1. T. Arano, "Software Reuse Activities in NTT," ICCI '1992, Computing and Information,IEEE Computer Society Press, 1992

2. V.R. Basili, "Experimentation in Software Engineering," IEEE Trans. on Software Eng., Vol. 12, No. 7, July 1986, page 733-743

3. V.R. Basili, "Viewing Maintenance As Reuse-Oriented Software Development," IEEE Software, January 1990, page 19-25

4. T. Biggerstaff, and C. Richter, "Reusability Framework, Assessment, and Directions," IEEE Software, March 1987, page 41-49

5. R.E. Brooks, "Studying Programmer Behavior Experimentally: The Problems of Proper Methodology," Communications of the ACM, Vol. 23, No. 4, April 80, page 207-213

6. S.R. Brown and L.E. Melamed, "Experimental Design and Analysis," SAGE Publications, 1990

7. B.A. Burton, R.W. Aragon, S.A. Bailey, K.D. Koehler, and L.A. Mayes, "The Reusable Software Library," IEEE Software, July 1987, page 25-33

8. B. Curtis, "Measurement and Experimentation in Software Engineering," Proceedings of the IEEE, Vol. 68, No. 9, Septermber 80, page 628-640

9. G. Fischer, "Cognitive View of Reuse and Redesign," IEEE Software, July 1987, page 60-72

10. G. Gruman, "Early Reuse Practice Lives up to Its Promise," IEEE Software, November 1988, page 87-91

11. J.W. Hooper and R.O. Chester, "Software Reuse Guidelines and Methods," Plenum Press, 1991

12. P. Hsia, "Software Reuse Activities in NTT," ICCI '1992, Computing and Information, IEEE Computer Society Press, 1992

13. T.C. Jones, "Reusability in Programming: A Survey of The State of the Art." IEEE Software, April 1984, page 488-493

14. G.E. Kaiser, and D. Garlan, "Melding Software Systems from Reusable Building Blocks," IEEE Software, July 1987, page 17-24

15. M. Lenz, H.A. Schmid, and P.F. Wolf, "Software Reuse through Building Blocks," IEEE Software, July 1987, page 34-42

16. J.A. Lewis, S.M. Henry, D.G. Kafura, R.S. Schulman, "On the relationship between the object-oriented paradigm and software reuse: an empirical investigation," Joop, July/August 1992, page 35-41.

17. S. Mamone, "Empirical Study of Motivation in a Entry Level Programming Course," ACM SIGPLAN Notices, Vol 27, No. 3, March 1992, page 54-60.

18. Mayer, R.E., "The Psychology of How Novices Learn Computer Programming," ACM Computer Surveys, March 1981, page 121-141

19. T.P. Moran, "An Applied Psychology of the User," ACM Computer Surveys, March 1981, page 1-12.

20. R. Prieto-Diaz, "Software Reuse: From Concepts to Implementation," NEC America, Inc. 1991

21. R.G. Reynolds, "Future directions in software reuse," ICCI '1992, Computing and Information, IEEE Computer Society Press, 1992.

22. SAS/ETS User's Guide SAS Institute, Inc. 1984.

23. T.A. Standish, "An Essay on Software Reuse," IEEE Trans. on Software Eng., September 1984, page 494-497

24. I. Toda, "How to prevent the coming software crisis," IEEE Software, May 1992, page 14.

25. G.M. Weinberg, The Psychology of Computer Programming, Van Nostrand Reinhold, 1971.

26. S.N. Woodfield, D.W. Embley, D.T. Scott, "Can Programmers Reuse oftware?" IEEE Software, July 1987, page 52-59.

A Practical Approach to Teaching Software Reuse

Captain James E. Cardow
Air Force Institute of Technology

William D. Watson, Jr.
The Charles Stark Draper Laboratory, Inc.

Abstract:

For software reuse to become a reality, the concept of reuse must be presented in a practical context. A practical context must focus on the use of reusable components to develop systems in well understood domains. "Write-only" software libraries will do nothing to accomplish the potential gain of reuse. Generic libraries of components will also provide little gain. This paper discusses a five lesson section covering reuse in a software generation and maintenance course. The course is part of a program designed to educate working professionals in software engineering. The reuse lessons focus on all aspects of reusing software components, from the development of a domain model through to the construction of systems. This paper also describes the homework and project tasks used to reinforce the lesson material.

1 Introduction

In 1986 James W. Canan, Senior Editor of Air Force Magazine, wrote an article [1] titled "The Software Crisis." In that article he stated that "software will soon account for 10 percent of the USAF budget." He also correctly pointed out that "there are problems of cost and quality, but the biggest problem is that demand for software exceeds supply by a dangerous margin." Changing political climates have reduced the demand, however, demand still exceeds supply. More importantly, problems of "cost and quality" are still prominent; possibly more prominent due to the shortages of resources, especially people.

The Air Force recognized this as a critical problem. As such, it was a problem to be solved, not by buying more technology, but by a better educated work force. In 1989 the Air Force launched a new educational program, the Software Professional Development Program (SPDP). The purpose of the SPDP is to provide graduate-level software engineering courses to a wide variety of practicing software professionals. The program consists of five two-week courses, developed with support and guidance from the Software Engineering Institute (SEI). (Development of the program is chronicled in Mead [2].)

One of the five courses adopted a goal specifically addressing Canan's issues. The Software Generation and Maintenance Course's (AFIT Course WCSE-474) prime focus would be to "comprehend the process of generating software from properly created design and the process of maintaining the system upon delivery." The course developers realized that these goals could only be attacked by placing major emphasis on the area of software reuse. This article describes the method used to present software reuse to the Air Force's future software engineers.

2 Software Reuse

Skepticism on the potential for reuse abounds. Mary Shaw of the SEI was quoted as correctly predicting that "software reuse will be the expert system of the 1990's." The students taking AFIT's course have the same skepticism. Reuse is often proposed; and it often fails. Part of the failure can be attributed to focusing reuse efforts on code; clearly the level of reuse expected in a generation and maintenance course. However, Prieto-Diaz [3] pointed out that reuse involved "the use of previously acquired ideas and concepts in new situations." In the past the emphasis was on "acquired ideas and concepts" in reality the emphasis should be on "use." The point being, learning about reuse must enforce the notion of having components available to support system development, first, last, and always. That is the focus of reuse in this course.

To scope the course (and this paper) some assumptions must be made concerning software reuse. The assumptions are:
- Reuse is a viable option for addressing productivity and quality issues in software.
- Reuse involves more than just the code.
- Reuse without domain analysis will offer little gain in productivity.
- For software reuse to work, the emphasis must be on the system development, not the reuse development.

These assumptions are addressed in a series of five lessons (covered in six hours), plus extensive project work and a homework exercise. The five lessons are discussed below.

2.1 Introduction to Software Reuse

What does software reuse mean? What aspects of software are reusable? What are the costs and benefits of reuse? These are some of the questions presented to the students during the introduction to the section. The purpose is to get the skepticisms out in the open, to address the student's doubts and misunderstandings. Often the students are presented with arguments that shake their preconceived notions of reuse. Arguments such as "software reuse libraries should not contain source code." This argument is especially effective in making the students rethink the potential for reuse. Barnes [4] argues that "the defining characteristic of good reuse is not the reuse of software per se, but the reuse of human problem solving." Biggerstaff [5] also presents a strong "potential versus payoff" argument for code level components. These, along with the cost of coders versus designers and the percentage of time spent coding versus designing and testing are used to formulate examples of why higher level constructs are more valuable in a library.

With these arguments in mind, the students are presented with a model (figure 1) of a reuse process. The process has four, totally interconnected sides consisting of domain analysis, component and tool construction, library management and construction, and system construction. This model was adopted from Holibaugh's model [6] for introducing reuse into an organization. The model has some very definite strengths. It places emphasis on early analysis of the domain as well as focus on system development and it allows for incorporation of new proposals to support reuse in a consistent approach. The major modifications to the model were to make it continuous and to provide interconnections between all points. This removed the sequential, circular path and created a reflective model with support from all activities.

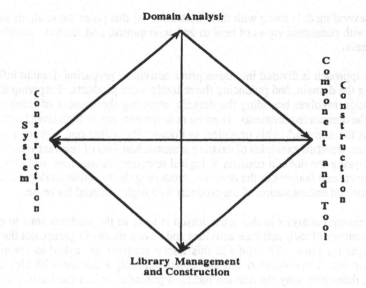

Fig. 1. Reuse Process Model

The model is covered in the next four lesson areas.

2.2. Introduction to Domain Analysis

Throughout the five courses in the SPDP the students are reminded of the importance of understanding their domain. Now they are presented with a much more complex problem; how to analyze the domain. Understanding is a matter of recognition. Analysis involves the problems of bounding (separating this domain from others), selecting sources of information (software engineers are generally not domain experts), creating taxonomies (organization and relationship of information), and storing the products of the analysis for reuse. What is discovered during the software reuse lesson is that domain analysis is the keystone of the reuse process. If "reusable" software is developed during a project without attending to the domain, the project builds libraries of components useful for building identical systems. Identical systems are seldom required; similar systems are often required and therefore provide a payoff for reuse. For that reason, reusable products must be initiated at the system concept level, the domain.

During this lesson, the students gain some ideas about defining domains. The examples used depend on the instructor, but a typical list of domains might include communications, control, electromagnetics, and thermodynamics. This is only a very simple subset of all possible domains, but it does provide a framework for consideration. The students need to understand that domain does not imply implementation. Domain analysis then is truly understanding the common characteristics of objects in the domain, especially systems.

A formal structure or process model is needed to explain all of these procedures properly. Prieto-Diaz's [7] model of domain analysis was selected to fill this need. Note, this is not necessarily the single best approach to domain analysis, but it does serve well. In fact, given more time to present the material, a more effective approach could be the presentation of several models along with their tradeoffs. At this point the students need to be presented with consistent views of how to gather, organize, and store the information about the domain.

Prieto-Diaz's approach is divided into three prime activities: preparing domain information, analyzing the domain, and producing the reusable work products. Preparing the domain information involves bounding the domain, selecting the sources of information, and defining the domain requirements. Domain requirements are a "high level breakdown of activities in the domain." This provides, as Prieto-Diaz points out, a set of potential areas to analyze, standard examples of existing systems, and lists of relevant issues in the domain. Analyzing the domain consists of logical selection, abstraction, and classification of the objects and features in the domain. Producing the reusable work products involves selection and encapsulation of the products with high potential for reuse.

The value of domain analysis in this reuse lesson is to have the students start to recognize the commonalty of their software activities and have a means to group, not the code, but the concepts for reuse. To reinforce this lesson students are asked to complete a homework exercise. The homework has the students identify a domain with high potential for reuse, determine why the domain has high potential, select the leading components within the domain for future reuse, and provide selection rationale for choosing among similar instantiations of the components. The purpose of this exercise is to have the students think about a domain, and to recognize that a *good* domain should have maturity, stability, and commonalty. Generally, the students select a domain from their area of expertise. This allows them to use the material in the context of their home organization's activities and makes it more practical in nature.

Note that the domain analysis process is system and technology independent. Once the domain analysis is complete, the same process needs to be carried into the development of specific systems. This is where the next level, Component and Tool Construction, comes in.

2.3 Component and Tool Construction

A very detailed domain analysis process was presented to the students in the first lesson. The process provided a way to organize the information, use it, and store it for reuse. Now, as the students are faced with building specific systems, they need a way to continue the process. For each of the development stages (requirements determination, design, and implementation) the process is the same. Each has a "prepare information" step, "conduct *activity* (requirements, design, or implementation)" step, and "produce reusable work products" step. The point of going through this is to demonstrate, clearly, where the added cost and potential savings from reuse will occur. The students are shown that the conduct *activity* steps are the typical development activities and should have minor negative impact from reuse, along with major positive impact. The two outer steps of preparing information and producing reusable work products do have a cost. This cost is the added cost of reuse and must be part of the *return-on-investment* strategy for doing reuse.

Since this is a generation course, the implementation stage is explored in detail. In addition, the code level activity of producing reusable work products is given special attention. The purpose here is to highlight the need for good guidelines for styles and standards. An emphasis at this point is that good guidelines are needed whether the code is "built-from-scratch" for immediate use or built for reuse.

This lesson's purpose is to have the students understand the relationship of the reuse process to the building of systems. The students need to see where the potential to draw components for system use and identify components for future use fits within system development. The students will not have this area directly reinforced, but the styles and standards aspects are part of delivering the course product. Once the students understand the construction of components, they need to know how and where to store the components. This is where Library Management and Construction comes in.

2.4 Library Management and Construction

The value of this lesson is getting the students to recognize the difficulty of putting components into and getting components out of a library. Generally the students have some experience in attempting to draw components from a library. They are asked to explain the problems (finding components, determining the purpose and quality of components, getting the components to do what is expected). With these issues in mind, the students are presented with a *wish list* for a library from Cardow [8]. The *wish list* includes easy access/retrieval, support for incomplete information, multi-level review capability, certification, and control of components. Essentially the students must understand that having a library can not overwhelm the system development effort. These issues are explored in relation to the system development so that the students can see the connections with the processes they were shown in the last lesson.

The students understand why libraries of software have been difficult to use. Now they need to see a better way to organize the information presented to them by the library. To accomplish this they are asked to consider the way information is gathered while doing research in a book library. With a model of *deselection of alternatives* in mind, they are presented with a model of organizing software information. This organization presents the more important information first; adding more details as fewer choices are left to consider. This approach, called the *onion-skin*, was developed for this course. The *onion-skin* has four layers of information: functionality, design, quality, and the artifact. Two layers of the approach (functionality and design) were examined in detail in Siebels [9].

From this lesson the students see ways to organize the reusable information so that is can be found, and used, in system development. This lesson is reinforced by project work. The students have a system, without an interface, that they have been previously asked to reverse engineer. Now, they are presented with the task of choosing among five menu interfaces. They are given the requirements and an example (look and feel demo), but not any of the source code. Their task is to define a process and criteria for selecting among the five choices. Then, they are asked to follow through with their plan. At the same time, they are asked to define how they would package the menu component selected for future reuse. This project covers several topics: 1) the students learn the difficulties of selecting components including the need for tradeoffs in functionality and quality, 2) they learn the difficulty of determining the information necessary to make the selection, and 3) they learn to use the selection criteria to build the packaging notation. If something makes selection easier, it should be used for packaging. If a criterion did nothing to help in the selection process, or it obscured the process, then why use it to store a component? The parallels between selection and storage are a critical lesson.

The final stage of the process is the use of components in building systems. This is covered in System Construction.

2.5 System Construction

The easiest concept to accept at this point is "I'm going to take a component, as is, and place it directly into my system, with 100 percent fit." Unfortunately, this will rarely happen. The point of this lesson is to have the student examine the issues of modifying components to meet requirements of the system and evaluating the needs of the system to accept reusable components. The first part is pretty clear; the second is difficult. The point is not to change the requirements of the system. The point is to recognize the tradeoffs between optimized, built from scratch components and readily available parts. An analogy can be drawn by looking at the tradeoffs in having a hardware chip developed from scratch versus selecting one from a catalog. Will the component support building of the system or not? If so, then accept something less than optimal to achieve cost and quality. This lesson is short, but important. This is one area where reuse fails miserably. If system developers will not *use* the parts stored in the library, then nothing accomplished during component construction or library management will be of any use. Too often we have built "write-only" libraries.

This area is reinforced in the project by joining the selected menu component and the reverse engineered system. The students must deliver a final, complete product.

3 Software Reuse Example

This block of lessons contains a considerable amount of material. The reuse process model helps the students maintain the idea of connectivity between the four sections discussed above; however, the students still need to see the model work. To solve this problem, an example is worked. The example is from Lee [10]. The domain of aircraft engines is analyzed and the process is carried through to the implementation level. By using this domain the students see an example with parts that relate to physical engine components and see the components become source code.

The example is started by explaining the selection of the domain and the scaling to an appropriate subdomain. In this case, the aircraft domain of simulation was selected along with the subdomain of engines. The simulators are mature in that they have been used since the 1940's to train pilots. They are stable in that there are seldom radical changes in the basic aircraft architectures simulated. And finally, they have commonality across different types of aircraft used by the Air Force. These three characteristics significantly increase the potential for reuse.

The same reasoning can be applied to the subdomain of engines to justify performing a domain analysis at that level. Keep in mind that what is being built is a software simulation of physical components, the engine. Once this domain area is understood, it must be analyzed.

The first steps in analyzing the engine domain are to bound the limits, select the sources of information, and define the domain requirements. This results in a domain region with its external interfaces defined. The next step is to identify the major components of the domain having further reuse potential. Figure 2 is an example of the results of these early steps. From here, the components with high potential for reuse (e.g., the rotor) can be packaged for storage in the reuse library as a domain object.

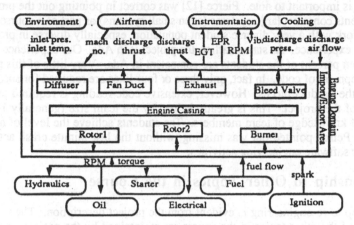

Fig. 2. Simulator Engine Domain and Components

Once the domain analysis is complete, the information can be used to construct specific implementation of the engine system. In this example, the process is continued using figure 2 to show a specific instantiation of the engine. To accommodate this, the internal interfaces are defined and Booch package diagrams are created to represent the system level architecture. The system level architecture is then refined down through the software architecture to detailed design and on into package specifications for the code.

While the example is relatively short (covered in about 30 minutes) it does provide the students with a concrete way to view the principle concepts in an application that they can visualize.

4 Project Support

Most of the aspects of the project were already discussed in section 2; however, some illumination might be beneficial. The total project uses the SEI artifact EM-1 [11]. This is a Documented Ada Style Checker system that will evaluate the style of Ada source code. In earlier parts of the course the students are learning maintenance tasks, especially re-engineering. As part of earlier project efforts they are asked to reverse engineer one of the ancillary functions (help, dictionary, etc.) of the system. For this portion of the course they are asked to select and attach the front-end menuing system. In the final portion they are asked to produce the final product, complete with an acceptance test, and packaged reusable components of the selected menu and reverse engineered ancillary piece. The menus available for selection were all developed for early versions of the course by student teams. Since all five of the menu choices were developed under similar development strategies, they all meet similar requirements. Unfortunately (for the students), they all have varying degrees of quality and consistency. This makes selection difficult. A choice in favor of functionality may have a penalty in quality. A choice in favor of quality might have a penalty in functionality, and possibly changeability. The purpose of having the process and criteria for activities presented before seeing the source code is to force thinking on the process, not the product. Generally, this makes the students uncomfortable, but the results are better thought out.

One point that is important to note. Pierce [12] was correct in pointing out the problems in having students construct large systems (even small systems) as part of a course. This project must work with a very diverse student population, especially diverse in programming language experience. As stated earlier, the project is in Ada. Our experience shows that less than ten percent of the students are competent in Ada. Very little of this project requires development of code. In fact, only three or four lines are required for successful integration of the product pieces. However, extensive code reading is required to work many aspects of the project. This is greatly helped by the team size (generally 10) and the diversity of knowledge of team members. The students achieve the level of accomplishment that Peirce pointed out was missing, without the last minute crash activities that foster poor software engineering activities.

5   Relationship to Other Topics in the Course

The relationship to re-engineering is evident from the project description. The relationships to many of the other topics in the course are maintained by the project. Students must draw on the metric's lesson for selection criteria. They must draw on the risk analysis process in performing the planning (how far can you go with a bad menu choice?). Quality assurance is enforced by delivery of the final product. The maintenance change process is used in adapting the component to work with the system. In all, this project very effectively combines the concepts of reuse with the notion of maintaining and generating systems, effectiveness that has been cited by numerous student comments on the course exit critique.

6.   Evaluation of Reuse Material

This section of reuse material is extremely effective at conveying the major concept to a class of working software professionals. The strength of the material is that it provides a process to follow addressing most areas of reuse. The focus is not limited to specific topics. The biggest weaknesses are that there is not sufficient detail to answer all questions (this is not a cookbook solution to reuse) and serious questions arise over optimal techniques. The issues on techniques will require further evaluation and experimentation. The biggest questions is, which domain analysis process is best. However, these weaknesses do not detract from the topic; they only serve to increase awareness of research opportunities.

The material in this course has been used for full-time graduate courses in software engineering and in part for seminars and tutorial presentations. In each case it has worked well. The material has not been used in undergraduate course work and may not work as well for inexperienced software practitioners. That remains to be explored.

7   Conclusion

The purpose of the reuse portion of this course is to present to practitioners, the concept of reuse and a way to make it work. This model and the material developed for the lessons works very well at achieving the goal. The students (over 200 so far) have had very positive comments about the presentation of reuse, often stating that it was the first clear approach they had seen. The benefits of the model are definitely a strong focus on system development and the necessity of analyzing the domain before establishing storage of components.

References

[1]   Canan, J. W. "The Software Crisis." *Air Force Magazine* (May 1986), 46-52.

[2]   Mead, N. R., Patricia K. Lawlis. "Software Engineering: Graduate-Level Courses for AFIT Professional Continuing Education." *Software Engineering Education, SEI Conference*, J.E. Tomayko, ed. New York, NY: Springer-Verlag, Oct. 1991, 114-126.

[3]   Prieto-Diaz, R., and Freeman, P. "Classifying Software for Reusability." *IEEE Software 4*, 1 (Jan. 1987), 106-116.

[4]   Barnes, B. H., and Bollinger, T. B. "Making Reuse Cost-Effective." *IEEE Software 8*, 1 (Jan. 1991), 13-24.

[5]   Biggerstaff, T., and Richter, C. "Reusability Framework, Assessment, and Directions." *IEEE Software* (Mar. 1987), 41-49.

[6]   Holibaugh, R., Cohen, S., Kang, K., and Peterson, S. "Reuse: Where to begin and why." *Proceedings of Tri-Ada '89*. Oct. 1989, 266-277.

[7]   Prieto-Diaz, R. "Domain Analysis for Reusability." *Proceedings of COMPSAC 87*. Oct. 1987.

[8]   Cardow, J. E. "Issues on Software Reuse." *Proceedings of NAECON - 1989*. Piscaway, NJ: IEEE Computer Society Press, May 1989.

[9]   Siebels, P. D., Capt, USAF. *Examining a Layered Approach to Function and Design Representation for Reusable Software Components*. Master's Th., Air Force Institute of Technology, Wright Patterson AFB, OH, Dec. 1992.

[10]   Lee, K. L., Michael S. Rissman, Richard D'Ippolito, Charles Plinta, Roger Van Scoy. *Paradigm for Flight Simulators, 2nd Edition*. Technical Report CMU/SEI-88-TR-30, Software Engineering Institute, Carnegie Mellon University, Pittsburgh, Pa., Dec. 1987.

[11]   Engle, C. B., Ford, G., and Korson, T. *Software Maintenance Exercises for a Software Engineering Project Course*. Educational Materials CMU/SEI-89-EM-1, Software Engineering Institute, Carnegie Mellon University, Pittsburgh, Pa., Feb. 1989.

[12]   Pierce, K. R. "Rethinking Academia's Conventional Wisdom." *IEEE Software 10*, 2 (Mar. 1993), 94-95,99.

Introducing a Software Reuse Culture in Practice

THOMAS GRECHENIG   STEFAN BIFFL

Department of Software Engineering,
Vienna University of Technology,
Resselgasse 3/2/188, Vienna,
A-1040 Austria

EMail: Grechenig@eimoni.tuwien.ac.at
Tel.: ++43-1-58801-4082
Fax: ++43-1-504 15 80

Abstract. The following paper deals with experiences derived from an industrial consulting project for designing a reuse model. The model is oriented towards actual use in practice and therefore also towards different levels of reuse intensity. It was outlined for a company employing more than 200 software engineers who primarily develop software for bank services and bank administrations. The field of investigation on hand is connected with a lot of vital software engineering (SE) questions for any larger developer: heterogeneity in age of software, heterogeneity of applications, heterogeneity of development environments as well as different levels of software engineering consciousness and of knowledge among the software engineers. The model presented is drawn from state-of-the-art suggestions in reuse research which were adapted to meet local constraints of time and costs. The model can be taken as a recipe for reuse in practice as it is providing three different levels of reuse intensities/investments, and thus returning three different levels of reuse maturity.
Level I reuse maturity in practice is to achieve maintainability: Many older programs turned out to be widely undocumented; often requirements and/or abstract design were missing, the programs do not meet basic criteria of maintainability.
Level II reuse maturity is represented by balance within similar projects: We define a group of software systems as balanced, if there is a clear top-down structure from the general to the specific in documents concerning analysis, design, code and test. A new but similar system can be designed reusing upper level software document components and adapting lower level ones.
Level III reuse maturity affords several technical and organizational efforts to establish a true reuse culture. Making a reuse culture work needs developing, providing and enforcing of standards. On the technical level this requires the use of repositories for all phases of development as well as the application of quality assurance methodology. On the organizational level cooperation among people responsible for the development of standards (metric analysis, quality check through reviews) as well as those coordinating the reuse environment is required. The roles for a reuse culture as well as the educational prerequisites are defined.
The value of the presented work lies in mapping the reuse state-of-the-art to often appearing financial and organizational restrictions consciously, thus opening possibilities beyond the "total reuse or no reuse" advice.

Keywords: software reuse, reuse model in practice, industrial experience, maintainability, standards, quality assurance, management issues

1 Introduction

Finding an appropriate and tested procedure within a pool of available software, instead of "inventing" it anew, is the idea of any reuse activity. The reuse of software documents has been suggested since the early eighties. Many suggestions have been made, some industrial experiences have been reported, tools have been designed so far (see chapter 2), such as repositories, CASE-tools, or the object-oriented paradigm, which all promise and proclaim some kind of reuse. Beyond these efforts it is obvious that successful reuse is a goal that requires technical and organizational preconditions: an ideal environment for reuse is more or less equal to an environment necessary for an ideal process of software engineering. Excellent software engineering will necessarily result in reusable software (because a fully conscious approach will anticipate many future uses and changes). Nevertheless it is a common experience that the everyday industrial development is different. There is no time and money for redesign, the requirements are incomplete, documents are already inconsistent within one project, design gets lost over time.

This article is about experiences in implementing reuse activities within an industrial environment. It can be regarded as a case study answering the question: What can reuse theory provide within reasonable time/cost constraints once you come across an existing software development situation? "Reasonable" in the context on hand means primarily the cost an average middle manager can be persuaded to invest. Within the decision space of this person (see fig. 5) any large investment proposed by a person of engineering competence is regarded as mere technical purity and aesthetics.

The reported research project is a supervision of a general company's effort towards a fundamental change of software structure, making a shift from a mainly mainframe-oriented software development and data processing structure to a dominant off-line structure. Within this new concept applications will run on workstations and central processing will be limited to data transactions.

Apart from the change in hardware configuration and hardware clustering towards a client-server-host architecture the whole software development strategy has to be redesigned. The object-oriented paradigm has been chosen to be the future development approach for front-end and server applications. Academic consulting has been required for the introduction of OO and reuse. The client was sure that OO development does not achieve reuse by itself. Because of the business area on hand the following constraints are important: independence from other software suppliers, continuity of development environment support, secrecy of actual software system details.

The goal of the paper is to report on conclusions for introducing software reuse in practice drawn from our consulting experiences. The second chapter provides a survey on the various reuse tools, concepts, and methods. Chapter three outlines intensity level I and II of reuse in practice. Level I is represented by reuse within one single project. Level II reuse can be established within a group of similar projects (a branch). In chapter 4 level III reuse is proposed as a (rather) ideal reuse culture. Level I is equivalent to maintainability. Level III includes definition and assurance of standards as well as a maximum of document reuse in any phase of development. The second level includes an effort towards a domain-restricted balance of projects lacking a special reuse and standardization management.

2 A Survey on Approaches to Reuse

2.1 General Remarks and Experiences

Productivity gains and quality improvement are at the core of effects expected from re-using software products. Moreover, reuse seems to be simple in the eyes of the beginner:

> "*Just take a piece of existing software and put it into a new product; that's what all good programmers do anyway*" (see [23]).

There are well known difficulties with this sort of naive reuse: There is usually a lack of "critical mass" of reusable components to start spontaneous reuse and keep it up as a regular practice. Normally the management is not willing to take the charge of necessary initial investments to help create reusable parts, and last but not least the average programmer seldom trusts of other people's code (see [8]).

The same author states that reuse success needs management commitment to the proper capitalization of software engineering (SE) infrastructure as well as organizational standards for design, programming, and reuse activities. [15] observes that all successful reuse projects had support from upper management. The working of reuse concepts needs a sound SE framework as basis; even extensive reuse investments will not cure a too-immature SE environment and will fail unless a certain level of consciousness is attained.

2.2 Some Reports of Industrial Reuse Efforts

[13] early reported on an insurance reuse project. The goal was to promote the reuse of COBOL code by supporting the research on the exchange of code, training, and support to eliminate highly redundant steps during code creation. The assessment and communication of code is made by a Reusable Code Review Board which consists of one member per application programming division.

[19] reports on a reuse level of 60% to 80% of COBOL source code lines by reducing the usual redundancy of code in commercial programs through employment of generic code-skeletons.

[11] describes The Reusable Software Library (RSL) a component library where code fragments labeled with keywords can be retrieved. He states that up to a third of the code can be reused trading off higher productivity in programming for lower performance of the resulting program.

[30] analyzed a set of moderate to large projects for unmanned spacecraft control (Quantitative Study of Spacecraft Control Reuse at GSFC). He found out that on the average a third of the source code could be reused or modified from previous projects. The modules that were reused without revision turned out to have less interaction with other modules or the user, to have simpler interfaces and more comments per source line than modules which were newly developed or revised.

The effort of the SEI domain analysis experiment had as a result that proper domain scoping is critical to success, there are no global but only local domain experts, and model representations may be domain-specific as well.

All case studies deal with quite specific environments and focus primarily on the reuse of source-code. The reported degree of possible code reuse depends on the diversity of the domain and ranges from 30% (broad domain) to 70% (narrow domain). Wherever authors claim to do a certain document reuse, the detailed working conditions for that reuse are missing. The guidelines which are applicable in a more general way resemble general wisdom of good SE practice.

2.3 Current Approaches in Practice

A company-wide reuse program is set up to improve the productivity and the quality of software production starting off from an already well-working SE environment. Thus a program of that kind will need more extra training and stimulus of the participants than new fancy tools. [33] underlines the importance of incentives to raise personal efforts for reuse activities: He suggests the assignment of the creator's name to a reuse unit as well as cash rewards for good reuse ideas or the recognition of reuse issues by management and the inclusion of reuse actions in the design and the project debriefing phase. What is equally important for any company on its way towards reuse is the communication about it. Communication among developers can be supported by including the reuse idea in basic training for beginners, in special training for advanced developers, in publishing new reuse material in the house newspaper as well as in providing an on-line catalogue of available reusable stuff (with index and query language).

	Management	Requirements	Design	Code	Test
Concept	Process Models [3] (PBO) Quality Assurance (PBO) Incentives [33], [15] (BO)	Domain Analysis [1] (Bo) Requirements Apprentice [28] (Pb)	Design Apprentice [34] (Pb)	Application Generator [7] (p) Problem Oriented Language [7] (p)	reuse of test cases (P)
Method	Software Factory [21] (PBo) Cost Estimation Models (Pb) Project Evaluation Metrics (PBo)	Draco [24] (Pb) OOA (PBo) expert advice, training of novices (PBO)	OOD (PBo) Parameter-ized Pro-gramming [17] (pBo) Generalized Components [29] (Bo)	Coding for Portability (PB) Component Classificatio n Schema [16], [27] (pBO)	Conf. Mngmnt. of test suites [6] (Pb) limiting the testobject by reusing well-tested parts (Pb)
Tool	built-in process model of a CASE-Tool (P)	general domain model in an OOA-Tool (Bo)	module templates (pBo) OO-class library (Pb) SE-environ-ment (PBo)	Component Library [13], [11] (PBo) CASE-Repository (P)	capture/ replay tool [4] (Pb)

Tab. 1. Concepts, methods and tools for reuse in practice:
The level of usual efficiency of a measure in a class is indicated by the size of the corresponding letter: impractical: no letter at all, some efficiency: small letter, high efficiency: capital letter project-wide (P), branch-wide (B), organization-wide (O)

Programmers often fear being deprived of their special skills as a consequence of reusing other peoples artifacts and adhering to more or less stringent standards. [5] favors an opposing view: The integration of reuse practices into the software engineering process will lead to a shift in the profile of a programmer's skills from writing lines of source code to the engineering skills of finding and integrating existing solutions as an answer to a new problem.

Table 1 lists keywords of examples in literature dealing with concepts, methods, and tools which can be used in the industrial practice. These means of reuse are arranged into the categories of the management of the SE process plus the four basic steps of development and maintenance (requirements, design, code, and test). The levels on which know-how can be reused efficiently are divided into the classes project-wide (P), branch-wide (B), and organization-wide (O). The most widespread reuse-tools are Component Libraries, object-oriented (OO) environments, and CASE-tools. Component Libraries ([2], [11], [12], [14], [16], [18], [26]) range from simple databases for pieces of code, along more elaborate systems with version management to systems especially tailored to a company's reuse procedures and needs.

OO environments ([20], [23]) are tempting due to their built-in inheritance/late binding/reuse possibilities. These features are a blessing in conjunction with strict ad-herence to common standards and design models; otherwise the programmer will be lost in a web of ill-defined objects and unclear roles of these objects in the system without any overview ([31]).

[21] considers CASE tools as the ideal basis for reuse. They provide a repository, built-in methods, guidelines, and process-models. This might be true if that particular CASE-tool was built with modern reuse techniques in mind. If that CASE-tool was designed without a clear reuse intention, all the built-in features will have a strong counter-effect.

Since the pay-off of code reuse is moderate compared to the reuse of designs and specifi-cations, the representation of reusable designs is a strong research issue. According to [8] the problems in the reuse of design documents are: Intermingled domain-specific and implementation-specific decisions which cannot be reconsidered each on its own easily any more. Final specifications which contain too many specific details which keep the specification as a whole from being reused - although the more general parts were good candidates for an immediate reuse if the details could be stated in a fuzzy way.

Having a look at the SE history one can find an unbroken thread of implicit reuse by the migration of individual expert know-how from concepts to methods and finally into tools then. The implicit reuse of the huge amount of experience necessary to build a state-of-the-art SE environment is only rarely recognized by programmers who work with tools of that quality every day unless they have to use a less advanced tool from time to time.

3 A "Return of Investment" Reuse Model for Practitioners

After having made a decision towards a fundamental change in the hardware and the system software environment our client realized that most of the established strategies for in-house software development should be questioned and redesigned, too. Apart from a general rise in consciousness in real software engineering the basic aim was to go towards object orientation. (A comparable competitor in the same business field decided to move towards non-OO CASE-development. This will result in a completely different strategy). There was also a strong will in the medium management to enhance the reuse of software, and it was intuitively obvious to them that OO promises new possibilities of reuse but does not ensure them.

This frankness was the beginning of our consulting project. There was not much more than some imprecise wish of "reusing as many components as possible that have worked well already". For four months we did nothing but interview software engineers, programmers, project managers. The interesting problem at hand was heterogeneity with respect to age and range of applications, to the range of development environments, to software engineering consciousness as well as to the level of knowledge among software engineers.

Software is mainly written for the developer's own use. It is vital to have a reliable support of the development environment. As a result of our inquiries we divided our task into two different projects:
- work out reasonable suggestions for reuse of existing software
- work out a plan for a reuse culture adapted to the new OO development

The answers to these consulting and research questions are outlined in the following three chapters. From the viewpoint of reuse the minimum quality level is maintainability of a project. Maintainability is a precondition for the quality level of balance, which includes a clear structure of software documents from general to specific ones within a certain domain. The most advanced level we title "standardization". Maintainability and balance are preconditions for standardization. The title was chosen because of the fact that within a SE culture of "searching, selecting and putting together" software document components obviously have to be standardized to a high degree.

3.1 Maturity level I: Maintainability = Reuse in one single Project

Large data processing companies that have been on the job for 25 years now have a wide-ranging supply of applications which often have been designed for different types of operating systems and work with different generations of hardware, too. Quite frequently working software systems are ported onto a new hardware/operating system environment with the help of emulations. If software systems have been developed very carefully, requirements in some cases still fit to the actual code even after 10 years. Others are perfectly doing important services, but are not documented at all. Most of the information has flowed informally during development and maintenance. Re-engineering was never regarded important. Developers of these programs often still work in the company and enjoy the benefit of their irreplaceable position.

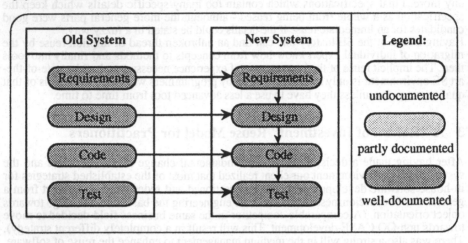

Fig. 1. Reuse level I: Conscious maintenance of a well designed software system
(adapted from [3])

It is not software engineering, but it is reality. Software engineering, though, should try to have an emphasis on predictable risks rather than on adventurous travels.
Figure 1 shows the ideal reuse of requirement definitions, design documents, code and testing experience, in case some new requirement enforces a change in the old software system. In the best case change of the requirements will result in a change in the subsequent phases, while reusing the contents of the corresponding documents of the old system. In this sense good reuse within one single project is just good maintainability. [3] has pointed out this connection by "design for maintenance is design for reuse".

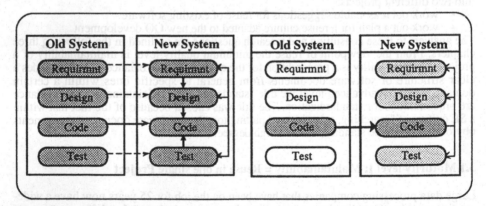

Fig. 2. Reuse level I: Typical quick maintenance of a normally designed software system (left), conscious quick maintenance of an ill designed (though not untypical) software system (right)

Figure 2 shows what usually happens to a software system when being maintained. Either there is a quick fix of the code satisfying the new requirements. This allows a quick delivery of the new system. Afterwards the documents of the other phases are adapted to the changes in the code. Though this does not match good style of software engineering (fig. 1), it is rather practical and much better than the "maintenance ignorance" towards informal information flow. Moreover, from this "quick fix maintaining process" one can retrieve a cost/time efficient reuse activity for ill designed software (fig. 2, right side). Whenever changes are made, these changes are made at the code. Afterwards maintaining stuff should start a short re-engineering activity, using their momentary insight for producing documents on other phases reporting on the changes they made as well as on the insight they had to gain about the whole system. This can lead to a software system which is "a little less ill designed". (A purer solution would be, of course, to start a complete re-engineering of the software system on hand. Nevertheless, often you cannot enforce that for the reasons described before).

In the client's case especially older programs turned out to be nearly undocumented. Often requirements as well as abstract designs were missing. These software components have been developed during the last 10 years, some will be used for the next 5 to 10 years to come. They come from programmers to whom at that time anything but code is "non-productive theory". The according project managers regarded documenting as hindering countable progress. High maintenance costs had no negative effects on them.

For software of that (non-)quality an overall redesign is much too expensive. For those pieces of software that are frequently maintained or those which are likely to be changed it is reasonable to assure maintainability.

A large number of assembler code pieces (some 2000) written between 1977 to 1985 providing application-oriented data transactions in the host environment was a typical example in the investigated environment.

In general, this maintainability level of reuse should be regarded as a minimum level. It is reasonable and appropriate also for uncommon new projects, too, where the high starting efforts for reuse are not (yet) justified.

3.2 Maturity level II: Balance = Reuse within similar Projects

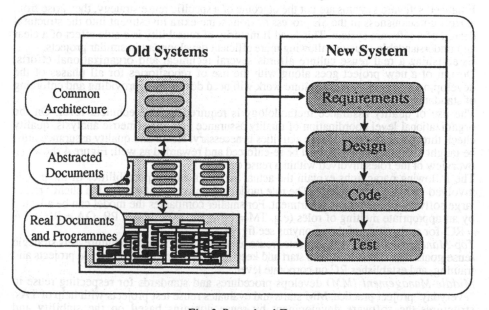

Fig. 3. Reuse level II:
Development of a software system using well structured and balanced information
on requirements, design, code and test from similar projects

Maintainability means that some software system can be modified within limited and predictable efforts. Nevertheless a maintainable system is not necessarily well prepared for a major change in requirements. Any broader range of reusability requires a more general design. Any software system contains specific and general components. More general documents are more likely to be reused in similar projects than more specific ones. We define a group of software systems as balanced, if there is a clear top-down structure from the general to the specific in documents concerning analysis, design, code and test. This balanced structure can be achieved by a consciousness during development or by redesign investment during maintenance.

There are several ways to gain the level of balance: E.g., a senior programmer who is experienced within a branch of applications can design a skeleton of documents and modules that serve as a sort of abstract language dealing with data structures, file structures and procedures for the domain at hand. Balance comes along with conscious redesign and abstraction as well as with retrieval of general components. Good (old) modular design of a software system results in a balanced structure, too. Obviously good OO analysis and OO design have to result in a balanced structure.

The client's older software systems (see 3.1) afford considerable extra efforts to gain a balanced software structure. Within our sample environment we found a group of approx. 5000 small to medium sized PL/I batch services, which might be restructured requiring an estimated investment of 6-8 person years.

What makes this level of reusability different from the following reuse culture is its mere domain-specific balance without a special design towards reuse. Standardization management is missing. In a newly developed project a balanced structure can originate from an extensive domain analysis. The level of balance ensures maintainability and time/cost reasonable reuse within similar projects.

4 Level III: Standardization = Reuse Culture in Practice

Balanced software systems are not the outcome of a specific reuse strategy, they arise from apriori consciousness in the SE process or from some extra investment into the structural design of a software system. This level II maturity of reusability is a side effect of a clear and understandable structure allowing more efficient development in similar projects.

Establishing a real reuse culture affords several technical and organizational efforts. Design of a new project goes along with the use of repositories for all phases of the development. Making a reuse culture work will need developing, providing and enforcing of standards.

The use of quality assurance methodology is required on the technical level. On the organizational level coordination of quality assurance activities (metric analysis, quality check through reviews) and reuse activities is necessary. Reuse and quality assurance must be taught to programmers. It must be re-enforced and rewarded as well. Figure 4 shows an overview of the roles involved within a reuse culture.

The following paragraphs explain the actual activities and responsibilities of the people involved within a reuse culture. The role model presented is suitable for the client's rather large software development department. For smaller companies the model can be adapted by an appropriate melting of roles (e.g. TM = MM, BL = TL, GL = PR, QA = RE = TA = RC, for explanation of the acronyms see fig. 4).

Top-Management (TM) communicates reuse as part of the company's culture, sets strategic reuse goals. TM enforces MM to start and keep up reuse research, funds reuse projects and training, and establishes RC on corporate level.

Middle-Management (MM) develops procedures and standards for respecting reuse in "everyday" project practice. MM starts and evaluates reuse test projects with help of TAs, structures the software development by reuse domains based on the stability and importance of the organization's activities in each domain, and allocates REs to project groups. MM provides incentive rewards to reuse participants, finds a solution to legal issues of potential liability and partial ownership for reuse software in contracts, establishes with the help of QA a central database for the financial data of software development, maintenance, and reuse for all projects, requires reuse within related projects.

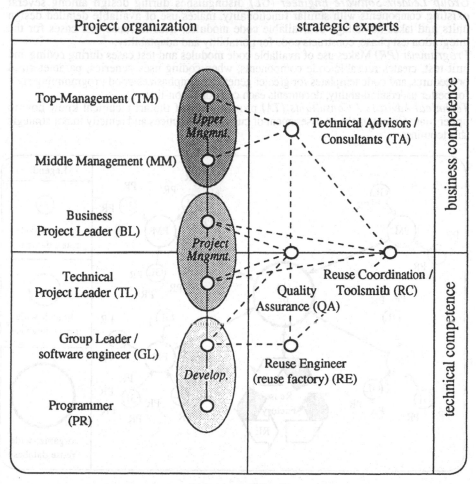

Fig. 4. A taxonomy of roles with respect to
a) project level and strategic level , b) technical and business competence

Project Management (PM) enforces reuse with all project participants.
Business Project Leader (BL) seeks contractual means to encourage contractors to create reusable software and to reuse software, tries to alter project funding approaches with help of MM to encourage the creation of reusable software.
Technical Project Leader (TL) emphasizes in his project effective and consistent methods for all aspects of software development and maintenance with GLs and PRs, establishes strong connections between future maintenance and reuse, makes use of available requirement components and takes advantage of existing high-level designs to create reusable requirements components, keeps the software reusable within the maintenance phase, states the reuse of software and the creation of reusable software as a requirement, evaluates the possible use of OO approaches or an application generator, establishes a set

of organizational guidelines for code development, parameterizes specifications that are dependent on the machine environment, emphasizes the use of metrics to assess adaptation effort.

Group Leader/ Software Engineer (GL) distinguishes during design among several existing components with similar functionality, makes use of available detailed design units and takes advantage of available code modules, tries to reuse test cases for the integration test phase, constructs code for portability and adaptability.

Programmer (PR) Makes use of available code modules and test cases during coding and unit test, creates reusable code components, when coding uses generics, parameterized procedures, and code templates for greater generality, emphasizes good programming style for better understand-ability, documents each component on-line.

Technical Advisors / Consultants (TA) provide state of the art technical know how to upper management, make an assessment of current SE practices and remedy major strategic shortcomings.

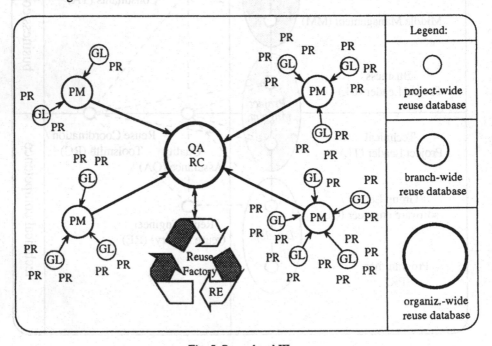

Fig. 5. Reuse level III:
Collecting and integrating information for reusable documents, code and standards
(PR = programmer, GL = group leader, PM = project manager,
QA = quality assurance, RC = reuse coordination)

Quality Assurance (QA) enforces the technical standards of MM on the developed software and development process, checks software which is to be stored in the organization-wide reuse database for fulfilling the requirements for reusable components.

Reuse Coordination (RC) uses domain analysis results as a basis for identifying reusable components, takes advantage of existing system engineering analyses, provides domain analysis results via REs to project groups, assesses to decide whether the development of a reusable software component by the reuse factory is advisable, sets standards to be met by all central library components, determines approaches for classifying and storing components, develops and implements a mechanism for search and retrieval in the database with a user-friendly interface, gets feedback from users of components.

Reuse Engineers (RE) REs in the Reuse Factory are responsible for the creation and maintenance of components in the organization-wide database. Moreover they act as advisers for individual projects to keep up information flow between the reuse-oriented developing staff an project-developers, record and supply adaptation suggestions with a reusable component.

The model in figure 5 assumes three levels of reuse databases: Within a project the GLs identify those pieces of software which are of use for the participants in the same project. These components are stored and communicated via the project-wide database. A PM can promote software from this database to the branch-wide database. The branch-wide databases are used by PMs from similar projects and are controlled by the RC. The RC looks for components of general interest which are worth 'polishing' for organization-wide reuse. These components have to correspond to reuse standards. These standards are maintained by the QA who reviews all components which are suggested for incorporation into the organization-wide database. If there are violations of standards the component is handed to the reuse factory for upgrading.

The purpose of this hierarchic promotion of reusable components is to assure that a component require the appropriate reuse investment (according to its distribution scope). Only few components migrate to the organization-wide database thus needing closer observance of QA, RC, and REs.

Software engineers reuse elements from local, branch-wide, and organization databases. A more local component is closer to the people who created it. The more widely available a component is, the more general, well tested, and standardized it is.

This three-level database model is a practical compromise between the common 'put all components into one big pot' reuse approach (which leads to indigestible hot-pot) and the common "drawer-reuse" in which every programmer and designer reuses software from previous personal only or 'trusted' experience.

Currently the client is implementing the new software developing strategy as well as most of the ideas presented in this paper. Two level II projects have been started. Stuff has been hired as well as in-house developers have been trained to cover the roles of a reuse culture. Several prototypes of applications are developed. By now we are not able to provide the reader with systematic results.

5 Conclusions

Within this article we reported on a software reuse model for a rather heterogeneous software development environment. We identified three levels of maturity for reuse in practice. These levels have been deduced from a detailed study of theoretical research contributions as well as from the organizational, political, technical and educational situation we identified during our consulting interviews. Beyond these results that are valid to a very local extent only we want to generalize our experiences by the following theses:

- A simple reuse activity - which should be and can be applied whenever an old piece of software is changed - is (re)establishing maintainability.
- Projects which are similar to each other, systems within a homogeneous domain, are well suited for redesign extracting a "balanced hierarchy" of software documents. Balance results in a sort of domain language providing working components on different levels of abstraction. Nevertheless this reuse effort is done without the cost of explicit quality assurance and reuse management.
- Strategic reuse efforts - the most mature approach - afford a general technical management of these efforts which can be established in a cost/time efficient way for newly developed software only. It will demand fixed investments in quality assurance, standardization, and reuse techniques. Moreover, a completely different style of programming is required from every software engineer for the development of software.

A working reuse culture can be established and maintained most easily with the help of good tools. Nevertheless, CASE-tools today do not provide satisfying reuse facilities. So far, the only way to succeed seems to concentrate the task force of your most experienced as well as your most innovative software engineers; make them define and standardize an environment big enough to serve as a beginning. Make them develop and guide the development of several "real" projects and adapt your environment permanently. Finally, when you start spreading "the new religion" within your company do not forget to integrate persons who were in important positions before the changes and adapt formerly significant standards to the new tasks.

Be aware that nobody might use your environment, unless you award

- coding by finding (in the reuse databases)
- coding and delivering (to the reuse databases).

There is still a long way to go in practice from the conventional development approach for an application to the "discovery" of an application within a reuse environment.

References

1. G. Arango: Domain Analysis: From art form to Engineering discipline. ACM, pp.152 - 159 (1989)
2. S.P., Arnold, S.L. Stepoway: The Reuse System: Cataloging and Retrieval of Reuse Software. Proceedings of COMPCON 1987, pp. 376-379
3. V.R. Basili, H.D. Rombach: Support for comprehensive reuse,. Software Eng. J., Sept. 1991, pp. 303 - 316
4. B. Beizer: Software Testing Techniques. Van Nostrand Reinhold, 2nd ed., (1990)
5. L.A. Belady: Foreword. in: Software Reusability (vol. I), Concepts and Models,. Addison Wesley, p. vii-viii (1989)
6. H. Berlack: Software Configuration Management. Wiley 1992
7. T.J. Biggerstaff, A.J. Perlis: Foreword (Special issue on software Reusability). IEEE Transactions on SE, Sept. 1984, pp. 474 - 476
8. T. Biggerstaff, Ch. Richter: Reusability Framework, Assessment, and Directions. IEEE Software 4(2): 41-49, March 1987
9. T. Biggerstaff: Design recovery for maintenance and reuse. IEEE Computer 22(7): 36-49 (1989)
10. T.J. Biggerstaff, A.J. Perlis: Software Reusability. ACM-Press 1989
11. B.A. Burton, R.W. Aragon: The reusable software Library. IEEE Software, July 1987, pp. 25-33
12. G. Caldiera, V. Basili: Identifying and Qualifying Reusable software Components. IEEE Computer, Feb. 91, pp. 61-70
13. M. Cavaliere: Reusable Code at the Hartford Insurance Group. in: T. Biggerstaff and A. Perlis: "Software Reusability - Vol. 2, Applications and Experience". Addison Wesley and acm Press, 1989, and in: Proc. of the ITT Workshop on Reusability in Programming, Newport R. I., 1983,
14. P. Devanbu, R.J. Brachman: LaSSIE: A Knowledge-Based software Information System. CACM 34(5): 34-49, May 1991
15. R. Fairley, S. Pfleeger et al.: Final Report: Incentives for Reuse of Ada Components. vols. 1 through 5, George Mason University, Fairfax, Va., 1989
16. W.B. Frakes, B.A. Nejimeh: An Information System for Software Reuse. Proceedings of the Tenth Minnowbrook Workshop on Software Reuse 1987
17. J. Goguen: Principles of Parameterized Programming. in: T. Biggerstaff and A. Perlis: Software Reusability - Vol. 1, Concepts and Models. Addison Wesley and acm Press, 1989 (ext. vers. of IEEE TR-SE, Sept 84)
18. G.E. Kaiser, D. Garlan: Melding Software Systems from Reusable Building Blocks. IEEE Software, July 1987, pp. 17 - 24

19. R.G. Lanergan, Ch.A. Grasso: Software Engineering with Reusable Designs and Code. IEEE TSE SE-10(5): 498-501, Sept. 1984
20. J.A. Lewis, S.M. Henry, D.G. Kafura: An Empirical Study of the Object-Oriented Paradigma and Software Reuse. ACM Sigplan Notices, OOPSLA '91, p.184-196
21. Y. Matsumoto: A Software Factory: An Overall Approach to Software Production. Proc. of the ITT Workshop on Reusability in Programming, Newport R.I., 1983 and in FREEMAN P.: Tutorial "Software Reusability"; IEEE-CS Press, 1987
22. B. Meyer: Reusability: The Case of Object-Oriented Design. IEEE Software 4, 2: 50-64, March 1987
23. W. Myers: We Want to Write Less Code. Computer 23(7): 117-118, July 1990
24. J. Neighbors: The Draco Approach to Constructing software from Reusable Components. IEEE TSE, SE-10(5), p. 564 - 574, Sept. 1984
25. R. Prieto-Diaz, P. Freeman: Classifying Software For Reusability, IEEE Software 4, 1: 6-16, 1987
26. R. Prieto-Diaz: Domain analysis for reusability, Proc. of COMPSAC 87, Tokyo, Japan,. pp. 23-29
27. R. Prieto-Diaz: Making software Reuse work: an implementation model. ACM SIGSOFT SE Not. 16(3): 61-68, July 1991
28. H.B. Reubenstein, R.C. Waters: The Requirements Apprentice: Automated Assistance for Requirements Acquisition. IEEE TSE, Vol. 17, No.3, March 91, pp. 226-240
29. R. Riehle: Software components - designing generalized components by creating abstractions. Programmers J., pp. 75-78, Nov./Dec. 1990
30. R. Selby: Quantitative Studies of Software Reuse. in: Software Reusability: Vol. II Applications and Experience, ed. T. Biggerstaff and A.J.Perlis, 213-33, 1989
31. D. Taenzer, M. Ganti, S. Podar: Object-Oriented Software Reuse: The Yoyo Problem. Journal of Object-Oriented Programming 2(3):30-35, 1989
32. W. Tracz: Reusability Comes on Age. IEEE Software, July 1987, pp. 6-8
33. W. Tracz: Software Reuse: Motivators and Inhibitors. Proceedings of COMPCON S 87, pp. 358-363
34. R.C. Waters, Y.M. Tan: Toward a Design Apprentice: Supporting Reuse and Evolution in Software Design. Software Engineering Notes 16(2): 33-44, 1991

Session 13:
Software Engineering Education Meeting Industry Needs

Meeting the Needs of Industry: SMU's Master's Degree Program in Software Engineering
Frank P. Coyle, Edward Forest and Murat M. Tanik,
Southern Methodist University, Dallas, Texas and
Dennis J. Frailey, Texas Instruments, Inc., Dallas, Texas

How Mature is Your Software Process?
William B. McCarty and G. Thomas Plew,
Azusa Pacific University, Azusa, California

Using a Multi-User Dialogue System to Support Software Engineering Distance Education
William A. Bralick, Jr. and John S. Robinson,
Air Force Institute of Technology, Wright-Patterson
Air Force Base, Ohio

Introducing Megaprogramming at the High School and Undergraduate Levels
Mary Eward and Steven Wartik, Software Productivity
Consortium, Herndon, Virginia

Meeting the Needs of Industry:
SMU's Master's Degree Program
in Software Engineering

Frank P. Coyle, Edward Forest, Murat M. Tanik

School of Engineering and Applied Science
Southern Methodist University
Dallas, TX 75275

Dennis J. Frailey

Texas Instruments, Inc.
Dallas, TX 75265

Abstract. In response to industry demand, the Master's degree program in software engineering at Southern Methodist University (SMU) was established in 1993. Drawing on the strengths of the university, the regional business community, and the Software Engineering Institute (SEI), SMU's curriculum addresses the software engineering process from both a technical and management perspective. The SMU curriculum affirms the tenet that software engineering must be a well-managed discipline supported by an underpinning of science and technology.

The SMU program is discussed in the context of existing graduate programs in software engineering as well as SEI's recommended core curriculum for graduate education. In addition, we establish critical links between the graduate curriculum and business requirements by mapping course offerings to SEI's Capability Maturity Model (CMM), a framework for project management and quantitative control of the software process. These linkages form the basis for the program's ongoing self-evaluation with respect to its goals and objectives.

1 Introduction

The software development process has undergone considerable advancement over the last forty years. Programming has progressed from the small job-specific problems of the 1960s, to the large-scale development projects commonly seen today. In its early stages, software development was basically an *ad hoc* process, utilizing the skills of experts. It was not until the mid 1960s that a scientific basis for software development began to emerge. The 1970s witnessed advances in generalized theories guiding the use of algorithms and data structures and by the 1980s large-scale software projects were commonplace, made possible by developments in language theory, compiler construction and structured programming techniques.

However, the ability to build new software systems has not been able to keep pace with the increasing demand for advanced products. Partly because of the lack of adequate resources and partly because of poor product management, software systems suffer from poor design and the inability to maintain programs following product release.

The Software Engineering Institute. In response to the difficulties existing in the software engineering field, and the critical nature of this field to the economic welfare of the nation, the Software Engineering Institute (SEI) was established in 1984. SEI has profoundly influenced software engineering, effectively defining the field and making numerous significant technical contributions in the short time of its existence.

The primary objective of the SEI is to improve the commercial practice of software engineering within government and industry, by promoting the evolution of software engineering from an *ad hoc*, labor-intensive activity to a well managed discipline supported by an underpinning of science and technology. SEI also provides significant support for software engineering education. SEI's educational efforts include curriculum reports related to trends in software engineering education, models of curricula for both undergraduate and graduate programs as well as written materials, videotapes and diskettes that are made available in support of instruction and course development.

The Capability Maturity Model. SEI has defined a general framework known as the Capability Maturity Model (CMM), a five level classification scheme that allows organizations to improve their software engineering practice. The CMM provides for the classification of organizations along five levels of maturity or effectiveness, based upon their software development practices [1]. As a direct result of the CMM, the Department of Defense now evaluates contractors against a consistent standard. Most leading defense contractors and many commercial organizations use the CMM as a basis for internal improvement efforts. The CMM has become the industry yardstick for organizations in this field. Figure 1 illustrates the progression of steps along the five level process maturity model.

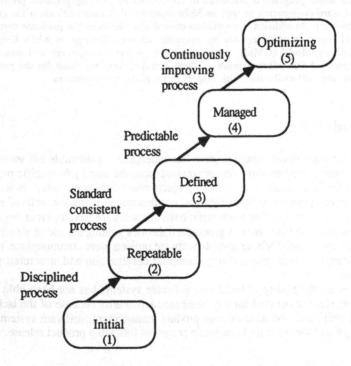

Fig. 1. The Five Levels of Software Process Maturity (from [2])

The five CMM levels, as defined by SEI, represent incremental attainable goals, which organizations are using to model their software process improvement efforts. Level 1 organizations tend to operate without formalized procedures, defined cost estimates or functional project plans. Level 2 or *Repeatable* organizations incorporate some project control procedures and complete software as a result of having accomplished closely related work in the past. However, firms at level 2 face major challenges and risks when undertaking different types of projects. Level 3 or *Defined* organizations have documented or institutionalized their processes while Level 4 or *Management* organizations possess "production" capabilities, in that they are able to set criteria and analyze performance data, as well as improve the software process by feeding-back information to the development staff as well.

Level 5 or *Optimizing* organizations have only a slight, but significant difference from Level 4. Organizations at Level 5 exhibit a consistently demonstrated practice of self-improvement. These companies have a strong management focus toward commercialization, and interpret software problems as originating from failures. Analysis of the failures lead to changes in the process and the way business is conducted.

2 Software Engineering Education

Universities and computer science and engineering departments have generally not been responsive to the educational needs of the software industry. The rapid growth of software engineering has resulted in too few practicing professionals with a deep understanding of the software process. The problem is exacerbated by the fact that many universities are not equipped to handle non-traditional part-time education and are hampered by an educational value system which does not place high priority on professional education.

Trends with respect to computer science enrollments offer some insight into the nature of the problem. The number of students graduating each year with undergraduate degrees in computer science, although substantial, is beginning to show signs of saturation. The leveling trend is more apparent at Ph.D. granting universities. Bachelor degree production from Ph.D. granting universities in the computing sciences has been relatively flat since 1987 [3].

The number of master's degrees granted during this same period suggest that somewhat less than 20% of bachelor's graduates eventually obtain this degree. It is understood that a substantial portion of the master's students in computer science have bachelor's degrees in fields other than computer science. A significant statistic is that only 5% of the computer science graduates in 1984 and 1985 were enrolled as full-time graduate students in 1986 while this number is about 25% for the sciences as a whole.

The total number of master's graduates is estimated to be about 100,000 as of 1992 [4]. Doctorate degrees granted in computer science and computer engineering as of 1992 are estimated at only about 4,000. Assuming double counting of about one-half between the bachelor's and master's graduates, the number of computer scientists working in industry must be of the order of 500,000. An additional equal number of engineers and scientists working in this field would place the current work-force at approximately 1,000,000. The very substantial number of qualified computer scientists, and well educated scientists and engineers from other fields working in this area, suggests that reasons for the difficulties facing software development are other than the number qualified workers. It is in fact more likely that the problems facing software development are truly unique and of exceptional difficulty.

However academic computer science has not been particularly responsive to the problems of industry. Computer science education is often focused around individual contribution rather than the managed group effort that is the norm in industry [5]. Because the ability to develop and complete complex software packages has lagged significantly behind the general capabilities of traditional engineering, the pressures on computer science departments is not expected to diminish over the next ten years. As Shaw points out, if computer science departments fail to respond to emerging needs, they risk being irrelevant [6].

2.1 Existing Graduate Program Overview

Although the need has been great, relatively few graduate programs in software engineering have been established. Currently, only about fifteen universities offer master's degrees in software engineering and of these, the majority are geared to the day-time on-campus student. A listing of the software engineering programs and programs offering an emphasis in software engineering is found in Figure 2.

University	Program Title	Comments, Date Initiated
Graduate Software Engineering Programs		
Miami University	Master of Systems Analysis	Related to Soft/Eng., Fall 1990
Rochester Institute of Technology	MS in Soft. Dev. and Mgmt.	Soft/Eng. Degree, Fall 1987
Boston University	MS of Soft. Systems Eng. MS in Systems Engineering	Soft/Eng. Degree, Fall 1988 Emphasis, Spring 1980
George Mason University	MS of Soft. Sys. Engineering	Soft/Eng. Degree, Fall 1989
Carnegie Mellon University	Master of Soft. Engineering	Soft/Eng. Degree, Fall 1989
Seattle University	Master of Soft. Engineering	Soft/Eng. Degree, Fall 1979
Andrews University	MS in Soft. Engineering	not reported
Georgia Institute of Technology	MS in Soft. Engineering	Proposed
Monmouth College	MS in Soft. Engineering	Soft/Eng. Degree, Fall 1986
National University	MS in Soft. Engineering	Soft/Eng. Degree, Summer 1985
University of Sterling	MS in Soft. Engineering	not reported
Univ. of Houston-Clear Lake	MS in Soft. Engineering	Soft/Eng. Degree, Fall 1990
University of Pittsburgh	MS in Soft. Engineering	Soft/Eng. Degree, Fall 1989
University of Scranton	MS in Soft. Engineering	Soft/Eng. Degree, Fall 1990
University of St. Thomas	Master of Soft. Design and Dev.	Soft/Eng. Degree, Spring 1985
Air Force Institute of Technology	MS in Soft. Systems Mgmt	Soft/Eng. Degree, June 1990
Texas Christian University	Master of Soft. Design and Dev.	Soft/Eng. Degree, Fall 1978
Graduate Software Engineering Emphasis Programs		
Miami University	Master of Systems Analysis	Related to Soft/Eng., Fall 1990
University of West Florida	MS in Computer Science	Soft/Eng. Emphasis, Fall 1989
Florida Atlantic University	Master of Computer Science	Soft/Eng. Emphasis, Fall 1989
The Wichita State University	Master of Computer Science	Soft/Eng. Emphasis, Fall 1988
Florida Atlantic University	Master of Computer Science	Soft/Eng. Emphasis, Fall 1989
Air Force Inst. of Technology	MS in Computer Science MS in Computer Systems	Soft/Eng. Emphasis Soft/Eng. Emphasis

Fig. 2. Graduate Software Engineering and Emphasis Programs

Surveying the existing programs indicates a substantial variation with respect to curricula. The differences, in part, reflect the newness of the discipline, the absence of a generally accepted definition of the important subject areas and the different faculty skills and resources at the various institutions. Many of the programs incorporate existing courses, mostly from computer science departments. As can be seen in Figure 2, a notable point of variation among the programs are the differences in program titles. This is partially attributable to the fact that some programs, derived from computer science departments not part of an engineering school, were unable to use the title "Software Engineering" because of resistance from the engineering school.

The preferred undergraduate degree for admission to these programs is the bachelor's degree in computer science. However, none of the master's programs restricted admission on this basis and, in fact, approximately 40% of the students enrolled in these programs did not have undergraduate degrees in computer science.

In our survey of existing graduate programs, at least one to two years of strong relevant experience was required for admission. Computer science graduates without experience were not considered qualified for admission into any of the schools interviewed. The average experience of the students, cited by the schools, was three to five years. Regardless of educational background, students were required to be familiar with data structures, algorithms, compilers, programming languages, database systems, and operating systems. Students were generally required to have a working knowledge of at least one high level language such as Ada, Pascal, or C, one assembly language and a course in discrete mathematics. In general, a computer science background equivalent to a sophomore level was required. Articulation was a common requirement for students with excellent experience but limited academic exposure. Semester-long leveling or foundation courses, stressing algorithms, data structures, and operating systems were cited as one way to insure proper background.

3 The SMU Software Engineering Program

The Master's degree program in software engineering at SMU was established in 1993 in response to industry demand for high-quality software engineers. Drawing on the strengths of the university, the expertise of the regional business community and the educational guidelines of SEI, the SMU curriculum addresses the software engineering process from both a technical and management perspective. The SMU curriculum affirms the tenet that software engineering must be a well managed discipline supported by an underpinning of science and technology. Its goal is to provide students with a body of knowledge that prepares them to assume positions of responsibility within an organization.

3.1 Organizational Structure

The Software Engineering program is situated within the Department of Computer Science and Engineering, where the skills of the faculty and the course offerings are closely related to software engineering. A Board of Advisors composed of full-time SMU faculty, academic faculty from other institutions, and industrial professionals guides the direction of SMU's involvement in software engineering and has a significant role in determining the nature and direction of the program as the field continues to evolve. While key leadership personnel for the program come from within the Department of Computer Science and Engineering, three to four experienced adjunct professors are associated with the program on a continual basis, contributing to the long term vigor and relevance of the program. In addition, the engineering, legal, and business management orientation of this program points to meaningful collaboration with faculty from the departments of Electrical and Mechanical Engineering, as well as SMU's Cox School of Business, and the School of Law.

3.2 Curriculum

Students are required to complete ten courses, covering thirty semester credit hours. All students must enroll in four required core courses and select at least three electives from a set of six preferred in-depth software engineering management and technology courses. Individuals may choose three free electives from either the preferred set of courses or any other courses offered by the Computer Science and Engineering Department. The student however may select other graduate courses offered by the School of Engineering and Applied Science, with advisor and program director approval.

Articulation Course	
CSE 5311	Foundations of Computer Science
Core Courses	
CSE 5312	Systems Engineering
CSE 5313	Software Requirements and Design Engineering
CSE 5314	Software Testing and Quality Assurance
CSE 5315	Software Project Planning and Management
Preferred Elective Courses	
CSE 6312	Software Generation and Maintenance
CSE 6313	Object Oriented Analysis and Design Methodology
CSE 6314	Software Metrics and Quality Engineering
CSE 6315	Software Acquisition Practices, Legal & Economic Issues
CSE 6316	User Interface Design
CSE 6340	Advanced Software Engineering

Fig. 3. The SMU Software Engineering Curriculum

The subject emphasis of the four required core courses are the underlying principles and methods of effective software development and commercialization. Both management and technical issues are integrated into each of the core courses. The core courses offer the basic knowledge and procedures common to the development of all software and software systems. Much of the subject material of the core, can be traced to the curriculum recommended by the Software Engineering Institute. The preferred set of in-depth elective courses, stressing both management and technology in greater detail, draw from faculty skills in law, business, management science, and technology, and enable students to focus with respect to particular interests.

3.3 Admission Requirements

The admission requirements for entrance to the program are:

(1)   A bachelor's degree in one of the quantitative sciences or mathematics, computer science or one of the engineering disciplines.
(2)   An undergraduate GPA of at least 3.0/4.0.
(3)   At least one year of college level calculus.
(4)   Competence or satisfactory completion of courses in Data Structures, Algorithms, and Discrete Mathematics. Substantial deficiency in these areas will require the student to satisfactorily articulate *CSE 5311 Foundations of Computer Science.*
(5)   Working knowledge of at least one general purpose programming language such as C, or Pascal, and at least one year experience in software development and/or maintenance.
(6)   At least one year of relevant industrial software experience.

3.4 The SMU Curriculum and the SEI Core

The SMU program is organized around SEI's core curriculum units [7]. The reason for SEI's emphasis on core units is threefold. First, not every topic area contains enough material for a typical university course. Second, combining course units can be accomplished in different ways to meet the specific needs of organizations. Third, this structure allows the units to evolve and reflect changes in software engineering practice while maintaining the overall curriculum structure. Figure 4 lists the individual core units of SEI's suggested curriculum.

Core Unit	Description
1	The Software Engineering Process
2	Software Evolution
3	Software Generation
4	Software Maintenance
5	Technical Communication
6	Software Configuration Management
7	Software Quality Issues
8	Software Quality Assurance
9	Software Project Organization and Management
10	Software Project Economics
11	Software Operational Issues
12	Requirements Analysis
13	Specification
14	System Design
15	Software Design
16	Software Implementation
17	Software Testing
18	System Integration
19	Embedded Real-Time Systems
20	Human Interfaces
21	Professional Issues

Fig. 4. The SEI Core Curriculum

These units provide a partial *specification* for the SMU program. In our curriculum design, an effort was made to address each of the SEI core topics in at least one course. The traceability from academic program to the SEI core provides a basis for course implementation similar to the role of software specifications for software implementation. Figure 5 indicates the mapping of each SEI core unit to the courses in the SMU curriculum.

SMU Courses	SEI Core Curriculum Units

SMU Courses	1	2	3	4	5	6	7	8	9	10	11	12	13	14	15	16	17	18	19	20	21
CSE 5312 Systems Engineering	X	X												X			X	X			
CSE 5313 Software Req. & Design Eng.	X	X												X		X			X		
CSE 5314 Software Testing & Qual. Assurance	X	X	X	X		X	X										X	X			
CSE 5315 Software Proj Planning & Mgmt	X	X		X	X	X			X	X	X										X
CSE 6312 Software Gen & Maintenance				X	X										X	X	X				
CSE 6313 Object Oriented Analysis & Design	X		X										X	X	X	X	X	X	X	X	
CSE 6314 Software Metrics and Quality Eng.	X	X					X	X													
CSE 6315 Software Acq. Practices											X										X
CSE 6316 User Interface Design																			X		
CSE 6340 Adv. Software Engineering	X	X			X		X														

Fig. 5. The SMU Curriculum and the SEI Core Units

The SEI Capability Maturity Model. In an effort to establish a relationship between the SMU curriculum and the requirements of industry, critical linkages were established between SMU's software engineering courses and the SEI Capability Maturity Model. In the context of the SMU curriculum, the Capability Maturity Model serves to (1) define the relevance of the program to industrial needs and (2) provide a basis for self assessment as the field of software engineering continues to evolve. The five levels of maturity defined by the Capability Maturity Model represent a well-defined evolutionary path that organizations can follow to achieve a mature software process.

Each maturity level is composed of several key process areas that must be addressed by organization in order to receive certification at that level. Figure 6 shows the mapping of the key process areas at each maturity level to courses in the SMU curriculum where coverage of these topics is provided. Such a linkage serves to (1) provide industry with data that is useful in evaluating our program (2) contribute to course objectives, and (3) provide a basis for developing course-specific evaluations. In effect, these linkages provide objectives against which we can measure the effectiveness of our curriculum and insure the continued relevance of our courses.

Course Offerings

CMM Key Process Areas	CSE 5312 Sys Eng	CSE 5313 Soft Req/ Dsgn	CSE 5314 Soft Test/ Qual	CSE 5315 Proj Plan	CSE 6312 Gen Maint	CSE 6313 OOA OOD	CSE 6314 Met- rics	CSE 6315 Acq. Legal	CSE 6316 Usr IntFace Design	CSE 6340 Adv SE
Level 1: INITIAL	-		-	-	-	-	-	-	-	-
Level 2: REPEATABLE	-	-	-	-	-	-	-	-	-	-
Requirements Mgmt.	X	X		X		X			X	
Soft. Project Planning				X			X			X
Soft. Project Tracking	X			X			X			
Soft. Subcontract Mgmt.				X				X		
Soft. Configuration Mgmt.			X	X	X					X
Soft. Quality Assurance		X	X	X	X	X	X	X		X
Level 3: DEFINED	-	-	-	-	-	-	-	-	-	-
Peer Reviews		X	X		X	X				
Intergroup Coordination	X		X	X	X					
Soft. Product Engineering	X	X	X		X	X			X	X
Integrated Soft. Mgmt.	X			X						
Training Program				X						
Org. Process Definition				X						X
Org. Process Focus				X			X			
Level 4: MANAGED	-	-	-	-	-	-	-	-	-	-
Soft. Quality Mgmt.			X	X			X			
Quantitative Process Mgmt.				X			X			
Level 5: OPTIMIZING	-	-	-	-	-	-	-	-	-	-
Process Change Mgmt.				X			X			
Technology Change Mgmt.	X			X						
Defect Prevention		X		X			X			X

Fig. 6. The SEI Capability Maturity Model and the SMU Curriculum

During the development of the SMU program, both the CMM model and industrial participation provided a basis for structuring the curriculum. For example, our core course in systems engineering was the result of both industrial feedback and the recognition that more key process areas needed coverage in our core curriculum. Thus, the mapping of maturity process areas to course offerings served to (1) structure the curriculum (2) placed it in the context of a widely accepted framework and (3) provided a basis for establishing benchmarks against which we will be able to document SMU's educational process.

Using the objectives associated with each key CMM maturity level process area, we plan to create a series of course-specific evaluations to be completed by students at the end of each semester. The feedback from these evaluations will be used by the advisory board to insure the relevance of our course offerings. We believe that the education and training process itself must be validated against objectives in order to insure that the program remains consistent with its intended goal of preparing individuals to meet the critical challenges within the software industry today.

4 Summary

The SMU Master's degree program in software engineering was developed in response to the need for competent software engineers who are prepared to assume positions of responsibility within industry. Designed to cover the software engineering process from both a technical and management perspective, the SMU curriculum draws on the strengths of the university, the regional business community, SEI's recommended core curriculum for graduate education, and SEI's Capability Maturity Model. We present a mapping from our course offerings to both the SEI core curriculum and the Capability Maturity Model. This mapping is used to provide a structure for our program as well as a foundation for directing and evaluating our own educational efforts.

Acknowledgements

Thanks are extended to Jeff Kennington, Chairman of the Computer Science & Engineering Department. Several appreciative conversations of exceptional value were held with Dr. Gary Ford of the Software Engineering Institute and Professor James E. Tomayko of Carnegie Mellon University. Appreciation is also extended to Dr. Raymond T. Yeh, President, ISSI Inc., Austin TX. for curriculum suggestions.

Helpful telephone conversations were held with many directors and faculty members of academic software engineering programs: James R. Comer, Texas Christian University; John Beidler, University of Scranton; Rod Brown, University of Houston; Erich Frankel, Seattle University; Mike McCracken, Georgia Institute of Technology; and John W. Brackett of Boston University.

Special thanks go to Dean André Vacroux for his strong support of this program.

References

1. W.S. Humphrey: "Characterizing the Software Process: A Maturity Framework," IEEE Software, March 1988.

2. M.C. Paulk, B. Curtis, M.B. Chrissis, C.V. Weber: Capability Maturity Model for Software, Version 1.1, Software Engineering Institute (CMU/SEI-93-TR-24)

3. D. Gries, D. Marsh: "The 1989-1990 Taulbee Survey," Comm. ACM 35, 1 (Jan. 1992), pp. 132-143.

4. National Science Foundation: Science and Engineering Indicators: 1991, NSF, Washington, DC, 1991

5. F.P. Brooks Jr.: "No Silver Bullet: Essence and Accidents of Software Engineering," Information Processing 1986, pp. 1069-1076.

6. M. Shaw: Informatics for a New Century: Computing Education for the 1990s and Beyond. Software Engineering Institute (CMU/SEI-90-TR-15)

7. G. Ford: 1991 SEI Report on Graduate Software Engineering Education, Software Engineering Institute (CMU/SEI-91-TR-2)

Appendix

Articulation Course Description

CSE 5311 Foundations of Computer Science
A comprehensive foundation course covering the major aspects of computer science. The course will cover hardware and software fundamentals, operating systems concepts, data structures, discrete structures, algorithms, programming languages and specification languages. The course will also address issues related to software engineering and object-oriented programming. This course is intended to prepare non-CSE students for the Master's program in Software Engineering.

Core Course Descriptions

CSE 5312 Systems Engineering
The objective of this course is to develop an appreciation of software as a component of complex systems. Topics include system requirements analysis, specification techniques, tools, structured and object-oriented methodologies, the relation of design to system testing, as well as validation and maintenance. Also examined are issues relating to subsystem and user-interface design, hardware vs software trade-offs, system integration and performance prediction.

CSE 5313 Software Requirements and Design Engineering
This course examines software requirements and design methodologies. Topics include defining software requirements, interacting with end-users to determine requirements, and identifying functional, performance and other requirements. Techniques to support requirements are studied and include prototyping, modeling and simulation. The course will address the relation of requirements to design, design in the system lifecycle, hardware vs software tradeoffs, and subsystem definition. Examples of design paradigms will be presented and will focus on fundamental issues such as data abstraction, information hiding, modularity and reuse.

CSE 5314 Software Testing and Quality Assurance
The relationship of software testing to quality is examined with an emphasis on the role of testing in the validation of system requirements. Topics include module and unit testing, integration, code inspection, peer reviews, verification and validation, statistical testing methods, preventing and detecting errors, selecting and implementing project metrics and defining test plans and strategies that map to system requirements. Testing principles, formal models of testing, performance monitoring and measurement are also examined.

CSE 5315 Software Project Planning and Management
The issues associated with the successful management of a software development project are addressed. This includes planning, scheduling, tracking, cost and size estimation, risk management, configuration management, quality engineering and process improvement. The course is centered on the concept of a Software Engineering Process and includes discussion of life cycle models for software development. The SEI software process capability maturity model (CMM) and other process standards are included.

Preferred Elective Course Descriptions

CSE 6312   Software Generation and Maintenance

Techniques for generating software and maintaining revisions to existing software will be examined. Topics include alternatives to coding, the use of program generators and very high-level languages, CASE tool, component re-use and the role of standards in the generation of software. Also covered are issues related to maintenance as a part of software evolution, the impact of the design process on long-term software maintainability, software re-engineering and the planning of release cycles.

CSE 6313   Object-Oriented Analysis and Design Methodology

Object-oriented design methodologies and their role in the software development process are examined. Data modeling and design principles such as data abstraction, information hiding, modularity and coupling are viewed in the context of the object-oriented paradigm. Concepts such as abstract classes, inheritance and polymorphism will be examined in the context of object-oriented languages. The strengths and weaknesses of different design methodologies will be contrasted and compared using case studies. Issues relating to making the transition from design to implementation will be examined.

CSE 6314   Software Metrics and Quality Engineering

Techniques of software quality engineering with emphasis on the role of metrics are addressed. The approach is drawn from practical experience and uses many examples from industry. The psychological and behavioral aspects of quality and quality assurance are included. Metrics and quality are presented in relationship to the software process and software process maturity models. Selection of quality metrics is addressed in terms of the goal/question/metric paradigm as well as various quality models. Methods of storing data for historical purposes, analyzing, and presenting data to others are included.

CSE 6315   Software Acquisition Practices, Legal and Economic Issues

Issues relating to software procurement, contract law, specification and control of product processes are examined. Topics include factors that affect cost, cost estimation, cost/benefit analysis, and risk analysis and legal implications with respect to ownership and use. Techniques and models of cost estimation are studied in detail.

CSE 6316   User Interface Design

Issues related to the design and implementation of viable user interfaces including design guidelines, tools, and techniques of evaluation, are examined. Topics include standard tool kits, portable window systems, User Interface Management Systems (UIMS), statistical testing strategies and protocol analysis.

CSE 6340   Advanced Software Engineering

In-depth study of specific software engineering techniques, methodologies and issues. Software development process models, rapid software prototyping, CASE tools and techniques. Object-oriented design and programming. Software metrics, and software engineering of knowledge-based systems.

How Mature is Your Software Process?

William B. McCarty, MBA
G. Thomas Plew, PhD

Department of Computer Science, Azusa Pacific University
Azusa, CA 91702

Abstract. We describe how a study of the SEI's Capability Maturity Model led us to change the structure and content of a project-intensive introductory graduate course sequence in software engineering. A brief review of the Capability Model is followed by an assessment of our software process as it previously existed. We then present some of the changes that were introduced and how they seem to have benefited the students.

1 Introduction

Azusa Pacific University's graduate program in Applied Computer Science and Technology requires all students to take a two-term, project-intensive course in software engineering. This paper describes the evolution of the structure and content of that course through the influence of the SEI's Capability Maturity Model. These changes have both improved the student's understanding of the software process and increased student satisfaction with the course.

2 The Capability Maturity Model

The Capability Maturity Model (CMM), based on the work of Watts Humphrey [Humphrey90], is intended to provide guidance to organizations seeking to achieve improved control of their software production process. It was developed at Carnegie Mellon University's Software Engineering Institute (SEI) over a period of several years. The CMM is well known within the Aerospace-Electronics-Defense (AED) sector. A recent conference for teams applying principles of the CMM within their organizations drew over 500 participants. The CMM is less well known outside the AED; it seems to be only rarely known within academic circles.

2.1 Key Process Areas (KPAs)

The CMM establishes a five-level ordinal scale for describing the maturity of an organization's software process. Within each level, the CMM identifies a set of Key Process Areas (KPAs), which assist an organization in focusing its software process improvement efforts on the issues that are most critical at the organization's current state.

A brief survey of the KPAs of the CMM is included in appendix A. For further information, the reader is referred to [Paulk93a] and [Paulk93b].

2.2 Measurement Methods

The SEI has developed two methods for measuring an organization's software process maturity: software process assessments and software capability evaluations.

Software process assessments are essentially self-studies conducted by an organization to enable it to better understand its software process strengths and weaknesses, often as an early step in the initiation of a software process improvement program. Software capability evaluations resemble audits. They are conducted by or on behalf of an outside agency to provide that agency with information about the subject organization's software process capabilities. This is typically done in connection with bid evaluations or contract administration.

3 Self-Assessment of Software Process

Not having the resources to initiate a full-scale software process assessment, and not being subject to a software capability evaluation, we embarked on an informal self-assessment of Azusa Pacific University's software process maturity in its project-intensive graduate course. The fact that both authors have personal responsibility for instruction in one or both of the sequence of courses added an element of subjectivity to the assessment, but eliminated many problems of gathering data. The software engineering sequence prior to the curricula of 1992-93 was assessed by the model as a base-line. The improvements in the 1992-93 curricula are then discussed relative to the model. In addition, future direction for the further implementation of CMM strategies are mentioned.

In his recent book on Software Quality [Weinberg92], Weinberg presents a model of software process "patterns." Weinberg's model includes five patterns that roughly correspond to the five maturity levels of the CMM and one additional pattern. Weinberg's patterns are:

Pattern 0: Oblivious
Pattern 1: Variable
Pattern 2: Routine
Pattern 3: Steering
Pattern 4: Anticipating
Pattern 5: Congruent

Our assessment of APU's software process, as used in its project-intensive software engineering class was that we were somewhere between "oblivious" and "variable." A good descriptive word for our state at that time would have been "chaos" (cf. [Olson93]). Basically the courses and subsequent capstone project were an exercise in program development rather than software engineering. Introduction to process issues were part of the course, however, project development activity did not allow a viable vehicle for practicing these techniques. A brief summary of the assessment and the corresponding KPA follows:

3.1 Level Two Process Assessment

Projects prior to the 1992-93 curriculum were individual projects which followed the student through the two course sequence and on to their master's project. Since many of these projects were "imaginary", the lack of a client did not permit the student to practice requirements management. (KPA 2.1.1). In fact, many of the projects were de-scoped when the programming phase was entered, some with approval and some in hopes that no one would notice. Intensive documentation accompanied this process. Part of this documentation included a project plan. Many of these plans showed no basis for their estimates and resource assignments were generally not included (KPA 2.1.2). Consequently, project tracking was almost entirely lacking. (KPA 2.1.3). Quality assurance in this period was synonymous with testing and debugging. While an acceptance test plan was developed as part of the project, consideration of quality was not a concept which spanned the entire process (KPA 2.1.5). Software configuration management was non-existent during this period. A project journal was required for completing the project, however, often this journal was developed post-hoc in order to meet the requirement. No project engaged in preventive measures by using the available software configuration management tools (KPA 2.1.6). The remaining level two areas were either not applicable to the APU course sequence or totally nonexistent.

3.3 Level 3 Process Assessment

Our course sequence having performed so poorly in level 2, we were reluctant to examine the Level 3 KPAs. After all, only about 7% of organizations can claim to have achieved Level 3. However, hoping for some unexpected encouragement, we pressed on. We found our organization process focus to be almost entirely absent. Some of our faculty are almost hostile to software engineering technology. Others are simply oblivious. We found little evidence of an organization-wide process focus (KPA 2.2.1). Since the inception of our program, our software process has been defined in terms of the outputs of each stage of the development process. In other words, we've followed a traditional document-driven approach. No attempt has been made to introduce more modern methods of process definition such as entry and exit criteria. Neither have the work processes themselves been defined (KPA 2.2.2). Actually doing software product engineering was the focus of our courses and master's project. However, this could have been more easily defined as program production rather than software engineering. Students worked individually on projects that were sometimes trivial. Many of our students have never participated in a software development project and many plan careers outside software development. Our software product engineering was, therefore, a highly variable process in terms of product quality and process economy (KPA 2.2.5) Although reviews at various points in the life cycle had long been a part of our program, management's (i.e., the instructor's) presence in these reviews had so influenced the process that they were entirely ineffective. Students were reluctant to point out even the most obvious defects in the work of their peers, lest they fall victim to critical retribution (KPA 2.2.7). The remaining level three areas were either not applicable for the APU course sequence or totally nonexistent.

Having found little basis for hope in the Level Three KPAs, we resigned ourselves to the opinion that our software process was inescapably flawed. Having thus confessed our sins, we were prepared to seek out the necessary means of rehabilitation.

4 Software Process Improvement Program

Our first step toward software process improvement was to obtain information. We re-read several familiar sources, this time from a new and more vital perspective. Sources we found particularly helpful include [Humphrey90], [Tomayko87], and [Weinberg92]. Curricular changes are noted relative to the course in which they were tried.

4.1 Software Engineering I

Software Engineering I serves as a survey course to introduce the student to concepts and process. To facilitate learning, a project is initiated in team structures which is passed to the succeeding course. In an attempt to focus the learning on process, several changes have been made to this course. The changes included:

- Project work in teams rather than individual
- Larger project proposals completed by all the teams taking a given portion
- Greater emphasis on the process of software engineering and a reduced emphasis on the product
- Implementation of peer reviews that were non-threatening
- Increased emphasis on quality assurance encompassing more than testing
- Incorporation of software tools which require the teams to think in terms of resources and planning in the estimation process
- Incorporation of projects with "real clients" rather that imaginary cases

Thus, an attempt was made to introduce students to the basic components of a level two and three process environment. Software Engineering was redefined as a process that is managed over time rather than a product that emerges in a given amount of time. The team approach allowed us to enlarge the scope of the projects, consider the possibility of "real clients" and expose students to the difficulties of working in an interdependent environment. The use of a client allowed us to explore the management issues of requirements control, yet the nature of our relationships did not yield contractual obligations.

Our assumption for these changes was that it is difficult to understand the process of working on a large project team if you have never experienced some of the frustrations of team project development. All of our teams worked on the same project with each team completing a portion of the functional specifications of the software requirements. This increased the need for inter- and intra-group communication which promoted discussion of the process. The standard "waterfall" model was kept intact, however, class discussions focused more on the process of software engineering rather than the products.

Peer reviews have increased in importance. Since teams receive a single grade which is shared by all, team members are more inclined to critique a team decision rather than let it slide. In addition, teams are required to provide written comments on the documents of other teams as part of the course process. Comments received on these peer reviews reveal that students are willing to give input if the vehicle is non-threatening and unstructured.

Quality assurance is still lacking in the course. While greater emphasis is placed on defining quality at earlier stages and peer reviews are expected to comment on the quality attributes of other's work, an understanding of the process of quality control is still shaky.

4.2 Software Engineering II

In the second of the two course sequence an attempt was made to break teams out of product functionality-based teams to process-based teams. We proceeded to divide the class into the following functional groups:

- Project administration
- Software design
- Quality assurance
- Configuration management
- Testing

We determined that each student would prepare a functional specification of one module, code one module and unit test that module. In addition, no student would code a module for which he/she had prepared the functional specification.

Since the course text had already been ordered, we could not introduce a text with a better emphasis on software process. Instead, we prepared handouts from journals and texts and provided each functional group with a package of material. In addition we pointed each group to a number of software tools that might facilitate their work.

Our classes are scheduled to meet once per week for 4-1/4 hours. We cut down on lecture material and reserved about 2 hours per class meeting for project-related reporting and discussion. We stressed to students the importance of raising questions about unclear portions of the text since there would not be sufficient time to walk through the text together. In order to make this point more operational, we increased the credit allocated to class participation to 20% of the course grade.

Since the subject course is the second of the two-term sequence, we "inherit" a project from the first term in the form of a system requirements specification and a user interface design. In order to reduce the scope of implementation work, we instructed the software designers to recommend to the class by the second meeting a de-scoped project they believed would be do-able within available time constraints.

Each week the various functional groups report on problems and progress. Formal inspections are conducted under the leadership of the quality assurance group. Where necessary, the project plan is adjusted. This is done on-the-spot by using in the classroom a computer equipped with a projection display. Occasionally, roles are shifted or exchanged to facilitate progress on the project and provide for more comprehensive learning by the students.

In order to ensure that students gain exposure to all aspects of the development process, the project is repeatedly de-scoped as necessary so that at least *some* portion of the system is put through integration and system testing.

5 Conclusions

Software Engineering, as a viable academic discipline, must move from a programming product emphasis to a process emphasis. The expected character of a product developed in an eighteen week course sequence will either be trivial in scope or lack quality. However, understanding the process issues by working on parts of a large project seems encouraging. The following has been noted with the changes instituted.

The total volume of work done by individual students in the course sequence has been reduced without reducing instructional objectives. Pressure to begin coding in order to meet deadlines has been almost eliminated as has the need to constrain one's project to something that is doable by a single individual. Meetings of project teams outside class have also been greatly reduced in time and energy. Extensive work is completed in class project meetings and individual assignments can be completed without the problems of scheduling additional sessions. Student satisfaction, as evidenced by comments, is increased. This may be due to Hawthorne effects, but we will gladly accept any increase in student satisfaction. In addition, comments in project journals have become more process rather than product oriented. A review of these journals indicate that students are focusing on what makes these models work rather than the documents that need to be completed to finish the course.

We estimate that our courses, as now constituted, are at least in tune with Level two concepts of software development. We might not be doing all the details well enough to achieve certification at that level, but we think the students could successfully work within a level two organization without experiencing "culture shock."

Our process is still "variable" in the sense that we have very few documented standards and procedures. It is part of the student's learning experience to discover the need for these and to recommend appropriate standards and procedures for adoption by the project team. In the long run, the variability of the process is constrained since we see to it that the students "discover" any necessary technology that their own reading has failed to disclose. Our view is that extensive documented standards and procedures would, by eliminating the joy of discovery, inhibit learning in this course.

Beginning Fall '93 we plan to institute further changes intended to add at least the flavor of some of the level three KPAs. Specifically, we plan to add a software process functional group and a software metrics functional group. Students participating in these groups will be specially chosen from among those students selecting a program emphasis in software engineering and will receive special training to prepare them for their roles in the course. Alternatively, we may use student interns for this purpose. A CASE tool will also be incorporated in the beginning course to further reduce the time requirements of generating the products of software engineering. This and other tools will then be used to focus attention on the process. Finally, newer texts which emphasize the process aspects of software engineering are being adopted. This will reduce the need for extensive handouts which must be integrated with a product-oriented text.

Our journey toward improved process maturity is not unlike that of many commercial organizations. It is a bumpy and difficult road, filled with self-doubt and resistance from many quarters. Having made the first step, however, we are fully determined to continue the journey and invite others to journey with us.

References

[Humphrey90]   Humphrey, Watts S. *Managing the Software Process*. Reading, Mass.: Addison-Wesley.

[Olson93]   Olson, Dave. *Exploiting Chaos: Cashing in on the Realities of Software Development*. New York: Van Nostrand Reinhold.

[Paulk93a]   Paulk, Mark C., et al. *Capability Maturity Model for Software, Version 1.1*, Software Engineering Institute, CMU/SEI-93-TR-24, February 1993.

[Paulk93b]   Paulk, Mark C., et al. *Key Practices of the Capability Maturity Model*, Software Engineering Institute, CMU/SEI-93-TR-25, February 1993.

[Pierce93]   Pierce, Keith R. "Rethinking Academia's Conventional Wisdom," *IEEE Software 10(2)*, March 1993, 94-95, 99.

[Tomayko87]   Tomayko, James E. *Teaching a Project-Intensive Introduction to Software Engineering*, Software Engineering Institute, CMU/SEI-87-TR-20.

[Weinberg92]   Weinberg, Gerald M. *Quality Software Management*. New York: Dorset House.

Appendix A
Key Process Areas

1 Level 2 Key Process Areas
1.1 Requirements Management

Requirements management is the process whereby the customer and developer enter into and maintain a common understanding of the customer's requirements that are to be addressed by the project. This involves documenting an agreement that encompasses both technical and non-technical (e.g., schedule and cost) aspects of the project and updating the agreement as necessary during the conduct of the project.

1.2 Software Project Planning

Software project planning includes the estimation of the effort associated with the project, creating an appropriate work breakdown structure and assigning resources and staff to the project.

1.3 Software Project Tracking and Oversight

Software project tracking and oversight addresses the ongoing control of the project. It includes measurement of actual progress and results against plans and adjustment of plans based on actual progress and results.

1.4 Software Subcontract Management

Software subcontract management deals with the selection of capable subcontractors and the management of their project-related work.

1.5 Software Quality Assurance

Software quality assurance strives to provide insight into the software development process and related products during the course of the project. Software quality assurance uses reviews and audits to assess the quality of the process and its work products.

1.6 Software Configuration Management

Software configuration management aims at preserving the integrity of work products by establishing a baseline of configuration items that are placed under change control. Revisions are made under the authority of a change control board.

2 Level 3 Key Process Areas
2.1 Organization Process Focus

Organization process focus fixes organizational responsibility for software process improvement. Most organizations desiring to improve their software process establish a software process improvement group to guide and assist the organization in working toward that end..

2.2 Organization Process Definition

Organization process definition involves the careful specification of elements of the organization's software process with a view to establishing a process assets library of re-usable process elements. These elements can be selected and tailored in designing the software process for a specific project.

2.3 Training Program

The training program aims at identifying and satisfying the training needs of individuals so that they can perform their functions efficiently and effectively.

2.4 Integrated Software Management

Integrated software management involves the use of the organization's defined software process to manage a software development project.

2.5 Software Product Engineering

Software product engineering is the process that actually produces software work products. It includes such tasks as analysis, design, coding, and testing.

2.6 Intergroup Coordination

Intergroup coordination provides a means for software engineers to work cooperatively with engineers of other disciplines in constructing a product to meet a customer's specifications.

2.7 Peer Reviews

Peer reviews are an important method of identifying and removing defects early in the software life cycle. Walkthroughs and inspections are examples of peer review processes.

3 Level 4 Key Process Areas

3.1 Quantitative Process Management

Quantitative process management is concerned with using process measurements to control and improve the conduct of the software process.

3.2 Software Quality Management
Software quality management involves the definition of quality goals, along with organizational mechanisms for achieving them.

4 Level 5 Key Process Areas

4.1 Defect Prevention

Defect prevention involves tracking defects and analyzing them to detect patterns, leading to the taking of action to prevent such defects from occurring.

4.2 Technology Change Management

Technology change management is an organized approach to technology transition, including the identification of candidate technologies, their pilot implementation and dissemination throughout the organization.

4.3 Process Change Management

Process change management involves defining process improvement goals and implementing changes designed to achieve these goals.

Using a Multi-User Dialogue System to Support Software Engineering Distance Education

William A. Bralick, Jr.* and John S. Robinson

Air Force Institute of Technology,
Wright-Patterson AFB OH 45433-7765, USA

Abstract. Multi-User Dialogues (or Dungeons), (*MUDs*) provide a convenient, low-cost vehicle for conducting software engineering seminars and project work with a diverse, geographically distributed group of students. We couple the *MUD* metaphor with a powerful management simulation engine to provide students experience with different scenarios typical within software engineering management.

1 Introduction

Telecommuting and distance education are two ideas whose times have come. One of the most serious problems confronting distance education in software engineering, however, is the accommodation of the necessary group project work that much software engineering education entails. Unless the student population clusters in a few work centers, few or no students would be able to participate in group project work in any given course. Recent research (e.g. [RCM93]) has looked at cybernetic metaphors of the work environment in advanced human-machine interfaces. Hill, *et al* state that "one could think of a shared computer application as a multiperson virtual meeting space accessed from computer terminals. Instead of meeting in a physical conference room ... conference participants meet in a virtual space, communicating via videophone and shared electronic charts, models, and whiteboards." [HBP+93] We agree; the computational resources and communication bandwidth needed to produce these effects, however, are prohibitive especially in today's climate of shrinking educational budgets.

Our work seeks a compromise between the power of cybernetic metaphors of the work environment and computer-supported cooperative work systems with lower cost (i.e. free) approaches to distance education. We believe that the human imagination properly stimulated with text can do much of the work of the more expensive graphical interfaces. Curtis and Nichols [PaCu93] have also looked at a serious use of *MUDs*. We desire a system that provides a metaphor of the work environment, an interactive capability, and the capability to coordinate different groups of geographically separated students under the supervision of

---

* Supported by an equipment grant from The Pennsylvania State University.

an instructor. The ideal system will provide an infrastructure for the student to work cooperatively with their team-members on projects even if they have never met face-to-face.

In what follows we begin with some background on *MUDs* in Section 2. In Section 3 we describe our adaptation of existing *MUD* technology to the problem of distance education in software engineering. In section 4 we describe the application of *MUDs* to the specific problem of software engineering management education. We conclude with a summary and a synopsis of our planned future work in Section 5.

2   Multi-User Dungeons *(MUDs)* – Background

Multi-User Dungeons or Multi-User Dialogues, *MUDs*, grew out of adventure games wherein a player traversed a virtual maze acquiring treasures and gaining experience points. A multi-user dungeon is an adventure game wherein more than one player shares the same virtual maze. The players are able to communicate with each other and cooperate within this virtual maze. Indeed, some tasks can only be accomplished with more than one player cooperating in the task. *MUDs* have been called "network-oriented databases of objects" [Ran91] wherein the attributes associated with each object are used by the *MUD* server to control the description of the player's environment.

We characterize *objects* as identifiable collections of attributes. These objects can be manipulated, moved, or carried about by other objects. An actor is a character object controlled by a human. The actor can be a cyborg, a robot, or a mere human being. Rooms are objects which can contain other objects. Doors are objects which link rooms. Teleporters are objects used to teleport within the *MUD* – i.e. move between different sections of the *MUD* without traversing the intervening rooms. This can only be done by an actor who has *a priori* knowledge about the different rooms in a given *MUD*.

There are several different kinds of *MUDs* extant. Some are "social" in orientation – participants meet and discuss things. Others are more faithful to the adventure/role-playing paradigm – participants engage in quests, fight monsters (as well as each other), and acquire treasures. One important distinguishing characteristic among *MUDs* concerns whether and how participants are permitted to extend the existing structure by building rooms, doors, etc. Another important characteristic is whether the *MUD* has a usable programming language. Finally, some *MUDs* can connect directly to each other through "cyberportals" allowing a single dungeon to extend across different physical machines on the internet. The game is then made available to participants on the internet by providing a telnet port to which a limited number of participants can connect using either *telnet* or one of the more powerful client programs described below in Section 2.1.

2.1   Servers and Clients.

A *MUD* consists of at least one *MUD* server running on a host machine and any number of *MUD* clients running on the players' machines. As in any server-client programming model, the server accepts connections and coordinates the activities of all the participants. The client programs provide the direct support of the player.

Servers. A representative server structure (that of UnterMUD) is illustrated in Figure 1 [Ran91]. The server manages the object database, the rules and policies, the players, and the time. The object database maintains the rooms, objects, and actors used within the *MUD*. Besides the maintenance functions, the server executes the various commands issued by the players. Many *MUDs* run entirely out of main memory and do not use the file system to checkpoint or retain the game state. Those *MUDs* which do use the file system are referred to as "disk-based" *MUDs*.

Table 2.1 contains a representative sample (from AberMUD) of the commands available on the server to the participants. These particular commands are clearly oriented toward playing an adventure-type game. Any commands can be substituted for these, however, and coupled with the appropriate actions as suggested in Section 3, adapts this paradigm to be a powerful educational tool.

Movement in our adaptation of teh *MUD* paradigm requires naming the door through which the participant wishes to pass, thus door labels can describe what lies beyond them rather than merely the cardinal directions as in Table 2.1. Upon entry into a room, the room is described along with its contents.

Table 1. AberMUD User Commands [Abe91]

Moving around				Communication			
N E S W U D		GO	JUMP	MSG	SAY	SHOUT	
LOOK	EXITS	SIT	STAND	TELL	WISH	CONVERSE	
Items				**Informational**			
GET	DROP	WEAR	REMOVE	ACTIONS	COUPLES	CREDITS	HELP
GIVE	STEAL	INVENT	PUT	INFO	LEVELS	MAXUSER	MUDLIST
EXAMINE	LIGHT	UNLIGHT	PLAY	NEWS	PN	USERS	VALUE
PUSH	TURN	OPEN	CLOSE	VERSION	WHO	WIZLIST	
LOCK	UNLOCK	EAT	EMPTY	JUGGLE			
Combat				**Utility**			
FLEE	KILL	WIELD		!		BECOME	BUG	COLOR
				QUIT	PROMPT	SAVE	SCORE
				TIME	TYPO	UPDATE	GLOBAL

Figure 2 illustrates a representative server control flow (again, that of UnterMUD). The software is neither complex nor particularly innovative, reusing existing paradigms (sockets, layered architectures, etc.) where appropriate.

The *MUDs* are generally classified into three categories: social, miscellaneous, and combat. Below, the description of each follows [Smi93b]. Examination of the various *MUD* source codes suggests that they have not been developed according to commonly accepted software engineering practice. Their application to the business of education should not be eschewed merely because they are fun

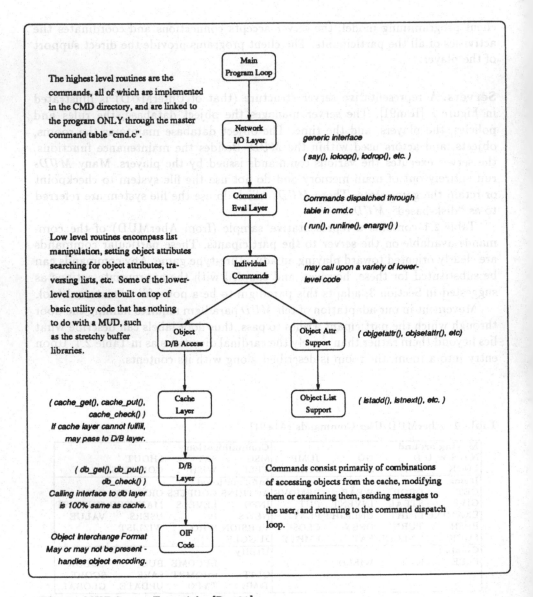

The highest level routines are the commands, all of which are implemented in the CMD directory, and are linked to the program ONLY through the master command table "cmd.c".

generic interface

(say(), ioloop(), iodrop(), etc.)

Commands dispatched through table in cmd.c

(run(), runline(), enargv())

Low level routines encompass list manipulation, setting object attributes searching for object attributes, traversing lists, etc. Some of the lower-level routines are built on top of basic utility code that has nothing to do with a MUD, such as the stretchy buffer libraries.

may call upon a variety of lower-level code

(objgetattr(), objsetattr(), etc)

(lstadd(), lstnext(), etc.)

(cache_get(), cache_put(), cache_check())
If cache layer cannot fulfill, may pass to D/B layer.

(db_get(), db_put(), db_check())
Calling interface to db layer is 100% same as cache.

Commands consist primarily of combinations of accessing objects from the cache, modifying them or examining them, sending messages to the user, and returning to the command dispatch loop.

Object Interchange Format May or may not be present - handles object encoding.

Fig. 1. *MUD* Server Essentials. [Ran91]

and poorly documented. Re-engineering the prototype *MUD* serves as a useful software engineering project in its own right.

Social *MUDs*. Social *MUDs* are those whose main purpose is to provide a vehicle for interplayer interaction. These *MUDs* also allow the participants to build onto the *MUD*. The *MUDs* in this category include: TinyMUD (original by Jim Aspnes) where players can explore and build, but not teleport; TinyMUCK, a

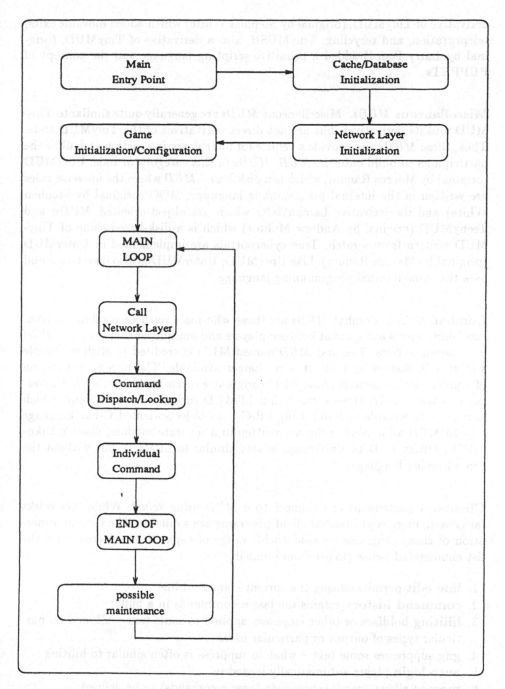

Fig. 2. *MUD* Flow of Control [Ran91].

derivative of TinyMUD, (original by Stephen White) which added movable exits, teleportation, and recycling; TinyMUSH, also a derivative of TinyMUD, (original by Larry Foard) added a primitive scripting language and the concept of PUPPETs.

Miscellaneous *MUDs*. Miscellaneous *MUDs* are generally quite similar to Tiny-MUD and its derivatives, but are not direct derivatives of the TinyMUD code. Thus, these *MUDs* also provide a vehicle for interplayer interaction and allow the participants to build onto the *MUD*. *MUDs* in this category include: UberMUD (original by Marcus Ranum) which is a disk-based *MUD* where the universe rules are written in the internal programming language; MOO (original by Stephen White) and its derivative LambaMOO which are object-oriented *MUDs*; and TeenyMUD (original by Andrew Molitor) which is a disk-based clone of Tiny-MUD written from scratch. True cyberportals are implemented in UnterMUD (original by Marcus Ranum). Like UberMUD, UnterMUD is also disk-based and uses the same internal programming language.

Combat *MUDs*. Combat *MUDs* are those who main purpose combines a treasure hunt, quests and combat between players and non-player characters, (*NPCs*) or between players. The first *MUD* named MUD is credited to Richard Bartle and Roy Trubshaw in 1979. It is no longer available. The present generation of combat *MUDs* include: AberMUD (original written at Aberstywyth University) in which only wizards can build; LPMUD (original by Lars Penj) which also permits wizards to build using LP-C – an object-oriented C-like language – in LPMUD all universe rules are written in a separate module, *mudlib*; Diku-MUD (written at Diku University) is very similar to LPMUD, but without the programming language.

Clients. A participant can connect to a *MUD* using *telnet*. While this works fairly well, more sophisticated client programs are available. The current generation of client programs provide a wide range of capabilities selected from the list enumerated below (taken from [Smi93b]).

1. **line edit** permits editing the current command line
2. **command history** retains the last n commands in a buffer
3. **hiliting** boldface or other emphasis applied to some text – allowed on particular types of output or particular users
4. **gag** suppresses some text – what to suppress is often similar to hiliting
5. **auto-login** player automatically logged in
6. **macros** allows macro expressions (new commands) to be defined
7. **logging** MUD output recorded in a file
8. **cyberportals** automatically reconnects the player to another MUD server
9. **triggers** certain actions on the MUD automatically cause events
10. **file upload** capability to upload a file

11. **command upload** capability to upload a command
12. **screen mode** some sort of screen mode on some terminals
13. **shells** escape to O/S
14. **multiple connect** connection to multiple MUDs
15. **regexp** UNIX-style regular expressions supported, e.g. to select text to hilite

The existing UNIX-based client programs offer different capabilities as shown in Table 2.1. TinyFugue provides perhaps the most robust environment and has formed the basis of our first generation *MUD* client (SEAFugue).

Table 2. UNIX-based *MUD* Clients' Capabilities [Smi93b]

Client	Target	Features
LPTalk	LP-MUDs	3-7
PMF	LP-MUDs	1, 4-7, 9-10
	TinyMUDs	(X-window interface, Sparc sounds)
SayWat	TinyMUDs	3-4, 6-10 (rudimentary xterm support)
TINTIN	TinyMUDs	6, 9, 14 (tick-counter)
TinyFugue	TinyMUDs	1-12, 14-15
TinyTalk	TinyMUDs	1-7
Tinyview	TinyMUDs	1-2, 6, 12, 14
VT	all types	(C-like extension language, windowing)

3 Software Engineering Activities MUD (*SEAMUD*)

Because software engineering is a cooperative process, any social *MUD* could have provided the baseline functionality for conducting distance education in software engineering. When more technical processes are taught different capabilities must be added as described in Section 5.2. Due to the complexity of the systems we build and the complex inter-relationships among contractors and sub-contractors, we were driven to UnterMUD as the baseline system.

3.1 Architecture

SEAMUD is a hybrid derivation of the functionality of AberMUD, UnterMUD, and, by derivation, TinyMUD. AberMUD contributed extensive non-player character interaction. TinyMUD contributed a robust, buildable environment. UnterMUD contributed a full, server/client-based cyberportal capability.

Figure 3 illustrates the conceptual object structure of *SEAMUD*. Teleporters, **O**bjects, **A**ctors, and **D**oors along with rooms and each of their attributes

572

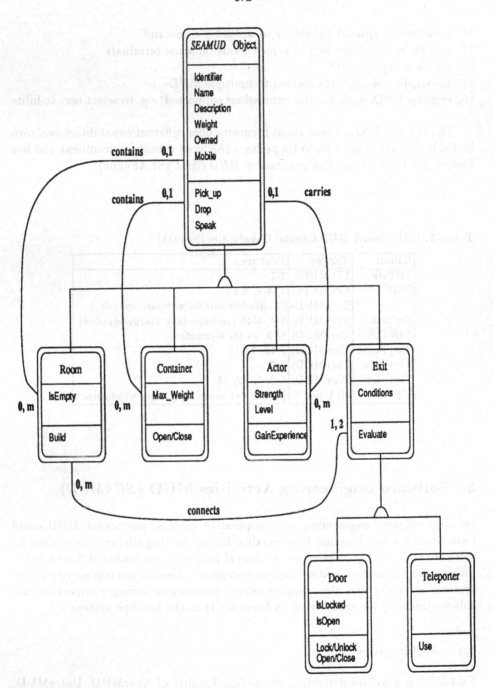

Fig. 3. *SEAMUD* Conceptual Object Layer.

comprise the basics of the *MUD* idiom. Although there is (at least) one self-consciously object-oriented *MUD* extant, *viz.* MOO, our discussion of the different characteristics of *MUDs* should not lead the reader to conclude that *MUDs* in general or *SEAMUD* in particular are objected-oriented in nature.

The *SEAMUD* server maintains a class system for the students. The *teacher* class is the same as the *wizard* class on traditional *MUDs*. We have added a class (relative to UnterMUD) to distinguish builder students from non-builder students. This will permit players to extend the *MUD* in a controlled fashion. Initially, we selected Tinyfugue as the baseline client program due to its complete set of features. As we indicate in Section 5.2, we plan an X-windows-based client that will provide a *WIMP* interface for the client.

3.2 CyberClass and CyberLab

There is a natural tendency to try to solve every problem with a single solution. We resist that temptation in the use of the *MUD* paradigm. There is little utility to including a lecture hall, however, a guided discussion could be conducted with good effect. Case studies and simulations (as described in Section 4) can also be presented using this method. The *MUD* itself becomes a project laboratory as we describe in Section 5.2. Here we examine the use of a *MUD* for a guided discussion.

Guided discussion. A guided discussion [AFM84] is a pedagogical method where an instructor poses a series of questions attempting to elicit certain responses from the students. The guided discussion is useful for attaining comprehension-level cognitive objectives. The questioning begins with a lead-off question and a set of anticipated responses against which the instructor checks the students understanding. Students can often surprise the instructor with unanticipated responses. The objectives of the lesson are established and questions are cast in order to achieve the learning objectives set by the instructor.

A sample session. In the subsequent example, **Durin** is the instructor. All others assumed to be students. Note that the students may have never met in "real life;" the extent of their contact with their classmates may well have been solely within the context of the *MUD*.

Following is a sample of a part of a guided discussion covering the question of the prioritization of requirements. Although the three points of view must be presented here one subsequent to the other, during the actual guided discussion the three would be occurring asynchronously on three different terminals. A double quote mark begins a statment by one of the participants which is then relayed to each of the other participants. Note, the "whispered" exchange between Neinor and Turin. This conversation was not seen by Durin. A colon (:) begins a description of an activity engaged in by a participant, e.g. sitting down, which is also relayed to the participants.

Durin

Seminar Room
You have entered a single-room building with comfortable chairs
gathered in a semi-circle around a fireplace.
Players:
turin
nienor
Obvious Exits:
out
nienor has arrived.
turin has arrived.

⋮

"One of my former students told me that her project scope was a
   superset of the project need which was a superset of the project
   urgent needs which was a superset of the project's funding.
You say, "One of my former students told me that her project scope
   was a superset of the project needs which was a superset of the
   project urgent needs which was a super set of the project's funding."

⋮

"Well, Turin, how would you recommend my student isolate those
   requirements that are most necessary to implement?
You say, "Well, Turin, how would you recommend my student isolate
   those requirements that are most necessary to implement?"
turin says, "I'd go to the customer and tell them that they have to
   prioritize their requirements."
"How?
You say, "How?"
turin says, "What do you mean, how?"
"How do you get them to prioritize their requirements?
You say, "How do you get them to prioritize their requirements?"
nienor raises hand.
turin says, "I dunno, I'd just ask them."
"Nienor?
You say, "Nienor?"
nienor says, "I'd use a wideband delphi method to asign numerical
   priorities to each of the identifiable requirements. Once they
   are costed out then the customer can do a cost-benefit analysis
   on the list."

⋮

                                          Turin

Seminar Room

You have entered a single-room building with comfortable chairs
gathered in a semi-circle around a fireplace.
Players:
Durin
nienor
Obvious Exits:
out

:

nienor whispers, "What are you doing after class?".
whisper nienor "I was going to extend the SafeHome DFD ...
  wanna come along?"
You whisper, "I was going to extend the SafeHome DFD ...
  wanna come along?" to nienor.
Durin says, "One of my former students told me that her project scope
was a superset of the project needs which was a superset of the
project urgent needs which was a super set of the project's funding."
Durin says, "Well, Turin, how would you recommend my student isolate
  those requirements that are most necessary to implement?"
"I'd go to the customer and tell them that they have prioritize their
  requir ements.
You say, "I'd go to the customer and tell them that they have to prioritize
their requirements."
Durin says, "How?"
"What do you mean, how?
You say, "What do you mean, how?"
Durin says, "How do you get them to prioritize their requirements?"
nienor raises hand.
"I dunno, I'd just ask them.
You say, "I dunno, I'd just ask them."
Durin says, "Nienor?"
nienor says, "I'd use a wideband delphi method to assign numerical
priorities to each of the identifiable requirements. Once they are
costed out then the customer can do a cost-benefit analysis on the list."

:

Nienor

Seminar Room
You have entered a single-room building with comfortable chairs
gathered in a semi-circle around a fireplace.
Players:
turin
Durin
Obvious Exits:
out
turin has arrived.

:

whisper turin "What are you doing after class?"
You whisper, "What are you doing after class?" to turin.
turin whispers, "I was going to extend the SafeHome DFD ...
wanna come along?".
Durin says, "One of my former students told me that her project scope
was a superset of the project need which was a superset of the project
urgent needs which was a super set of the project's funding."
Durin says, "Well, Turin, how would you recommend my student isolate those
requirements that are most necessary to implement?"
turin says, "I'd go to the customer and tell them that they have to
prioritize their requirements."
Durin says, "How?"
turin says, "What do you mean, how?"
Durin says, "How do you get them to prioritize their requirements?"
:raises hand.
nienor raises hand.
turin says, "I dunno, I'd just ask them."
Durin says, "Nienor?"
"I'd use a wideband delphi method to assign numerical priorities to
 each of the identifiable requirements. Once they are costed out
 then the customer can do a cost-benefit analysis on the list."
You say, "I'd use a wideband delphi method to asign numerical priorities to
each of the identifiable requirements. Once they are costed out then the
customer can do a cost-benefit analysis on the list."

:

If text or limited graphics is sufficient for the learning objectives desired then
dialogue, guided discussions, case studies, and simulations can all be conducted
through a *MUD*.

4 Software Engineering Process Simulation

Rationale. The value of simulation-based instruction in the development of
complex problem solving skills has been well recognized for years [Sol93]. The
airline industry and the military for example, rely heavily on the use of simulations to train their pilots. Pilots gain the experience and expertise through many
simulated flights, providing a safe and cost effective approach to learning.

This same logic has been applied to the management of software projects.
Approaches taken by [AHM91] and [PR91] model the software development environment through the use of a system dynamics language (DYNAMO). When
used for training managers, these models, in conjunction with case studies can
be used to demonstrate the side-effects and long-term consequences of management decisions as well as showing the effects of factors such as quality, rework
effects, requirements creep, and schedule compression. The model described in
[AHM91], for example, uses over 100 interacting variables to model the software

development process. Software managers typically learn about these complex interdependencies through work experience, however, many of the complex software development projects we have problems with may span 10 years or more. The FAA's Air Traffic Control upgrade and the Air Force's C-17 avionics software are just two examples of projects with lengthy development cycles. As a side note, IBM stated that the Advanced Automation System will not be completed until well after the year 2000, making it at least an 18 year development cycle! [Ush93] Thus, it may be difficult to find project managers that have experienced more than a couple of these projects in their careers. The use of simulations can compress these timelines drastically. Potential program managers can experience the pitfalls of large system developments, learn what works, what doesn't, and most importantly, accomplish these educational goals within a realistic time-frame.

Background. Computer simulations of the software process in an academic classroom environment have already been used with some success. The Software Engineering Institute's (SEI) Interactive Video Code Inspection Laboratory provides students an opportunity to experience an interactive code inspection, playing different roles and receiving immediate feedback on their actions [Chr92]. This environment has many advantages over the traditional classroom lecture – primarily increased student interest and motivation. Current educational research shows that when students are "engaged in active exploration, interpretations, and construction of ideas", the learning process is much more effective. [Haw93] Hawkins points out that moving away from the traditional lecture toward a project-based and seminar discussion curricula will support these goals. Among others, [AFM84] and [Adl83] both stress the need to bind educational objectives with teaching methodology.

The interactive video approach isn't without its drawbacks, however. The SEI code inspection laboratory uses a 386-based computer to control specialized interactive video equipment. Students interact with the simulation through a graphical interface which triggers various video responses based on a sequence of student actions. Although video and sound greatly increase the realistic feel of the simulation, they can be expensive to create, to store, and to reproduce on the computer because of the file sizes and specialized equipment involved. We feel it is possible to achieve many of the advantages of the classroom simulation without the expense by using simple text as the primary interaction medium.

Application. The MUD framework described earlier can provide a useful tool to build software project management simulations. MUDs provide several advantages over the multimedia approach. First of all, since it is text based it provides both low cost and a high level of portability. It doesn't rely on expensive hardware and is easily customizable by the user. Interactive video requires new scenes to be scripted and shot, actors hired, etc., then integrated into the simulation. A new CD or videotape must be produced and changes to the software must be accomplished to hook the video scenes to the proper actions. Secondly, when running on a multiuser platform, MUDs also allow several users to interact simultaneously. Using the multiplayer characteristics of a MUD, we can extend the realism of the simulation by having a group of students take on various roles in the project's development, forming a project team which must solve a series of software problems together.

The course instructor can participate and guide students through the simulation, stopping periodically and discussing the results of each situation with the students within the simulation itself or discreetly observe student interaction. By integrating a system dynamics model of the software development process with the MUD, we can gain the additional advantages of the dynamic model and use the MUD as a scenario-based interactive case study. The MUD, serving as the front end handles the first order effects of decisions (effects which are immediate) as well as providing for the set up of the problems or scenarios to be solved at that level. The dynamic model handles all time-delayed integrative effects. Other computer based learning environments have done similar integration, combining dynamic models with interactive teaching. [Pre90]. This combination provides a higher fidelity simulation while still gaining the advantages of the computer interaction.

The interactive simulation begins by positioning each student at the beginning of the simulation. The student team then completes a series of scenarios achieving defined educational objectives along the way. As a team students can meet, discuss and use various tools off-line or while meeting on-line under a window-based environment. Background information on the project such as related readings, requirement documents, software development plans, etc., are provided to participating students prior to the use of the simulation. Students synthesize what they have learned off-line and apply it in the simulation.

The educational objectives which can be incorporated into this environment are only limited by the imagination of the instructor. Typically, the objectives will consist of the completion of a series of tasks which themselves are made up of a series of individual actions. Completion of a defined set of tasks moves the students to the next level in the simulation. Unlike traditional case studies, the interactive simulation described here provides the capability to relate all actions to the subsequent scenarios; case studies are not usually time interdependent. In other words, results and decisions arrived at from one case study are not usually fed into the next. With this environment, the data generated at the previous level is fed into a dynamic simulation, such as [AHM91] or [PR91], generating a new MUD configuration customized to the input data. Moving to the new level thrusts the students forward in time to experience the effects of decisions made on the previous level. Level I for example, handles requirements analysis situations. Level II would handle early design activities, etc. Each level then represents progress in the development of the project with the dynamic model providing data resulting from the effects of the students' decisions. Currently the instructor runs the dynamic model manually to enter the data into the next level MUD. Future implementations will automate this process.

5 Conclusions and Future Work.

5.1 Summary and Conclusions

This paper has presented a convenient, low-cost vehicle for conducting software engineering education with a diverse, geographically distributed group of students. Although we have presented several applications of *MUDs* in the education domain, the potential is still largely untapped for applying this technology to practical software engineering projects. There is no reason to assume that this idea need be limited to the classroom. While it is less attractive than multi-feed video/audio it is available now at low/no cost to any institution connected to the internet.

5.2 Future Work

Flexible MS in Software Systems Engineering. One problem facing practitioners is how to continue their employment while attending graduate school. Many universities offer flexible Master's programs for working students. A severe problem with this approach is the compression of in-class hours over specified weekends. This limits the types of laboratory and in-class exercises that can be given the student. Limitations of this sort can be overcome if the various meetings and conferencing which needs to occur can do so in cyberspace.

Graphical Clients. Work is already proceeding apace on the production of graphical *MUDs*. Our real needs are much more limited, *viz.* we need to be able to transmit and receive different directed-graph-oriented diagrams and mixed English/non-English text. To this end we have begun work on X-window-based *SEAMUD* client which will be capable of displaying these diagrams as well as providing a convenient mechanism for accessing the more typical *MUD* features.

Software Systems Engineering from Within. Our current research direction focuses on building a metaphor of the process of model-building by providing the student/practitioner with specific tools for building onto the *MUD* in a controlled fashion. Part of the *MUD* itself then becomes a model for the software system under development. Thus, for example, equipped with a *dataflow* tool, the student/practitioner can add data stores or processes as rooms and dataflows as doors between them. A simple dataflow diagram – the SafeHome example from [Pre92] has already been modeled in this fashion. Figure 4 is the portion described in the following description.

```
Obvious Exits:
SafeHome
safehome
SafeHome

Obvious Exits:
erm
dfm
oom
dfm
SafeHome:0
```

SafeHome software enables the homeowner to configure the
security system when it is installed, monitors all sensors
connected to the security system, and interacts with the
homeowner through a keypad and function key.

```
Obvious Exits:
cp
s
cpd
a
tl
s
sensors

Obvious Exits:
ss
look ss
sensor status
ss
monitor sensors

Contents:
pspec
Obvious Exits:
si
at
tnt
lvl2
look lvl2
```

The level 2 DFD that refines the Monitor Sensors process.

```
get pspec
```

Monitor sensor process takes the configuration information
and sensor status and asseses against the set-up. If an
alarm condition has occurred an alarm signal is generated,
sensor id is displayed and an emergency phone number dialed.

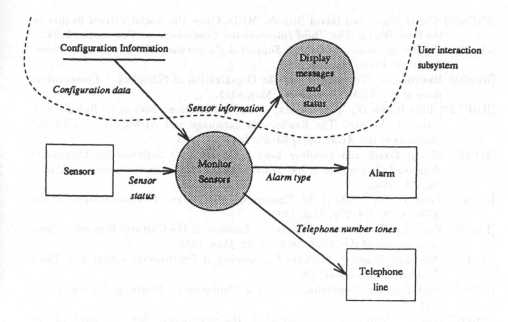

Fig. 4. *SafeHome* Level 1 DFD. [Pre92]

Given the cyberportal capability one team can work on a subsystem design on one machine which can be linked with another subsystem on a different machine. Similarly, different models can be used and synchronized via the doors that link them. A map generator can then serve to communicate the design among the participants. Technical design meetings in this paradigm will give a new and more literal meaning to the concept of a design walk-through.

References

[AHM91] Abdel-Hamid, T. and S. Madnick. *Software Project Dynamics, An Integrated Approach.* Prentice-Hall, 1991.

[Abe91] University of Aberstywyth. AberMUD Documentation Set. Archived on ftp.math.okstate.edu(139.78.10.6) in /pub/muds/servers, June, 1991.

[Adl83] Adler, Mortimer J. Paideia Problems and Possibilities. Macmillan, New York, 1983.

[AFM84] Department of the Air Force. Handbook for Air Force Instructors. Air Force Manual 50-62, January, 1984.

[BB91] Bowers, John M. and Steven D. Benford, editors. *Studies in Computer-Supported Cooperative Work: Theory, Practice, and Design.* North-Holland, New York, 1991.

[Chr92] Christel, Michael. Experiences with an Interactive Video Code Inspection Laboratory. *Lecture Notes in Computer Science 640: Software Engineering Education Conference Proceedings, (October 1992, San Diego, CA.),* Springer-Verlag, Berlin, 1992.

[PaCu93] Curtis, Pavel and David Nichols. MUDs Grow Up: Social Virtual Reality in the Real World. *The Third International Conference on Cyberspace*, 1993.

[Gre91] Greenberg, Saul. *Computer-Supported Cooperative Work and Groupware.* Academic Press, London, 1991.

[Haw93] Hawkins, J. Technology and the Organization of Schooling . *Communications of the ACM*, 36(5):30–35, May, 1993.

[HBP+93] Hill, Ralph D., Tom Brinck, John F. Patterson, Steven L. Rohall, and Wayne T. Wilner. The Rendezvous Language and Architecture. *Communications of the ACM*, 36(1):63–67, January, 1993.

[MB92] Marca, David and Geoffrey Bock. *Groupware : Software for Computer-Supported Cooperative Work.* IEEE COMPUTER Society Press, Los Alamitos, CA, 1992.

[Pre90] Press, L. SIGGRAPH '89, Tomorrow's PC Today. *Communications of the ACM*, 33(9):274–279, Mar, 1990.

[Pre93] Press, L. Technetronic Education: Answers on the Cultural Horizon . *Communications of the ACM*, 36(5):17–22, May, 1993.

[Pre92] Pressman, Roger S. *Software Engineering: A Practitioner's Approach, Third Edition.* McGraw-Hill, 1992.

[PR91] Pugh-Roberts Associates. *Program Management Modeling System Guide.* 1991.

[Ran91] Ranum, Marcus J. UnterMUD Documentation Set. Archived on ftp.math.okstate.edu(139.78.10.6) in /pub/muds/servers, June, 1991.

[RCM93] Robertson, George G. and Stuart K. Card and Jock D. Mackinlay. Information Visualization Using 3D Interactive Animation *Communications of the ACM*, 36(4)57–71, April, 1993.

[Sch93] Schank, R. C. Learning via Multimedia Computers. *Communications of the ACM*, 36(5):54–56, May, 1993.

[Smi93a] Smith, Jennifer "Moira". [rec.games.mud]: FAQ #1/3: MUDs and MUDding. Archived on ftp.math.okstate.edu (139.78.10.6) in pub/muds/misc/mud-faq, May, 1993.

[Smi93b] Smith, Jennifer "Moira". [rec.games.mud]: FAQ #2/3: MUD Clients and Servers. archived on ftp.math.okstate.edu (139.78.10.6) in pub/muds/misc/mud-faq, May, 1993.

[Sol93] Soloway, E. Reading and Writing in the 21st Century . *Communications of the ACM*, 36(5):23–27, May, 1993.

[Ush93] Usher, Chris. Flying in Place: The FAA's Air Control Fiasco. *Business Week*, April 26, 1993.

Introducing Megaprogramming
at the High School
and Undergraduate Levels*

Mary Eward and Steven Wartik

Software Productivity Consortium, Herndon, Virginia

Abstract. This paper discusses a project to introduce software reuse, in the form of megaprogramming, to high school and university students. The project is working with high schools and universities to develop course materials and curricula incorporating reuse. These course and curricula are based on a version of megaprogramming called Synthesis. We have developed a one-to-two week pilot course that is being taught in several high schools. This course, while not an attempt to teach students systematic techniques for software reuse, introduces the students to key reuse concepts and shows them the importance of reuse. We are using feedback from the course offerings to help us continue developing the course and curriculum material.

This paper recounts some of the issues encountered by the project in working with the high schools and universities, and outlines our current strategy for teaching reuse at these levels.

1   Introduction

Software engineering educators often complain that current computer science curricula introduce crucial concepts of software development too late. Some educators introduce such topics as abstraction, reuse, software processes, and group projects in early courses, but students often perceive them to be of secondary importance to their programming assignments. Students learn a develop-from-scratch mentality, rather than viewing reuse as a viable strategy to increase productivity.

The U.S. Department of Defense (DoD) has a vested interest in this problem. The DoD has observed that most graduates entering industry are ill-prepared to employ reuse strategies when developing software. To achieve the productivity required to meet its mission, the DoD would like to see people entering the work force with more exposure to modern software development paradigms.

The Software Productivity Consortium has been tasked by DoD's Advanced Research Projects Agency (ARPA), through the Virginia Center of Excellence for Software Reuse and Technology Transfer, to develop curricula that introduce software reuse in high schools and introductory college computer science

* This material is based in part upon work sponsored by the Advanced Research Projects Agency Grant #MDA972-92-J-1018.

courses. Specifically, we are basing our curricula around megaprogramming, an ARPA-sponsored initiative that encourages and facilitates software construction through component assembly (Boehm and Scherlis 1992). We are building a curriculum and course materials that are based on a version of megaprogramming called Synthesis, a reuse-driven software development process developed by the Consortium. The intent is to train students to think of building software from existing components whenever practical.

This paper is a summary of our progress to date. We first present some background on the project. We then explore the issues we face in introducing reuse, and present our strategy. We conclude with a description of the first course we have developed under this project.

2 Project Background and Progress to Date

The Virginia Center of Excellence for Software Reuse and Technology Transfer (VCOE) was formed by the Software Productivity Consortium and the Virginia Center for Innovative Technology in 1992 through a grant by ARPA. The Megaprogramming Curriculum Project is working through VCOE to develop and transfer a curriculum and supporting course materials for high school and university students based on megaprogramming concepts.

The project has developed a one-to-two week long "Overview of Megaprogramming" course targeted for high school students. Five high school teachers (four from Fairfax County, Virginia, and one from Morgantown, West Virginia) are consulting on the project to develop the course material and to learn megaprogramming concepts. These are the same teachers who have taught early offerings of the course. As we learn more about how to teach these concepts to high school students, we will be continually improving the course and expanding it to go into more detail on megaprogramming concepts. We also plan in the short-term to get the course ready to be picked up by any high school teacher who wants to teach the material.

Early project efforts have focused on high schools. Though progress with universities has been slower, it has been no less promising. The project has held discussions with James Madison University, the University of Virginia, and West Virginia University. Through these interactions, we hope to begin teaching megaprogramming concepts to university students in the spring of 1994.

3 Issues in Introducing Reuse

There are many issues to be considered, both technical and non-technical, in introducing reuse into a computer science curriculum. This section is a summary of those we have encountered. Our approach to introducing reuse, discussed in Section 4, addresses many of these issues.

3.1   Displacing Existing Material

There is a vast amount of literature on software reuse. The field now has regular conferences and workshops, IEEE tutorials, and books. Researchers and practitioners are actively generating fresh insights. Since the field is evolving at a rapid pace, some of the literature is in conflict with other literature on the subject. One could easily devote an entire course to the topic. However, our goal is to incorporate reuse into existing curricula, without (at least in the near term) significantly altering their format.

We believe that introducing reuse in early courses is a necessary component of a student's overall computer science education. Given the growth of the field and the frequency with which reuse is being beneficially used in industry, students need to develop a mindset of reuse as opposed to a mindset of "develop-from-scratch" early in their education. In addition, though the inclusion of reuse in early computer science courses may displace some material from those courses, we believe the students will gain time in subsequent courses by routinely reusing software in their later courses. The time saved on mundane parts of programs can be spent concentrating on the central themes of a course.

The need for reuse in early courses is also present in the software needs for other disciplines. For example, educators in other departments may expect students to be able to develop a certain degree of software proficiency in a single semester computer science course. However, reuse benefits all disciplines and could be used in all disciplines; educators in other fields can use this knowledge to their advantage.

3.2   Disconnect with Current Curricula

Current computer science curricula tend to focus on programming expertise at the expense of covering material on other aspects of the software development process (e.g., concepts of processes, requirements, reuse, and working within a team). However, the average industrial software developer spends at least as much time on the non-programming aspects of software development as on programming itself. It is ARPA's and VCOE's goal to bridge this disconnect through the megaprogramming curriculum.

3.3   The Reuse Mentality

Reuse emphasizes use of others' work. This mode of education runs counter to the typical computer science model, where students are explicitly forbidden to copy others' work. However, in a course stressing reuse, one could argue that the student who finds a previous project that exactly satisfies a homework assignment is the one who best understands reuse!

3.4   Existing Components

For a student to reuse software, there must exist a suitably large set of available components. Libraries of small parts are readily available (and their use should be encouraged), but they generally perform fairly elementary functions (sorting, elementary data structures, etc.). In addition, there is a need for reusable educational components as opposed to reusable components in general. The reusable components that are available are often for a problem area in which the average student does not have expertise (making them hard to understand and use). Reusable educational components could have a full set of supporting educational materials and be in a problem area that is intuitively understandable by the average student. We have started such a set of reusable components for our "Overview of Megaprogramming" course laboratory exercise, discussed in Section 7.2.

3.5 Realizing the Value of Reuse

Students must see the value in reuse or they will not practice it. If they just invoke existing reusable components in the same way they make calls to built-in routines, students will not realize the benefits of reuse and therefore will not be motivated to either develop components for reuse or search for and use reusable components. Students need to understand why and how reuse is an effective technique for developing software.

3.6 How Does Reuse Fit In?

Although reuse is an important tool for software development, it is not an end in itself. The goal of a software curriculum is to teach students software-oriented problem solving. Reuse is simply one tool that students should know how to apply as they develop solutions.

As such, reuse is grounded on many other concepts and technologies. Most significantly, it is one part of a software development process, which indicates when to reuse components, when to develop reusable components – and when reuse is inappropriate. Students should be encouraged to reuse software whenever possible, but they must still be proficient at programming, and must be able to recognize when it is appropriate to create components from scratch. In addition, since the best "reusers" will be those who are most proficient at all aspects of software engineering, students will need to become proficient at all stages in the software development process.

Abstraction, which is showing up earlier and earlier in curricula, also plays a key role in reuse. Indeed, verbatim reuse of components through function or procedure calls is easily taught by simply introducing such components. Abstraction also plays a central role in teaching students how to develop components that are likely to be reusable. Object-oriented systems also promote reuse, and offer interesting solutions to the problems of representing variation in a component, increasing its reusability.

Learning reuse, then, requires learning other concepts and technologies. However, one must also consider and establish a proper context in which reuse can occur. In industry, a company's business area provides this context: companies accumulate libraries of software components that are proven useful for the types of systems they are accustomed to developing. Educational institutions need to establish an analogous context in traditional disciplines.

3.7 Transfer Issues

Short-term transfer issues involved in getting high schools and universities to teach reuse include:

- Deciding when the material can be taught during the school year.
- Deciding in which course the material should be presented.
- Getting the instructors familiar enough with the concepts to feel comfortable teaching the material.
- Making the material suitable for all the varying environments that exist in schools today.

In high schools, deciding when the material can be taught is of special importance since most schools offer two computer science courses: introductory computer science and advanced placement (AP) computer science. In the AP courses, most of the year is devoted to teaching the topics that are on the national-level AP exam. We plan to work with the College Board and the Educational Testing Service to integrate megaprogramming into the AP exam. However, to get around that constraint for the near-term, our pilot courses are using the time between the end of the AP exam and the end of the year. We have found that most teachers are interested in introducing special topics during this time. For the introductory computer science courses, where there is no standard exam, we have found teachers willing to add a topic, even during the middle of the school year, that isn't too time-consuming. Universities have shown interest in teaching reuse early in an undergraduate's computer science education; specific times during their school year have been less of a concern.

The project had to decide if the material should be taught in introductory courses, in AP courses, or both. The high school teachers we have been working with felt strongly that the material should be taught at both levels to establish the right mindset in the students from the beginning. Therefore, the "Overview of Megaprogramming" course is the same for both levels, with coverage for the introductory students possibly taking more time than for the AP students.

Familiarity with the reuse course material is less of a problem than we had envisioned. For the high school teachers, we spent a series of two-hour meetings briefing them on megaprogramming concepts and organizing the logistics of having them teach it to their high school students. By the third meeting, the teachers were making significant inputs to the course material and by the fourth meeting the teachers announced that they felt comfortable teaching it.

High schools and universities have varying hardware and software environments. We have had to take several optimizing steps to get the laboratory exercise developed for the "Overview of Megaprogramming" course to work on some of the slower computers. (We will also have to work with high schools without computers in the short term.) In general, the universities we have talked to and have visited have faster equipment than what is in the high schools, so we expect to have less of a problem in those environments.

The short-term issues listed above involve transfer efforts from the bottom up; that is, those efforts that focus on working with high schools and universities one at a time to teach megaprogramming. To get megaprogramming taught on a more national basis, we need to do transfer from the top down; that is, work with curriculum developers at the national level to get megaprogramming and reuse concepts integrated into national-level computer science curricula. We expect to do this by working with existing curricula, such as "Computing Curricula 1991: Report of the ACM/IEEE-CS Joint Curriculum Task Force" (Tucker and Barnes 1991).

We also realize the need to work with government, industry, and university-sponsored efforts aimed at improving the educational materials and environments for students. One example is George Mason University's effort to put in place a nationwide very-high-speed networking structure and workstation environment. Their scope of work includes establishing that infrastructure and populating it with components for students (and researchers) to use. However, they do not identify specific techniques for reuse. We have discussed with them the possibility of combining our efforts such that at least some of the components would be developed using megaprogramming. This would complement our work by helping us disseminate our material, and complement their work by increasing students' ability to reuse components.

4 Approach to Reuse

The issues in Section 3 convey the breadth of the problems in introducing reuse. To make the problem tractable, we believe it is important to introduce a specific form of reuse, not general notions. We are building a curriculum based on reuse that:

- Is set in the context of a larger method for problem definition and solution. This allows us to establish a rudimentary (but well-defined) process for the students to follow, both in developing reusable assets and in building applications. It also motivates why assets are needed, how they would be made available, and why students would want to develop assets for future use.
- Encourages reuse of entire components, rather than reengineering. This decision, while eliminating a broad and certainly useful category of components from a student's reach, encourages abstraction on the student's part by forcing him or her to think about the component as a single, indivisible unit with a carefully-conceived interface.

The reuse vision we are introducing is based on megaprogramming (Boehm and Scherlis 1992). Megaprogramming is an ARPA-sponsored initiative to encourage and facilitate construction of software through component assembly. Megaprogramming is well-suited to our needs for several reasons:

1. Megaprogramming provides the students a useful, realistic approach to software development that is of interest to software development professionals. A computer science curriculum must include a more complete picture of the range of activities that occur as part of a normal software development effort. The activities necessary for megaprogramming help present such a picture.

2. We believe that megaprogramming can be taught meaningfully to students just learning computer science. Though megaprogramming is intended to address problems that arise in programming in the large, and emphasizes reuse of large, complex components, there is nothing in megaprogramming that precludes development and use of small components, and it appears likely to work equally well at that level.

3. As will be discussed in section 6, megaprogramming is consistent with our ideas on how reuse should be taught to students.

4. Although megaprogramming technology is not fully mature, it can be taught to students if certain constraints are added.

Synthesis We are using a version of megaprogramming called Synthesis (Software Productivity Consortium 1992, Wartik and Prieto-Díaz 1992). Synthesis is a process for developing a product family, rather than a single product. ("Product" includes requirements, design documents, and other non-executable items routinely written as part of producing software.) In Synthesis, reuse is targeted to a particular product family or "domain" – that is, a class of (software) applications related by a set of common concerns but distinguishable by well-defined variabilities. The following summarizes Synthesis concepts.

Synthesis, shown in Figure 1, is a reuse-driven software development process that splits software development into two activities: Domain Engineering, where a product family (that is, the members of a domain) is developed, and Application Engineering, where individual applications satisfying specific problems are developed by reusing components from the product family.

Synthesis emphasizes understanding a domain in terms of families. Dijkstra (1972) defines a "program family" as "a set of programs that are sufficiently similar that it is worthwhile to understand their common properties before considering the special properties of individual instances." This notion readily extends to entities other than programs. Domains are generally modeled in terms of the problems and solutions associated with them. Understanding a domain therefore requires considering:

– What is common among all problems that are associated with the domain.
– How individual instances of those problems vary.
– What is common to all solutions associated with the domain, and how the commonality can be maximized.
– How individual instances of solutions vary.

In other words, students performing domain engineering must consider how to describe all problems and solutions in the domain. Ideally, they also describe the relationship between problems and solutions. By doing so, they learn what

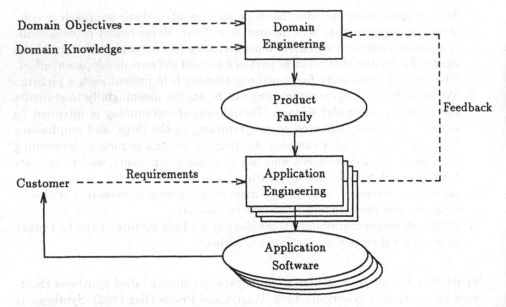

Fig. 1. The Synthesis Reuse-Driven Software Development Process

components to reuse when solving a given problem. They therefore develop mechanical processes to build part or all of a system within a domain.

Synthesis' focus on a domain is important to the development of the curriculum and course materials for the following reasons:

- It motivates why an application should be developed. Currently, students take their instructor's word that the set of requirements they are given is a statement of a useful problem to solve. A domain ties a problem to the real world.
- It provides a long-term context. A domain in an established science or engineering field has enough problems to span several semesters. Students have the opportunity to reuse existing components as well as to develop components that they can later be asked to reuse.
- It provides a coherent area of focus. In some domains, it may also provide a body of laws, allowing students to apply rigorous analysis techniques to verify and validate their designs and implementations.
- It introduces standardization among the problems the students will consider. The students will be asked to reason in terms of, or to derive, laws of the domain. This encourages them to think more deeply about the nature of the problem they are defining and solving than if they solve a single problem with no domain-specific context.
- It introduces domain-specific architectures. The students must reason about standardized solutions as well as standardized problems. Papers on megaprogramming recognize the importance of domain-specific architectures: they provide the conceptual "glue" that shows students how to integrate reusable

components (e.g., Boehm and Scherlis 1992, Belz, Luckham, and Purtilo 1992). Lacking such an architecture, integration is a much more complex task.

5 Classroom Model for Reuse-Oriented Software Development

We envision software development in a class occurring along the following lines:

1. The instructor gives the students a general statement of a problem in a domain with which they have, or are given, some familiarity. The type of domain depends on the students' level. More advanced students could be expected to use domains chosen from their major area of study. Less advanced students would need to use familiar examples from everyday life (traffic light control) or domains with some simplifying assumptions (such as the robot control domain described in Section 7.2).

Domain Engineering Steps
2. The students define the family of problems that are part of the domain. (The instructor may need to help them analyze the commonalities and variabilities if they are not familiar with the domain.)
3. The students define a family of solutions to the problems in the domain. The instructor could use this opportunity to introduce algorithms and programming paradigms that are important in the domain. The students would be asked to identify several alternative designs. They would need to consider the viability of each design both as a general solution for all problems in the domain, and as a solution to specific problems.

This paradigm introduces another important principle into software development: design evaluation. Most courses covering software design mention that the student should consider several alternative designs, but student projects seldom reinforce this concept. Studying solutions for an entire domain makes considering more than one design mandatory. Students are also asked to reason about what makes a design "best."
4. The students implement a family of solutions that solve all problems in the class they defined in step 2. In this step, they are developing reusable components that they will later use to solve the problem they were originally assigned in step 1. The emphasis is on having them adopt a reuse mentality early in the development process.

Application Engineering Steps
5. In steps 2 through 4, the students performed a domain engineering role. They now undertake application engineering. They return to the original problem definition they were given in step 1 so they can solve a specific problem. Their first objective is to precisely state the problem. This is not, as is usual in software development, done by writing a software requirements specification. Because of their work on the entire domain, they only need to

describe how their problem differs from other problems in the domain. Along with the commonalities they have identified, this description unambiguously describes the single problem they are to solve. They are therefore performing reuse in this step – not reuse of executable software, but of the concepts they developed.

6. The students now implement a solution to the problem they stated in step 5. They do so using the reusable components they developed in step 4. If they have performed step 4 correctly, they can construct a solution solely from those components.

(The above steps are a complete software process for developing a product family. Instructors will want a student's very first introduction to software development to be gentler. They could do so by having the students perform only the application engineering steps. From this, students see an idealized picture of software development as problem definition and solution using existing components. This is the approach that we adopted for the "Overview of Megaprogramming" course.)

So that students truly appreciate the value of reuse, the instructor must give subsequent assignments in the same domain. Students will perform essentially the same steps, but they will modify the domain rather than create problems and solutions from scratch. The assignments should allow students to reuse components they created as part of step 4, reinforcing the idea that previous work can play an important role in software development. Assignment sequences should also encourage students to use iterative software development – to use refinement in creating both domains and individual applications.

The intent is that students see reuse not as a special technology, but as a natural, obvious part of software development. Working within a domain on several assignments (common in industry yet relatively rare in classrooms) communicates the proper context for reuse. Reuse is relatively straightforward when Domain Engineering is performed. The reasons why it can be done, and the reasons why it should be done, are clear once one has seen the variety of problems in a domain and the similarities among solutions.

6 Analysis of this Approach

Teaching reuse early is not a new idea (e.g., Samanthanam 1990), although interest in doing it has increased considerably in recent years. Megaprogramming is arguably one of the more ambitious forms of reuse, however, and teaching it is perhaps more involved than teaching (for instance) reuse of small, domain-independent components.

Focusing on a domain mitigates many of the issues raised in Section 3. We believe it is especially important for students to perceive a need to create reusable components, and that they can see this much more easily if they are working in a coherent domain. There must be a motivation for reuse. Studying the complete set of problems in a domain makes one see how solutions can be applied in situations beyond that of a single problem.

This emphasis on studying the problem area also appears to be gaining in popularity – witness textbooks such as Clancy and Linn (1992). Synthesis adds to this a complete software development process. We believe that students must be aware of process concepts so they can differentiate between stating problems and solving them – a distinction that is sometimes blurry to them. The process we have outlined above is not deep; it only separates problems from solutions, and emphasizes the iterative nature of software development. It also helps students understand reuse by showing them the appropriate times to perform the creation and reuse of components.

Moreover, focusing on a domain is likely to yield reusable components that have a clearly defined need and are therefore more likely to be used by the students. The reason is that there are only so many domain-independent components one can create. Furthermore, many of the useful ones are data-structure oriented, and are beyond the scope of the first few courses in a computer science curriculum.

Introducing megaprogramming potentially increases complexity. Megaprogramming in general, and Synthesis in particular, relies on creating components that are highly adaptable; this adaptability increases their reusability. It also increases the size and complexity of components. We believe this can be handled in the near term by choosing the correct examples. Variation among problems and solutions in domains must be such that students can represent it in straightforward ways.

We are still investigating the correct long-term approach. Traditional languages used for teaching (like standard Pascal) lack the necessary flexibility for representing variations among data-oriented abstractions (e.g., the data type of a family of stacks). Languages such as Ada, with generic facilities, are an improvement, as are object-oriented languages. However, neither of these are widely used for undergraduate or high school instruction. Moreover, they are as yet only programming technologies, and megaprogramming requires creating adaptable requirements, designs, etc. Technologies such as metaprogramming (Cameron 1987, Campbell 1989) provide general-purpose solutions but may prove too complex for novice computer science students. Most likely, students should learn multiple techniques and the proper circumstances for applying each one.

7 Status of Curriculum and Course Material

Early project efforts have primarily been on developing the "Overview of Megaprogramming" course material. Considerable time has been spent studying existing computer science curricula and formulating ideas for a megaprogramming curricula, and actual development was initiated during the second half of 1993. Both tasks will involve instructors and curriculum developers from the educational world. This section covers our ideas and progress for the course material.

7.1 "Overview of Megaprogramming" Course Material

The "Overview of Megaprogramming" course is organized into four units and takes approximately one to two weeks to cover. Below is a brief description of each unit.

Unit 1: Software Development. Since the students attending the course will have varying backgrounds in computer science, we need to lay a common foundation before presenting megaprogramming concepts. Therefore, the first unit is devoted to covering important concepts in the practice of software development, including process and requirements. These concepts are used to motivate the need for reuse and megaprogramming. The students are introduced to a top-level chart of the megaprogramming process so that they can put the rest of the course in the proper context. The goal for the in-class exercises for this unit is to have the students understand how difficult the requirements step is by having them write complete requirements for simple, everyday problems. Students are also introduced to an example used throughout the course: developing a vending machine for the high school. For their homework assignment, they come up with a complete set of requirements for a vending machine they want in the school.

Unit 2: Concepts of Megaprogramming. This unit introduces software development as analyzing a problem and implementing a solution, defines domains, and shows how domains support reuse. The student is then re-exposed to the megaprogramming process, with more detail, in order to define domain engineering and application engineering. In-class exercises for this unit have the students identify whether or not simple, everyday classes of applications are domains. For the vending machine problem, the students combine their requirements, identify similarities and differences among their different vending machines, and identify those components that can work for all vending machines. For homework, they identify what components they need for their own vending machine.

Unit 3: Application Engineering. This unit steps the students through the application engineering process. The students are shown how to precisely state a problem, how to validate that problem statement, and how the domain is used to generate a solution. In-class exercises have the students discussing whether or not each student was able to generate a complete list of components for that vending machine. After this unit, the students are given their first laboratory exercise, described in Section 7.2.

Unit 4: Domain Engineering. This unit covers domain engineering concepts (although, given the course's time constraints, at an extremely high level). The unit covers how domain engineers define a domain, and aspects of the support domain engineers provide for the application engineer, mainly decision-making processes and domain-specific architectures. This unit does not go into detail on how these steps are actually done. The exercise for this unit is focused on getting the students to see how megaprogramming can be used in the development of vending machines.

7.2 Laboratory Exercise

The laboratory exercise at the end of unit 3 asks the students to carry out an application engineering process in a domain based on a hypothetical company that builds software-controlled robots. The students build the software for three customers: a farmer who needs corn harvested, a representative from the Alaska National Guard who wants search-and-rescue robots, and a National Park Service Ranger who wants robots that can pick up litter. The application engineering process the students follow shows them the commonalities among the software requirements for these seemingly disparate robots – although it also calls their attention to the specific differences. The software solutions they generate are constructed purely from reusable components. They integrate these components according to a domain-specific software architecture, and can therefore see the similarities and differences among implementations as well.

Robots in this domain are all similar in that they search autonomously for some type of object. However, they differ based on such characteristics as the terrain they search (field, tundra, or forest), the types of objects for which they search (corn, people, or litter), the action they take on finding an object (pick up and return, locate only, continue indefinitely), their search strategy (zigzag or sweep), and their initial amount of energy (in joules). The application engineering process asks the students to reason about robots in terms of these concepts. Students must also make quantitative comparisons of robots based on a cost model we provide them and an execution environment that simulates the time and energy needed to perform a mission. Students vary certain quantities, and see the relative effects on a robot's cost and the time needed to complete a mission.

The laboratory exercise is built on top of the Karel-the-Robot concepts developed by Pattis (1981). We have added a front end to an existing Karel implementation that asks the students to make decisions that differentiate one robot from other robots within the domain as described above. Based on the decisions, the students then use the environment to generate robot software from the reusable components within the domain, and to simulate the robot moving through the specified terrain performing the specified mission.

8 Conclusion

We are in the early stages of our goals to develop course and curriculum materials based on megaprogramming, and to transfer them to high schools and universities. However, our results to date have been extremely encouraging: every educator we have talked to has been open and receptive to working with us and has shown great interest in improving the way computer science is taught to their students. In addition, we believe that introducing reuse and megaprogramming concepts early in a computer scientist's education can have a large impact on the way they think about and develop software. Much work is still needed to improve what we have done and to carry it through an entire computer science curriculum. However, the potential benefits resulting from industry-wide improvements as properly-prepared students enter the work force is incalculable.

References

Domain Engineering Guidebook. Technical Report SPC-92019-CMC, Software Productivity Consortium, Herndon, Virginia (1992).

Frank Belz, Dave Luckham, and James Purtilo: Application of ProtoTech technology to the DSSA program. In *Proceedings of the DARPA Software Technology Conference*, Los Angeles, California (1992).

Barry Boehm and William Scherlis: Megaprogramming. In *Proceedings of the DARPA Software Technology Conference*, Los Angeles, California (1992).

Robert Cameron: Software reuse with metaprogramming systems. In *Proceedings of the Fifth Annual Pacific Northwest Software Quality Conference*, Portland, Oregon (1987) 223–232.

Grady Campbell: Abstraction-based reuse repositories. In *Proceedings of AIAA Computers in Aerospace VII Conference*, pages 368–373, Monterrey, California (1989).

Michael Clancy and Marcia Linn: *Designing Pascal Solutions: A Case Study Approach.* W. H. Freeman, New York, New York (1992).

Edsgar Dijkstra: Notes on Structured Programming. In O.J. Dahl, E.W. Dijkstra, and C.A.R. Hoare, editors, *Structured Programming*, Academic Press (1972) 1–82.

Richard Pattis: *Karel the Robot: A Gentle Introduction to the Art of Programming with Pascal.* John Wiley and Sons, New York, New York (1981).

Viswa Samanthanam: Teaching reuse early. In L. Deimel, editor, *Software Engineering Education*, Springer-Verlag, New York, New York (1990) 77–84.

Allen Tucker and Bruce Barnes: Computing curricula 1991: Report of the ACM/IEEE-CS joint curriculum task force. Technical report, Association for Computing Machinery, New York, New York (1991).

Steven Wartik and Rubén Prieto-Díaz: Criteria for Comparing Reuse-Oriented Domain Analysis Approaches. *International Journal of Software Engineering and Knowledge Engineering*, 2 (1992) 403–431.

Formal Methods for Software Engineering

Mahesh H. Dodani
The University of Iowa
Iowa City, Iowa

Abstract. This tutorial introduces formal methods in software engineering. The main objectives of the tutorial are as follows:
- Introduce the notion of formal methods, and show how it is used in practice for specifying and verifying software.
- Describe "industrial-strength" formal methods for specifying and verifying the object, dynamic, and functional models of software.
- Discuss various approaches to showing consistency between the three models of software.

This approach to formal methods is innovative compared to current practices of introducing theory for software engineering (as exemplified by tutorials based on [11, 17, 18]), overview of formal methods (e.g. tutorials based on [8]), or in depth study of software engineering methodologies (e.g. tutorials based on [1, 15]).

There exists many formal methods for each software model. The following criteria characterize the formal methods used in the tutorial:
- The formal method is based on logic. This criterion facilitates establishing a common thread in specifying and especially verifying software.
- The formal method is used in industry. This criterion facilitates exposure to usable and well defined methods.
- The formal method has been successfully extended to address a recent change in software engineering practice. The most interesting recent change in software practice i s the use of Object-Oriented (OO) techniques.

Teaching Logic as a Tool

David Gries and Fred Schneider
Cornell University
Ithaca, New York

Abstract. The typical discrete-math course has a unit on formal logic, but is concepts and notations are rarely applied in other units of the course. Instead, logic is viewed as an isolated topic, perhaps motivated by an application or two. Not surprisingly, students develop a negative view of logic as a topic that is of academic interest only.

This tutorial presents our experiences in teaching another view: logical manipulation can be a powerful and versatile tool for the practicing mathematician and computer scientist, and students should be taught to use this tool skillfully. Armed with this tool, students have an easier time mastering other discrete-math topics, as well as later topics in the computer science and mathematics curriculum.

The Capability Maturity Model for Software: A Tutorial

Mark C. Paulk
Software Engineering Institute
Pittsburgh, Pennsylvania

Abstract. This tutorial provides an overview of the work being done at the Software Engineering Institute (SEI) on the capability maturity model for software (CMM). The CMM describes the ability of organizaitons to develop and maintain software; it is a model of organizational improvement. It is based on the process management work of quality gurus such as Deming, Juran, and Crosby and can be applied by organizations to improve their software process via software process assessments and by acquisition agencies to select qualified software vendors via contractor evaluations. The tutorial briefly discusses the principles underlying process and quality management and performing assessments to improve the software process and evaluations to improve the supplier base. The bulk of the discussion is on understanding the five maturity levels and the key process areas that characterize them. The tutorial is based on Version 1.1 of the CMM, released in February 1993.

The audience for the CMM tutorial includes software managers, practitioners. and members of process groups, who are interested in improving the software process.

Lecture Notes in Computer Science

For information about Vols. 1–680
please contact your bookseller or Springer-Verlag